D1557834

Live Yankees

THE SEWALLS AND THEIR SHIPS

W. H. Bunting

Tilbury House, Publishers
Gardiner, Maine

Maine Maritime Museum
Bath, Maine

Tilbury House, Publishers
103 Brunswick Avenue, Gardiner, Maine 04345
800–582–1899 • www.tilburyhouse.com

Maine Maritime Museum
243 Washington Street, Bath, Maine 04345
207–443–1316 • www.mainemaritimemuseum.org

First hardcover edition: May 2009
10 9 8 7 6 5 4 3 2 1

Library of Congress Cataloging-in-Publication Data

Bunting, William Henry, 1945-
  Live Yankees : the Sewalls and their ships / W.H. Bunting. -- 1st hardcover ed.
      p. cm.
  Includes bibliographical references and index.
  ISBN 978-0-88448-315-1 (hardcover : alk. paper)
 1. E. & A. Sewall Company (Bath. Me.)--Correspondence. 2. Sewall, Arthur, 1835-1900--
Correspondence. 3. Shipbuilding industry--Maine--Bath--History-=-19th century. 4. Square-riggers--
Maine--Bath--History--19th century. 5. Shipping--Maine--Bath--History--19th century.
6. Businessmen--Maine--Bath--Correspondence. 7. Ship captains--United States--Correspondence.
8. Merchant ships--United States--History--19th century. 9. Seafaring life--History--19th century.
10. Ocean travel--History--19th century. I. Title.
  VM301.E325B86 2009
  387.5065'73--dc22
                                    2008045206

Jacket design by Geraldine Millham, Westport, Massachusetts
Copyediting by Genie Dailey, Fine Points Editorial Services, Jefferson, Maine
Scanning by Pure Photographic Goodness, Portland, Maine
Printed and bound by Maple Vail, Kirkwood, New York

Title page photograph: Mid-1890s. The ship Sterling *at South Street, New York. A veteran of the Cape Horn trade, she was built by the Sewalls in 1873, and sold in 1881 to John Rosenfeld of San Francisco— here she flies Rosenfeld's house flag. The boxes on the lighter alongside are possibly cases of oil—each containing two five-gallon tins of kerosene—from an East River refinery located above the Brooklyn Bridge. The barrels may contain lubricating oil.* Peabody Essex Museum
Part openings: The decorative engraving of Shenandoah *was used on vessel register certificates and officer licenses issued by the U.S. Department of Commerce and Labor circa 1897 and 1899, respectively.* Maine Maritime Museum

For Andrew "Andy" Nesdall
The man who loved square-riggers

———⋈———

"Live Yankees" were a nineteenth-century strain of New Englander known for their enterprising hustle in the pursuit of the almighty dollar. The extreme clipper ship *Live Yankee*, built at Rockland, Maine, in 1853, was the most notable of the vessels named in their honor.

Live Yankees are chuck full of character and sizzling hot with enterprise and curiosity. . . . The beauty of a river to him is its capacity for a steamboat; its sloping banks checker into building lots; and its poetry waters might do the drudgery of a cotton mill. . . . If you would save your pride from being sand-papered, risk it not in a dicker with Jonathan.*
—*Henry Wheeler Shaw (Josh Billings), 1818–51*[**]

*   Jonathan was a term for an American, especially a New Englander.
** Walter Blair and Raven I. McDonald, *The Mirth of a Nation* (Minneapolis: University of Minnesota, 1983), p. 155.

CONTENTS

APPENDICES

SOME PRELIMINARY CONSIDERATIONS

The Ship has Saled vary hevy & dull

Live Yankees resulted from an invitation to the author, tendered by members of the Sewall family and the Maine Maritime Museum, to attempt to weave a story both readable and able to withstand scholarly scrutiny from the more than 315 linear feet of documents in the Sewall Family Papers, one of the world's great family archives. Donated by family members to the museum in 1992, the heart of the collection concerns the business activities of the shipbuilding and ship-owning firms of Clark & Sewall, c. 1827–66; E. & A. Sewall, c. 1854–79; and Arthur Sewall & Co., 1879–1932. In essence, this vast accumulation of letters, bills, casualty reports, official documents, logbooks, telegrams in code, and so on, is really a collection of stories, large and small. This book presents a selection of those stories.

Notice is hereby given that spelling and punctuation of passages from letters, and in some instances even newspaper items and other sources, have been edited for readability. No words have been added or deleted, other than as may be indicated.

Most of the letters quoted from were written by sea captains who first went to sea at a young age. On the whole, the teachers who taught these future captains the basics at the little district schools did very good work. That said, even the better educated at this time commonly dispensed with periods, often not even capitalizing the first word of what rightly should have been the following sentence. Which is not to say that writers did not enjoy freely employing capitals elsewhere, seemingly as the spirit moved them.

Not unreasonably, many words were spelled phonetically, yet it is surprising how long it can take to tumble to what is meant by some alternative spellings of even a common word. And nautical terms, which are confusing enough to many readers, are that much more difficult to translate when spelled phonetically with a Down East accent, as in the case of "horse chalk" for "hawes chock." Even in the very common and also obvious case of "hole" for "hold," the flow of the sentence is interrupted. Unorthodox punctuation and spelling is far more noticeable—and more obstructive—when set into type. To cite an admittedly extreme example, consider a passage from a letter written in December 1859 by Captain Robert Jack, the longest-serving Sewall captain, reporting the arrival of the ship *Valentia* at New Orleans:

I Arived at the Barr Sat 3rd at 11 clock Nite Came over the Barr 4th None & Arrived at Town 6th 6 P M I have jist entered ship hasd 58 days passage to the Barr the Ship has Saled vary hevy & dull & she is the Slowest Sailing Vessel I have ever ben in especaly this passage, hir Bottom is vary fowl & had she ben put on the gridiron [dry dock] in Liverpool & hir Botom Cleened I think I Could made the passage in 45 Days. (To Give you some ideer From the Tortuges to the Barr 7 ships 1 Bark 1 Brigg & 2 chooners Came up & passed ous, & went out of Site a head of ous in 25 howers

(In truth, Captain Jack's style is so original that, if used in the text, it would either have been left as is, or paraphrased.)

Common nineteenth-century practice used no commas in numbers, e.g., 10000 rather than 10,000. Commas have been added in the text. Also, dollar signs, often placed after the number, e.g., 10000$, have been put in front, as in $10,000.

The use of the word "ship" can be very confusing. When used as a prefix, as in "the ship *Molly Sue*," it tells us that the *Molly Sue* was a full-rigged ship, being square-rigged on all three masts. However, "ship" also refers to any large vessel, as in "the bark *Peggy Sue* was a very good ship to ship in."

Traditionally, a "voyage" included a homeward passage, with some leeway given as to the definition of "home." A "passage" is a journey between two points. Thus, by this definition, the ship *Molly Sue* sailing 15,000 miles from New York, around Cape Horn, to San Francisco, has made but a passage—and legally, a coasting passage, at that! She will not have completed a voyage until she has returned to the East Coast, even if she has to do so by way of Hong Kong or Liverpool. To merchants, underwriters, shipowners, and the like, however, a voyage involved a single commercial engagement. For their purposes, the *Molly Sue* completed a voyage when she entered the Golden Gate.

Tonnage numbers cited are gross registered tonnage. The tonnage given on a ship's register is a figure intended to reflect the ship's capacity derived by a measurement formula, with one ton equaling 100 cubic feet. Net tonnage was gross tonnage minus certain spaces. (The formula in use before 1864 assumed depth equal to one half the beam, resulting in the "kettle-bottomed," narrow-beamed rule-beaters particularly popular in the cotton trade. All things being equal, under the pre-1864 system hulls measured somewhat larger.)

Trying to determine the relative value of the dollar over time, depending on the methodology employed, results in a wide range of conclusions. For example, using various accepted measures devised by expert economists, the $7 million cost of digging the Erie Canal between 1817 and 1825 translates in today's dollars to $147–160 million, 1.6 billion, 4.3 billion, or 114 billon. Therefore, no such comparisons will be attempted. Even simply calculating accumulated inflation (or deflation) over a period of time is of limited utility, since the relative value of various commodities can vary widely independently of that rate. Comparing values within a certain limited period, however, reveals significant information. All that said, the post–Civil War dollar was very close in value to the pre–World War I dollar; obviously in the hundred years since, there has been very great inflation.

Even salty nineteenth-century writers did not always obey the "proper" literary conventions. According to rigid traditionalists (and some editors), the name of a ship is only to be preceded by "the" if it is a person's name. Someone forgot to instruct the Sewalls and their captains of this rule, but we will observe it, as it pleases our editor to do so. All names of ships have been italicized, whether or not that was the case in original material.

Writing a book such as this is fundamentally a matter of selecting certain information while excluding a great deal more. Not only is subjectivity unavoidable, but it is precisely what the author is supposed to bring to the table. Broadly speaking, the material selected for this volume was that which the author found of interest or else deemed of essential importance. Thus, while researchers enthralled by the history of late-nineteenth-century federal shipping legislation will find rich material in the Sewall Family Papers, little has been included here, in part because, for all the efforts made, relatively few such bills became law, or were particularly effective, and in part because such matters put the author to sleep. Researchers made of sterner stuff are called for. Likewise for the extensive documentation of the marine insurance industry, and other such material.

The Sewalls did business with a great many people, and inevitably some of them, rightly or wrongly, were made unhappy enough to write nasty letters or to file lawsuits. Lawsuits and court cases can be very informative and interesting, and for that reason several are considered. Of course, most people with whom the Sewalls came into contact did not end up in a dispute with them, and the vast majority of the thousands of passages made by Sewall ships were completed without any untoward incidents that we are aware of. But a book listing satisfied customers and humdrum passages would be of very little interest. And while the first obligation of the historian may be to understand what was normal, the reactions to, or participation in, matters of an unusual nature can be far more revealing as to the character of the players. It devolves upon the reader to maintain some perspective in these matters.

The members of the Sewall family who have so generously supported the writing and publication of this book, to their great credit, made it clear that they were not interested in funding a vanity volume. Some may argue that the results reflect an excessive commitment to meeting their wishes; there is no doubt but that in at least several cases the result has been to present persons as being far more complex than they have heretofore been characterized.

It is important to bear in mind that whenever the life of anyone who lived at a time and in a place not our own is being considered, it is our obligation to attempt as best we can to do so within the context of these differing circumstances. For example, while we recognize today that slavery was a great evil, not all slaveholders—whose numbers included George Washington and Thomas Jefferson—were therefore evil people. Indeed, even within a single lifetime, strongly held beliefs and social mores may greatly change. People of the past must also be allowed to work their way through the callow-ness of youth, and also to become with old age a senile shadow of their former active and consequential selves, as will happen to many of us. We are obliged to investigate with thoroughness, and then to judge with care.

Late-nineteenth-century America is both an entertaining and an instructive era to study, thanks to blatant social hypocrisies, of both comical and tragic nature, which serve to illuminate those of the present day, the immensity and audacity of which likely would have sore amazed even that most jaded of nineteenth-century social cynics, Mark Twain. And it is all too easy, while condemning our ancestors for their various and sundry sins of commission and omission and delusion, to overlook their many remarkable achievements, their ingenuity, their abilities, their toughness, their courage, their acts of kindness, and their characteristically artful melding of aesthetics with prac-tical considerations. And perhaps nowhere was this clash of cultural characteristics better reflected than in the building, ownership, and operation of a fine and lofty Yankee ship.

Abbie Sewall had the idea for a new book about the Sewalls and their ships, and then raised the funds, largely from generous fellow family members. Earl "Bud" Warren suggested my name for author. Director Tom Wilcox of the Maine Maritime Museum ironed out the details of the museum's participation, and his successor, Amy Lent, has continued the support. My sincere thanks to all these folks for having provided and entrusted me with the opportunity of a lifetime.

Ralph Linwood "Lin" Snow, a former director of the museum and Bath's foremost historian, shared the fruits of his own research on Captain Jim Murphy and family—a more generous act hath no writer. And one bright and crisp late fall day Lin gave me a memorable memorial tour of Maple Grove and Oak Grove cemeteries, where many of the players in the Sewall saga are buried.

During the many months that I was underfoot in the museum's library, Senior Curator Nathan Lipfert's patient helpfulness never wavered, despite my frequent inva-sions of his inner sanctum to share the latest interesting discovery. Nathan's deep pas-sion for the library's extraordinary and growing collection, with the Sewall Family Papers as its centerpiece, was quickly apparent.

I began this project anticipating having the guidance of old friends Andrew "Andy" Nesdall; Captain W. J. L "Lew" Parker, USCG Ret.; and Captain Harold Huycke, the reigning authorities on the late-nineteenth-century American sailing marine. Alas, Lew and Harold passed over the bar before I had even begun to write, and Andy's unique fund of knowledge was slipping from his grasp. Nevertheless, I wrote the book as if for their approval, and their influence is writ large.

Lin Snow, Bud Warren, Nathan Lipfert, and Abbie Sewall, along with Dr. Charlie Burden, Captain Doug Lee, Ed Coffin, and Prof. Bill Jordan, all reviewed the manuscript

—some while meeting other pressing demands—and made important corrections and suggestions. Their efforts have significantly reduced the likelihood of my having to endure serious post-publication depression, for which I am immeasurably appreciative. As is my wife. I take full responsibility for all errors and shortcomings which remain.

Thanks to the extraordinary efforts of editor/publisher Jennifer Bunting to produce quality books, all Tilbury House authors, including her husband, receive a level of forbearing assistance now all but unknown in the business.

Many other folks have contributed in various kind and helpful ways to this effort. Among them Anne Cough of the Maine State Library, Bill Barry of the Maine Historical Society, Dr. Josh Smith, D'Arcy James, Gene Reynolds, and members of the MARHST Internet discussion group deserve special mention. Others are recognized in the appendices. My sincere thanks to all.

W. H. Bunting
Whitefield, Maine

The success of a ship is necessarily and chiefly due first to a rigid keeping down of all her expenses and to strict economy both in and out of port, and next to her being placed in charge of a good captain and crew, and the adoption of a model which would save taxation was a natural proceeding. It must be said, however, that the burdens of port charges and taxation in its various forms never weigh hard on shipping unless trade is dull, freights are low, and competition is sharp. No matter how big and costly a ship, no matter what wages are paid or how expensively she is run (and a ship *is* an expensive investment, spending money right and left with a prodigality known in few forms of business), she can carry every burden if trade is good and freights are profitable, and spend from 20 to 45 percent of her value, as she does, every year, without feeling it. When a ship does make money, it makes it rapidly.
—Henry Hall, 1842*

* Henry Hall, Special Agent, *Report on the Ship-Building Industry of the United States*, Tenth Census (Washington, D.C., 1884), p. 66.

Abbreviated Family Line of the Maritime Sewalls
(descended from Dummer Sewall)

Dummer Sewall, 1737–1832, and Mary Dunning had ten children, forty-six grand-children.

Joseph Sewall, 1770–1851, the sixth child and second son of Dummer, had twelve children by three wives. He was active in "maritime affairs" of which there is no record.

William Dunning Sewall, was the second child and second son of Joseph. William had a brother named Joseph, 1795–1851, who would be the grandfather of *Captain Joseph Ellis "Joe" Sewall*, 1854–1925.

William Dunning Sewall
1797–1877

Harriet   Marcia   *William D., Jr.,*   *Edward*   *Arthur*   Franklin   Alice

Edward Sewall
1833–1879

Samuel   Oscar   Edward (Capt. "Ned")   Frederic   Mark   *Frank*   Blanche

Arthur Sewall
1835–1900

Harold   William

Full names and dates for the maritime offspring are: William Dunning Sewall, Jr., 1827–1851; Samuel Swanton Sewall, 1858–1935; Oscar Trufant Sewall, 1860–1914; Edward Robinson Sewall, 1863–1924; Frank Lewis Sewall, 1869–1930; Harold Marsh Sewall, 1860–1924; William Dunning Sewall II, 1861–1930.

PART ONE

We first meet Arthur Sewall, the most notable of the maritime Sewalls. We receive an overview of the history of the Sewall fleets and follow the course of the great Kennebec River, upon which Sewall ships floated to the sea and on whose shore lay Bath, the City of Ships. We review the history of the storied Sewall family in America, and we meet William D. Sewall, founder, with partner Freeman Clark, of the Sewall shipbuilding and managing dynasty. Clark & Sewall would build over two dozen ships before being succeeded in the business by William D.'s sons, Edward and Arthur, who form the E. & A. Sewall Company.

Take your hatchet, Mr. Preble. . . .

In the spring of 1939 the old shipbuilding town of Bath, Maine, lost two unique voices when Dr. Edward E. Briry—old "Doc" Briry—and his parrot Charlie were buried in the same grave. Charlie, while making a loud pest of himself during the funeral service at Doc's Grove Street home, was shut up in a closet, where he promptly bit the telephone wires that ran through it. It was decided then that Charlie and Doc should go on ahead together.

That Doc had expired without first having had his memories downloaded was a signal tragedy. The son of a veteran Bath physician, a graduate of Bowdoin College and the Boston University School of Medicine, Doc Briry delivered more than one thousand Bathites. He served as city physician, secretary of the board of health, on the school board, and as the boarding officer of the port. He also owned and sold shares in many Bath schooners—including the four-masted *Edward E. Briry*—and was very knowledgeable about maritime affairs, having, he claimed, salt in his veins from his mother's seafaring family. A sharp-eyed, sharp-eared, dry-witted observer, he was ideally equipped to observe both the tragedy and comedy of the local human condition, which, in Bath, often had a maritime aspect.

In 1938 journalist Mark Hennessy's book, *The Sewall Ships of Steel*, was published with the support of members of the Sewall family, whose forebears had built and managed ships at Bath for nearly a century. It is a unique and remarkable book, presenting in detail the history of the final generation of Sewall vessels.[1] The Sewalls were the only shipbuilders in the United States to build steel square-riggers and were the last American firm to operate a fleet of square-riggers employed in deepwater, worldwide trade. Doc Briry enjoyed the book so much that, in a badly palsied hand, he wrote Hennessy three letters. In the first, he reported:

> I have been holding your *Sewall Ships of Steel* in one hand while my land hand palm is supporting one side of a queerly aching head. Aching probably because of the angina in my heart. Within that aching head is another ship book—my Book of Memory—my Book of Life. I could not loan it if I so wished. It will go with me when I make my last voyage on that "one way ferry which lands one on the shores of that beautiful Island of Some Where."

Hennessy's book, based on voluminous family papers which the Sewalls, unlike other old shipbuilding families, had, in good part, not dumped into the Kennebec River, was a remarkable and unique achievement. Yet it was clearly intended not to offend, and, as Doc Briry noted: "Mr. Hennessy, You have said not one unkind word of anybody in your whole book." Doc then proceeded to tell a few stories that helped to round out the picture. One story concerned Arthur Sewall, the moving force of the Sewall dynasty after the Civil War, and the destruction of a piece of fine furniture built into the cabin of the ship *Indiana*.

Probably no one ever called Arthur Sewall "Art," much less "Artie." Even as a young man Arthur Sewall appears to have been imbued with the gravity and aura of authority of one much older. Arthur Sewall was also an ardent Democrat, and, anticipating victory in the 1876 presidential election of "Pitchfork" Sam Tilden and his running mate, Thomas Hendricks, the Sewalls had named *Indiana* in honor of Hendricks's home state, which was expected to deliver the key electoral votes. Alas, although the Democrats won the popular vote, the Republicans, by hook and also by crook, obtained enough electoral votes to put Rutherford B. Hayes in the White House, turning the new ship's name into a bitter reminder. Twenty years later, in another consequential election, Arthur Sewall himself, dubbed "the Maritime Prince," would be the Democratic Party's vice-presidential candidate.

Also in 1876, responding to high freight rates in the California wheat trade, Bath shipyards launched ten full-rigged ships—Cape Horners—along with six barks (at least two of which were Cape Horners) and fifteen schooners. Three of the ships, *Indiana*, *Reaper*, and *Thrasher*, were built by E. & A. Sewall, *Indiana* being the thirty-fourth or thirty-fifth vessel built by brothers Edward and Arthur Sewall since they had formed their partnership in 1854.

According to Doc Briry, *Indiana* was to have been commanded by Captain John Delano of Woolwich—a town lying across the Kennebec River from Bath. Captain Delano, forty-nine (Arthur was then almost forty), was Arthur's brother-in-law and a well-respected shipmaster who, for many years, had commanded ships of Bath's Houghton fleet.

Cleveland Preble, the Sewalls' longtime master joiner, or finish carpenter, many years later told Doc Briry that Captain Delano had asked him to build an elegant black-walnut "book secretary" into his cabin aboard *Indiana*. Down East ships in general, and Bath ships in particular, were noted for their large, well-appointed, and finely finished after cabins, which included the captain's cabin. Masters-to-be of a ship under construction, who had usually bought a captain's share—typically an eighth—in the ship, and who might wish to take their families to sea with them, were normally consulted in the design of the cabin. Glowing descriptions in the local press of the exotic woods and luxurious features found in the cabin of the latest ship to slide into the Kennebec helped to fuel cabin envy among builders and captains alike, and even the parsimonious Sewalls, known for the economical finish and outfit of their ships, were not immune. But apparently there were limits.

Arthur Sewall, Doc Briry wrote, rarely missed a daily stroll about the shipyard, but "He did not climb on board very often, I think because of some stiffness in hips and crotch—no one ever saw Mr. Sewall run."[2] On this particular day, however, something had induced Arthur to climb the steep ramp and board the nearly completed *Indiana*, whose great bulk dominated the shipyard. Entering the cabin, and —"as Mr. Preble soon noticed to his sorrow and disgust"— spying the tall, handsome secretary, Arthur, in his "slow and rather stern voice"—Sewall was said to speak in a low, measured monotone—addressed Cleveland Preble:

"Who told you to do that?"

"Captain Delano told me to make it."

"How much is it costing?"

"I figure it is going to cost around one hundred and twenty-five dollars. We have done a cabinet-maker's job, and we have used the best of walnut." Preble quickly added that Captain Delano had instructed Preble to send the bill to him.[3]

"Captain Delano will do no such thing. I do not allow such ornaments in our Sewall ships. We do not intend our captains to be reading story books at sea. We intend our captains to spend their time on deck reading the weather and trying to make quick passages. Take your hatchet, Mr. Preble, and convert that thing into kindling wood and charge the materials and labor to A. Sewall & Co. [*sic*]."[4]

Preble told Briry that right then he felt like telling Mr. Arthur Sewall to "go to the hot place," and that he, Preble, was "done with the Sewall shipyard."[5]

Captain Delano never took command of *Indiana*. Perhaps, upon discovering the fate of his secretary, he stalked off the ship and out of a job. He was soon back in command of the Houghtons' ship *Austria*. By the time of *Indiana*'s launching, Captain John Drummond, formerly of the Sewalls' ship *Humboldt*, had been named as her master.

Launched today at eleven o'clock, from the yard of Messrs. E. & A. Sewall, a fine ship of about 1,500 tons, called the *Indiana*. She is to be commanded by Capt. John Drummond, and will take four or five hundred tons of ice as ballast to Baltimore, there to load for San Francisco. The *Indiana* is built in the thorough and workmanlike manner which characterizes all the ships built by that enter-prising firm. —*Bath Daily Times*, October 31, 1876

Was it a happenstance that Arthur Sewall boarded *Indiana* that day? Or did he wish to replace Delano with Drummond, and, having caught wind of the secretary, hatched a plan likely to serve his ends. Arthur Sewall was not known for losing his temper, and if this was planned, surely the other owners—brother Edward; their father, William; and silent partner Thomas M. Reed—were also in on it.

If, on the other hand, Arthur's reaction was spontaneous, it indicates that he was then really running the Sewall show. Yet if he rarely boarded ships under construction, it may be presumed that Edward was more involved in the everyday business of the shipyard—it also indicates the great confidence placed in master builder Elisha Mallett.

Arthur Sewall does not appear to have been a man who held grudges. Captain Delano served as a director of the Bath National Bank, known as "the Sewall bank," of which Arthur was president, and after Delano's death Arthur was asked to step in to protect the assets of the estate from a spendthrift son.

After further reflection, Doc Briry wrote, "This book-case incident brings up a thought—was Mr. Sewall himself much of a reader, much of a book-man in his own house?" He had never heard any discussion regarding Arthur Sewall's early education, although Arthur's sister Alice had attended "the old Bath Academy, the highest seat of learning." Arthur's 1896 campaign biography stated only that he attended the "common schools" in Bath, and that "Mr. Sewall is a student, but studies from actual contact with men of affairs and events rather than from books."

In essence, was not Briry posing the question, "Who really was Arthur Sewall?" Indeed, Arthur Sewall, one of the notable figures in the history of both American ship-building and ship-owning, was something of an enigma in his day and has remained so. A better understanding of Arthur Sewall must entail a better understanding of other maritime members of the Sewall family, of the Sewalls' business, of the people they employed or routinely did business with, and of their world and of their times. And the best, first place to look for evidence regarding all these matters is in the Sewall Family Papers, lined up in boxes on over three hundred feet of shelving in the library of the Maine Maritime Museum at Bath.

There is, as well, the enduring fascination of ocean-borne commerce propelled by wind and sail, a combination which to some degree and in some form may yet be returning to the seas. If the Sewalls had built steamships rather than sailing ships, we probably would not be so interested in who they were.

Although Doc Briry had seen Arthur Sewall often in passing, and although Briry's Uncle Jim Murphy was—at least in Murphy's mind—the commodore of the Sewall fleet, Doc Briry only met Arthur Sewall, to speak to, one time:

Mr. Arthur Sewall owned where his father Mr. Wlliam D. Sewall did, a wide hay-field extending from High Street to Dummer Street. Midway of this field was a flat interval, overflowed in winter by water . . . where in the summer months nothing more than bull-suckers grew. . . . It offered a place for boys to play ball. . . . [With] a playmate, Charlie Jordan—we were grammar school boys at the time — wandering up High Street one summer forenoon—in vacation time. We noticed some boys our age playing ball on this dry clay patch in Sewall field. Charlie Jordan and myself very naturally wandered down and were invited to play.

We had knocked out but few balls when Mr. Arthur Sewall suddenly was among us. Before we hardly realized it . . . [Mr. Sewall] walked very slowly—almost heavily—and yet walked gracefully and thoughtfully—and very dignified.

Said Mr. Sewall: "Boys, what are you doing in my hayfield?" very slowly and with dignity, removing his cigar at the same time. We boys made no reply. Then Mr. Sewall asked our names—one at a time—and who our parents were. He made a few notes in a little book—and slowly walked away. Noticing my classmate Ed McAullife leaning over his [backyard] fence, I stepped over and asked Edward how often Mr. Sewall visited his hayfield. Edward replied: "Just about once a year."

Makes money every year

The general outline of the history of the maritime Sewalls is well known. For nearly a century members of the family built and managed a fleet of more than one hundred merchant vessels, mostly stout deepwater square-riggers. No family has been more intimately associated with the history of the city of Bath, which was then among the most productive shipbuilding communities of any size in the world. And there was, as well, a cosmopolitan nature to the Sewalls that set them apart from many of their fellow, more down-to-the-chips, shipbuilders. That Bath's Sewalls were members of the greater American family of Sewalls—long a notable tribe—adds additional interest to their story.

Beginning in the 1820s, the Sewalls, along with many other New England shipbuilders, ship owners, and mariners, participated in the great flowering of the American merchant marine, culminating with Yankee ships leading the world's merchant fleets. The role played in this era by America's maritime people—primarily New Englanders—in providing markets for domestic goods, in obtaining foreign goods and exchange, in creating wealth, and in spreading American influence, was of fundamental importance to the growth of the nation.

Quickly moving beyond the West Indies trade, the traditional nursery of American maritime enterprise, the Sewalls and their Bath neighbors helped pioneer the carriage of cotton from southern ports to Britain and Europe, a trade which grew to immense proportions and international importance. Conservative in everything but the size of their ships, the Sewalls made a name for themselves in 1841 by launching likely the largest merchant sailing vessel built up until that time, the 1,133-ton "cotton box" *Rappahannock*, more than twice the size of the average full-rigger of the day.

During the brief clipper-ship era of the 1850s, the Sewalls, like other shrewd and conservative Bath shipbuilders, resisted the mania for "clippers," ships of extreme model and rig designed for speed over capacity, and built none.

The Civil War greatly accelerated the decline of the American deepwater merchant marine, which had begun with the panic of 1857. (On the other hand, coastal shipping greatly expanded.) By war's end, all members of the two Sewall fleets—Clark & Sewall and E. & A. Sewall—had been disposed of. Although even many of the ship owners who had survived the war were now winding up their fleets, young Edward and Arthur Sewall jumped back into the fray. An 1874 credit report described E. & A. Sewall & Co. as "a wealthy concern, makes money every year, prompt, careful & in excellent credit."[6]

With the cotton trade extinguished during the war and afterwards taken over by British steam, Sewall ships rounded Cape Horn to join the growing San Francisco grain trade, which inspired a temporary but notable revival of the American deepwater sailing fleet. During a slump in the grain trade in the 1870s, the Sewalls resorted to the unsavory Peruvian guano trade. And, as before the war, voyages were made by Sewall ships to Calcutta, Burma, Australia, Russia, Chile, and elsewhere.

Coal, a problematic and dangerous cargo, was often carried westward around Cape Horn by Sewall ships bound for Acapulco, San Francisco, and other ports. The "case oil" trade from Philadelphia and New York, mostly to the Far East, provided another lease on life for the Sewall fleet, as did the turn-of-the-century Hawaiian sugar trade.

In the early 1890s, against all odds, the Sewalls built four of the largest wooden square-riggers ever constructed. Then, quickly converting their shipyard, they constructed the first American steel square-rigger, a four-masted bark, to be followed by seven near sisters (plus a bark and a five-masted schooner) before the yard closed in 1903. The Sewalls sold their last remaining tonnage during the World War I shipping bubble, but not before their four-masted bark, the *William P. Frye*, became the first American merchant vessel lost in the war.

Often overlooked is the Sewalls' fleet of fore-and-aft-rigged coasting schooners, built primarily to transport southern hard pine, a vital shipbuilding timber, from the Southeast to Bath. Sewall schooners ranged as well to the Caribbean, to South America, to the Mediterranean, and one sailed around the Horn and back, while two others—one a steel five-master—sailed around the world by way of the Cape of Good Hope.

As the owners of the last surviving important fleet of American square-riggers engaged in worldwide trade, it was the Sewalls' fate to draw the curtain on this most significant epic of American economic enterprise. No family had worked more assiduously, more stubbornly, or with more enterprise to delay the arrival of that day. That said, the Sewalls, as shipbuilders first, strongly opposed all efforts to open up American registration to foreign-built ships, which presumably would have expanded the American-flag fleet while retarding American shipbuilding.

The Sewalls shunned steam to the end, believing that there would always be cargoes for sail in certain long-distance trades. Ironically, had the Sewalls not made the move to steel, they very likely would have been among the founding owners of the gloriously profitable American–Hawaiian Steamship Company, which, at the turn of the century, crowded American sailing ships out of the protected intercoastal trade. The combination of the Panama Canal and World War I finally killed the world's deepwater sailing fleet, which, only a decade earlier, had included about four thousand square-riggers under a number of flags. It was a remarkably quick death.

Despite a veneer of old-fashioned formalized civility, international shipping in the late 1800s and early 1900s was a highly competitive, low-margin, and often cutthroat business. The Sewalls' reputation as tireless, tiresome tightwads was well deserved and likely carefully cultivated. Hard bargaining was a reflexive reaction in any transaction, be it over the price of a ship or the salary of a stenographer. They never tired of nagging or browbeating their captains to practice the strictest economy, to the penny. While shipping people reacted in different ways to the Sewalls' often brusque manner, they could not ignore them.

Although Sewall ships were known for their plain finish and lack of extras—remember Captain Delano's bookcase!—the Sewalls took great pride in them and did not skimp on cordage, sails, and other material essential for efficient operation. Outspoken complaints by their captains when stores were found to be spoiled indicate that, like most American ships, Sewall ships usually fed their crews well. Yet no fleet experienced worse publicity regarding alleged shipboard abuse and brutality toward sailors, an all-too-common characteristic of American ships.

In the palmy, profitable, pre–Civil War years, ownership of Sewall vessels was primarily held by the firm partners, and a few additional family members and insiders. As shipping became less profitable, and as ships became larger and more expensive, a different strategy evolved, and the percentage of ownership held by the partners became smaller, while increasing numbers of "dry" or "outside" owners were recruited. As managers, the Sewalls charged an annual fee per ship ($250) and collected on various commissions, split-commissions, fees, rebates, and such, some presumably kept off the books. When a partner attended to a ship's needs in port, the ship paid the firm. When a partner testified on behalf of the fleet's interests at Washington, the ships paid the firm. The partners thus made money even from ships which were earning their owners no dividends.

While the clear intention of the partners in later years was to sell all but a very small portion of each vessel, the Sewalls routinely falsified ships' registrations to place unsold "vessel property" with certain out-of-state friends and relatives so as to avoid high Bath property taxes. And there is some irony here (in addition to Arthur Sewall's reputation as a great local booster), since the reason that Bath's property taxes were so high was due to the huge debt that the city had incurred backing the Knox & Lincoln Railroad, a money pit promoted by Sewalls.7

Once having sold an interest in a ship, only under the most extraordinary circumstances would the Sewalls ever agree to buy it back, and then usually only at a deep discount.

Bath's maritime Sewalls—with the notable exception of one of the two Sewalls who actually went to sea as a career—all appear to have retired very comfortably, no small feat considering the declining state of the American deepwater shipping industry. Making money was of prime importance to them all and indeed served as a strong link among family members. Rare indeed is a letter from one Sewall male to another that does not include mention of business.

The Sewalls invested heavily in nonmaritime securities and speculations, as was also the case with other Maine and New England shipbuilders and ship owners (sometimes to their sorrow). Unlike hard-shelled wealthy Yankee misers, Sewalls openly enjoyed the pleasures afforded by their good fortune—Arthur Sewall kept a separate accounting of "luxuries"—including much travel at home and abroad.

When I was a boy, I lived by a river

Arthur Staples, a boyhood friend of the sons of Edward and Arthur Sewall, became a Lewiston newspaperman. He never forgot growing up by the Kennebec:

> When I was a boy, I lived by a river and I know what an influence big rivers are apt to exert upon boys. Rivers reach out with abounding imagination, to youth. . . . Many boys that we knew went off in the ships and came back perhaps in a year or two for a little stay in town, swaggering a good deal and telling strange tales of spice-lands and strange foreign cities—of Lima and Callao, and "Frisco" and South Seas, and adventures in the "Roaring Forties."
>
> The river was alive. It touched our emotions and awakened them. We lived in it and upon it. We used to go down to its wharves in days of storm and lie in the soft shavings of the ship-yards and hear the waves beat up under the piers and dream and sleep, awaking to hear the song of the river, dreamful, mystical, world-calling. . . . Equally did we love it in calm summer-days. It lay like a mirror, broken only by the leap of the sturgeon whose mighty splashes have awakened me on many a summer Sunday morning. We fished in the river, swam in it, learned to sail boats on it, traded in crude boats in boys' coin—such craft as punts and skiffs, out of which the harvest of drowned boys was appalling. . . .
>
> The person born and reared where ships come and go, gets something of a new faith. He counts no ship that he saw launched and sail away as ever lost. To him they still sail the seas, with gay flags flyin'—ever going and coming. . . . [8]

All the stories in *Live Yankees*, in essence, flow out of the Kennebec River. The passage from the mouth of the river up to Bath is very brief; so we will go by the longer route from the headwaters, Moosehead Lake.

Maine's largest lake, Moosehead lies about twenty miles to the east of the center of the state. Over a hundred square miles in size and draining a large forested watershed, Moosehead is more than 1,000 feet above sea level. From there to the Gulf of Maine the river flows nearly 170 miles, running through, or by, eighteen "unorganized" forested townships—including Misery Gore, Indian Stream, Squaretown, West Forks, and Moxie Gore—and thirty organized towns and cities. Tributaries, most notably the Dead, the Sandy, and the Sebasticook Rivers, join along the way. The Dead was once an important contributor to the long log drives; the Sandy is still known for

1898. The view down the Kennebec from South Gardiner, towards Sands Island. A tug tows two three-masted schooners, come to load ice, upriver. At left, a four-master loads at the Commercial ice houses at Goodwin's Point, Pittston; very likely she will sail for Philadelphia. Down river, beyond the second towed schooner, Haley's ice house, on the Richmond shore, coincidentally, served the Richmond, Virginia market. Beyond the island we can glimpse ice houses in the town of Dresden. In the foreground, the log boom of Lawrence Brothers' mill is filled with pine and (mostly) spruce logs from the distant Moosehead and Dead River watersheds. Note the open upland farmland of Pittston and Dresden, famous for producing prime hay for the Boston market. MAINE HISTORIC PRESERVATION COMMISSION

the prime "intervale" soils of its flood plain.

Principal communities located at dammed falls —where countless generations of Indians once speared salmon—include Madison, Skowhegan, Waterville, and Winslow. Ticonic Falls, between Waterville and Winslow, was the dead end for any upriver navigation. Augusta, the state capital, grew where a trading post was established by the Pilgrims—yes, *those* Pilgrims—in 1628, to acquire furs. In the early 1800s, at times of low water, wading ox teams hauled flatboats upriver from Augusta to Ticonic Falls. Remarkably, from the early 1800s into the 1850s, over a hundred seagoing vessels, including full-rigged ships and barks, were built along that shoal stretch of river.

Hallowell, just below Augusta, became the practical head of navigation, and for many years before the arrival of railroads was the principal river port, doing an extensive trade with the interior. In addition to maintaining large trades to the West Indies and Boston, the Kennebec Valley in the early 1800s was an important source of supplies for the huge whaling fleets of Nantucket and New Bedford, exporting stores, spars, oars, and such, while importing Quakers.

Gardiner, a mill town built on either side of the falls of Cobbossee Stream, which drained a chain of lakes, became the terminus of the Boston steamer. Passengers aboard steamers in the late 1800s wrote of the picturesque scenes of orderly agricultural prosperity lining both sides of the river, with green pastures, sear fields of oats, and well-kept farmsteads. Among steamboat men, the Kennebec Line was called the "Hay Line" for the large cargoes of "pressed" (baled) hay it carried to Boston. South Gardiner was a major steam sawmilling center.

Beginning during the Civil War and reaching its peak in the 1890s, the lower Kennebec Valley, primarily from Gardiner south to Dresden, was the site of a huge ice industry. Ice cut from the river and housed in mammoth icehouses was shipped in the summer, mainly by coasting schooner, primarily to Philadelphia, Baltimore, and Washington, D.C. In 1891 the Kennebec's icehouses, built of upriver spruce, had a capacity of 1.2 million tons, and the thousands of arrivals and departures of ice schooners during the shipping season reportedly made the river the busiest in the nation.

Just north of Swan Island, off Richmond, was where river tugs could replenish their boiler water without fear of saltwater contamination. Just south of Richmond, long a very active shipbuilding town, lies the estuary of Merrymeeting Bay, a famous resort for waterfowl. Here the Kennebec is joined by the Eastern, the Cathance, the Muddy, the Abagadasset, and the mighty Androscoggin Rivers. The Androscoggin, fully as long as the Kennebec, with headwaters high in northern New Hampshire, was once among the most industrialized rivers in America.

The runoff from the vast combined watersheds of these rivers flows from Merrymeeting Bay through the narrow "Chops" and then through the tight passage between Day's Ferry in Woolwich and Telegraph (now Thorne) Head, at the north end of the North End of Bath. And here, as if according to some great plan, the river suddenly expands into magnificent, deep Long Reach, a basin about half a mile wide and four miles long, bordered to the east by the evergreened shores of Woolwich and Arrowsic Island, and to the west by Bath, whose shore was once lined with shipyards—the Sewall yard, at the foot of a bluff, was among the northernmost.

From this grand, deep basin, normally ice-free, thousands of vessels built on the Reach, on the bay, and along the rivers, rounded Doubling Point and headed south into Fiddler's Reach, passing by Bluff Head, Squirrel Point, Parker's Head, Cox's Head, Gilbert Head, and various islands, about twelve miles to the sea.

The river's mouth, with sandy-beached Popham to the west, granite-ledged islands to the east, and high, beaconed Seguin Island standing guard three miles offshore, is both profoundly dramatic and deeply historic. The waters right off the mouth can be notoriously lumpy, or "cobbly" when the determined ebb tide flowing out of the river meets a strong southwest breeze. The powerful effect of the river can be noticed by passing navigators well outside of Seguin.

The narrow point of high land lying to the west of Seguin, Small Point, would become the summertime resort of half a dozen generations of Sewalls.

The first European mariners to enter the Kennebec were likely forgotten Norsemen, or else fishermen from the Bay of Biscay. George Waymouth, on his 1605 exploratory voyage, left an ambiguous description of his travel up a "Mane river"

Early 1890s. The tide-streaked mouth of the Kennebec from Cox's Head, Phippsburg. Two tugs head upriver, while a third tows two schooners—no doubt carrying ice—to sea. Popham, with its fort, is to the right; Bay Point, Georgetown, is to the left. The most distant island is Seguin. Small Point, with its then nascent summer colony, lies four miles to the west— to our right—of Seguin. DAVID E. KENNEY

which long was claimed by Bath boosters to have been the Kennebec, but which was more likely the Penobscot, far to the east. The European explorer who surely did enter the river was the redoubtable Samuel de Champlain, in 1605.

In 1606 two separate English companies were formed to establish American colonies, one to the south and one to the north. The following year the Virginia Company's three ships arrived at Jamestown, and the Plymouth Company's two ships arrived at the mouth of the "Sagadehock." Landing at present-day Popham—so named for leader George Popham—members built a fort, houses, and a church, while ship-wrights began the construction of a thirty-ton "pynnace." Named the *Virginia*, she would be the first ship built in Maine.

A hard winter, George Popham's death, and a dearth of gold or silver led to the abandonment of the colony in 1608, with the colonists returning to England in a sup-ply ship and the *Virginia*. The able little *Virginia* is known to have been at Jamestown in 1610. Given the thousands of ships later built on the river that would pass out to sea by Popham, the "pretty Pynnace" *Virginia* was a fair harbinger indeed.[9]

The Kennebec would produce as well a race of mariners known as "Kennebeckers," said to fear nothing but God and Cape Cod, a reference to the peril faced by an outward bounder in a rising easterly gale. A great many Kennebeckers became shipmasters.

His fruitful vine, being thus disjoined

A family pedigree is usually only of interest to members of that family. But to properly understand the maritime Sewalls, it must be understood that they knew themselves to be members of a singular Yankee family, the term "Yankee" being a more precise term in New England than, say, in Havana, or below the Mason–Dixon Line.

New England Yankees, a distinct race that evolved during the colonial period, were, to quote Samuel Eliot Morison, a "new Nordic amalgam on an English Puritan base."[10] To the degree that any such broad generalization has validity, Yankees were a restless, tough, ambitious, and enterprising people who believed in education and the individual. Hard-working, they could be hard-headed, hard-nosed, hard-boiled, and hard-shelled. And there was surely as well a strain of hard-heartedness. The influence of Yankees on the course of this nation, and indeed the world, arguably mostly for the good—at least as defined by their terms—is beyond calculation.

The Sewalls were planted in America by Henry Sewall, of Coventry, Warwickshire, born in 1615, and his wife, Jane Dummer, also from Coventry, born circa 1627. Both were Puritans. Thanks to the magic of compounded generations, there are now—to coin a Down East Yankee phrase—a "skinny million" descendants, many named Sewall and many not, who trace back to Henry and Jane. That many of them have led notably successful and useful lives suggests that they picked their ancestors well.

Henry Sewall was, by all accounts, a man of high character, respectful of his obligations to family, church, and community. To differentiate him from his father Henry and grandfather Henry we will call him Henry the Dutiful. Henry the Dutiful's grandfather, a linen merchant, or "draper," a large landowner, and two-time mayor of Coventry, was the source of the family's wealth. We will call him Henry the Prosperous. Henry the Dutiful was the only son of his father Henry, who we will call Henry the Disagreeable, an irascible, sometimes violent, and possibly slightly deranged man. Henry the Disagreeable had "at sundry times" so "offended" his mother Margaret that his bad behavior was mentioned in both of his parents' wills, Margaret leaving him but eighteen pence despite writing that she forgave him.

Jane Sewall's parents, Stephen Dummer and Alice Archer, were also Puritans from Coventry. Prominent Dummer relations included William, a governor of Massachusetts, a benefactor of Harvard and founder of an academy which until recently bore his proud name, before it was replaced by a name thought less likely to be misconstrued.

Puritanism, largely a middle-class religious and social movement, arose in the sixteenth century within the Church of England and became a powerful political force in the seventeenth century. Puritans held that the church's doctrines violated New Testament rules, and they objected to elaborate hierarchy and rituals, the hedonism of popular entertainments, violations of the Sabbath, and such. Although religious fundamentalists, the Puritans believed in education and literacy, ultimately a fatal tenet for the continuation of a doctrinaire sect, and vital for building a dynamic new hybrid culture.

The Pilgrims were the first group of English religious malcontents to come to America intending to create a model society. In 1630, under the Massachusetts Bay Colony charter, a much larger and better prepared group of over 900 Puritans, arriving in seventeen ships, began the settlement of Boston. By 1640 the white population of the Bay Colony numbered over 21,000, although only a small minority were church-going Puritans.

In 1634 twenty-year-old Henry the Dutiful, along with neat cattle, servants, and provisions, arrived at Boston aboard the ship *Elizabeth and Dorcas* after a difficult passage during which thirty passengers died of disease. A scheme for establishing a stock farm had been underwritten by Henry the Disagreeable and several associates. Young Henry settled his outfit in Newbury, becoming one of the very first settlers of that interesting town. Here, extensive marshes provided ready forage for the stock, although one wonders what mighty oaths even the most devout Puritan may have uttered when attacked by the vicious greenhead flies that there aboundeth in hideous multitude.

Henry the Disagreeable arrived at Newbury about a year later, having emigrated due to his dislike of the English hierarchy. He would fare little better under the strict eye of the Bay Colony, where even the picking of peas on the Sabbath was a punishable offense. One of his several appearances in court stemmed from charges that he had beaten his (second) wife, from whom he had already obtained a legal separation. He moved to neighboring Rowley after a dispute regarding the relocation of the Newbury meetinghouse, but feuded there as well.

Henry the Dutiful, by contrast, was a model citizen. In 1646 he married Jane, the daughter of Stephen Dummer, a partner in the cattle scheme who had emigrated to Newbury with his family. As a wedding present, the Dummers gave the couple 500 acres back at Coventry, it likely being no coincidence that the Dummers, by then wearied of cold New England winters, had decided to join the many Puritans now returning to Old England, then under the Long Parliament. The near cessation of emigration to New England collapsed cattle prices, making it easier for Henry and Jane to leave as well. Once back in England, Henry the Dutiful became a minister.

In 1657 Henry the Disagreeable died, and in 1658 son Henry dutifully sailed back to New England to settle his father's estate, which included 500 acres in Newbury. With the monarchy restored soon afterwards, Henry sent for Jane and their five English-born children. Three more children would be born in New England. Henry the Dutiful died in Newbury in 1700, Jane, the next year, or, as the inscription on their tombstone reads, "His fruitful vine, being thus disjoined, fell to the ground January following."

The most famous of their children—and doubtless the author of the gravestone inscription—was Massachusetts Chief Justice Samuel Sewall, keeper of America's most famous diary, notorious for his role in the Salem witch trials, and celebrated for his subsequent apology. Judge Sewall was a pioneer abolitionist and a friend to the Indians. He was surely also the first Sewall to view the future site of Bath, arriving on the

Colonel Dummer Sewall, 1737–1832, attributed to Benjamin Greenleaf.
MAINE MARITIME MUSEUM

Sagadahock—as the lower reach of the Kennebec (then spelled Kennebeck) River was then known—in August 1717 aboard HMS *Squirrel*. He was there as a member of the governor's party which met for three days with Indian leaders. Squirrel Point is yet named for the location where the HMS *Squirrel* briefly grounded.[11]

Henry's son John was a farmer. Of John's seven surviving children, two, Nicholas and Samuel, moved to York in the south of the Province of Maine. Three of Samuel's fourteen children—Joseph, Dummer, and Henry—would settle in Georgetown along the Sagadahock at "the Reach," on land that would lie in the future town of Bath. Another son, David, later judge of the District Court for Maine, was a member of the legal team that secured disputed land titles in Georgetown, including those to his brothers' properties.[12] Another son, Samuel, built an innovative bridge at York and the Charlestown Bridge at Boston. He was also a skilled cabinetmaker, and one of his high-boys is in the collection of the Maine State Museum, another at the Saywood-Wheeler House in York.

Son Dummer, truly a man for all seasons, was a rare piece of work and would embellish any family tree. Enlisting in the Provincial Army at age nineteen, he participated in the epic capture of the great French fort of Louisbourg at Cape Breton in 1758. As a lieutenant he fought under General Amherst in 1759, then under General Wolfe at the climactic Battle of Quebec, when, on the Plains of Abraham, Britain wrested Canada from France. In 1760 Dummer married Mary Dunning, the "hand-somest girl" in York.

In 1761 Dummer and brother Henry bought land at the Reach, and in 1762 Dummer built a cabin on what would become High Street, Bath. Dummer became the little community's driving force, and, among other good deeds, played a principal role in establishing the school system and a church.

In 1773 Dummer was one of six signers of a letter supporting Boston patriots after the Boston Tea Party. At the outbreak of the Revolution, Dummer, selected as a committee of one, backed up by fifty armed men, convinced a gang of men hewing masts for the Royal Navy to cease and desist. During the war Dummer served as Maine's muster master with the rank of lieutenant colonel.

In 1781, when Bath was set off from Georgetown, it was Dummer, fittingly, who named the town which he had done so much to create. In 1787 he was a delegate to the convention in Boston that ratified the federal constitution. Other civic activities included, but were not limited to, being a special justice; a senator from Lincoln County; an overseer, trustee, and treasurer of Bowdoin College; and the first postmaster of Bath.

Dummer died in 1832 at age ninety-five. He left the 130-acre homestead, a mahogany table worth $1.50, a spinning wheel worth $1.50, a large maple chest and an old warming pan, each worth $.25, one yoke of six-foot (girth of each) oxen, five cows, twenty-five sheep, and one wig (hair), no value. The estate was valued at $1,128.70. He also left six of his ten children. His wife Mary had died nine years earlier.[13] His High Street house is still in the family.

Their situation attracts attention

In what was basically an agrarian society, most of the sons of farmers had either to seek new lands to settle, join a profession or trade, or go to sea, since subdividing the family homestead was usually not economically feasible. In 1753 Dummer and Henry Sewall, of York, purchased from Nathaniel Harmon, also of York, the so-called York Lot along the Kennebec at Long Reach, for their brother Joseph. In 1761 Henry and Dummer bought two adjoining properties north of the York Lot for their own two farms. All of the properties had river frontage.[14]

Presumably the Sewall brothers bought these tracts because others from York, most notably Captain Nathaniel Donnell, having secured titles, were then settling at Long Reach. Surely it was not because of prime agricultural soil, of which the area had none. Lying below an upland spine, running north and south parallel with Long Reach, however, was a broad plateau with the proper declivity for launching ships—the angle at the Sewall riverfront was in fact a little too flat—adjacent to deep, sheltered, ice-free water. The lots were heavily wooded with good timber. While there is no record that the brothers foresaw the prospects of extensive shipbuilding, it certainly cannot be ruled out.

The practice at the time was to build ships at almost any location where a set of ways could possibly be constructed handy to a good timber supply, rather than to transport timber to a consolidated shipbuilding center. Indeed, ships were often bull-headedly built at sites far from ideal—launching ways at upriver Pittston were constructed with bed logs of uneven length, so as to heel the launching vessel on its side so that it might reach deep water before it righted.

In 1789 Dummer was selected to travel to the Sandy River settlements, west of the upper Kennebec Valley, to make an inventory of settlers' lots for the resolution of claims by the Commonwealth. As part of the deal, Dummer and two associates bought the remaining unclaimed lots in the township—which would become Farmington in 1794—for £400.[15] Apparently Dummer also then received title to 8,000 acres which he already owned in neighboring Chester (present-day Chesterville) and where his son Dummer and several other Sewalls—most notably the famous missionary Jotham Sewall, who delivered an estimated 12,500 sermons—had settled in the early 1780s.[16] Dummer thereby came into possession of a certain lot in Farmington which, as the residence of his son Joseph, would later be known as the Sewall Farm.

Joseph, born in 1770, was a carpenter before becoming active in business and "maritime affairs." He was said to have been a man of "magisterial prominence," and a "gentleman of the old school, of strong personality and integrity of character." About 1804 he moved downriver to Popham (then called Hunnewell's Beach), where he built a large white house known as the White House (houses painted white being uncommon at the time). A year after the move, his wife Lydia died following the birth of a daughter. Son William, then about eight, went to live at his grandfather Dummer's farm at Bath, where he would remain.

In 1806 Joseph married Hannah Shaw, a daughter of Major Joshua Shaw, who fought at Quebec and in the Revolution, and commenced a second family. After Joseph suffered severe financial loss during the War of 1812, Dummer gave him a life tenancy of the Farmington property, and in April 1816 Joseph contracted with one Nathan Backus to "convey in his stage coach the family of said Sewall consisting of the 3 grown females and 3 children together with 250 lbs. weight of baggage" from Hallowell to Farmington for nine dollars. There, Joseph cleared the land, built buildings, and farmed—all very much easier to describe than to do![17]

Hannah died in 1830. Joseph's third wife, Catherine Shaw, was Hannah's younger sister. When they married, Catherine was thirty-five and Joseph was sixty-nine. They had one daughter and two sons. Joseph had twelve children altogether. His eldest son, Joseph, a lawyer and Civil War general, became adjutant general of Maine and customs collector of the Port of Bath. His second son, William Dunning Sewall, would be the first of the Sewall shipbulders. A son by his second wife, George Popham Sewall, a lawyer and prominent public figure, founded a distinguished branch of the family at Old Town, Maine.[18] Although rich in children, Joseph did not prosper at farming, and, afflicted with palsy and poverty, suffered a long and difficult descent to his demise. Catherine, who was six years younger than her stepson William Dunning Sewall, wrote to him in May 1846 on her husband's behalf:

His health he wishes to say to you is declining, although he does not suffer much pain yet the shaking of his left side produces a degree of nervous irritability and depression of spirits at times almost insupportable. . . . It will . . . be a great alleviation to his feelings to have his children visit him and to hear from old friends, for he has lost none of his parental or social feelings.

In February 1851 Catherine wrote William that she had had to read a much welcomed letter from him three times to Joseph, and that she supposed that in his imagination Joseph was helping William "contriving and assembling" the second floor then being added to William's Bath house, which house Joseph had once helped to frame. Despite two comforters, a heavy woolen quilt, and maple fires around the clock, they could not keep the old man warm.

On April 3 of that year Catherine wrote that Joseph rejoiced at the news that his grandson, William's son William, who had joined the Gold Rush, had returned from California. Joseph, she wrote, would be very much gratified to receive a letter from his grandson describing California and the mines.

Joseph died that November. A document pertaining to his estate—son William was the executor—from the Lincoln County judge of probate (Sagadahoc County was not created from Lincoln County until 1854) listed seventy-seven claimants, with debts totaling $26,536.12—a huge sum. The net assets after the sale of real estate—it is unclear what property this was—were $5,937.07, to be distributed among the creditors "in proportion to the sums unto them respectively due and owing. . . ."[19]

William, along with his half-siblings George and Mercy—Mercy had married into the prominent Cony family of Augusta—had helped support the Farmington household while Joseph was alive. After his father's death, however, William's assistance apparently ended, he and Catherine evidently having had a falling out. What modest amounts he later sent went by way of George Popham, as did Catherine's letters of thanks to him. A letter from George to William in November 1856, in which George enumerated the very liberal sums that he had sent to Farmington over the previous couple of years, described dire conditions on the farm:

A sense of duty requires me to suggest to you that you ought to do something to aid those three small children of our father at Farmington. They are poor, very poor. The oldest [boy], about 12, has worked away from his mother some 2 or 3 miles all summer for his board and scanty clothing and the other two are destitute of winter clothes. . . . The farm has run out and yields a meager support. The winter storms whistle through the old house and during the storms of last winter those two small boys did all the work, taking care of fires, etc. Would this not be hard if your children or mine were compelled to do it? I have given her the use of the farm as it was necessary to save her children from the poor house and the support, if given, would by law fall on you & me. At any rate the disgrace would come upon us of family pauperism. . . . I see not why the obligation falls not on you as well as on me to aid them. . . . If I don't hear from you I shall have to trouble you again . . . for they must not starve nor be helped by the town. . . . Their situation attracts attention at Farmington.

In another letter to William, year unknown, George apologized for troubling William for "a small sum" for the suffering children who "must have a little pittance in order to get through the winter." In January 1859 Catherine wrote George asking him to thank William for his "handsome New Year's gift" of ten dollars. She also wrote that she had never before known what it was like to go without bread. The boys had worked hard and had raised 106 bushels of corn, forty bushels of oats, and five and a half of wheat, but the potatoes had all rotted, and the hay crop was but half of the usual, so she had to sell a good cow. And so on. Her sons Bradford and Arthur—William's half brothers, of course—were then fifteen and twelve years old respectively.

In November 1872, a year after Catherine had died, George Popham wrote William once again to inquire whether he could "afford" to send to Bradford, either by way of George or directly, as he pleased, "a little assistance," as Bradford was discouraged. Bradford had been working very hard on the farm, had bought out with his own money the shares of several half-siblings—brother Arthur had gone to live in the West—and George had been helping him as much as he was able to. In 1871 Bradford had only put in eleven tons of hay and had had to sell his stock.

We don't know if William answered the call or not, but he certainly could have afforded to. In any event, Bradford remained on the farm. A clever mechanic, he won several farm-related patents. Like his father, he later suffered "palsy," and ended up living in Iowa with Arthur. Arthur, a contractor, had built the largest part of the town of Dysart, Iowa, and served as its first mayor. The Sewall Farm passed to him, and in 1917—he would die in 1922—he was said to be keeping it for sentimental reasons, rather than for profit.

There was a strange fascination about that place

When, in 1919, Arthur Staples recalled the shipbuilding and ship-owning Bath of his boyhood, those memories were of a time and place far more distant than the passage of years would indicate:

> Boys of Bath used to infest . . . the ships as they lay at the wharves making ready for sailing off to sea, never to return. We swarmed over them, down in the holds, in the dark places along the keelson; between decks where the ship smelled of tarred rope and of the hard-pine; thru the forecastle and the after-cabins, here and there as we willed provided we kept out of the way; and often we were given a chance to take a turn on the huge capstan-bars and help a crew warp up a main yard to the music of a chantey.[20]

The great test of a Bath boy's courage was to "cap" the main truck, placing one's cap on the gilded lignum vitae ball atop the mainmast of a newly rigged ship. Staples could hardly recognize either the daring boy he once had been, or the city of Bath, in that seemingly faraway time.

Bath's great epoch of wooden shipbuilding rose and fell within about a hundred years. In the late 1760s, there being no market for ship timber, Dummer Sewall cut and hauled out the best hardwood on his Long Reach farm for sixty-two cents a cord, to be loaded aboard a coasting vessel. Quite possibly it was bound for Boston as firewood, there to go up in smoke.

The early importance of transport by water cannot be overstated—sailing a cargo of cordwood to Boston was, in some respects, less complicated than transporting a single woman by land. In 1771 the Reverend Winter traded a horse in Boston for a small two-wheeled chaise to carry his fatigued wife home to Long Reach. Two Negro axemen went before them, and at obstructions the vehicle had to be taken apart. Once home, Mr. Winter was obliged to sell his prize, it having been deemed by his flock as too ostentatious a possession for a simple shepherd of the Lord.[21]

Jonathan Hyde, a Connecticut trader, wisely chose to make the trip to Long Reach by coasting vessel:

In 1792, all below Bath on the river and seaboard, the islands were all covered with trees. Seguin was like a dark forest standing high in the ocean. . . . [One] could see a good many single-deck schooners and sloops passing up and down, deeply loaded with lumber, all of which, on coming in from the sea, had a very romantic appearance. Bath did not appear much like a village; a few stores and a very few houses were near the river, and a few houses were scattered along on the country road which is now High Street . . . it was chiefly pasture where the city now is, considerably covered with trees and bushes. . . .

The inhabitants at and near Bath were generally industrious, rather rough in their manners, though kind, civil, and hospitable, fond of getting together and having a row; a great proportion would work hard through the day and be drunk at night; a few were reputable, some were very pious. The females were civil to strangers; were kind and somewhat agreeable; not generally very handsome and not overstocked with neatness; a few were quite accomplished; such were generally from other parts. There were but few schools and little preaching, mostly Methodist.[22]

In the late 1700s Wiscasset, on the Sheepscot River to the east, was the region's booming seaport, its great houses (where, it is still said in outlying towns, the residents "fart through silk") reflecting its trading ties to London. Much of the hewn pine timber carried away by its ships was rafted from the Kennebec. Rather than Long Reach, the New Meadows River to the west was then the site of shipbuilding, yet within the lifetimes of persons then alive, Bath would become the world's greatest wooden shipbuilding center.

Nearly all of the eighty-odd vessels launched at Bath from 1780 to 1800 were locally owned, thus beginning the flow of wealth into the town and establishing the tradition of locally owned and family-owned fleets.[23] Bath, however, lacked the hinterland that was necessary for extensive development as a mercantile port, and, while shipbuilding increased, its vessels engaged in more distant trades. In 1854, often considered the high-water mark of American maritime enterprise, Bath launched 33,222 tons of shipping. According to historian Henry Owen, "Among American ports, none excelled Bath either in the quality of its ships or the ability of its ship owners and shipmasters." Bath also featured streets of fine homes, many occupied by people of culture and refinement.[24]

In 1875 the tonnage owned by the district of Bath was exceeded only by that of New York, Philadelphia, Boston, and San Francisco, and included 76 ships, 26 barks, 10 brigs, and 112 schooners.[25] (And if truth be known, the actual figure was probably considerably greater, as many Bathites were said to have put their ownership in the names of out-of-state relatives, to avoid local property taxes.)[26]

Bath became a "city"—as opposed to a "town"—in 1847, and in 1850 its population was about 8,000. After a decline in the 1860s, the population rose to 8,700 by 1890. Per capita, Bath surely contained an inordinate number of independent and strong-minded individuals, shipbuilders and captains in particular. Socially, Bath remained a small town, and, unlike Maine's largely French-Canadian mill towns, remained essentially Yankee, despite an influx of shipwrights from the Maritimes. As with any socially inbred community, but perhaps even more so, since Bath never did anything by halves, Bathites knew all the family ties and tensions.

A journalist from the nearby textile-weaving city of Lewiston, visiting Bath in 1882, observed:

> Bath is essentially marine. The current of life flows sluggishly in its commercial streets. There are no screeching whistles or clanging bells to awake one in the morning. There is no whirring of machinery, or none of the steady rattling of wagons over pavements which gives noisy animation and bustle to other towns. . . . Bath has been given over to the sea. . . . To a stranger, who might spend a forenoon among the quiet stores . . . the city would seem to be taking a quiet nap; but this misapprehension is speedily removed the moment he nears the North End and his ears catch the first cheery clicking of the ship-yards; and the rapping and chafing and pounding of the thousands of adzes and mallets and broad-axes and planes and hammers, with the hissing and steaming of the ship-yard mills, and the buzzing of their saws, and the dinging of the blacksmiths' shops,—as all these and many other conflicting sounds swell into a roar about his ears, and he stands under the shadows of the mighty ribs of oak, his ideas suffer a transformation; it grows upon him that Bath is one of the busiest of busy places. . . . [27]

There were at the time twenty-four vessels on the stocks, and in that boom year Bath would launch over seventy vessels, including eight ships, three steam auxiliary barks, nine schooners, thirty-two three-masted schooners, and three four-masted schooners, the construction of large coasting schooners more than taking up the slack created by the decline of the deepwater square-rigger.

In 1882 the transactions of Bath's shipbuilding interests with the great London banking house of Baring Brothers was said to rank third in America, even ahead of Boston and Baltimore.[28]

In 1894 someone calculated that from 1781 through 1892 Bath had launched a vessel every ten days.[29] Up to 1910, within Bath itself, there were built at least 604 full-rigged ships, 147 barks, 215 brigs, 819 schooners, as well as assorted sloops, steamers, and barges. Other communities within the Bath custom district, in total, built roughly as many vessels in number, although Bath led by far in tonnage.

Shipbuilding was a boom and bust business, boom years including 1854, 1877, 1882, 1890, and 1899, whereas busted years included 1861, 1878, 1887, 1893, and 1910—in 1910, the year after the launching of the immense six-masted schooner *Wyoming*, the largest wooden merchant vessel ever built, Bath built but one wooden craft, a fifteen-ton motor boat. It is worth noting that *Wyoming*'s gross tonnage of 3,730—gross (and net) tonnage is a measure of capacity—was one ton greater than that of the entire fleet of Bath's Jonathan Davis family of 1785–1819, which consisted of twenty-one vessels in all—eight ships, five brigs, one snow (a brig variation), four schooners, and two sloops.[30]

Despite the spectacular bust of 1910, shipbuilding was far from finished at Bath, although wooden shipbuilding was about done, and the string of old yards, where once, in the morning before sunrise, carpenters wended their way, and where, with first light, "the day-long chorus of the strokes of the broad axes and the thumps of the mauls would be heard," were now empty and overgrown with grass.

Bath Iron Works today builds guided missile destroyers of a technological complexity that is almost unimaginable, but the culture of the community is no longer "essentially marine," and small boys do not play on the river and infest the shipyard. Yet Bath remains the the "City of Ships." In 1914 Henry Merryman, a ship carpenter who took his first job in a Topsham shipyard in 1847 and moved to the Sewall yard at Bath in 1851, recalled:

> I remember one winter I went up to Pittston and worked on a brig, but as soon as she was finished I was back to Bath again. There was a strange fascination about that place and ship carpenters all liked to get there to work.[31]

So happily connected with you in the business of life

In 1859, when William Dunning Sewall begrudgingly sent some small relief to his suffering half-siblings in Farmington, he was among the wealthiest of Mainers. And as pictured in a portrait—tight-lipped and steely eyed—he looks the very image of a miserly, no-nonsense Dickensian skinflint. His letters, however, if somewhat pedestrian, paint him as an affectionate father on good terms with his children, in no way overbearing or mean-spirited.

As a leading citizen of Bath, William D. Sewall—as he has been designated by the family—held various respectable business and civic positions, including those of state representative, state senator, banker, and railroad director. He was an active member of the Maine Historical Society and a founder of the Bath Old Ladies' Home. He was well-read, widely traveled, and an eager extemporaneous speaker. In one respect, however, William was something of a radical, leaving the Congregational Church—the church of the New England establishment—to help found Bath's Swedenborgian, or Church of the New Jerusalem, to which he gave much money and support.[32]

As a shrewd businessman, William was likely a good judge of character, and wise to a swindle—perhaps he suspected that his young stepmother, Catherine, exaggerated her financial difficulties. And one might well surmise that William's keen interest in making and keeping money—a sentiment fully instilled in his two sons—may have been fired by his father's prolonged state of poverty and large debt, a shameful fate to be avoided at almost all costs. One might also wonder if William's relationship with his father, and with his father's later children, was colored by his having been sent away from his family when so young.

In 1821, when William D.—as we will call him when necessary to differentiate him from subsequent William D.s—was twenty-four and married Rachel Trufant, he was still living at his Grandfather Dummer's farm, which he had been managing for some time and would continue doing so for several more years. Soon after, he built a small house across High Street from Dummer's house. Several years later he "began trade" with Front Street storekeeper Freeman Clark, who had come to Bath from Massachusetts in 1807. In 1827 a "co-partnership" between the two was announce, under the name Clark & Sewall, offering textiles; barreled pork, beef, and mackerel; butter; cheese; West India goods; groceries, feathers; seine twine, and so forth.[33]

While storekeeping might today seem an odd choice of career for an ambitious young man, in the early 1800s storekeepers, or merchants, were key drivers of the economy. Coastal stores have been called the "parents of ships," since many vessels were built by or for storekeepers as an adjunct to their business. Vessels carried local produce taken in trade to Boston or the West Indies, returning with stock-in-trade and "West India goods"—sugar, molasses, and rum. (In similar vein, upcountry storekeepers early organized drives of cattle to Boston's Brighton Market as a means of liquidating livestock taken in trade.)

About 1830 William bought the York Lot, by then belonging to two maiden ladies in York. Lying along the southern boundary of his grandfather's farm, the York Lot was covered with excellent ship timber. This purchase put William on the path toward "the great business of his life, shipbuilding." Initially, William's involvement consisted of selling timber to his shipbuilding neighbors, and dealing in timber would long remain an important business for the Sewalls.

When Clark & Sewall commenced to build ships, the timber came from William's land, and the ships were built on William's land. Workers were paid with "store credit," allowing the partners to recoup as much of the wages as possible. This arrangement, common among shipbuilders and other industrialists, was especially advantageous

A detail from the posthumous portrait of William Dunning Sewall painted (along with a portrait of his wife, Rachel Allen Trufant, 1795-1876) by Philip Spencer Harris to the order of Arthur Sewall. It is evident that Harris based this likeness on the photograph of Sewall. In June 1878, Harris wrote Arthur from his Brooklyn studio that "The portraits have been brought to a point from which their completion can be best effected under the eyes of intimate friends. . . . The pictures and frames will be boxed & sent on Saturday. . . . I shall . . . reach Bath Wednesday. . . ." Harris, 1824–84, a Massachusetts native, had lived in Bath painting portraits of local notables in the 1850s before moving on to fame and much greater fortune in New York.
MAINE MARITIME MUSEUM

William Dunning Sewall, 1797–1877
MAINE MARITIME MUSEUM

given the tempting opportunity to mark prices up, a law that tied debtors' custom to the store to which they owed money, and the very generous repayment terms offered by Boston wholesalers.

Although neither Clark nor Sewall had evidently ever worked in a shipyard, there were ample opportunities to have absorbed sufficient knowledge to set up as "ship-builders," the hiring of a capable master builder to take charge of the actual construction being a key decision. Setting up a shipyard itself required but little capital.

In a common Down East method of financing the building of a vessel, subcontrac-

Freeman Clark, 1795–1861
MAINE MARITIME MUSEUM

tors and vendors accepted shares in the vessel as payment for services, or for the privilege of supplying goods or material. Indeed, it was humorously suggested that anyone—especially a store owner—could build a ship by such arrangements. Clark & Sewall, however, preferred to hold their ships themselves, along with members of a small group of well-off local investors, invariably including Thomas M. Reed of Phippsburg. Freeman Clark and William usually held an eighth, sometimes a quarter, apiece. The captain was commonly in for an eighth as well. This suggests that the principals had the necessary means, that the ships were being built economically, and that the ships were making money.

The identity of the first vessels in the original Sewall fleet is not certain, although the 1823 brig *Diana,* the 1824 brig *Orbit,* and the 1825 brig *Lewis* have long headed the list. The first vessel unquestionably built by Clark & Sewall was the brig *Dummer* of 1826, while the first vessel for which William was the registered owner was the schooner *Emulous* of 1829, a Boston–Bath packet, which would be a logical vessel for storekeepers to build. Confusion may stem from the fact that Benjamin Robinson was master builder not only for the three early brigs—in which Sewalls possibly only held shares—but also for the first seven vessels clearly of the Clark & Sewall fleet.

From 1833 to 1854 the firm would build another seventeen ships, one brig, and one bark; Stephen Larrabee and Benjamin Small were the principal master builders during this period.

A naive "port painting" of the Clark & Sewall cotton ship Ville De Paris *with tanbarked sails. Built in 1837, measuring 537 tons, she is shown leaving Havre. The French artist has taken the liberty of redesigning Old Glory to suit his own taste.* PATTEN FREE LIBRARY

In 1836 Clark and Sewall sold the store business to devote their full attention to building and managing ships. After Clark's death in 1861, the management of the surviving Clark & Sewall vessels was handled by E. & A. Sewall, the partnership formed in 1854 by William's sons Edward and Arthur, who also took over shipbuilding at the yard, building and managing their own fleet.

Freeman Clark, the senior partner in the Clark & Sewall firm, is the largely forgotten man in this saga. Glimpses of him can be gleaned from letters to William and to captains—at least from those in which his seemingly neat but deceptively illegible handwriting can be deciphered. In December 1845 he jotted down notes for what reads almost like a sermon regarding the evils of intemperance—alcoholism being a widespread social ill closely linked to the ready supply of cheap rum available in stores large and small:

> In social visits, decline [treats of rum] as far as possible, avoid them entirely in retail stores . . . let no one slip amidst the whelming tides of intemperance! Let us do what we can to promote virtue to discourage vice. Let your habit of thought be cultivated & encouraged. Let the idle become industrious. Let the time spent in the bowling alley . . . or idled away in . . . the bar of some hotel or grog shop be devoted to reflection.

If a business partnership can be compared to a marriage, Freeman Clark and William Sewall were evidently a very congenial couple. On December 2, 1859, Freeman wrote William from Boston:

> We had a pleasant Thanksgiving, it being over 50 years since I spent one in Mass., in fact I never have since I left the state when 13 years old. And now to look back upon over half a century the changes are really very great. I then was a boy and now am a man, a father, & even a grandfather. And I by no means forget that more than over half of that span has been so happily connected with you in the business of life.

1. Mark W. Hennessy, *The Sewall Ships of Steel* (Augusta, ME: Kennebec Journal Press, 1937).

2. Letter written to Mark Hennessy, January 24, 1938.

3. Cleveland Preble's bill for "joining" the ship was $3,500.

4. Should be E. & A. Sewall & Co.—a forgivable error.

5. Letter dated February. 11, 1938, from Edward E. Briry to Mark Hennessy, Hennessy Collection, MS-53, Maine Maritime Museum library.

6. Maine, Vol. 19, pp. 266–67,R. G. Dun Collection, Baker Library Historical Collections, Harvard Business School.

7. The November 6, 1885, Bangor *Industrial Journal* reported that it was a frequent practice for Bath ship owners to place vessel property in the name of out-of-state relatives to avoid taxes. This sometimes led to exposure when a creditor of the relative attempted to attach the vessel property. The registrations of the Sewalls' steel ships printed in Mark Hennessy's *Sewall Ships of Steel* are inaccurate and deceptive, and, not surprisingly, have led historians, such as William F. Fairburn, astray.

8. Arthur G. Staples, *Just Talks on Common Themes* (Lewiston ME: Lewiston Journal Publishing Co., 1919), p. 157.

9. There is a vast literature concerning early activities of Europeans in Maine waters. A very good synopsis is found in the opening chapters of William Avery Baker's *A Maritime History of Bath, Maine, and the Kennebec River Region,* vol. I (Bath, ME: Marine Research Society of Bath, 1973).

10. Samuel Eliot Morison, *The Maritime History of Massachusetts, 1783–1860* (Boston: Houghton Mifflin Co., 1921), pp. 21–22.

11. Henry Wilson Owen, *The Edward Clarence Plummer History of Bath, Maine* (Bath, ME: Bath Area Bicentennial Committee, 1976), p. 59.

12. The vanquished land-grabber was the Kennebec Proprietor Dr. Sylvester Gardiner. By one account—Arthur Sewall's 1896 campaign biography—three lineal descendants of Henry became chief justices of Massachusetts, and two others were judges of the "highest court of the province and commonwealth." A son of colonial attorney general Jonathan Sewall, a great-grandson of Henry and a royalist, became chief justice of Quebec.

13. Sewall Family Papers MS22-1-1. See also monograph *The Sewall Genealogy* by Rev. Charles N. Sinnett, Fertile, Minnesota, at Maine State Library; Rev. N. H. Chamberlain, *Samuel Sewall and the World He Lived In* (Boston: De Wolfe, Fiske & Co., 1897); Ola Elizabeth Winslow, *Samuel Sewall of Boston* (New York: The Macmillan Co., 1964); Richard Francis, *Judge Sewall's*

Apology (New York: Fourth Estate, 2005).

14. Owen, *Plummer History of Bath*, pp. 92–93.

15. "History of the Sewall Family," *Lewiston Journal Illustrated Magazine*, September 23, 1917. Richard P. Mallett, *The Early Years of Farmington, 1781–1860* (Wilton, ME, 1994), pp. 6–7.

16. Ben Butler, *Father Sewall and His Zion's Hill Neighborhood* (Farmington, ME: Farmington Historical Society, 1967).

17. *Lewiston Journal Illustrated Magazine*, September 23, 1917.

18. Two other Maine Sewall lines were descended from Dummer's brother Henry. Henry's son, the Reverend Samuel Sewall, settled on Wilson's Stream, south of Farmington. His son Levi moved to Island Falls, then a frontier area. His son William W. Sewall was Teddy Roosevelt's wilderness guide, mentor, and companion in the West. Samuel's son Deacon Rufus founded the Wiscasset line.

19. Sewall Family Papers, 547/19.

20. Staples, *Just Talks on Common Themes*, pp. 211–12.

21. Parker McCobb Reed, *History of Bath and Environs* (Portland, ME: Lakeside Press, 1894), p. 479.

22. Owen, *Plummer History of Bath*, p. 101.

23. Reed, *History of Bath*, pp. 75–76.

24. Owen, *Plummer History of Bath*, p. 136.

25. Owen, *Plummer History of Bath*, p. 201.

26. *American Sentinel*, June 13, 1889.

27. *Industrial Journal*, November 6, 1885.

28. *Industrial Journal*, August 11, 1882.

29. *Industrial Journal*, July 13, 1894.

30. Owen, *Plummer History of Bath*, p. 467.

31. *Bath Daily Times*, May 21, 1914.

32. Disciples of Swedenborg were admonished to shun evil and to perform "good actions" in life, but of course these were judgment calls. Emanuel Swedenborg, 1688–1772, was a Swedish scientist, philosopher, and mystic. His scientific work alone, which covered many fields, would have made him a figure of historical renown. In middle age he proclaimed himself to have been chosen as the spokesman of the Lord, who communicated with him directly. Beginning in 1847 he wrote voluminously on Scriptural interpretation, and his thinking influenced that of Coleridge, Robert and Elizabeth Browning, Henry Ward Beecher, and Thomas Carlyle. Although Swedenborg did no preaching and made no attempt to found a sect, believing that the New Church was open to members of all churches, his followers formed the New Jerusalem Church based on his writings.

33. Baker, *A Maritime History of Bath*, vol. I, p. 296.

PART TWO

We learn of "family fleets" of Bath besides the Sewalls', something of the building and outfitting of ships at Bath, and also something of Bath captains. We get a taste of trading to the West Indies, which laid the foundation for Maine and New England shipping. This was succeeded by the large and profitable carriage of cotton from southern ports to Britain and Europe, which in turn was supplemented by the carriage of Irish, British, and European emigrants on the cotton ships' westward passages.

All four bloomed in concert

When Bath historian Parker Reed wrote in regard to his brother Thomas's long association with Clark & Sewall, "Thomas M. Reed built largely . . . with this firm," by "built" he meant "invested." As Bath historian Henry Owen pointed out, in the heyday of the sailing ship, the term "shipbuilder" might have been applied to every businessman in Bath who had invested in her ships. He calculated that a complete list of Bath "shipbuilders" would likely number upwards of 300 individuals, firms, or corporations, which could then be boiled down to perhaps 100 firms and individuals who were of significant historical importance to Bath shipbuilding.

Even shipbuilders who actually were practical shipbuilders commonly engaged a master builder, or "master mechanic," to oversee the construction itself. It was usually, but by no means always, the master builder who signed the customhouse certificate after a completed vessel was officially measured.

Bath's four most important family-built and -managed deepwater fleets were those of the McLellans, the Pattens, the Houghtons, and the Sewalls. All four bloomed in concert with the great flowering of the American merchant marine in the early decades of the nineteenth century. The McLellan fleet began with a store kept by James McLellan, who moved into shipbuilding in 1810. By 1864, when the McLellans closed up business, they had built or managed at least fifty-one vessels—ships, barks, brigs, and schooners. Their square-riggers were most heavily employed in the cotton trade.[1] Winthrop Farrin was their principal master builder.

Deacon Levi Houghton arrived at Bath from Boston in 1802 at age nineteen and began business with a one-room store. By 1819 the size of Levi's business was such that he began building vessels for his own account in his own yard. Eighteen vessels were built under his instigation. As the shipping business grew, the store business was given up, save for the importing of salt, much of which Bath builders used to pack the frames of ships as a preservative. Under the management of Levi's four sons, the fleet would number forty-four vessels, almost all ships, employed in the cotton, guano, and grain trades. A father and son named Wildes successively served as master builders. The firm lasted until World War I.

When Captain John Patten died at age ninety-seven in 1887 he may no longer have been Bath's wealthiest citizen, but he surely remained its most beloved. Captain J. H. Drew recalled that when, as a boy, he joined a Patten ship, Captain John helped him to carry his sea chest aboard—it would be difficult to imagine William D. or Arthur Sewall doing this. Although John did not go to sea until age twenty, in short order he was captured by the French, the British, and then twice by American privateers. About 1815 John joined his brother George shipbuilding at Topsham; in 1820 they moved to Bath. Captain John commanded each new vessel in turn.

In 1830 Captain John retired from the sea to concentrate, with George, on the business of the yard and the fleet. G. F. & J. Patten built one or two vessels a year, initially concentrating on the West Indies and cotton trades, then entering the California and other long-distance trades. After the friendly dissolution of their partnership in 1860, both brothers continued to build ships separately, each launching his last in 1869. All told, the Pattens produced fifty-eight ships, with but a handful credited to master builders other than George, John, or the firm.

When the Pattens moved their shipbuilding operations to Bath they were the first builders to pay their workers in cash, rather than in store credit redeemable only at a shipyard or a confederate store, thus giving their workers a considerable advantage in buying power. Although it took many years, the old system of "store credit" was eventually ended at all yards.[2]

Three more famous fleets, contemporary to the Sewalls, hailed from Thomaston, Maine's second great shipbuilding and ship-owning center. (There were, of course, other fleets from other ports, but none surpassed those of Bath and Thomaston.)

Edward O'Brien, of Scotch-Irish descent, a practical shipbuilder, began building for his own account at Thomaston in 1827, eventually building over one hundred vessels. Unlike nearly every other Maine shipbuilder/owner, O'Brien sold no shares in his vessels and owned his fleet in its entirety, being the country's largest individual ship owner. He often owned the cargoes as well. O'Brien's ships were full-modeled, no-nonsense bulk carriers, and many were employed in the guano trade.

After O'Brien's death in 1882, his invalid son Edward inherited the fleet. The 2,157-ton ship *Edward O'Brien*—the third ship of that name—which was on the stocks at the time of the old man's death, was the last ship built for the fleet.

Samuel B. Watts, who at one point was a partner with Edward O'Brien in a general store and in shipbuilding, was nineteen years younger than O'Brien. He built his first vessel for his own account in 1862, and thereafter built sixteen big square-riggers before shifting to schooners. Captain Alfred Watts, Sam's brother, was the longtime master builder. Watts's ships were finer-modeled and loftier-rigged than were O'Brien's.

The premier fleet of post–Civil War American square-riggers was that of Chapman & Flint, a firm which began as a store in Damariscotta, expanding into shipbuilding and ship-owning at Thomaston in 1842. Isaac Chapman and Benjamin Flint were brothers—Benjamin was raised by an uncle and took his name. In 1858 they moved to New York, the better to manage their fleet. After 1853 their shipbuilding was overseen by John McDonald, who had been a foreman for clipper builder Donald McKay at Boston. In 1867, after the Knox & Lincoln Railroad was routed through the Thomaston yard, McDonald moved his operations to Bath. In 1880 Chapman and Flint separated the management of their vessels, picking the names of ships from a hat. John McDonald continued to build ships of unsurpassed quality for Flint & Co.

On a hot day, it was enough to kill a man

While the Sewall Family Papers are a treasure-trove of information concerning certain aspects of shipbuilding in the early 1800s, they do not contain firsthand accounts. For these, we must look elsewhere.

In 1894 historian Parker Reed wrote of earlier days of Bath shipbuilding, evidently referring to the late 1700s and early 1800s:

> The timbers, planks, and ceiling [inner planking] had all to be carried to place on the shoulders of the workmen instead of moved as at present by oxen or horse with a tackle. But the timbers were vastly larger than those now used for the same size vessel. Instead of sawed in the yard mill, the planks were sawed by whipsaw in the saw-pit. Less iron fastenings were in use and treenails ["trunnels"] were utilized for that purpose. These were made by hand with the broadaxe from pieces rifted from white oak blocks. This light work was mostly done during stormy days under cover. . . . The bolts and spikes were made by hand. The blacksmith would heat the end of a flat bar of iron, which he would split the length of a required bolt, cut off the pieces and shape the bolt on the anvil. Spikes were made in a similar manner. When bolts were to be fastened by nuts, the screw on the small end of the bolt would be made by hand, as likewise was the nut.

The history of the early use of half models for designing a vessel and determining the shapes of its timbers is murky, and indeed Reed stated that models were not then used. Framing the hull, he wrote, was begun amidships and filled in fore and aft, as "lined out" by the "master workman." Frame timbers were selected for their natural bend, hewn only on two sides, and frames were set up as much as two-and-one-half feet apart. The stern flared so much that the mizzenmast was stepped on the end of the keel. At the launching, the keel blocks were cut away from bow to stern, the reverse of the much safer method used later.

> The time was when at a launching a man would set astride the farther end of the bowsprit and when the vessel was sliding from the ways would call out the name that had been given her, at the same time breaking a bottle of rum over the bowsprit, first drinking from the bottle.[3]

In 1907 William Rogers, then the dean of Bath shipbuilders—over a fifty-five-year career he had launched 102 vessels—recalled:

> The first ship that I built was the *Arlington*. It was 600 tons, 123 ft. in length, 31 ft. beam, and about 21 ft. in depth [of hold]. The launching occurred October 14, 1847. . . . The *Arlington*, as was the case with all ships built 50 or 60 years ago, required about nine months for construction. . . . The frame was of oak and hackmatack from the forests of Maine and it had a hard[wood] bottom, composed of beech, birch, and maple, which the growth of this state provided.[4]

If exposed to moisture and air, beech, birch, and maple were very prone to rot, but when used where they were always wet, they lasted well and did not contain the acid of oak, which corroded iron fastenings. This shipbuilding practice was long followed at Bath, and much timber cut locally was delivered by water via "gondolas," as the indigenous sailing scows were called.

> The lower futtocks were of hardwood and the upper of oak and hackmatack.[5] The frame generally was what we called "picked up," that is, we gathered wood in lumber operations in various parts of the state and used those which we knew were best adapted for ships. Sometimes we would have sections waiting for a long time before they were needed, held over until just the right places for them were found. We used for the planking, ceiling, and beams southern pine, and usually the same for lower masts, although a good deal depended on what we had on hand from the Maine forests. Whenever any straight, sound [white pine] trunks were cut, which looked good for masts, we put them aside and kept them. Therefore, it frequently happened that we found sticks from the Maine forests just the right thing; but we had to count on the southern grown for the lower masts generally.[6]

Southern "hard," or "yellow," longleaf pine lower masts were usually "built" masts, assembled from sections banded together. The use of southern hard pine at Bath began about 1837 when William D. Sewall and his waterfront neighbor, George Patten, contracted for a shipment. The extraordinary old-growth yellow pine of the vast coastal forests of South Carolina, Georgia, and Florida—along with the white oak frame timber of Virginia and Maryland—would become the mainstay of New England shipbuilders. The Sewalls became shippers and dealers of hard pine.[7] Rogers continues:

Our spikes came from the mills in Massachusetts and we bought most of our iron in Boston, although we had several good iron stores in Bath and excellent workers in the metal also. It was principally Pennsylvania iron, but occasionally we got that which was rolled in Massachusetts mills, and, I suppose, came from abroad.

Labor was cheap in those days, compared to the wages paid today. For skilled workmen the average rate per diem was $1.25, although less experienced hands drew $1 and $1.10; and some of the more expert got as high as $1.50. The men usually worked from sunrise to sunset, and they kept at their undertaking very steadily. Today from $2 to $2.50 per day is paid, and the men work 8 hours in a day. . . . Everything was done by hand, and when timbers were too heavy for a gang of men a yoke of oxen was used. We had no electric hoists or steam cranes; the men and oxen pulled, hauled and struggled until they succeeded in getting things where they wanted them. Yet, we turned out ships that challenged the admiration of all nations.

According to ship carpenter Henry Merryman, who came to Bath from Topsham in 1851, at Topsham yards the work went from sun to sun, with two hours off at noon, but at Bath they worked sun to sun in the winter, but only ten hours in summer. This was one reason why Bath was a popular place to work.[8]

In 1907 Captain Sam Percy, of the electrified shipyard of Percy & Small, recalled that the broad axe was once "the most important tool in a ship carpenter's outfit. It was used on nearly every piece of timber that went into a vessel. . . . 'Beating out' hackmatack knees [was] a [particularly] tedious job. . . . Power borers are now beginning to make the holes which once were the test of a strong man's arms, for holes from 4 to 8 feet in depth put through solid hard pine and oak meant the expenditure of no little power."[9]

Indeed, while there are many accomplishments that our ancestors routinely performed which we today must stand in awe of, from mowing a farm by scythe to felling a forest by axe, surely none is more impressive than the hand-boring of the tens of thousands of holes—many located in very cramped quarters—required to fasten a large vessel. The tool used until 1855 or so was the half-turn (no crank) "bare-foot" (no guide screw) pod auger, which had to be started with a gouged hole and withdrawn to clear chips. Our ancestors must have been adept at producing a very sharp edge on their cutting tools.

On a cold December day in, 1895—with the country and the shipbuilding industry deep in a depression—several old-time ship carpenters were overheard conversing around the stove in a Bath store:

"There was a time when men got from $2.50 to $3 a day and some even more with all the work they could do. Now they get $1.25 or about that a day and have to hustle to get a job at that price. I tell you its no wonder Bath merchants say that business is dull . . . ."

A man in the corner, who was occupying a soap box and whittling shavings, remarked that Patrick Welch had told him that in the palmy days of shipbuilding he had earned some days as much as $12 boring holes [by piecework] in timber at ship yards.

"I don't doubt it a mite," remarked an individual in a leather jacket. "Pat Welch was a mighty smart borer and made good money, but he couldn't hold a candle to Bob Scott. He was the fastest borer that ever grew up in these parts. He used to take contracts to bore small schooners at about $100 and would average $8 or $10 a day. He used to take his auger and file it a certain way so that it took hold better than an average one and could turn work off a good deal faster than most men."

Another remarked that vessel boring was about the hardest work that a man could do, and as the men sat there discussing hard times and wishing for this, that, or something else, their fellow men were out on the cold timbers of some craft along the waterfront working to earn an honest dollar to keep their families well clothed and fed.[10]

About 1924, an old man who started working at General Berry's Georgetown ship-yard as a boy in 1850, recalled to an interviewer: "'Fastenin' off' was a tough job! Lifting all them heavy plank and borin' all them holes by hand and sheetin' all them trunnels home with a big heavy beetle! Now that was desp'rite. On a hot day, it was enough to kill a man."[11]

Fit for sea in a workmanlike manner

In a notebook kept by William D. Sewall in 1854—in that boom year, Bath launched thirty-one ships, two barks, five brigs, and a schooner—one finds brief contracts made to build the 1,099-ton ship *Holyhead*. The main agreement is that with Daniel Small to "build a new ship about 1,000 tons the present summer meaning to do all the car-pentry work excepting the spars . . . to do all the sawing with the exception of the plank. In fact to do all carpenter work and fit for sea in a workmanlike manner for nine dol-lars and seventy-five cents per ton government measure." Daniel Small was clearly responsible for hiring and paying the carpenters.[12] (William Sewall evidently signed the master carpenter's certificate, which may or may not be of any significance regard-ing his level of oversight.)

Likely Small was expected to cut the half model for a ship of the desired tonnage and form, from which the lines defining the shape of the hull were expanded and lofted full-size. Wooden patterns, called "moulds," for various parts of the ship's skeleton were "taken off" from the lofted lines. Moulds were taken into the woods to select appropriately proportioned timber, which was then hewn, or "beat out," with a broad-axe. Beginning in the 1850s it became common for frames of Virginia white oak to be "got out" by Maine contractors who loaded moulds, men, tools, camp supplies, and their oxen aboard a schooner and headed south to spend the winter getting out frames.[13]

An agreement with George Spear covered all the blacksmith work required for the hull, spars, rigging, and blocks (pulleys), excepting the deck nails, for one dollar and twenty-five cents per ton, "with a discount of six pence per ton if I use the patent blocks." It was agreed with Elbridge & Soule to "joiner" the new ship, i.e., do the finish carpentry "to the satisfaction of the owners," for two dollars and sixty-two cents a ton. James Patten agreed to furnish the iron. J. C. Tallman was to "grain & polish" the cabin, and do "all gilding and find [supply] material." And so on.[14]

The brevity of these contracts is remarkable. Obviously William knew these men and trusted their work, and they knew him and trusted him as well. Evidently few—if any—mechanics were hired by the shipyard, i.e., the "builder," as the ship was built entirely "by the "job" or "by the ton." In fact, the yard, or "builder," may not have hired many men beyond the yard teamster and watchman. This evidently had not always been the case with Clark & Sewall during the years when the store was operating, since historian Parker Reed wrote that workers then were "paid largely in goods."[15]

There were a great many aspects of building a ship to be dealt with beyond building the ship, foremost being the timely acquisition of the staggering amount of materials and supplies needed to build and outfit even a relatively plain and simple "cotton box."

Timber for the 715-ton ship *Adriatic*, launched by Clark & Sewall in 1850, was purchased from half a dozen local parties (including W. D. Sewall), much coming from Georgetown and Phippsburg, and "gondaliered" by scow or rafted to the yard by water. Knees and other timbers were delivered by the schooners *Hillsborough* (likely from the Maritimes) and *Peace*. Southern hard pine was ordered through Charles Buck of Boston. A good deal of timber was bought from neighboring shipbuilders, indicating a state of cooperation that benefited all—indeed, *Adriatic*'s lines were "drafted" in the loft of the Moses shipyard, which was made available for ten dollars. All timber and spars had to be inspected by a trusted surveyor, who, in this case, was spar-maker Andrew McFadden.

Adriatic's spars were all of local timber, her lower masts doubtless of white pine, being seventy-one feet by twenty-seven inches, sixty-nine feet by twenty-seven inches, and sixty-seven feet by twenty-two inches. They were towed to Bath from Portland, and thus possibly came from the Sebago region, or from Canada, Pennsylvania, or Michigan, delivered to Portland by the Atlantic & St. Lawrence Railroad.

Boss blacksmith Elliot Smith charged $834.17 for making ironwork, with materials supplied by the owners. The vitally important anchors and anchor chains, and also lesser chains and various rigging fittings, were imported from Liverpool by way of Boston aboard the ship *Sunbeam*, and carried to Bath by schooner—the story of smoky, dismal English chain-making villages is a fascinating subject unto itself.

Local iron foundries supplied numerous castings and forgings, including hawsepipes, deck irons, chocks, quarter blocks, bushings for chain sheets, davit steps, belaying pins, and so on, and also two capstans. A local brass founder supplied many items, including rudder braces, sidelights, scupper spouts, and so on. Donnell's Bath ropewalk supplied 22,435 pounds of cordage. *Adriatic*'s rigging was not done by the job; rather, nine riggers were paid for having worked between seventeen and twenty-four days apiece.

An itemized bill for $132.67 was presented by F. H. Morse for carving billet-head, taffrails, hawse chocks ("horse chalks"), "quarter rail stopps," eight "festoons," twenty-four "caps," and "one pair head boards 16 letters with ornamental ends." The billet-head was gilded by S. C. Sawyer, who also painted, grained, and gilded the cabin interiors, which had been built by master joiner David Mitchell. Other expenses included Thomas Bradley's bills for ox teaming in the yard ($110) and for carting goods to the yard. After the hull seams were caulked by master caulker L. C. Litchfield and his gang ($643.50), the hull was "watered" for $20 by the Torrent (Fire) Engine Company to check for leaks. Grease for the launching ways—165 pounds of tallow—cost $13.24.

Sails were made by Arthur Brown for $291.08 from 108 bolts—the owners supplied the material. Other items included mast coats, capstan cover, and tarpaulin. William Fell was paid $15 to "bend," or install, the sails.

A pair of twenty-foot yawl boats and one twenty-four-foot surf boat were built by Henry Delano for $250. Brass rowlocks were extra. Cooper Charles Murphy supplied twelve water casks, the largest eight holding 200 gallons apiece; two "harness casks" for salt beef and pork; a dozen wooden buckets; a "tunnel" (funnel); and copper pipe.

And the list goes on—sandpaper, chalk, brooms, oil, saw file, brushes, hooks, nails, tacks, padlock, lamp black, red lead, spirits, log lines, crowbar, grindstone, pump leathers, tables, looking glasses, writing desk, cabin chairs, plush trimming, stools, cushions, table covers, wool and oilcloth carpets, mats, mattresses and pillows, blankets, quilts, sheeting, damask, the ship's medicine chest, stoves, cabin dinnerware, tableware, teapot, trays, decanter, eggbeater, three spittoons, "chambers" with covers, lamps, butter tubs, dirt pan, brush, pickle dishes, gravy dishes, lanterns, sperm and tallow candles, binnacle lamp, wicks, numerous carpentry tools, matches, a Bible and twelve Testaments, and more.

Three hundred and five tons of stone ballast, and also 301 tons of "English"—meaning timothy—hay, and 17,000 feet of boards—common cargoes for a cotton port—were loaded in her hold for her maiden passage south, and the stevedores needed to be paid. The provision list included four barrels of pork (two of "mess" quality, two of prime); seven barrels of mess beef; two barrels of flour; one barrel mackerel; one-half barrel of cod tongues and sounds; a barrel of rice; one barrel of beans; one barrel dried meal; one barrel vinegar; one barrel green apples, three barrels turnips; two barrels of beets; six barrels of potatoes; one-half barrel carrots; 727 pounds of navy bread; one-half barrel of crackers; and so on, including also cabbages, molasses, codfish, sugar, coffee, tea, Boston hams, split peas, cucumbers, twenty dozen eggs, tapioca, macaroni, cranberries, vermicelli, raisins, tomato ketchup, walnut ketchup, pepper, pepper sauce, nutmeg, ginger, pimento, cloves, sage, thyme, sweet oil, cassia, Irish moss, English mustard, mixed pickles, salt, onions, lemon extract, crushed sugar, cocoa, lard, cheese, cream of tartar, caraway seed, squash, fancy soap, brown soap, rosewater, peach water, lavender water, "one load" of cider, and other items too numerous to mention.

Other incidental expenses included insurance on the ship while under construction;

the cost of boarding Captain John H. Lowell, who was from Phippsburg; shipping-master fees for hiring a crew; and the costs of piloting and towing the ship to sea. (The departure of a square-rigger from the river under sail was so rare after the availability of steam towage as to be noted in the newspapers.)

For all the effort and expense that went into building a ship and putting it to sea, ships typically did not last very long—between disaster and deterioration, ten years might be considered a fair average.[16] Hence the great pressure on captains to make profitable voyages. *Adriatic* remained with Clark & Sewall for seven years, spent primarily in the North Atlantic working the "cotton triangle"—sailing from a northern port to a southern cotton port to a British port (usually Liverpool) or a European port (usually Havre).

In March 1857 Captain Lorenzo Parker of Bath (he would die at New Orleans the following year of fever) was sent to Bordeaux to meet *Adriatic* in order to relieve Captain Albert Jewett of command and to try to sell the ship. Jewett had displeased the owners by getting into costly difficulties following a grounding at the River Plate, South America, and then a voyage to Calcutta under what proved to be a defective charter. The final straw was his tardiness in submitting accounts. Captain Parker reported finding Jewett to be in a poor state mentally and physically, with his wife and three children living on board. The cabin was also in a bad state, and "there is no provisions at all on board & not much of anything as even to knives & spoons."

Captain Parker soon determined that *Adriatic*'s hull was badly "wormed" by teredoes above the copper sheathing, and that part of her keelson was rotten, among other deficiencies. He proceeded to paint her up in good shape, and wrote Clark & Sewall regarding the application of a veneer of boards over the wormed planking: "If the ship is covered with oak I think I can sell her, if pine it will be difficult." He bought more ballast in order to hide the rot in the keelson, and was able to bribe a surveyor to give a good report to a prospective buyer. *Adriatic* sold for 120,000 francs.[17]

They had him going and coming

Coastal New England once constituted one of the world's great maritime communities. However, as S. E. Morison observed, the Yankee maritime culture never produced a deep-sea proletariat: "High wages and the ocean's lure pulled the Yankee boys to sea; but only promotion—or rum—could keep them there."[18]

Lord Lindsay, a large English ship owner, wrote:

During the first half of this century the masters of American vessels were, as a rule, greatly superior to those who held similar positions in English ships. . . . American ship owners required of their masters not merely a knowledge of navigation and seamanship, but of commercial pursuits, the nature of exchanges, the art of correspondence, and a sufficient knowledge of business to qualify them to represent the interests of their employers to advantage with merchants abroad.[19]

In 1910 the retired Boston clipper-ship master Captain Arthur C. Clark wrote:

Taken as a class, American sea captains and mates half a century ago were perhaps the finest body of real sailors that the world has ever seen, and by this is meant captains and officers who had themselves sailed before the mast. . . . They were the first to establish discipline in the merchant service, and their ships were the envy and despair of merchants and captains of other nations.[20]

One hundred ninety-two shipmasters who served aboard Sewall vessels are represented by documents in the Sewall Family Papers. The vast majority were Maine natives, most of them Kennebeckers. Many who were active in the post–Civil War era learned their trade in the storied prewar days when American ships led the world.

The Sewalls insisted that captains write them as soon as they reached port, and frequently thereafter until their departure. These letters are not travel letters—there are no descriptions of moonlit tradewind nights at sea, of exotic foreign ports, or local cultures—but, for the most part, matter-of-fact business letters.

Captains routinely reported on the passage just completed; on the condition of the ship, of crew problems, on freight rates, on the state of business, and so on. Most letters are no longer than they had to be. Some, particularly from younger captains, are obsequious. Dry humor, of which Mainers were normally past masters, is rarely detected—these were letters to The Boss. Most are reasonably legible—on the other hand, one can well sympathize with captains in distant ports puzzling over letters written by Arthur Sewall.

Typically, a captain, raised alongshore or along a river, first went to sea at age fourteen or so for a summer aboard a small coasting or fishing schooner as "boy," or possibly cook. Perhaps after a second such summer he left school to join a larger schooner or brig trading to the West Indies. As a young man—perhaps with some chums—he shipped as a sailor aboard a Maine-owned deepwater square-rigger. While most of his friends' wanderlust was thereby satisfied, he had an aptitude for seafaring, and went back for more.

Being an American—a legal requirement to be an officer—and bright and ambitious, before long he was tapped to be second mate. Although now a responsible watch officer, living aft in Dana's "world of knives and forks," and called "Mister" by the mate and the captain and "Sir" by the men, he was still part sailor and was expected to lay aloft to reef and furl and to dip his hand in the tar bucket. Mistrusted by the forecastle and but tolerated by the mate and the captain, he was neither fish nor fowl. On Sundays he studied navigation.

In due course, through a lucky break, he advanced to first mate, an office vastly elevated from that of second mate. "The mate" had legal standing, and, upon the death or incapacitation of the captain, took command. He was the ship's chief operating officer. The captain spoke to everyone else aboard ship (except the steward) through him. He kept well posted on the condition of the ship and on everything that happened aboard her. He supervised all the work and saw that order and discipline were maintained—

and on a Yankee ship, "work" and "discipline" had a special meaning. Notoriously prickly, mates were likely to become indignant if the captain interfered with, or appeared to be monitoring too closely, areas of the mate's responsibilities. Although the mate and the captain ate together at the cabin table, there was no expectation of familiarity between them, and, while there were certainly many exceptions, often they dined in silence.

Eventually, an ambitious mate wanted his own ship. Before 1898 there were no federal licensing requirements for mates or captains of American sailing vessels (as opposed to steam vessels), and even then, only sailing vessels of 700 tons or more came under the law. (Master mariner certificates had been issued to veteran captains by the American Shipmasters Association.) Barring a "yellow fever promotion" in a distant port, the naming of a master was the owner's decision, subject to acceptance by the underwriters and legalized at the customhouse.

Even in the palmy days, when ships were plentiful, there were always more mates than there were opportunities for command. With the decline of the fleet after the Civil War, ship owners had their pick of veteran shipmasters—indeed, some were so desperate that they offered to make a voyage for the Sewalls without pay to prove their worth. It thus became much more difficult for a mate to ever obtain a command, and many able mates left the sea, leaving behind drunks and drones. Captain George Goodwin, a Sewall mate who eventually, by good fortune along with much ability, gained a captaincy, wrote of those times:

> It was almost impossible [for a mate] to get command unless you had money enough to buy a captain's interest, which is one-eighth of the ship. If a mate did get command it was because [the owners] could not find a purchaser, and if they did find one later, the mate had to get out. If he went in debt to the owners for an interest he might just as well be in the hands of a New York loan shark, as the average down east shipbuilder. They had him going and coming. The agony might be prolonged a little longer than in the case of the loan shark, but the result would be just the same at the end of the chapter. I have known several careers of this kind.[21]

For one who gained a command—albeit, perhaps, of a small and ancient bark long employed as a plodding nursemaid for fledgling captains—his life was changed even beyond his imagining. He was deferred to by all on board, and flattered by merchants and supplicants on shore. For the first time since going to sea, once safely offshore, he discovered that he had leisure time. Initially he sharpened his navigational skills and studied up on commercial law, but he inevitably discovered that he had time to kill, which was often taken up with reading or hobbies, from conchology to needlepoint.

Despite being lord and master, by custom the captain was largely confined to the cabin and the poop. Any meandering about the ship would unnerve the sailors and annoy the mate. Sailmaking, usually performed on the poop, was the one activity having to do with the upkeep of the ship in which the captain was free to participate without giving offense, and many captains became experts.

For the captain sailing without wife or family, loneliness was all but a given; many kept singing birds in the cabin for company. The very real hazards of the sea could fill a captain's long nights with foreboding. Failure to fulfill the owners' expectations was a source of worry. Some captains—including a few Sewall captains—committed suicide. And some—also including some Sewall captains—became alcoholics, recluses, petty-minded scolds, or fearsome tyrants.[22]

The line between the enforcement of necessary discipline and tyranny was sometimes hard to distinguish, as was the line between sane, but severe, and psychotic captains and mates. Indeed, one of the rare occasions in Maine courts where a murderer was found innocent by reason of insanity was the 1858 case of Captain John A. Holmes of Wiscasset, who was tried for the murder of a sailor named George Chadwick aboard the ship *Therese*.[23]

The English writer Frank Bullen, once a chief mate in British sailing ships, experienced the breakdown of discipline aboard a British ship wherein the master was reduced to begging the contemptuous sailors to obey orders. He thus had some appreciation for the very different American approach, but also recognized its pitfalls when carried to an extreme:

Now such a scene as that would be unthinkable on board either an American or a "Blue-Nose" (British North American vessel). There the traditions are all on the side of stern discipline, which is not based upon law, but upon force. The foremast hand, whoever he may be, that signs in an American ship, realizes at once that it is dangerous to play any tricks with his superior officers. . . . He must at all times hold himself at the disposal of his officers, and whatever work they consider it necessary to undertake he must, on the word being given, throw himself into it as if it were a matter of life and death. Theoretically this is the case in all ships, but it is nowhere carried out as it is in American vessels. It is their tradition, and they have a pride in its maintenance. What it means to the sailor under the despotic rule of a bowelless master and iron-fisted officers it is impossible to convey to anyone who has not seen the process. . . . We are much too slack in our discipline; the Americans, as a rule, are far too severe. Of course there are exceptions on both sides but I speak of the rule.[24]

Interestingly, Bullen wrote that the treatment of boys aboard American ships was far better than aboard British or European ships.

Captain George Goodwin, sailing for the Sewalls, wrote:

We have to keep discipline on ship-board and we cannot call on the police to do it for us. . . . We have to do it ourselves and at times we get some very stubborn men to handle. . . . I have been a deep water sailor for forty-five years and have read more in the newspapers about the ill-usage of sailors than I ever heard or saw anywhere else. The greater part of it is gotten up by the shyster lawyers and crimps, after the ship had arrived in port. There may have been some useless fellow who had been pushed out of the way when things had to be done in a hurry, with which to start the case.

But Goodwin condemned captains who "starved and bulldozed" their crews:

I heard one [captain] make his brags that he sailed a ship between Europe and the Chincha Islands for ten years and never paid a crew. He made it so hot for them that they were glad to jump the ship as soon as they could and when his papers were taken before the consul, they were recorded as deserters. . . . His portage bills were small and therefore he was a fair-haired boy with his owners.

While deploring those captains who would do things that "would make a high-wayman blush," Goodwin stated, "I am safe in saying that ninety per cent of the men that command ships are men with self-respect, professional pride, personality and consideration for others that will compare favorably with any class of men on earth."[25]

Some broad-beamed señorita

When Captain Peleg Curtis of Harpswell, Maine—Curtis was later a longtime Sewall captain—assumed the command, his first, of a brig in 1844, his friend Washington Garcelon advised him:

Let your whole mind be bent upon your business. . . . But by all means look well to your own health when you have a freight offered, look to the influence that the peace will probably have upon your health, for when you once impair your health and run down your constitution, that will be a final winding up of your business affairs, if not your life. . . . Be gentlemanly and courteous to all whom you deal with. . . . Be kind and humane to your men, and not constantly glabing with them, be sure and request nothing of them but what is right and then see that your commands are obeyed, and you will soon gain their esteem. . . .[26]

Although no two letters of instruction to a master from the Sewalls were evidently exactly the same, the boilerplate was very similar, containing such language as:

We wish you personally to effect and attend to the business of the ship, exercising strict economy in your disbursements, making all possible dispatch in *Port and at Sea* settling all her bills and accounts before leaving port, sending copies of same with Duplicate, with corrections, if any, from next port, writing us as often as once a week while in port and keeping us fully advised of all your proceedings. [And so on, for three pages or so. See Appendix 3.]

Charles R. Flint, scion of an illustrious Thomaston maritime family, recalled from his time serving as a broker and agent in the 1870s:

> In Peru I had an excellent opportunity of becoming intimately acquainted with the shipmasters of different nationalities. We were agents for French, Germans, Scandinavians, Italians, English, and Americans. . . . I do not hesitate to say that . . . the American shipmasters were usually superior to those of other nations. They were generally part owners and had full authority to conduct the business of the ship, while the captains of European vessels were for the most part only sailing masters, and we as agents received instructions on important matters direct from the owners.[27]

The Sewalls well understood that no decisions they made were more important for the success of their enterprise than the selection of suitable captains. A captain who made good passages and profits, kept out of costly difficulties, maintained his ship in good order, corresponded regularly, and posted his accounts promptly was otherwise allowed considerable latitude. The Sewalls typically did not get involved in the captain's selection of mates or other members of a ship's company. And while it might seem remarkable that the Sewalls often did not know the names even of mates who had long been in their employ, it is just as remarkable that captains often knew very little about the mates they engaged for long voyages only just before sailing.

In the pre-telegraph years, captains beyond reach of timely communication were left largely to their own devices, and to local advice, when seeking a cargo. And even after cable communications were available, the Sewalls commonly left to their captains the final responsibility for chartering their ships.

As was evidently (and conveniently) the "custom of the port" at Bath, the Sewalls ordinarily paid square-rigger shipmasters but twenty dollars per month in wages, plus five percent "primage," or five percent of the freight income, minus commissions. (New captains commonly received half-primage; first mates made fifty dollars per month.) A captain sailing on wages received up to a hundred and fifty dollars a month. The Sewalls' insistence that the ship share in the receipts of the "slop chest"—the shipboard store maintained for the sailors—may also have been a custom at Bath, but was a tra-ditional—and much prized—perk for captains sailing from other ports. Likewise, the receipts for sales of " junk"—old rope and such—traditionally considered to be a perk for the mate, were expected by the Sewalls to be credited to the ship.

Even though a captain might own a larger share in his ship than did the Sewalls, they held power over him through proxy, and he needed their permission to bring fam-ily members along for a voyage. The Sewalls charged four dollars a month for the wife's board; children were extra. A new captain was wise not to ask to bring family members aboard for a voyage or two. Wives were not to interfere with the ship's business in any way.

Being keen students of the habits and foibles of the *genus captainis*, the Sewalls were only too aware of the many opportunities presented to captains to skim from, or hide, expenditures, and to pocket various commissions and "rebates"—some of which the Sewalls surely coveted for themselves. Even the most veteran and trusted captains' accounts were subjected to rigorous audit, with the most petty discrepancy questioned. This sort of scrutiny could backfire, as Charles Flint recalled:

> The captains in foreign ports often compared notes as to how they had been treated . . . [and] got even . . . by retaining commissions. . . . In one case a captain included in his expense account a suit of clothes, which the owner refused to allow. The next time the captain returned home and rendered his account, the owner said: "I see that you left out the suit of clothes this time." "Oh, no," replied the captain, "it's there, but you can't see it!"[28]

Alert to exaggeration, even from half a world away, the Sewalls had no reluctance questioning a captain's judgment concerning the alleged dire condition of a mast, or the poor state of his copper sheathing. And they never gave the slightest indication that they might be at any disadvantage in making such judgments for never having gone to sea themselves.

Sewall square-riggers were supplied with one chronometer as part of the ship's outfit, and most captains owned or rented an additional timepiece. Captains provided their nautical instruments, barometer, charts, and nautical books—no small outlay, as an ocean "directory" could cost thirty dollars—and also their own bedding. A captain relieving a regular captain for a voyage made arrangements for the use of books, charts, chronometer, and such.

The Sewalls customarily charged 6 percent to lend money to a captain to buy his required captain's share. The pinch came when paying the high insurance premiums captains felt obliged to incur to cover their loans in a period of falling freights and primages.

The consequences of an ill-advised charter could result not only in a poor return or loss for that voyage, but could place a ship out of position for a good charter by tens of thousands of miles and many months' time. From the owners' perspective, having an expensive ship depreciate daily while lying idle or sailing on a fool's errand, its crew headed toward a big payday while devouring costly stores, was a situation that could not be tolerated indefinitely. Captains guilty of poor judgment or bad luck entered port with the fear of finding their replacement awaiting them at the caplog—consider the letter from distraught Captain John Dillingham of Brunswick, master of the ship *Macedonia* from January 1855 to June 1856, written from Bordeaux in July 1855:

> I suppose you have been expecting to hear from me for a long time but I had no heart to write. To think I bound myself to lay here so long and then to get nothing for it. I did all that lay in my power to be let off after I chartered. I offered them all that belonged to me, more I could not give and to go I did not know where but anywhere could not have been worse than laying here so long on so much expense. . . . It is wretched business and unpardonable.

On a lighter note, Captain P. A. McDonald—*not* a Sewall captain—recalled of late nineteenth-century captains:

Generally speaking, the sailing ship and her captain of some thirty or more years ago was a colorful figure. He usually done his own business in foreign ports, knew the cost of stevedoring, the price of mutton & hemp. Also understood "cumshaw." Aye, "cumshaw." The skipper took his drinks in a private bar, sometimes, it is said, in the company of some charming barmaid or a broad-beamed senorita. . . . The captains were not as a rule "judges of pulchritude," their choice usually being tonnage in preference to delicate beauty. Invariably these ladies carried considerable canvas, and when all "rattled down" and all glad rags bent upon their spars, they were dazzling to the eye of the young and gullible sailorman.[29]

They did not like the smell of powder

Beginning in colonial days, no trade was more important to the early development of what would become the United States in general, and to New England in particular, than was the West Indies trade. For many generations the effect of trade to the West Indies figured heavily not only on the coastal economy, but extended deep into the hinterlands.

The trade typically employed small vessels, which, in Maine, well into the early decades of the nineteenth century, sailed forth from ports large and small, carrying salt fish and products of the forest and the farm, and returned with West India goods—molasses, sugar, rum, coffee. (In later years, fruit, coconuts, salt, and dyewoods were additional returning cargoes.) The trade was a great nursery of mariners, introducing generations of coastal boys to the sea and to the wider world beyond the horizon. The gradual consolidation of Maine's West India trade at Portland would be a major factor in that city's rise, and it would remain an important element in the city's commerce throughout the nineteenth century.

It was in the West Indies trade that Bath's great family fleets cut their teeth before expanding into the cotton trade. Sugar and cotton, both commodities of incalculable importance and sources of great wealth, were both also founded on the labors of millions of enslaved Africans. West Indian sugar would engender warring over tiny islands by great European powers, and the American cotton culture by slave labor would be the root cause of the horrific American Civil War. Northern maritime enterprise was a vital component of both epics.

Although trade to the West Indies was legally defined as foreign trade, in practical terms it was but an extension of the coasting trade, and was engaged in by relatively small vessels (and even some *very* small vessels), mostly sloops, schooners, and brigs. The brig, the handiest, or most maneuverable, of all rigs, was well suited for West Indian trading. With her lofty royal catching the tradewinds blowing above the forest canopy, a brig under a skilled pilot could work her way, backing and filling, up a winding Caribbean river. She could also be readily employed coastwise, or even sent to Europe.

In the 1820s Clark & Sewall built at least two brigs likely intended primarily for West Indies trading. Their only other brig was the *Marcia*, built in 1848. Papers concerning the earlier brigs have not survived, but some relating to the *Marcia* have. The brief sea letter to Captain Thomas Merryman, a Brunswick native, in October 1848, directed him to proceed to New Orleans and there to "dispose of the [lumber] cargo . . . to the best advantage, and be very careful in disposing of same, as we know not whom to put confidence in. . . ." He was to then "engage the brig in such business as can be obtained and of which you will be able to decide, being on the ground yourself. Possibly business may be found . . . to Cuba or West Indies or in the bay." Presumably the "bay" was the Bay, or Gulf, of Campeche. Merryman was engaged for twenty dollars a month plus 5 percent primage.

The brig arrived at New Orleans after a "long and unpleasant" passage of twenty-nine days, and the lumber was quickly sold but at a low price. As freights were low and the river rising, Captain Merryman took a charter for the shortest trip possible, taking a cargo of sugar—Louisiana was a major sugar producer—for Philadelphia, where the *Marcia* arrived after a rough passage of twenty-eight days. A broker proposed sending the brig to London with "wet provisions"—presumably barreled salt beef and pork—but Merryman thought the freight too low for the brig's small capacity. He ended up taking an undisclosed cargo to Boston, encountering along the way three heavy, snowy gales which strained the brig, ripped sails, and damaged the galley.

Business offered at Boston included ice for Wilmington, North Carolina; box shook—sugar box parts—for Havana with empty barrels on deck; or ballast to "the south side of Cuby" with molasses back. Hearing nothing from Clark & Sewall, on February 28 he chartered the brig for "Trinadad de Cuby" with shook and hoop poles out—hoop poles were shaved saplings used to hoop barrels—and molasses back.

And so it went. Arriving at Havana in December, 1849, Merryman reported finding between eighty and ninety American vessels in port. While on the passage he fell in with the Panama steamer *Crescent City*, disabled with engine problems, and relieved her of seven discontented passengers.

———

The great scourge of the West Indies sailor was yellow fever. In June 1856 Clark & Sewall's 549-ton ship *Lady Franklin*, built in 1853 and named for the heroic wife of the explorer Sir John Franklin, lay at the Cuban port of Matanzas. Having discharged a cargo of ice from Boston, Captain William Leavitt reported loading 3,809 boxes of sugar for Trieste. Yellow fever had broken out, with one sailor dead, and another and the mate sick—fatally so, as it developed—in the hospital. The dead sailor, William McLoud, was owed thirteen dollars, and Captain Leavitt suggested that the money be sent to Mr. Littlefield, the Boston shipping master, who might be able to locate McLoud's widow. Leavitt intended to sail as soon as possible, although he would be without a mate.

On July 7 Captain Leavitt wrote from New York, having "broken passage" after the fever had spread to nearly all of his crew and also to his wife, who was dangerously ill.

One sailor died on the night of arrival. Leavitt blamed the cargo of ice for "all the mischief," but did not explain. Additionally, the ship was leaking a good deal, probably through the upper works, which he thought should be corrected before leaving port. Two weeks later the ship was ordered moved to the Lower Bay on account of the death of a ship keeper, and also the second mate's having fallen ill. "I fear we have a long and difficult job before us," Captain Leavitt wrote. He asked to be temporarily relieved, so as to be able to better care for his wife, who did survive.

In September the quarantine lifted and the ship was dry-docked. Captain Mitchell Trott of Bath, who had relieved Leavitt, wrote Clark & Sewall that the ship's topsides had been caulked, that she had been found to be very open under the counter, and that she had some "bad splits and rents forward." The cargo, which had been discharged, was now being reloaded, but Trott doubted whether the stevedores would be able to fit all the boxes back in, "as they do not understand stowing sugar here as well as in Cuba."

———

On November 17 Captain Leavitt, who had returned to take the *Lady Franklin* to sea, wrote from Boston:

I have to inform you of the total loss of the *Lady Franklin*. On the evening of the 20th of Oct. in Lat 41.30 Lon 50 in a heavy gale from E. S. E. she sprung a leak and at midnight when the gale abated . . . the lower hold was nearly full of water. She soon settled over on her beam ends and we were obliged to heave everything movable off deck and cut away the masts to prevent her turning bottom up. We hove cargo overboard every opportunity from the between decks. We laid on our beam ends 10 days when having thrown seven hundred boxes overboard she righted and we freed her from water. The sugar in lower hold was no doubt all dissolved.

The ship had been stricken when about one third of the way across the Atlantic. When she "fell in" with a schooner it was decided to abandon ship. When the schooner fell in with the bark *Volunteer*, from Marseilles to Boston, some of the *Lady Franklin*'s people, including Captain Leavitt, shifted to the bark. He wrote that he planned to return to Portland, his home, and would come to Bath soon after to settle up accounts.[30]

———

Violence and also sharp practices were common to West Indian voyaging. In April 1859 Captain James Nichols, a Portlander, of Clark & Sewall's ship *Champion*, wrote from Havana:

The most of my crew have been boarding on shore for a few days in prison on their own expense on account of mutinizing on board. My mates are hardly worth the room they occupy on board the ship.

In November he wrote from Falmouth, England, to report that he had put into the port partially dismasted and in distress, having been run down in the dark of early morning by "a large ship which came near carrying us all down to the bottom in a pile." He thought the hit-and-run ship had been a New York packet.

On November 10, 1860, Captain Nichols wrote from Key West:

I dare say you will be much surprised in getting a letter from me from this port. . . . I left Havana on the 30 of last month as I wrote you in my last letter I intended to do after procuring for the ship stores necessary for the voyage. When only 6 or 8 miles outside of the Moro Light the crew ris and took charge of the ship, threatening to kill me or any one else that interfered. I was not born to be tampered with in that manner. . . . Though the life of myself and family was at stake as soon as I did interfere with them unless I commenced in a desperate and determined manner which I did and they were only made to yield and give up the command & become obedient to my orders by the discharge of a musket among them. The sight was a sickening thing to behold yet a very necessary one. Two of the offending party were shot. One fell dead on deck, the other wounded. By this operation I brought them to their senses for they did not like the smell of powder nor the sound of shot whistling among them. Knowing it was unsafe to proceed farther I went again into Havana in tow by a steamer. I immediately applied to the consul for assistance & the result of the whole matter so far is we all, officers and crew, [were] taken out of the ship & sent to this port for trial.

Champion had been bound for the island port of Remedios, to load sugar for Europe. Before being taken to Key West, Nichols arranged for a Captain Forsythe, of New Orleans, who was highly recommended by the consul, to take charge of the ship, and had shipped a new crew for him. On January 7 Nichols, who had been released, wrote from Remedios, describing himself as having been driven "nearly mad" upon discovering that Forsythe was in fact an "infernal scamp" who had soon become drunk, had run the ship aground and lost her kedge anchor, and had run up bills amounting to about $2,300.

The insidious tunneling of the shipworm, and the cancer of dry rot, were all-too-common consequences of West India trading. In May 1862 *Champion*, found to be too rotten and worm-eaten to be sold by private treaty, was disposed of at auction at Liverpool by Captain Arthur Prince for but £2,500 cash "as she laid with all her faults & failings."[31] The E. & A. Sewall ship *Kineo* also sold at Liverpool that week, bringing £5,850.

Oh, Captain, pay me dollar

For thirty-odd years before the Civil War the carriage of cotton from New Orleans, Mobile, Savannah, Charleston, and other ports—including New York—was the staple employment for America's deepwater merchant marine, which eventually carried two-thirds of all cotton exports. A great fleet was also employed carrying cotton coastwise; much was carried to New York for transshipment.[32] The Sewalls, and other Bath and Maine ship owners, were in the thick of it.

On November 27, 1858, of 116 ships and barks lying in New Orleans, 95 were American and 21 were foreign-flagged. Sixty-six, amounting to 60,872 tons, were built or were owned in Maine. At Charleston, fifteen of sixteen American ships were built or owned in Maine, and in other cotton ports Maine ships were also "largely represented."[33] From September 1858 to August 1859 over three million out of a total crop of 3,851,481 bales—a bale weighed about 500 pounds—were exported, with over two million going to Great Britain.[34] Since plantation owners customarily paid off last year's debts with this year's crop, the role played by British capital in the American cotton business was very large.[35]

Despite Britain's interest in, and dependency on, American cotton, American ships, and not British ships, dominated the trade. One reason for this was because foreign-flagged ships were not allowed to carry cargo in the coastal leg of the "cotton triangle," from a northeastern port to a cotton port. Also, many of the cotton brokers were northerners, with ties to northern shipping houses and captains. And the builders and owners of the American cotton fleet—especially those at Bath—specialized in the building and management of ships designed for the trade. These "cotton boxes" were big, beamy, shoal-draft, bluff-bowed rule-beaters, designed to lift a large cargo over the bars that blocked deep vessels from the entrances of southern river ports, and to capitalize on loopholes in the official tonnage measuring formulae which resulted in reduced port fees and taxes. The bigger the ship the bigger the advantage, and Clark & Sewall's monster (for her day) *Rappahannock* avoided paying port fees on nearly half of her actual tonnage.[36]

Ship carpenters of later years wondered how their predecessors managed to bend even well-steamed four-inch oak planking on bows as blunt as a canal boat's. Indeed, so abruptly did the ends of some cotton boxes conclude that, to coin an old saw, they looked as though they would bunt a barrel across the Atlantic while simultaneously drawing along a bundle of shingles tossed in their wake. Many were fitted with a long poop which made for even more untaxed cargo space and created a social hall for passengers when carrying emigrants on the western leg of the triangle.

Given a cotton bale's low weight-to-volume ratio, a roomy ship could not be overloaded with cotton, even with additional ballast, and with the bales "screwed" in the hold as tightly as possible. As a result, loaded cotton ships tended to be "crank," sailing "on their sides." Of course, these ships were also general freighters and carried many other cargoes. While some were like E. & A. Sewall's notorious *Valentia*—which, according to one captain, did not "take much notice of light winds"—many were said to sail well.[37]

During the height of the winter cotton-shipping season the levees of New Orleans were lined with shipping. The cotton was delivered from upriver by wood-burning, spark-spewing steamboats—one wonders why they didn't all burn up. Bales were

The first Rappahannock, 1841, *represented, perhaps, the ultimate development of the very full-modeled "cotton box." This portrayal does not do justice to the bluntness of her bow, which resembled that of a canal barge. The false gunport motif, originally intended to confuse pirates, had become a common decorative style and would survive on British and European ships to the final days of sail.* MAINE MARITIME MUSEUM

rolled by gangs of roustabouts, mostly slaves, up the ship's staging, then tumbled on deck and lowered down into the hold. Because freight money was based on weight, the bales were jammed into the smallest possible spaces by gangs of tough "cotton screwers," who were specialists at the business. Using screw jacks braced against hickory posts set against deck beams, the cotton screwers forced three bales into a space that would otherwise be occupied by two. So tightly were cargoes compressed that decks were sometimes sprung; it might take a gang of over a dozen men with two tackles an entire hour to break out the first six bales at the port of discharge.

Screwing cotton was said to be the hardest work ever performed aboard a ship; five men composed a screwing team. In New Orleans and Mobile, at least before the Civil War, the cotton screwers were a rough set of hard-drinking and hard-fighting English and Irish sailors, and also Irish and French Canadian timber stevedores from the Gulf of St. Lawrence, who chose to spend the winter sweating in the holds of cotton ships.

Loading a ship could take a month; bales were often also jammed into the carpen-

Cotton bales on Atlantic Wharf, Charleston, South Carolina. From a stereographic photo taken after the war. Maine Maritime Museum

ter's shop, into the "boy's room," under the topgallant fo'c's'le, and one might serve as the cabin table. In October 1872 Captain Fred Bosworth of the ship *Freeman Clark* complained to E. & A. Sewall from New Orleans that the springy bales they were loading—the "ugliest" he had ever seen—would not compress satisfactorily, even though the deck had been lifted off the stanchions "nearly fore and aft." To load a paying cargo, he was going to put a bale "in every corner that one can go."

At the end of the season, the screwers, fleeing hot weather and Yellow Jack (yellow fever), shipped as sailors to Liverpool or London, there to spree away their hard-won earnings. A cotton ship sailor recalled the screwers:

> The gang, with their shirts off, and handkerchiefs tied about their heads, take hold
> the handles of the screws, the foreman begins a song and at the end of every two
> lines the worm of the screw is forced to make one revolution, thus gaining per-
> haps two inches. Singing, or *chanting* . . . is an invariable accompaniment to
> working in cotton, and many of the screw-gangs have an endless collection of
> songs, rough and uncouth, both in words and melody. . . . One song generally suf-
> fices to bring home the screw, when a new set is got upon the bale, and a fresh
> song is commenced.

> Oh, we work for a Yankee Dollar,
> Hurrah, see —man—do,
>   Yankee dollar, bully dollar,
> Hurrah, see—man—dollar.
>   Silver dollar, pretty dollar,
> Hurrah, see—man—do,
>   I want your silver dollars,
> Oh, Captain, pay me dollar.[38]

Letters from captains indicate that often a large fleet, covered up from the sun with
awnings and old sails, lay in New Orleans awaiting an acceptable freight rate. When the
price finally rose, the singing by hundreds of gangs of cotton screwers could be heard
all along the riverfront.

In February 1858 Clark & Sewall's ship *Sarah G. Hyde*, Captain George Bailey,
sailed from Mobile to Havre with young Arthur Sewall aboard as observer. Arthur had
just familiarized himself with the New Orleans market and now was to learn something about going to sea—likely this was the only lengthy passage he ever made under
sail. The *Hyde* loaded 2,951 bales weighing 1,525,382 pounds at the rate of 15/16 penny
per pound, excepting 666 bales at 7/8 penny per pound. Freight and primage amounted
to $14,785.56, and expenses amounted to $5,723.14.[39]

In October 1861 young Captain James Lincoln of the bark *Frank Marion* wrote
Clark & Sewall from Kronstadt, Russia:

> I like her [the bark] very much, but she sails very dull, but that was doubtless
> owing partly to the cargo being screwed in too tight. Also to being too near on an
> even keel, as well as having no copper on her bottom where it fouled very much,
> there are barnacles on her bottom over an inch long.

That a ship must be permitted to "work" in order to sail well was a common
belief—or at least a common excuse for a slow passage. Many ships sailed best when
trimmed slightly by the head.

A new ship leaving the Kennebec for a cotton port often shipped young locals in her crew. First-timers marveled at the impossibly clear water when the ship anchored on the Bahama banks awaiting a favorable slant of wind. Working through the Florida Straits, against the Gulf Stream, was an inherently risky and difficult business—in December 1875 Captain P. H. Taylor of the ship *Tabor*, long held up by headwinds, wrote that he doubted there was a "crook or hole where there is three fathoms of water from the Hole in the Wall to Key West that I haven't been in to."

At a cotton port many young New Englanders first saw slavery in the flesh, a sight which surely shocked some, although Arthur did not comment on it.

New Orleans–bound ships "took steam" in large tows off Southwest Pass, over one hundred miles from the city. Outbound ships often anchored for weeks at the bar, awaiting a southerly wind which would push up enough water to allow them to be towed through the mud. Flooding and also disease frequently occurred; in June 1849 Captain Thomas Melcher of Brunswick arrived aboard the Clark & Sewall ship *John C. Calhoun* and reported "nearly one half the city is covered with water. The cholera still prevails. . . ."

Ships at Mobile anchored thirty miles below the city, and cotton was lightered down the bay to them.

At Liverpool (and at Havre) cotton ships entered massive stone docks at high water through lock gates. Just as San Francisco's harbor would later be dominated by English grain ships, so the Liverpool docks were once crowded with American cotton ships. Only these great granite docks, required by the large range of tide, allowed Liverpool to become a major port. Extreme precautions were taken in the docks against fire, and no open flame of any kind was permitted on board. All lights had to be out early. Watchmen patrolled ceaselessly, and all hands were boarded ashore. Aboard ship, hard-boiled eggs from ashore were standard fare.

Liverpool was the sailor's paradise, offering cheerful "singing houses," donkey races, and other forms of amusement and hospitality. It was famous—or notorious—for its many sailor's tailors, whom American ship captains often appointed as bankers for their crews. The tailor only extended credit in the form of clothing; and as Jack needed spending money, the tailor was happy to tack five dollars onto the bill, for a suitable fee. Thus, the tailors made out well, the captains received a free suit, and poor Jack was cheated once again.[40]

Female beggars were common, often attempting to enter the cabin to relate their sad tales, the common ploy being to sell their wedding rings. Men selling unbreakable chinaware from baskets threw a "sample" to the deck but would not allow anyone else to try. Jolly parties of captains and their families chartered big carriages for tours of the English countryside, inspecting Roman ruins and grand estate houses, and sampling the refreshments at inns.[41]

The carriage of cotton under sail ended with the installation in the 1870s of the Eads jetties, designed by the great engineer James B. Eads, at the mouth of the Mississippi. Employing the river's current to scour out the channel, the jetties finally opened the commerce of a considerable portion of the continental United States to deep-draft ocean steamers.

Sewall cotton ships were active in the pre–Civil War transatlantic emigrant trade. The peak years of transatlantic passenger traffic from Europe to the United States under sail, spurred by the Irish potato famine in 1847 and European political unrest, occurred in the 1840s and 1850s. The large majority of this traffic was carried by American sailing vessels.

These years also represented the heyday of the American merchant marine, as led by the crack North Atlantic packet ships and culminating in the California and Australian clipper ships, all developed to carry passengers and high-value cargoes. Although these would also be remembered as the "palmy days" for the Sewalls, they owned neither packets nor clippers, but rather typical "cotton box" freighters.

By the late 1840s and 1850s the scheduled North Atlantic packet ships (primarily built and owned in New York, although commanded by New England Yankees) were carrying increasing numbers of steerage passengers along with cabin passengers. Most emigrants, however, took passage aboard "regular" and "tramp" traders, especially homeward-bound cotton ships fitted out with primitive temporary accommodations. Many were chartered by European operators as the need arose, to sail in so-called "lines" existing only on posters.

Conditions aboard an emigrant ship of the 1840s were not much different from those enjoyed by Henry Sewall and fellow Puritans in the 1630s. The first American regulations concerning passengers aboard American ships became law in 1819 and limited their number to no more than two persons per five tons. Additionally, ships departing from any port on the continent of Europe were required to have secured under deck certain amounts of water, salted provisions, bread, and vinegar per passenger, no matter what provisions were provided by the passengers themselves or others.

Due to high death rates, in 1847 new regulations required "fourteen clear superficial [i.e., square] feet" in the lower deck to be apportioned to each passenger in a temperate zone, with but two tiers of six-foot berths allowed. In 1848 more regulations required a house structure over the hatches, ventilators, and better cooking facilities for the passengers, who did their own cooking, and further adjustments of space.[42] More comprehensive requirements, including the provision of privies, and separation of family groups and single males and females, did not arrive until 1882, long after the transatlantic passenger trade under sail had virtually ceased.

At ports of embarkation other requirements were mandated by local government inspectors, usually including the addition of boats and "life boys."[43] The boats were not lifeboats in the usual sense, since they were by no means of sufficient capacity to provide accommodations for the entire ship's company, but were intended to facilitate the transfer of persons to a nearby shore or ship in the event of an emergency.

The command of a ship on any long passage was invariably a taxing responsibility, and the addition of from 200 to even 500 passengers (as aboard Clark & Sewall's big *Rappahannock*) would complicate any captain's life considerably. Nevertheless, as ships engaging in the emigrant trade were doing so before the transatlantic cable, the decision to take passengers was usually the captain's, although often it would seem that taking passengers was a matter of last resort to save having to make a passage in ballast or with a very low-paying cargo.

Captain Thomas Purington, the wordy letter-writing master of the Sewalls' bark *Frank Marion*—"it takes a great many words for me to come at a little"—preferred a non-paying passage in ballast to carrying passengers. However, in September 1866, at Bordeaux, he turned his own cabin over to two ladies, two servants, and five children, as cabin passengers for New Orleans for five hundred dollars. He wrote: "I think I can father this lot from here to N. O. without any room for slander [although] these things have to be taken into consideration now days."

One must read a great deal between the lines of most captains' letters to grasp what conditions were really like on board a crowded emigrant ship. About 1850 Captain J. H. Drew, then a young sailor, sailed in a New York packet ship, and also in the Patten ship *Caspian*, carrying emigrants. He later wrote that most of the steerage passengers in the packet were Irish, with people of various nationalities in the first and second cabins. At Havre, *Caspian* took on Belgians, and Germans from Saxony, Bavaria, and Wittenburg, along with Hungarians, "Polanders," and also "Israelites," which Drew described as "those national nobodies who are everywhere."

Drew deplored the hardships faced by the women, exposed to all kinds of strangers in the 'tween decks. The daily water allowance was but three quarts per person, with which all cooking—making gruel, tea, and coffee—and washing, had to be done. For a woman with several children, some of them always sick, "amusing" tactics were sometimes used in attempts to obtain more from young Drew, who was assigned to dole it out. The women, he wrote, were invariably more cheerful, enduring, and smarter than the men, some of whom never came up on deck for an entire passage.

At midnight it was his task to take a lantern and make the rounds of the 'tween decks, the only way below being through a house built over the main hatch. In the dead of winter, when all was closed up, a single lantern hung under the hatch provided all the light for hundreds of people. The 'tween decks were fitted with a double row of three-tier bunks amidships, and one row along each side, for the length of the ship. Five people in a family might sleep in one bunk.

"One can imagine the fetid atmosphere coming from so many wretched beings, half of them, perhaps, seasick and vomiting," Drew recalled. As he passed along on his patrol "sometimes a woman's head would emerge from a berth looking more like a swab than a head" and ask:

"Ah, sailor, would you tell us of the night?" "It is a heavy gale," I sometimes had to reply, as I slipped about in danger of breaking my neck. "Ah! d'ye hear that now," she would say, tugging at her husband, a feeble grunt would be the response. By this time a dozen female heads would be sticking up in the gloom, and it would be, "Tell us, sailor, is there danger?" "It is a heavy gale," I would say. "The topgallant masts went over the sides a short time ago." "Oh, we shall all be larst!" "There is no danger yet. I will let you know; keep quiet. You will be in New York in a week."

When the weather was fine, family groups would gather on deck, mourning for the fatherland, thinking about America, and singing songs. Sometimes diamonds could be glimpsed among rags, and gleaming arms in half-opened chests. "There was flirtation and coquetry and love, and all that which served to make the passage spicy."44

They died very suddenly

Despite the manifest opportunities for contagion and the lack of any understanding of the role of microbes in disease, emigrant ships sometimes crossed the North Atlantic in a month or more without any deaths. Then again, the same ship on its next voyage might experience heavy mortality. Matter-of-fact letters from masters reporting multiple deaths state nothing more than the basic facts, even after what must have been a most gruesome and grievous experience. But then, such deaths were common enough on shore as well, and, in plain fact, the ship owners did not require detailed information—no one was going to sue them.

The ship *Rio Grande*, sailing in the cotton/emigrant triangle, experienced passages demonstrating both extremes. In April 1848 Captain David Ryan wrote to Clark & Sewall from New York's quarantine anchorage that *Rio Grande* had arrived from Liverpool in thirty days, with all passengers well.45 From New York, Ryan sailed to New Orleans, having filled the leftover extra water casks for ballast.

At New Orleans *Rio Grande*, awaiting better freights, was "well covered up" to keep her from drying out. In July Ryan refused an offer to carry a thousand cotton bales to Boston at twenty-two dollars per bale in the expectation of carrying Mexican War troops to Boston at twelve dollars per man, and thirty-five dollars per officer. When this deal fell through, he loaded 716 hogsheads of tobacco, sixty barrels of bread, and four steerage passengers for London, having in mind good prospects for passengers at Bremen or Havre. The passage to London was completed on October 28, despite a hurricane which lay the ship over with her lee rail under water, and shifted the cargo. One man was lost to yellow fever.

On December 6 Captain Ryan wrote Clark & Sewall from London that his ship was lying wind-bound at Gravesend, bound for New Orleans with 186 German and twenty-three English passengers, including two infants. There were also three cabin passengers. Complying with the inspector's wishes, Ryan had had a hatch house built over the fore hatch, and had installed ventilators and ten deck lights. He had also been required to buy a new longboat. He ended his letter thusly: "I shall go down to the ship this evening and proceed to sea the earliest opportunity. Hoping to meet your advices at New Orleans. Capt. Gaskins of your ship the *Roger Sherman* arrived here this morning. He will proceed to Havre."46

On February 2, 1849, Captain Ryan wrote from New Orleans reporting that he had made a passage of forty-four days from Deal:

I beg you will pardon me for not writing before but the ship has been quarantined having lost 24 passengers and 2 of the sailors. I had to come to at Slaughterhouse Point, discharge the passengers and smoke the ship out. . . .
I think I had a few cases of cholera as they died very suddenly some of them.

Ryan later wrote that most of the passengers who died had done so during the first two weeks at sea. On one day four had died, on another day, three. And a sailor had just died after falling between the ship and another, making "28 persons that I have buried since I left here." He had whitewashed the hold from the keelson up to the lower deck, thinking it would "have a tendency to cleanse the ship and kill any disease that might remain on board her."

Cholera was a ghastly disease to suffer or to observe under the best of circumstances, and likely few venues could be more demoralizing than the dark and fetid confines of the 'tween deck. In serious cases the victim rapidly loses fluids due to vomiting and copious diarrhea; death follows from severe dehydration.

In September 1850, departing Liverpool with passengers, *Rio Grande* was raked by a fierce gale which caused the main topsail yard to fall to the deck, which was a scene of mayhem with water casks, boat, and galley all adrift. One man was lost overboard. The heavy casks, rolling about the deck like loose cannons, had to be staved in to be subdued. Casks of water in the hold were also lost, necessitating a return to port, for which Captain Ryan apologized profusely.

On a passage from Cardiff to Philadelphia in the winter of 1852, in a gale off the American coast, it was necessary to caulk *Rio Grande's* hatches "so tight that it nearly caused a suffocation to take place among the passengers."

On January 20, 1849, Captain Thomas Melcher wrote from Liverpool of his arrival aboard Clark & Sewall's ship *John C. Calhoun* after a very rough passage of thirty-six days from Baltimore:

I have not obtained any business for the ship yet. Business is very dull, there is nothing at all doing without passengers either to the north or New Orleans. Liverpool is full of ships, and most of them are going to New Orleans. . . . If I should take passengers it will cost around £25 to ventilate and build houses over the hatches.

On January 25 Melcher wrote that he had chartered the ship to New York to take passengers for £900, and also cargo. On February 23 he wrote that he was about ready to sail; his next letter, dated April 2, was from the quarantine anchorage off Staten Island, New York. On the passage he had lost twenty-one passengers and one seaman to sickness, two children having died that very day. Other than that, he wrote, "I have had a very pleasant passage for the time of year. Left Liverpool the 27th Feb. and arrived off the bar and took a pilot the 30th of March." On April 7 the *Calhoun* was still lying at quarantine, and Melcher wrote:

I have no sickness on board except one boy who is deranged but I am afraid if we are kept here much longer we shall all be deranged. The sickness that we have had on board was the cholera in a mild form, but we have had nothing of the kind for the last two weeks. Those that have died since that time were not much better than dead when they came on board.

Bills included $5 for James Edgerton for "conveying dead ashore," and $30.75 for the steamer *John Jay* for "fetching 242 passengers" from Quarantine to New York.

Some other Bath emigrant ships suffered far worse losses than did Sewall ships. In 1853 the ship *Sagadahoc*, fifty-three days out of Gothenburg for Boston, spoke the ship *Havre* and reported fifty passengers dead of cholera, with fourteen, including the captain's wife, "in a low state." The worst emigrant disaster involving a Bath ship was the loss of the ship *New Era* on its maiden voyage, in November, 1854. After the ship went aground at Deal Beach, on the New Jersey shore, about 240 German emigrants lost their lives.[47]

Such horrors notwithstanding, taking passage on a relatively big and fast American ship headed for an American port—as opposed to taking a small, slow British ship to a Gulf of St. Lawrence port—was likely the wisest choice that a would-be emigrant could make.

1. Bath *Anvil*, April 25, 1908; William Avery Baker, *A Maritime History of Bath, Maine, and the Kennebec River Region*, vol. I (Bath, ME: Marine Research Society of Bath, 1973) p. 287.

2. Baker, *A Maritime History of Bath*, p. 312; *Bath Commercial*, July 7 1877. For a history of the Pattens, see Kenneth R. Martin and Ralph Linwood Snow, *The Pattens of Bath* (Bath ME: Maine Maritime Museum and Patten Free Library, 1996).

3. Reed, *History of Bath and Environs*, p. 144–46.

4. Bath *Anvil*, November 6, 1907.

5. Futtocks were the individual sections that, fastened together, made up a frame or rib.

6. Bath *Anvil*, November 6, 1907.

7. There is a family connection between the Sewalls and the hard-pine business. Dummer and Mary Sewall's daughter Mary married Captain Daniel Buck of the Penobscot River town of Bucksport. About 1830 a family member, Henry Buck of Bucksport, pioneered in exploiting South Carolina's hard pine for use as ship timber. The Sewalls were customers of the Bucks.

8. Bath *Daily Times*, May 21, 1914.

9. *Nautical Gazette*, August 8, 1907.

10. Bath *Enterprise*, December 14, 1895.

11. *Georgetown Tide*, vol. 10, no. 4, November–December 1984.

12. The costs for carpenter labor for E. & A. Sewall's 678-ton 1865 bark *Frank Marion*, excluding whipsawing, was $4,893. Although there was no item listed for compensation for her master builder, Daniel Small, there was an unidentified $3 per ton "commission." If this, in fact, was Small's pay, the combined amount, $6,297 would be in the ballpark with *Samaritan's* rate, adjusted for the tonnage. Fastening, however, was jobbed out separately at $1,300.

13. This process is well covered in Virginia Steel Wood, *Live Oaking* (Boston, MA: Northeastern University Press, 1981), pp. 106–07.

14. Sewall Family Papers, Box 42/Folder 6.

15. Reed, *History of Bath and Environs* , p. 178.

16. Testimony before the 1869 Lynch Committee regarding the average lifespan of American ships ran from eight years to twelve or thirteen years. That of Provincial ships was considerably shorter. *Causes of the Reducation of American Tonnage. . . .* (Washington, D.C., 1870), pp. 102, 140.

17. In March 1880 Captain Robert Jack, while trying to sell the ship *Hermon* at Havre, wrote (his spelling now vastly improved) to Arthur Sewall: "Everything works slow in this port except the French Veritas surveyors. . . . I had the keelson covered with ballast in hopes it would escape him and only exposed the top as we done in New York but it was no use. He was too smart for me. I can assure you it has made me sick and I wished for you to be here on the spot. I think we have got off pretty cheap as I know her main keelson is a good deal worse than the top. . . . The leak aft I wrote you about I find is caused by worms. I have puttied them up and blacked her over so it is impossible to detect them." One wonders if anyone appreciated the irony of selling a ship named from the Bible in somewhat less than a virtuous manner.

18. Morison, *The Maritime History of Massachusetts*, p.106.

19. W. S. Lindsay, *History of Merchant Shipping and Ancient Commerce* (New York: AMS Press, Inc., 1965), vol. III, p. 15.

20. Arthur H. Clark, *The Clipper Ship Era* (New York: G. P. Putnam, 1910), pp. 123–24.

21. From Goodwin's unpublished autobiography, Maine Maritime Museum library.

22. Much of the foregoing has been adapted from the writings of "The Kennebecker," Hallowell's Captain J. H. Drew—writing being his shipboard pastime—which appeared in various New England newspapers of the 1870s and 1880s.

23. The *Maine Medical and Surgical Reporter* (Portland, ME: November, 1858), pp. 273–76. My thanks to Bill Barry for this.

24. Frank T. Bullen, *The Men of the Merchant Service* (New York: Frederick A. Stokes Company, 1900), pp. 38–39, 264–65.

25. Goodwin, unpublished autobiography, pp. 22–23, 56. Maine Maritime Museum library.

26. Courtesy of David C. Garcelon.

27. Charles R. Flint, *Memories of an Active Life* (New York: G. P. Putnam's Sons, 1923), p. 52.

28. Ibid, p. 53.

29. In a letter to Mark Hennessy, 1930. Captain McDonald, best-known as master of the four-masted bark *Moshulu*, was believed by some to have been of Scandinavian nativity and to have assumed the identity of a deceased partner during the Klondike gold rush.

30. The *Lady Franklin* was the only Sewall vessel that Captain Leavitt commanded. After forty-seven years at sea he retired to Portland, going to work for the Portland shipbrokers and agents Chase, Leavitt & Co. He died in 1911 at age eighty-seven.

31. *Champion* was built at Harpswell by P. R. Curtis, and purchased by Clark & Sewall that year.

32. John G. B. Hutchins, *The American Maritime Industries and Public Policy, 1789-1914* (Cambridge, MA: Harvard University Press, 1941), pp. 264–65.

33. *Eastern Times*, December 17, 1858.

34. *Annual Report of the Chamber of Commerce of the State of New York. 1850–1860* (New York, John W. Amberman, 1860), p. 339.

35. Dr. Jacques M. Downs, *In the Golden Ghetto* (Bethlehem, PA: Lehigh University Press, 1997). A remarkable study of American opium traders at Canton, regarding bills drawn by American China merchants from agents of mostly London merchant banks, most notably

Baring Brothers. "The bills, sold in Canton to opium traders who brought their drug from India and Turkey, ultimately returned to England via India and were cashed against the drawers' accounts. These accounts were kept in funds through American exports to Britain. Thus Americans drank Chinese tea paid for by Southern cotton through the medium of London bills and Asian opium." P. 111.

36. Baker, *A Maritime History of Bath*, vol. 1, p. 488–90.

37. Henry Hall, *Report on the Shipbuilding Industry of the United States* (Tenth Census, Washington, D.C., 1882), pp. 64–67.

38. Charles Nordhoff, *The Merchant Vessel* (New York, Dodd, Mead & Co., 1877), p. 41. See also Frederic William Wallace, *In the Wake of the Wind-Ships* (New York, George Sully & Co., 1927), pp. 64–66; Captain John D. Whidden, *Ocean Life in the Old Sailing Ship Days* (Boston, Little, Brown & Co., 1909), pp. 96–100.

39. From Havre the *Hyde* returned to Mobile and loaded cotton for Trieste, freight and primage amounting to $13,955.76, although Bailey had had to have a new mizzenmast stepped, running expenses up to $7.000, "which takes all the profits off." Letter to Arthur Sewall, July 4, 1858.

40. Nordhoff, *The Merchant Vessel*, pp. 66–67.

41. Kate Baker Chase, in Mildred P. Paine, *Harwich Men of the Sea* (Harwich, MA: Harwich Historical Commission, 1977), p. 47.

42. John G. B. Hutchins, *The American Maritime Industries and Public Policy, 1798–1914* (Cambridge MA: Harvard University Press, 1941), p. 320.

43. A letter from Captain Robert Jack of the ship *William D. Sewall* at Liverpool, March 5, 1850, reads: " My ship chandler bill is higher than usual it includes two life boys & a fitting up a lifeboat as by the last English laws." In December 1856 the *W.D.S.* departed Liverpool for New Orleans with 250 passengers. On the fifty-eight-day passage five died of smallpox, and a sixteen-year-old boy named Riley was lost overboard. In the 1850s many English Mormons were emigrating to the West via New Orleans.

44. Clipping from the *Boston Journal*, condensed for readability.

45. Harnden & Company, the New York charterer of *Rio Grande* on the previous passage, from Baltimore to Liverpool, in a letter dated February 29, claimed that they had been assured that the ship would carry the equivalent of 8,500 barrels of flour in bulk, when in fact she carried but the equivalent of 7,200 barrels, allegedly wiping out their profit. Referring to Clark & Sewall's reputation for doing business "upon principles of the highest honor," the New Yorkers wished to know "what you think equity requires." A letter dated May 23 revealed that Harnden had withheld a portion of the freight money, and that in response "Mr. Sewall gave us the pleasure of suing him here" rather than seeking a settlement "in a spirit of friendship and liberal compromise. . . . Had the ship been as represented, the profit would have been over $1,000 to us." Evidently the dispute was resolved amicably, as Harnden would soon charter the ship again.

46. The *Sherman* had had an eventful year, having been in great danger of sinking on a passage from New Orleans to a port of refuge, Falmouth. After much caulking and re-rigging she had loaded 170 passengers for New York. Arriving at New York on May 28 with all well, Captain Gaskins wrote Clark & Sewall, "I left Falmouth under rather unpleasant circumstances, that is in leaving all of my bills and vouchers behind me. I hope they have been sent on by the American consul from that place."

47. Baker, *Maritime History of Bath*, p. 240.

PART THREE

We first consider William D. Sewall's entanglement in the risky web of early railroad finance. We move on to the story of his oldest son William's experiences in gold-rush California and his tragic death. In the 1850s two of William D.'s other sons, Edward and Arthur, enter the family business. During the Civil War the Sewalls dispose of their ships, but after the war Edward and Arthur rebuild the E. & A. Sewall fleet, finding employment in the guano trade and the California grain trade, which had replaced the cotton trade.

I had rather sink every dollar I have

William D., Edward, and Arthur Sewall were all involved with Maine railroading. William, like many other shipbuilders of his era, helped to usher in the age of the railroad. Arthur became one of the leading railroad men of New England; Edward's railroading activities, on the other hand, were most unfortunate. We are concerned here with William D.'s involvement in a famous Maine railroad controversy.

Lawyers were prime beneficiaries of early railroad-building, along with the shrewd capitalists who picked up the pieces after the dreams of the initial investors had gone to smash. The revolutionary (no pun intended) practical economies produced by rolling a wheel atop a rail, coupled with inexperience, blinded promoters to the true costs and difficulties of construction and operation, frequently resulting in legal and financial chaos.

The history of the Kennebec & Portland Railroad, organized in 1846, was a case in point. Chartered to run from Augusta to Yarmouth (where the "narrow gauge" K & P would meet the "broad gauge" Atlantic & St. Lawrence), along with a branch to Bath, the road was opened in 1848. Among the largest stockholders were the Bath shipbuilders and shipowners George and John Patten, in for 125 and 105 $100 shares respectively, and William D. Sewall, in for 40 shares. The Pattens invested another $50,000, and William Sewall, $2,000, in a separate stock sale required to complete the Yarmouth portion of the line. The purchase of mortgage bonds totaled $49,000 for the Pattens, and $9,000 for Sewall. This was very serious money for the day.

Construction costs were greatly underestimated. As but one small example, while the value of the Bath land taken from Joshua and Charles Sewall was set at only $100, extraneous damages, including damage to mowing fields caused by having to pasture cattle in them, and the clearing of stones in fields after blasting, amounted to an additional $523.75.

The road's key promoter and president, former United States senator Reuel Williams of Augusta, shouldered much of this extra burden. By 1855, in return for monies he had advanced to the railroad, for his endorsements of the treasurer's bills, and as a means of fending off suits seeking to attach railroad property, the road had been largely mortgaged to him. In a January 1856 letter, Williams wrote director Marshal Hagar, a Richmond lawyer and shipbuilder, reporting that he had borrowed $25,000, and "taken up" personal notes amounting to $13,000, in a desperate move to keep the road afloat:[1]

> I have borrowed all the money I can get & paid as high as 9 pc for part of it & must pay back as fast as I can get it. . . . The notes due in Feb., March, and July I must depend on you & Mr. Sewall to meet. . . . I want you to show this to Mr. Sewall & have him prepared to help.

The previous June, Hagar, Sewall, and Patten had signed an agreement with Williams which Williams interpreted as being a promise to help him weather just such a situation. Hagar, Sewall, and Patten, however, had either had a change of heart, or else—as was claimed—believed that Williams had not fulfilled certain obligations to them in order to qualify for assistance. In February 1859 the three responded to Williams's plea: "We do not admit that our liabilities to you under the paper of June 1855 which you hold are such as you desire. . . . Before we do anything now we wait for some developments which time only can make known to us."

Williams was not placated, and pressed in vain for a meeting with the three. In June a frustrated Williams wrote to William Sewall:

> I have a letter from Mr. Hagar saying that he has written to you requesting you to make as early an appointment for a meeting at Augusta as you can so that you may have a calm mind and not feel hurried up & pushed into a meeting before you are ready for it.
>
> I do not understand this unless he or you think I am unreasonably persistent in endeavoring to get a settlement, but when you reflect [it] is more than 4 years since you assumed a liability for my indemnity & three years since I had to pay the money I cannot suppose that you blame me for urging an early settlement especially when I supposed we had made one a year ago.
>
> My necessities require that I should have what is due me & our age admonishes us that what is to be done should be done quickly. I would be glad to meet you as we used to do, but if we must meet on other terms, the sooner it is over the better for all of us.

In 1857, after the K & P had defaulted on the interest on its second mortgage bonds, the trustees of the bondholders took control of the road. In 1859 the three trustees— including Hagar and Patten—caused a foreclosure of the road, operating it themselves until 1864, when a new company, the Portland & Kennebec Railroad, was formed. The rush of war business had reversed the road's fortunes, earnings having increased from $8,000 in 1858 to $103,000 in 1863. But back in 1859, when Williams wrote his letter, that all lay in the future.

In March 1860 Hagar, to Sewall, wrote of Williams: "He is a powerful antagonist. He has wit & craft & will & leisure to plan . . . & we must do our best to get ready for the contest." In a brief to the Maine Supreme Judicial Court, Hagar argued that the agreement was not as was represented by the plaintiff, maintaining that Williams had promised that the funds required would save the defendants' stock value. In February 1861 Hagar wrote William Sewall that the case would soon come to trial, however, "Judge Rice is negotiating with Mr. W."[2]

Judge Richard D. Rice, a justice of the Maine Supreme Judicial Court, was negotiating the purchase of Williams's controlling securities in a deal that would wipe out Williams's claim against Hagar, Sewall, and Patten. A week later, Hagar wrote Sewall: "We all regard his mortgage bonds as the most valuable securities in his suit. I do not wish to be led away blinded by my desire to get Mr. Williams's claims out of the way. I think therefore $100,000 is all we ought to pay him for his whole list clear. . . ."

A most revealing letter to Sewall from Hagar in October 1861, marked "Confidential," reads:

> Judge Rice has not made to us such a proposition as my conscience approves. I do not want to act merely for the sake of making a few dollars & I had rather sink every dollar I have of railroad property than force my conscience to do what I feel to be positively wrong. I do not know as he intends his proposition as an ultimatum. . . . It is so different from all the talk we have ever had upon the subject.

In 1862 Williams and Hagar both died, Hagar having been killed alighting from a train, no less. At the urgings of Colonel Darius Alden, who had conceived the scheme forwarded by Rice to gain control of the K & P by obtaining Williams's securities, Rice had left the bench the better to get rich.[3] Lo and behold, when the P & K emerged out of the wreckage of the K & P, Judge Rice was president.

Not surprisingly, these goings-on led to a lawsuit by the wiped-out stockholders, and it became one of the most celebrated and prolonged of the era. The plaintiffs charged that the foreclosure had all been a sham resulting from a conspiracy among certain directors. When Williams put his securities, representing a mortgaged value of $500,000, up for sale for $113,000, the trustees, according to the plaintiffs, had an obligation to obtain them for the benefit of the road, rather than letting them fall into the hands of Rice and his associates, who purchased them through an agent. Williams, they claimed, had only made the sale believing that it would assist the railroad.[4]

Rice and his friends were accused of having paid for the securities with earnings from the road. If so, it happened all over again when Rice sold the securities to the P & K for $119,456, plus $12,304.36 in interest. The road also picked up the tab for $66,161 in past due coupon payments paid to bondholders.[5] Although the court found no evidence of wrongdoing, it tempered this finding by admitting that, due to the passage of time, the trail had become very cold. In 1926 railroad historian Edward E. Chase concluded that: "The merits of the controversy cannot now be accurately analysed."[6]

From presidency of the P & K, Rice moved to the presidency of the Maine Central Railroad when, in 1870, the latter—an 1862 creation formed from two existing railroads—leased itself to the Portland & Kennebec. P & K stock was exchanged for Maine Central stock, which, by 1873, was worth sixty dollars to seventy dollars per share. When in that same year, the Eastern Railroad purchased a majority interest in the Maine Central, Rice received a special price of a hunded dollars apiece for his 1,600 shares.[7] Darius Alden received 2,670 shares. And William D. Sewall, a director of both the K & P and the P & K, received 450 Maine Central shares.

In 1873 Judge Rice left the Maine Central to become the manager of the Northern Pacific Railroad just in time for the bursting of the Northern Pacific's "bubble," resulting from the failure of the great financier and promoter, Jay Cooke, to sell its securities. This set off the Panic of 1873. Rice's influence with U.S. Speaker of the House James G. Blaine, of Maine, had earlier garnered exceedingly generous federal favors for the project, and his reputation had persuaded many New Englanders, to their sorrow, to invest in the railroad. He resigned from the wreckage in humiliation, his health broken.[8]

William D., however, emerged with nothing to complain about, his reputation evidently intact, and his portfolio much enhanced by valuable Maine Central stock.

I shall try to be good

At age twenty-three William Dunning Sewall, Jr., stood five feet seven inches; had a high forehead—a distinctive Sewall family characteristic to this day—hazel eyes, an ordinary nose, a small mouth, auburn hair, and an oval face. Such, at least, is the description on his certificate for protection—a sort of letter of introduction that Americans traveling in foreign lands could request from a consul—which he obtained on January 26, 1851, at Acapulco, Mexico, where the steamer he was aboard called for bunkers. William was headed home via the Isthmus of Panama after two profitable years in gold-rush-era California.

William D. Sewall, Sr., and his wife, Rachel Allen Trufant, had eight children, of whom seven survived infancy. Two daughters, Harriet and Marcia, were followed by William, an unnamed infant, then Edward, Arthur, Frank, and Alice. In July 1840 William Jr., age thirteen, wrote William Sr., who was probably attending to business in New York:

Mr. Clark has had the store painted blue, the windows yellow, and the door white. It rained yesterday forenoon a little we had about four ton of hay out in it but as it was very green it did not hurt it much. . . . Dear Father, please get me a small fowling piece or a pair of small pistols and I will try and be a good boy.

The letter was written on campaign stationery headed by a cut of the Whig candidate, General William Henry Harrison, and the icon of his campaign, a log cabin with cider barrel by the open door, with two soldiers and the cabin's owner enjoying a convivial glass. Earlier that year Harrison, on a visit to Bath, had visited the Clark & Sewall yard to marvel at the ship *Rappahannock*, a huge vessel for the day, then on the stocks.

For his secondary education, William was sent to North Yarmouth Academy. North Yarmouth being an active shipbuilding and ship-owning community, it is not surprising to read in an 1843 letter, presumably from the headmaster, that William's course of study should enable him "to go through Bowditch's [*New American Practical*] *Navigator* in a few weeks."[9] That fall he joined the Clark & Sewall bark *Detroit*. His father wrote Captain Mitchell Trott:

Allow me to ask of you to devote to him all that attention and care which you may think a youth of his age & inexperience may need, to protect him from the many evils incident to the life he [is] about entering on. Also that you will give him such instruction & advice as you may at any time think will tend to aid him in a course of usefulness & happiness both in this world and the future. . . . In case you may think it ——— for him to attempt to do the duty of a foremast hand, if convenient & agreeable to you I should wish you to give him the privilege of living aft, that he might be kept from too intimate association with such as he might possibly find in the forecastle.

In March 1845, back at Bath, William wrote to his traveling father: "I have been considerably troubled not being able to decide what course to pursue. I have at last concluded to follow the sea for a living (with your consent)." He suggested that he might sail "before the mast"—evidently he had ended up in *Detroit*'s cabin—aboard the ship *Roger Sherman*, which was bound to Europe, and that perhaps "in the future I should be capable to take a 1st or 2nd mate's berth."

Instead, he joined the ship *Macedonia*, writing home from Liverpool in March 1846 that the ship, after arriving from New Orleans, had been four weeks in the dock, and was now bound for the James River via New York. To pay expenses she would carry passengers to Staten Island, laying there but forty-eight hours. Still undecided as to his future, he wrote: "I want you to advise me what to do. [I] should like very much to stop at home with you this summer and go in the new ship in the fall for I think that . . . *if I am going to sea* I had better go steady and may not have another such chance as the present coming summer for some years to come." He ended by stating that he was "about tired of Liverpool and of going to sea."

On December 5, 1848, President Polk announced the discovery of gold in California, and William, back at home, decided—against strong family objections—to join the rush. In response to his letter seeking advice, Richard P. Buck, the New York ship broker, a Sewall relative and business associate, wrote that the steamers to the Isthmus were all booked until March, and thus a passage made "outside," under sail around Cape Horn, would be much less expensive and also less risky—"Isthmus fever" took more lives than did Cape Horn "snorters"— and would arrive at about the same time. He further advised:

> If I were you I would get a fine vessel of 300 or 400 tons & put in 20 house frames & boards enough to cover them & if you will come along this way I will get the balance of your cargo at $2 per barrel as fast as you can take it in. . . . In my opinion the California Boys will be very hungry & —— gold won't satisfy hunger.[10]

Indeed, Buck was then loading just such a vessel himself. But William, writing to Bath from New York several days later, was not to be put off. He was not going to go around the Horn, and had, in fact, secured a passage in the steamer *Crescent City*. He had also obtained several letters of introduction from prominent New Yorkers, and had found a traveling companion. "Now Father & Mother, try & not be anxious for me. . . . I shall try to be good and if I should be taken away before I see you again in this world, I hope I shall be prepared to go & that in Heaven we may meet again."

The steamer *Crescent City* was the first vessel of the United States Mail Line, but recently established to provide the Atlantic portion of a subsidized steamer service, via the Isthmus, between New York and San Francisco. William was aboard for her inaugural run to the Isthmus, leaving New York on December 24, 1848. On January 2, 1849, William wrote home from Chagres (later to be called Aspinwall, and then Colon) after a pleasant passage. About 280 people, delivered by a steamer, a bark, and a brig, were already there, waiting to cross overland, a far cry from the rumored 6,000. About 300 people were said to be in Panama awaiting the arrival of the steamer *California*, the first vessel of the Pacific Mail Line, which had left New York in October, before there had been any talk of gold.

William's next letter, from Panama City, dated January 13, described how he and three companions had spent two days lying on their backs in small, tippy canoes, ascending the Chagres River. It rained nearly continuously. At a "negro village" about twenty-five miles upriver, they remained for three days before continuing on horseback, over mountains and through rivers, to Panama. William remained in good health although six Americans had been "taken away" on the journey from Chagres. Two ships and a schooner were ready to depart for San Francisco, and evidently William took passage on one of them.

There is usually little wind to be found after departing Panama, and William finally arrived at San Francisco in April, writing that it had been a "long & most tedious passage of eighty days." Ashore, all was confusion. After a brief pause to gain his bearings, he accompanied friends to the gold diggings on the San Joaquin River, about 240 miles away. Despite the fact that one miner in one day "took out" gold worth $1,100, William remained but two days, having decided, astutely, that it would be easier to extract gold from miners and would-be miners in San Francisco than from the mines themselves.

Despite its climate, which he described as being "without exception the most disagreeable one that ever I was in," William returned to San Francisco, where shiploads of gold seekers were now arriving daily. With his traveling companion, Augustus Arnold, William threw up a frail store of boards and cloth covering on a rented lot and entered the grocery business. For operating funds, he tendered a note drawn on R. P. Buck & Co., which he would quickly redeem. By 1850 the business had evolved into the successful house known as Robinson, Arnold & Sewall, wholesalers in provisions, fish, groceries, liquors, building supplies, and "miscellaneous" goods. (William had arrived at San Francisco with a letter of introduction to Robinson, who was the San Francisco agent for Howland & Aspinwall, leading New York owners of California clippers. Both Robinson and Arnold may have been Bath boys.)

On May 1, 1849, William wrote home predicting that the market for pine lumber and house frames would remain strong. He ended by advising his father to "be sure and keep Ed at school another year, never think of sending him here —— you want him ruined altogether." As if by way of further explanation, in August he wrote:

This is certainly a hard country to live in, every kind of temptation & vice completely surrounds you & oh Father I hope you will pray to our Father in heaven that he will keep me from them & permit me in his own good time to return to those whom I love. I see by the last papers that the [California] fever is still raging in the states. People are crazy to come out here but mark my words, Father, there will [be] thousands of young men who left good situations at home ruined here, I see them every day.

In July Captain Gaskins of the ship *Roger Sherman,* lying at Antwerp, wrote Clark & Sewall that he was "about concluding" to take a charter from there to California and return for twenty thousand Spanish dollars. Conservative William D. was in no way in favor of such a distant venture, but his scolding letter arrived too late, and the *Sherman* would become the first Sewall ship to "double the Horn"—sailing from 50 South to 50 South—and to arrive at San Francisco.

In September William wrote of his disappointment at not receiving any invoices (by mail via the Isthmus) for a lumber cargo en route:

San Francisco continues to flourish & increase very rapidly. Great numbers of buildings are being put up of all descriptions for churches, theatres, gambling houses, stores, dwellings, etc. . . . Ships are arriving very fast. The harbor is now nearly full, as near as I can judge there are now 300 sails in port. What they are all going to do this winter no one can tell. There is nothing for them to do here. Their crews leave immediately on their arrival. No law here can keep them on board. . . . I hope you have not any large vessel of your own coming here. The brig I think I could sell at a fair price, or perhaps get her some business but for a large vessel or ship there is nothing they can do and here they will have to lay I am afraid until they rot.

1851. The fleet of abandoned ships at San Francisco. Maine Maritime Museum

Evidently the idea of sending a small brig out with lumber had already been broached. In October Father William, becoming bolder at last, wrote that he had shipped "one heavy old carriage" which he hoped would bring a fair price—it would bring three hundred dollars—by the ship *Hampton*. Also, Clark & Sewall had bought, with Captain Pinkham, the brig *Almira*, 137 tons, which they were now loading for San Francisco. She would be carrying a mixed cargo including house frames with window frames and sashes, doors, shingles, nails, brick, planed pine boards, and also pork, pickles, and butter.

On May 18, 1850, William wrote that both the *Roger Sherman* and the *Almira* had arrived. *Almira's* arrival was well timed, since there had just been a most destructive fire that made the lumber market brisk for a few days. Her cargo was expected to net $5,000. (Remittances were sent to New York in the form of gold nuggets and dust.) *Almira* and the *Sherman* were sold for $4,600 and $5,000, respectively, the *Sherman*, old and strained, was evidently not thought worth sending home, particularly at the very high wages sailors were demanding.

Clark & Sewall had by then also dispatched their ship *Macedonia*, Captain Joseph Snow of Brunswick. Arriving in August, Captain Snow wrote that since leaving Boston he had not seen land for 157 days, and that his chronometer had been an excellent investment. He hoped never to find a place that he disliked more than this—with 400 to 500 sail in port, many of them deserted, and no harbor regulations, vessels were daily swinging foul of each other and being damaged. *Macedonia* was chartered to proceed to Calcutta.

Returning home in April 1851, well satisfied with his adventure, William was made a partner in Clark & Sewall. He also got married. In September he was killed by an all-too-common shipyard accident. In an obituary for *The New Jerusalem*

Magazine, the Reverend Dike, of the Swedenborgian church, wrote:

> He was followed [to California] with intense and prayerful interest by his family and other New Church friends, both on account of the dangers besetting his path and natural life, and also, the danger to which he seemed exposed from the love of wealth, so liable to be strengthened and confirmed by its gratification.. . . . After prosecuting a successful business for three years he returned, professing that his *anxiety* for the possession of money had left him. . . . Full of life, happiness and hope, he was . . . engaged in showing some gentleman a ship, the building of which he had been personally superintending, when, by a misstep, he was precipitated from the staging a distance of twenty-two feet, and survived the fall only about five hours. . . . On the Sabbath before his demise, he spent some time in reading from the treatise on Heaven and Hell, what is there said on the states of departed souls, and conversing with his wife on the same.

Shipyard staging, being a temporary structure erected by subcontractors, was usually built to be just good enough, and with little thought to safety.

William's son, William Dummer, was born after his death and died in September of 1856 of the croup.

Very active and industrious

In 1854 the operation of William D.'s shipyard was transferred from Clark & Sewall to E. & A. Sewall—that is, to Edward and Arthur Sewall, who celebrated their twenty-first and nineteenth birthdays, respectively, that year. "Wm. D. Sewall & Co." and "Wm. D.

Sewall & Sons" appear on correspondence that year, and occasionally later, and William D. Sewall is listed as having signed the customhouse documents of both ships launched in 1854, *Samaritan* and *Holyhead*.

Some confusion attends the transition. Tradition places *Holyhead* at the top of the E. & A. Sewall fleet list, although the contracts to build her were made by William D., and her captains' letters are addressed to Clark & Sewall. This would indicate that the 1855 ship *Kineo* was in fact the first E. & A. Sewall vessel. *Kineo* would be followed over the next twenty-three years—until Edward left the partnership in 1879—by thirty-one ships, three barks, one brig, and two schooners.

While the mantle had been passed, the shift may have been so seamless as to have even been invisible to some. William D. was still on hand to give advice—indeed, he would do so for the rest of his life—and the small nucleus of loyal investors, including William D. and Thomas M. Reed, who supported the Clark & Sewall fleet, now invested in the E. & A. Sewall fleet. Master shipbuilder Daniel Small, who had been building ships "by the ton" for Clark & Sewall, continued doing so with E. & A. Sewall. Indeed, carpenter Henry Merryman, interviewed in 1914, who in 1854 returned to the Sewall yard—he had worked there on *Erie* in 1851— to work for Daniel Small, did not then recall that Edward and Arthur had taken over until 1860, with the building of *Ocean Scud*. Of the boom shipbuilding year of 1854, Merryman recalled:

> That may be called the golden period of shipbuilding in Bath. There were many yards. . . . As soon as one [ship] was launched the keel of another one was placed and the work went constantly on. At that time no one ever thought that the business would ever die. Not only was the city a bee hive of human industry but the farmers for miles around were constantly coming in with timber, masts, and hackmatack knees which found a ready sale. Then we gradually commenced to get timber from Virginia and this came in vessels making the harbor a lively place. Large crews of men went south every fall to cut timber. . . . In 1860 I was with Wm. D. Sewall and Clark for a time and then came the Sewall boys, Arthur and Edward, who took charge of the business. . . . When I worked for Daniel Small in the Sewall yards, I received $3 per day as a carpenter much of the time, and when I left there I was getting $1.25 a day. That was because there was but little doing.[11]

It is also possible, of course, that his interviewer misunderstood him. In any event, Merryman had nothing but good things to say about the Sewalls specifically, and also generally about other shipbulders of the era. He also said that there were no labor troubles or strikes.

One notable change in how E. & A. Sewall conducted business was in the manner of drawing up agreements. Whereas William D. contracted to build a ship with but the equivalent of jotted-down handshakes, agreements between E. & A. Sewall and contractors and others were considerably longer and more detailed, leaving little opportunity for possible misunderstanding. For example, a simple sales agreement with Captain Timothy Everett, dated August 1855, regarding his purchase of one-eighth of

*Arthur Sewall, 1835–1900, and Emma Duncan Crooker (Sewall), 1836–1919,
possibly about the time of their marriage in 1859.* MAINE MARITIME MUSEUM

the ship that would be *Kineo*, to be "in all respects equal to any of the ships Messrs Clark & Sewall have built within the last two years," consumes the entirety of a large sheet of writing paper.

According to the local snitch for R. G. Dun's New York credit agency, in May 1856 Edward and Arthur were both considered "very active & industrious." Both were still single, had perfect credit, and if necessary would be assisted by their father, as plenty of credit was available "right at home."[12] Indeed, the two boys had enjoyed the most advantageous possible circumstances for learning all aspects of the business.

At age sixteen, Arthur traveled to Prince Edward Island buying hackmatack knee timber. In the winter of 1857, at age twenty-two, he traveled to New Orleans to learn the cotton business, and later sailed to Havre aboard a cotton ship. We don't know what Edward might have done to broaden his practical education. While Arthur's 1896 vice-presidential campaign biography would claim that he was capable of performing "every part of the work" of constructing a ship, this was surely an exaggeration for political reasons, but no doubt both boys became thoroughly familiar with every phase of vessel construction.

The entrance of these two ambitious, smart, harmonious, detail-oriented, and persevering young men into the family business at this particular juncture was most timely. The Civil War, on top of the already depressed state of shipping in the late 1850s, would deal a crippling blow to the American merchant marine just at the time when its greatest generation of shipbuilders and owners was growing old and passing from the scene. While most of their sons looked elsewhere for more promising opportunities, Edward and Arthur chose to stem the tide.

Catching up with Sewall family matters, in 1856 Edward married Sarah Elizabeth Swanton of Bath, who was always called "Sade." In 1859 Arthur married Emma Duncan Crooker, who came from an old Bath shipbuilding family.

Eldest sister Harriet married Abram Lowe Cutler of Brookline, Massachusetts, owner of a paint and glass business. She had nine children, and owned shares in a number of Sewall vessels. Older sister Marcia married Joseph Ropes, an artist from Salem, Massachusetts. She lived in Italy after her marriage and had three children.

Frank, their younger brother, married Thedia Gilchrist, who bore him five daughters. A Bowdoin graduate, the Reverend Frank became a distinguished Swedenborgian theologian. A man for all seasons, he was an educator, artist, architect, prolific author, and a dogged investor in the Sewall fleet.

Alice, the youngest, never married. She lived in Bath all her life and owned in Sewall vessels.

And set him on fire

The sudden ending of the cotton trade by the outbreak of the Civil War dealt a severe blow both to Northern shipowners and to English textile mill owners and their suddenly destitute workers. The shipowners' situation was made very much worse by the activities of Confederate raiders, two of which were built in Britain with the support of powerful Southern sympathizers who accused the North of interfering with Britain's special relationship with the cotton-growing South. (Teddy Roosevelt's Confederate uncle, Captain James Bullock, played a central role in this affair.)

The raiders destroyed 239 vessels, but did even more serious damage to Northern shipowners by raising insurance premiums. As a result, from 1861 to 1865, about 801,300 gross tons of shipping—out of 2,500,000 tons registered for foreign trade—were sold to foreign buyers, chiefly British, usually at fire-sale prices.[13] While a number of owners continued to operate their re-flagged tonnage as agents, many others, including the Sewalls, sold out for the best deals they could get, and America's loss was Britain's gain. Clark & Sewall had already sold two vessels in 1860, and disposed of four others during the war. (*Holyhead*, whose ownership is a matter of question, was condemned and sold at auction in 1865.)

During the war E. & A. Sewall sold six vessels and lost one, not counting four ships, a bark, and a brig built during the war, with all but one either sold on the stocks or within a short time after launching. (The exception, the bark *Volant*, was sold days after Appomattox.) It would appear that the only vessel remaining in their fleet at the end of the war was the ship *America*, built for them by Johnson Rideout at his yard, and launched in November 1864.

Maine emerged from the Civil War with a well-deserved reputation as a solid Republican state with an unsurpassed record of support for the Union cause. No less than 800 Bathites served in the army or navy during the war, and 109 lost their lives.

But the story was not as simple as that. In the months leading up to war there was considerable support, from both Republicans and Democrats, for making concessions to the South to keep the peace. Indeed, the Bath *Times* favored allowing South Carolina to secede from the Union. Shortly after Lincoln's election a group of leading Maine Republicans, including such luminaries as Portland's sugar king J. B. Brown and plutocrat W. W. Thomas; Bangor lumberman General F. C. Hersey; and even the progressive writer and thinker John Neal, advocated the suspension of state "liberty laws" which made it difficult for slave owners to regain their runaway property.[14]

Democrats divided into "War Democrats" and "Peace Democrats," with many degrees thereof between. War Democrats backed fighting to preserve the Union if it came to that, and some, like Samuel Cony—who was married to William D. Sewall's half-sister Mercy; Mercy's sister Margaret was married to John Cony, Samuel's cousin—became Republicans with the outbreak of war.[15] Cony was elected governor as a Republican in 1861, and in 1863 was reelected as a Unionist, a label Republicans adopted in an effort to attract War Democrats to their fold.

Peace Democrats—known to foes as "copperheads"—opposed Lincoln and his policies, and were sympathetic to the South's position on states' rights. Not surprisingly, many Maine ship owners, including William D. and apparently his sons as well, were of this persuasion, no doubt because of their strong economic and social ties to the South. (In Thomaston, a shipping town said to be composed largely of Southern sympathizers, feelings were so strong even after the war had ended that two well-known ladies reportedly danced upon hearing of Lincoln's assassination.)[16]

William D. blamed abolitionists and Lincoln for driving the South into a corner, and supported the Southern position on states' rights. The naming of the 1847 ship *John C. Calhoun*—one of the few Sewall vessels to be embellished with a figurehead[17]—honoring the firebrand pro-slavery and states' rights advocate, raises questions as to what degree this represented a shrewd marketing ploy for a ship that did frequent business in Southern cotton ports, or her owners' heartfelt sentiments.[18] In March 1861, a few weeks before Fort Sumter was fired upon, William wrote of his concerns to his cousin, New York shipping broker R. P. Buck.[19] Buck responded:

> Friend Sewall, Your remarks in your last to me require a word in reply. You speak continuously or repeatedly of interference by the North with the South. Now it appears to me this has nothing to do with the question at issue. The fact of a Northern state passing a law obnoxious to the South is no excuse whatever for rebellion against the Federal Government. Revolution for cause grows out of a party in power oppressing the party ruled. . . . The U.S. Supreme Court decisions are all favorable to the Peculiar Institution [slavery], as it is called, and until the U.S. government as a ruling power oppress, or in some manner abridge the right of the states I cannot conceive what right a state has to break off its allegiance. . . .

Buck thought the true cause of secession was the loss of power by the South. He was sorry to see the seceding states leave the Union, but would let them go without a fight. He thought that Lincoln was trying to be reasonable, and that he would not be surprised if within two years Lincoln would be as popular with William as he would be with "all good patriots north and south." But in September 1864, in a letter to his sons, William was as yet unpersuaded, and noting the strong support for Lincoln and the abolitionists in the coming election, saw no hope for relief from "the present state of political misrule for another four years, and all the consequences that are to result from such."

In May of 1861 E. & A. Sewall wrote Captain Fred Bosworth aboard their 1859-built ship *Vigilant* at Bordeaux. Bosworth was advised to cease long voyaging, and indeed to sell *Vigilant* at a fair price if possible:

We presume you are fully aware of the status of the country, that civil war is upon us, and that we cannot expect otherwise than a severe struggle between the sections of this [country this] coming summer, or at least before a settlement, if not a long ruinous war.

In November 1861, *Vigilant,* Captain Peleg Curtis, while bound from New York for the guano island of Sombrero in the West Indies, was captured and burned by the Confederate raider *Sumter* under Commander Semmes.[20] Commander Semmes's journal read in part:

Tuesday, Dec. 3—A fine clear day, with a light breeze from the S.E., freshening. At 6:30, "Sail ho!" a point on the starboard bow. At 7:30 the sail, which was standing in nearly the opposite direction from ourselves, approached us within a couple of miles. We hoisted French colors, when she showed United States. Took in all studding sails, hauled by the wind, tacked, and fired a shotted gun. The stranger immediately hove to. Lowered a boat and sent a lieutenant on board of him. Stood on and tacked, and having brought the stranger under my guns I began to feel sure of him (our smokestack was down and we could not have raised steam in less that two hours and a half). He proved to be the ship *Vigilant* of Bath, Me. . . . Captured him, took from on board chronometer, charts, etc., and a 9 pounder rifled gun, with ammunition, etc. and set him on fire, and at 3 P.M. made sail. This fine, new ship . . . was worth about $40,000. . . . [21]

From the "beautiful bonfires" he created, Semmes kept captives aboard his ship until conditions became too crowded, at which point they were put aboard a prize to return to the United States.

On January 12, 1862, Captain Arthur Prince of their ship *Champion*[22] wrote Clark & Sewall from Sombrero Island: "I understand you chartered the *Vigilant* to load here and she has been so long coming they have given her up as lost." Word on the island was that war with England was certain. Captain Prince wanted advice, as he was chartered to Liverpool.

Of course, disagreeing with policies that brought on the war, and deploring the continuation of the war, was not to suggest that the Sewalls hoped for defeat of the Union. The ship *Vicksburg*, launched in July 1863 and quickly sold by E. & A. Sewall to a British buyer for a handsome profit, was obviously named to celebrate the recent Union victory. (The appearance of the name of the former Confederate general "Wade Hampton" on Arthur's postwar lists of possible ship names likely had more to do with Democratic politics of the time.)

As was commonly done, Edward and Arthur both hired draft substitutes; Edward's, in 1863, being Francis Kelly; Arthur's, in 1864, Francis Sullivan.[23]

The Sewalls would eventually receive some restitution for the loss of *Vigilant* in the *Alabama* claims settlement.

It is plain she is not seaworthy

In December 1860, with the fears of impending war closing in on the shipping people of New Orleans like a vise, there was rising pressure to get one last cotton cargo out, and to not have ships stranded there when worse came to worse. On the 8th, agents Cammack & Converse wrote William D. Sewall asking what should be done with the ship *Sarah G. Hyde*. Her captain, George Bailey, had rejected a cargo of tobacco for Spain because, he said, it would not stow well in her 'tween decks. He had also turned down a cotton cargo for Liverpool, looking instead for something to the Mediterranean.

The *Hyde*, as it turns out, had badly wormed planking around her load waterline, and evidently Bailey feared that his ship was not fit for northern winter waters. Apprised by Bailey of the situation, William D. wrote back that the only "wise & proper" course would be to "dispose of her" at New Orleans. Bailey responded that she could not stand to be sold subject to examination, and advised that the best plan would be to "let them look at the ship and make their own offer and take her for better or worse."

Cammack & Converse then wrote:

At the request of Capt. Bayley [sic] we have advertised the *Sarah G. Hyde* for sale. . . . South Carolina having voted herself out of the Union, we suppose other Southern states will soon follow & when the end of this is to be no one can tell. We would much like to see this political trouble settled as it is interfering very much with all branches of trade.

They then suggested to Bailey the possibility of sheathing over the wormed planking with boards. Bailey wrote Bath:

The only way she can be made tight is to sheath with boards. By [just] re-nailing the copper it would make her more safe but I have my fears she would not be tight and would require much pumping which is difficult to keep secret and [would] be the cause of anxiety and trouble. What the expenses may be to sheath with boards [to] the depth of 4 feet from stem to stern I cannot tell until I find a carpenter [who is] the right sort of a man to do such work and is not interested for the insurance people. She will not require docking. Can be careened enough to sheath all that will be required.

Captain Bailey found a carpenter who had often done such work, but worried that the underwriters would find out and would then order the ship docked and thoroughly inspected:

In case they should get wind of it no doubt they would order the *plank* taken off & that would not be the end. The next move would be to examine inside and that would not bear inspection. The consequence is we would be obliged to place many new timbers which would cost more than the ship is worth. . . . One great trouble is if the crew and officers find considerable pumping they have an excel-lent excuse to leave after receiving large advance and it is a hard matter to find an officer that will not turn *traitor* no matter how well he is treated.

On December 26 Bailey wrote that the carpenter advised against sheathing, as the underlying planks were too badly wormed. He had also made some borings in timbers, which were found to be sound, and judged that the frame was good. Bailey suspected that the carpenter was keeping the agents informed of the situation, and that some friends might well buy her. Then Bailey discovered that the mainmast head was rotten.

On January 3, 1861, Bailey wrote of a rise in freight rates, but three days later warned: "If she should go to sea and never arrive in port again as many a good ship never does, the question is whether the insurance [people] would not find some hole to crawl out." He suspected that his former mate, despite having been used "like a brother," might cause trouble, and paid him to leave town.

I cannot see any possible way to do it [the sheathing] and not have it publicly known. Therefore I have almost concluded to load . . . and trust to fortune there-after. . . . One thing is certain. If the copper once started she will go down. All the pumps in the world could not keep her free and to put on the sheathing is impos-sible to do and keep the underwriters from knowing it.

On the 14th Bailey wrote that he would only sheath the vessel under direct orders: "I have come to the conclusion if we cannot load her after re-nailing the copper and get out of this place soon as possible before it is too late. To all appearance government troubles is growing worse and worse every day."

That letter crossed paths with one from William D.: "If the ship is in the situation you have represented in your letters, it is plain she is not seaworthy and of course it is not proper to engage in the freighting business and must be made seaworthy before engaging in any business." The options he laid out were to sell her for no less than $8,000; to make adequate temporary repairs, if possible, in the $1,000–$1,500 range;

make substantial repairs not to exceed $5,500; or, if all else failed, to lay her up.

On January 16 Captain Bailey sold the *Hyde* for $12,000 "as she stands without any guarantee as to her soundness or good qualities. The gentlemen that bought are New Yorkers and as near as I can find out deal in old ships for they have one loading now here some twenty years old."

On the 17th, Cammack & Converse concluded: "We look upon dissolution as inevitable. There seems to be no chance to save the Union. Although there are many good men yet left, the abolition fanatics seem determined to drive the South to the last extremity." A few days later they expressed hope that E. & A. Sewall's *Villafranca* and *Valentia* would arrive in time to benefit from the high freights being offered.

Records show that the *Hyde* received some major repairs in 1861. Ten years later she was sailing yet, under the British flag, as the *Trowbridge*, of London. Evidently her frame had yet been sound, as the carpenter had judged.

In 1889 Arthur Sewall received a letter from Philena N. Bailey of Pittston:

Some years ago one of your father's ships was the birthplace of a baby girl. She was christened in honor of the ship, Sarah G. Hyde Bailey. The letter G we have never known what name it represents. In a few days she will change her maiden name and we would like to know her whole name. I have thought you may know something of it as your father was one of the principal owners. . . . .

Sarah G. Hyde was Freeman Clark's third wife.

Irregular, unjust, and not strictly legal

Arthur Sewall's campaign biography in 1896, when he was the Democratic candidate for vice president, stated that no Sewall ships—that is, while under Sewall ownership— were put under a foreign flag during the Civil War. This was presumably an attempt to blunt any attack on Arthur's patriotism for his lack of a personal war record. However, a Clark & Sewall ship was briefly put under a foreign flag, although not with the firm's foreknowledge. But neither did the firm object.

In January 1862 Captain Isaac Preble of Hallowell, aboard the ship *Erie* at Montevideo, Uruguay, having found it impossible to get a charter while under the American flag, wrote Clark & Sewall:

I suppose that you will be surprised to hear what I have done with the *Erie*. I have made a [switch?] of her and put her under the Montevideo flag. I got the papers engrossed back to Mr. Coelho with a power to sell and want you to have the insurance policies made out for the ship *Dona Plisa* of Montevideo. Had to change the name of the ship to make everything legal and I hope you will approve of what I have done in our troublesome times. . . . As soon as I changed my flag I got a full cargo of talc and salt hides [dunnaged with bones] for Liverpool and I am loading and I think I shall get away from here in 20 days. . . . We have had a report here today that England was going to war with the United States but we can't tell whether it is true or not but they will not ship by English ships today.

A month later *Erie* was still in port, all loading having been suspended awaiting further news of war or peace. Preble wrote: "I have taken a power of attorney and a letter book stating all the particulars of sale and ownership, that the sale was made to change the flag, that she belongs [to] the original owner. . . . You can get the policies endorsed & on the register is the name of Joseph Coelho and you can have her insured in his or your name."

From Bath, Clark & Sewall wrote Captain Preble:

We have your favor . . . advising of the changes in name & nation of the ship *Erie*. This arrangement is of course all new to us but we trust it will be for the best, at any rate we have no doubt you acted from the best of motives. . . . Our wish is to dispose of this ship at the best advantage [at Liverpool] as she is of an age that will be constantly requiring repairs. . . . We presume she can be closed at a fair price.

Captain Preble was advised to put the ship's business at Liverpool in the hands of Messrs. James Brown & Co. On August 2 Captain Preble wrote from Liverpool that he had entered her as the ship *Erie*, had placed her on the market for £3,000, and thought he might get a taker at £2,400. If not, he might have a freight to Nassau. On August 30 he wrote that he had accepted a charter carrying coal to Rio de Janeiro, then to go to the Chincha Islands for guano, to return to Rotterdam or Hamburg. He had put the ship on the gridiron [dry-dock] and found her bottom sound, although some timbers on the port side were rotted halfway through. These had been repaired by removing the ceiling and installing graving pieces, reinforced by pointers.

On September 20 Clark & Sewall sent a letter to await Captain Preble on his arrival at Rio:

We regret you had not placed the ship in the hands of Messrs. James Brown & Co. as we directed you as we had given them directions to dispose of the ship to the best advantages without any hesitation and had said the same to yourself as this ship was well advanced in age. . . . This engagement you have made we are sorry to say is not at all satisfactory as the ship cannot possibly pay her expenses being too small entirely for such business. As the affairs now stand we have thought it necessary to send a new master to take the charge of the *Erie*.

A letter was also written to Captain Jabez Minott of Brunswick instructing him to take passage on the next vessel bound from the U.S. to Rio, there to take charge of *Erie* and to collect her freight and charter money.

Now enters Mr. L. Watson Webb of the United States Legation at Petropolis—the temperate mountainous summer capital of Brazil. Clark & Sewall received a copy of a letter from Webb, written December 8, to George Barrett, the acting United States consul in Rio, informing Barrett that Captain Preble had been to Petropolis to see Webb regarding Preble's removal from command:

> He says it is in contemplation to turn him adrift without furnishing him with the means of returning to the United States. . . . It does not appear that there is any charge of fraud or intended fraud or embezzlement made against him, and it would undoubtedly be a very hard and unjustifiable proceeding if the owners were to leave him in Rio in a destitute condition and without the means of getting home.

Webb could take no official action, but urged Barrett to read the letter to the consignees of the cargo, who had not yet paid the freight, and also to Preble's appointed successor, to see if some amicable solution could be worked out. The consul had no authority to send Preble home at government expense.

On December 20 Captain Preble very belatedly wrote Bath that *Erie* had arrived on November 25, forty-nine days out from Cork. When ten days out Captain Preble had broken his leg, and had suffered much, and was not yet well. Three days after the ship's arrival Captain Minott showed up, but Preble had only given the ship up to him the day before, as the consignee wished for Preble to deliver the cargo. Preble had now finished discharging, and had put 150 tons of ballast in her, and had then given over the papers to Captain Minott. Preble then again wrote Clark & Sewall:

> Gentlemen, I have always done everything I could for your interest but I may have made mistakes. We are all liable to err in judgment. The *Erie* is a strong ship and will make the voyage as well as the best of ships with care. She had ought to bring back 750 tons for I have landed 711 tons of coal. The ship will be ready for sea in 3 or 4 days.

A letter to Clark & Sewall from Consul Barrett dated December 29 reported that the ship had been turned over to Captain Minott, and noted that had Captain Minott been given a "full and perfect instrument for power of attorney there would have been fewer difficulties, and Captain Preble would have been better satisfied."

> As it is, he thinks the effort to remove him from command in a foreign port irregular, unjust, and not strictly legal. . . . Captain Preble claimed a balance in his favor of twelve or thirteen hundred dollars, and although Capt. Minott did not feel authorized to settle with Capt. P. he accepted the only terms upon which he would yield up the ship and her papers. But I would do Capt. Preble the justice to say that he evinced a disposition to do what he considered *fair* and *right*, and in conclusion I will only add that in my efforts to carry out your wishes in this matter I trust I have not done injustice to either party.

In 1863 *Erie* was sold at Hamburg for £1,600, and was renamed *Argentina*.

Frank is no more

With the sudden cutting-off of Southern ship timber, builders were forced to look to mid-Atlantic, northern New England, Canadian, and local sources.

The 1860 acquisition by Bath shipbuilders of the just-completed and yet already bankrupt Androscoggin Railroad would soon prove a wise investment. Although the Androscoggin's roadbed was so full of "humps" and "hollows" that a locomotive's big, spark-arresting stack disappeared from sight from the caboose monitor, and progress was frequently interrupted by numerous farmers' bar-ways, the road opened up a new territory of ship timber at a critical juncture.

Likely along its winding path to Farmington there were many "pasture oak"—solitary old trees too big to have been worth the effort to chop down just for firewood, and which had been doing duty providing shade for livestock. Many such trees no doubt contained within their trunks a good stem, or a sternpost.

In December 1863 Mr. James S. Nash, of Livermore, was cutting a ship frame of "grey" oak for E. & A. Sewall, to be delivered across the frozen Androscoggin River to the railroad. As Nash was evidently short of skilled help, the Sewalls sent him some men, who pleased him much, and who he promised "to return in good condition if cider and apples will keep them so, together with such other living as we can pick up for them." Livermore was indeed good cider country. In November 1864 Nash was sawing out oak planking when he wrote to the Sewalls:

> I suppose you have received 2 car loads of lumber from me this week. The cars came for me to load on Saturday last so as to load on Sunday but I received the sad news on Saturday evening of the death of my oldest son who was shot in the battle of [Wednesday ?] under [General] Sheridan. My neighbors went over and loaded the cars. I thought I would try and come down to see you but my feelings is such and my health altogether I thought I would drop you a line now and come down when I feel better if I ever do. . . . If you will send me what may be due me now by express to Livermore Falls you will much oblige me as I am going to send and try to get the remains of my son. I don't feel as if I could live and have his remains lay out there. Say to Mr. Small and Garcelon if you see them that Frank is no more. He has fought his last battle. Please send so I can have it tomorrow and you will oblige one in affliction.

The people up here are peculiar

Wooden shipbuilding supported a small army of tough, colorful woodsmen who "cruised" the forests looking for stands of timber or regal spar trees, and contracted to make delivery of same. Rail connections were vital for making inland hardwood ship timber available. Spruce spar timber was delivered both by rail and by river. Below are some snippets from woodsmen's correspondence with the Sewalls.

From J. W. Coffin & Co., Cherryfield, Maine, January 23, 1870:

> We have a vessel frame for sale. Yellow birch & rock maple all moulded for 500
> to 550 tons with keel, kellson, stern & stem —— and a hackmatack top moulded.
> The frame is all of old growth and the hardwood is seasoned.

The Sewalls were offered a number of ship frames—in pieces, of course. A few were located in Boston, the plans to build the ship there having evidently fallen through, while others appear to have been cut on speculation. Some were said to have been made from the moulds of a successful vessel.

From G. S. Libby, writing from Fryeburg, Maine, June 20, 1873, on a contracted job cutting a frame for the Sewalls:

> As the most of the hardwood is square hewing, shall endeavor to get along with
> ordinary broad axe men. But shall *have* to have a man from your yard when we
> come to the hack. . . . Mr. Larabee is moulding the frame.

Hackmatack, or larch, was often used for the top timbers of a vessel frame, it being more rot-resistant and also lighter than oak, thereby increasing the ship's stability and carrying ability and possibly its longevity.

From G. S. Libby, writing from West Charleston, Vermont, January 9, 1874:

> The moulds are reduced to a mere armful . . . but Young found a bundle at
> Bangor Depot last week (counter timber) which we did not know anything
> about. . . . They have arrived at Island Pond.

Libby was explaining that the frame has been almost all cut, excepting timbers for the stern, their moulds—patterns—having just been discovered at a railroad station.

From Libby again, writing from West Charleston, Vermont, January 21, 1874:

> I have succeeded in getting 20 teams . . . this involves a heavy additional expense.
> Please therefore to send me $200 to Island Pond. . . . *Don't fail to send it* as the
> teamsters are strangers to me & from 3 or 4 different towns, and my *word* as well
> as credit is at stake.

Mr. Libby had hired local teamsters to move the hewn timber from the woods to the nearest Grand Trunk rail siding and wanted to be sure to be able to pay the men promptly.

From Libby, Island Pond, Vermont, January 28 , 1874:

> I have just begun hauling timber, have been waiting for *Snow.* Have tried to haul
> on *wagons* but while the fields & hills are bare the hollows & woods are a sheet

of *ice* & the wagons slide into the ditch & upset. Can get it all [with sleds] in 3 days after snow. . . . Please forward [$300] at once if you have not already done so, as the people up here are peculiar like the "Heathen Chinese" & won't let their timber leave their land till every cent is paid on it.

From the legendary timber cruiser, frame-timber moulder, and spar contractor James Larrabee, who was said to have an uncanny ability to see a spar in a standing tree, writing from Stark, New Hampshire, November 23, 1878:

Gents, are you in want of any spruce spars this winter or next summer? If you are I can accommodate you at a reasonable price. Please drop me a line and I will bring you some spruce gum when I come.

Spruce gum, exuded from a wound in the bark, was America's first chewing gum. It was a commercial commodity, collected in the forests by the wandering members of the motley tribe of gum-pickers, and used in the manufacture of chewing gum produced in largest part by the John B. Curtis Company at Portland, Maine.

From W. A. Manning, of Manning & Soper, suppliers of "Domestic ship lumber of all kinds," from Newport, Maine, December 4, 1875. The timber was being hauled out seventeen miles to the railroad:

Every stick of the frame is out & they are hauling it but there is not much snow. . . . I have bought 2 good barrels of cider for you but those barrels you sent are not fit to put it in. I have tried my best to clean them . . . they are musty still. Shall I buy some good barrels?

On December 27, 1878, Manning wrote:

I have sent by freight 2 barrels of cider. . . . They are both extra. I don't think there is any choice in them. I have also sent jar of butter 62 lbs, 22$^1/_2$ lbs jar, leaving 39$^1/_2$ lbs butter. This butter was all made last June from one cow by my wife. It is possible that the top layer is not as good as the rest as that is usually the case.

From Sturgis, Lambard & Co. of Augusta, Maine, November 14, 1884:

We have got in our [Kennebec River log-holding] boom here a very nice pine log about 45 feet long, 3 feet through at the butt and nearly holds its size to the top. It is smooth and sound, and I should think would make a magnificent bowsprit for a ship. Do you want it?

From the Bisbee Brothers, vessel frame contractors from West Camden, Maine, writing from their winter headquarters at New Kent Court House, Virginia, on December 31, 1888:

I notice in paper that you are having a mould made for a very large ship to be built next summer. If you have not purchased the frame we —— cut it for you. We are cutting a schooner for Thomaston parties that is nearly cut and we are going to cut one for Storer for Waldoboro.

Turds of foreign birds

The July 31, 1857, Bangor *Whig & Courier* printed a list of eighty-five American ships that had loaded guano cargoes and sailed from, or were loading or awaiting loading at, Peru's three small Chincha Islands in the ninety-six days previous to June 22, 1857. Some of the ships had been waiting since December—lengthy delays were common in the trade. No Sewall ship was among this fleet, but E. & A. Sewall's ship *Kineo* would arrive from Melbourne in October.

In 1857 the London firm of Gibbs & Co., until 1861 the largest concessionaire of the Peruvian guano business, dispatched 477 ships from the islands.[24] A famous sailor's ditty went "The House of Gibbs that made its dibs / By selling the turds of foreign birds."

The fleet listed in the *Whig & Courier* included Maine-built ships launched at Bath, Thomaston, Biddeford, Castine, Farmingdale, Pittston, Richmond, Yarmouth, Rockport, Harpswell, Kennebunkport, Stockton, Freeport, Brunswick, Hampden, Damariscotta, and Bowdoinham. All were launched in the 1850s; some were genuine clippers. The monarch of the fleet was among the most celebrated of all American ships, the East Boston–built 3,387-ton *Great Republic*. Such was the importance of the guano trade. Many of these ships were returning from San Francisco, and likely Melbourne, having sailed to the Chinchas in ballast.

Among the listed ships was the *Rochambeau*, Captain George Gilchrest of Thomaston. Aboard this ship young Irishman William R. Grace, then clerking aboard a floating chandlery located off the islands in a moored hulk, met his future wife, eighteen-year-old Lillius Gilchrest. The store hulk was an annex of the Lima firm of John Bryce & Co., later Bryce, Grace & Co., agent to the Sewall guano ships. William R. Grace, later mayor of New York, was the founder of W. R. Grace & Co., which would grow to vast proportions.[25]

Peruvian guano was composed of the excrement of cormorants and seals, and the carcasses of same, having fed upon the teeming schools of little *anchoveta* fish that thrived in the rich, cold Humboldt current sweeping northward along the coast from antarctic waters. Accumulating for countless centuries in a rainless climate, the guano was the world's best fertilizer, very high in nitrogen and phosphorus, and even small amounts had a spectacularly salubrious effect on crops growing in the worn-out soils of Europe, Britain, and certain regions of the United States, and elsewhere.

The shipment of guano to Britain and Europe began about 1840, the trade growing to great importance to shipping, to agriculture, and to Peru. Borrowing £30,000,000 against its guano reserves, the Peruvian government—controlled behind the curtain by the American Henry Meiggs—assumed an ever-increasing foreign debt while buying off revolutionaries and building Andean railroads, and ultimately squandered its bargaining power, despite its guano having sold for $600,000,000.[26] Conveniently, the House of Gibbs also functioned as Peru's banker.

While not quite the most objectionable of all cargoes, guano was surely in the running. Aside from the dust and the eye-watering, acrid stench, guano cargoes induced dry rot, especially in new ships; strained hulls as it solidified; destroyed iron on contact; and drove legions of rats out of the hold and into the cabin, where they died behind panels and drowned in water pitchers.

Supplying workers to the hot, barren, waterless islands was a challenge, and when convict labor proved insufficient, thousands of Chinese coolies, sold a rosy bill of promises, were crammed aboard ships and brought to the islands. Having survived the miseries of the voyage, the wretched men now received no relief. Indeed, here they were virtually enslaved in a state of constant misery, required, under the threat of the lash, to perform hard labor seven days a week. Many committed suicide, and none, it was said, ever received the promised return trip home.

After the major maritime nations forbade their ships from engaging in the Peruvian coolie trade, fast ships were purchased, renamed, and put under the Peruvian flag. Two ships found in the *Whig & Courier* list, the splendid clipper *Oracle*, built by John MacDonald at Thomaston, and the clipper *White Falcon*, built on the Kennebec at Pittston, were to be so fated. In 1866 the latter ship, as the *Napoleon Canavero*, was fired by coolies who, in an uprising, had been battened down below, and faced suffocation. The crew left the burning ship in the boats, leaving the 650 coolies to die a most horrible death.

For New England captains and their families, however, aside from the obvious drawbacks, the months spent lying at the Chinchas brought constant rounds of socializing among seldom-seen seafaring friends and neighbors. Open house for captains and their families was held on a loaded ship ready to depart, while sailors from the fleet, singing chanties, helped the crew to raise the anchors and make sail.[27] But no such charming accounts are to be found in the no-nonsense letters posted to Bath by the captains of Sewall ships. Captain William Kennard, of E. & A. Sewall's ship *Hellespont*, loading at the Chinchas in September 1860, wrote of loading guano from the launches: "I shall hire a horse to hoist it in. I can get one for less money than it will cost to pay two men & keep them."[28]

Reporting the arrival of his ship *Samaritan* at Callao in November 1863—ships had to call at Callao both when arriving and before departing—Captain Frank Stinson of Woolwich reported that he had lost two men and strained the ship some in heavy weather off Cape Horn. Faced with the compulsory official survey and inevitable order for expensive recaulking by the guano authorities, which he thought "a perfect swindle," he planned to pay a $300 bribe instead.

In January 1869 Captain James Morse of Phippsburg, contemplating having to wait ninety-three days for the ship *Hermon* to be loaded while only being paid his twenty-dollar-per-month base salary, almost wished himself "in our institution [the state prison] at Thomaston for life." In March he reported that four young

Ship Samaritan. *It was a common for artists to depict the subject of a ship portrait in two or three perspectives, thus giving the customer full value for his money. This painting has been attributed to either Liverpudlian R. B. Spencer or Londoner John Hughes.*
MAINE MARITIME MUSEUM

British captains in the anchored fleet had suddenly sickened and died.

In March 1869 Captain Joseph Small of the ship *America* wrote from another Peruvian guano island, Guanape: "I have been here thirty-seven days and have not got one pound of guano on board. Nor can I find out when I shall get it & expect to load the most of my cargo on demurrage. There is here twenty ships . . . and about fifty more expected. . . . There is about fifty Chinamen here at work. There is no chutes fit to work. Unless they get more chutes at work I sha'n't get loaded 'til the first of June." Demurrage was money owed them for undue detention after a vessel's "lay days," or allotted time for loading, had expired.

The chutes were long canvas tubes (some were wooden), held open with wooden hoops, which were rigged from the cliff-tops down to the sea. Guano dumped in at the top was deposited, among great clouds of acrid yellow dust, into launches, or, in some instances, directly into the holds of ships carefully moored below. Launches were purchased by arriving captains from departing captains. In 1875 the resourceful Captain

John Arey, of the ship *Matterhorn*, converted a twenty-seven-foot boat, obtained in a trade for lumber in Liverpool, into a suitable launch on the outward passage.

Due to the relatively thin Clark & Sewall records in the Sewall Family Papers, we do not know when their ships first entered the trade, but it would seem that they were later players in the game. The frequent appearance of Sewall ships in the 1870s presumably reflected the depression of 1873, the decline in San Francisco grain rates due to the competition of British iron sailing vessels, and the loss of the cotton trade to British steam.

By this time, the once-vast deposits of the Chinchas, over a hundred feet deep in places, were approaching exhaustion, and ships were dispatched to smaller deposits at more dangerous locations in the Ballestaas, Lobos, and Guanape Islands, and islets and cliffside plateaus at Pabellon de Pica, Huanillos, the Bay of Independencia, and other points. It is ironic that the locations where this wondrous fertilizer was found were completely barren and devoid of vegetation.

In August 1872 Captain Joseph Small, of the ship *Eric the Red*, having just arrived, wrote that he had lost one man off Cape Horn, and had six laid up sick. From Callao he was dispatched to Guanape Island, where seventy-five ships were ahead of him. From there he wrote: "I want to get this voyage over and start anew. I suppose it was an error of judgment in me for taking it but it was all I could do at the time."

In January 1875 Captain Arey of *Matterhorn*, having arrived at Callao, wrote that he and the captain of the ship *North Star* had "offered Messrs. Dreyfus & Co.—the newly installed French concessionaire—thirteen hundred dollars apiece—bribes—if they would send us to Lobos. . . . We are going to offer three hundred dollars to go to Pabellon de Pica. On account of there being a few vessels at Pabellon de Pica and such a large fleet being at Huanillos."

On February 5, 1875, Captain J. B. Minott of the ship *Hermon* wrote from Lobos Island: "This is a very good place to load at with one exception. The ship is rolling her rails to the water all the time. . . ." In April 1878 Captain Prince Taylor, of the ship *Tabor*, wrote from Pabillon de Pica:

> I came very near getting into trouble with the ship a few days ago. Our stern moorings unshackled in the night & ship swung around but we managed to get her back before doing any damage. We are all jammed up in a heap. . . . We have earth quakes most every day & some are quite heavy & on every full & change of the moon we have heavy surf days & it is not at all pleasant. I wish we had our load & was away out of this.

In May 1875 Captain William Dunphy arrived at Pabillon de Pica aboard the ship *Occidental*, and from there was ordered to Point Lobo, where an anchor chain soon parted:

> This is one of the worst places that I ever saw for a vessel to come to. I should not be surprised if half the fleet be lost. The risk after the vessel leaves here is

nothing compared with laying here. There is no shelter whatever. I should advise you to get the ship fully insured while laying here. I shall request my brother Frank to get his interest and mine fully insured.

Occidental would not depart until January, trouble having arisen between government officials and Dreyfus. Captains were tempted to "buy time" for quicker loading, or else to give up their claims for demurrage. (A "charter party," or written contract, for a guano voyage, consisted of three pages of very fine print doubtless intended to confuse anyone less expert than a Lima lawyer.) Dunphy concluded that the government was bankrupt, having sold more guano than it possessed, and that "going to law" in Lima over demurrage would be a "bad business." Tons of rocks were picked out of the guano.

In June 1875 Captain Bill Lincoln, lying at Lobo Pont in the ship *El Capitan*, wrote:

There are some 110 to 115 ships here, mostly of large size. Some of them have been here from 50 to 60 days and not an ounce of cargo yet. The facilities for loading are very bad, indeed, can only work on an average about 3 days out of a week. This is one of the most dangerous places . . . that I ever saw for a ship to lay in. . . . vessels lying here are exposed to the open Pacific . . . and a very heavy long swell running all the time.

Captain Dunphy had ordered a spare anchor and chain to be sent out from Callao. In June 1878 Captain Taylor wrote: "In the event of the *Tabor*'s not going to a home port from Antwerp I should like to be relieved if convenient to you. I shall have been five years away from home & my affairs need a little looking after, as well as my boys." From a letter from Captain John Arey of the ship *Matterhorn* written at Queenstown, Ireland, in March 1877, after a passage from Pabellon de Pica:

When we first left . . . the ship was as tight as a bottle. After being out four or five weeks she commenced to leak. . . . I commenced to get quite uneasy but after about two or three weeks we only pumped her out every twelve hours. . . . I have come to the conclusion that when we left Pabellon de Pica that the felt under the copper was fairly baked on the wood & when the water had been to it some four or five weeks, softened it, so the water went through it. The seams being opened & treenails shrunk up was the cause of it. . . . After the water had got to the wood she swelled up.

In May 1877 many ships on the Peruvian coast, including some Bath ships, were sunk or damaged by a powerful tidal wave. No Sewall ships were involved, but *Oriental*, Captain Albert Otis of Brunswick, arrived several months later. His young daughters, Alice and Carrie, were initially frightened by the sight of the barren island, made even more forbidding by the sight of the masts of sunken ships, of a ship thrown up high and dry, and of word that there were no other children in the anchored fleet.

But they soon discovered themselves the object of the fleet's attention—one English captain painted up a dinghy to the colors of their choosing, painted their names on each oar, and would fetch them for a row whenever signaled by the hoisted American ensign.[29]

They know how to find new cruising grounds

Merchant ships, intended to make a profit, were usually built for a particular trade, or trades, and in response to a rise in the respective freight rates. A significant revival of the deepwater American marine after the Civil War resulted from the rising demand for tonnage to carry West Coast—mostly California—wheat, primarily to Liverpool. This trade played a key role in the story of Bath and the Sewalls.

San Francisco, during the heyday of the wheat trade, was perhaps the world's most hospitable port for captains. Captain J. H. Drew, a Kennebecker, master of the Boston ship *Sea Witch*, wrote to the *Boston Journal* from San Francisco in 1878:

> There is no place in the world where the sea captain has so much notice taken of him as in San Francisco. The managers of the Merchant's Exchange send him a card of admissions before the anchor is down. . . . Let us . . . go to the "Exchange" and see these captains. . . . Here are all the grain men, ship-brokers, commission merchants, owners, captains, and if I'm alive, here are two shipowners from Richmond, Me. They left the Kennebec just a week ago, and have come out to see the Pacific coast and look after their ship's interests. . . . At the next table are four or five captains of Bath ships; they're part owners and know what they are about. Ten years ago you seldom saw one here, but rather looked to New Orleans for them, but King Cotton played it on them and has gone over to steam, but they know how to find new cruising grounds and know to a cent what it costs to sail their ships. Standing around that column are half a dozen Thomaston captains, great stout fellows. Ten years ago they were to be found in the guano trade. . . .

The great grain fleet added significantly to maritime San Francisco's activity, prosperity, and rough-and-ready character. Sailors, lured off the hundreds of incoming ships by the oily seductions of the rum-treating "runners" working for the boarding-house masters, or "crimps," were spirited off to the "Barbary Coast" district of saloons, whorehouses, and sailors' boardinghouses. In a perennially tight labor market, the crimps extorted high "advance" payments on sailors' wages, in addition to "blood money" bonuses, from captains anxious to be underway. Drunken or doped sailors—in some instances only just hours arrived in port after a four-month Cape Horn passage—were unceremoniously dumped on the outward-bounder's deck.

California wheat farming began shortly after the gold rush in the rich Sacramento and San Joaquin Valleys, which were connected to the port of San Francisco by water; rail connections would later extend to Salinas. The trade began shortly after the war and lasted for about thirty-five years; by 1868 fully one-third of the United States'

Launching day for the ship Harvester, *September 4, 1875. During the mid-1870s, with a new vessel sliding into Long Reach about every ten days on average, launchings were attended with little ceremony, and often but minimal mention in the local press. A-shaped sheerlegs have been erected preparatory to stepping* Harvester's *mainmast. Beyond,* Reaper *is under construction—* Harvester, Reaper, *and* Thrasher *were evidently built from the same model, while* Indiana, *next in the sequence, was built from her own model. Note the yoke of oxen posed at* Harvester's *forefoot.* MAINE MARITIME MUSEUM

wheat exports passed out the Golden Gate. The addition of cheap California wheat to other American and also Russian wheat imports proved to be the final straw, as it were, for British "corn" farmers. By the final decades of the century Washington and Oregon were also exporting large quantities of wheat.[30]

The key to the trade was reliable and economical transport of the heavy, perishable, and valuable cargo, by sail, for some 16,000 miles—including a doubling of Cape Horn and two equatorial crossings.[31] The trade demanded superior ships, and the American "California" ship, at its best, was arguably the most highly evolved large wooden ocean carrier ever devised, and one of the most handsome. Loftily rigged, and of artful "medium clipper" model full on the floor, but with a good bow and a fair run, it was capable of superior performance.[32]

More such ships were built at Bath than anywhere else, a number by the Sewalls. In 1887 Bath ship owner Captain Parker Whitmore said of these ships:

It has been the experience of people in this city that short spars and long masts give the greater speed. The large amount of elasticity inevitable in a long mast is productive of this result. . . . In cotton [carrying] times we tried small ballast and short masts, but found it a poor experiment and returned to the tall masts.[33]

The fastest ship was not necessarily the most profitable ship—a damaged cargo was remembered long after a quick passage had been forgotten. In the long run, the most profitable ship delivered big cargoes in good order in the most economical fashion, and thus fuller-ended, and more conservatively rigged ships, were what the Sewalls usually built.

The trade also inspired the construction of a huge fleet of British iron and steel ships—British grain ships always outnumbered the Americans. Many were among the best and also handsomest examples of their type ever built. But they were not without their critics, as ships of the "narrow gutted" British model were dangerously wet on deck when deeply laden in heavy weather. Also, their painted bottoms were much more liable to be fouled by dragging marine growth than were the copper alloy–sheathed hulls of wooden ships. (Ferrous metal hulls could not be coppered due to the destructive reaction of the dissimilar metals.)

The wheat trade defied easy organization, requiring ship owners to send ships on their way, often from halfway around the world, before the tonnage needs of a new crop were known. The man credited with ensuring that sufficient tonnage would arrive in a timely fashion was grain merchant Isaac Friedlander, a German Jew, who made his first fortune by cornering the wheat market during the gold rush. Prior to his 1877 failure, Friedlander's ability to predict harvests by means of an elaborate crop intelligence network, along with nearly unlimited credit, gave him unrivaled power.

Hard-grained California wheat was very well regarded by British and Irish millers. Arriving at the end of the season in one-hundred-pound bags (to prevent cargo shifting) rather than in bulk, and calculated by weight rather than by the bushel, it had its own market identity. With San Francisco's grain trade brokered by British merchants and bankers, insured by British underwriters, filling her bay with British ships and her waterfront dives with their sailors, San Francisco became an outpost of Her Majesty's Empire.

American wooden ships were severely discriminated against by British shippers and underwriters, despite statistics said to demonstrate that they were faster, safer, and delivered better cargoes than did British metal ships.[34] However, in obtaining good-paying outward cargoes to carry to San Francisco, first-class American ships enjoyed a distinct advantage, having the sole privilege under federal law of carrying cargoes out from the East Coast, legally considered a protected coastal trade.

In the record season of 1881–82, 550 ships sailed from San Francisco carrying wheat and flour (with nine more carrying just flour). Likely another hundred sailed from Portland, Oregon. Over $16,000,000 was paid in wheat freights from San Francisco.[35] In the four years ending June 1885, out of 1,533 ships participating in the trade, 761 were British "iron" (including steel); 198 were "British" wood—doubtless overwhelmingly from Nova Scotia and New Brunswick—and 418 were American wooden ships, along with five American iron ships. The remainder were mostly German, Norwegian, French, and Italian wooden ships, in that order, along with one Russian.[36] By 1892 only thirty-nine American wheat ships cleared from San Francisco, as opposed to 234 foreign ships. In the early 1900s, a flock of heavily subsidized steel French "bounty" ships played a significant spoiler's role. In 1901 only ten American ships sailed as against 149 foreign ships, of which 103 were British.

Freight rates from San Francisco to Liverpool reached a peak between 1872 and 1874, at about 95 shillings per long ton, and fell sharply after 1883 with the oversupply of British steel tonnage. Between 1891 and 1894, with a great world surplus of tonnage created by depression, rates fell to as little as fifteen to twenty-five shillings, and many once profitably sized ships were rendered obsolete. Captain George Goodwin dated the beginning of the end of the American fleet to the drop in freights in 1883:

> They [the owners] had been so used to getting from sixty to one-hundred shillings. . . that when the price dropped to fifty shillings they would not accept it and so their ships were laid up, some of them for two or three years, and then these far-sighted owners accepted twenty shillings less than they could have gotten before the ships were laid up. Some of the finest wooden ships in the world laid up in San Francisco Bay until they dried up, became worm-eaten and their gear rotted, and then were sold for a song. . . . Quite a number of shipping firms failed and the captains who would have kept their ships going for what they could get, lost their life savings.[37]

The Sewalls preferred to keep their ships at work; in the 1870s they sent them into the guano trade, and in the 1880s put them into the difficult coal trade from British Columbia. Even if the ships were earning little or no profit for their owners, as managers, the Sewalls continued to make money from fees and commissions, and the ships did not dry out. Also, they sold ships and built bigger ones to replace them.

By the turn of the century, low international wheat prices, combined with declining fertility in the California wheat lands and the demands of a rising local population, led many farmers to change to other crops, and the once-great trade largely faded away.

Got 90 gallons of beautiful oil

On October 5, 1867, Captain Warren Morse of the ship *America* wrote Arthur Sewall "a few lines in a kind of a private way"—Morse and Arthur obviously were good friends—from Acapulco, where *America* had arrived from New York. After the standard complaint about the bad crew that he had been stuck with, and so on, Morse wrote:

> Thirteen days out there was a whale seen a short distance off. It being most calm & smooth at the time we got the boats out and gave chase for him, captured and had him alongside in less than an hour ["a nower"], took his pelt off and got

90 gallons of beautiful oil. I have decided —— [to give the] ship one third lay and I think of selling the balance to rise some spending money. That is more than some fellows has got that have spent their thousands for petroleum—how does Edward get along with the railroad? Will he be ready to send me any order for a cargo of iron? Remember me to him.

A "lay" was a portion of a whale ship's profit. While merchant ships often carried harpoons for catching the occasional porpoise, they were wholly unequipped for killing, cutting up, and processing even a very small whale. The reference to failed investments in petroleum—the Sewalls had invested in the Pennsylvania oil fields—suggests that Captain Morse was engaging in some dry Maine humor over the Sewalls' dry Appalachian holes.

Morse was married to the daughter of Johnson Rideout, the Bath shipbuilder who had built *America*. He was evidently a good enough friend of the Sewall brothers to accuse them, in the same letter, with possibly having supplied the ship with inferior "damaged stores," perhaps bought at half price.

In 1866 Morse smuggled in thirty-three rifles and ninety-one muskets to Forbes & Company at Shanghai, on a speculation shared with the Sewalls. The guns were transferred under cover of darkness into a small boat fifteen miles downriver from the city. Morse invested the modest proceeds from the gun-running—the rifles brought $150, while the muskets were taken on consignment at a valuation of $3 Mexican apiece, profits to be split with Forbes & Co.—at Manila on coffee and cigars.

Once upon a time a captain in the East Indies spice trade or the China trade made small fortunes with his own "adventures" stowed in the cabin.

1. Hagar was a brother to the better-known shipbuilder, James Hagar. Both Hagars were financier shipbuilders, building ships with the pen, not the plane.
2. Sewall Family Papers, 547/30; 548/16, 17, 18.
3. *Kennebec Reporter*, November 30, 1889.
4. *Kennebec & Portland Railroad Company in Equity v. Portland & Kennebec Railroad Company and Others*, Maine Supreme Judicial Court, 1870; Edward E. Chase, *Maine Railroads* (Portland, ME: A .J. Huston, 1926), pp. 25–26.
5. *Sixth Annual Report . . . of the Kennebec and Portland Railroad Company*, Augusta, 1863. p. 12.
6. Chase,*Maine Railroads*, pp. 25–26.
7. Edward Chase Kirkland, *Men, Cities and Transportation*, vol. II (Cambridge, MA: Harvard University Press, 1948), pp. 8–9.
8. *Maine Mining Journal*, September 14, 1883. The fine Thomaston ship *R. D. Rice*, built in 1883, was surely named for Rice, although he was by then deceased.
9. Named after Cape Cod's Yarmouth, to the southeast. The town had not yet divided itself into coastal Yarmouth and backcountry North Yarmouth.
10. R. P. Buck arguably had a shrewder mind for business than even the Sewalls. In January 1848 he tried to persuade Clark & Sewall to send the ship *Macedonia* around the Horn to Panama

with a cargo of good steam coal, and then carry passengers from Panama to San Francisco, at $100 to $125 a head, on prepaid tickets sold by the Pacific Mail Company at New York.

11. Bath *Daily Times,* May 21, 1914.

12. Maine, Vol. 19, pp. 266–67,R. G. Dun Collection, Baker Library Historical Collections, Harvard Business School.

13. John G. B. Hutchins, *The American Maritime Industries and Public Policy, 1789–1914* (Cambridge, MA: Harvard University Press, 1941), pp. 322–23.

14. Louis Clinton Hatch, *Maine: A History* (Somersworth, NH: New Hampshire Publishing Company, 1974), p. 430.

15. Actually the family tree was even more tangled. Caroline Sewall, daughter of Charles Sewall, who was the son of Revolutionary War general Henry Sewall (who was great-grandson of Henry the Dutiful's son John), married James Manley, whose son Joseph married his cousin Susan Cony, who was Mercy Sewall Cony's daughter.

16. Aubigne Lermond Packard, *A Town that Went to Sea* (Portland, ME: Falmouth Publishing House, 1950), p. 4.

17. The full-length figurehead, carved by Freeman H. Morse of Bath, cost $100. The complete bill, including fashion pieces, one pair of trailboards, headrail halves, two nameboards with ornamental ends, forty corner blocks, taffrail, and "caps," and (looks like) "tongues," was $247.50, with $2.50 discounted for cash. Morse was a colorful figure, serving in the legislature and three terms in Congress. In 1861 he was appointed U.S. consul general in London by Lincoln, serving until 1870. Due to questions regarding the disposition of consular funds, he remained in England, becoming a British citizen and dying there in poverty in 1891. Baker, *A Maritime History of Bath*, p. 660. *American Sentinel*, February 12, 1891.

18. In 1859 T. J. Southard built a ship named *Southern Rights.* Southard reportedly later claimed he named his ship this to protect her from Southern raiders in the war that he anticipated. "Jeffie" Southard was a phenomenon, a pint-sized practical shipwright born in Boothbay who built more than one hundred vessels at Richmond, a Kennebec River town which he did much to develop.

19. The Bucks, from Bucksport, Maine, as mentioned earlier, were an interesting family. Henry Buck founded the sawmill town of Bucksville, South Carolina, on the Waccamaw River, about 1830. He came to the region to exploit its vast hard pine timber supplies for shipbuilding timber. His son, William, a strong Unionist—although his two sons fought for the Confederacy— freed 600 slaves after the war. At the start of the war Lincoln sent a gunboat to rescue William's daughter-in-law and her children. She was the daughter of Searsport, Maine shipbuilder and owner William McGilvery.

20. *Vigilant* was owned by William D. Sewall, Edward and Arthur Sewall, Thomas Reed, Captains Fred Bosworth and Peleg Curtis, and George Prince.

21. Baker, *Maritime History of Bath*, pp. 478–79.

22. *Champion* was built in 1854 by P. R. Curtis of Harpswell, and purchased in that year by Clark & Sewall. She was sold in England in April, 1862.

23. Report of the Maine Adjutant General, 1864–65.

24. W. M. Mathew, *The House of Gibbs and the Peruvian Guano Monopoly* (London: Royal Historical Society, 1981), p.122. Gibbs did not control North American shipments.

25. Marquis James, *Merchant Adventurer—The Story of W. R. Grace* (Wilmington, DE: ER Books, 1993) pp. 34–36.

26. Charles R. Flint, *Memories of an Active Life* (New York: G. P. Putnam's Sons, 1923), pp. 53–54.

27. Frederick Jordan Ranlett, *Master Mariner of Maine* (Portland, ME: Southworth-Anthoensen Press, 1942), pp.132–36.

28. Charles R. Flint, a partner in Flint & Co., wrote that his uncle, Captain James Chapman, once bought two ponies at Acapulco after most of his crew had deserted. The ponies, he claimed, were used to help work the ship to the Chinchas, where they loaded a full cargo of guano, and then were sold for a profit. Flint, *Memories of an Active Life*, p. 19.

29. *A Young Girl's Life at Sea, or The Experiences of a Young Girl under Sail being an Autobiography of Carrie McElroy Otis Moulton* (Portland, OR: Averhill Press, 2003), p. 4.

30. See Rodman W. Paul, "The Wheat Trade Between California and the United Kingdom," *The Mississippi Valley Historical Review*, vol. 45, no. 3. (December 1958), pp. 391–413.

31. A single rounding of the Cape, from 50 South to 50 South, was said to be a "doubling."

32. Henry Hall, *Report on the Shipbuilding Industry of the United States*. From the Tenth Census (Washington D. C.: 1884), p. 93. The California ships were the prime examples of a generation of ships which have become known as "Down Easters," which, while a convenient classification, was not a specific term applied to these ships during their careers. The term, as applied to these ships as a type, will not be found in Hall, or in Frederick Matthews' two-volume history of the vessels, or in the literature of the day. It may have first been so utilized by the English writer Basil Lubbock.

33. Bangor *Industrial Journal*, May 6, 1887.

34. William W. Bates, *American Marine, The Shipping Question in History and Politics* (Boston, MA: Houghton Mifflin, 1892).

35. Paul, "The Wheat Trade," *Mississippi Valley Historical Review*, p. 252.

37. Goodwin unpublished autobiography, pp. 73–74.

PART FOUR

We first follow the saga of ship Matterhorn, *which nearly sinks in the South Atlantic and then becomes notorious for cruelties practiced aboard her. We then take a wider look at the all-too-common abuse of sailors aboard American ships, a subject which would fester to the end of sail, tarring the Sewalls' proud name. We will end with a visit to the hard-pine forests of the coastal Southeast, the source of vital timber for New England shipbuilders. In the 1870s the Sewalls built the first members of their fleet of three-masted schooners, which supplied their shipyard, and others, with hard pine.*

Ship shrank up very bad

To be launched—Messrs. E. & A. Sewall will launch from their ways at 10 o'clock this forenoon, the ship *Matterhorn* an entire White Oak Ship, 1,350 tons, owned by the builders, W. D. Sewall, Thomas M. Reed, and Captain Peleg Curtis, who will command her. This ship will class A1 for nine years in French Lloyd's and is now in the market for sale, freight, or charter.[1]

—Bath *Daily Times*, May 26, 1866

Captain Curtis, born in Harpswell, Maine, in 1818, was a trusted veteran of the Sewall fleets, having previously commanded the ships *Erie, Leander, Vigilant, Villafranca, Vancouver,* and *Holyhead.* His first wife (of three) was lost in 1858 when *Leander* was sunk in a collision with the steamer *North American* off the coast of Ireland.[2] *Vigilant* was burned by the Confederate raider *Sumter.*

On her maiden voyage *Matterhorn* carried cotton from New Orleans to Liverpool. Curtis wrote from Liverpool that it had been a bad mistake not to have taken a cargo of coal from Philadelphia to San Francisco instead, as the ship could have earned a freight of $70,000 carrying California wheat to Liverpool. She then carried iron to Philadelphia and took coal to San Francisco, entering the Golden Gate after a fearfully slow passage of 169 days. She loaded wheat for Liverpool, arriving in March of 1868. She was then chartered to carry coal from Birkenhead for Bombay, to return with rice for Falmouth or Cork for orders. "A small year's worth [of] work," groused Curtis.

From Bombay, where Curtis wrote that after discharging the dusty cargo "the whole ship's company would [pass] for Congo Negroes in Cuba," *Matterhorn* sailed in ballast for Akyab, Burma, bucking the Northeast Monsoon in the Bay of Bengal, to load her cargo of rice. Rice could be a very problematical cargo. It was heavy, and once in the hold—particularly early in the season—it could heat severely, sometimes even combusting. The hot "steam" opened seams and loosened fastenings, while condensation rained down from the underside of the deck. A rice cargo typically lost from 2 to 10 percent of its weight during a voyage, particularly when infested by weevils. If a ship sailed on one tack for an extended period, the settling rice often imparted a dangerous list. The stench of rice dregs in bilge water was said to be "almost unbearable." Adding injury to insult, the shipworms found in at least some Burmese rice ports were said to be particularly voracious, even consuming the wooden stocks of anchors.3

On June 22, 1869, *Matterhorn*, deeply laden with a cargo worth £50,000, and leaking badly, approached the island of St. Helena, a speck of the British Empire in the South Atlantic Ocean. Measuring but ten miles by eight miles, the mountainous island was visible in good weather from sixty miles off. A sailor aboard a British ship recalled a dawn approach:

> With the growing light, we could see the highlands and mountain-range soaring to the clouds. Their lower slopes caught the first rays of the rising sun and shone in vivid emerald patches. Shadowed chasms and ravines wound down the mountain-sides and the whole upland appeared to terminate at the edge of fearful cliffs, which fell perpendicular into the white fury of the surf below.4

These cliffs reach to 1,800 feet. Located in the "strength" of the southeast trade winds, for hundreds of years St. Helena had served as an important port of refuge for plodding homeward-bound East Indiamen. From 1651 until 1834 (excepting the years of Napoleon's exile) the island was a mid-ocean fiefdom of the British East India Company, which introduced black slaves and Chinese coolies as agricultural workers. In the palmy years of empire, thousands of ships called annually—watercress growing in an inland spring was noted in pilot books as an effective remedy for scurvy. But with the opening of the Suez Canal in 1869, the rise of steam, and improvements in food preservation, the island's importance declined drastically.

The exposed anchorage at Jamestown, the island's only settlement, although located on the leeward side, was subjected to violent wind eddies and gusts which could lay ships caught athwartship almost on their beam ends, and to heavy "rollers" which burst furiously on the shore and wrecked ships anchored on the steep-to bottom. Nevertheless, the sight of the island must have appeared as a godsend to Captain Curtis and his pumped-out sailors.

On June 26 Captain Curtis sent a letter via a Liverpool-bound ship addressed to agents Ross, Skofield & Co., requesting that they cable the Sewalls. On July 6 he sent a letter to the Sewalls with the passing ship *Bengal* to New York:

Gentlemen, We arrived here on 22nd ship leaking 1,600 strokes per hour. By sounding here we find she made 9 inches per hour on even keel. We began discharging the 25th late evening; 26th had 2,000 bags out and leak increasing. Now making 7,500 strokes in four hours or 1,875 per hour, gained since here 275 per hour. . . . [The ship] made no water until 33 days out then in the NE trades all sail set began with 150 strokes per hour and less until we passed the Cape, slowly increasing then up to about 450. Since then June 4th until 22nd increased to 1,650. The last four days out the leak gained some 100 per hour every 24 hours. If we had a steady leak even to that I should [have] tried to ship extra men and get the ship to Falmouth, but the leak increasing so fast she might go down at any time.

Curtis added that the ship was lying in a bad place. The ship would have been fitted with a double-barreled, double-flywheel pump, mounted within the main pinrail, producing two lifting strokes per revolution, with up to four men on two handles, unless supplemented by additional men pulling on lines.

By July 8 half of the 21,400 bags of rice—a bag weighed about 165 pounds—had been discharged. The leak had increased to 3,200 strokes per hour, and six islanders had been engaged to help pump. A live fish two inches long had been pumped out. On July 12, with about 14,000 bags discharged, the leak had slightly relented. Along with wrinkled copper sheathing, a number of sprung lower-deck hanging knees gave evidence that the ship had been strained.

On July 27, with 19,500 bags discharged, a rush of water was discovered coming from the outer garboard seam, with about four inches of oakum, and the copper covering it, gone. Two fish, three inches long, were pumped out. The leak was stopped from the inside with caulking and tar. Curtis wrote:

I am now in strong hopes we may take in the cargo and proceed on the voyage and get away in six weeks. . . . I think it's perfectly impractical to heave the ship down here with only six carpenters in this place and swells that heave around the island at all times, sometimes quite heavy.

With the fortuitous arrival on August 4 of an unnamed man-of-war with diving apparatus, the leak was caulked and coppered. The local insurance surveyor insisted that the copper sheathing above the waterline be stripped and the exposed seams recaulked. On August 12, Curtis wrote: "I am in hopes either to see you here or receive a letter of credit . . . do not think I can negotiate draft on you but will have to give a bottomry bond on ship and cargo at 30 percent and to be met at Cork or Falmouth."

A "bottomry bond" was a distressed shipmaster's last financial resort, in which the value of the ship, freight, or cargo was pledged for funds to be used exclusively to continue the voyage. The bond was only repaid if the voyage was completed, and interest rates, accordingly, were usually very high.[5]

On July 26 Arthur Sewall, in New York, received the news of the *Matterhorn*'s difficulties by wire, and immediately wrote Barings's New York agent to arrange a bond. Then a letter was sent to Captain Curtis informing him that the ship was but half insured, the freight, not at all. "Be careful in your protest & surveys [that] no mention is made of any defect in ship—frequently surveyors [find] decayed wood or worms in planks even when there is no occasion for it." It would not be until September 11 that Curtis would receive this letter, along with a letter of credit from Barings. A week later, *Matterhorn* was ready for sea. Expenses at St. Helena had amounted to £3,448.14.1, less £584.14.0 from the sale of some rice.

On November 24 *Matterhorn* arrived at Antwerp, her port of discharge. A letter awaited Curtis from the Sewalls: "Our opinion is that the ship does not require any work inside of her nor any fastenings and that all that is absolutely necessary is to thoroughly recaulk, felt & metal and repair any planks that may be wormed." The ship was to make a long voyage at once.

However, the damage was far more severe than the Sewalls could divine from Bath, and Curtis replied on December 9: "Ship shrank up very bad, waterway seams in some places are 1/2 inch. All between decks are very open. I could hardly credit so much shrinkage without seeing it." A survey would recommend that forty knees in the lower hold needed refastening or replacement, the shrinkage of the wood having started bolts or split the wood making the bolts useless.

Curtis also wrote that he was feeling "about sick," and that his wife, who had joined him, was possibly consumptive, and "so low [I] do not think it's safe to leave her or take her to sea." A new captain would have to be found, while Curtis, looking after the ship's affairs, chartered her to load coal at Cardiff for Callao, Peru, to load guano. On February 18 Curtis wrote that with all the bills paid and accounts settled he had remitted to Baring Brothers £1,194.12.2 for the owners. He did not expect to return home until late May, after taking a well-deserved rest in the south of France.

These fellows have made up a yarn

A new master was required for *Matterhorn*, and in short order, for the ship was proving a very poor investment. The name of William Frazier, first mate of the Sewalls' bark *Frank Marion*, due shortly at Liverpool from New Orleans, was suggested by Arthur to Edward. Frazier had come to their notice in May 1869, when the *Marion* arrived in the English Channel from Batavia with first mate Frazier in command, young Captain James Lincoln having died during the passage, probably of appendicitis. (Two years previously Captain Lincoln had replaced Captain Thomas Purington, who died of yellow fever in New Orleans.)

Captain E. Thompson had briefly taken command of the *Marion*, followed by Captain Samuel Duncan, while Frazier remained her first mate. Although Edward was concerned about Frazier's inexperience, Arthur's offer of command was awaiting Frazier when the *Marion* arrived at Liverpool on January 6, 1870. This development could not have been more timely for Frazier, who had killed a sailor on Christmas Day, and accordingly quickly left town, one step ahead of the law.

Captain Duncan reported to the Sewalls that the trouble had begun when a sailor refused to turn-to because it was Christmas. When the mates attempted to put him in irons the sailor seized a belaying pin, whereupon Frazier struck him on the side of the head with a capstan bar. The sailor died that evening. The Sewalls expressed their regret, but judged Frazier's actions justified.

On February 8 the Sewalls wrote Frazier, who had sailed *Matterhorn* to Cardiff, a most unusual letter:

Mr. Allen your 1st mate takes the steamer from New York the 9th to join you. . . . We have full confidence in him & doubt not that he will please you. From Capt. Duncan's last letter it would seem just possible that you may have [crew] trouble in Cardiff or on leaving. . . . In case you should thereby have cause for detaining the ship we now instruct you that rather than the ship should be detained or in the event of delay we wish you to place Mr. Allen in charge for the voyage under similar instructions to your own.

"Mr. Allen" was red-haired Zaccheus Allen, the late mate of the Sewalls' ship *America*, which had been sold. Born in 1843 in Bowdoin, Maine, he had grown up in nearby Richmond, then a very active shipbuilding center. After graduating from high school, he had gone to sea in Bath's Patten fleet. Frazier responded:

Mr. Allen has arrived here on the 23rd and what I have seen of him a good mate. The ship is loaded got in 1,602 tons and will get away Monday. . . . I don't think I shall have any trouble here on account of that *Christmas breakfast* but if I do, I will place Allen in charge as you wish.

Almost five months later, on June 16, having doubled Cape Horn and sailed two-thirds the way up the west coast of South America to Callao, Peru, Captain Frazier wrote:

The *Matterhorn* arrived in this port yesterday after a passage of 100 days and considering the time of year off the Cape I think it a very good passage. I had very heavy weather from the River Plate round to 35 [latitude] in the Pacific. There is no ship here that has beat it. . . . The ship is looking finely and is in good order.

On June 27th Frazier wrote the Sewalls another similarly chatty letter. On July 15, however, Arthur's old friend and brother-in-law, Captain Fred Bosworth, master of the Sewalls' ship *Freeman Clark*, which was lying at Guanape Island, wrote to inform the Sewalls of news "of rather an unpleasant character" regarding *Matterhorn*. Two men, it seemed, had been killed on the passage out, and the consul would be sending the Sewalls a copy of the evidence, which looked bad. Mr. Allen had been taken out of the ship, put aboard the USS *Kearsarge*, and would be sent to San Francisco for trial. "One

The ship Freeman Clark, *built in 1865, lying at a Peruvian guano port.* Matterhorn, *built in 1866, had nearly identical measurements, and probably was built from the same model.*
MAINE MARITIME MUSEUM

mistake [Frazier] made was in not reporting it to the consul on arrival and think he said that he had not written you anything about it which is no doubt owing to some bad advice and *inexperience.*"

In a letter accompanying the evidence, Consul Williamson wrote that the charge against Allen was that of "cruel and unusual treatment of the crew," although the U.S. district attorney at San Francisco might "consider the offense to be one of much greater character, and may have him indicted for manslaughter." Captain Bosworth later wrote that it was only due to his influence with the consul that Frazier had not been removed from the ship as well.

Consul Williamson took testimony from First Mate Allen; Second Mate Martin, who was a native of Ireland; Third Mate Nickerson, a twenty-year-old Mainer; the cook, twenty-two, from French Guiana; the ship's boy, a twenty-one-year-old Mainer; the carpenter, a twenty-seven-year-old German; and half a dozen sailors, including natives of England, Maine, and Baltimore. Nearly half the sailors and the cook and the steward were black. All of the black sailors, along with a few whites, were members of the port watch, under Mate Allen. Allen testified:

My name is Zaccheus Allen, twenty-six years of age, born in the State of Maine. I joined the ship *Matterhorn* of Bath at Cardiff . . . on the 5th day of March 1870. . . . On the 19th of March I came on deck about 1/2 past 4 o'clock in the morning and went to the forecastle and saw a seaman named Moses Blake who was lying asleep. I got a small lantern called a "Bull's Eye" in order to see who was in the forecastle. I ordered Blake on deck, he got up on his feet but did not start to go out. I then put my hand on his shoulder and gave him a push when he said "Don't you put your hand on me," and then said if I put my hand on him, he would "cut my guts out," and put his hand behind him as though he was going to draw his knife.[6]

Allen stated that he left the forecastle and picked up a capstan bar, being followed by Blake. Allen swung the bar at Blake, who jumped back into the forecastle while holding his knife. Blake refused Allen's order to come out, so Allen went aft to his room and got his revolver, which he put in his pocket, and started forward again. He met Blake nearing the main hatch, and stepped up onto the hatch. Blake then drew his knife and jumped for Allen, holding the knife over his head. Allen jumped off the hatch. At this point Captain Frazier arrived at the scene. Allen fired a shot at Blake, who continued to advance, and then fired again, simultaneously with a shot fired by the captain, at which point Blake fell to the deck. Allen thought that his first shot hit Blake in the arm.

Blake, unable to stand on his own, was "triced" up, in irons, for about a half or three-quarters of an hour. He was then let down and his wounds dressed and was put on top of the after house. At night he was put down in the lazarette; during the day, he was kept on the after house, in irons, except for meals. On the 31st at about 5:00 P.M. Blake was missed, and it is presumed that he jumped overboard. The steward told Allen and Frazier that Blake had asked for a knife with which to "cut out their guts" and then he would go overboard.

Allen also claimed that a sailor, Frederick Hill, said that Blake and a sailor named Alfred Morris had been planning since the first day out of Cardiff to mutiny and take over the ship. Morris allegedly had "had charge" of his last ship, the *Ida Libby*. Allen claimed to have once overheard Blake talking about cutting him and the captain. He said that he had never had a problem with Blake, who had always done his duty, albeit in "an off handed independent kind of way."

As well, Allen stated that he had had problems with a German "who was no seaman" and who always complained of being sick. One night off Cape Horn when he did not obey an order, Allen knocked him down, and he fled to the forecastle. Allen met him coming out carrying a large stick; the captain, who had gone into the forecastle after the German, also came out, and said that the German had "had him by the throat." Allen then gave the German a beating with his fists. When the sailor grabbed a belaying pin, Allen took it away and "struck him over the head two or three times." The German was later discovered hiding in the lazarette and was sent to the forecastle; he caused no more trouble after that.

Allen said that he had had no trouble with the steward Emanuel until one day when he caught him drawing drinking water for the cabin into a dirty bucket. A few days later Allen saw him dump dirty water and slops from the bucket and then fill the bucket again. When he denied it, Allen "caught hold of him and choked him. He appeared to be about half crazy and was guilty of masturbation."

On another occasion, when spoken to by the captain, the steward appeared to be ready to take up a large carving knife when the captain restrained him. After being put in irons he caused no more trouble. He was never struck. "One day he left the cabin with a dish and first we heard was, 'A man overboard.' I saw him astern myself; we hove the wheel down, back'd the yards as soon as possible, but could see nothing of him."

On cross examination, Allen was asked whether he had struck Blake with the capstan bar. Allen replied that Blake went down but he wasn't sure he had hit him, although he was trying to. He said that he shot Blake because he felt threatened, and also to set an example. He said that he had been warned at Cardiff that the colored sailors intended to take charge of the ship. When asked if Moses Blake was triced up again when the *Matterhorn* met the bark *Anna Kimball,* and if Captain Frazier had called attention to Blake to the captain of the bark, Allen replied that he did not recollect if Captain Frazier had done so, but knew that he himself had not.

Asked whether he had said that it would be necessary to get rid of Blake before reaching Callao so that he would not cause trouble, Allen answered, "No, sir." "How long have you been an officer of a ship?" "About eight years." "Were the crew of the ship *Matterhorn* treated as well as is customary with crews of vessels that you have been in as an officer?" "Yes, sir."

In response to their request, on September 16 Captain Frazier finally wrote the Sewalls a letter giving his account of the events. He concluded:

That is all the trouble we had to my knowledge. I guess the mate struck some of them when they needed it. I have seen twice the trouble on a passage before and nothing thought of it but these fellows made up a yarn and all swore to it. . . . I see now I did very wrong in not reporting it to the consul but I was working for the ship's interest. . . .

I am going to make an example of him

The versions of events given by crew members differed in significant points from those given by Frazier and Allen, and all were in general agreement with each other. Seaman Alfred Morris, thirty-five, of Maine, was the only witness who testified as to what took place in the forecastle:

On the 19th of March last a Seaman named Moses Blake came into the forecastle and layed down upon his chest, about 5 o'clock in the morning. I was in the forecastle to get a piece of tobacco. The mate, Mr. Allen, came forward and said "What are you doing here, you son of a bitch asleep," and caught hold of Moses and told him to go on deck. Moses said, "Don't strike me." . . . The mate went out of the forecastle, took a capstan bar and hit him over the shoulder as he was coming out of the door, when Moses stood back in the doorway. The mate struck at him the 2nd time, which split the door of the forecastle about 4 feet. The mate then said, "Oh you won't come out, you black son of a bitch," and then went aft and got his revolver and a large fid about 18 inches long. . . .

According to Morris, Moses left the forecastle to be met by the mate, who hit him twice over the head with the fid. Moses said, "You will hit me, will you?" and started toward the mate, who ran aft. Moses followed him to the cabin door and raised his hand, when the captain, who was in the doorway with a cutlass and revolver in his hands, cut Moses badly on the arm with the cutlass. The mate then turned around and fired at Moses, and the captain did also. After Moses fell to the deck the captain fired at him again. The captain and the mate then handcuffed Moses and triced him up, and the mate played salt water from the wash-down hose on him.

After lowering Moses, the captain and the mate beat Moses with a small iron block and a rope until his face was so swollen he could hardly see, the captain saying, "Kill the black son of a bitch." The mate then kicked and jumped on him. A sailor called "Italian Joe" was ordered to sew up the cuts on Moses's head with a palm, sail needle, and twine. Moses was then triced up to the crojack yard by one arm, where he was left all that day. At night he was made fast to a ring bolt. When put to work scraping a spar he was chained to a heavy "devil's claw" chain stopper. He was fed only bread and water. And so on. Morris testified that he could not swear whether Moses had had a knife in his hand or not.

Peter Williams, a twenty-year-old sailor from Santo Domingo, testified that Moses had drawn his knife when he advanced on the mate, but had not raised it up. He said that one bullet had gone through the body, one entered the body near the left breast, the third grazed the head.

Frederick Hill, a sailor from Baltimore, who was on lookout on the forecastle, testified:

About 5 o'clock A.M. Mr. Allen the chief mate came forward and went to the forecastle door and looked in. I did not hear him say anything but he went aft. When he came back he had a dark lantern in his hand. He took a capstan bar out of the rack and set it up alongside of the door of the forecastle and then went into the forecastle and says to Moses Blake, "What are you doing here, you black son of a bitch. . . ." He then stepped out of the door and picked up the capstan bar and waited for Moses to come out, and when he stepped out he struck him a very heavy blow across the shoulder. . . . The mate told him to come out and as Moses came again to the door he struck him and split the door . . . about 3 feet. The mate then took up his lantern and walked aft and Moses came out of the forecastle and went aft . . . as he was ordered to come aft. I did not see him have anything in his hand, and I did not see him have his arm raised up.

Hill thought that there was one bullet hole near the shoulder blade, the ball having passed through Moses's body. "At about 10 or 11 o'clock a bark bound to New Orleans came near us and . . . the captain ordered Moses to be triced up by one arm clear from the deck, and hailed the bark and pointed to Moses and said, "There's a specimen. I am going to make an example of him before I get to Callao." Moses disappeared on the 31st during the port watch's supper, after the captain had ordered him unshackled. When the ship was being searched, Mr. Allen, who had earlier said that he would kill Blake before reaching Callao, said that it was better for Blake if he had jumped overboard.

Regarding the steward Emanuel, Hill, like Morris, said that the steward's face was badly cut open after a beating, and that he told Hill that both the captain and Mr. Allen had hit him with brass knuckles. Hill did not think that Emanuel was crazy. He claimed that the captain and the mate often beat Herman, a slow old German of fifty or so. Hill, who had by then been made steward, said that one day the captain came into the cabin to wash blood from his hands, and said to Allen, "What do you say, Mr. Allen, let us go and kill that Dutchman, he is no sailor. He is a damned old soldier." Hill said that Mr. Allen lifted the man up while the captain hit him in the head. When released, Herman fell to the deck, whereupon they stripped him of his clothes, leaving him naked. The next morning he was found lying naked in the 'tween decks on the coal. "It was very cold that night. I sent him a pair of pants and a shirt to put on him."

Additional gory details of the abuse of Blake, the steward, and the German were offered in other accounts. The cook stated that he had been hit in the head and cut by the captain's brass knuckles for breaking a dish worth one shilling, but none of the other crew members claimed to have been abused, and they had no complaints about the food. All who were asked said that they had never before seen such abuse aboard a ship. Although they had signed a statement on April 3 absolving the captain and the mate of any blame for Blake's death, they testified that they had only done so in fear of their lives.

Some money had to be used outside of counsel fees

On August 13, 1870, the Sewalls sent "sundry papers" to George Howe & Co., San Francisco, of Howe's Dispatch Line of Clipper Ships, attesting to the good character of their Mr. Allen, a prisoner aboard the U.S. steamer *Saranac* on passage from Callao to San Francisco. In the name of the Pattens—Allen had sailed in a Patten ship before coming to the Sewalls, and evidently Howe was tight with the Pattens—they asked Howe to support young Allen "in his hour of need."

Included was an affidavit in which E. & A. Sewall, William D. Sewall, and Thomas M. Reed certified that Mr. Allen had been the first officer of their ship *America* for between four and five years, and that from their long and extensive experience as ship owners they employed only officers in whom they had "strong confidence as to their habits and qualifications." They expressed full confidence in Mr. Allen's "truthfulness, integrity, and humanity," and did not believe him to be a man of "cruel disposition or of uncontrolled passion."

Under their signatures was a second statement, attesting to the foregoing signers' status as "merchants and gentlemen of high standing," over the signatures of Joshua L. Chamberlain, the hero of Gettysburg and governor of Maine; Richard D. Rice, creator of the Maine Central Railroad and vice president of the Northern Pacific Railroad; Joseph Howard, a justice of the Maine Supreme Judicial Court; James G. Blaine, of Augusta, Maine, the Speaker of the U.S. House of Representatives; Lot M. Morrill, United States senator from Maine; and William G. Barrows, judge, Superior Judicial Court.

These were heavy hitters, indeed, attesting to the reach of the Sewalls' political pull. George Howe responded that such testimonials would be of no use in the trial, but might be helpful at sentencing. "We feel that Mr. Allen is in a very unfortunate situation and unless all the protection is given him that can be, we fear it will go hard with him." On September 9 Howe reported the arrival of *Saranac* with prisoner Allen on board. The grand jury being in session, Allen was quickly indicted on five charges, including one of murder:

> We have visited him twice at the prison, he appears quite contented and says the imprisonment he can stand, but for Capt. Frazier to neglect him in the manner he has, when he repeatedly promised him to assist him, is very hard for him to hear.

A Dr. Eliot, a cousin of Allen's living in the area, wrote to the Sewalls after visiting the prisoner. The doctor believed that Allen was the victim of a conspiracy between Captain Frazier and the consul. "If the captain had kept out of the affair there would have been no trouble." Only when the "mutinous murderous Negro, knife in hand, was prostrated on the deck" did the captain rush in, "sword in hand, like the hero of Cervantes." Dr. Eliot saw no reason to delay the trial—one of the *Matterhorn* witnesses had "gone off," and of the two remaining, only one "was a bad one, and him we are trying to reach and mollify as far as possible."

The two remaining witnesses were being held in jail, the standard procedure for guaranteeing the appearance of a sailor witness in court. "One is a boy," wrote the doctor, "I have just found his father who lives here and is allowed to visit them. I found the father and all the family *very* much interested in Mr. Allen's favor. . . . Mr. Allen's counsel, Mr. [Cutler] McAllister, and I, called on the district attorney. He seemed much inclined in favor of the mate and said he did not understand why the captain was not sent here instead. He . . . will not push the prosecution more than his duty absolutely requires."

The three witnesses who had been brought north were Henry Bowman, a German and the ship's carpenter; Percy Boutelle, the ship's "boy"; and Baltimore sailor Frederick Hill. At the trial, the testimony of Bowman and Boutelle substantially repeated the outline of events as given by crew members to Consul Williamson. The only witness who could testify as to how the altercation began, Frederick Hill, had sailed to Oregon aboard a steamer—one might suspect that he had been bought off. The district attorney moved for a continuance until the steamer returned; Mr. McAllister

Captain Zaccheus Allen, 1843–1914, at left, likely posing with brother captains or—if he was still a mate himself—other mates. (A captain would never socialize with a mate.) Allen gained his first command, the Sewalls' ship Humboldt, *in 1874.*
<small>MAINE MARITIME MUSEUM</small>

objected. Judge Hoffman agreed with McAllister, opining that he didn't think that Hill's testimony would be important.

On November 3 Andronicus "Dron" Chesebrough, an East Coast shipping agent who was a friend to the Sewalls, and who had just arrived at San Francisco to join the firm of Williams, Blanchard & Co., wrote to Arthur:

I have just returned from the Court Room where I heard Mr. Allen's sentence. The judge spoke beautifully to him, reviewing the case beginning to end, and finally closed by saying that the prisoner was acquitted of *every* charge except several kicks given to Moses Blake. Pitched into the Consul for sending Mr. Allen here at such an expense while, to use his own words, "the great culprit judging from the evidence, remained at Callao." He then said that Mr. Allen had undergone quite enough punishment at Callao, onboard the man of war & in prison here & he would fine him $10. So ends the matter. . . . Mr. Howes saw the judge yesterday & had a long talk with him. . . . Quite a number of masters & mates were present to hear the sentence & I judge all were surprised.

The judge concluded:

The whole moral aspect of this case depends upon a state of facts of which, so far as evidence discloses, I am in ignorance. If the affray began on your part, and if the man only acted to protect himself against some brutality or violence on your part, then your deed, of course, would be viewed in a far different light. . . . I can only express my astonishment that the American consul, having these facts before him, should, at the expense of the United States, have sent you up here for trial, while the greater culprit, the captain, is permitted wholly to escape. . . . 7

Judge Hoffman had instructed the jury not to consider the charges against Allen regarding the steward and the German sailor, for lack of evidence.

Mr. Howe wrote the Sewalls: "The expenses of this case we expect will be pretty heavy as some money had to be used *outside* of counsel fees." He thought that young Mr. Allen was a very fortunate man. The lawyer's bill came to $734; the bill from Howe to the Sewalls for all expenses associated with the suit was for $1,000, which was the amount of the Sewalls' letter of credit to them. This included Allen's ticket home. We will meet up with "Zack" Allen again.

On April 28, 1870, Captain Samuel Duncan of the bark *Frank Marion* wrote the Sewalls of his great surprise, upon arriving at New Orleans, of being rather "roughly used" and arrested, along with his mate, and charged with "murder on the high seas." They were refused bail and committed to the parish prison, where they lay for forty-eight hours before "friends" succeeded in getting them bailed out. "We finally ascertained that the charges had been made against us by that contemptible scoundrel Dudley, consul at Liverpool, for aiding and abetting Frazier for murder on the high seas—Frazier goes Scot free and we suffer for his conduct." This, of course, referred to the Christmas morning murder aboard the *Marion*.

Captain Frazier remained in command of *Matterhorn* through most of 1871, his last voyage being a round trip from Philadelphia with oil to the Mediterranean, returning with fruit, for a net profit for the owners of $6,000. He was then replaced by Captain Peleg Curtis, who returned to his old command for about one year.

In May of 1872 the Sewalls received a letter from Mr. Alvin Frazier of Lisbon Falls, Maine: "As there is no doubt of the loss of my son William with the Bark *Andaman* it becomes my painful duty to look after his business affairs." Frazier still owed the Sewalls for a note, which he had probably taken when buying 1/16 of the bark when he had surely believed—on what basis we can only speculate—that he would continue in command. Owning—or, as in this instance—owing for an interest in his vessel, gave a captain no security against being removed at the Sewalls' pleasure, and no guarantee that he could sell his interest back to the Sewalls.

The ill-fated *Andaman* was a small Bath bark. *Matterhorn* was sold at Hamburg in 1877 for £8,000 to A. W. Wappans, a major buyer of American ships. Many old American ships sailing under German colors sailed in the "barreled oil trade" from Philadelphia and New York to Europe. These ships, as a rule, were very well liked by their German captains.

You've got bloody Jack Halyard to deal with

The unique legal status of the seaman—a citizen who, when signed aboard a ship, assumed a role not unlike that of the soldier—was predicated by the necessity that authority must reside with the captain and officers. Such power, of course, too often corrupts. And even worse than the corrupted bully was the psychotic madman.

In the 1870s America was still living in the aftermath of a brutal civil war that had taken half a million soldiers' lives. It was not a society of brotherly love. In 1874, J. Grey Jewell, M.D., having returned from several years as U.S. consul at Singapore, published a passionate book, *Among Our Sailors*, concerning brutality aboard American ships, including the case of the Sewalls' ship *Matterhorn*.

A consul was a bonded federal officer posted in a foreign port and charged, among other duties, with upholding the navigation laws of the United States, particularly as they pertained to the welfare of American seamen—any seaman serving aboard an American ship was considered to be an American seaman. Having entered a foreign port, shipmasters were required to surrender their ship's papers to the consul, who returned them after the ship had been properly cleared for departure.

Jewell's introduction to shipboard brutality began with his passage to the Far East aboard a Boston ship that was commanded by a sadistic boor who also was a bad navigator, and with mates cut from the same cloth. Jewell described his frustration at being powerless to intervene when hearing the screams of sailors being cruelly punished in the night. The steady stream of sailors calling at the Singapore consulate seeking relief compounded his outrage. He wrote in his preface:

> I have vainly examined many libraries in the hope of discovering some work deprecating the unjust expectations which ship-owners, underwriters, and consignees have of the officers commanding their ships; some work that would denounce the unmerited, unmerciful, and cruel punishments inflicted upon American sailors, when at sea, in the merchant and naval services; some work that would expose the defective and unjust laws which enslave the sailor and screen his oppressors. . . . This hope having failed, I determined to write what I know about these things. . . .[8]

With over a million men serving in the British and American merchant services (about a third were under the American flag) and the average career of a sailor being but twelve years, it was apparent why British and American merchant ships—unlike those of any other countries—were manned in large part by foreigners. According to

Jewell, everyone serving at sea, even the seemingly all-powerful captain, labored under the thumbs of superiors.

Captains were expected by owners to make fast passages, but could be black-balled by underwriters if they ran into trouble doing so. In port they were often responsible for doing the ship's business. They must always reduce expenses. If the ship was for sale they were expected to "swear that a leaky old hulk was as tight as a bottle." If the crew had been shipped at a high-priced port, captains were expected by many owners to "get clear of them" by driving them out of the ship.[9]

According to Jewell, most owners—Maine owners, at least after the Civil War, were evidently exceptions—did not allow captains' wives to join them at sea. Thus, after perhaps a month's vacation at home resting after two years at sea, a captain would receive a telegram to join his ship immediately for a voyage that might last one year or possibly three. Upon returning home his children would not recognize him. But many eager candidates were ready to take his position.

Jewell wrote that some captains were "as good men as I have ever known," and conceded that "sailors are not angels, afloat or ashore. Some of the very worst specimens of mankind are to be found among our sailors." Although most captains had little education, Jewell found them, as a group, very shrewd, but that only one in ten was what he called "a proper man—one who sets a good example to his men and officers—a just and conscientious man." More common was the "knock-down" type of captain whose typical speech at the outset of a voyage went something like this:

Men, my name's Captain Halyard; I'm master of this ship, and I want to be square with you. We've got a long voyage before us, and there's plenty of work to be done. I want you to understand, I'm great on discipline, and you can have hell or heaven on board, just as you please. . . . If you do your duty, it will be all right; and if you don't, it will be all wrong. The first man that disobeys my orders, I'll put daylight through him [damned] quick, and here's the little joker I'll do it with. [Exhibits a revolver.] If any of you men try to make trouble aboard of this ship, I'll make it [damned] hot for you; I'll make mince-meat of some of you quicker 'an hell'd scorch a feather! I hear that some of you are from the *White Swallow*, where you gave much trouble. Well, this is not the *White Swallow*, and you've got bloody Jack Halyard to deal with. Now you know who I am, and what you've got to expect. Go forward!"[10]

Jewell found that very few of the countless instances of abuse of seamen ever went to trial, and of those that did, far fewer resulted in any punishment. Trials cited included one regarding charges of brutality aboard the Boston clipper *Fearless* in 1869; the 1870 "shanghaiing" of crew members aboard the ship *Bengal* in 1870; charges of brutality involving the New York ships *Old Colony* and *Neptune* in 1870 and 1871 respectively; and aboard the Sewall ship *Matterhorn*.

The *Old Colony* case involved two men allegedly "shanghaied," or kidnapped, from Valencia, Spain, and who were then beaten, kicked, suspended in the rigging, set upon by a vicious dog, starved, and otherwise abused. New York police found the two emaciated men confined in a small and filthy space, suffering fearfully.

The captain of the ship *Neptune* had been in court before on charges of cruelty against both seamen and passengers. Approaching the American coast in February in very cold weather he ordered sailors aloft to perform an allegedly unnecessary task and kept them there until they were badly frostbitten. One sailor later had a finger drop off. When New York police entered the small, unventilated forecastle they found the sailors moaning and crying with intense pain. The stench was unbearable.[11]

Both cases, tried in federal court at New York, resulted in acquittals thanks to an 1835 statute which required proof not only that cruelty was employed, but that it involved "malice, hatred, or revenge," a nearly impossible standard to meet. The *Neptune's* captain, however, was later found guilty and fined by New York City's unique Marine Court.

Citing two cases where crews that had mutinied in self-defense were acquitted, Dr. Jewell suggested that this would have been the proper course for the crew of *Matterhorn* to have followed. He did not explain how the sailors would have been able to navigate the ship with the officers in irons.

Pointing to a recent increase in vessel losses, Jewell charged that ships were not being built as well as in years past, and that some builders were guilty of fraud, including using iron bolts with coppered heads. Also, ships were routinely undermanned, overloaded, and overinsured.

In this regard, surely the Sewalls deserved a passing grade, since they built good ships and generally sold them before they had become too ripe or wormed. They could not be accused of overinsuring their ships, although overloading them was a different matter. They appear to have usually "fed" well. But the case of *Matterhorn* was just one of many cases of alleged abuse aboard a Sewall ship. No doubt a number were groundless, or at least exaggerated. But there is no evidence that the Sewalls were ever very concerned about the problem beyond the nuisance, expense, and bad press that resulted.

Jewell's otherwise somber jeremiad is relieved by some humor. A Swedish sailor is quoted telling a story regarding the ship "*Andelobe*" [*Antelope*], Captain Crashpie [Crosby], when about to depart for Boston from Angier, the stepping-off port from the East Indies. Not realizing that the captain had already ordered "wegetubles" [vegetables] for the passage, the crew, fearing scurvy, and egged on by a "sea lawyer," was contemplating mutiny:

> Vell, de mate call us all aft, und he make us stand in a line on de port side, near de cabin-house. . . . Bimeby [By and by] Capen Crashpy comes up on deck, und at first he didn't say a vord; but he valks along de line right straight to Pill [Bill] Jones [the sea lawyer] first one. He puts a revolver pistol in Pill's face, und den he makes a little speech; but it vos a very short von. Says he: "Do you vish to go to hell, or to Boston?"
>
> "I vish to go to Boston," says Jones, very quick.
>
> "Vell," said Capen Crashpy, "you go on de starboard side."

Captain Crosby then put the same question to every man, receiving the same answer from each.

As the last man goes over, Capen Crashpy he sings out to de mate, "Man de windlass, Mr. French," und de men run forward mit a will—de anchor coomes up mit a run, de bum-boats mit de wegetubles und stores make fast to de channels, und ve sail away for Boston.[12]

Captain Crosby had made his point.

Some Interesting Letters

On June 6, 1868, Arthur wrote Edward from Baltimore:

Yours of 6th at hand, and you are already advised of safe arrival of *Hermon*, etc. Tonight we have her ballast all out & 60 tons of coal in for stiffening & have put on 7 courses of metal from top down to shore staging on the r[ail]way. I never hope to copper a vessel here again & you will think so when you see the bill for this job. We started with a colored crew, had a riot with whites & blacks, killed one man & are now doing it with whites, a most miserable set of fill-ins you ever saw. Please not say anything to Emma about this trouble

Translation—*Hermon* had arrived without cargo, "in ballast." The ballast had been removed, and sufficient coal—sixty tons—had been loaded to give the ship a safe margin of stability. She had then been hauled out on a marine railway to have her bottom covered with copper alloy sheathing as protection against shipworms and to retard marine growth. On June 9 Arthur and Emma had been married just over two months. At Baltimore, blacks—both slaves and freemen—had dominated the caulking trade since before the war..

On April 25, 1870, Edward wrote Arthur from Boston:

Nothing of interest to advise. Have consulted a 2nd Dr. and find they both agree as to my treatments & shall follow Dr. Derbes proscriptions & shall hope sooner or later to regain at least a part of my sight, the Dr. wishes to see me each day for the next week or ten & then I shall probably return. Neither Dr. would advise any Water Cure treatment or Turkish Baths so I shall not go to North Hampton at least for treatment. Was glad to be advised of safe arrival of *Frank Marion*. . . .

The *Frank Marion* had just arrived at New Orleans from Liverpool. "Water cure" treatments included various applications of cold water, sometimes including the use of tightly wrapped wet sheets, to address various ailments. The fact that the letter looks to be in Edward's own hand is puzzling. Among a number of forms of temporary sight impairments was what was then called "hysterical blindness," now called "temporary vision loss," and considered to be of psychological origin.

Of the two brothers, Edward was the more unsettled, as would become increasingly evident. Arthur, by contrast, had all the mental fragility of a granite boulder. And in 1870 Edward was facing some very worrisome concerns. The Sewalls built no vessels that year, the shipping business being in a slump, but what was much more likely to have been causing Edward sleepless nights was the unfolding financial disaster known as the Knox & Lincoln Railroad, in which Edward had, with reckless enthusiasm, deeply entwined himself.

—

In November 1871, while on a passage from Göteburg, Sweden, to Boston with iron, the bark *Frank Marion*, Captain Samuel Duncan, likely having been held up by headwinds, ran low on provisions and was in danger of having to "break passage" and put into a port to resupply, a costly matter. To Captain Duncan's great good fortune the *Marion* fell in with the bark *Alexander McNeal* of New York, Captain Killean, from whom supplies were obtained. On January 25, 1873—three years later—Thomaston attorneys Gould & Moore wrote the Sewalls trying to collect payment for the supplies provided by the *McNeal*. Responding to a request from the Sewalls for an itemized bill, the lawyers wrote back:

> We presume with some trouble a bill of items could be provided of the bill of the ship *McNeal*. . . . We met Capt. Killean & named to him what you say. He is willing to furnish items so far as he can, yet he feels indignant that the vessel that he furnished with provisions *at sea*, to keep her on her voyage, should hesitate about paying that small sum. Especially since it appears, by the capt.'s letter which we have that he sent you the amount of the bill and directed its payment. Your captain says he wrote Capt. K. Moreover Capt. Duncan says he got the costs & weight in Boston & sends Capt. K. the amount which he, Capt. Duncan, also says he sent you & being same amount we sent you.
>
> Capt. Duncan only allowed the *actual cost to Capt. K. in Boston*, and didn't consider him anything for shipping them and carrying them to sea. . . . Your bill was furnished Nov. 15, 1870.
> $41.18
> Interest 5.60
> $46.78
> Interest 5.00
> $51.75

The Sewalls' end of the correspondence has not been discovered. There are several other such bills for reprovisioning at sea in the papers—one having been due for over two years—but no other where payment was denied pending an itemized list.

———

In January 1871 Captain Alpheus Boyd of Wiscasset, of the Bath bark *Niphon*, owned by F. O. Moses, wrote the Sewalls a chatty letter from Liverpool:

> In the short time that I have been here I have seen enough to convince me that it is useless for us to build any more wooden ships in America when a first-class iron ship with an East Indian outfit which includes two suits of sails, three anchors, and chains, spare rigging & twenty years class can be bought for twelve pounds per ton. The Englishmen are getting out of wooden ships fast as possible and going into iron and steamers. . . . Am sorry to write so discouragingly but perhaps it is better to know it sooner than later what we have would bring very little more than half the cost. I was talking with Donnal Mackay [Donald McKay] in London four days ago. He is of the opinion that there will not be many more wooden ships built in the United States.

"Donnal Mackay," of course, was Donald McKay, the great East Boston clipper builder, who was also among the pioneering American iron shipbuilders. In 1869 McKay and other shipbuilders (not including the Sewalls) testified before the Lynch Committee in Congress regarding the harmful effects of the very high tariffs on imported material used for shipbuilding. In 1872 a drawback of duties for imported materials used in the construction of registered tonnage went into effect, restricting the participation of such vessels in coastal shipping—not including the Cape Horn inter-coastal trade—to two months in a year, unless the "rebated" duties were paid.

———

On January 26, 1870, Frederick Howes of Boston wrote E. & A. and W. D. Sewall:

> I notice your good Ship *Hermon* laying at Charlestown with Howes' rig upon her—and that she was rigged *before* my patent expired—I will send you the bill for the same—by remitting the amount you will very much oblige.

On June 11, 1871, Howes wrote again:

> You say that you are of the party of the combination that was gotten up in Bath to contest the suit against J. P. Morse & others. I am aware of that fact, and have every name connected with it. This arrangement was that all that joined that ring was to adopt the Constitution or Bath Rig. And was not to be molested with by me. And I never have. But the ring was not satisfied with the Bath Rig. And went and adopted my regular rig. . . .

Captain Howes, a Cape Codder, obtained a patent for a double-topsail rig—which divided the big topsail into two more easily manageable sails—in 1854. It was a major improvement, all but universally adopted, and he spent many years trying to collect royalties of ten cents a ton, thirty cents if he had to sue. A dunning letter was sent to William D. back in 1857 regarding the ships *Kineo* and *Hellespont*.

The mystic balsamic odor of the pine

Between 1873 and 1891 the Sewalls built and managed ten three-masted schooners and two four-masted schooners. The three-masters, in large part, were employed carrying southern hard-pine ship timber to Bath. The Sewall Family Papers are surely the greatest source of documentary evidence regarding this distinctive trade.

While "registered" deepwater square-rigged tonnage shrank precipitously after the Civil War, the "enrolled" coastwise tonnage, composed in large part of fore-and-aft-rigged schooners of increasing size, grew dramatically. Although much aided by the exclusion of foreign competition from coastwise commerce, the American schooner evolved, as well, to became a highly efficient carrier that dominated many trades over steam.

In his scrawled 1938 letters to Mark Hennessy, Doc Briry expressed the hope that in a second book the hard-pine schooners would not be forgotten. Of those schooners he noted: "It took good seamanship and great courage to steer a heavily loaded vessel in winter months over Frying Pan Shoals and then past Hatteras. Some . . . never got by, never were heard from."

The schooners of Bath's hard pine fleet—Bath businessman James P. Drake managed another—were said to be the "smartest" on the coast. When entering the Kennebec they eschewed pilots and, if at all possible, tugs. The sight of several pine schooners sailing into the river hard by the beach, at close quarters, on a flood tide in the quiet of a gentle summer evening, with their long-boomed spankers "wung out" to catch the last of the dying southwester, was long remembered by residents of Popham. The voices of the bowler-hatted, pipe-smoking skippers could be distinctly heard discussing their passages as they leaned on their taffrails.[13]

The hard-pine trade was a part of the epic slaughter of millions of acres of old-growth "longleaf," "hard," or "yellow" pine, stretching from Virginia down the southeastern coast and west along the Gulf Coast to Texas. Among the first to appreciate the superior qualities of this golden-hearted timber were northern shipbuilders in the 1830s. Most of the pioneering lumbermen of the coastal hard-pine business of the Southeast were Yankees, Englishmen, and Scotsmen. Among the Yankees were the Bucks of Bucksport, Maine, and the Baileys of Woolwich. As Doc Briry recalled:

A Woolwich-born man by the name of Bailey . . . established large mills on the Satilla River, Georgia. One of the best known of the Sewall fleet of small schooners was named the *Satilla*. A captain [Parker T.] Rivers commanded the *Satilla*, a daring captain he was, too. Winter months did not frighten Captain

Rivers. It was nothing unusual to see the *Satilla* come in from sea loaded . . .
high on deck with those heavy and long pieces of Southern pine.

Sadly, Captain Rivers's employment with the Sewalls ended in the fall of 1880, following reports from Jim Bailey that *Satilla's* dispatch was often delayed by the good
captain's "frollicking" in Brunswick, Georgia, in the company of a certain "fast
woman."

The rivers of South Carolina, northern Florida, and especially Georgia provided the
mills with access to timber from far inland. The best description of a visit to one of
these river mills comes from Captain Alfred Green, the young yet already stuffy
English captain of the small British Nova Scotian–built bark *Mertola*, after loading pine
fully forty miles up the narrow, sinuous St. Mary's River in December 1889. (The St.
Mary's forms the boundary between Florida and Georgia):

> Such a ridiculous little river it now seems to drag a ship into, the branches all but
> seem to interlace across it. . . . This is really quite a unique experience, sailing
> through a forest in a ship, brushing showers of dried leaves and twigs upon the
> deck as the yard arms sweep among the branches, now gliding along a shadowed
> avenue, where the serried ranks of tall pines press closely upon the bank at either
> side, and the still air is fragrant with the mystic balsamic odor of the pine. . . . [14]

The remote sawmill settlement of Orange Bluff, the bark's destination, was little
more than a clearing in the woods, where lived three white married brothers in three
pretty houses, some young orphans a little ways off, and twenty or thirty black
employees living in log cabins in the woods. Captain Green found few diversions until
the arrival of the three-masted schooner *Susie P. Oliver*, of Bangor, Maine:

> Almost all American vessels are named after some individual (an abominably
> tasteless fashion), and every name must of necessity include the initial, as *Joel F.
> Hopkins, Amanda K. Jones.*[15] They are great institutions, these same schooners,
> for, owing to their simplicity of rig, they can sail a vessel of 900 tons capacity
> with eight hands all told. They sail well, shift without ballast, use but little gear,
> and rarely exceed 13 feet in draught. Perhaps the first thing that strikes a
> stranger's eye is their enormous beam . . . but they seem to get along all right
> and undoubtedly sail like foam balls.

Captain Green was envious of the schooner's palatial cabin as compared to his own
cramped quarters. And to his great surprise he found the elderly, dry "Daun East" skipper of the *Susie P. Oliver* to be very good company: "As it turns out, this same solemn-
visaged, slow-of-speech, old Yankee salt is as full of fun as a kitten, and as tender
hearted as a child. A slow, halting delivery that he is always lamenting simply makes
his constant drolleries perfectly irresistible. . . ."
Green was far less impressed by the run-of-the-woods local whites: "Such a jaun-

diced, lean, and bloodless crew! . . . And nine out of every ten of them ruminating like so many cows, only with a difference in the cud that reflects very favorably to the cows." He was more favorably disposed toward the "darkies," who he found good-natured and sociable, if childishly credulous. Green would likely have felt more at home among the coastal upper class of Darien, Georgia. Mrs. Lillian Sinclair, a member of society there, recalled:

> The social life of Darien during the eighties and nineties was most delightful. A number of the old families were still living, together with the lumber merchants, who were English and Scotch—made a charming society. We often spent the day with each other—always had three balls each year. . . . We could always count on a mask ball at the Hiltons and a dance of some kind at the Fosters. . . . They would floor over a big lighter (which would be towed by a tugboat); on this they danced. We would go to St. Simons, Fernadina, Frederica, and Brunswick. We always got stuck in the mud, going and coming, but we didn't mind as it only made the trip longer.[16]

Vast quantities of pine were exported, much as squared timber. Much was shipped to the Argentine, some going by schooner, and also to Britain. In the 1880s up to eighty foreign square-riggers each would sometimes be anchored in Georgia's Dobey and Sapelo Sounds. Too deep-drafted to cross the river bars, they were loaded at anchor by gangs of black stevedores—very fit men, indeed. Wooden vessels would first be loaded with the heavy timbers brought aboard through bow ports. The son of a mill owner recalled:

> Each gang of stevedore hands had a leader, who sang a line of a chanty song, the others coming in on the short chorus, then, with a "ho" all heaved together on a big stick in perfect time. This same system of singing when the combined effort of a gang was needed to move heavy timbers, was used in loading coastwise vessels also, and I never heard of a boss stevedore interrupting it.[17]

The shoal American schooners usually loaded right at the mills, although often when departing deep-loaded they were delayed in clearing the river bar, and sometimes "thumped" several times when crossing over.

James S. Bailey, the Satilla River lumberman, was born in Woolwich in 1837. Two older brothers, William and John, preceded him to the river, and they in turn were following an earlier group of Mainers who, in 1839, had built the first steam sawmill in the region.[18] The "Jim Bailey" mill and the "John Bailey" mill were located about thirty-four and forty-one miles, respectively, up the narrow, winding river. When, in April 1872, the Sewalls complained about the high rate asked by a Thomaston schooner to fetch a cargo from "Bailey's Mills," New York ship broker J. W. Elwell advised them: "Captains decline generally to go to Bailey's Mills to load & we have hard work to find vessels to go there excepting St. George & Rockland vessels." By "St. George" vessels he was likely referring to vessels from both Thomaston and the adjacent town of St. George, both lying on the St. George River.

No doubt the fact that they could drive a hard bargain with the remotely situated Bailey attracted the Sewalls like flies to honey, and it is apparent that the Sewalls' reflexive cheese-paring irritated Bailey, especially when it disrupted his operation. In April 1871 a frustrated Jim Bailey wrote the Sewalls:

> Do you think lumber grows already sawed? The W. Y. [*J. F. Willey*] vessel is here and it is already probable she will have some demurrage and if this be the case you shall pay it. We have paid enough on your account. It appears to us that you do not care one snap as long as you get the lumber how much trouble you place us to or the expense. If this be the case we had better finish your memo and play quits for it is useless for us to work and pay all the profits away in demurrage. The *J. F. Willey*[19] will be off next week . . . Charter no other vessel until you hear from us under no circumstances. . . .

On May 22 Bailey wrote:

> The captain of the [brig] *Collins* yesterday refuses to take your masting. . . . We have borne the expense of getting your masting ready in accordance with your orders. Now by your own neglect or carelessness you have failed in chartering your last two vessels to mention your masting in their charter party. This gives no chance at all. . . .

"Masting" normally consisted of long component timbers for a "built" mast, but on this occasion Bailey had found a single log "straight as a gun barrel," seventy-two feet long and twenty-seven inches through at twenty feet from the butt, which could serve as a mizzenmast. Because a captain would have charged extra for carrying such a spar if it were listed in the charter party, the Sewalls had not mentioned it, hoping that a captain would bring it along anyway, if only to get it off of Bailey's wharf. In his next letter Bailey complained: "You have screwed us down now until we hardly make a living. . . . We cannot live at the present prices." On July 6 he wrote:

> You say you had to furnish Messrs. G & S [Bath shipbuilders Goss & Sawyer] the 2 large sticks at a considerable loss. Whose fault is this? Why did you not charter your vessels in such a way that we could have compelled the captains to have taken these large pieces? In your twisting around to get out of a little freight you have got into this and now try to pack it off on us. And furthermore we note you have charged us with commissions on your last order. This will not do. . . .

Beginning with *Satilla*, launched in 1873, the Sewalls began to build their own schooners.[20] The advantages were obvious. First, they no longer were dependent on independent Thomaston captains. And with their own schooners they could enjoy other benefits of vertical integration, including additional opportunities to profit from the building of ships. And the schooners were also largely paid for by other people. Jim Bailey became a large owner in the fleet by supplying ship timber, and three schooners, the *Ada Bailey, Nora Bailey,* and *Carrie S. Bailey,* were named for his daughters.

Many years later, Doc Briry met Nora Bailey, who told him that her father was shot and killed by a sawmill worker, and his son was unable to carry on the business, thus the sudden cessation of business done with the Baileys. Jim Bailey's Satilla River holdings were then bought by the Hilton Timber & Lumber Co. of Darien.

The first Hilton, a representative of a mill machinery firm, came to Georgia from England in the 1840s. The Hilton Timber & Lumber Company did most of its business on the Altamaha River. Hilton & Dodge, a later iteration, was long a major supplier for the Sewalls, with whom they enjoyed a relationship characterized by frequent squabbling and discord.

By the early 1900s the forest along the hard-pine rivers had been well cut back, and transitory little logging railroads extended into the back lands, with logs skidded to the cars by steam-powered winches. After most of the old-growth longleaf pine had finally been cut off, Thomas Hilton, a grandson of the founder, recalled what it had been like in the great forest that was no more, with the tops of the trees forming a canopy that kept the ground at their feet open for easy travel, "allowing the sunlight to splotch through on the ground. . . . A light breeze through the tops sounds like surf in the distance."[21]

1. *Matterhorn* cost $96,331.21. A register dated September 5, 1866, listed her owners as Arthur and Edward Sewall, partners with 3/16; William D. Sewall, 4/16; Thomas M. Reed, 4/16; Peleg Curtis, master, 2/16; William S. Cutler, 3/16.

2. The letter from the Liverpool agents Jones & Longey & Co., February 12, 1858, informing Clark & Sewall of *Leander*'s loss, stated in part: "The vessel it appears went down in 5 minutes. Although we have to deplore the loss of Mrs. Curtis & 9 seamen we rejoice to be able to add that Capt. Curtis, his son & remainder of the crew have been saved. We assure you we deeply sympathize with Capt. Curtis in his loss, whom we have found so truly intelligent in matters of business."

3. Robert White Stevens, *On the Stowage of Ships and Their Cargoes,* (London: Longman's Green, Reader & Dyer, 1878), pp. 517–22. Chas. H. Hillcoat, *Notes on the Stowage of Ships* (New York: Colonial Publishing Company, 1919), pp. 190–96.

4. H. C. De Mierre, *The Long Voyage* (New York: Walker and Company, 1963), p. 129.

5. A close cousin, a bond of respondentia, was given to raise money on the cargo, or a portion of it, so as to allow a ship to continue its voyage. If the vessel was lost but sufficient cargo was salved, the bond had to be paid.

6. Most serious shipboard violence involved sheath knives. Since 1868 it had been illegal to wear (not simply to possess) a sheath knife aboard an American ship, captains being obligated to enforce the statute or face a fifty-dollar fine for every omission. But despite this severe penalty it is unlikely that any shipboard regulation has been more flagrantly ignored. Ship slop chests offered sheath knives and also the belts to hang them on.

7. *Daily Alta California,* October 30, November 1, November 4, 1870. See also *Daily Morning*

Call, November 4; *San Francisco Chronicle*, October 30, November 4; *Daily Examiner*, October 31.

8. J. Grey Jewell, M.D., *Among Our Sailors* (New York: Harper & Brothers, 1874).

9. With several exceptions, since 1803 a captain discharging a seaman in a foreign port was required to pay an extra three months' wages. (Two months' worth was paid to the seaman after he signed aboard a departing ship, the other third was retained by the government to help fund the return of displaced seamen.) The 1872 shipping act provided that wages due a deserter were forfeited to the government (in the person of the consul).This was later amended to require the captain to pay wages and three months' extra pay if the consul was persuaded that an apprehended deserter had fled by reason of cruelty. (Deserters could be arrested and detained without a warrant and were ordinarily liable for expenses associated with their apprehension and return). In 1884 this was reduced to one extra month's wages. The payment of extra wages to "any seaman" whose contract had expired in a foreign port was left to the discretion of the consul who could, "if he deems it just," discharge the seaman without awarding extra wages—see Sec. 4583 of the Navigation Laws of the United States. Thus we find Captain Minott of the Sewalls' ship *Hermon* writing from Liverpool in January 1873 after arriving from high-wage San Francisco: "I had a very hard passage . . . and a bad crew to make it with . . . . I have paid off 13 of them yesterday. There is three ways of getting clear of them here. Some give one third of their pay [presumably as extra wages]. Some pay the consul one month's extra pay. Others pay the same but charge one half of it to the men. I have done so. I think it the least expense to the ship and decidedly the safest way. I take a protest for the extra pay. . . . All of our articles was given by a government official and read to be paid off in Liverpool."

10. Jewell, *Among Our Sailors*, p. 46. In fact, we have an eyewitness's account of the captain's welcome as recalled by Benjamin Albertson, who, as a recent school ship graduate, joined the four-masted bark *Erskine M. Phelps*, Captain Robert Graham, in 1906: "Some of you look familiar, some I don't recall but most of you know *me*. This ship feeds about the same forward as aft only for what I pay for. When my officers speak to you, you will reply with a 'Sir.' We do not overwork ourselves but when you get an order don't walk to obey it and don't run but God damn, you fly. That's all."

11. Jewell, *Among Our Sailors*, pp. 108–17.

12. Jewell, *Among Our Sailors*, pp. 191–92.

13. As described by the late J. Arthur Stevens to his son, the late James P. Stevens, who relayed it to the author.

14. Alfred J. Green, *Jottings From a Cruise* (Seattle: Kelly Printing Co., 1944), pp.132–44.

15. The classic example was perhaps the three-master *Alfaretta S. Snare*, built at Bath in 1880. No doubt Alfaretta was a lovely person, but her surname would surely give any young would-be suitor serious pause.

16. Thomas Hilton, *High Water on the Bar* (Savannah, GA: privately printed, 1951), p. 19.

17. Hilton,*High Water*, p. 10.

18. See Alex S. McQueen, *History of Charlton County* (Atlanta, GA: Stein Publishing Co., 1932).

19. Three-masted schooner *Jennie F. Willey*, of Thomaston.

20. In 1890 *Satilla* was sold to David Trubee of Bridgeport, Connecticut, for $11,000 cash. After the sale had been completed the Sewalls billed Trubee an additional sum as a commission. The indignant Trubee responded: "I thought it very small potatoes & few in a hill for you to even claim or say a word to me of the kind, *when I had your written price $11,000*."

21. Hilton,*High Water*, p. 17.

PART FIVE

We are introduced to ships' agents and brokers, including Andronicus Chesebrough, long the Sewalls' vital helpmate in San Francisco. We accompany Edward Sewall in the great port of New York while he looks after the interests of Sewall ships sailing "on the line" for San Francisco. We meet Joe Sewall, a cousin who would become a skilled yet notorious captain, and meet also Joe's mentor and brother-in-law, Captain Bill Lincoln. Finally, Captain Dinsmore, of the ship Undaunted, *while claiming innocence, skips town to avoid arrest.*

You need not depend on us

Shipping agents and brokers were the cogwheels of the shipping business, and correspondence with them comprises a large portion of the Sewall Family Papers.

A "shipping agent" assisted captains with all manner of transactions in a port, business and otherwise, and, particularly in a foreign port, engaging the services of an agent was essential. Agents also sometimes acted as double agents. In 1908 agent J. Williams of Montevideo, Uruguay, informed the Sewalls regarding Captain Henry St. Clair: "We consider it our duty to inform you that the captain of the *Benj. F. Packard* during his stay here was all the time under the influence of drink; had he attended to his business the vessel could have sailed yesterday morning."

The job of a "ship broker," or "commission merchant," was to introduce a shipper (often a dealer of a commodity) to the ship owner (often in the person of the captain, acting as the owner's agent) for which service the broker was paid a commission by the ship, known as "brokerage." "Split commissions" shared by brokers with other brokers involved in "fixing" a ship were routine, and explains why the Arthur Sewall & Co. letterhead identified the firm as being commission merchants. Secondarily, it identified them as being "agents," meaning that they served as agents for the ships they managed, and not that they were general shipping agents.

The usual brokerage commission was 5 percent of the net freight, although in some trades it was higher, particularly if more brokers or other intermediaries were normally involved—some participants might be paid a small fee per ton of cargo rather than a part of the commission. In some trades the broker was expected to give back a "return commission" to the ship, no doubt a case where an inducement had become an entitlement.

Formal distinctions aside, brokers were also commonly termed "agents," or "general agents," when they also performed agent services. If no extraordinary tasks were required, no extra charge was made for these services, although it was expected that the ship owner would give the broker preferential consideration when chartering. And likewise, the ship owner expected preferential treatment from the broker, and expected the broker to take a financial interest in his new ships. In some cases—the New York and San Francisco clipper trade being a prime example—brokers could also be the charterers, while serving as both the agents for the line and for the ship—a recipe for disputes.

Stevedores, who loaded and discharged the cargo, technically were hired by the ship, i.e., the captain, although often there were undercover alliances with the broker or agent and also the managing owner that ended up determining the selection.

An important part of a broker's job was to be informed, through various sources and networks, of the latest shipping intelligence and prospects, be it of the rice crop in Burma or the wheat crop of California. Brokers kept track of where scores of ships were presently located, or where they were bound for and when they were expected. They were familiar with ships' reputations and also the qualities of their captains. Some brokers specialized in particular trades, or in business to particular ports, or in ships of a particular flag, and other brokers would send such business their way for a split of the commissions.

Brokers were supposed to be experts in the laws of commerce, in dealing in different currencies, and with the arcane financial instruments of the day. When a captain "entered a protest"—in essence a protest against the ship or its owners being held liable for an expense or damage beyond their control, and which should be shared by all participants in a voyage—brokers participated in the negotiations of the "average adjusters" whose job it was to apportion liability.

Brokers followed not only the weather and the resulting crop prospects halfway around the world, but also kept well apprised of international politics—nothing quite set their hearts aflutter as did the rumor of an impending good old-fashioned war in Europe.

The introduction and expansion of long-distance and transoceanic telegraph in the later 1800s greatly altered the relationships between broker, captain, and owner, bringing the owner into the decision-making process even when a ship was on the other side of the world.

The Sewalls, along with many other American ship owners engaged in foreign trade, maintained an account with the great international banking house of Baring Brothers, of London, and it was to the Barings that captains made their freight remittances from foreign ports. When, in 1890, the Barings suffered an "embarrassment"— they were promptly bailed out by the Bank of England—the Sewalls noted that they had had an account with the Barings for over sixty years, and were carrying a balance at the time of £8,000.[1]

New York brokers with whom the Sewalls often did business included Sutton & Co.; R. P. Buck—Richard Buck was a Sewall relation from Bucksport, Maine; J. W. Elwell & Co.—James Elwell was a Bath native; and, most particularly, D. B. Dearborn & Co—David Dearborn was a Kennebecker from East Pittston. At Boston, John S. Emery was yet another Mainer with whom the Sewalls often dealt. A brother of James Elwell was a partner in the Philadelphia firm of Darrah & Elwell; the Portland, Oregon, firm of Sutton & Beebe was a branch house of Sutton & Co.

David Dearborn, born in 1832, apprenticed to an uncle who was a New York ship chandler. In 1851 Dearborn went to San Francisco as purser of the steamship *Pacific*, the first steamer to traverse the Strait of Magellan. In 1854 he founded in New York what became a series of partnerships in the brokerage business. Like most brokers, he had his ups and downs, once declaring bankruptcy during the Civil War.

The Dearborns (David and son George, later also a partner) acted as the New York agents for Sewall ships, owned in Sewall ships, and allowed the Sewalls to hide much of their ownership in their ships from the Bath tax collector by placing interests under the Dearborn name. George Dearborn, who became very wealthy in the early 1900s, joined the Sewalls' Small Point summer community in a most ostentatious manner. The Sewalls' 1889 four-masted schooner *Douglas Dearborn* was named for George's son, who died in infancy.

Perhaps because they were both Kennebeckers, and thus "family," David and Arthur freely expressed themselves when one felt slighted by the other. In May 1885 Dearborn, upset about not having received the consignment of the *Thomas M. Reed*, wrote: "I think I have more interest in the care of your ships than any charterers can have. . . . I have some pride in your ships being reported to me as I am supposed to be your agent." In March 1892 a letter from the Dearborns was deemed by Arthur to have been "abusive" and "impertinent." He wrote in response: "Many a shipowner has been growing poor year by year while our New York friends have been making fortunes out of their ships."

In February 1894 Arthur wrote David:

I am thoroughly disgusted with the dispatch of the *Susquehanna* and *Roanoke*. The idea of the *Susquehanna* consuming eighteen days taking out her ballast is entirely inexcusable. I am reminded of the time when I was doing your work in New York for our ships, the ship *Tabor* arrived with a full cargo of sugar and hemp. I chartered her for Endeberry Island and the 14th day after arrival she went to sea. . . . You will excuse my plain expressions, but if you realized the daily cost of a ship as I do . . . you must agree with me.

The Sewalls were then secretly helping to underwrite the acquisition by the Dearborns of a California "line," and were suffering hurt feelings when they felt that their ships were not being properly favored over others.

In general, communication between shipping people was conducted in the most civil manner, no matter the often contentious disputes. In August 1885 an exasperated

Ship broker David Bailey Dearborn, a native of East Pittston, Maine, and a descendent of Revolutionary War general Henry Dearborn, in his New York office. Above his desk hang a portrait of Arthur Sewall, a reproduction of a painting of the four-masted bark Shenandoah *in a heavy gale, and apparently a photo of one of the Sewall steel four-masted barks.*
MAINE MARITIME MUSEUM

John Rosenfeld, a San Francisco broker, wrote the Sewalls regarding their wish to back out of a deal: "If the *Harvester* charter at $2^1/_2$ is not satisfactory to you it is not too late to cancel it . . . and I would be only too well pleased thereat." In January 1889 a Rosenfeld son wrote: "Referring to our conversation between your Senior and our Mr. John Rosenfeld re. building a new ship we take this opportunity to say that you need not depend upon us to take any interest." In the end, however, genial "Johnny" Rosenfeld took a $1/_{64}$ interest in the ship *Rappahannock*.

A Sewall ship was named for John Rosenfeld, and another for his young son Willie, who had died. Arthur also named a ship for San Francisco broker Andronicus "Dron" Chesebrough, long-time partner in Williams, Dimond & Co. of San Francisco.

Williams, Dimond, successor to Williams, Blanchard & Co., was long the Sewalls' San Francisco anchor and played a vital role in the operation of the Sewall fleet. And the Sewalls, as well as bringing much business to Williams, Dimond, had some of their

Andronicus Chesebrough, c. 1838–1914
MAINE MARITIME MUSEUM

own family members planted within the firm—Edward Sewall's son Oscar went to work for Williams, Dimond in 1879, becoming a partner in 1889 (along with David Dearborn's nephew, Warren Clark). Arthur's son William and Edward's son Frank both spent some time with the firm.

While Williams, Dimond's substantial role in the Hawaiian sugar trade initially had much to do with bringing vital employment to the Sewall fleet, ultimately the firm's key role in the creation of the American–Hawaiian Steamship Co. (Oscar was a director and "Dron" Chesebrough was a director and vice president) helped to bring about the inevitable end of the Sewall fleet.

Dron Chesebrough, and also Liverpool broker Charles T. Russell, rate individual attention.

Your ships are in mind, first, last & all the time

In July 1881 Charlie Russell, Arthur Sewall's favored Liverpool broker at the time, was visiting San Francisco. After meeting Andronicus Chesebrough, the San Francisco broker also favored by Arthur, Russell wrote: "I am having a very nice time here & must say I like Mr. Chesebrough better than any other man I have met. Next to him Mr.

Williams. Mr. C is a live broker & does business as a broker. The only man here that does do it."

Andronicus Chesebrough was born in Baltimore in 1838. Details are sketchy, but from about 1868 until 1874, when he moved to San Francisco for good, Chesebrough was involved in the ship-brokering business at Baltimore, San Francisco, Philadelphia, and New York. In 1870 Chesebrough was a guest of the Sewalls at Bath, and theirs would be a long and mutually beneficial friendship. Later that year Chesebrough made his first trip to San Francisco, where he was associated briefly with Williams, Blanchard & Co. May 1872 found him returning to San Francisco, leaving behind a debt in Philadelphia. He wrote Arthur of the view from the train window of the vast wheat fields of the San Joaquin Valley, stretching as far as the eye could see in all directions. The San Francisco grain trade would be the glue of their relationship.

Returned to Williams, Blanchard & Co., Chesebrough flaunted the friendships he had developed with the Sewalls and other shipping men at Bath. He reported to Arthur:

> I handed the memo given me by you to Mr. Blanchard. . . . The matter of commissions will be made satisfactory to you. In this connection I would remark that I told Mr. B. the conversation held between *us*, what *your* feelings have been & are still toward me, in few words, *what friends all of your name in Bath are to me.*

However, the following year Chesebrough was again back east, serving as co-agent of Comstock's Regular Line of Clipper Ships for San Francisco at New York. In August 1874 we find him riding herd on visiting cousins Oscar and Will Sewall, fourteen and thirteen years old respectively:

> Your sons are very anxious to return via Boston & I have told them all right, so they will go Thursday & take the "boat" Friday night in care of Mrs. Dunphy. Yesterday they went to Greenwood [cemetery in Brooklyn] with Capt. D. & his wife. Today they go to Hell Gate with me, then to David's house to stay all night. Tomorrow they will "do" Prospect Park Brooklyn. . . . You would have laughed had you been here when your telegram was rec'd last week. Neither wanted to go, so Willie said "I know that's not my father writing," then Oscar took it & made a like statement.

Captain William Dunphy, of the ship *Occidental*, was a Kennebecker, born in Gardiner. "David" was doubtless broker David Dearborn; Hell Gate was the notorious tide-roiled channel connecting the East River with Long Island Sound.

That November Chesebrough returned to Williams, Blanchard & Co. at San Francisco. Two years later, in 1876, he formed his own firm, secretly funded by a loan from Arthur. In January 1877 he assured Arthur that "your ships are in mind, *first, last & all the time*, yet you will probably see others fixed before them, if of smaller capacity." In July 1878 Chesebrough responded to the news that a ship just launched by the Sewalls bore his name:

Words fail me to express my surprise & gratification at the *great* honor you have seen fit to confer upon me. . . . What have I done to merit it? If my attentions to your large interests in this port have been satisfactory to you & Mr. Reed I am *quite* content. . . . May your good ship meet with success wherever she may be.

In 1879 Mr. Blanchard retired, to be replaced as a senior partner by William Dimond, and Chesebrough returned to the firm, soon to be renamed Williams, Dimond & Co., as a partner. Also joining the reorganized firm was Oscar Sewall. By 1891 Chesebrough had taken over much of the firm's management, and with Mr. Dimond's retirement in 1896 became senior partner. By this date Williams, Dimond & Co. had become a most substantial organization, controlling a large portion of the Hawaiian sugar business, and as agent to the Sante Fe and Mexican Central Railroads.

Dron Chesebrough wrote Arthur many chummy letters combining business with personal news. He named his son Arthur Sewall—one of about half a dozen boys so dubbed. While Arthur's side of the friendship was the more reserved, so was Arthur. But one also suspects that Arthur's sentiments were guided at least as much by cool financial calculation as by warm affection. In a letter written from his Boston Eastern Railroad office (Arthur was then president of the Eastern) to nephew Sam in March 1884, before a visit by Chesebrough to Bath, Arthur wrote: "[I] hope [Elisha] Mallett will make some show in the yard, would like to see 25 or 30 men at work. . . . "

A connoisseur of wines, perhaps somewhat of a hypochondriac, Chesebrough summered at San Rafael, then a magical Eden on San Francisco Bay. He retired very well off in 1912, and died two years later. His son Arthur became a broker as well, to do business, if not very happily, with Will and Sam Sewall.

From a baby carriage to a locomotive

A ship put "on the line" loaded general cargo at New York's South Street for San Francisco (or Portland, Oregon), sailing on one of several lines, including Sutton & Co.'s Dispatch Line; Comstock's Regular Line; W. R. Grace & Co., George Howe & Co.'s—later John Rosenfeld's—Dispatch Line; Van Vleck & Co.'s—later Dearborn's—California Line, and various iterations of some of the aforementioned under different agents. Some ships made the reverse passage, but not as many. All of the lines either had West Coast branch houses or else worked in league with other West Coast firms.

Sutton's Dispatch Line, founded in 1849 by Effingham B. Sutton, was the oldest. With the onset of the gold rush, Sutton, then a textile merchant, astutely chartered the ship *John Q. Adams* and sent it to San Francisco loaded with supplies for the miners. His new business grew rapidly; New York's posh Sutton Place was named for him. Son Woodruff later managed the New York office; son Allen, the San Francisco office; son Theodore, the Philadelphia office. Nephew George Beebe managed the branch house of Sutton & Beebe at Portland, Oregon.

Only the best of American ships were employed "on the line," and since the Sewalls built good ships, had a young fleet, and employed able captains, they were very much involved in the trade. Although the Sewalls had wisely not joined the mad rush to build California clippers in the booming 1850s, their ships would see the California trade out.

At New York, the latter-day California clippers (so-called in a holdover from the days of the true clippers in the 1850s) loading at South Street was among the notable sights of Gotham. Their lofty rigs—yards perfectly squared and bright masts shining—towered above the warehouse roofs, while horsecars trundled along beneath their overhanging jibbooms. Their sailings were advertised by garish posters and pasteboard "sailing cards" (now very collectable) which proclaimed even moderately sharp ships as "A1 Extreme" clippers.[2]

Frederick Perry, who in the late 1870s served as mate aboard the Sewall-built ship *Continental* (owned by DeGroot & Peck of New York), wrote that "general cargo" loaded in a California clipper consisted of everything imaginable, "from a baby carriage to a locomotive." The cargo lists for newly arrived ships appearing in the San Francisco papers bear him out. According to Perry:

> Loading a vessel is always a puzzle to the average landsman; he cannot understand how the piles and piles of boxes, barrels and cases of merchandise that disappear each day down the ship's hatches never seem to fill her up. The bulk of the goods lying on the piers always seems to total at least three times the capacity of the ship's hold. Successful loading is the secret of the stevedore's art. . . . The whole cargo had to be stowed and blocked off so that it could not shift, no matter how heavily a ship might roll or pitch during the voyage, and at the same time it had to keep her on an even keel and properly trimmed.[3]

Captain George Goodwin, in retirement, bitterly recalled the "puffed up clerks" placed as freight agents for lines who accepted goods with no regard to their fitness aboard a ship. It was important to keep separate any items which might by their proximity damage other cargo—damaged cargo resulted in expensive arbitration and reclamation, and put a mark against the ship's name. Also, the captain's primage was cut up to 5 percent of the value of the damage, yet captains who complained about agents or stevedores were, he claimed, censured for being interfering.

Goodwin blamed an incompetent stevedore forced on his ship by an arrangement between the charterers and the Sewalls for a cargo that shifted after he had made his fastest passage to Cape Horn. It took three days' continuous hard work in the hold to set it right as the ship drifted to the eastward, unable to turn her "lame" side to the sea. The lost chance to round the Horn with favoring weather delayed his arrival in port by three weeks.[4]

While the first gold rush clippers had the very profitable San Francisco freight market to themselves, very soon the mail and people traversed the Isthmus of Panama, which was served on both sides by steamers of the Pacific Mail Line. After the opening of the Panama Railroad in 1855, much high-value freight would follow. The 1869 opening of the heavily subsidized Union Pacific transcontinental railroad was a development of very great and grim importance to the lines, since the railroad took a great deal of freight from the Cape Horn route, and, in effect, controlled Cape Horn shipping rates.

Nevertheless, the clipper lines survived, buoyed by the San Francisco and Oregon grain trades, which provided an east-bound cargo, and by the protection from foreign competition afforded American-flag ships sailing intercoastal. Whiskey headed west and wine headed east would become important cargo items. Despite declining profits, to its end, the so-called California clipper trade would rank as the most prestigious of any engaged in by American ships.

Ships sailing "on the line" were either chartered by a line on the basis of dead-weight capacity, and loaded to a certain draft—usually the maximum allowed by the underwriters—or else were provided with a cargo assembled by the line for a fee. In either case, except for certain prepaid freights, the freight money would be collected by the line's West Coast agents. In June 1878 Simonson & Howes, agents for the California Line, wrote the Sewalls regarding the ship *Occidental*:

> If you will accept a charter of $17,500 or a guarantee that she shall exceed $20,000 freight subject to 10% commission, returning $2^1/_2\%$, and in the event of not making the guarantee we to return you all the commission we have for loading, we will take the ship after getting Messrs Williams, Blanchard & Co.'s approval by wire.

At San Francisco Williams, Blanchard & Co. would collect the inward freights. The dead-weight carrying capacity of a ship sailing on the line, as indicated by her draft, was calculated to the inch—indeed, sometimes even to the half-inch. In August 1885 Van Vleck & Co. wrote the Sewalls regarding a draft dispute:

> In reply to your letter . . . regarding our claim against [the ship] *T. M. Reed* would say that we can only repeat our former statement [of the] facts, "You chartered us the ship for $20,500 agreeing to load her to 24 ft 9 inches. . . . The captain refused to allow us to load her to the agreed draft & to cover up his tracks lowered the ship's top figures [draft numerals] $3^1/_2$ inches so while apparently the ship was only 2 inches light, she was actually $5^1/_2$ inches inside the agreed draft. . . . We are losing 100 tons capacity or $745 (pro rata charter). . . . The captain's timidity must have been occasioned by the fact that he was chartered by the ton.

When the Sewalls claimed that the old marks had been wrong by three and a half inches, Van Vleck's responded that the explanation had been "duly noted though not appreciated," but that they saw no opportunity for "making any headway by correspondence," and hoped to resolve the matter with the expected arrival of one of the Sewalls in New York. Draft marks—numbers cut from sheet lead—were adjusted as the sheer of a ship straightened with time. Captains watched their drafts as a check upon the charterer's claims of weight, sometimes demanding that the cargo be reweighed when discharged. In his usual state of high dudgeon, Joe Sewall wrote from aboard *Susquehanna* at San Francisco in June 1893:

> There is great dissatisfaction here amongst masters and others interested in Am. ships about the line business, and opinions are freely expressed that ships are not receiving their just dues. For instance the barque *Adolph Obrig* received some $7,000 less than her actual freight. . . . The ship *Conqueror* will weigh her cargo unless Grace & Co. pay for weight she is said to have, and Sutton & Co. will have to pay on *Edward O'Brien* or weigh the cargo. Of course you heard that Grace & Co. paid the *Gen. Knox* for 88 tons rather than have her cargo weighed.

Hot-tempered Joe was all for tying the fleet up until satisfaction was won. Not surprisingly, there was little love lost, or cooperation practiced, between certain lines unless they were secretly joining forces either to defraud the government or the shippers and ship owners, or to gang up on a mutual rival. In November 1881 Sam Sewall, who was then interning with Van Vleck's, wrote Arthur:

> [Sutton] paid us today $500 to bid under him on 1,000 tons government coal to be shipped, not knowing that we had not been asked to bid at all, and he hinted at making some sort of combination with us to keep up freights. When will more A & P rails be opened to bids? We wish to make him [Sutton] take some more at a ruinous figure unless he will divide with us.

In 1891 there was alarm that cargo was being sent from the East Coast to the West Coast via Europe for a mere five or six dollars a ton, when Sutton considered seven dollars the break-even price. The cry was to have such trade declared illegal by the Congress. In 1893 Sutton and the Dearborns—with whom the Sewalls then were allied financially and otherwise—although heretofore not notably friendly rivals, entered into a price-fixing combination "for the protection of mutual interests in the carrying trade between U.S. Atlantic ports and U.S. Pacific ports." Given that three years later the Suttons were out of business, it had evidently not been a great success for them.

The passage of a clipper to San Francisco usually took about four months, with the ship actually sailing 15,000 or more miles. After making sail off Sandy Hook the outward bounder laid a course to the eastward in the general direction of the Cape Verde Islands, off Africa, heading for a position about latitude 35 degrees north, longitude 45 degrees west, from where the ship should be able to sail a couple of points free before the northeast trades, and comfortably clear Cape St. Roque on the bulge of Brazil. At about 10 degrees north latitude the trades played out as the ship entered the equatorial doldrums, where she might spend a few weeks tediously working through fitful, slatting calms, while a well-worn suit of sails was bent in place of the good suit required to safely make the offing from the coast.

Most ships planned to cross the equator at about 25 degrees west longitude, where they might sight the small island of St. Paul's Rocks to check their chronometer. At about 10 degrees south latitude the southeast trades hopefully began to blow, giving the ship a fair slant to the Horn. It was then time to bend on the ship's heaviest suit of sails in preparation for the Cape Horn gales of the "Roaring Forties," not to mention the fierce River Plate "pamperos"—sudden, vicious gales bred on the hot pampas of South America. The veracity of Cape Horn's evil reputation, particularly in the southern winter, and the great difficulties often encountered when doubling the Horn sailing from east to west against the prevailing westerlies, are well documented by many a captain's letter and "track chart"—course charts which Sewall captains were to fill out, ostensibly to aid in the planning of future voyages.

The long run northward from the Horn to San Francisco, again featuring the southeast trades, the doldrums, and the northeast trades, was largely devoted to obsessively and compulsively putting the ship into tip-top condition. When finally coming to anchor, or when tying up along the Embarcadero, she would be scrutinized by a jury of mariners and merchants who included some of the sharpest-eyed and tartest-tongued critics ever to pass judgment on a work of man.

"Undaunted" to the eye would perhaps take better

In the summer of 1872 Edward and Arthur had been enjoying what appears to have been an unusually affectionate and harmonious business and personal partnership for eighteen years. Although each was about to move to fancier digs, the two brothers still lived with their families as nextdoor neighbors in modest homes. In this year they acquired the adjoining George Patten shipyard, which—with the 1877 purchase of the Wiliam Moses yard, south of the Patten yard—became their South Yard. Acquired with the Patten yard was the small Italianate building which became the Sewall office, later simply known as 411 Front Street. Master builder Elisha Mallett, who had started building for the Sewalls by at least 1869, was well on his way to becoming a fixture at the yard, where he would continue for another twenty years.

Arthur was now president of the Bath National Bank (called the "Bath Bank" or the "Sewall Bank"), and Edward had high hopes for his Arctic Ice Company, located on Nequasset Pond in Woolwich. Ice cut on the pond would be shipped by way of the Knox & Lincoln Railroad to Long Reach, from where it could be shipped year-round.5 The oldest ship in their growing fleet was but seven years old, and the newest, which would be named *Carrollton*, after a Baltimore hotel, would be launched in the fall.

We find Edward staying in New York to look after their ships in the great port. Picking July 24 at random, that day there were lying in the vast harbor thirty-eight ships, one hundred and eighteen barks, seventy-two brigs, ninety-eight schooners, and fifty-four steamers, not to mention hundreds of tugs, lighters, ferries, excursion steamers, and other assorted harbor craft.

There were seamen enough in residence in New York to man all these vessels, most of them residing in seedy-to-vile sailors' boardinghouses. And there were also to be found along the waterfront pilots, merchants, clerks, chandlers, sellers of cheap sailors'

South Street, East River, New York, August 1896. At center, the Sewalls' ship Iroquois
*is loading "on the line" for San Francisco. The Sewall house flag flies at her main truck.
Beyond her lies the Sewalls' lofty, three-skysail ship* W. F. Babcock, *also loading "on
the line" for San Francisco. At right is the barkentine* Mersey Belle, *a West Indies
trader built at Liverpool, Nova Scotia, and loading for Port au Prince, Haiti.*
ANDREW NESDALL

clothing, saloonkeepers, shipwrights, riggers, blacksmiths, longshoremen, lightermen,
canal boat men and canal boat families, towboat men, sailmakers, teamsters, horses,
street cleaners, pickpockets, harbor pirates, crimps, pimps, prostitutes, watchmen, cops,
waterfront reporters, and dreamers, not forgetting the corpses fished out of the eddied
flotsam by the busy harbor police.

Many Mainers were to be found in maritime New York. In addition to captains,
mates, sailors, and other transients, there were transplanted Down East shipowners,
agents, brokers, chandlers, and so forth, along with active and retired captains, many of
whom lived in Brooklyn Heights, across the East River from South Street.[6] South
Street, running along lower Manhattan's East River waterfront, was the epicenter of
maritime New York.

When staying in New York, Edward "stopped" at the old Metropolitan Hotel on
Broadway, once the toast of the town, but now getting thin in the carpet, having fallen
under the management of Richard Tweed, son of "Boss" William Marcy Tweed. Back in
his room after a day on the waterfront, Edward wrote Arthur long letters discussing
matters of business. Despite the separation from his wife and brood of seven children,

Edward appears to have enjoyed his days in the great port, daily meeting the steady flow of challenges inherent in a dynamic and problematical business.

On July 30, 1872, three Sewall ships, *Tabor*, *Undaunted*, and *Matterhorn*, lay in the port. Edward spent the day on South Street, keeping an eye on the loading of general cargo aboard *Tabor*, which was chartered "on the line" for San Francisco by Sutton's Dispatch Line. That evening he wrote Arthur:

> I told Sutton this A.M. that if he would give me the ship ready for sea next week I would give him $500. . . . To day I am painting ship & with cargo going in both hatches am quite contented. . . . The ship certainly shows the vigilant care of some officer & I hope [first mate] Mr. Rich may continue in the ship if we have nothing else to offer.

He had also visited a dry-dock to take a look at the ship *John Watts*, built at Bath in 1859, and appearing to be quite sound for her age. Nothing ventured, nothing gained, he offered $10,000 cash for her as she lay, calculating that even at $15,000—reflecting the cost of getting her "reclassed," i.e., repaired to meet insurance standards—she should be able to make money in the North Atlantic barreled petroleum and cotton trades. But her owner thought she was worth $20,000.

Elsewhere on the planet, the brothers' ship *Freeman Clark* was bound from Sunderland to New Orleans; *Hermon* and *Humboldt* were at San Francisco to load grain for Liverpool; *Eric the Red* was en route for Callao to load guano; the bark *Frank Marion* was headed from Boston to New Orleans; and the bark *Wetterhorn* was sailing from Cardenas, Cuba, with sugar to Falmouth, England, for orders.

Turning the calendar ahead four months to November 21, 1872, we find Edward, again in New York, writing Arthur of *Carrollton*'s maiden arrival from the Kennebec. Her master was their old friend (and Arthur's brother-in-law) Captain Fred Bosworth, and Edward's fourteen-year-old son Sam was aboard for the brief passage. The ship was to be dry-docked when she arrived to have her bottom coppered:

> I telegraphed you this P.M. of safe arrival of *Carrollton*. I had sent 5 letters down [the harbor] by different steamers & had ordered the ship to Pierpont St. [in Brooklyn] & berth all ready to discharge ballast. . . . I hardly expected the C. and was on board *Undaunted* and at 1 o'clock was looking through Buttermilk Channel, thinking of *C*, as one ship was reported in tow outside at 8:30 this A.M. & making out our white *S in Blue* [the Sewall house flag] boarded her just before the Governor Island as Capt. B. had just dropped his anchor. . . . Capt. B. seems in good spirits & *Sam* has I think had a fine trip, lost but one meal. . . . The C. looked finely as I pulled off to her. She looked a little short sparred up & down, nice [finished] outside but a little *new* on deck. I shall not . . . be ashamed to put her alongside of any outside of our own ships in New York. I think the *Undaunted* to the eye would perhaps take better.

Edward added that he had also been working to charter a "pine vessel," a coasting schooner, to deliver a cargo of Southern hard pine to the Bath yard, but "all decline Kennebec at the season of the year." He would keep looking, and he thought that the recent "Boston fire [Boston's Great Fire] will largely increase orders."

On November 24 Edward reported that *Carrollton*'s metaling was finished. A leak had been caused by a sheathing nail hitting a "hard shake"—an internal defect—in a plank next to the garboard just aft of the fore chains—likely this leak was discovered by "watering" the ship, pumping in water to flood her bilges.

> Took Capt. B. this morning & visited the fleet ☐ S ☐ I think we both enjoyed the day & perhaps both learned something. The *Carrollton*'s deck particularly from main hatch aft is I think the coarsest deck we ever laid & it looks bad on such a ship, the first thing that strikes the eye & you know 1st impressions go a good way sometimes or at least invite inspection. Otherwise she is all right and looks well. I only mention this as the *least worthy of notice* by parties viewing the ship and I would not advise the economy if any in this kind of decking. Capt. B. *does* and *should* feel pride in his ship.

Captain Bosworth informed Edward that his wife wished to join him for this voyage, if that were acceptable. As Mrs. Bosworth was Arthur Sewall's sister-in-law, this was but a formality, but Edward groused to Arthur that they would be having a number of "lady *boarders*" this winter at four dollars a week. "I have very comfortable quarters on 1st floor from the *top* @ $4.50 per day. If we could place our families as comfortable we should save about 50%—I trust our masters will appreciate this diff[erence]."

I have had quite enough of Landerkin

On December 6, 1872, at the end of a difficult day, Edward wrote Arthur a long letter. The bark *Wetterhorn*, Captain Landerkin, had finally arrived from Greenock. Landerkin had been in *Wetterhorn* since 1869, but Edward had decided that he was "not the man we want" due to how he "attended to the bark." Edward wished to replace him with John Rich, former mate of the ship *Tabor*. Captain Landerkin became very unhappy with the news:

> Landerkin understands fully that owners are not satisfied with his management and no actual dividends from the bark for past three years; this is the reason I have given him. . . . He pleads hard, says he has no money & with his nice little family to lock his capital up [in the bark] he says will deprive him of all the means he has to support them.

The Sewalls were under no obligation to purchase Landerkin's one-eighth interest in the bark, but, in consideration of the family Edward was disposed to do so, providing that they could agree on the bark's worth. Landerkin had bought in on the basis of $40,000 valuation, and was willing to settle on a basis of a $32,000 valuation. Edward made no counter offer, but assured Landerkin that he would receive fair market value.

The bark, Edward wrote Arthur, was in need of a good deal of upgrading, but appeared to be sound "both inside and out, with my knife." To test the market, he had offered the bark to a Boston ship owner at $32,000, with no response, but allowed that he would rather have her himself than sell her at that price. He wondered if he and Arthur should "for policy" trade with Landerkin for their own interests—they each owned 5/32—at the price on account. But he would let Arthur make the final decision.

The next day Edward took a closer look at the bark and hardened his position. "She appears sound, a little started on rails, planksheer & waterways. Rails opened . . . in scarfs 3/8 inch. Between decks & wales outside looks well. Hatch combings & deck soft. Running rigging about gone." Landerkin begged to be bought out to "let him go home as a man with money," and offered to settle at $24,000 valuation. Edward countered with $22,000. He reported to Arthur: "Today has been a lonely day for him 2 miles from anywhere and how he will feel tomorrow I cannot say."

On December 9 Edward wrote that he had bought Landerkin's interest at $24,000 valuation, payments to be $500 cash, $500 in sixty days, and balance of $2,000 in six months, no interest. This was, he observed, a most satisfactory outcome for the owners and E. & A. Sewall. Nor was he feeling any regrets on Landerkin's behalf:

> I have had quite enough of Landerkin. . . . I find Landerkin has been selling from vessel without my advice & I therefore placed Capt. Rich in charge at once. . . . I bought this small interest on E. & A.'s account & you will make such disposition of it . . . as you see fit, but don't let it increase our taxes.

In other words, their new ownership would appear under the name of someone not a Bath resident. On December 23 Edward wrote that he had towed down to Sandy Hook, at the entrance of New York Harbor, aboard *Carrollton*, where she had anchored to await a favorable wind to be off for San Francisco on her maiden voyage..

> Ship drawing 21 ft., cargo 2,760 tons. She looked finely loaded & I would only suggest one change *viz* at 21 ft. she is too full aft. I think 8 to 12 inches off at mizzen chains would be an improvement. . . . I received a $20,000 batch of [Knox & Lincoln] notes to-day from Mr. Moses for my signature. It was not at all pleasant. . . .

Regarding the shape of the hull, Edward was suggesting that at twenty-one feet of draft the waterline, beginning at a point about beneath the mizzenmast chainplates, turned too abruptly in toward the sternpost, thus creating excessive drag. He was arguing for an "easier run" on the next ship. While the shape of the stern played second fiddle to that of the bow in most casual observers' eyes, it was every bit as critical to performance, if not more so, balancing the requirement for vital buoyancy in extreme conditions against excessive drag and ease—or not—of steering.

Naval architecture was a pleasant distraction for Edward compared to signing notes for the Knox & Lincoln Railroad. On November 12, the road's treasurer, L. S. Alexander, had written Edward: "We have been sailing along very easy, borrowing money on our bonds and paying it out until we have got down to twenty-five thousand in bonds and $7,000 cash and still melting away. . . . As you know, we have $43,000 due in a few days."

The K & L, running from Bath to Rockland—a ferry shuttled cars across the Kennebec—was a result of Maine's post–Civil War railroad mania. Whereas other Maine railroads ran north and south along river valleys, the Knox & Lincoln ran cross-grain to the glacial path, thus confronting streams, swamps, rivers, and ledge in abundance. Despite tortuous twists and turns to avoid obstructions—it was said that when the K & L met a cow it went around her—it could not avoid ruinously expensive cuts, trestles, and bridges.

Costs for construction, financed by the credit of the towns along the route through the sale of high-interest bonds, were nearly double the original estimates; meeting interest costs all but bankrupted some towns—and did bankrupt Wiscasset. Because of its railroad debt, which was not paid off until 1960, the city of Bath operated under the most stringent economy for decades, the situation only exacerbated by the fraudulent avoidance of taxation for vessel property.

Edward, an active promoter of the Knox & Lincoln, along with president Oliver Moses, was one of two directors from Bath. Locomotives named for Edward and father William were manifestations of their heavy involvement. Edward had also pledged funds for an associated steamboat line, which line and which funds never materialized, leaving a legal entanglement for Arthur to deal with after Edward's untimely death in 1879.

Edward spent Christmas of 1872 at New York, apart from his large family. On December 27 he wrote Arthur:

> Christmas was a severe cold day here & more like Sunday than a holiday. Nothing done here & all that could enjoyed their day at home. I was on board *Undaunted* with Sam [Captain Samuel Dinsmore] where we did the best we could. I suppose you all had a merry time at home. . . . I have a most urgent call by tele[graph] this morn from Mr. Moses & Gould on the Hogen matter. . . . It seems I am summoned and sued for $30,000. . . . I shall sign no more K & L notes until our finances are conducted more to my mind. . . . We have had a most severe snow storm & streets are completely blocked. Nothing can be done here until the snow has been carted from the streets. . . .

Hogen, a construction contractor on the K & L, no doubt wished to be paid.

Edward's letter to Arthur on December 30 indicated that young Mr. Rich's mastership of *Wetterhorn* was in jeopardy. Rich, without the means to buy into the bark, was to sail on salary, and the possibility that some captain might wish to buy into the bark at a valuation of $32,000 (Edward's figure) or $40,000 (Arthur's figure)—the bark's value had appreciated most wonderfully since Captain Landerkin had sold out his interest—had to be considered. Two candidates, a Captain Allen, and a Captain Waite from Freeport, Maine, who were both then located nearby, had been contacted.

A few days later Edward reported that Captain Waite was willing to buy a half or quarter of the bark, but at no more than $25,000 valuation. Captain Allen, on the other hand, would buy an eighth at $35,000 valuation, but only if he was promised a quick move into a bigger ship. Edward had heard that Allen was not "a lucky man," but left the final decision to Arthur.

In the end, to Edward's satisfaction, fledgling Captain Rich kept his new command. Edward wrote Arthur: "Rich wanted a set of studdingsails which I gave him & I think he will use them." Studdingsails were set from booms that extended the width of the yards, the implication being that Rich would make fast passages.

On January 6, a severe northeast storm having passed, sails were being bent on *Wetterhorn*, and stores put aboard for her passage to San Francisco—it was thought that she might do well in the Pacific lumber trade and there attract a buyer. She had required a great deal of stores: "You would hardly believe a vessel could be so bare—there must have been a good deal sold or stolen from her." A crew was shipped at low wages, four sailors at twenty dollars a month and four at twenty-five dollars, and Edward boasted that he had received five dollars per man "blood money."

Normally "blood money" was a bonus extorted from captains by the "crimps" in addition to an advance on one, or sometimes two, months of the sailor's future wages, which usually went to pay the sailor's inflated board and outfitting bill. But since seamen were then in surplus in New York due to severe winter weather, and the boardinghouse masters were eager to get rid of some long-time boarders, they were willing to sweeten the deal with a five-dollar rebate per man. Of course, the five dollars would doubtless unknowingly be paid by poor "Jack."

On her way to sea, *Wetterhorn*'s cargo would be topped off with fifty tons of gunpowder offloaded from the "powder boats"—powder being a common part of California-bound cargoes.

I feel sorry to part with this good ship

On June 4, 1873, Captain Bosworth aboard *Carrollton* wrote the Sewall brothers from San Francisco:

> We arrived here last evening safe and all well after a tedious long passage of 162 days. There seems to have been a great difference in the passages of ships here now but I can only say that I never tried and worked harder to make a passage in my life. The *Carrollton* is a noble good ship, not very fast but an average sailer. The *Freeman Clark* will beat her with a free wind, but this ship is better by the wind and if the *Clark* had spars as heavy as these she would beat her any way. She steers very well & works well, drags the water a little under the mizzen

Believed to be June 1873, with the ship Sterling, *launched on May 26, fitting out at the E. & A. Sewall yard in Bath's North End. The vessel in frame would thus be* El Capitan. *The two anchored coasting schooners may be delivering ship timber. The buildings in the foreground are in the Goss & Sawyer yard, which occupied the old Johnson Rideout yard. In 1873 the Sewalls purchased the George Patten shipyard, their neighbor to the south; in 1877 the William V. Moses & Sons shipyard, abutting the old Patten yard, was purchased as well. Altogether, over five hundred ships were built along this short stretch of riverfront. The North End's shipyards are long gone, and the remains of many of its shipbuilders, ship owners, and shipmasters have long since been buried at Maple Grove and Oak Grove cemeteries—the latter occupying land once owned by William D. Sewall. But many of their fine homes still stand, and the North End remains a district of great historical significance and charm.* MAINE MARITIME MUSEUM channels when there is a strong breeze and she is going quick.

When we left New York she made considerable water but gradually tightened up until it does not amount to over 15 minutes spell [at the pumps] in a day . . . after leaving New York and getting into the [Gulf] Stream we took a severe gale and I certainly thought we should lose our masts. The rigging was so slack that it was frightful to see the masts sway before we could get it tightened, . . . [from the equator] to 50 South had very light winds and from there to 50 North the Pacific nothing but NW and W gales 41 days and that was where our passage was spoiled.

A ship's maiden voyage was always risky because of the stretch in the rigging. Captain Bosworth's remark about *Carrollton* dragging water under the mizzen chains bears out Edward's observation made when the ship was towing out of New York.

Carrollton would not remain long under the Sewall house flag. She had been chartered for San Francisco by Sutton's Dispatch Line for a lump sum of $31,000. From San Francisco she was chartered to Liverpool with wheat at £4 per ton, or £8,194.1.1—about $40,000—plus the freight on 2,000 cases of salmon and some redwood pieces. Upon returning to San Francisco after another slow passage, caused by nearly a month of calms, Captain Bosworth was informed that the ship had been sold to Boston owners for $96,000, or, $15,000 over her cost. Along with her high freights, she had netted her owners a substantial profit.

Captain Bosworth was disappointed at having to give *Carrollton* up, and wrote:

I feel sorry to part with this *good ship*. She improves on acquaintance and it was said by many that she is the finest looking ship in the best order of any that has come in this season, but as it is so I must submit to it as one of the chances & changes which occur to us through life, and trust that all will turn out well in the end. . . . There has been the largest arrival of ships here the past few days that ever was known and berths are scarce. The *Eric the Red* is not in berth yet, and she arrived a day before us. . . . Capt. Lewis wants [Mate Chase] very much to stay, and he may do so. . . . He is a very superior man. I never had a better mate, and such mates nowadays are not picked up often.

Captain Edward Lewis, a Cape Codder, would sail in *Carrollton* for twenty-two years.7 In May 1877 *Carrollton* narrowly escaped destruction by the great tidal wave that struck the Peruvian coast. At Huanillos, seventeen guano ships, including the Houghtons' ship *Geneva*, were destroyed. At Pabellon de Pica, *Carrollton* and the Bath ship *St. Joseph* were set ashore and badly damaged, but were refloated. (*Carrollton* was wrecked for good on Midway Island in 1906.)

I don't think we better allow him to pay more

A look at the building account for the ship *Eric the Red*, launched in September 1871, shows that "carpenter labor," i.e., the building of the hull (not including caulking, joinery, spars, etc.), was contracted out to master builder Elisha Mallett, who hired the crew. Mallett was credited with $12,415.36 for 5,333$^1/_3$ days of labor at $2.25 a day, and 184$^6/_{10}$ days of Sunday labor. Presumably the labor rate included Mallett's profit.

Although Mallett did his own hiring, it would be naive to think that the Sewalls did not have the final say over wages. In March 1884 Arthur wrote Sam Sewall regarding Mallett's hiring of a crew to build *Rainier:* "He [Mallett] has no need to fear about getting all the men he needs at $1.50 & I don't think we better allow him to pay more except for extra men."

Cleveland Preble did the joinery, or finish carpentry, on *Eric the Red* for $3,500. Blacksmithing, sparmaking, rigging, caulking, carving, sailmaking, and "blocking" (supplying blocks, i.e., pulleys) were contracted out. Four painters, however, were hired individually by E. & A. Sewall. Bills for rafting and "gondaloing" of timber, trucking and teaming, "watching," surveying, "machine labor," i.e., machine planing and sawing, and so on, along with all material—a long list—were also paid for directly by E. & A. Sewall. The cost of the 1,580-ton ship was $75, 657.07.

The system employed in 1865 to build the bark *Frank Marion,* under master builder Joseph Small, was more complicated. The billing for hull construction—not including fastening, caulking, joining, or use of a trunnel- [treenail] shaping machine—was divided into eight different "jobs," including making and erecting the frame; making and erecting stem, stern, and rudder; planking; making and installing chocks, channels, and hatches; whipsawing; and also "carpenter labor," let out to at least five different contractors.

Small was listed as the owner of $^1/_{16}$, valued at $2,815.42, and as there is no other item for him, one presumes that this was his pay. The other owners were William D. Sewall, $^1/_4$; Thomas M. Reed, $^1/_4$; and E. & A. Sewall, $^7/_{16}$. The bark cost them $45,046.66.

No smarter captain ever sailed out of Bath

Joseph Ellis Sewall, Bath-born in 1854, was the son of General Frederick Sewall, a lawyer, who came out of the Civil War as a brevet brigadier general. He, in turn, was a son of Joseph Sewall, also a lawyer, who served as Maine's adjutant general and was collector of the port of Bath. This Joseph was the older brother of William D., both being children of their father Joseph's first wife, Lydia Marsh. Joseph Ellis Sewall was thus a second cousin of Will, Harold, Ned, Oscar, Sam, etc. Of this Joe Sewall, Doc Briry—who knew him all of his life—wrote:

A more vicious boy than Joe Sewall was never born at Bath. . . .[8] Boys younger than Joe Sewall himself seemed to be objects of his hatred, and upon whom he was all the time playing or attempting to play cruel pranks. He would yell at us many younger boys in the neighborhood. Would throw rocks and snow balls at us, in snow ball season. Some vicious boys in those days would make their snow balls from soft damp snow one day, then leave them on a board to freeze solid

Left: Joseph Ellis Sewall—"a more vicious boy than Joe Sewall was never born at Bath,"
according to Doc Briry—and his sister Lina. Joe was born in 1854, Lina in 1858.
Right: Captain Joseph Ellis Sewall, 1854–1925 MAINE MARITIME MUSEUM

over night. One or two such snow balls Joe Sewall had in an overcoat pocket when he walked down Washington Street after dinner one day. . . . A small boy by name of Freeman was coming out of Drummond's Lane. . . . Joe Sewall was always lean, and his muscles were strong. Taking aim, Joe Sewall shot one of his frozen balls at this unsuspecting Freeman boy. The snow ball hit the mark, hit the Freeman boy on side of temple. The Freeman boy dropped in his tracks, and later died from concussion of brain. It took some of General Fred Sewall's money . . . and some tricks of law to keep Joe Sewall in Bath, and out of Thomaston [State Prison].

One mean trick I recall he used to play on me and other boys and even girls. We used to go to the William V. Moses and Sons shipyard at close of work and fill our wheelbarrows with chips for parents' stoves. We carried these chips, large and small, by the armful from hold of ship through a low port hole to our barrows . . . and while we were on our way back to ship for our second armful of chips, Joe Sewall used to place big rocks—even place dung and other dirty things—under these first chips, which we would not discover until we reached home and tipped our load. I often used to wonder what made my wrists ache more than usual. It was the ballast of rocks he had put in.

Young Joe had no intention of going to sea, and he entered Bowdoin College as a member of the class of 1876. However, as he told Doc Briry many years later, he fell in with a fast crowd and after but a few weeks realized that his father could ill afford to cover four years' worth of gambling debts and drinking expenses. For this reason and no other, he left college and, the following year, began a career at sea as one of four "boys" on the next new Sewall ship, *Sterling*.9

Sterling was launched in May 1873. Under command of Captain James Baker, she was chartered to load deal timber—heavy planks—at St. Stephen, New Brunswick, for Liverpool, arriving at Liverpool on August 8. On August 15, Captain Baker wrote the Sewalls: "This morning my crew were all missing with the exception of the boys. Joseph Sewall fell during the passage and bruised himself severely & has not got over it yet. Thinks he would like to leave & go home but I tell him he had better continue on to New Orleans and if he wishes to go home from there I shall let him do so. . . . "

Sterling was instead chartered to take barreled oil from Philadelphia to Antwerp. The next word on Joe is found in a letter dated March 15, 1875, to the Sewalls from Dron Chesebrough at San Francisco:

This A.M. your telegram of 13th reached me reading "Has Joe Sewall joined either ship. If not arrange for him on *Occidental* or *Sterling* as he prefers. Answer." The *El Capitan* sailed yesterday Sunday. . . . Captain Dunphy . . . informed me that Mr. Sewall joined the *El Capitan* after being idle about two days & has gone to sea in the ship. . . . I was not aware of any troubles or would have mentioned the same in my letters to you.

Joe had arrived aboard *Sterling*, and, for some reason—perhaps he had been second mate and had had sailor trouble—had left her at San Francisco. *El Capitan* having given up on receiving a satisfactory grain charter due to the competition from British iron ships, was bound for Callao, Peru to load guano. Her master, Captain William Lincoln, wrote his mother that the ship had not made a dollar in eighteen months.

El Capitan, 1,493 tons, was launched in 1873. Her name was suggested by William D. after a trip to Yosemite, where he had seen the spectacular monolith of that name. Her master, Captain William Lincoln, of Bath, was the younger brother of Captain James Lincoln who had died aboard the bark *Frank Marion*. Bill Lincoln, a bachelor with three unmarried sisters under his wing, was a bit of a fusspot. By May 1877, Joe was *El Capitan's* mate. In a letter probably written in October 1878 responding to a request for an appraisal of Joe's abilities, Bill Lincoln wrote E. & A. Sewall:

His *honesty, sobriety, & industry* are unimpeachable. . . . His seamanship is as good as can be expected considering the short time that he has been following the sea, in fact *better* than the *majority* . . . he has had no easy school to learn in, and the only point he has disappointed me in is that I fear he has not the real tenacity and go ahead spirit I would wish. . . . I think he is fully as capable to take command now as he ever will be until the full responsibility is thrown upon him.

Of Joe's career as a shipmaster, Doc Briry wrote:

No brainier, no smarter captain ever sailed out of Bath. He was a past master in the use of his chronometer, and was figure perfect when adding up his latitude and longitude. . . . When making the land he was always exactly where he figured he ought to be. Captain Joe never plunked a ship ashore, as several Bath captains had done because of errors in their . . . figuring. Captain Joe's knowledge of forecasting the weather would have entitled him to position of chief weather forecaster on shore, had he applied for that position. It took brute courage to make the Cape Horn passages. It took brains to navigate a ship through the many narrow treacherous straits and seas to China and Japan where Captain Joe sailed often, but he was equal to it.

But we are getting ahead of the story.

The expense of maintaining his three sisters, "Celia," Mary, and "Sadie," in the manner to which they were accustomed, was a great annoyance to Bill Lincoln. While urging them, on the one hand, not to stint themselves in any way, on the other hand he predicted that he would likely have but "a few months' enjoyment this side of the grave" thanks to how his money seemed to "slip away."[10]

According to Doc Briry, Celia, the eldest sister, was both homely and somewhat peculiar, and Bill had little hope of ever being relieved of her. Both Mary and Sadie, however, were attractive and good company, and Bill hatched a plan, inviting them to join *El Capitan* for a long voyage in the hope that balmy tropical nights would weave their magic, luring Joe into a trap. And so it happened that Joe proposed to Sadie, breaking Mary's heart. After the engagement, Bill wrote Sadie wanting a report on how she had been received by Joe's parents:

Now you *know* that I never want you to marry with any family where you can not be accepted upon the most cordial and friendly terms and at the same time not to feel that there is a barrier between the two families or that they feel as though it was any condescension from their part by an alliance with their son. . . . I would rather you would remain single all your life than feel that you were any but my own darling sister Sadie. . . . [11]

No doubt.

In September 1881, with Sadie set to marry Captain Joe at San Francisco, Bill Lincoln wrote Mary and Celia, his "poor little things," and urged them to get out and about more, lest they become "dried up old maids." Bill Lincoln's sadistic streak went beyond writing needling letters to his sisters, and Joe was evidently a willing helper. Doc Briry wrote of an alleged incident aboard *El Capitan*:

Captain William P. Lincoln, 1842–84

A sailor one day reported aft to Captain Bill Lincoln and mate Joe Sewall that he was not getting food enough and the little he did receive was damned poor quality. Captain Lincoln is said to have sent for this sailor to come aft. The sailor came and was invited to a chair on the after house. The cook soon appeared with a large basket of ship food. . . . Joe, as mate, told this hungry sailor to get busy and to keep busy until he was told to stop eating. It is said Joe Sewall and Captain Bill took turns hitting that sailor under the jaw with a belaying pin every time that man's jaw stopped moving. They made him eat steady for three days. The man became almost —— and as white as a ghost. He tried to beg off. It is further stated that it took all the Epsom salts in the medicine chest to thaw out that sailor's intestines.

In 1884 Bill Lincoln died of Bright's disease complicated, according to Doc Briry, "by a most obstinate constipation" which a mixture of castor oil and croton oil failed to relieve. One can but wonder if the dying Bill Lincoln had some appreciation for the sufferings of that poor sailor he and Joe had force-fed like a Strasburg goose.

The arrival at San Francisco in September 1874 of the ship *Undaunted*, Captain Fred Dinsmore, 140 days from New York, would put another Sewall ship in the headlines. In early November second mate Joseph McArdle was arraigned for trial in the United States Circuit Court on charges of beating and wounding seamen. The allegations included knocking men down with handspikes or belaying pins for amusement, and kicking a seaman (who took hold of the wrong line) in the "most vulnerable portion of a man's body," incapacitating the man for several days. McArdle, who had escaped prosecution in Baltimore for stabbing a seaman in the back, pled guilty to one count, and was sentenced to two years imprisonment at the state prison.

Testimony at the trial having implicated Captain Dinsmore, a warrant was issued for his arrest.[12] On November 10 the San Francisco newspaper *Alta California* predicted that if the evidence against the captain was conclusive, he would "undoubtedly have to stand a severe sentence." On the 13th it was reported that the trial had been postponed on account of the failure of the witnesses to appear, although the United States marshal and his deputies "had been scouring the city. . . . It is presumed that the complainants have been sent away, and if this is the case the captain of the *Undaunted* need not fear a trial." On November 16 Williams, Dimond & Co. telegraphed Bath that if Dinsmore did not sail on the ship "his conviction and imprisonment [were] certain." They elaborated by letter:

> As a rule shipmasters think themselves best qualified to settle their sailor difficulties (and possibly they are), but it often happens that they keep the matter . . . to themselves until it comes to the climax of their entanglement and they call in their consignee [the ship had been consigned to Williams, Dimond Co. for its services as broker/agent] who comes into a muddle that they know nothing about. The first we knew of this case was that the Grand Jury had indicted the master and that arrangements were in progress to "settle" with the complaining witnesses.

The deal was that if the men kept out of sight until twenty-four hours after the ship had sailed with Dinsmore aboard, they would then get paid. If Dinsmore did not leave, the men could testify against him. Captain Dinsmore wrote to the Sewalls:

> On the passage out, we had some little trouble, but nothing serious. On arrival here both mates left in the stream, and after being here six weeks the 2nd. mate was arrested and as I would not employ a lawyer for him, he plead guilty . . . and said that it was all done by my orders and in my presence and with the evidence of the only three remaining out of the crew they arrested me and I was freed under $2,000 bail. As I was without any evidence on my side I thought it best to get the men out of the way, supposing that if there was no evidence they would throw the case out, but they have postponed it four times, and the last time until

December or until they find the witnesses. So I shall forfeit the bail if they ever find them. . . . The ship was ready for sea Saturday night but I thought by waiting three days I could save $2,000. We sail Wednesday morning.

Bond had been posted by Williams, Dimond & Co. It was reported in the November 19 *Alta California* that the case against Dinsmore had been indefinitely postponed on account of the failure to find the witnesses, and that same day *Undaunted* sailed. On December 4 Williams, Dimond & Co. wrote that one of the witnesses had been found and arrested for safekeeping for trial, raising the possibility that the bond would be declared forfeited. "There is only this consolation, namely, that if [Dinsmore] had been tried, his state prison sentence was a certainty."

On January 25, 1875, Williams, Dimond & Co. wrote that they had made a "settlement of the matter" for $2,125.40. "Much regretting that your captain should have placed himself in so unfortunate a position."

Captain Fred Dinsmore was a Kennebecker from Richmond. (*Undaunted*'s first master, Captain Samuel Dinsmore, may have been a cousin.) Fred's wife, their son George, and daughter Gertrude made some voyages aboard *Undaunted*. In 1934 Gertrude recalled a time when stevedores at San Francisco, knowing that the ship would be at sea on the Fourth of July, gave Captain Dinsmore a large box of fireworks:

Amongst the night display were a number of tissue paper balloons about six feet high, shaped like regular balloons. They were made with some sort of a metal holder at the bottom in which you put an oily rag and when this was lighted . . . they would rise to quite a height. . . . Being made of colored tissue paper they were quite pretty lit up by their own fire.

Knowing that the ship would be passing close by Pitcairn Island, the home of the descendants of the *Bounty* mutineers, Captain Dinsmore saved three balloons which he sent up in the evening just as the islanders were rowing ashore, singing a hymn, as was their custom. "Several years afterward when Father passed there on some other ship they remembered him and asked about the balloons and had him explain what made them go up."

Of 1,722 tons, *Undaunted*, launched in 1869, was an unusually big ship for that time. She was also a three-skysail-yarder, a rarity in the Sewall fleet, and very well built. Her name reflected Edward Sewall's insistence that she be completed despite a downturn in shipping that had all but put a stop to shipbuilding at Bath. Sold by the Sewalls in 1889, she was "barged" in 1903 and lost with her crew of five in December 1913, off the Jersey shore.

More Interesting Letters

October 12, 1872, a letter for E. & A. Sewall from James W. Elwell, New York shipping and commission merchant, i.e., agent and broker (and Bath native):

We are glad to hear that your new ship is so near completion, and you ask us about a name for her. We would suggest, in case you intend her for the California trade, that you call her some name that will sound clipperish, for instance *Gazelle*, *Skylark*, *Stormy Petrel*, *Antelope*, *Ocean Foam*. Or, if you wish to give her a geographical name, *San Francisco* or *Vallejo*. For a strong name we would suggest *Sampson*, *Hercules*, *Ocean Monarch*. For a fancy name, *Red Jacket*. How would you fancy the name of our next president, *Horace Greeley*?

The Sewalls named her *Humboldt*, after the California county.

———

Two letters, dated March 28 and April 1, 1874, from David Brown, a Liverpool broker who catered to American ships, are of interest. The following is a combined excerpt:

Our underwriters in London have suffered so heavily by the Suez Canal steamers that the insurance premiums are now as high by this class of tonnage as by sailing ships via the Cape. . . . While sailing ships in the Indian trade have for the last 12 months been doing well. . . . owners of steamers are suffering most disastrously, and a great many boats are now lying idle. The prosperity of steam tonnage a few years ago had the effect of inducing a very large number of persons to become steam shipowners without any practical knowledge. . . . The consequence has been fearful losses (as many as 20 steamers being reported "foundered" or "missing" during the last few months) resulting in a great measure from overloading and other preventable causes. . . . Proposals are now being considered [in Parliament] for marking a loadline upon all vessels.

———

April 10, 1878, from San Francisco stevedore "Commodore" Theodore H. Allen to E. & A. Sewall:

I saw Mr. C. [Chesebrough] yesterday and he said he had [received?] a letter from you. Now I hope you will do me the favor not to speak to no ship owners nor capts. about our contract. I would not like for any of your capts. to know about the $100 that I will give to Mr. C. on every ship [whose business I receive] and he will remit it to you privately. Because you know it would make trouble for me with Mr. Howes and other ship owners so please never mention it to any one.

A native of Bridgeport, Connecticut, and the son of a Liverpool packet captain, "Commodore" Theodore H. Allen was one of the most prominent men in San Francisco shipping. A partner in the stevedoring firm of Allen & Young, he held shares in most of the important American ships and had infallible judgment when wagering large sums on their passages. Sailing in the transatlantic trade until 1849, he arrived at San Francisco as sailing master of a bark and immediately began a lightering business. The fine ship *Commodore T. H. Allen* was built by Southard at Richmond, Maine, in 1884.

———

A letter from Bath manufacturer (Torrey Roller Bushing Co.) and future collector of customs, Francis B. Torrey, to Arthur Sewall from San Francisco, November 17, 1878:

> I arrived here Wednesday night & found [Captain John P.] Reed [of the Sewalls' ship *Bullion*, and Richmond, Maine] had sailed the day before. There was a Capt. Smith who came here on business for some whalers that occupied the upper berth in my section. The passengers were telegraphed from Omaha and this Capt. Smith came next to my name and Capt. Reed saw it. He told Chesebrough that he was sure that I was bringing this Capt. Smith to take his place in the ship . . . therefore, he said, he should sail at once.

———

A letter received by the Sewalls from Mr. John Hawkins, Shaftsbury Cottage, Plymouth, England, dated June 15, 1873. It represents other such letters, mostly from the United Kingdom, from family members seeking information about a missing husband, brother, or son. In some cases the missing mariner was the sole support of a family.

> After weating a very long time since I wrote and have not received any answer I take the liberty of writing again the third time . . . respecting my son John George Hawkins that joined your Ship at Cardiff the latter end of 71 and saild to Rhio—and from their to Calcutta I receivd a letter from your office in 72 to say that the Ship saild from Calcutta July 2-72 for new york and that a letter addressed to the ship at that port would find him if on board I sent two letters to the ship at that port but receiving no answer I received a letter from him dated June 4–72 Calcutta and as I informed you in my last that he was sick and not able to do his work but he hoped he would in a day or two but I have never herd from him since nor have you answered my letters. . . . I hope you will answer this as soon as you can and inform me if the ship arrived safe at new york and if he was on board or if he died on the passage or any information you would give would be most thankfully received.

1. Edward O'Brien, the great Thomaston shipbuilder and owner, built the fine ship *Baring Brothers* in 1877. The names of the eastern Maine towns of Baring and Alexander [for Alexander Baring, later Lord Ashburton, of the Webster-Ashburton Treaty) are relics of the

marriage of two sons of Sir Thomas Baring to two daughters of Senator Bingham of Pennsylvania, owner of extensive wild lands in Maine, and for whom the town of Bingham was named.

2. On January 1, 1878, Simonson & Howes' Line issued a circular reading in part: "We take much pleasure in informing you that we are now loading some of the finest clipper ships ever built, and we point with pride to the fact that during the year just ended, we were able to dispatch a fleet of ships which have never been surpassed, even in the early days of the celebrated clippers. We have on the berth, the New Extreme Clipper Ships *Thomas M. Reed* and *Pharos*, with the *Valiant* to follow. This ship made her last passage in 114 days. . . ."

3. Frederick Perry, *Fair Winds & Foul* (Stanfordville, NY: Earl M. Coleman, 1979), pp. 3–4.

4. Goodwin, unpublished autobiography, pp.104, 126–27. Maine Maritime Museum library.

5. On March 6, 1872, however, the river froze over, halting the ferries, and allowing people to cross between Bath and Woolwich on the ice.

6. Montague Terrace, located atop the riverside bluffs in Brooklyn Heights, was developed by the transplanted Thomaston ship-owning partners, brothers Isaac Chapman and Benjamin Flint. Each owned identical Montague Terrace corner townhouses.

7. Frederick C. Matthews, *American Merchant Ships, 1850-1900*, Series 1 (Salem, MA: Marine Research Society, 1931), pp. 57–59.

8. Mark Hennessy's able scholarship and great contributions to the record of the maritime history of the Sewalls and of Bath are beyond dispute. It is thus disappointing to read in his draft for the book never completed about the Sewall wooden fleet, written in light of Dr. Briry's letter: "There probably never was a Sewall more vigorous as a boy than Joseph E. Sewall." He continued: "It is known that he played baseball in the 1870s at 'Dead Horses,' a field at the end of Center Street, and Grinnell's Field as a member of the Fleetwings."

9. Letter from Dr. Edward W. Briry to Mark Hennessy, received January 28, 1938.

10. Lincoln's letter book is in the Hennessy Collection, Maine Maritime Museum library.

11. This and other excerpts from the William Lincoln letter book, Hennessy Collection, Maine Maritime Museum library.

12. *Alta California*, November 6, 8, 1874.

PART SIX

Edward Sewall has a carriage accident and goes to court. Old Captain Arey has bitter bones to pick with the Sewalls, and young Captain Curtis loses his prize first command due to weakness of the flesh. The firm of E. & A. Sewall is dissolved. Edward dies, and Arthur Sewall & Co. is formed. Cousin Joe Sewall takes his first command, and sailors on the dismasted Nora Bailey *are reduced to trying to eat seaweed.*

Your insolent letter of this date is just received

On March 14, 1875, at about eight o'clock in the evening, Mrs. Amos Larrabee of Phippsburg was driving her horse and wagon on Washington Street, Bath, heading for the house of Mr. Frank Moses, there to meet her husband. Mr. Moses was a retired shipbuilder; his father, Oliver—a shipbuilder, industrialist, and president of the Knox & Lincoln Railroad—was closely associated with Edward Sewall in the struggle to keep the railroad afloat. Mrs. Moses was Mr. Larrabee's sister.

Mrs. Larrabee later testified that she was driving very slowly, reining her horse toward the sidewalk, when, just past Grove Street, the left rear wheel of her wagon was hit by the left front wheel of an oncoming chaise being carelessly driven on the wrong side of the street by Mr. Edward Sewall. Mrs. Larrabee was thrown over the dash to the frozen ground and dragged. She was helped into Mr. Moses's house by Mr. Littlefield, Mr. Moses, and Mr. Sewall, where she was examined and treated by Dr. Milton Briry. She was later diagnosed as having damaged the main trunk of her sciatic nerve, causing great pain, introversion of her foot, and permanent lameness.

Upon legal action being brought against him on August 1, Edward Sewall paid the Larrabees $1,500, and the Larrabees signed a prepared release absolving Edward Sewall of any further liability. Mrs. Larrabee thereby acknowledged that the accident was inevitable, and that her carelessness had been a contributing factor.

Upon further reflection, however, the Larrabees changed their minds, claiming that the settlement had been obtained through the undue influence, over-persuasion, and fraud of Mr. Moses and a Mr. Marr, who were secretly acting as agents of Edward Sewall. Mrs. Larrabee's attempt to return the $1,500 to Edward Sewall was rebuffed.

The money was then deposited with the court, and a suit instituted.

On August 10 Attorney Moore, of the Thomaston firm of Gould & Moore, doing his lawyerly duty to his client, wrote Edward:

I have been reflecting upon some things of which I was informed today. Dr. Payne said that he had the impression that the injury was inflicted upon Mrs. Larrabee by being dragged upon the ground on her knees; and Mr. Moses said she was dragged considerable distance by holding upon the reins. Moses also told me that the horse was nervous. I would like to have you ascertain as much as you can about the character of the horse, and of the harness. . . . It is probable that the darkness of the night is your best defense.

One week later, Attorney Moore wrote again:

Before leaving home Mr. Gould looked carefully into your case and I have given it diligent attention since. I certainly don't find much encouragement, and cannot give you much. . . . You will today be able to get a list of the jurymen from the clerk of courts. You should get such list, and find out all you can about them, where they live, *what church* they attend, and their friendly connection. The right kind of jury is often important.

The trial lasted nine days. The Larrabees testified that over the course of two days Mr. Moses dissuaded them from consulting a lawyer, telling them that he was acting under the advice of mutual friends; that Mr. Sewall would fire any employee who testified against him; that Mr. Sewall would corrupt jurors and was hiring witnesses; and that he, Moses, had seen a large number of witnesses who saw Mrs. Larrabee "in an unseemly place." His arguments were bolstered by Mr. Marr's "pretended knowledge and experience in matters of law and law suits, and his avowals of disinterestedness . . . well calculated to win the confidence of the plaintiffs, throw them off their guard, intimidate, mislead, and deceive them."[1]

The Larrabees were awarded $3,000 and costs in excess of $300. The verdict was appealed to the state supreme court, which, in May of 1877, affirmed the decision of the lower court, and it thus became case law.

On September 8, 1876, Lawyer Gould wrote Edward:

We are mortified at receiving a word from J. D. Pulsifer, Auburn, that you haven't sent him the $75 due him for a report of the case of *Larrabee & w v. you.* It is his due and you must sometime pay it, and why not now and save your credit. It places us in a false and very unpleasant position, and such as no client before ever placed us in.

On November 21, 1878, Gould wrote again:

Your insolent letter of this date is just received.[2] Its characterization is such and its statements of fact so differing from the truth, that I should have believed three years ago you were incapable of writing it; and should so believe now, but from some circumstances that have been recently communicated to me. Dr. Garcelon attended the court on your account, and your denial of this fact can only be accounted for upon the supposition of a loss of memory.[3] This suggests to me, and the whole tone of your letter suggests, that you may have forgotten that I was your counsel in the suits of Amos A. Larrabee and wife against Edward Sewall, and Amos A. Larrabee against Edward Sewall, and that you are not therefore aware that you owe my firm a bill for services in those cases. . . . The balance due is $933.25.

The circumstance referred to was surely Edward's worsening alcoholism. Perhaps alcohol had played a role in the accident as well.

Passage and board of a cow from Cardiff

In October 1853 Captain John Arey departed Boston for San Francisco in command of the extreme clipper ship *Spitfire* on her maiden voyage. Launched from the yard of James Arey & Sons, Frankfort, Maine, *Spitfire* was judged one of the most beautiful of clippers. Two weeks out her fore and main topmasts and bowsprit were badly sprung, and, thirty-four days out, she put into Rio for new spars. She would arrive at San Francisco in just under a hundred sailing days, a splendid record.[4]

Twenty years later, Captain Arey took command of the ship *Matterhorn*, taking a quarter interest at least partly paid for with loans from the Sewalls. Over the next four years Arey distinguished himself by his extraordinary efforts working for the interests of the ship. His final voyage aboard *Matterhorn* was very difficult. He had nearly been drowned going ashore to file his demurrage claim. When the ship arrived at Queenstown from Callao, John Dawson, ship's agent, wrote the Sewalls that Captain Arey was "pretty much worn out," having had a very troublesome first mate who was a "great villain." At Queenstown the crew had "knocked off" and demanded to be discharged. The ship, however, looked "in splendid order."

From Queenstown *Matterhorn*—the crew having relented—sailed to Hamburg, where the ship was sold. Captain Arey wrote the Sewalls of his unhappiness when he was denied authority to help sell the ship, thus being deprived of any portion of the commission. Not only was he certain that he could have "worked" a better price, but he had recently lost heavily with the failure of the Continental Life Insurance Company:

I am sorry, and feel hurt, to think you did not send the power of attorney direct to me. . . . I have never worked harder to get the ship in order as I have for *Matterhorn*. I sold for Mr. Hammond one ship in Liverpool, and have had power of attorney . . . every year for four years trying to sell the clipper ship *Spitfire*. I have now been master 40 years this month. I have never had a ship to touch bottom nor carried a spar over the side, and I have made some of the quickest passages on record. I have exerted myself to sell the ship to please the owners. . . . I have been nearly two years on this last voyage, and you can see for yourself what my wages has amounted to sailing by month and primage.

Upon reviewing his settled accounts Captain Arey, who had retired to Cambridge, Massachusetts, discovered that the Sewalls had not paid him primage on the guano demurrage payments or on the earnings from a coffee speculation, amounting to a total of £119. They had also neglected to reimburse him for his steamer fare home.

The Sewalls responded that the settlement was final, but agreed to pay Arey primage on the coffee profits and to reimburse him for the steamer fare, amounting to over $600, but they would not pay primage on the £1,308 guano demurrage. And they added that if the books were to be reopened they would demand payment by Captain Arey for various unstated rebates and other charges, which they estimated at $1,000. Captain Arey wrote back that he had polled several Boston captains and owners and all agreed that paying primage on demurrage was standard practice.

In April 1878 Captain Arey's lawyer named $2,500 as the price which Arey would settle for. The Sewalls' attorney, L. S. Dabney, responded that his clients would pay at most $1,000 just to "get rid of the labor of answering and the annoyance." Captain Arey responded that he would settle for $1,500, but no less. In September 1878 Mr. Dabney wrote his clients:

Mr. Somerby and I agree in thinking it is specifically desirable that no claim shall be made in your suit with Capt. Arey, on your behalf, which shall have the slightest appearance of being in any wise unreasonable or excessive, and it also seems to us that the sums which . . . you instructed us you wished to claim for passage of a woman from Cardiff to Rio and for passage and board of a cow from Cardiff to Rio and San Francisco ($500 for each) might be open to comment as high; so much so that we think it desirable to ask your attention to the matter once more.

A letter from Dabney to the Sewalls in August 1878 revealed that the Sewalls, who had acted as Arey's insurance agent, had not credited Arey's account with a considerable sum of "insurance scrip"—presumably Arey was invested in a mutual insurance company which paid dividends. But the Sewalls chose to play tough, and Dabney complied:

I have changed the answer to conform . . . to your views, so that it will read thus: "and it is well known and understood that the ship's agents are to have, as part remuneration for their services, such insurance commissions and scrip, and this was so in the case" re. The knowledge and understanding meant is not Capt. Arey's but that of people generally, who are conversant with the business.

The Sewalls were blowing smoke. In September Dabney reported that Captain Arey's lawyer had suggested that an offer to split the difference between the Sewalls' proffered settlement of $1,000 and Arey's price of $1,500 would be accepted. The correspondence ends with a rather pathetic communication, dated January 1880, from Hyde Park, Massachusetts, addressed to Arthur Sewall:

> Capt. Arey who resides here wished for me to write you a few lines in regard to his health. He is very much broken down in health. His nervous system is very much injured, should think, from the loss of property. He was anxious that I should write you about his condition.
>   F. L. Gerald, M.D.

———

A retired Cape Cod shipmaster who gloried with the wonderful name of Elkanah R. Crowell, and who, when he was Captain Arey's first mate on *Spitfire*, had announced that the only sailors he wanted must be willing to jump over the foreyard before breakfast, had long owned an interest in the Sewalls' ship *Benj. F. Packard*. In March 1894, in final response to several inquiries from Crowell regarding selling his interest, the Sewalls sent a version of their standard letter:

> In reply to yours of the 27th inst. would state there will be no dividend on ship *B. F. Packard* from her last voyage. We do not know of anyone at present desiring to purchase an interest in this ship and are not in position ourselves to buy tonnage except at a price much under its real value ought to be. Should you conclude to sell and care to name a very low figure we will consider same if put before us.

The sad condition of affairs at home

In 1875 the Bath informer for R. G. Dun's New York credit agency lumped Edward and Arthur together in his praise: "1st class men & in high credit. OK in every respect." His word the following year: "Reliable in every way with $125m at least." In 1877 they were still: "Reliable as ever."[5] But the story was becoming more complicated.

Edward was not yet sixteen when older brother William warned William D. not to let Edward come out to wild gold-rush San Francisco lest he be "ruined altogether," suggesting that Edward was already exhibiting evidence of an addictive or unstable personality. Arthur, although younger, took the lead in business decisions, although Edward appears to have had a better understanding of ships, and also perhaps of the common man—he was particularly popular with the men in the yard. In a letter to Arthur written in July 1877 from Philadelphia—then the epicenter of perhaps the most violent labor uprising in American history—Edward recognized the plight of the laboring class:

Edward Sewall, 1833–79
MAINE MARITIME MUSEUM

It has been so fearfully hot that men [stevedores] cannot do much. We should be thankful that our property here has not been destroyed. I think now the main trouble is over but it has so discouraged things it will be hard for labor to find work. No lack of labor here for city or [railroad] work at .80 to 1.00 per day. It is low pay for a man with a family to pay his bills & be honest.

In January 1877 William D., who had continued to advise his sons and to invest in their ships, died at age eighty. Dun's Bath agent's estimate that William D. left an estate of some $500,000, and that Edward and Arthur "no doubt" each had $150,000 outside of their inheritances, likely overshot the marks somewhat.[6]

To put these figures in perspective, however, a common goal for young China trade merchants in the 1840s, whereby they could leave Canton and return to America to spend the rest of their lives in great comfort, was $100,000; adjusted for inflation this would have been about $130,000 in 1870.[7]

With national economic difficulties continuing into 1878, the decision was made—presumably by Arthur and Thomas Reed—not to build a ship that winter. Tradition has it that Edward, as a result, decided to build a ship for his own account to provide employment. Launched after his death, the ship was named *Solitaire*. While there are other traditional explanations for this name, the memorial homily below suggests that the ship was named to honor Edward.

On March 11, 1879, the twenty-five-year partnership between Edward and Arthur was dissolved, with Arthur assuming sole management of the yard and the fleet. The breakup, according to Dun's Bath snitch, was caused by the "intemperance"—alcoholism—of Edward Sewall.[8]

Edward was now president and treasurer of the Free Trade Coal & Ice Company, formerly the Citizen's Coal Company, a Bath firm which he had bought in 1878. The Arctic Ice Company, on Nequasset Pond, of which Edward had been president and the largest owner, had never amounted to much, and had been long dormant when its buildings burned in 1885, likely from a spark from a passing Knox & Lincoln locomotive.

In June 1878 the Reverend Frank Sewall—Edward and Arthur's brother—wrote Arthur from Urbana, Ohio: "I am very sorry indeed to hear what you say about Edward." On March 3, 1879, Frank wrote:

[Sister] Alice writes me something in very general terms —— the sad condition of affairs at home. . . . We are not a little troubled . . . the more so perhaps for knowing so little definitely about the state of affairs and being so unable to offer any assistance. If there is anything you want to impart to me or consult me about I beg you will do so with all frankness. . . . I feel a great deal of distress for my poor brother himself and his family. may the Lord lighten their burden and bring them now brighter days.

Death of Mr. Oscar [*sic*] Sewall

The remains of Mr. Oscar [Edward] Sewall, who died yesterday from the effects of a fall over the balustrade at the Windsor Hotel on Thursday, were transferred to the custody of his wife and brother yesterday afternoon. Mr. Sewall was 50 years of age, and a native of Bath, Me., where for many years he followed the business of ship-builder. Although his injuries were not at first pronounced serious by Dr. Markoe, who attended the case, it was thought advisable before he recovered his consciousness to telegraph to his friends in Bath. The shock to the system tended, however, to a fatal result, and, after a short rally, he sank rapidly on Thursday night. Mrs. Sewall and the brother of the deceased responded immediately to the summons, but did not arrive in time to see Mr. Sewall alive. The remains, under their direction, were enclosed in a handsome casket and transferred to the Grand Central Depot in time for the 10 o'clock train last night by way of Boston. The deceased was a man of considerable estate and influence.

—*New York Times*, March 23, 1879

This account would seem to lay to rest any suggestions that Edward committed suicide. However, falling over a balustrade would be much more likely to occur if one were inebriated.

Memorial
Edward Sewall
Solitaire

Solitaire a French word, definition an
Individual who is doing a good work
without any sympathy from his fellow
beings is Solitaire. Therefore our Savior
when on this earth in the flesh was
Solitaire. He looked and Behold there
was no man. His own arm brought
Salvation.

Let your light shine before
men that they may see your good works
and glorify your Father which is in
heaven.

Coals and its appurtennencees [*sic*] are
the highest external Representation
of the Lord's true Church for they impart
both heat and light.

George Stevenson an Individual
who built the first locomotive and Rail
Road of any Account in England from
Liverpool to Manchester without any
sympathy from his fellow scientists
he was *Solitaire,* an external development of the Lords true Church
Read his Life.

The instructions accompanying this rather edgy screed stipulated that it was to be "printed and put into a neat frame about two feet by eighteen inches and presented to the family to be hung in the house in a conspicuous place that every visitor may see and read it." It was to be topped by a framed portrait of Edward Sewall and flanked by framed pictures, one of the coal yard premises at left, and of the ship *Solitaire* at right, forming the shape of a cross. The respective captions were to read "Coal yard and premises bought by and rebuilt under the direction of Edward Sewall (alone)

September and October 1878," and "Ship *Solitaire* built under the direction of Edward Sewall (alone) October 1878–March 1879." *Solitaire* was among Edward's best memorials. In March 1886 Captain Fred Bosworth wrote Arthur: "The *Solitaire* is without any exception the most perfect ship I have ever sailed."

Edward left his widow, Sade, and seven children. In 1879 Sam would be twenty-one; Oscar, nineteen; Edward, or Ned, sixteen; Fred, fifteen; Mark, twelve; Frank, ten; and Blanche, eight. Arthur would take them all under his wing. Of Sam and Oscar, who had shoreside maritime careers, on the Atlantic and Pacific coasts respectively, and of Ned, who became a captain, we will have much more to say further along.

Fred, like Sam, a Yale graduate, owned Sewall Paint & Glass Company in Kansas City. Frank, after working first for Fred, and then under Oscar at Williams, Dimond & Company, grew oranges on a ranch in California.

Mark, after attending a business college, doing a brief stint as a cowboy, and working for the Maine Central Railroad, bought back his father's coal company, which had been sold after Edward's death. M. W. Sewall Company, involved in petroleum products and commercial real estate, not only survives but thrives today.

Blanche married and lived in Portland and Connecticut.

In November 1886 Oscar ended a letter to Uncle Arthur thusly:

I look back on my eastern trip with much pleasure & I have you to thank for most of it & I *fully appreciate* all you have done and are doing for our family. It is more than the ordinary interest of an uncle & although we cannot repay you it will give me the greatest pleasure when I can serve you in any way.

His other hand belonged to his cigar

On May 1, 1879, brief notices were mailed out to captains and interested parties announcing the establishment of Arthur Sewall & Co., displaying the firm's official signature, and providing its cable address, "Sewall Bath."

The fleet then consisted of the ships *Solitaire, Bullion, Challenger, Chesebrough, El Capitan, Eric the Red, Harvester, Hermon, Indiana, Occidental, Oriental, Reaper, Sterling, Tabor, Thrasher, Undaunted*, the bark *Wetterhorn*, and the schooners *Carrie S. Bailey* and *Satilla*.

Along with Arthur and master builder Elisha Mallett, the most important person associated with the new firm was James Mulligan, clerk, who managed the office and had been there for a couple of years. In February 1880 Arthur made a trip to Liverpool, likely in part to confer regarding the libel suit against the ship *Tabor* for having sunk a French bark, which, no doubt to the delight of the lawyers, had become an international legal tangle. And no doubt he was looking for business, such as the importation of English rails. And for Arthur Sewall, making two North Atlantic steamer passages in February and visiting the great port of Liverpool likely qualified as a holiday.

Mulligan was instructed to write Arthur a letter every day; a typical brief update read:

Arthur Sewall, likely taken on his visit to
San Francisco in 1882, when he was forty-seven.
Maine Maritime Museum

Enclosed find copy of letter from J. S. Bailey & Co. The *Carrie [Bailey]* finished discharging today. Mr. Reed was up this afternoon and tells me everything is all right at the bank and all your other businesses that he knows anything about. Everything else going along all right.

Mulligan assured Arthur that he could stay abroad as long as he wished and hoped he was enjoying himself. In the shipyard the second *Thomas M. Reed* was then under construction, but Arthur requested no updates regarding the doings of the semi-autonomous Elisha Mallett.

A letter written by Arthur in May 1893 to the assistant secretary of the Treasury, regarding Mulligan's attempt to be appointed Bath's United States shipping commissioner—shipping commissioners oversaw the engaging and discharging of seamen—tells us more about Mulligan, who was then doing business at Bath as a stevedore:

The information you have received while in part correct is in the main decidedly incorrect and unfair. Mr. Mulligan has been in my employ since he left school some 16 years ago, and I ought to know him better than anyone. He is capable, honest and entirely trustworthy. The last six years in our employ he was our office cashier and entrusted with large disbursements and money. My firm has every confidence in him today and have signed his bond. His one out was that occasionally, not more than perhaps once a year, he would drink to excess. He did so in September last, and under the impulse of the moment the firm discharged him, which they afterwards regretted, and to show our interest and confidence in him a few months later started him in business, and assisted in furnishing his capital. If his old position was vacant in our employ today we would gladly take him back.

Arthur Sewall & Co. as yet had no partners, but two young men were in the wings, namely, Samuel Swanton Sewall, Edward's eldest, born in 1858, and Arthur's youngest child, William Dunning Sewall II, born in 1861. Doc Briry recalled playing with Sam, Will, and the other Sewall boys as a youngster:

Harold and Will Sewall, rather dignified boys, were below me in classes in high school times. These two boys were seldom seen in the Sewall shipyard and always took their baths at home. NOT so the sons of Mr. Edward Sewall. All these several Sewall boys took baths in the Kennebec river, together with us local neighbor boys. These Edward Sewall boys were democratic—not aristocratic. Boys took their baths in those days in their birthday suit, so called. We never wore tights. Samuel Sewall and myself were very chummy. We went gunning together—we went boating together—I furnishing the row boat, which my father had made for me.

After Yale, Sam apprenticed with the New York shipping firm of Robert B. Van

Vleck & Co., and later with Charles T. Russell & Co. in Liverpool. A quick study, Sam joined Arthur Sewall & Co. as a partner in 1882. In 1883 Sam married Marcia R. Houghton, a daughter of Captain Silas Houghton, one of the four sons of shipbuilder Levi Houghton who composed the notable Bath shipbuilding and owning firm of Houghton Brothers. The Samuel Sewalls had a son, Edward, and a daughter, Marcia.

From the evidence, Sam was a diligent, no-nonsense, hard-nosed businessman, with little tolerance for human foibles. He reviewed captains' accounts to the penny, even taking to task the venerable (and very wealthy) Thomas M. Reed for missing one day's interest by depositing a commission check on a Saturday. It is not surprising that his ideas didn't always mesh with those of Elisha Mallett—Mallett's "inexcusable blunder" referred to in a February 1889 letter to Arthur evidently had to do with his meeting the demands of unhappy ship carpenters: "We must crush them this time," wrote Sam. Arthur's calmer and shrewder course was simply not to build any ships during this period of unrest. Sam's was an early voice to be done with wooden ships.

When Will, Arthur and Emma's younger son, left home to attend Worcester Polytechnic Institute in 1882, his letters suggest that Emma took nearby lodgings—a not uncommon practice among well-to-do families concerned about the well-being of a son going away to school. Will did very well at Worcester and subsequently attended Johns Hopkins University, apparently also for one year. He briefly joined Arthur Sewall & Co. before going to San Francisco to spend three years with Williams, Dimond & Co., where his cousin Oscar was employed.

A photo of Will as an adult shows a very slender man. In January 1885 his cousin Ned, just arrived at San Francisco as mate of the ship *John Rosenfeld*, wrote to Arthur: "Will looks a good deal better than when I last saw him, has fattened up and has more color in his face. I think the Pacific coast agrees with him." Will—as with many ship-masters, in fairness—was prone to seasickness, and altogether, one is left with the impression that he was not physically robust. Will was made a partner in Arthur Sewall & Co. in 1886, that same year marrying Mary L. Sumner, of Worcester. They would have four children—Arthur, Margaret, Dorothy, and Sumner. Will was for many years the president of the Bath Savings Institution and sat on a number of local boards.

Will left the least obvious record—it was Sam who most often went to New York or Philadelphia to look after ships, and was thus the more prolific letter writer. But in the 1890s Will likely wrote much of the general correspondence which appeared over the firm's official signature, and thus Will may have disappeared while in plain sight. The style of these letters might be termed "skinflint Yankee," always coolly correct and with nary a superfluous word.

In addition to 411 Front Street, with its wall of cabinets with ships' names labeled in gold, "the Senior," as Arthur was called, also kept an office at the Bath National Bank, of which he was president. The bank was located downtown near the customs house and the railroad station. Doc Briry's strongest memories of Arthur Sewall were of seeing him traveling to and from the bank, as he did frequently, driving a "pretty slow-going old horse hitched to an open side spring wagon—a 'Concord wagon' so called, and much used by business men. . . . Mr. Sewall would drive holding reins loose with one hand, while his other hand belonged to his cigar."

Having a bank in the family—or in his pocket—was obviously very useful to a businessman who lived and breathed money. Writing to a Boston banker with whom he was involved in railroad schemes, Arthur described the Bath National as "in one sense my bank, I owning the majority of its stock." He had proposed borrowing back at 5 percent a large deposit he had placed in the Boston bank that was returning 4 percent interest. The Boston banker was confused, but Arthur no doubt had his reasons.

A financial scorecard of sorts, casually jotted down on a half-sheet of paper, and dated by the fact that the 1880 schooner *Belle Higgins* is the last name on the list, places Arthur's equity in eighteen vessels at $68,480; in stocks of five banks, $29,750; in real estate, $26,200; and horses, carriages, etc., at $3,770, for a total $128,200. Not listed are his many other securities invested in railroads, mills, mines, and the like.[9] In 1883 Bradstreet's credit bureau (not yet allied with Dun) reported that Arthur Sewall's net worth was estimated at more than $200,000.[10]

Not a blush came to her cheek, nor did she move

In May 1879 young Captain George H. Curtis of Brunswick, formerly first mate of the first *Thomas M. Reed*, and a favorite of Thomas M. Reed himself, was given command of the new ship *Solitaire*.

The *Reed*, Captain Joseph Small of Bowdoinham had been lost on the second passage of her maiden voyage in January 1879, when, in the dark of night, she went ashore on the coast of Wales. The seas made a clean breach over the ship, which immediately began to break up. It was fifteen hours before the coast guard discovered the wreck and got a line aboard her. With great difficulty all safely made it ashore by way of the line, excepting the second mate and a sailor, who were swept away. Rescuers pulled survivors out of the surf and hurried them by horsecart to farmers' cottage fires.

Captain Small was an old stager, having been first mate of Clark & Sewall's ship *Macedonia* from 1847 to 1850, back when she made her voyage to gold-rush San Francisco. He later commanded the ships *Wm. D. Sewall*, *Samaritan*, *Ocean Scud*, *America*, *Freeman Clark*, and *Eric the Red*. He had been badly hurt in a fall aboard the *Reed* when off Cape Horn, from which he never fully recovered, and with her loss his long career came to a sad end.[11]

Solitaire's maiden passage was from Philadelphia with coal to San Francisco. An undated note from Captain Curtis to Arthur Sewall, handed to the pilot as he left the ship off the Delaware, read: "Ship works well, steers splendidly. Crew all right and orderly. Everything looks favorably."

In December Dron Chesebrough wrote Arthur from San Francisco:

Since *Solitaire's* arrival I have taken *special* interest in Capt. Curtis knowing that he's a young man & wishing to see him do well. . . . Captain Robert Simpson . . . said he saw him in company of a man of questionable character & that if I would send Curtis to him he would talk to him & warn him which he did & Curtis thanked him. . . . I dined here & in the evening went to the theatre, a thing I have not done for six months. Curtis came in with a woman & as I noticed them I asked my friend Hooper (who was with me) if he knew her which he did & he says a woman of easy virtue.

Soon after, ostensibly to see if Curtis had settled some accounts, Dron Chesebrough boarded *Solitaire* in the midst of a pelting rainstorm, "and who should I find there but the very woman who was with him at the theatre, sitting on the side of his berth. I took them unawares yet not a blush came to her cheek nor did she move." Curtis, who was suffering from a bad cold, later admitted that he had drawn a large amount of money in small sums; exactly how it was spent he could not recall:

I then questioned him about the woman & he informed me she was virtuous. I questioned that to him, saying that no virtuous woman would have been found sitting alongside of a man in bed & not showed signs of a blush, not to say continued sitting there. To this he could not reply.

Chesebrough "begged him to tell me if he had given any amounts of money to any woman"—if so, he would "take immediate steps to recover some." Curtis assured him that he had not, and had spent it in "a general way." He had drawn a total of $2,200; his wages were but $100 a month. Despite Curtis's pleading that he wait a few days, Dron wired Arthur the news, and in a postscript to a follow-up letter, added:

Since writing the foregoing I have thought that I must tell you just how Capt. Curtis appears to me. He is in bed, *completely broken down* & I cannot tell as yet what the result may be. He has a severe cold & a doctor attending him. Mr. Snow [the mate] feels equally bad as Curtis has told him same to me—I truly hope you may let him go on in the ship. I know it will be a *severe* blow to your goodselves & Mr. Reed. Then again think of his dear mother & he an only son—I added to my telegram *"Deal gently* with *him."*

Oscar Sewall, writing to Arthur on January 5, expressed much the same sentiments:

If I went by my feelings should like to see him have another chance for think it would be the making of him. Do not think he really intended to be dishonest. . . . The whole story is this: He got in with a crowd of bad fellows and wanted to keep up with them & together with fast women was led on. Women had much to do with it. Find that when he has been here before he has paid considerable attention to them. He sees his mistake now and of course feels very badly. Is still confined to the house waiting your orders, which if favorable will make him well; if not I fear the consequences. . . . He says he would rather have his brains blown out than have his mother know of this affair & I think he means what he says, so you can see how he feels.

Captain Curtis was replaced by first mate Snow. On January 26 Oscar wrote Arthur that Curtis had finally left for the East by rail, traveling third class, which would take him about thirteen days. A friend was accompanying him. And *Solitaire* had sailed:

Think Capt. Snow did well while here. . . . He took his second mate [for first mate]. . . . Was sorry to hear an account the watchman gave, who was the last to leave the ship, that belaying pins were flying around at a great rate. Also says there was no cause for it, but probably the capt. could give his reasons. Only know he had a first class crew and they had been on board over night so were not drunk.

John Henry Snow, a Bath native, gained notoriety in 1876 as mate of the Bath bark *C. O. Whitmore*, Captain Thomas Peabody, who was Captain Bill Lincoln's young English-born cousin. When the *Whitmore* arrived at Hong Kong the crew accused Peabody and Snow of extreme brutality. The crew claimed that second mate James Elwood had been demoted and then cruelly punished for not joining in the abuse, and had subsequently died in shocking circumstances, likely from an open crotch wound resulting from his being bound straddling the narrow keel of the upturned longboat. Peabody and Snow denied all the crew's charges, and claimed that Elwood had been demoted and punished for disobeying orders, and that he had died of a sexual disease.

In June 1878 Snow was arrested at San Francisco while serving as mate of the *Thomas M. Reed*. He was later found not guilty for lack of credible witnesses. Peabody stood trial at Boston in April 1879 with similar results. The testimony taken at Hong Kong was not taken into consideration. Peabody's reputation as a hard-case captain followed him throughout his lengthy subsequent career. The watchman's account of the flying belaying pins aboard *Solitaire* under Captain Snow was all too reminiscent of that of the *Whitmore*'s crew, as related in the *Boston Journal*, March 18, 1878:

The testimony of all agree substantially one with another, and the story told by Charles Wright gives an idea of its character. He relates the circumstances of joining the vessel at Cardiff in May 1876, with all hands, and says the crew had not been on board three hours before they were struck with belaying pins by the chief mate, [John] Henry Snow, of Bath, Me.

Snow made but one passage in command of *Solitaire* and was then given command of the ship *Tabor*, replacing Captain Jabez Minott of Brunswick. Snow's successor aboard *Solitaire* was the gentlemanly Captain Albert Otis of Brunswick, who took a piano and his family to sea with him.

Captain Minott, whom Albert Otis described as "the thickest headed man about I ever saw," and whose ship, the *Tabor*, Otis described as "about the worst looking ship I ever saw," had been a central figure in a prolonged and expensive legal battle. In 1879 the *Tabor* sank a French bark in a nighttime collision. The case was moved to England, where, in 1880, a court found the *Tabor* at fault for not having her lights lit. The Sewalls' ship *El Capitan* had initially been arrested at Havre and held hostage as security against possible damages, but was allowed to depart under a small bond when the French authorities were satisfied that the two ships, while under the same management, shared but few owners.

The easiest happy go lucky ship

Captain Joe Sewall's first command was the ship *Oriental*, of 1,625 tons and built by E. & A. Sewall in 1874. He joined her in May 1880 at Baltimore, relieving Captain Albert Otis, who was promoted to the command of *Solitaire*. At Baltimore *Oriental* loaded coal for Acapulco, under charter to the Pacific Mail Steamship Company, operators of steamers between San Francisco and Panama.

As it happened, *Oriental*, *Occidental*, and *Chesebrough* showed up together at Acapulco in August, all with coal for Pacific Mail. The talk among the three captains was surely of the loss of *Thrasher* at Nanaimo, British Columbia. Captain Dunphy of *Occidental* was heavily invested in *Thrasher* and was very anxious to learn if his interest had been covered by insurance—the Sewalls brokered his policies—before the ship had been sent to that dangerous "hole."

The three ships departed Acapulco within an hour of each other, all bound for San Francisco, sailing close-hauled, in ballast. After nine hours *Oriental*, which had many fast passages to her credit, led *Occidental* by seven miles, and within twenty-four hours the *Chesebrough* was hull-down to windward of *Occidental*. *Oriental* won the race with a twenty-nine-day passage, beating *Occidental* by four days and the *Chesebrough* by seven.

Acapulco during the rainy season was considered a damnable pest hole, and both Joe and Captain Dunphy left with sailors down with "the fever." Dunphy, with long experience treating the disease, reported that his sailors had all recovered under his care, but aboard *Oriental* three men became very sick, and one died. Of the other two, Joe reported: "I got the two sick ones out of the ship before the quarantine officer made his visit. They ran away."

At San Francisco *Oriental* loaded 2,405 tons of wheat for Queenstown for orders. Edward Sewall's son Ned was signed on, likely as third mate. Joe wrote that he hoped that on the next voyage he might be permitted "the privilege of taking a wife with me." *Oriental* departed on November 13 and arrived at Queenstown March 14, 1881. Joe wrote that heavy gales in the South Atlantic revealed that the ship had been loaded too heavily—indeed, Captain Otis had written as much to Arthur from San Francisco. Off the Western Isles *Oriental* had rescued the crew of a waterlogged Norwegian lumber bark from Pensacola. At the end of his letter Joe made Arthur a bold proposal he would regret:

If you intend to make any changes in the *Indiana* is there any possibility of placing the one you tend for her in the *Oriental* and allowing me to take the *Indiana*? . . . To speak plainly, I am getting afraid of the *Oriental*, she acts so in bad weather. I think she is the worst sea boat you have amongst all your ships and sometimes it seemed to me she would take everything [the rig] out of her and I know she was loaded as easy [not too stiffly] as she can be. The worry and the anxiety made me sick, and I have been poorly in health besides. I hope you will not think me ungrateful for all you have done for me . . . but it would relieve me of much anxiety if I had a ship I wasn't fearful of some disaster every gale.

On March 15 Joe wrote that he had received his orders for the English port of Hull, but that the crew had refused to work. On April 15, arrived at Hull, he wrote:

As I have never fully explained the trouble I had in Queenstown I will now do so. The day after arrival . . . the whole crew refused duty. . . . The men said they wished to go ashore to see the consul to prefer complaints of abuse and ill-treatment, etc. I ordered them to work, but they refused, and being in English waters, I could not use force. Same day the consul, Col. Brooks, came off to the ship. . . . He deemed their complaints without foundation and he ordered them to duty. They refused to obey him and said they would not go to sea again in the ship. There it rested until we received orders.

Had the consul ruled that the men had good cause to be discharged, the ship would have been liable for three months' extra pay per man. The men continuing to be "defiant and stubborn" even after a second visit by the consul, Joe put them in irons, locked them in the carpenter's shop, hired a crew of runners, and proceeded to Hull.

I fed them on bread and water, and not much of that, and would not allow them out on deck or give them any bed clothes. They stood it for three or four days and then begged to be released, but we kept them there till we docked, when they all cleared out. The consular agent here had instructions from c. general in London to afford them no relief. . . . It has not cost the ship one penny for the money they had due them more than covers all extra expenses entailed. I will not deny that some of them were corrected on the passage, but they were not abused, and as long as I have charge of lives and valuable property I am determined to maintain strict discipline. . . . If Col. B—— had been so disposed he could have caused me much trouble.

The crew's imprisonment had lasted ten days. Before they were able to speak with the consul at Hull, Joe had already done so, leaving a "gratuity" of £4. Regarding Consul Brooks at Queenstown, Joe had written: "I had to 'gratuity' consul here but not much, £2, though he may want more. I talked political influence in Washington [to him] . . . and now he says he should like a better consulate. He wants some Sewall who has influence in Washington to mention him to Secretary Blaine. Please don't mention this to anyone."

At Queenstown, Captain Dunphy, aboard *Occidental*, had written Arthur backing up Joe's position:

> You know in order to keep our ships in good order we have a great deal of work to do and sailors nowadays will do but as very little as they can. Consequently a little pressure has to be brought to bear to get the work done. The consul wished

Three interesting images of steering gear and binnacles—one aboard the long-lived 1874 ship Oriental (below) many years after her sale in 1881; one aboard the hard-luck 1877 ship Challenger (upper right) taken after she had been sold to New York owners in 1892; and one taken aboard the 1876 ship Indiana (lower right) in her Hollywood days in the 1920s, with actor William Boyd—later known as Hopalong Cassidy—at the helm. The Oriental photo shows Captain J. Youngren at the wheel, with his daughter in the foreground, while the ship was owned by the Alaska Packers Association. The Challenger view, taken in the 1890s, shows her master, Captain William H. Gould of Kennebunkport, Maine, at right, and his son-in-law, Captain Robert Tapley, Brooksville, Maine, master of the outstanding Flint & Co. bark St. James. (They are looking aft.) Note the time-tested and simple rope-and-spindle steering gear, with tackles mounted on the aft-facing white tiller—the rudderpost head is in the fore-ground in the Challenger view. Note also the binnacle stands which appear to have doubled as skylights. Challenger's compass is protected by a removable wooden binnacle box which no doubt contained two small lanterns for use at night. ANDREW NESDALL

me in my letter to you to mention that he thought he exceeded his authority and if he should receive any censure for you to bear him out if it lays in your power as he was anxious to get the ship away to her port of discharge.

In response to an evidently chastising letter from Arthur, Joe wrote a "personal and confidential" letter to his "Dear coz. Arthur" apologizing for his undiplomatic proposal to be given *Indiana*:

I feel sorry that I ever asked you so preposterous a question, and have thought ever since I sent the letter that you might well consider me ungrateful and unstable. I will try and speak plainly and frankly. On the first passage the *Oriental* encountered no very severe weather and also was not so deep. . . . In S. F. I felt that she would carry 2,400 tons easily. . . . The ship herself is strong enough to carry much more than that, I think, but it puts her too deep. I firmly believe her to be one of the strongest vessels afloat, but she is a very hard one on herself. . . . I know my request was unreasonable and will you please forget it. I should like a different vessel for a permanent one, but will wait till you are ready to change me. . . .

At Hull, Ned Sewall left the ship for home under something of a cloud. We will deal with Ned's career in detail further along. Mark Sewall's wife, Rachel Fannie Thompson, the daughter of Captain Joseph Thompson of the fine Bath ship *Gatherer*, many years later described a deep-sea encounter with Joe Sewall, presumably aboard *Oriental*:

It used to be good fun to speak ships at sea. . . . Father would call down, "Fannie, come up and read the flags, you've got just the eyes for it." . . . I remember one morning early I heard our shepherd dog barking furiously and when I went up on deck, there was Captain Joe Sewall of Bath, close to us with distress signals hoisted. He was out of leather . . . he wanted the leather for his pumps. He had sprung a leak and his pumps were going all the time. He followed us into San Francisco a week late, and never stopped pumping from the time he got that very necessary leather.[12]

Oriental was then sold into the West Coast lumber trade. (Later joining San Francisco's Alaskan salmon-packing fleet, seasonally freighting men, supplies, and canned salmon, she was laid up in 1925.)

In April 1882 Joe Sewall was given command of *El Capitan*, Bill Lincoln having left the sea due to Bright's disease, from which he would die in 1884.

Loaded with railroad iron at Philadelphia, with Ned Sewall back aboard, now as second mate, "*El Cap*" arrived at Astoria, Oregon, late in December, after having spent two weeks standing off the Columbia River bar as gale followed upon gale. On January 2, 1883, Joe wrote: "It has been a most unfortunate passage, and we had a wretched crew diseased with syphilis, scurvy, and I don't know what. I expect trouble, in fact, Mr.

The 1873 ship El Capitan *is backed away from a Baltimore coal dock by a tug. She is very likely bound around Cape Horn for San Francisco. While the date of the photo is unknown, it was surely made after her 1884 sale to a New York firm. In 1897* El Capitan *departed Baltimore with coal for San Francisco, meeting hurricane-force winds off Cape Horn which shifted her cargo and destroyed her cabin. For two weeks the crew worked to right the ship, eventually putting into Montevideo, where the ship was condemned.*
PEABODY ESSEX MUSEUM

Sewall, the steward, and myself are under bonds for assault and battery. . . . " On January 12 he elaborated:

> As yet nothing more serous than a charge of assault has been preferred . . . but the sailors held as witness, four in number, allege all sorts of cruelty, starvation, etc., and the stories have got into the papers. Unfortunately we lost four men on the passage. . . . These witnesses say that the men lost were beaten and abused on their death bed, etc.

According to Joe, when six weeks out a sailor had fallen from the main royal yard and drowned, despite efforts to save him. Off Cape Horn two men had died, one from syphilis, the other from consumption (tuberculosis). West of the Cape, while furling the fore upper topsail, two men had fallen on deck, and another had broken his arm. One of the two fallers had later died, while the other two men were laid up for the rest of the passage. By the end of the passage only eight men were left fit for duty. Five were laid up, two with tertiary syphilis, two from falls, and one from consumption.

> For 115 days I have doctored two men with sore legs that would make one sick to look at them. . . . I can honestly say that the ship has been this passage the easiest happy go lucky ship I ever went to sea in and all these stories of abuse, etc., as far as I know are utterly false.

He added: "PS. If my father or mother hears of this will you please reassure them. They don't understand these affairs." After all charges were dismissed, Ned left the ship for a brief stint working ashore for a San Francisco chandler.

In January 1884 Arthur wrote David Dearborn regarding selling *El Cap*, pricing her at $52,000. Dearborn responded that the prospects for selling ships "that are approaching age" was not good, especially given the ominous fact that steam tramps had recently joined the North Atlantic barreled oil trade. For years the "barrel trade" had been largely in the hands of Canadian and German sailing vessels, a great many of the latter being old American ships. "No more old ships for Germans," Dearborn predicted.
. A week later *El Cap*, which was on a passage from Philadelphia to Hiogo (Kobe), Japan, with case oil, was purchased, with her freight money, "sunk or afloat," and sight unseen, by the New York firm of DeGroot & Peck for $50,000, on their "great confidence" in the Sewalls' "ability to build a first class vessel," and their faith in the Sewalls' assurance that *El Capitan* was "sound, well found, and in good order." When she arrived in New York they complained about several things, among them that the ship had been "run out" of rope and spars. Also, Captain Sewall had evidently neglected to inform them of the customary charge for his wife's board. On his next trip to New York "our Senior" would call on them in order to reach a satisfactory resolution on these matters.

Joe, remaining in *El Capitan*, left the Sewalls' employ for six years. We will rejoin his story then.

I feel as if I was a machine

If a man can be judged by his friends, Arthur's lifelong friendship with his well-spoken brother-in-law, Captain Fred Bosworth, must surely be taken into account.

Frederic S. Bosworth was born in Bath in 1835, his father Robert having commanded the Clark & Sewall ship *Girard*. Fred's older brother Robert commanded the Sewall ships *Freeman Clark*, *Thrasher*, and *Reaper*. In 1860 Fred married Juliette Crooker, Emma Sewall's sister. His career as a Sewall shipmaster had begun in 1859 with the ship *Vigilant*. He then commanded the painfully slow *Valentia* with dry good humor. His subsequent commands were the ships *Freeman Clark*, *Carrollton*, *Continental*, *Harvester*, and *Solitaire*. He retired from the sea to become a marine surveyor and broker in Portland, Oregon. He died at Bath in 1913.

From the cabin of *Harvester* at sea in November 1880, bound from San Francisco toward Queenstown, Bosworth wrote Arthur a letter. The passage out to San Francisco had featured a full month of heavy westerly gales off Cape Horn and had been the most prolonged and difficult in his experience. He had been in the ship for five years and was weary of the life:

> I hope you won't all get tired of my letters . . . but I want to do something and what else is there to do? . . . I have now been right here in the same surroundings five years last month, looking at the same grey haircloth furniture, sitting in the same chairs, promenading the same little quarter deck (how many hundreds of miles I must have walked) until I know every knot & splinter in them, eating about the same things off the same table at precisely the same hours every day, and going through about the same routine every day, that I feel as if I was a *machine* and that the machine was getting loose in the joints and needs to be stopped for a while & screwed up & tightened up & lubricated and started afresh.
>
> There has been some changes in the surrounding faces from time to time but most of the trials and vexations to be endured is connected with these same changes of faces, especially officers. There don't seem to be any of the old stamp going now and you have no idea what we have to put up with not to be in a *row all* the time. Last passage I thought if I got in to port with the hull safe, and had enough left of the sails, spars, & rigging, for a starting point, I should be lucky. I never got quite so badly sold on officers as that time and got so tired of seeing everything go wrong that I almost concluded at last that, as Cooper says, "Disgust concealed is at times proof of wisdom, when the fault is obstinate and cure beyond all reach."
>
> This passage is better in some respects so far as officers is concerned, but it is awful annoying to see them so slack in discipline. I do like to see sailors jump round when they are spoken to and they *won't* unless the mates set the example and are lively themselves, which is far from the case at present. . . . I should like to stay at home a voyage if no more, to get civilized a little, if you think I can stand the pressure.

One of the most memorable passages in Captain Fred's long career was on *Harvester's* first voyage, from New Orleans to Liverpool with cotton, arriving in November 1875. Loading a ship with its first cotton cargo could be an education, and it was in this instance. *Harvester* was so crank, or unstable, that Bosworth had to jettison the deck load to gain some control over the ship. Shortly afterwards a heavy gale lay the ship over until the entire rail and the *upper* deadeyes were underwater. The ship was over a week in the St. Georges's Channel, where, according to Bosworth, he had never gotten a worse "drubbing."

After getting the Liverpool pilot on board, a heavy gale from the north-northeast commenced to blow, with the ship but five or six miles off a lee shore and drifting broadside. The pilot said that there was just one chance for them, and that was to try for Beaumaris, a small Welsh port to leeward. Bosworth wrote from Liverpool:

Captain Frederic S. Bosworth, 1835–1913
Maine Maritime Museum

We took that chance and kept away for it. The entrance was very narrow and a
terrible sea on. It did not look wider than the length of the ship, the lighthouse on
one side and the rocks on the other, the sea running right over the lighthouse. I
thought the *Harvester*'s time had come, as it was so difficult to steer so straight in
such a sea, and in the narrowest part it threw her bow around almost across the
channel, but she recovered in time & shot through and in five minutes more was
in safety with I hope a few thankful hearts on board. . . . She is a splendid ship. . . .
She sails well and steers well and everything about her is just right.[13]

A "circular" letter, dated November 4, 1880, from Arthur Sewall & Co. to the captains of the Sewall fleet:

> We desire to call your attention to the fact, that during the past three years we have totally lost *four valuable Ships,* all through the error of the Master in incorrectly judging his distance in approaching land, these Ships were run on shore in reasonably fair weather.
>
> You are aware that we carry no insurance on Ships or Freights, and while we have the utmost confidence in the construction of our Ships and we are perfectly contented to carry the risks at sea, *we do expect our masters* to keep them *off the land,* and we hereby caution you not to take *any chances* in approaching [paper missing].
>
> A few days saved in your passage is unworthy of your consideration compared with the safety of your ship and cargo.

The lost ships were *Granger,* wrecked on a reef in the China Sea;[14] *Thomas M. Reed,* wrecked on the Welsh coast; *Eric the Red,* lost on a reef off Cape Otway, Australia; and *Thrasher,* towed onto a reef in British Columbian waters (*Thrasher's* loss was not really her master's fault). There is ample evidence that the Sewalls did sometimes insure their interests in ships and freights but did not inform the captains, preferring that they did not know—some policies may have required this. *Granger's* master, Cape Codder Captain Uriel Doane, wrote the Sewalls from Hong Kong after *Granger's* loss: "I also hope to hear the *Granger* was insured tho you have always written me to the contrary." Alas, the Sewalls' interest in *Granger* apparently was not covered on this voyage.

Settle with them for 50 percent

The 448-ton three-masted schooner *Nora Bailey* was launched in June 1882. Her captain, Daniel Barker, had previously commanded the schooner *Satilla.* At the completion of the *Nora's* maiden passage to Savannah, Captain Barker reported:

> I made ten knots & a half per hour from off Cape Romain to Tybee light. I overhauled a fleet of about 25 to 30 vessels off Cape Hatteras & passed them all one after another. She is a first class sea boat. I don't think you can build another vessel to beat her.

Barker, born in Bath in 1835, had his rough edges. On a passage a short while later he chained two sailors to stanchions in the hold, promising them nothing but bread and water, and soon "made first class men out of them."

In October 1883 the *Nora Bailey* arrived at St. Johns, Newfoundland, with a cargo of hard pine. Barker wished next to take a cargo of hard pine south to the River Plate, and suggested having the schooner's bottom copper-sheathed. On the coast he preferred a painted bottom, given the many snags encountered in southern rivers, and he suspected that once arrived at the River Plate the schooner could lie in a freshwater tributary, but he feared having an accident on the way which might force the schooner into a port where the worms "will almost eat the anchors." As the schooner was very foul, and as the dry-dock at St. Johns was too small for her, it was decided to sail her empty the short distance to Sydney, Cape Breton—presumably a three- or four-day passage—where there were adequate facilities to dock her.

The *Bailey* sailed from St. Johns on the 5th of November, with captain, first mate, second mate, six sailors, and a black cook, and was promptly blown far offshore by heavy northerly gales. A letter mailed to Bath on December 24 by John S. Emery, the Boston broker, relayed the information that the schooner *Isabella Helen*, which had arrived at Halifax on December 11, had supplied provisions to the *Bailey* 150 miles east of St. Johns. The *Bailey* had suffered loss of sails but was trying to return to St. Johns, no easy matter in her foul and unballasted condition.

On December 30 the steamer *Galilee* arrived at Boston carrying the crew of the British brigantine *Blanche*, which had been abandoned in sinking condition on December 25 after a terrible gale on the 22nd. On the 21st the *Blanche* had provided the *Bailey* with provisions about 100 miles off St. Johns.

On January 8 the schooner *Satilla* arrived at Darien, Georgia, from Tusket River, Nova Scotia, after a very hard passage of twenty-one days. Regarding the missing *Nora*, Captain Skofield wrote:

> I don't know as we would [have] got here at all if we had no ballast. I know she would not lay-to light. If Capt. Barker had such weather as we did he never can get back to St. Johns light. His only chance is to get into warm weather & get to St. Thomas or some Southern port which I think he has or will.

However, in that furious gale of December 22 which had fatally damaged the *Blanche*, the *Nora* had been dismasted, with her boats and water tanks smashed. On February 1, Sam Sewall, in New York, wrote Arthur:

> Dear Uncle, I wired you the P.M. of the loss of the sch. *Nora Bailey*. Barker cable from Gibraltar reads *Nora Bailey* abandoned. All masts bowsprit gone crew saved." Hard lines! Capt. Barker owes us some $2,800 and the sch. had only about $1/5$ paid for herself. I feel very badly for some of the small owners. . . .

Working amidst blinding snow and hail, the crew had constructed a jury rig, and Barker had shaped a course, so to speak, for the Western Islands—the Azores. Sixty-nine days after leaving St. Johns the crew was taken off by the schooner *Excelsior*, of Brixham, England. The *Bailey* was abandoned, but not before six days had been spent attempting to tow her. On February 3 the British ship *E. J. Spicer* came upon the hulk and fired her as a danger to navigation.

On February 2, Captain Barker wrote Arthur Sewall from Gibraltar:

I hope if I have done wrong in regards to the *Nora Bailey* you will over look it for I tried every thing in my powers to save her but failed. I acted just as if I owned the schooner myself and it almost breaks my heart to think that I lost her for she was one of the ablest schooners that ever went out by Seguin and I was very proud of her and had her in good order until I lost the masts, and even then I would have saved her if I had provisions enough as I sailed her 680 miles under jury masts towards the Western Islands. . . . I know how much hardship a man can endure & I can solemnly swear that my crew could not endure but very little more. . . .

On February 26, 1884, the *Bath Times* published a remarkable letter from the crew, posted from Gibraltar and signed by the mates and six sailors, in which they praised Arthur Sewall & Co. for having built such a strong vessel, and Captain Barker for his inspired leadership:

When we were almost in despair, hungry and exhausted, he managed to give us new hope . . . and when we grumbled about the smallness of our allowance of food, he would say: "Boys, you may think it hard of me, but I am doing the best I can, and you will thank me for it before we part. . . . "

Reduced to skin and bones themselves, they noted the terrible toll that the ordeal had taken on Captain Barker. During the forty-two days until the dismasting he had been on deck almost constantly trying to take advantage of any wind shift. The schooner had been but eighteen miles from Cape Spear, Newfoundland, when the terrible hurricane hit them. Had it not been for the captain's discipline the crew would have devoured all the stores at once, and then starved. For ten days before rescue the daily allowance per man did not exceed two ounces of bread and one of beef, and for some days they had been eating seaweed. They wished also to call attention to two steamers which had surely seen them but had refused to stop.

One might well have thought that the members of the *Nora*'s crew deserved full and prompt payment of their wages—they certainly hadn't consumed many stores— but Arthur evidently thought otherwise. A letter dated February 28 from the office of the U.S. Shipping Commissioner in New York read:

William Boote and James Halston representing themselves respectively as mate and seaman of the late schooner *Nora Bailey* of Bath and owned by you have today applied to me to collect the wages due them from that vessel. They state that they abandoned this vessel in mid-Atlantic Jan. 20th and were carried to Gibraltar from which port they were sent here. Mr. Boote states that he joined the vessel on the 5th of Nov. at St. Johns NF at $35 per month and received $15 advance and claims a balance of $69.16. . . . Halston says that he joined the vessel at Darien Sept.18th at $15 per month and had but $2 (at St. Johns) and 1 lb of tobacco and he claims a balance of about $56. The men are entitled to wages up to the date of abandonment. Asking a reply at your early convenience for the men are entirely destitute.

On March 6 Arthur wrote a New York law firm—despised "sailor lawyers," no doubt—that was representing the steward, Mr. Taylor Johnson, in his claim for $107 wages, that there was "no occasion for any action," that Captain Barker had just arrived and that as soon as he had made up his accounts the crew would get all that was due them. On March 16 Captain Barker reported back to Arthur from New York:

I settled with the mate for $40, a little more than half the amount due him. You told me not to give them only half the amount due them but Mr. Dearborn advised me to settle for that with the mate. The others I could not get hold of as the boarding master had them stowed away. I left . . . articles and accounts with Mr. Dearborn with instructions to settle with them for 50 percent. . . .

In July a Boston lawyer visited Arthur in his president's office at the Eastern Railroad regarding $82.23 due sailor Frederick Foss, who had arrived in that port destitute. Arthur assured the lawyer that the matter would be attended to. On September 23, after having ignored several letters from the New York lawyers representing the steward, Arthur responded with more smoke:

Captain Barker some time since went to N. Y. for purpose of making settlement with his crews of sch. *Nora Bailey*. He effected settlement with some of them and we understood arranged with Mr. D. B. Dearborn . . . for settlement of other claims. We are writing him re. the matter by this mail & think you had better see him.

There is no indication that the sailors ever received their pay.

On September 21 Captain Barker, now in command of the Sewalls' schooner *Carrie S. Bailey*, had just arrived at Smithsville, Georgia, from Aspinwall. He had several sailors down sick with "the fever," but bluffed the quarantine doctor by painting their sallow faces with pink tooth powder.

Barker was next given command of the new schooner *Ada Bailey*, but was relieved in New York by Sam Sewall following a prolonged voyage to the River Plate, during which there was much crew trouble, a death of disputed circumstances, and possible irregularities—Barker may have shortchanged his crew on provisions, presumably pocketing the difference. The record is unclear, but it would appear that he was arrested and charged with cruelty, but there is no indication that he was convicted.

In 1888, bold as brass, Barker wrote Arthur from Darien, Georgia, where he had set up in business as a stevedore. He claimed that he could give better results than did the "darkie" stevedore that the Sewall vessels patronized, since he had four winches, and could expropriate men from the gangs of black stevedores as needed. Also, he claimed sailors resented taking orders from a "darkie" boss, and ended up running away. If Arthur used his services, Barker said he would also put part of his fee toward paying off his outstanding debt on the *Nora Bailey*.

1. *Amos A. Larrabee and Wife vs. Edward Sewall,* Maine Supreme Judicial Court, May 31, 1877, p. 385.

2. Note same-day mail delivery from Thomaston to Bath!

3. In 1878, during a political crisis, Dr. Alonzo Garcelon was elected governor by vote of the state senate.

4. Octavius T. Howe, M.D., and Frederick C. Matthews, *American Clipper Ships* (New York: Argosy Antiquarian Ltd., 1967),. pp. 610–11.

5. Maine, Vol. 19, pp. 266–67, R. G. Dun & Co. Collection, Baker Library Historical Collections, Harvard Business School.

6. Ibid. In January 1870 William D. had added up his assets and his liabilities and arrived at the figures $191,210 and $3,751 respectively. To that was to be added $21,900 for "Estimate of ships' earnings & non-paying stock"—he owned in seven E. & A. Sewall vessels, amounting to $74,500. He anticipated gaining 450 shares of Maine Central Railroad stock in exchange for his Portland & Kennebec stock, which he estimated would be worth $25 a share, although that proved to be less than half what they would soon be worth.

7. Jacques M. Downs, *The Golden Ghetto* (Bethlehem, PA: Lehigh University Press, 1997), p. 85.

8. Maine, Vol. 9, p. 356, R. G. Dun Collection. A notice for the "Dissolution of Copartnership" printed in the Bath *Daily Times* on April 29, 1879, read: "The copartnership heretofore existing under the style of E. & A. Sewall, is this day dissolved by mutual consent. Arthur Sewall is authorized hereafter to use the firm name in settling up the Copartnership affairs. Dated at Bath this 11th day of March, A.D. 1879. Signed, Edward Sewall, Arthur Sewall."

9. Sewall Family Papers, 22-586-5.

10. Sewall Family Papers, 22-558-18.

11. Frederick C. Matthews, *American Merchant Ships, 1850-1900*, Series 1 (Salem, MA: Marine Research Society, 1930), pp. 319–22.

12. Undated, unidentified newspaper clipping of column by Richard Hallet, in Small Manuscript Collection, Maine Maritime Museum.

13. See also the account in Matthews, *American Merchant Ships*, p. 144. Bosworth recalled to Matthews that the cliffs were lined with spectators.

14. Albert Joseph George, *The Captain's Wife* (Syracuse, NY: Syracuse University Press, 1946).

PART SEVEN

We go back to 1873 so as to follow the career of Captain Jim Baker, beginning with the ship Sterling. *We meet the Baker family and First Mate George Goodwin, who rises to the command of* Sterling. *We consider the long and perilous career of the schooner Alice Archer. The case-oil trade to the Far East rose to great importance for deepwater sail and* Rainier, *a case-oil ship on her maiden voyage, is wrecked among alleged South Sea cannibals. We meet Edward Sewall's son Ned, the source of much frustration and sorrow, and we attend the launching of Captain Baker's big ship, the* John Rosenfeld, *built during the last surge of square-rig construction at Bath.*

We had to hunt them with lanterns

> Launch—From the yard of Messrs. E. & A. Sewall an A-1 ship of 1,900 tons was launched last week. She is named the *Sterling* and is owned by the builders, Thomas M. Reed, and others.
> —[Brunswick] *American Sentinel*, June 5, 1873

In 1873 Bath launched nine ships, four barks, twenty-three schooners (fourteen were three-masters), and four small steamers. The minimal news coverage reflects how ho-hum Bath ship launchings had become.

Command of the new Sewall ship *Sterling* was given to Captain James G. Baker, who had first written to the Sewalls inquiring about her mastership in February from Liverpool, where he was completing the sale of his old command, the venerable clipper *Asa Eldredge* of the William F. Weld fleet of Boston, once the nation's largest. Baker wrote that he was in no position to buy an interest, and was not impressed by the $150 per month wage, but he accepted it. "Although it is rather small pay for a ship of her class, however I trust at some future time to satisfy you that my services are well worth the money."

Baker further wrote that it had long been his ambition to command a new ship, and having sailed for the Welds was proof that he knew how to keep a ship "in proper order." He figured that if he gave "fair satisfaction" the job would become a permanent one. When Weld partner Richard Baker died two years later, the fleet of about a dozen remaining ships was divided and many were sold off. As a result, former Weld captains swallowed their pride and applied, hat figuratively in hand, for a chance with the Sewall fleet. But Jim Baker had beaten them to the poop.

Jim Baker, a Cape Codder, was born in South Dennis in 1834. Like so many boys from that great sandy nursery of seamen, he went to sea by age fourteen. Wife Mary, a fellow Cape Codder, was from West Harwich, where the Bakers made their home on a small farm. Captain Baker, Mrs. Baker, and their three children, Rufus, Susan, and Katherine, made many voyages together.

The Bakers hit it off with the Arthur Sewalls. When *Sterling* left Bath on June 17 for St. Stephen, New Brunswick, to load a cargo of deal timber for Liverpool, twelve-year-old Will Sewall was aboard for the brief passage, to return with Mrs. Baker. Signed on as "boy" was nineteen-year-old Joe Sewall, then at the very beginning of a notable seagoing career. In 1880 Susie Baker, leaving the ship in Liverpool to return home for school in Boston, accompanied Arthur and Emma, who were returning from a European trip, aboard a liner. With Susie's marriage to nephew Ned Sewall in 1886 the two couples became virtual co-parents-in-law.

Captain Baker remained aboard *Sterling* for nine years, during which time he completed thirty passages. Aside from an 1880 voyage to Rangoon, *Sterling* was confined to North Atlantic and San Francisco voyages. Baker often expressed his great affection for the ship, as well as his pleasure in sailing for the Sewalls. Under Baker *Sterling* suffered no great mishaps, with passages differentiated primarily by the nature of the crew and the weather.

Departing the Delaware in November 1873 for Antwerp, with 11,943 barrels of oil stowed in every possible nook and cranny, Baker wrote:

> Our sailors came on board as usual in fighting trim. Some would not man the windlass & one fellow collared the Mate & I never saw a sailor whipped so quick in my life. The 2nd Mate cut one man over the head pretty bad and frightened the rest. They got hold of the capstan & went to work well satisfied that they were not the best men & this morning they fly around in great shape. So I don't apprehend any more trouble. The man the Mate handled is now in rather bad condition, both eyes dressed in deep mourning.

A passage from San Francisco to New York completed in January 1876 was notable for a succession of heavy westerly gales met after departing the Golden Gate, including one of near hurricane force that blew sails out of their boltropes, and also by "the most miserable lot of men that ever went on board of a ship."

> Many of them never had been to sea before & nights when we shortened sail, they would stow themselves away & we had to hunt them with lanterns & drive them aloft with a rope's end. . . . The very next time we shortened down they would repeat the same thing over again.

One man went missing and was thought to have fallen overboard until hunger flushed him out of the hold. At the time of writing, another man had disappeared, and was assumed to have hidden himself in the cargo. "Our cargo is such that they crawl in underneath & between the casks and it is impossible to find them. I write you all these things that you may know what we have had to take care of this ship with the last passage."

Writing from Liverpool on February 10, 1877, Captain Baker was very pleased with a passage of 114 days, pilot to pilot, from San Francisco. This was as good a time as made by some of the "*celebrated* American and English clipper ships" that left with him, by which he meant the *America* and the *Barrowdale. Glory of the Seas* had beaten him by eight days, but "take the different sailing qualities of the two ships, I think any disinterested party would call the *Sterling's* passage the best."

Baker's only complaint with *Sterling* was that she was too stiff, or stable, which he attributed to her broad beam and flat bottom. A ship that was too stiff had a quick roll which was hard on the rig and the people. The standard treatment was to make sure that sufficient weight of cargo, usually about one-third, was carried in the 'tween deck, and Baker wrote that filling the 'tween deck with wheat, and leaving space in the hold, "makes her just as she wants to be." All in all, he thought *Sterling* to be "one of the best grain ships afloat."

Arrived at Havre from San Francisco in February 1878, Baker described spending seventeen miserable and dangerous days from his arrival "on soundings," off the entrance of the English Channel, until finally making port.

> For nine days in succession we stood back & forth between the Scillys & Ushant . . . under three lower topsails and reefed foresail with sea enough to founder her—no observations day after day. It was the most anxious time I ever experienced at sea in my life. On January 31st at about 8 OC PM the Lizzard Lights broke out on our lee beam. . . . "

After this experience, he could well understand why so many ships came to grief in the Channel.

I am going to like you

On August 20, 1876, having just arrived at San Francisco, Captain Baker reported to Arthur Sewall on a "very tedious" 140-day passage from New York, plagued by calms:

> As regards the ship she has *as usual* performed admirably in all weather & the longer I go in her the more deeply I *fall in love with her.* . . . I had a very fair crew, better than average, although you thought I had a poor lot. But my officers have not come up to my expectations. My 2nd mate is a miserable man & Mr. Davis my mate I am not highly pleased with. He is smart enough and attentive but I do not like his ways as a disciplinarian.

As it happened, George Goodwin, also recently arrived at San Francisco, was looking for a mate's berth. Goodwin had left the Bath ship *Louisiana* "in the stream" along with the departing sailors because he could no longer stand her captain, an incompetent, cowardly bully and braggart who had gained his position by buying a master's share.[1]

George Goodwin was born Down East in Calais, Maine, in 1848, and in the fashion of the times went to sea as a boy. He would retire in 1909 from the Sewalls' four-masted steel bark *Dirigo* with a record few shipmasters could likely top, having "doubled" Cape Horn fifty-six times, circled the globe twelve times, and lived out of sight of land for an estimated twenty-five years.

From 1869 to 1874 Goodwin served from sailor to mate aboard three fine Newburyport, Massachusetts, ships managed by William and John Cushing, brothers of the famous diplomat, Caleb Cushing. Men of education and refinement, the Cushings were enlightened ship owners, believing that sailors should be treated by the philosophy of "live and let live." And they hired captains who suited their views. They owned first-class ships manned by first-rate seamen—their ship *Montana*, on which Goodwin sailed, carried fourteen studdingsails. Goodwin left the Cushings' ship *Nearchus* as second mate only because the fleet was set to be sold.[2]

Goodwin left *Louisiana* on a Saturday afternoon, and the following Monday morning, having received a message from Captain Baker at his hotel, walked aboard *Sterling*. She would be his home for the next eighteen years. As he recalled many years later:

> I went down on the dock just as Captain Baker was coming down the gangway . . . .
> I had taken a good look at him as he walked down the gangway, and then went up
> and introduced myself, and took the hand which he held out with a feeling that I
> had found a friend. We looked at each other from head to heels and my thoughts
> were, "I am going to like you.". . . We spent four years together, passed through
> many gales and calms, visited many ports, and everything was just the same.
> Captain Baker was a model shipmaster, and our friendship grew from that time I
> shook hands with him. . . .

When Goodwin joined *Sterling* a week later he spotted the two little Baker girls, Katie and Susie, taking turns peeping out of the cabin door at the new mate. They quickly became fast friends, as was also the case with Mrs. Baker. Goodwin wrote of her:

> She had one of the best dispositions of any woman I ever met, year in and year
> out, on board of a deepwater ship with nine months of the year at sea, out of
> sight of land. If that does not bring out all the little wrinkles in a person's disposi-
> tion nothing will. She stood that test and our ship's cabin was like a well-regu-
> lated home. She was brave in stormy weather and the life of the ship in pleasant
> weather; did all she could to make it pleasant for others and was methodical in
> everything. She had her school for the children, her work, and she was always
> doing something.

On August 29 Captain Baker wrote Arthur that the cargo was coming out in good condition save that rats had gnawed through the head of a barrel of cod liver oil and emptied its contents onto two barrels of whiskey. He did not know yet whether any had penetrated. The rats had also emptied three boxes of starch. Rats had troubled him a great deal on the passage notwithstanding the three cats shipped aboard which had "slaughtered a great number." He concluded: "I have discharged the mate Mr. Davis and have engaged another man by the name of Goodwin belonging to Calais, Maine. So far I like his performance very well. Mr. Davis had many good qualities but his bad ones over balanced."

On October 14 Baker wrote that *Sterling* was ready for sea. Mate Goodwin had been hit on the head by a falling slush bucket—"slush" was grease rubbed into masts— and had received a severe cut and was knocked senseless for a while. Baker sewed up the wound and trusted that in a few days Goodwin would be up and about.

Once at sea, Captain Baker saw that Mr. Goodwin was a mate after his own style, and he gave Goodwin a free hand. Although a believer in firmness, Goodwin was no bucko, believing that "the men will soon get on to the fact that when you give them all that belongs to them that you expect good work from them in return." He flourished aboard *Sterling*, and the ship reflected the results:

At that time there were a lot of young officers in the deepwater ships and we used to vie with each other to see who could take his ship into port in the best order. I have had Captain Pritchard, the dock master at the Waterloo Dock in Liverpool, say when we arrived, "Well Mr. Mate, all you want to do now is to put her into a glass case." . . . The *Sterling* was one of the show ships along South Street in those days and we had many visitors come on board and ask all sorts of questions. . . .

[In port] the captain and his family go on shore to live and the first mate looks out for the ship with only every other evening and every other Sunday to look around. . . . When the ship was ready for sea, Mrs. Baker and the girls came on board and we sailed away on another long voyage. We soon settled down to sea life and things went along as pleasantly as they did before and as they always do on board of a well-regulated ship where people have a little consideration for each other and the men are used like human beings. . . . We had very little trouble during the four years that I was mate of the *Sterling*.

Not to say that there was no trouble. On October 2, 1879, Captain Baker wrote Arthur from Oakland:

I wish to write you now in regard to a little trouble that we had on board here on the last passage. Early one morning Mr. Goodwin & the carpenter had some trouble & the c. used saucy language to the mate. Upon which he took the carpenter by the throat & choked him. The carpenter then took a knife from the cook & cut the mate a severe gash in the forehead. He then dropped the knife & came aft in after cabin. I then took hold of the carpenter & after a while managed to get him out of my cabin. While I was at work on the carpenter, the mate went to the galley & took hold of the cook & struck him with his fist for passing the knife to the carpenter. The cook then raised a knife to strike the mate but my son who was 3rd mate came up to the mate's rescue & knocked the cook down. So ended the affair.

If only. Shortly after the crew was discharged warrants were issued for Captain Baker, Goodwin, and young Rufus Baker. Goodwin and Rufus were advised by Baker to clear out of the city, and Baker insisted on an examination before the U.S. shipping commissioner.

Soon after my examination my *most bitter enemy, H. C. Pitman, stevedore...* went before Mr. Lovett the district attorney and told him I was the biggest *scoundrel* that ever walked a ship's deck. [That] I always had trouble with my crew every voyage, that I had to pay out hundreds of dollars to *bribe sailors* from having me arrested. And so much more too mean to put on paper. I can vouch for the truth of it for it came direct to me. But thank God I was never condemned to imprisonment for piracy on the high seas, as H. C. P. has been, the dirty low down scoundrel.

Eventually the three accused appeared before the grand jury, which refused to indict them. Nevertheless, after the ship was cleared and ready for sea, civil suits were filed, which Baker termed extortion. "The whole thing has been a put up job from the beginning to end & they have annoyed me ever since I have been here to my utter disgust. Our case I have left in the Frisco attorney's hands & I feel confident it will be looked after."

We had to chloroform them

In Harwich, Massachusetts, in 1949, Kate Baker Chase, writing of her childhood at sea, recalled that sometimes on tropic evenings Mr. Goodwin would sing to her, her favorite song being "Darling Nellie Gray."[3] The girls would sometimes go into his cabin, take everything out of his trunk, and put it all back in a different order. He never said a word.

Before a passage from Cardiff to San Francisco a doctor advised the Bakers that young Kate needed fresh milk every day. Accordingly, a little high-bred Jersey cow was purchased. A stall was outfitted for Molly in the forward house, complete with a spring floor and padded walls; during storms, which made her moo in fear, Captain Baker had a sailor with a lantern sit with her. In the tropics a "summer house" was built for her on deck, where she could be shaded during the day and sleep comfortably at night. During good weather she was allowed to wander about the deck, becoming a great pet for all hands. The sailors polished her hooves and her horns, and the girls braided her tail switch. Her coat shone like that of a racehorse.

Only Mr. Goodwin milked Molly. The carpenter made swinging shelves so that the cream would set. Butter was made off Cape Horn so that they could say it had been done. Molly was due to "freshen," i.e., to calve, before San Francisco was reached—she was indeed a *very* good milch cow not to have dried up. Goodwin wrote:

Many times I told the girls what a nice little calf I had stowed away in the fore peak, and if they were good girls and learned their lessons, I would bring it up and let them play with it after we rounded Cape Horn and were up in the fine weather. They did not seem to credit my story and wondered how Bossy could live down there in the dark. When the time did come and Bossy was born, I told them if they would not come on deck until four bells, I would bring Bossy up on deck. I went in and blind-folded the two girls, led them out on deck, stood one each side of the calf and took the handkerchiefs from their eyes. Their surprise and pleasure at seeing that little Bossy was something to be remembered. You could not make those two girls believe that I would say anything that was not so, after that.

Also on board were pigs and chickens. The chickens had a wing clipped so they could run about the decks and take sunbaths without flying overboard. The pigs were washed down every morning along with the decks and were white and bright, and, given free range, got into everything and were great pets. (On one voyage an officer made the girls a little cart which they hitched a pig to. On another, the sailors taught a pig tricks, and when it was time to kill it the Chinese cook balked, explaining, "I no kille that pig. Spose I killie that pig, sailors no eat him, how can do?" The pig was saved over for the next voyage when there would be a new crew.)

At San Francisco Captain Baker sold Molly and Bossy for a good price and decided to buy a milch goat for the next passage. The ship had been shifted to Vallejo to load grain, and one day Captain Baker met a boy leading a fat, sleek goat by a rope. A deal was struck and the boy agreed to deliver the goat to the ship. Mate Goodwin received a note from the captain to put the goat in the cow house when it arrived. The steward was assigned goat chore duty. The goat was not mentioned or thought of over the next few busy days, but when finally at sea Captain Baker asked if it wasn't time for the goat to freshen. Mr. Goodwin replied that the "days of miracles" were over, as it was a billy goat. "The deuce it was!" Captain Baker groaned.

Attempts to make Billy into a pet were sabotaged by his habit of eating the sailors' boots, and he finally sealed his fate by butting Mrs. Baker heels-over-head. Gamely chewing its gamy flesh, the sailors wondered if their boots would have made better eating, wrote Goodwin. Captain Baker was never allowed to forget about the goat.

Mr. Goodwin once bought two kid goats for Katie and Susie, to join their menagerie of pet rabbits and kittens. The boatswain, Richard Williams, was a big, kind-hearted alcoholic—when drunk on shore he called himself "One-Eyed Dick, the Terror of the Western Ocean," but when sober he would pick a fly out of water and put it in the sun to dry. He was very fond of the Baker girls and made Kate and Susie skipping ropes displaying all sorts of the old-time sailor's hitching, cross-pointing, and fancywork.

At Liverpool Williams went on a spree and ended up sailing back to San Francisco aboard another ship, arriving at about the same time as *Sterling*. On the passage the kid goats had developed sore feet from running on the hard deck, and, the condition of their feet worsening, it was finally decided to chloroform them and bury them at sea.

Arrived at San Francisco, the old boatswain set out to pay a social call on *Sterling* to visit the girls, but stopped at several saloons along the way. When he finally arrived at *Sterling*, displaying a "gilt edge," the girls happened to be ashore visiting friends, but Mrs. Baker came out on deck to exchange pleasantries. "How are the kids, Marm?" "Oh, " Mrs. Baker said, "They got such sore feet that we had to chloroform them and bury them at sea." The boatswain, dazed, looked at her for a moment, then exclaimed, "Good Lord!" and abruptly departed. They never saw him again.

Once, when *Sterling* was becalmed four hundred miles west of San Francisco after 130 days at sea, the smoke of an approaching steamer was seen. As everyone was anxious for news, Mate Goodwin persuaded Captain Baker to let him take the dinghy and row into the steamer's path to ask for a newspaper. The steamer proved to be the crack Pacific Mail steamer *City of Tokio*, bound for Japan. Upon discovering Goodwin's trivial request her captain was not amused until he learned that the ship's captain was Jim Baker, a friend and fellow member of a fraternal lodge. The boat was laden with fruit, vegetables, and fresh meat before being towed back to the ship—Goodwin wrote that one experience of being towed in a small boat behind a mail ship was enough for him.

I saw a ship with the Bath coat of arms

Sterling's 1880–81 voyage from Liverpool to Rangoon (likely she carried coal) then to London (via Queenstown) with rice was a long and tedious affair. Rufus Baker was second mate. The crew was the worst that Mr. Goodwin had ever experienced, made up of what he called "turnpike sailors" who would lodge in a boardinghouse until they were thrown out for refusing to join a ship, and then tramp elsewhere to play the same trick. Turnpike sailors gave the public the wrong impression of seamen, Goodwin held, just as the minority of bad captains gave all captains a hard name.[4]

The turnpike sailors came aboard with almost nothing but the clothes on their backs, worked indifferently, and fought amongst themselves. "On several occasions," wrote Goodwin, "some of the fight had to be knocked out of them." A wild plot concocted by the "crazy" Irish boatswain to seize the ship in the Bay of Bengal, kill the afterguard, take the ship's money, scuttle the ship, and then row ashore as shipwrecked seamen, was dashed. (Goodwin noted that the only ship he had ever sailed aboard that carried any amount of money was the bark *Walter Hallet*, a West Africa trader.)

At Rangoon—a hot and sultry port, particularly hard on the rigging and spars, where Captain Baker became very sick—all but three of the turnpikers deserted. They were replaced by sailors who had just arrived aboard English ships after long passages. Captain Baker had been unable to buy any vegetables before departure, and after about forty days at sea, the first of six cases of scurvy broke out. Captain Baker treated the men with "acids," i.e., ascorbic acid, and planned to stop at St. Helena for fresh provisions, but, arriving there just at dusk with a strong tradewind blowing, could not bear to lose eighteen hours of that wind, and so decided to "let her come."

In March of 1881, when *Sterling* arrived at Baltimore to load coal for San Francisco, Captain Baker wanted to "stop" at home for a passage, as it had been four years since he had been at his Cape Cod farm. The Sewalls had been thinking of giving Mr. Goodwin command of *Indiana*, but instead decided to let him take *Sterling* to San Francisco. Goodwin's brother, who had been mate on Chapman & Flint ships, would go as mate, and Captain Goodwin would have his new bride aboard. Four years earlier the two had met on a visit Goodwin had made "down home," but they had not seen each other since, and the joke was that Goodwin's sister had to accompany the bride to the wedding so as to identify her. The ceremony took place in Baltimore at the Carrollton Hotel, with a thrilled Katie Baker standing up with the couple.

Arthur Sewall came to Baltimore shortly before *Sterling* sailed and informed Captain Goodwin that the ship *El Capitan* had sailed for San Francisco from New York a few days before, that Captain Bill Lincoln was a hard man to beat, and that if Goodwin made as good a passage as *El Capitan* made he would be meeting expectations. Goodwin predicted that he would pass Bill Lincoln before the equator. *Sterling* sailed on March 31, with Captain Baker on board while towing down the bay, to return with the tug. Goodwin later wrote the Sewalls: "Capt. B. felt very bad at leaving the ship that had been so faithful to him so long. I hope she won't know the difference and will go along just as well for me."

An overcast night in the South Atlantic, with continual heat lightning playing on the horizon and a falling barometer, found *Sterling* between Cape Frio and the River Plate. This region was notorious for sudden, screeching gales called *pamperos* blowing off the hot Argentine pampas. Goodwin had a very good crew, and, with the men standing by, was carrying all possible sail before a fair wind when the lookout spotted a sail close ahead. Goodwin sheered off and passed *El Capitan*, snugged down under lower topsails and a reefed foresail, close aboard. Within a couple of hours the wind had changed and *Sterling*, too, was put under small sail, and by morning she was dealing with a howling gale. *El Capitan* was sighted there once again, and then once more off Cape Horn. Goodwin recalled the Cape Horn meeting:

> I came on deck at daylight and saw a ship with the Bath coat of arms about three miles astern, and recognized our friend. Bath ships, at this time, or the greater number of them, had their chain plates, bobstays, and back ropes painted red. Sailors used to say never go in a ship with the Bath coat of arms, or N S [Nova Scotia] or N B [New Brunswick] on her stern if you wanted to be treated like a human being. That was so in many cases, but some of the best and kindest hearted ship masters I ever knew sailed Bath ships.[5]

With Bill Lincoln in command, the Bath coat of arms meant what it said.

Sterling made the best passage of the fleet. In a letter written at sea, Goodwin described a freak sea off Cape Horn that washed four men overboard. Three of them caught hold of the mainsheet and were saved; one went overboard along with a section of bulwarks, and was then swept under the counter, which came down on him. He could not be saved. Also, the pipe from the cabin water closet—the captain's toilet—broke off, with water rushing in "all it knew how." Fortunately, Mrs. Goodwin was in the cabin and heard it.[6]

At San Francisco Goodwin learned that *Sterling* had been sold to John Rosenfeld. Rosenfeld was a San Francisco broker who, in 1880, took over the Cape Horn fleet managed by the venerable house of George Howe & Co. Most of the ships, which included the celebrated clippers *Young America* and *David Crockett*, were by then quite old and were quickly sold off, and newer tonnage was purchased.

Goodwin wrote Arthur Sewall that although he could remain as master of *Sterling*, he would prefer to sail for the Sewalls, because with them he could invest in a ship. From Liverpool in February he wrote Arthur: "My wife leaves me on the 2nd. I shall miss her very much. We have followed your advice and so far my married life has been very happy. I suppose when I get home I shall find a little tow head. I did not mean to but things will happen." He would later remark that although his wife never got seasick, she eventually became sick of the sea.

John Rosenfeld, according to Goodwin, was a man whose word was absolutely as good as his bond. He offered Goodwin a wage considerably higher than that paid by the Sewalls. Regarding the slop chest income, which the Sewalls insisted be split between the captain and the ship, Rosenfeld said that he did not keep a clothing store, only asking that Goodwin buy good clothing and price it fairly. As he did not wish to be dealing with sailor lawyers, the sailors were to have all that was their due.[7]

Although Goodwin was a candidate in 1883 for command of the Sewalls' new ship *Rainier*, he would remain in *Sterling* sailing for John Rosenfeld for more than twelve years. During these years *Sterling* became a favorite ship with the San Francisco shippers:

> We made good passages, delivered our cargoes in fine condition and did not call
> on the underwriters for anything. . . . I had a free hand to keep the ship in good
> order. We rejected all goods that would damage other people's goods and the
> result was there was no haggling over reclamations for damaged cargo. The own-
> ers of the ship were Jews, the shippers and consignees of the cargos were, the
> greatest part of them, Jews. All liberal fair-minded men with whom it was a
> pleasure to sail for and do business with. I cannot recall a thing these people
> ever said to me that they did not make good.

Although presently out of the Sewalls' employment, George Goodwin was by no means through with the Sewalls.

One other of the Sewall hard-pine fleet was the schooner *Alice Archer*, commanded first by Arthur Gibbs, later by his brother Sam Gibbs. The Gibbs boys drank hard. . . . But they delivered the goods and delivered the big schooner loads of hard pine *ON TIME*.

—Doc Briry

There is no record of Sam Gibbs having commanded the *Archer*, but Doc had it right about Arthur and his drinking, and also his good record for (usually) making port in a timely fashion—Arthur Gibbs was the General Grant of the hard-pine fleet.

A book could be written just about the Sewalls' schooner fleet. Although their fleet of square-riggers substantially outnumbered their schooner fleet, the Sewalls spent more time dealing with the schooners than they did with the square-riggers, since the schooners carried many more cargoes over the course of a year. The *Archer* has been selected to represent her sisters here not because of any unusual drama in her life, but simply because she was long-lived and spent her entire career under the Sewalls' management.

The three-masted *Alice Archer*, 447 tons, was launched December 19, 1882. Due to ice in the river, the lightly ballasted schooner, which had been completely rigged and outfitted on the stocks, was immediately towed down the river and sent on her way. Among the more than twenty owners, sawmill-owner Jim Bailey owned 4/64—possibly some of Arthur's out-of-state brother Frank's 14/64 belonged to tax-dodging Arthur, who was listed with only 2/64. The schooner was named for Frank Sewall's daughter, who in turn had been named for Henry the Dutiful's mother-in-law.

On December 28 the *Alice Archer's* captain, Reuben Fletcher, late of the schooner *Carrie S. Bailey*, wrote the Sewalls from Brunswick, Georgia:

We arrived here today. The vessel does very well and I think if [she] had more light sails could do as well as the *Carrie S. Bailey*. . . . While on our passage we lost a man overboard and drowned. The man's name was Thomas Libby of New York. . . . We was just six days from the river as far as Savannah, the wind being easterly had to keep offshore as it was not prudent to run in, so doing have been three days longer getting here. Shall get to work on cargo as soon as possible.

This was one of but very few instances when a drowned sailor was named—since the Sewalls normally wouldn't have known a dead sailor from Adam, there was, quite realistically, no reason for a captain to identify them.

In 1887 Joseph Williams, the *Archer's* mate, lost an arm while loading lumber at Darien, Georgia, and Arthur Sewall, then president of the Maine Central Railroad, gave him the position of flagman at Bath's School Street railroad crossing—normally such sinecures were handed out to maimed brakemen.

In 1889 Captain Fletcher moved into the new schooner *Talofa*, to be replaced by Captain Arthur Gibbs, a native of Bathurst, New Brunswick. A letter from Gibbs after arriving at Charleston in June 1889 reporting his first passage on the schooner, presumably with a cargo of Kennebec ice and/or hay, was typical of letters received from Sewall schooner captains upon reaching a southern port:

Arrived here today after a very hard struggle the latter part of passage. I got down off Hatteras six days after leaving the Kennebec and there I struck a heavy gale from SSE with a terrible sea. I had to heave-to and drifted back about one hundred miles. There I lay becalmed four days. Worked down to Hatteras again and struck the long south-wester. Was off there seven days in company with a large fleet of vessels and finally had a dead beat right down to the Bar. Lost foresail off Hatteras, bent an old mainsail . . . and blowed that to pieces. . . . I found the *Archer* to be a good sailer and a splendid sea boat but in moderate winds and a heavy sea she is awful hard on everything and in a calm with any sea I have to lower everything down on deck or she would slat herself to pieces.

Wide-beamed schooners had a quick roll under such conditions.

Southbound schooners beating around and beyond Hatteras against a southwest breeze stood in and out off "the beach," keeping inshore of the northbound Gulf Stream. With an easterly gale "the beach" became a deadly lee shore. Anchoring south of Hatteras could be problematical, especially on a "hand-puller" with no steam donkey engine—the Sewalls long did not believe in such extravagances—if the anchor became buried by the shifting sand.[8] Steamer traffic off Hatteras was very heavy and the visibility often poor in haze and fog—coastwise steamers, it was said, never altered their heading unless they absolutely had to, being loath to get off their timed compass course.

In winter nor'westers schooners were blown hundreds of miles offshore; schooners that became badly iced-up on the coast often sought the warmer waters of the Gulf Stream. Coming north, "should Hatteras let you pass," then there was Cape Cod to worry about. Typical was a telegram received from a vessel reporter at Chatham, on the Cape, on February 12, 1893: "*Archer* coming back from northward nine A.M. for anchorage north west gale has main boom fished no deckload in sight above mainrail [signed] nickerson."

The Sewalls' hard-pine schooners did much business in the Caribbean and Gulf of Mexico, carrying timber from Louisiana and Texas to sickly Aspinwall (Panama) when the French were attempting to dig a canal across the isthmus., and also south to the River Plate (Argentina and Uruguay). Heavily laden lumber schooners sailing "to the River" suffered shipworm holes in their deck planking under the deckload. In 1888 the *Archer*, lying in a Columbian bay loading mahogany from rafts floated down a river, rescued with her boat more than ninety persons thrown overboard from a small capsized steamer.

In 1889 the *Archer* delivered machiner, and a timber cargo including fourteen-by-

The three-masted schooner Tofa, built by Arthur Sewall & Co. in 1891 and sold in 1901—the slight "hog" to her sheer indicates that this photo was taken late in life. The late Captain W. J. L. Parker, USCG, calculated that while under Sewall management for a little over ten and a half years Tofa repaid approximately 180 percent on her initial cost of $45–55,000, or more than 17 percent per year. As a component of a system of vertical integration her value to the Sewalls would have been much greater. Over these years, in addition to timber, she carried coal, salt, sugar, cement, phosphate rock, asphalt, hay, stone, rails, pilings, and ice. Captain Arthur Wilson, from Prospect Ferry, Maine, commanded her throughout her career under the Sewalls. "Tofa" means "goodbye" in Samoan. Tofa was a sister to the schooner Aloha—meaning both "hello" and "goodbye" in Hawaiian—launched in 1890. Tofa was lost in 1915 in a hurricane while bound from Sierra Leone to Pensacola. MAINE MARITIME MUSEUM

fourteen-inch creosoted timbers forty-two feet long and "heavy like iron," and also forty-two-foot-long piling from Wilmington, North Carolina, to Greytown, Nicaragua. After being laboriously winched by hand out of the bowports, the timbers and piles were rafted over the bar. Gibbs wrote to the Sewalls:

> This is no place for vessels of this class or no kind of sailing vessel. The vessel has more wear and tear here this time than she would in any other trade in a year. My copper is all knocked to pieces clear down under the bilges and sides all

chafed up & it can't be helped the way a vessel pitches and rolls about in the sea that is always on the coast with a lighter alongside. No kind of fender is much good. . . . I would as soon lay anywhere off the American coast in the winter as lay here.

Schooners returning north from the Caribbean often carried "logwood," a crooked, hard-stowing wood used to make dyes. Other cargoes were guano from the island of Nevassa, salt from Turk's Island, or pitch from Trinidad. A pitch cargo oozed to leeward over a long passage and congealed in that plane when cold weather was reached.

In June 1890, lying at the Lower Bluff Mill on the Satilla, Gibbs reported "a very unpleasant affair":

A Portuguese sailor & the steward (who is a South American of Spanish & French blood) had some kind of a quarrel between themselves and the sailor threatened that he would kill the steward before morning. About midnight everybody on board was awakened by a pistol shot and the sailor was found close to the forward cabin door with a bullet in his brain and the steward in the entry with a pistol saying he killed him, there he is.

At Bailey's Mills in February 1896, Gibbs wrote that the lumber coming aboard being very heavy with pitch, he could only take 390,000 board feet comfortably: "Don't want to overload this time of year as it will be nasty on the coast when I get up there and I want to go safe & have the vessel in trim so I can handle her in case of getting iced up." Departing Charleston in October 1896 Gibbs signed an all-black crew: "I had to buy them about $25.00 worth of clothes. I could not carry them around Cape Cod without something to keep them warm."

Schooners leaving Maine often carried ice cargoes, even in the winter—in February 1894 Captain Gibbs wrote from Rockport, Maine, that the loading berth was ready but the schooner couldn't be moved as she was frozen-in solid. After loading at a Richmond, Maine icehouse owned by Charles W. Morse, the Bath-born ice and steam-boat robber baron, Gibbs smelled a rat when the bill of lading showed forty-two tons less than the schooner had previously loaded on the freshwater (and thus less buoyant) Kennebec at the same draft.

In June 1897 the *Archer* was loading granite at Rockport, Massachusetts, and Gibbs wrote: "I guess they will get us loaded all right in our time but we are getting a terrible shaking up, dragging & tumbling those big stones about in the hold gives her some awful jars. Its like striking a rock. And it don't do her any good." In April 1899 Captain Gibbs, at Savannah, wrote broker David Dearborn in New York apologizing, sort of, for his recent "bad" (i.e., drunken) behavior. But he did not think that he needed "the Keely [Keeley] Cure"—"I am personally acquainted with over 100 people that has taken that business and with the exception of one they are all a great deal worse today . . . ."[9]

In Philadelphia in July, Gibbs had considerable trouble getting a crew: "They want steam schooners, most of them," meaning schooners equipped with a donkey engine. Days later the *Archer* went ashore near Fernandina, Florida, and pounded heavily for thirty-five hours before a tug got her off. Remarkably, she was but little damaged. Gibbs blamed a strong northerly current for throwing out his dead reckoning, but perhaps the northerly current wasn't the only strong liquid flowing—in October 1899 Arthur received a letter from one A. F. Byers of Brooklyn, New York:

> You may think it funny that I take the liberty of writing you this letter. . . . I understand you are the owner of the schooner *Alice Archer*, a vessel worth thousands of dollars. And which in my estimation ought to be in [the] charge of a man who will not be 7 days a week intoxicated and in his bunk. . . . Captain Chase, the present mate of the *Alice Archer*, navigated that vessel around for the past 6 months, has attended to her in port & out of port. . . . If Captain Chase . . . has to be the captain pro tem why not give him the whole glory?

A letter from the Sewalls in December 1900, addressed to Gibbs at Brunswick, Georgia, referred to reports "of your behavior previous to your sailing. . . . We cannot submit to the continuation of such action. . . . You must put a stop to it at once, if you desire to continue in our employ. . . . "

But Gibbs was still with the old *Archer* on January 18, 1902, when, loaded with coal, she foundered in a gale, appropriately, off her old nemesis, Cape Hatteras. In a heavy cross sea she began to leak steadily; railroad iron on deck came adrift, breaking things up. With three feet of water in her, despite steady pumping, it looked "kind of blue," so when the schooner *John L. Treat* appeared out of the vapor it was decided to abandon the *Archer* to her long-cheated fate.

Over a career of nearly twenty years the *Archer* completed 229 passages. Her long survival in a trade that was both very hazardous and also brutally wearing—the large deckloads of heavy, green hard-pine lumber placed extraordinary strains on the schooner's hull—was a testimony to the skill of her builders, and of the ability, fortitude, and also very good fortune of those who sailed in her. Doc Briry was right to insist that the Sewalls' hard-pine schooners should be remembered.

My pantaloons are worn out

Beginning about 1870, and ending shortly before World War I, the case-oil trade, involving the shipping of five-gallon tins of kerosene, packed two to a wooden case, primarily from New York and Philadelphia to the Far East, was a major employer of large sailing vessels, including those of the Sewall fleet. Although several refiners were initially involved in the business, all became subsidiaries of the Standard Oil Company, which monopolized the trade.

Newtown Creek, a tributary of New York's East River separating Brooklyn from Long Island City, and once the center of New York shipbuilding, was the site of America's first petroleum (as opposed to coal) kerosene refinery in 1867. Refined from

Pennsylvania and Ohio crude oil, kerosene was an effective, clean, and safe illuminant, and a catalyst for vast social and economic change worldwide. It was also the basis for Rockefeller's vast wealth. Its production helped to turn Newtown Creek into a waterway so polluted that it corroded ships' bottoms; it remains highly polluted with oil to this day.

By the late 1800s over half of American kerosene production was exported as case oil. In 1886 the 12,244,300 cases shipped to "the East" were carried by nearly 300 sailing vessels, of which nearly 100 were American, the largest single fleet, and 27 steamers.[10] In the Far East empty oil tins were fashioned into many useful items. Case oil shipped to Asia and the Orient replaced plant-derived oils, freeing up vast areas of cropland for food production, and may have helped support a large growth of population.

Being homogenous and relatively light, case oil cargoes were notorious for making ships "crank," or insufficiently stiff, unless adequate ballast was loaded beneath the oil. Shippers and sometimes owners were notorious for sending ships out insufficiently ballasted, so as to maximize the cargo. Captain Joe Hamilton of the ship *Undaunted* wrote the Sewalls from Yokohama in 1883 after completing a case-oil passage, remarking that the ship had been so crank that, "The knees and seat of all my pantaloons are worn out [from] crawling and sliding about the decks."

Ships that loaded at Newtown Creek had to house their topgallant masts to get under the Brooklyn Bridge. For some reason it proved difficult for riggers to accurately measure the height above the water of the lowered topgallant mast, and several Sewall ships hit the span. The *Undaunted* was one, the housed main topgallant mast knocking off about 200 pounds of the bridge, including some bolts, one of which hit Captain Hamilton in the arm.

Breakers ahead!

There were captains who retired after many years at sea and had never lost a ship, nor some, even a man. Doubtless at least most of these men were very competent shipmasters, but there can be no doubt that they were also very fortunate, such was the nature of hazards at sea. And there were other masters, many at least as competent and as cautious, who suffered disaster more than once. When the Sewalls suspected that one of their captains was of the unlucky sort, they found a way to be rid of him.

Captain Samuel H. Morrison, born in Phippsburg *circa* 1830 (and the older brother of Captain Parker Morrison of the ship *Indiana*), by all accounts was a very competent shipmaster and a gentleman but had the misfortune to lose several fine ships, including, in 1883, the Sewalls' new ship *Rainier*.

In December 1877 under Morrison's command, the Bath ship *James A. Wright*, bound from Liverpool to Savannah, in ballast, went ashore on the coast of the Hebrides Islands, and was a total wreck. All hands made it ashore. In 1882 Captain Morrison took command of the handsome ship *Oracle*, 1,550 tons, built at Bath in 1876 by Hitchcock & Blair.

Oracle, a lofty ship rigged with double topgallants and fore and main skysails, proved to be a very smart sailer. On her first voyage under Captain Morrison she made a 109-day passage from New York to San Francisco, followed by a 111-day passage to Queenstown. For the whole round voyage back to San Francisco she averaged 153 miles a day.

In January 1883 *Oracle*, Captain Morrison, with Omar Humphrey of Yarmouth as mate, again departed San Francisco for Liverpool. According to an account given by Mr. Humphrey, at about 25 degrees south the ship encountered a series of heavy westerly gales, then a perfect hurricane. Seas smashed the wheelhouse and the after cabin, and washed a sailor overboard. Humphrey wrote: "Men were blown against the houses and held there impossible to move. They could only drop on deck and creep and lash themselves to keep from being blown overboard. The ship lay on her beam ends with the water up to the hatches. . . ." At midnight the wind moderated somewhat, showing land close on the lee beam, with seas breaking against high cliffs.

> Destruction seemed inevitable. . . . Only by the captain's great coolness and presence of mind were we saved. When close upon the breakers an opening in the land was discovered and the wheel put hard up. The ship sailed in between the land, towering up hundreds of feet, into smooth water but she then became unmanageable on account of the eddying currents. The anchor was got ready but no bottom could be found. . . . The ship struck with tremendous force . . . then drifted off. Boats were then made ready, officered, manned, made fast to the ship. . . . We had only time to secure a few clothes when our ship listed over and sunk entirely from sight, sliding off into deep water.[11]

They were stranded on an island located eight miles north of Cape Horn. After a week, Captain Morrison, Mate Humphrey, and five men set out in the longboat, hoping to reach the Falklands through the Strait of Le Maire, 359 miles distant. After two very difficult days they were picked up by a German bark. The German captain could not be persuaded to rescue the seventeen poorly provisioned men marooned on the island, but held on for Valparaiso, reached nearly a month later. There, the American consul immediately organized a rescue expedition, including Mr. Humphrey, which was quickly sent south and rescued the men.

Upon his return to Maine, Captain Morrison was given command of the Sewalls' fine new ship *Rainier*, 1,877 tons, launched that June. Morrison again chose Omar Humphrey, who had just become his son-in-law, for mate. At Philadelphia *Rainier* loaded 73,000 cases of kerosene for Hiogo, Japan. With the ship fully loaded and at anchor, Captain Morrison noted that with all the yards braced sharp-up she heeled over one strake, which he thought indicated good ballasting. The ship's company numbered thirty-two persons, including Mrs. Humphrey, the captain's daughter. The cabin furniture included a piano, a wedding present from her parents.

The ship's departure was delayed while repairs were made after a steamer struck her head rigging. When "running her easting down" (to round the Cape of Good Hope and run before the powerful westerlies towards the Indies or Australia) the crew began to fall sick, their illness suspected to be caused by fumes from leaking kerosene tins. On

Captain Samuel H. Morrison, 1830–1910
MAINE MARITIME MUSEUM

November 15, during a heavy southerly gale, *Rainier* overhauled and passed the smaller Thomaston ship *Pactolus*, which had departed from New York a few days before *Rainier* had sailed. Five days later the Australian coast was sighted, and soon after, the ship was headed north, up the Tasman Sea, toward warmer weather.

Because of continuing sickness among the crew, Captain Morrison decided to call at remote Norfolk Island to procure fresh provisions. Norfolk was formerly a prison island, but at that time was the home of the descendants of the *Bounty* mutineers, who had been relocated from Pitcairn Island. Learning that there was a lady aboard the ship, the island women sent out gifts of milk, strawberries, and bananas.

Soon after departing Norfolk, Mate Humphrey, the steward, the cook, and several men, fell ill to a fever. Becalmed, the ship drifted for twenty days, while slowly working by the Caledonia, Solomon, and New Hebrides Islands. On January 3 a gentle northeast breeze began to blow, then gained strength, and the spirits of all on board picked up. In the afternoon the island of Lae, in the Marshalls, was sighted. Mate

Humphrey came on deck for the first time in some weeks. At 4:30 the island was eight miles distant on the port beam. Returning on deck after consulting his chart, Captain Morrison gave the new course, northwest, and stated that there was nothing ahead to trouble them until reaching the coast of Japan.

The supper bell rang, and captain and mate went below, leaving instructions to keep a good lookout for breakers, with a second lookout at the masthead until dark. At eight bells, when Mr. Humphrey took over from the second mate, the night was black, the moon having set. Two lookouts were posted forward, and the captain remained on deck as the ship forged ahead under a heavy press of sail. Simultaneously, the white flashes of breakers were seen from foreward and aft. "Breakers ahead!—Hard a-starboard!" The port braces were let go, but it was too late, and the ship drove onto a reef.

Or so Mate Humphrey's account in his book reads.[12] Two letters from the captain to the Sewalls, written in the Marshall Islands, present somewhat differing versions of a more complicated navigational situation. In one, Morrison reported that the doldrums had left the ship several degrees to the east of where he had planned to pick up the trade winds. Having passed Margaretta, or Lao, Island, he had expected to see Lydia Island before dark. When it could not be seen from the fore-royal yard it was apparent that its position, as laid down on the chart, was incorrect. Out of caution, he then steered southwest. At 9:30 the ship struck a half-tide reef not laid down on his charts. He gave its position as L165½ E, Lat. 9 N.

The heavy seas striking the ship soon made it apparent that she was doomed. Provisions stored in the stern were moved to the more secure bow, as were the two quarter boats. It was not long before the ship began to break up, and by daylight cargo was floating out of her. As far as the eye could see in either direction was a white line of breakers, while dim in the distance a few islets could be perceived—these, according to Morrison, were also missing from his chart. The reef that the ship lay on was part of an elliptical atoll thirty miles long and five miles across.

Soon the sails of native canoes could be seen approaching the wreck. It was strongly believed by mariners at this time that the natives of this region were not only savages but possibly cannibals.

A Thanksgiving feast for the savages

The canoes were made fast to the coral, and the natives then approached up to the inside surf line and commenced to shout and gesticulate, which sent a chill of terror to the unfortunate mariners who clung to the wreck which soon must go to pieces.[13]

So wrote first mate Humphrey. With twelve rifles and plenty of ammunition at hand, it was agreed, if necessary, that they would make a stand "as long as life lasted." And there were indeed islanders in the region who killed white sailors, some to avenge the activities of white labor recruiters—"black birders"—who kidnapped innocent natives who boarded their schooners to trade. All hands aboard a ship that was wrecked on an island thirty miles away in 1882 were said to have been murdered.

To open communications, the gangway ladder, with a line attached, was floated to the reef through the surf. Two natives boarded it, were pulled out to the ship, and were hauled aboard with bowlines. Handed pipes, they smoked them happily. Quizzed in every language known by the *Rainier*'s polyglot crew, they responded with gibberish, but recognized the words "captain," "king," "schooner," and "whiskey," suggesting that they had contact with trading schooners. With this encouragement, the captain decided that the ship's company should go to their island, Ujea, which lay about twelve miles away.

> The natives who had been smoking now handed the pipes back, but when given to understand they could have them, held them high in the air and shouted with a hideous screech to their kindred on the reef, and so quickly did they observe the pipes that many rushed into the water and swam through the heavy surf, eagerly watched by the *Rainier*'s crew, who expected to see them dashed against the coral. . . . But they were perfect in their art, and on swimming alongside were hosted on board and fitted out as were their comrades, also with shirts and dungaree pants.

The evacuation of the ship was carried out by running one of the quarter boats on a taut line back and forth through the surf to the reef. Mrs. Humphrey, refusing a blindfold, was lowered in an armchair, her husband cutting the rope just as the lunging boat rose to meet it. Later, all three boats, loaded with supplies, were towed across the lagoon by the canoes, the flotilla arriving at the village at dusk.

> During all this time, the savages had been examining everything, and their wild, demoniac looks and yells accompanied all their movements, either swimming or on the canoes. They were clad only with a small mat fastened about the waist, with holes in their ears large enough to put one's hand in. . . . All this sent a thrill of terror through the stoutest hearts, as all hands only expected to be a Thanksgiving feast for the savages.

The island's king, however, graciously turned over his own hut of palm fronds to the *Rainier*'s people. It being very small, it was occupied only by the afterguard, along with the guns and valuables, while the men camped around it. There being no water on the island, the king had several baskets of coconuts brought for the weary and thirsty refugees.

Captain Morrison decided to outfit the longboat so that it could be sailed to seek help. Because Mate Humphrey was still ill, Second Mate Harry W. Drohan was to be in command, accompanied by four volunteers. A compass, sextant, and clock were provided; most stores were in the form of coconuts. On January 10 the longboat set sail. Later, Morrison, worrying that the boat might not have survived recent bad weather, decided to build a schooner. The carpenter had saved a few tools, although as Humphrey remarked: "As a Dutch [German] carpenter's tools are generally in poor condition, so these tools came fully up to the rule." For a grindstone, a piece of a sort of sandstone was mounted in a framework, and turned by a windmill devised by the carpenter.

A wormy fifty-five-foot drift log provided the keel and garboards. Frame stock was derived from breadfruit trees. All island material had to be paid for with articles of clothing, with the king soon rejoicing in a heavy overcoat and a sou'wester. *Rainier's* wreckage had been reduced to but some bulwarks and part of the deck; decking was laboriously ripped into planking stock with two saws, one broken in half and both dull. Deck spikes were used for fastenings. After seventeen days the frame was ready for planking—at this juncture, for reasons known only to them, the natives burned the remaining wreckage.

On March 13, after fifty-two days, the schooner, christened *Ujea*, forty-one feet on the keel and painted with an island dye, was launched. *Ujea* proved a handy sailer. Provisioned with coconuts, she was ready to sail by March 15, the same day that the steward, who had never recovered from his illness, died and was buried. The captain's health had also been fast failing, and he had largely lost the ability to speak. He decided to command the schooner himself, the quicker to receive medicine. His plan was to sail to the island of Jaluit, some 300 miles away, where the king had assured him there were "white kanaka," i.e., white men, presumably at a trading station.

The men who had departed in the longboat had had a very difficult time of it, but did reach civilization.[14] Mr. Drohan's intention had been to reach the island of Oulan, 300 miles away. Early on, the boat was nearly capsized by a squall, drenching the stores with salt water—the coconuts then began to rot and the canned goods to rust and burst. The only drink was sour coconut milk, and severely debilitating diarrhea set in. After twelve days they raised the island, and also spied the royals of a ship rising up from below the horizon. And the sickest sailor, Peter Dawson, died.

The approaching ship proved to be the iron bark *Catalina*, of London, Captain Williams, with coal from New South Wales for Saigon. Drohan wrote: "If ever true and honest hearts beat in sailors' breasts, it was in those of Captain Williams, his officers and crew. . . ." Williams, an old stager, said that if they had landed on Oulan Island they would have been killed by the natives. For four days the bark attempted to beat against the strong trade winds to reach Ujea, but her bottom was so foul that Captain Williams concluded that it might take her six months to do so, and turned-to for Saigon, arriving thirty-eight days later, on March 3.

News that some survivors of *Rainier* had been landed at Saigon was soon wired to Bath, but without details. Captain Jarvis Patten guessed that the rest of the crew was marooned on Ujea Island, and urged Sam Sewall to request that a U.S. warship be dispatched there. On March 6 Sam added an odd "by-the-way" to the end of a letter to Arthur: "I don't believe a request of that kind would diminish the uncertainty. The captain's family are nearly wild with anxiety about them & suppose them among savages, etc., and with no way of reaching the mainland."

There was no American consul at Saigon, but the British consul procured passage for the longboat's crew to Hong Kong on a steamer. Captain Williams paid their fares, in return for which Drohan gave him the longboat. Word was wired from Hong Kong to the sloop-of-war USS *Essex*, stationed at Canton, which arrived at Hong Kong on March 4. With Drohan aboard, the ship proceeded to Nagasaki for stores, and on March 14 set out for the Marshalls, 1,500 miles away.[15]

The schooner *Ujea*, meanwhile, departed her birth island with three cheers. So fully loaded was she with coconuts for stores, and oil tins for trade, that half the crew—we are never told exactly how many were aboard—had to sleep on deck, while the smell of kerosene made a berth below no great treat, either. Three of the company were Will Jackson, a smart young Mainer; the king's son—the prince—as interpreter; and the prince's servant.

Captain Morrison soon fell so ill that he could not sit up, and Jackson navigated by his instructions. After about five days the Bonam islands were raised. On one, the island of Jaluit, there was indeed a white settlement, including a German trading station, two saloons—"which the crew soon found, when their happiness was complete"—and an agency of a San Francisco trading firm.

The American consul, a German—"a fat, pussy [pusillanimous], Dutchman"—an unprincipled opportunist, immediately attempted to seize the schooner. The men were boarded in a hotel/saloon kept by a hospitable outlaw named Negro Tom. Morrison was required to mortgage the schooner and its cargo, chronometer, sextant, and even his clothes, to pay off the sailors. All appeals to the consul for assistance in the rescue of the people on Ujea were rejected; the many schooners calling were in the business of trading, not rescuing castaways.

Their luck changed with the arrival of the schooner *Lotus*, formerly a San Francisco yacht, owned by King John of the island of Alni Lap Lap. Commanded by the king's son, she had come to obtain medicine for the ailing king. A charter was arranged, and after delivering the medicine, the schooner, with Will Jackson in command of a crew of natives, was to sail for Ujea. But nothing was ever that simple in the islands, and only after many complications would Jackson eventually reach Ujea, albeit while being imprisoned below decks by the crew. When released, he was met by the king, now rejoicing in the uniform of an American naval officer, showing that *Rainier*'s people had been rescued.

The king, accompanied by all the able-bodied islanders, left aboard the schooner to visit King John, taking all their canoes with them and leaving Jackson on the island. After an interminable three weeks with nothing to read but an old almanac, Jackson was sprung from his prison by a trading schooner, eventually reaching Jaluit on May 11. On July 31 he sailed for San Francisco aboard the schooner *Klaluk*, arriving there on September 20.

Six months earlier, the searching *Essex* had been unable to find Ujea at its supposed location. Instead, she eventually came upon the island of Lae, which Mr. Drohan recognized, having been told by the king of Ujea to avoid its cannibals. Drohan knew that Ujea lay thirty miles to the west of Lae, and that is where they found it, along with the thankful remaining *Rainier* survivors.

When *Essex* steamed into the harbor at Jaluit looking for Captain Morrison, he had been reduced to a mere skeleton, unable to speak. "Father and daughter were clasped in each other's arms, and as Mrs. H. led him to a chair in the commander's cabin, many an eye was wet with tears. . . . " *Essex* arrived at Yokohama on May 5; from there the *Rainier* refugees took a steamer to San Francisco.

Although the crews' wages stopped when the ship was wrecked, Captain Morrison earned $525, at the rate of $150 a month, for "attending to wreckage." The proceeds from selling the schooner *Ujea* ($330) and other salvaged items at Jaluit amounted to only $435, which was considerably less than Captain Morrison had had to pay out for various purposes. On August 5, Sam Sewall wrote his Uncle Arthur:

> Captain S. H. Morrison has requested me to make a settlement with him saying he wishes to square up for his interest in [the new ship] *John Rosenfeld*. I have delayed doing so having ascertained that he received a portion of his funds after ship was lost from sale of the schooner he built from ship's material. . . . It strikes me that he should have credited ship with every cent rec'd from any source except his own property.

Relocating to the Santa Clara Valley, California, Captain Morrison recovered his health. Omar Humphrey wrote: "And here, surrounded by his family, contented and happy, the captain of the ill-fated ship *Rainier* has cast his anchor in a peaceful haven."

Alas, he should have remained at anchor. In February 1890 Captain Morrison relieved Captain Dexter Whitmore of the fine Bath ship *Parker M. Whitmore* at Tacoma, taking her to Avonmouth with grain, and departing from there for Philadelphia. On August 25 Captain Parker M. Whitmore, the ship's managing owner, received the following telegram from Lockport, Nova Scotia: "Ship *P. M. Whitmore* hopeless wreck on Arnold's Rocks; are stripping, landing at Lewis Head. S. M. Morrison."

To the credit of Morrison and the officers and crew of *Rainier*, there is no record of any discord. The sagas of the two boats demonstrated good seamanship, great ingenuity, and admirable fortitude. With hindsight it is easy to criticize Morrison for carrying too much sail after determining that his chart was inaccurate, but a shipmaster paralyzed by every risk would make very slow passages. The Sewalls' ships *Granger* and *Iroquois*, both under good masters, were lost on tropical reefs, one charted and one not, when luck ran out.

In 1945 Richard Hallet, a Mainer visiting Ujea, asked the islanders, through an interpreter, if anyone remembered the wreck of the ship *Rainier*. One old man stepped forth. "What was the name of the captain's daughter," Hallet asked, thinking of catching him in a lie. The old man thought a moment and said, " Emma." Mrs. Mark Sewall, who knew Emma when both met at San Francisco as ship captains' daughters, recalled many years later, "She was a harum-scarum sea-girl, good fun, with light hair and freckles—and plenty of courage."[16]

What follows is a curious, if very mature letter, dated November 1875, from Edward's twelve-year-old son Ned, written while apparently visiting relatives in Boston, addressed to "Dear Uncle." Any further comments would be speculative.

We have a change in the atmosphere here today. The ground is covered with a thin white covering of snow, a gentle reminder of what's coming. . . . Mother is washing and living on wishes and hopes that it will clear off so her clothing can dry. It is quite a matter of doubt if Sunday can repair the hard words to be said by the women of East Boston against the weather today. . . . Galen's washing was in a wretched condition but will be clean before you and Aunt see it and it will help stop scandal as the help in Bath love to gossip. I have the numbers of the pawn tickets now in Galen's possession, the first to be redeemed is on Dec. 5th. . . . I can advise you about them. I presume if he has lost the ticket for his watch he should give you the proper notice. The diamond stud pawned for twenty-five Dollars.

Arthur Staples, editor of the *Lewiston Evening Journal*, who, like Doc Briry, played with the Sewall cousins, recalled: "[Ned] Sewall was a terrifying sort of person . . . no one knew where or how he would break out into some dare-devil stunt or some instance of bullying. . . . He was a strange lad—many things lovable: all-powerful in physical strength; tall; raven-black hair; handsome in his way."[17]

In December 1877 we find Ned, evidently a handful at home, farmed out to his Uncle Frank in Ohio, enrolled in Urbana University—then a small Swedenborgian academy—of which the Reverend Frank was president. Ned, Frank wrote his brother Edward, was using tobacco, could not be trusted with money, and was "very impulsive and lazy and restless and fond of taking his own way."

In March Frank wrote that Ned had spent twice as much money as he received for allowance. In November—after again dunning Edward for payment of long past-due bills for tuition and board—Frank wrote of Ned that money was still "a temptation for misuse. . . . He must learn at some time that there is a limit to disobedience." By the following January Ned had left Urbana, and Frank wrote Edward: "You may inform Ned that I cannot commit to act as his agent in the redemption of his pawned watch: it is a kind of business that I do not engage in." After Edward's death in March 1879, Ned, along with his siblings, became, in effect, wards of their Uncle Arthur, who took his responsibility very seriously. Over many years none would receive more patient forbearance and assistance than would Ned.

Two weeks after Edward's death Ned left New York aboard the ship *Eric the Red*, Captain Zack Allen. We last saw Zack Allen, it will be recalled, at San Francisco, where he was fined ten dollars for his role in the troubles aboard the ship *Matterhorn*. In 1874 he had been given command of the Sewalls' ship *Humboldt*; in 1876 he was promoted to the larger *Eric the Red*. In September Captain Allen, writing from Yokohama, noted that the "two boys" were both good and smart, although Ned "would never follow the sea."

Returning home in April 1880, Ned joined the new ship *Thomas M. Reed* at Bath, and sailed to Baltimore with her, from whence she was to depart on her maiden voyage. A letter to the Sewalls from the *Reed's* Captain Abel Work at Baltimore ends with: "Edward [Ned] Sewall is waiting for a letter from home but tells [me] he intends to go to New York and go with Capt. Allen." On June 10, 1880, the ship *Eric the Red*, with Ned as third mate, departed New York for Melbourne, loaded with case oil and a mixed cargo including pianos, toys, sewing machines, tobacco, and items intended for display at an exposition in Melbourne.

Eric the Red ran her "easting down" under nearly bare poles, with decks awash, before a series of strong gales. She was but eighty-five days out—near clipper time— when, on a moonlit night the light at Cape Otway, marking the approach to Melbourne, was sighted, and shortly afterwards, all went to smash when she piled up on Otway Reef, three miles north of her presumed position. Zack was said to have been an able navigator, and his error was blamed on a low-lying haze. The ship broke up in a heavy swell in about fifteen minutes. Three men drowned. Ned, a strong swimmer, clung to his jettisoned sea chest until transferring to more substantial flotsam. Twenty-three survivors were picked up from floating wreckage by a small steamer that happened to be nearby.[18]

Ned came by steamer to San Francisco, where, in November, he joined Captain Joe Sewall in the ship *Oriental*—this was Joe's first voyage in his first command—evidently as third mate. Joe wrote to Arthur that he would "try to have a care of him in port as well as at sea." In April Captain Joe wrote Arthur from Hull, England: "Ned is . . . smart but I think lacks stability. He can if he chooses make a first class officer. He wants to go home but I am trying to reason him out of it. He thinks I keep him too short on money but I think he spends it foolishly and want him to save some."

After having given Ned money for his ticket home from Liverpool, Joe was not pleased to discover Ned still in town the following morning in the company of a woman, and having already spent half his money. Joe wrote Arthur: "I personally saw that he left the city for L-pool. I did not dare to trust him with money so I wrote Mr. Russell [the Sewalls' Liverpool broker and agent] to buy his tickets and pay his hotel bill and I would repay him."

In August Ned left for San Francisco planning to join Zack Allen aboard his new command, the ship *Harvester*, but arrived too late. Brother Oscar, now working in 'Frisco for Williams, Dimond & Co., thought that city a bad place for Ned—a concern reminiscent of young William Sewall, Jr.'s advice to his father not to let his brother Edward go to gold-rush San Francisco lest he be "ruined altogether." Ned then rejoined Captain Joe, now in command of the ship *El Capitan*.

In January 1883 Joe wrote home from Portland, Oregon, that charges of assault had been preferred "against Mr. Sewall, the steward, and myself." Following the dropping of these charges Ned left *El Capitan* for employment at Foster's chandlery in San Francisco, a position that Oscar had found for him. He quit soon after without informing Oscar, whereupon. Oscar wrote Arthur: "There are some things [about Ned] which I can explain better when I see you, but give me considerable anxiety."

Oscar thought that Ned would be best off sailing with Captain Jim Murphy, and Arthur evidently agreed, because the next word we have of him is from Murphy aboard the ship *W. F. Babcock* at Liverpool in January 1884. Having arrived at Liverpool after a long passage, Murphy wrote: "I like Ned very much. He is smart and ambitious and learning all about a ship except the most necessary part of navigation and figures these he would learn better as mate. I trust he will continue in the ship." However, £25 for a ticket to bring Ned home was wired to Liverpool in March. In July Captain James Baker, aboard the new ship *John Rosenfeld*, at Baltimore to load coal for San Francisco, upon learning that Ned would join his ship as second mate, wrote to Arthur (even when addressed to "Arthur Sewall & Co.," Baker's letters were always for Arthur):

I will take him with the greatest pleasure & I will do all that lays in my power to make a man of him. . . . The greatest mistake he ever made in his life was when he went with Allen. A shipmaster that would take a young man as Ned was then into the lowest & vilest of dens is not worthy of the name of Capt. That was a common thing for Allen to do, they would go off & drink & whore together. That I know to be a fact. It was then the first seeds of vice & intemperance were sown & Ned must have decision of character enough to stamp out the evil. . . . Whatever nautical instruments he requires I will get for him rather than let him have the money.

When the *Rosenfeld* arrived at San Francisco in January 1885, Captain Baker wrote Arthur:

Ned is the only good officer I have had. I like him very much & the only fault I find he likes to thump sailors too well for little or no reason, but he will soon learn better. . . . I have sent him away for a few days. . . . I thought it best for him to keep shady for a few days. Do not worry about him. I think I have the upper hand of him at last.

From his hiding place in the shade, the Auzerais House in San Jose, Ned wrote his Uncle Arthur that it had been a pleasant passage, that Captain Baker was the finest man he had been with yet, and his family was also very pleasant. With a little more practice he would feel capable of navigating by himself. He had "had a little trouble coming out" and was staying in the country for a few days until the thing blew over. "Well Uncle, I have been pretty wild the last few years and have troubled you a good deal but this passage has straightened me out and I am going for it in earnest this time." Upon his return to the ship, Ned was promoted to first mate, and Captain Baker soon wrote that Ned was doing "first rate. The only trouble I find he will spend his money. . . ." Several days later: "I think he will turn out yet the *smartest of the boys, no offense.*" The *Rosenfeld* then made a 118-day passage to Liverpool. In July, just before the ship's

The family of the late Edward Sewall, likely in 1886. Standing at far left is Samuel Swanton Sewall; his wife, Marcia Houghton, holding their son Edward Houghton, born in 1884, sits in front of him. Standing next to Sam is Oscar Trufant Sewall, of San Francisco. The woman standing in front of Oscar, displaying uneasy body language, is presumably Susan Baker Sewall, who in 1886 married Captain Edward Robinson Sewall—"Ned"—who is standing to her left. At far right are Mark Warren Sewall and Frederic Norris Sewall. Frank Lewis Sewall sits at lower left. Blanche A. Sewall, the youngest child, sits at center foreground. Their mother "Sade"—Sarah Elizabeth Swanton Sewall—sits at right, in front of Mark. The elderly lady is probably Sade's mother. MAINE MARITIME MUSEUM

departure from Liverpool, Baker reported having had crew trouble, and having fired the second mate, whom he blamed. He wrote Arthur the following day:

> Took a few riggers [along] to see ship safe over the bar. After pilot left us & ship well out, I called the boys aft & let them know the ship had but one master & gave them five minutes to make up their minds whether to go to work or have a free fight. Within the time specified they came to the wise conclusion to go to work & behave like men. . . . Mr. Sewall is & has been all I could wish. He wanted to have a good fight today, but was disappointed. The only trouble I have with him now is spending his money.

Looking east across Washington Street from the grounds of Arthur Sewall's mansion, likely in the 1890s. Mrs. Edward Sewall's house is at center, behind the tree. It was built as the residence of shipbuilder Johnson Rideout, who, in his day, was fully as well-known as was William D. Sewall. It was purchased by Edward Sewall in the early 1870s when Arthur and he moved from their modest adjoining residences at nearby 1065 and 1071 Washington Street, respectively. (Bath street addresses were numbered in the 1880s.) Sam Sewall later built a shingle-style house directly to the south of his mother's house, while Mark Sewall purchased the small Greek Revival house pictured at left. All three houses still exist. In the right-hand background the masts of a three-masted schooner mark the site of the old Rideout shipyard, later Goss & Sawyer and subsequent iterations, located north of the Sewall shipyard. On the horizon, the Woolwich shore lies across Long Reach. MAINE MARITIME MUSEUM

In November, from San Francisco, Captain Baker wrote Arthur: "I have had a poor miserable lot of men & petty officers. Mr. Sewall has been the only one I could place my confidence in." And a month later: "I was sorry to learn the other day that [Ned] had sent to you & had received credit for $500. What the boy wants of so much money is more than I or any one else can tell . . . it seems to have been born in him." Oscar, however, found Ned to be a changed man. He was spending all his free time with the Bakers, and he now deserved a ship of his own: "He has had a hard life and one different from the rest of us and I want to see him at the top of it. He is very anxious to be married [to Captain Baker's daughter] Susie when he returns from Nanaimo."

As will be described in due course, the *Rosenfeld* was wrecked departing Nanaimo. Ned returned to San Francisco in March, having been employed salvaging—called "wrecking"—gear from the *Rosenfeld*, and promptly went on a spree. Captain Baker urged Arthur to overlook it, explaining that Ned had fallen in with a "bad set" and was now very sorry. Of the upcoming marriage, Baker, who had lost all his savings with the loss of the *Rosenfeld*, wrote: "I meant to have done more for Susie than I am able to do now. He must take her as she is & I think she will make him a good wife, at least I know she will make him an economical one & help him save his money. The step they are about to take I trust will be the turning point in his life. . . ."

For wedding gifts, Arthur asked Oscar to authorize Ned to wire for $500, and to spend $125 for a gift for Susie in Emma's name. Oscar purchased a pair of diamond earrings. The couple honeymooned at Monterey.

I am the greatest sufferer of all

Four years before finding Captain Baker in command of the *John Rosenfeld* we saw him decide to "stop" at his Cape Cod farm while George Goodwin took the ship *Sterling* to San Francisco. Baker had expected to have the option of returning to the command of *Sterling*, but this was upset by the surprise sale of the ship to John Rosenfeld.

Captain Baker then believed that he would be given command of the Sewalls' newest ship, *Iroquois*, but, despite some backing and filling by Arthur Sewall, that was not to be. He was then promised the Sewalls' next new ship, but, as it happened, she was sold while on the stocks to sail under the management of New York ship owner William H. Starbuck. As the *Henry Villard*—Villard, a German immigrant, had secured control of the Northern Pacific Railroad, then under construction—she was to be employed carrying rails, locomotives, and so on, to the West Coast.[19]

Captain Baker, taking command of the *Villard*, took some pleasure in writing Arthur that he was to receive $175 a month salary, plus the right to take his wife with him at no cost, and also to keep all the profits from the slop chest. But he was not content for long—he wanted, he wrote Arthur, to be invested in a new ship. By having taken the *Villard*, Baker missed out on having the *Rainier*. In 1884 his wishes were finally answered with command of the "big ship," the *John Rosenfeld*.

On February 25, 1884, Arthur, in Boston, wrote Sam to say that he had sold John Rosenfeld 1/8 of the ship then being built, at fifty dollars per ton. The ship was to be named the *John Rosenfeld*, and was to be the pioneer ship of the new Rosenfeld Line to operate between New York and San Francisco in opposition to Sutton's Line. One month earlier, at least seventeen ships were either loading "on the line" at New York for San Francisco, or were on the passage. All but one was Bath-built, with ten owned by I. F. Chapman & Co. or Flint & Co.[20] (As it happened, none was one of Arthur Sewall & Co.'s fifteen ships, although seven were in passage from San Francisco to Queenstown, Liverpool, or Nanaimo.)

In November 1884, at his Bath yard, John McDonald would launch the *Henry B. Hyde*, 2,580 tons, the "monarch of all Maine ships," for Flint & Co. An incomparable vessel in all respects, the *Hyde* would put all other ships built at Bath in that notable year, including the Sewalls' big *Rosenfeld* and I. F. Chapman's superb *A. G. Ropes*, in the shade.

The *Rosenfeld*, at 2,374 tons, most certainly a notable creation, was scheduled to be launched in late morning, Saturday, June 21.[21] Three or four thousand spectators, many of them excursionists who arrived by train or steamer, gathered under the unusually

The ship John Rosenfield *ready to launch. It appears that economics trumped aesthetics in her design.* MAINE MARITIME MUSEUM

hot morning sun to see her slide. By 10:30 the sliding ways had been wedged up and the keel blocks knocked out, but the huge ship, towering over the crowd, refused to budge, the tallow lubricant having melted and been absorbed by the timbers of the newly built ways. (It was not reported if the tallow had been mixed with flax seed, a traditional measure for hot-weather launchings.)

Tugs, jacks, and rams were of no avail. The tide had been lost, and the weary, sweating shipwrights, reinforced by men from other yards, shored up and blocked the ship again, and added new tallow to the ways. That night, with her lofty masts disappearing into the darkness, and her towering white-leaded topsides reflecting the moonlight, the great ship was again wedged up to the thunderous volleys of the coordinated blows from the two lines of maul-wielding men laboring under her bilges, reportedly working by the light of hundreds of lanterns. At ten o'clock the *Rosenfeld* finally relaxed her grip, and, with a rush, slid into the Kennebec, leaving a great hole in the night. For those who had waited up to see her go, it was a night to remember.

Launching a big ship was an engineering feat fraught with danger and the specter of costly failure, or even disaster, and no one could have been more relieved to see her go than master builder Mallett. And in the aftermath of the loss of *Rainier*, the launching was surely a satisfaction to the Sewalls.[22] Yet no one could have been more pleased than Captain Jim Baker.

1886. Sightseers aboard the wrecked ship John Rosenfeld, *hard atop a reef in Georgia Strait, British Columbia. A steamer is tied up to her starboard side; the reef was at a depth of twenty-one feet when the ship struck. First Mate Ned Sewall was in charge of stripping the wreck of as much salable material as possible before it was auctioned off.* MAINE MARITIME MUSEUM

On July 4 the *John Rosenfeld* departed for Baltimore in ballast with a crew of Bath riggers serving as "runners." A rare summer nor'west gale blew her off the coast, and on July 21, when finally towing up Chesapeake Bay, Captain Baker wrote Arthur: "In regards to the good ship & indeed she is *good* she works like a *yacht* & sails *like the wind*. Made 12 knots with yards braced sharp to backstays." From Baltimore the *Rosenfeld* carried coal to San Francisco, then wheat to Liverpool, and then more coal to San Francisco, arriving there in November 1885.

Captain Baker had by now concluded that the ship, when loaded, would not move in light wind, the most common complaint of Sewall captains. "We have seen a large number of ships during the passage, but with no exception [in light wind] they could all get the best of us." Off Cape Horn Flint's *St. Stephen* had taken but ten hours from first appearing astern to disappearing ahead. But with a "full topgallant breeze" the *Rosenfeld* could turn the tables on them, and she performed admirably in heavy weather. And her hull was *too* tight, which made the bilges stink.

Baker had never before sailed on a ship fitted with a wheelhouse: "I can truly say that I like them very much, not only in one respect, but in all. Better steering especially in heavy weather, no trouble with binnacle lights. Lots of other advantages and I should put one in the next ship by all means." Baker's reference to the binnacle light is interesting, given that one argument forwarded by Britons for not putting wheelhouses on their vessels was the concern that if the binnacle lamps blew out when the ship was running before a gale the helmsman would be unable to feel the direction of the wind, possibly resulting in a fatal broaching-to.

From San Francisco the *Rosenfeld* sailed to Nanaimo Island, British Columbia, to load coal. Running to Nanaimo was a common employment for ships awaiting higher grain rates at San Francisco.²³ Although there was small profit in the business, and considerable hazard, a ship so employed did not dry out as did ships anchored for long periods in San Francisco Bay. On February 22, 1886, Captain Baker wrote Arthur from Port Townsend, Washington Territory:

Why should it ever have been for me to have to write what I have to communicate to you of the loss of the *John Rosenfeld*. I am in a state of mind now almost bordering on insanity. I am not fit to write a letter to you, must excuse me, but to begin.

When heading down Georgia Strait towing behind the tug *Tacoma*, with 3,905 tons of coal in her, just before daybreak and at the top of a spring tide, the *Rosenfeld* had been run onto a known reef. With the falling tide the ship was bilged, and was rendered a total loss. The tug had been far off course, Baker reported, her skipper in his cabin asleep. The mate, in the steam-heated pilothouse, had likely dozed off. Aboard the *Rosenfeld*, mate Ned Sewall had been on watch. Although he may have just returned to the poop from a trip to the galley, he was held blameless by Baker because his orders had been to follow the tug.

The *Rosenfeld* disaster was eerily similar to the loss of the Sewalls' fine ship *Thrasher* in 1880, which was towed onto an unknown reef—still called Thrasher Rock—when departing Nanaimo. The ship was under tow by two British Columbian tugs, and Arthur resolutely fought the case all the way to London, finally losing on the questionable grounds that there should have been a pilot aboard the ship. Family members were said to have lost heavily.

The interests of the partners in the *Rosenfeld* were at least partially covered by insurance, and her loss did not keep Arthur, as imperturbable as ever, from enjoying his travels with Emma and Will in California. On February 27 he wrote Sam from San Diego: "Have had a splendid trip so far, the only drawback has been the *Rosenfeld* loss, but we can bear it & it's no use to worry over losses beyond our control." After a brief visit to San Francisco, he wrote:

> Mr. Rosenfeld's loss does not improve any, expenses will be large. . . . Left the whole business with him and Oscar. Tug has been appraised at $24,000 & possibly we may recover this amount, but the expenses will take 25 to 50 percent of it. It's a hard loss for us, but it would have been much worse if it embarrassed us, but I don't see that it will. If Baker is free from blame I think Mr. R. will join us in getting up another ship for him. Ned I am sorry not to see. I think he had better be married after he gets thru with the wreck & then we must give him a ship. . . .

After a lengthy trial, the tug was held to be at fault, but its owners were only liable under the law for the value of the tug, set at $10,000, and $12,000 in costs.[24] Captain Baker had no insurance on his master's share; the high cost of premiums having led him to gamble with his life's savings.[25] He wrote Arthur:

> I am the greatest sufferer of all. What little I had is now swept by the board in one fell swoop. Not a dollar left, & what my wife & girls will do I know not. It is hard to think of it & all through no carelessness of mine. . . . I never in all my life knew what trouble was before. . . . When I turned my back on my ship I knew she must lay her bones there, one of the finest ships afloat. It was too cruel.

In January 1888 Captain Baker wrote Arthur from San Francisco: "You will doubtless be somewhat surprised when I tell you I leave for New York on Sunday 16th to take command of ship *C. F. Sargent.* Mr. Rosenfeld has purchased the ship on purpose to give me immediate employment & when shipping interest improves, we will see what can be done towards building another J. R. or one like her."[26]

When Captain Baker came east to take command of the *C. F. Sargent*, his daughter Susie, Mrs. Ned Sewall, was heading west to join Ned in his first command, *Solitaire.* Captain Baker persuaded the officials to stop the trains when they met, and he was given a few minutes to rush through the cars to find his astonished daughter, exchange a few words, and then rejoin his train.[27]

When the *Sargent* was subsequently sold, and Captain Baker moved on to the ship *Commodore,* Mrs. Baker and Kate returned to Cape Cod, having not been home for four years. Rufus Baker, who had served under his father as mate of the *Henry Villard,* succeeded in the command of *Commodore.* Rufus soon left *Commodore* to be first officer of the steamer *Advance.* In January 1892, at the port of Bahia, Brazil, Rufus, a highly respected mariner, died of yellow fever at just thirty years of age.

The hull of the *Rosenfeld,* stripped of everything of value, remained largely intact until March 1891, when it finally slipped off the reef and sank.

1. From Goodwin's manuscript autobiography, written after his retirement, in the library of the Maine Maritime Museum, a gift from Dr. Irwin Abrams. *Louisiana* belonged to the Houghtons. Her captain was Cyrus Oliver.

2. Freda Morrill Abrams, *Tall Ships of Newburyport* (Yellow Springs, OH: Free Wind Press, 1989). This book contains Goodwin's autobiography up to the time of his joining *Sterling*.

3. Mildred P. Paine, *Harwich Men of the Sea* (Harwich MA: Harwich Historical Commission, 1977), p. 39.

4. George Goodwin's autobiography in the library of the Maine Maritime Museum.

5. Chainplates were metal straps bolted to the side of the ship that anchored the side stays of the masts. Chain bobstays stayed the bowsprit from the stem. Chain "back ropes," otherwise known as "martingale backstays," stayed the dolphin striker, or martingale boom, from the bow. Goodwin might well have added "Thomaston" to his list of hard-case hails, and "Bluenose" ships (primarily from Nova Scotia, but from New Brunswick as well) were reputed to feature the starvation diet of a British ship with the harsh discipline of an American ship. Such a deal!

6. In his autobiography, written many years later, Goodwin confused this incident with a another hard time met off Cape Horn. Thirty feet of bulwarks, a skylight, and both quarter boats were lost on that second occasion, but no men were washed overboard. In 1888 rats gnawed through the water closet pipe of the ship *Occidental* and there was three feet of water in the pump well when it was discovered.

7. In his autobiography, Goodwin wrote that Rosenfeld did not charge extra for Goodwin's wife's board, because he was not "keeping a boardinghouse," and because "she will keep you straight. But do not forget to take along plenty of good things for her to eat." However, in Goodwin's first letters to Arthur after the change of ownership, Goodwin wondered why Rosenfeld would not allow him to take his wife, but his wife soon did sail with him again, presumably at no cost.

8. When one of their later donkey engine–equipped schooners had a broken engine, the captain was allowed to sign on one additional sailor—presumably a very mighty man.

9. References to the Keeley Cure often surface in the Sewall Family Papers. The so-called Keeley Cure for addictions, involving the injection of gold chloride, was the proprietary treatment devised by an Illinois doctor and promoter that achieved widespread popularity before eventually being exposed as a hoax.

10. Bangor *Industrial Journal*, 23 January, 1887. Ninety-eight were American, eighty-six British, forty-five Italian, nine German, five Austrian, three Dutch, and two Swedish. The separate North Atlantic "barreled oil" trade, carrying barreled crude and also refined oil to Europe, and returning with empty barrels, gave a second life to many older and smaller American-built square-riggers, called "Petroleum Klippers" by their proud German owners and captains. Many Canadian and Norwegian square-riggers were also employed in the trade.

11. Frederick C. Matthews, *American Merchant Ships, 1850–1900* (Salem, MA: Marine Research Society, 1930), p.253–56.

12. O. J. H.(Omar J. Humphrey), *Wreck of the Rainier* (Portland, ME: W. H. Stevens & Co., 1897). See also Matthews, Series 1, pp. 254–55.

13. Humphrey, *Wreck of the Rainier*, p. 29.

14. Humphrey, p. 125 *et al.* Also, from an interview in an unidentified clipping.

15. In May, when the *Catalina* arrived at Hong Kong, the boat was auctioned off and the proceeds, $95.00, were remitted to Arthur Sewall & Co.; presumably Captain Williams was reimbursed by the U.S. consul, Colonel J. S. Mosby, famed Confederate raider, said to have so many scars that he couldn't walk in a straight line. Mosby became a friend of President Grant and a rabid Republican after the war. As consul, he was notorious among seamen—especially black

seamen—for his dismissal of their complaints of shipboard abuse. He much enjoyed receiving the hospitality of the cabins of the many American ships that called at the port.

16. Undated, unidentified clipping of column by Richard Hallet, see n12, p. 175.

17. Undated clipping, probably from 1931.

18. An interview with W. A. Paul of Auburn, Maine, who had been ship's boy, may be found in the *Lewiston Journal Magazine*, March 18, 1931. See also Hennessy notes at library of the Maine Maritime Museum. The wreck story is also in the *American Sentinel*, October 21, 1880. A sign regarding *Eric the Red's* anchor, on display today at the base of the lighthouse at Cape Otway, states (erroneously, of course) that it "belonged to a clipper captained by the famous Viking Eric the Red." A section of a mast is also on display. My thanks to Peter Beeston for this intelligence.

19. The ship *William H. Starbuck*, built in 1882 by the Sewall yard's neighbor, Goss, Sawyer & Packard was also intended for this service. The Dearborns were evidently also owners, along with Starbuck and Villard. The *Villard's* history is confusing. Frederick Matthews wrote that she later came under the management of George Dearborn, although documents in the Sewall Family Papers would indicate that the Sewalls took her over.

20. From Bath *Independent* in the Bangor *Industrial Journal*, February 1, 1884.

21. An article from the San Francisco *Chronicle* quoted in the Bangor *Industrial Journal*, September 18, 1885, claimed that thirty-seven American "hardwood" ships carried 3,387 lbs. of grain to the registered ton, against 3,425 for thirty-nine iron ships. Nine Nova Scotian "softwood" ships carried 3,389 pounds, and seven English composite (metal-framed, wood-planked) ships carried 3,107 pounds. However, the *John Rosenfeld* topped them all, at 3,559 pounds.

22. In addition to the *Rosenfeld*, the Sewall fleet then consisted of the ships *Undaunted, Occidental, Harvester, Reaper, Indiana, Challenger, Chesebrough, Bullion, Solitaire, Thomas M. Reed, Iroquois, W. F. Babcock,* and the schooners *Satilla, Nora Bailey, Alice Archer, Belle Higgins,* and *Blanche Allen*.

23. Since Nanaimo was a foreign port, registered American ships were not penalized for engaging in domestic coasting for more than the limit of two months a year, as they would have been if carrying coal from a mine in Washington Territory. The penalty was a cancellation of, and payment for, the "rebated" tariff on imported materials (i.e., metal fittings, also copper sheathing) used in their construction, less depreciation. The intercoastal trade was exempted from the two-month limit.

24. These figures are from Matthews, *American Merchant Ships*, pp 186–87.

25. On August 28, 1888, Baker, having just reviewed the firm's final accounting with him, wrote: "In looking over it I see you have charged full interest on my notes 6 mos. & 1 year with [W.R.] Grace [& Co.], which is *not right*. You had in hand Aug.10, 1887, more than enough in my account to cancel these notes. . . . Again I see $830.16 amt. due underwriters from salvage as agreed. I want some enlightenment on that charge. I was not aware that I had any insurance on the J. R. That amt. of money would have insured my full 1/8 interest one year at least & cannot see the justice of that charge. No doubt you can enlighten me."

26. Although built in 1874 at Yarmouth, Maine, and no spring chicken, the *Sargent*, 1,704 tons, was a handsome and able ship with many good years left in her. As a favor to Rosenfeld, Captain Baker reluctantly transferred to the ship *Commodore*, built at Yarmouth, Maine, in 1879. She was said to have been so heavily constructed that only bulk cargoes could be carried profitably; she could not carry enough bagged sugar to keep from being crank. Matthews, *American Merchant Ships*, pp. 77–80.

27. Mildred P. Paine, *Harwich Men of the Sea* (Harwich, MA: Harwich Historical Commission, 1977) p. 43.

PART EIGHT

We meet the slippery Charlie Russell, U.S. consul, and learn something about Arthur Sewall's own shady business dealings. More sailor trouble. And we meet Arthur and Emma's oldest son, Harold (known as Harold Marsh), the family intellectual, and follow him to Liverpool and then to Samoa, where he becomes famous. Ned Sewall becomes captain of a square-rigger, and a schooner captain dies. And we learn of Arthur's career as railroad president.

Another Selection of Interesting Letters

To Arthur Sewall from his Bath friend Francis B. Torrey,[1] visiting in San Francisco, January 10, 1883:

> Your letter of the 3rd inst. is at hand and here let me say that in future if you would make words a little plainer and not leave so much to be inferred from straight marks you would save your friends considerable agony in trying to read your letters. You just imagine my agony after trying to read your letter until the pain in my eyes caused me to go to Chesebrough for help, to have him read.[2]

To Arthur Sewall & Co. from Captain Thomas P. Gibbons, aboard the fine three-skysail Bath ship *John R. Kelly*, lying at Port Costa, California, on August 31, 1883:

> A few days ago received a letter from my son saying he had not received any remittance or account from you of schooner *Carrie Lane* & cannot express my astonishment after a vessel has been 18 months, made several voyages, and had good freights. . . . Certainly a schooner must be a hard kind of a vessel to manage. I have friends who seem to get money out of them. I . . . went into the *Lane* with the idea that I could help young men along and make something out of the investment but it seems the young men ignore me entirely and I can get no money and don't even know where I stand. . . . I must say this is a new way to me. I think I have schooner enough. . . . Sorry to be compelled to write such a

letter as this to two young men that I have such respect for.

To Arthur Sewall from Van Vleck & Co., New York, shipping and commission merchants, September 21, 1883:

> We enclose your Adams Express Co.'s receipts for 3 bbls. whiskey to your address. Instructed our truck man to deliver to Am. Ex. Co. but as he has not suppose they will connect at Boston & it will reach you via A.M. [mail].

November 25, 1883, for Arthur Sewall from Warren Littlefield, Freeport, Maine, who had sold Arthur a cow for sixty dollars:

> I called at your place the other day, to see about the cow that I sold your wife, some three weeks ago, and she told me that you would arrange about settling for her. I have talked the matter over with my folks, and the cow was just as I represented her to be, and if by changing her from Freeport to Bath, she does not give quite so large a quantity of milk for a while, I think in due time she will get contented, and with proper attention and feed, she will come up to what I have said. When she started from here, of course, the money was due. . . .

A letter from (looks like) C. W. Mann of Freeport, Maine, July 12, 1884:

> Elmer Ridley told me you are in want of a pair of Cattle. I have a pair of Ship yard Oxen 7$\frac{1}{2}$ ft. They are fat. I think as good a pair as stands in this County 5 years old. I will sell them in about a week if you want them let me know by return mail.

Cattle weight was estimated by girth (or "girt") measurement behind the shoulders. An ox who girted 7$\frac{1}{2}$ feet weighed about 1,600 pounds. The shipyard owner was responsible for providing the team and driver. Oxen were long preferred over horses for shipyard work, generally being stronger, steadier, easier to keep, and content to stand in one place, chewing cud, when not needed.

Elwell will sweat blood

Charles T. Russell of Haddam, Connecticut, was a piece of work. Formerly associated with New York–Liverpool packet lines—in 1868 he had joined the ranks of shipmasters approved by the American Shipmasters' Association, but was without a command. At some point he entered the ship brokerage business at Liverpool.3 His relationship with the Sewalls dated from at least 1874.

In 1879 Russell came to the fore during the *Tabor* case crisis—the ship *Tabor* had sunk a French bark in a collision, and initially it appeared that no Sewall ships could enter a French port without being seized. He appears to have served the Sewalls' interests energetically and well, while losing no opportunity to blow his own horn. Possibly manic, and surely short-fused, Charlie Russell was in many respects temperamentally the opposite of Arthur, yet opposites appeared to attract. Arthur maintained the friendship, addressing Russell familiarly, long after he had every reason to have ended it.

The tangled web of notes and drafts of promiscuous origin that characterized financial dealing of the day is indicated by a letter from Russell to Arthur in November 1882:

> Liverpool took up my draft your order for £2,000 due on the 30th in London and the draft on Liverpool for £1,000 is due on the 7th. Now I want to keep Sam [Russell, brother and partner] in funds till my return & want you to sell for me £2,500, sending me cheque for $5,000 so I can use it on Monday to remit them £1,000 & the balance on Friday. I am sending you one draft on Liverpool for £2,000 which I prefer you use, but in case it suits you better I send you one for £1,500 on London & one for $1,000 from Liverpool.

Russell was desperate to make money, at one point badgering Arthur to invest in a New York hotel with him. In 1883 Russell's Liverpool firm became embarrassed thanks, allegedly, to the work of an embezzling bookkeeper named McQuaid, although Arthur wondered if it was indeed all McQuaid's doing. When Russell asked Arthur for a loan of £4,000 Arthur declined and Russell responded in anger, charging, among other things, that while young Sam Sewall had been treated most kindly when he interned in Russell's office, he had treated Russell like a "brute." And more:

> You probably have forgotten that some years ago we had thousands of pounds locked up in six months' paper for your accommodation. I refer to the grain ships on your account. We paid the losses, disbursed the ships & took or drew on you for the amounts at six months, and only since 1879. You had thousands of my money locked up for your accommodation in coal cargoes. You have done me two or three favors but you have taken care to have good security in every instance. You have always professed great friendship for me, but when I wanted a friend you refused me. . . .

Russell & Co. failed. In 1885, with President Cleveland in office, Russell's Democrat friends obtained for him the office of United States consul at Liverpool, long the plum of the consular service. (Nathaniel Hawthorne was his most distinguished predecessor.) Arthur, whose influence had been critical, became one of Russell's required bondsmen, and playing tit for tat, Russell appointed Arthur's son Harold as vice consul. That the American consul in the major foreign port of call for American ships—one of whose chief functions was to aid abused American seamen—should be a man whose career had been to advance the interests of ship owners and captains, and that his vice consul should be the son of one of America's largest ship owners, were evidently not matters of concern.

An undated clipping underlined and sent home by Harold Sewall:

There is rumor in London that the appointments of some of the foreign consuls in Great Britain, including representatives of the United States, are likely to become the subject of Parliamentary "questions." . . . *One consul is known to have barely escaped* [underlining by Harold] being refused recognition by the threatened protest of the merchants of the port to which he was appointed, and the feeling is so strong against him now that he is seldom if ever seen in society, which has always been proud to receive representatives of the United States. . . .

In January 1887 Russell wrote Arthur: "I am very much disappointed in regard to your refusal to let me draw on you for $600." In July 1887 Russell wrote Arthur that he had drawn on him for £1,200, and that an increase in the "oath fee" should allow him to repay it promptly. American consuls in large ports were, by this date, paid a salary instead of subsisting on fees—Russell's salary was a hefty $6,000. Along with an expense allowance, "unofficial fees" could amount to a considerable additional sum.4 Whereas Russell had once reported to Arthur that he expected the consulate to return $25,000, by September 1888, Russell wrote that his income no longer covered his expenditures: "When I came here in 1885 I found a very lucrative office. Today a living here . . . hardly exists." It was "simply and absolutely impossible" for him to pay off Arthur or anyone else—". . . our Democratic administration [has] simply ruined the consular offices for the benefit of a few Englishmen."

In October Arthur was contacted by the treasurer of the Democratic National Committee regarding an unpaid pledge of $1,000 made by Charlie Russell, described as the "*late* [emphasis added] Consul at Liverpool." Russell's departure from office for misappropriation of consular funds led to a judgment against Arthur Sewall, as a bondsman, for $3,118.41.

In February 1889 Russell wrote Arthur from London: "Just when I hope for daylight you allow a writ to be served upon me. I am unable to pay the £100 till I get some money from New York. Your action is a terrible ending of our years of friendship." And more of the same, ending with a plea for Arthur to intercede on Russell's behalf in another legal proceeding that would "jeopardize a company that I am floating here that will enable me to get on my feet."

Yet the friendship held. In February 1891, from London, on stationery of "The District Messenger Service & News Company, Limited," Russell wrote: "In regard to my making a trip round the world with you, it will be impossible for me to do so, as I am at the head of a syndicate to bring out a French company known as the Bi-Metallic Wire for telegraph and telephone purposes. It is without doubt one of the most wonderful and useful inventions of the present day, and in my opinion will be a tremendous success." He wished Arthur to accept a syndicate share, estimated to net a profit of at least £10,000, probably £15,000. When, alas, the enterprise failed, Charlie blamed politicians.

In 1894 the relief bill—which had been Arthur's idea, and had been shepherded by political operative Joe Manley (who we will learn more about in due course)—absolving Arthur from any liability for Russell's irregularities, finally passed Congress. Manley had written Arthur in May 1889 to assure him that his wishes regarding the accounts of the Liverpool consul would be carried out.

Some Portland lawyers who did work for Arthur billed $500 for their services concerning the matter, and expressed the hope that Russell would pay the bill. But after a meeting with Russell, a lawyer wrote Arthur: "Mr. Russell has been here but I cannot do anything with him. He evidently thinks he cannot pay on account at present and I am afraid the prospect of his paying it is as remote as his visions of future wealth."

In November 1897 Charlie Russell wrote that he was a candidate for New York dock commissioner. In January 1898 he wrote Arthur asking for support for his candidacy for governor of Sailor's Snug Harbor, an institution whose huge endowment must have shimmered in Russell's dreams. Later that month Payson Tucker (former general manager of the Maine Central Railroad) wrote Arthur that the word was out that Russell had mortgaged the same piece of Connecticut property to two different parties—a "state prison job" was how Tucker phrased it.

In June 1898 Russell wrote that he and others had purchased the rights to the Rapid Steam Generator, incorporated as the National Steam Beer Pipe Cleaning Company, and were doing a good business. About this time he was also embroiled in a bitter legal battle with New York ship broker James Elwell, a former partner with Russell in the Connecticut Granite Company. After Elwell had Russell arrested and briefly imprisoned on the charge of fraud, Russell wrote Arthur: "Elwell will sweat blood before I am through with him." Russell was absolved in court.

In May 1898 Russell's daughter Matilda wrote Arthur that her father "has got to have $2,000 right off." She acknowledged that Russell owed Arthur $600 "for some lawyer," but promised that if Arthur would send the $2,000 and take her note for it, she would pay it promptly. In December 1898 Russell wrote Arthur that he had accepted the position of president and manager of the Commercial Transportation Co. at a salary of $10,000 a year. But in July 1899 he wrote:

My health has entirely broken down and I am in a critical condition from diabetes & Bright's [disease]. The doctors give me no encouragement but say I must take a sea voyage and if possible take a course at Marienbad, provided I can raise sufficient money. I propose sailing on one of the slow Hamburg steamers the 20th for Hamburg and then go on to Marienbad. I have no hope of fully recovering my health but I hope to prolong it.[5]

Friends—creditors, one would imagine—had, according to Russell, invested in a life insurance policy for him which would leave $60,000 after his death to cover his debts. But any hopes for Russell's speedy demise were dashed when, risen from near death, he returned in the pink of health, having been "cured" by Dr. Schner's miraculous electrical bath treatment. This boon to humanity Russell now intended to bring to America:

Charles T. Russell, Esq., representing a syndicate for promoting and introducing in the United States a new electrical bath treatment for the cure of all nervous diseases and particularly paralysis, Bright's and diabetes, discovered and patented in the United States by the eminent specialist Dr. Emil Schner of Carlsbad, Austria.

Charlie's plan was to set up ten demonstration baths in New York City. The procedure involved the application of both galvanic and faradic currents, taken from a 110-volt—or 220—direct current circuit, said current being sent to any organ of the human body. No details were given regarding the means by which the application of electrical current was combined with the taking of a bath.

And that was the final word heard from Charlie Russell.

We can make a lot of money

On June 18, 1883, Wayne Griswold, a dealer in English and American railroad rails, still using the letterhead of his former partnership of Griswold & Field, sent Arthur Sewall a statement regarding their joint account in the sale of ten thousand tons of steel rails to the Mexican Central Railway. Griswold's commission was $9,537.75, which he split evenly with Arthur (after deducting certain expenses) for $4,738.89 apiece.

Arthur, as it happened, was a director of the Mexican Central, which was an off-shoot of the Atchison, Topeka, and Santa Fe, both roads being headquartered at the same Boston address. The president of both roads, Thomas Nickerson, a Cape Codder, had been a sea captain and a major Boston ship owner before turning to railroading. The Mexican Central, intended to carry ore north to a connection with the Sante Fe, instead became more famous for carrying Mexican immigrants to the United States.

Whether Wayne Griswold was related to the Griswolds prominent in New York shipping is not known. With Griswold's cooperation, Sewall ships had an inside line on getting cargoes of rails bought through him that were shipped either from Liverpool, where ship broker Charlie Russell was involved in the chartering, or from East Coast ports to the West Coast. In April 1883 Griswold wrote Arthur that he had arranged for his partner, Mr. Fields, to leave the firm. He continued:

> I hope we shall do a good business with Mr. Nickerson this year. If we can make the sales at prices quoted we can make a lot of money. I shall be just as well pleased if we do not make the sale to Nickerson till after the first of May as Fields would [otherwise] get half of the profit on the sale.

In January 1884 Griswold wrote Arthur that within the past two years he had lost over $84,000 in the stock market, and was in debt. Indeed, he was in such a fix that his "friends"— Arthur was one such —would have to wait to be repaid, but he had some "splendid things in hand" which, if he could pull them off, would make him "a pot of money." The rail business, however, was at a standstill. Griswold couldn't imagine why he had not heard from Arthur, unless it had to do with the money Griswold owed him.

In 1891 Griswold, who with one Jerome Gillette, was a partner in the investment firm of Griswold & Gillette, wrote Arthur, then president of the Maine Central Railroad, trying to interest him in buying a controlling interest in the St. Croix and Penobscot Railroad for fifty cents on the dollar. Although one of the oldest railroads in Maine, the St. Croix and Penobscot was a very short line indeed, with no rail connections to any other road, and Arthur was able to control his enthusiasm. In July 1897 Griswold & Gillette failed.

In April 1898 Griswold wrote Arthur begging for $2,600 to allow him to capitalize on a revolutionary firebox blower to which he had the rights. In August 1894 Arthur won a judgment against Griswold in the New York Supreme Court for a debt of $3,714.44, incurred in 1892. Arthur's lawyer demanded repayment by installments. In response, Griswold, then at the resort of Seabright, New Jersey, wrote to Arthur complaining that the case had been put in the hands of a man who would "take me by the throat and make me sign the document."

> Besides, I have made you a lot of money on the Mexican Central deal alone. When you was a director of that road I paid you thousands and thousands of dollars [in] commissions to help me get the rail orders for that road. And look at the thousands of dollars I made you in a legitimate way on other orders for rails which you helped me get, so that if you had lost all I owe you, you would have still been way ahead. . . . The last $500 I paid you I raised by pawning my wife's ear-rings which cost $2,000 for $700 out of which you got $500 (and poor Andy Gill $200 to keep him out of the poor house & he was never able to return it, poor fellow). . . . It was cruel after the money I have made you to . . . force me into law.

Nothing further was found pertaining to Wayne Griswold.

We are having too much of this

In October 1882 Arthur, en route to the West Coast, wrote Sam from the Boody House, Toledo, Ohio:

> Just arr. here. Recd Your telegram re. Tacoma ships, which was not *inspiring*. Have tel[agraphed Fred] Bosworth to fix *Challenger* at his discretion regardless of *crew trouble* & if required we would send out masters for one or both ships. We are having too much of this kind of work & we must take measures to stop it.

The ships having sailor troubles were *Harvester*, Captain Zack Allen, and *Challenger*, Captain Robert Mountfort of Brunswick, Maine. Mountfort had been first mate of *Challenger* for five years under Captain E. H. Thompson, also of Brunswick.

Thompson was taking a rest for a voyage, and Mountfort, accompanied by his wife and daughter, had taken the ship from Philadelphia to Tacoma with rails. As a result of his ships' troubles, Arthur traveled to Tacoma, too.

The record regarding *Harvester*'s case is slight—after the case was tried the ship was allowed to sail under bond. In June 1883 *Harvester* was at Liverpool, where Sam Sewall—Sam was then interning with Charlie Russell—wrote Arthur that Allen was doing "first rate," and that nothing would be gained by changing masters, as evidently had been contemplated. But he also wrote, "I have given Allen to understand that we cannot have any more crew trouble and he must get along without it. He says he can explain his Tacoma trouble to your satisfaction but I did not think it best to tell him all you heard at Tacoma concerning himself." In October 1883 Zack Allen was found not guilty on all charges by the district court.

The *Challenger* case was not so easily disposed of. The crew described a reign of terror during the whole course of the passage, as they, without cause, were wrongfully subjected to beatings, imprisonments, cruelties, and abuse by the first and second mate, with knowledge of the captain. One sailor suffered a broken jaw, another had been crippled for two weeks as a result of his injuries. Weapons used against them included belaying pins, "heavers," clubs, and boots. Seaman Francisco suffered a gashed head and a broken nose, and was hoisted halfway up the mainmast by a small line. And in a new wrinkle, a quantity of human excrement had allegedly been forced into his mouth while other crewmembers were compelled to hold him down. Several seamen had been driven to attempt suicide, but were restrained by their fellows.

The first mate, George Conway, found guilty of two of seven charges, was sentenced to five-and-one-half years' imprisonment. Second mate John Bennett, found guilty of five of eight charges, was sentenced to four-and-one-half years' imprisonment. Captain Thompson, who had come west, thought that the sentence given Conway was an "outrage," but had no comment regarding Bennett's treatment.

In a separate case the third mate and eleven sailors sued the ship, i.e., the owners, for damages and back pay. A district court judge found in their favor, libeling the ship for $7,700 and costs; $25,000 bond had to be posted so that the ship could leave. The judge reportedly told the owners' lawyers that he expected his judgment to be overturned on appeal, but had ruled as he had out of sympathy for the sailors. The lawyers wrote the Sewalls that they were confident that their appeal would prevail, else, "if the rule as laid down by Judge Greene gets to be the law, ship owners will rapidly go out of that business."

They were correct. The appeal was heard by the Supreme Court of Washington Territory in July 1885. On the question of liability, the court found that:

> The officers of the ship were the fellow servants of the Libellants engaged in the same common employment, and the owners of the ship cannot be held liable for their negligence unless they have been negligent in their selection and have retained them after their incompetency.

In 2008 this same basic issue came before the Supreme Court of the United States in a case brought against Exxon-Mobil regarding the awarding of punitive damages in the grounding of the tanker *Exxon Valdez* in Prince William Sound, Alaska. From news reports, it appeared that the case law cited by the oil company's lawyer had not changed since 1885.

Captain Thompson, who had provided key testimony regarding the competency of Captain Mountfort, later had his own bone to pick with the Sewalls. Noting that he had been summoned to Tacoma by the Sewalls in order to look out for the interests of both *Harvester* and *Challenger*, and to be prepared to assume command of either one depending on the trial outcomes, he had assumed that he would be reimbursed for his fare—$240—and also would be paid $100 per month for the four months that *Challenger* was detained. The Sewalls thought differently. Captain Thompson should have known better than to have made such an assumption.

I have a position to uphold

In September 1881 Harold Sewall, age twenty, home from his sophomore year at Harvard, wrote to his father, Arthur, who was out of town:

> I wrote you Saturday that Sunday morning I came down and found two pair of shoes that I had left for Dan [the household groom] had not been touched. I asked him why he had not blacked them and he said he could not get into the front part of the house at seven o'clock. I asked Mrs. Arnold if this was so and she said that it was not and that she and Clara were both up at that time. I told Dan so and he said it was not the case. I immediately said that somebody had lied and that I guessed it was not Mrs. A. This was all that was said,
>
> On my way home from church Dan met me and said he had left [employment]. I told him all right. I have Mike over to rub down the horses, milk, etc. Today was a wet day and he could not work at the yard so let him clean some carriages and harnesses and he has start enough now to do all that is absolutely necessary until we get a man.
>
> Dan came into the office this A.M. and asked Jim [Mulligan] to pay him off. I happened to be in the office and told D, I guessed he could wait until you came home. He was fearfully mad, said he did not come to the house to wait on me, etc. I am of course sorry to lose Dan for you, for as regards his work he is a first class man. I can never see him taken back while you allow me to live with you. As you know I do not much object to blacking my own shoes but since you have allowed me the privilege of having the man do it I wish it to be you and not a hired man who deprives me of that privilege.

This was signed not "Harold," and not even "Harold Sewall," but "Harold M. Sewall."

Doubtless Dan and Mike were Irish "help." Having received no response from

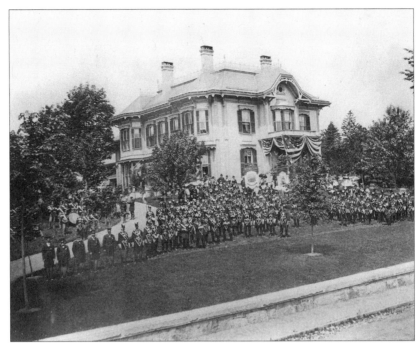

June 24, 1881. A gathering of the Knights Templar's Dunlap Commandery of Bath, and the St. John Commandery of Bangor, at the mansion of Sir Knight Arthur Sewall, 1180 Washington Street, Bath. "The United Religious, Military and Masonic Order of the Temple and of St. John of Jerusalem, Palestine, Rhodes and Malta" was a Masonic order. Mainers were inveterate joiners, and even the reclusive Arthur Sewall belonged to more than two dozen social organizations. The Italianate mansion was built in 1874 to designs by Maine's leading architect, Bath native Francis H. Fassett. The quarried granite stone from which the doorstep was fashioned measured 14 feet long by 8 feet wide, and reportedly cost $400 when landed at Bath. Unoccupied after Emma's death in 1919, the mansion was razed in the 1930s. The Grace Episcopal Church now occupies the site; only the granite wall in the foreground remains as a relic of an earlier era. The neighboring house to the north, still in the Sewall family, was the home of William D. Sewall. MAINE MARITIME MUSEUM

Arthur, and troubled that Emma was acting "very queerly" toward him for what he had done, Harold wrote Arthur a follow-up letter describing his actions as having been taken in their best interests. "I have always liked Dan, but I have a position to uphold and when Dan insults one of the ladies of the house by flatly contradicting what she has just told me, he is not fit to remain."

Harold Marsh Sewall was born in Bath in 1860, but clearly even when young had a mind very different from the average Bath boy's. According to his lifelong friend, Arthur Staples:

When I was a boy in Bath, he was my schoolmate. . . . He was the wonder of our school because he read the daily papers; knew all about politics and Congressional affairs, whereas most of us High School boys hardly knew what was a Congress.

Harold Marsh Sewall
as a boy and as a young man
MAINE MARITIME MUSEUM

He was early interested in history. Harold was a debater . . . whom none could surpass; he was a wonderful public speaker; a good scholar, an ambitious and scholarly man.[6]

It is a pity that the following note bore no date:

Harold is again in trouble. When he came from his recitation this morning he went outdoors, instead of coming direct to his room, and fired a pistol, for which action there is not the least excuse. He is losing recesses now for previous misdemeanors and I am at a loss how to punish unless I dismiss him from school. Yet I am desirous of saving him this disgrace if possible. . . .

Upon graduation from high school Harold received this telegram from Arthur: "Success is measured by industry & perseverance [was there ever a better motto for the Sewalls?] We congratulate you. A European trip this vacation is yours if you desire."

Harold was a member of the class of 1882 at Harvard, and was commencement day speaker. He then entered Harvard Law School. In 1884, on a summer vacation, he traveled overland to San Francisco scouting out possibilities for practicing law but returned home little enthused. A May 1885 letter to Arthur from one Edward Coolbroth, perhaps a porter at Harold's law school residence, only reinforces the earlier impression that Harold, while a man of small stature, possessed a well-inflated self-regard:

> Some months ago I wrote you stating that your son neglected to pay me a bill and received no reply but the young man met me afterwards and said he owed me nothing and called me a liar. I have asked him to pay an honest debt $1.75 and he has refused to do so and if all stories are true he can fool away money as fast as he pleases. . . . Only a few days ago I had business in a saloon and he stood at the bar drinking. Now I know the bill is small but if he is still smaller. . . . I very much dislike to write to you or any other Gent about such a thing but we often have such things to do. . . . Generally I have not much trouble to get my pay of students but he with a few others are bound to beat [me].

Harold did not quite graduate at semester's end, due, he explained to Arthur, to his not having turned over quite enough pages in one particular book. To his great relief, he passed a final exam that summer taken in Liverpool, where he now held office as the United States vice consul, a politically appointed position gained thanks to Consul Charles Russell.

Relations between Harold and Russell, who in turn owed his office in large part to Arthur's influence, blew hot and cold. Russell, according to Harold, had a "fearful temper," and while Russell's erratic personal history lends credence to the possibility, it is also not difficult to imagine that Harold just being Harold could provoke an outburst. In March 1886 Harold wrote Arthur regarding Russell:

> All the nice people I have met tell me frankly that it is a great detriment to me to be with him. The best Americans here will not have him in their homes and feel very bitterly disappointed that they cannot have a consul here whom they can associate with. . . . He doesn't know how positively detested he is by the people here with whom I care to associate. . . .

And again:

> CTR wants money more than anything else now and if there were only some good business position offered him either in the States or over here representing some American house, railroad, etc. I am sure he would get out of the way. I would gladly contribute my salary to bring this about.

In May Harold reported:

We had a slight rupture yesterday, Mr. CTR and myself over some courtesies I have arranged, as a Harvard graduate—not as vice consul—to extend to [visiting dignitary] Dr Oliver Wendell Holmes. He thought I was usurping his place. . . . *I do wish that* something could be done for him that would give me a chance to get this office. I would pay out my salary to bring about such an arrangement. . . . I do not want to retire from the service without first getting a consulate.

Chastised by Arthur, Harold promptly tacked ship and praised Russell for, among other favors, having obtained for him an invitation to a diplomatic affair in London. This allowed Harold to devote the greater part of his letter appraising the speech Gladstone made regarding Irish reforms.

In February 1886, after the loss of the *John Rosenfeld*, Harold wrote Arthur that he hoped he would not build a replacement: "Since I have been over here I have become convinced that the day of the wooden ship is over."

Harold had little regard for Captain Abel Work of the Sewalls' second ship *Thomas M. Reed*.7 In going over the ship's slop-chest accounts, part of the consul's duties when overseeing the paying off of seamen, Harold discovered that Captain Work had been grossly overcharging, and suspected that Captain Work was keeping two sets of slops books. Under recently passed regulations, only a 10 percent markup was permitted, yet Work had charged one sailor one dollar for a bar of soap which had likely cost five cents. Harold observed: "Any man who will cheat sailors as he does will naturally cheat the owners, too. . . . Hope Work will not disgrace your service longer."

Work had also broken the law by taking a San Francisco boy for the voyage who was not on the ship's articles, and who Work had angrily driven from the ship. Had the consulate been in different hands, Harold reported, heavy penalties would have been imposed. Regarding captains, Harold warned:

It has occurred to me re. your ships accounts that there is a chance of crookedness on the part of those of your captains who are open to it in the difference that might be made in the payment off of the crew at one rate of exchange and the charging the ship at the other rate. The rate at which they are paid off is at $4.86 to the £. If the ship is charged at $4.84 there is a little something saved for the captain.

Harold tried to make some money for himself on the side by "fixing" cargoes for Sewall ships until told to desist by Arthur. In January 1887 Russell, who was by then having his own money problems, wrote Arthur that Harold felt very badly for having spent $1,500 above his income, but that keeping up his position as a gentleman cost $4,000 a year. "I am on the lookout for any vacancy [as a consul] for him, which will come, I think, before many months."

Not long afterwards Arthur wrote Frank Jones, a well-connected Portsmouth, New

Hampshire, brewer, businessman, and Democrat: "When in Washington will you kindly see the President, Secretary [of State] Bayard in reference to promoting Harold M. Sewall (now vice consul at Liverpool) to a desirable consulate . . . ?" Arthur suggested Paris or St. Petersburg, but what Harold got instead was the tiny port of Apia in the far-distant Samoan islands.

In July 1887 a worried Charlie Russell, in debt to Arthur, wrote Arthur asking why he had not written him since Harold had returned home. No one, Charlie reminded Arthur, could have been a better friend to Harold than he had been. He had a letter from the State Department showing that he, and he alone, had been the means of Harold being appointed to Apia. "I retain this important letter for your perusal. We parted best of friends, and he has written me since his departure several nice letters, but your silence has troubled me."

To thrust a stick into the German wheels

In 1889 a Boston reporter described a sighting of the hero of the hour, the Honorable Harold Marsh Sewall:

A man of small stature with a little dab of very red whiskers on each side of his face and a stubby mustache, sat at a table in the reading room of Young's Hotel, last evening busily writing. No one seemed to pay him any particular attention, from the fact that few of the guests present were aware that the ex-consul-general to Samoa was in their midst.

Harold was the ex-consul-general to Samoa because Secretary of State Bayard, at the tag end of his term of office, had asked for Harold's resignation. He had had no choice, given Harold's highly charged testimony before a senate committee highly critical of Bayard's Samoan policies in response to a heavy-handed German power-grab. Harold even read from a recently received letter from Samoa that predicted that if the Germans were not stopped "the tortures of the Inquisition will be discounted" in comparison to the horrors planned by the vengeful Huns.

Harold had been provided with this bully pulpit by Maine's Senator Frye, although a Republican, a friend of the Sewalls. Like Harold, Frye was an avid Pacific imperialist. Harold's "secret" testimony, quickly leaked to the like-minded press, turned the matter into a partisan crisis, and Harold, although still a Democrat—he would later switch parties—was the fair-haired boy of expansionist Republicans.

When Harold, age twenty-seven, had arrived at the port of Apia on the central Samoan island of Upolu in 1887, the appearance of the sleepy, ramshackle town, fronting on a very poor excuse of a harbor, belied the strategic importance attached to the islands by Germany, the United States, and Great Britain—all jealously guarding their claims to rights regarding the islands.

The Germans, like the United States, late arrivals to the empire grab-bag, were busily scooping up unclaimed odds and ends of island groups in the Far Pacific and were by far the most aggressive of Samoa's suitors. Their vast island copra plantations, however, benefited the Samoans they had displaced not at all, while their heavy-handed attempts to reshape the leisure-loving Polynesians into obedient, hardworking, tropical Teutons were doomed to fail.

At the consulate Harold succeeded a man named Greenbaum, a former San Francisco clothing merchant, who had become so alarmed by German activities that he attempted unilaterally to turn the islands into an American protectorate. When Secretary Bayard dispatched Harold to calm the waters until cooler and wiser heads arrived at a diplomatic solution, he likely knew little of the prickly young man who had driven Dan the groom out of the household on a matter of petty principle.

It is the nature of islands that their politics are invariably complex and also inscrutable to outsiders. Samoan politics were further complicated by the interference and jealous maneuvering of the representatives of the foreign powers, typically operating through their native puppets. Shortly after Harold's arrival the German's puppet chief, Tamasese, in a coup backed up by naval forces, was made king. Harold, against his feisty inclination, was ordered to restrain the deposed monarch, Laupepa, from fighting back.

Dissatisfied with the responses from Washington to his warnings (wired from Auckland), Harold, in the fall of 1888, returned to the U.S. to argue for more forceful action against the Germans, whom he accused of planning to take over Samoa, in league with the British, who would also receive Tonga. The fate of Hawaii would then hang in the balance. In December, as matters escalated, twenty Germans were killed by supporters of the deposed king, led by a chief named Mataafa.

Robert Louis Stevenson arrived at Apia in 1889, about a year after Harold's departure—the two would not meet until Harold's return in 1890—but his account of the situation that Sewall faced in 1887 is classic. Neither the acting English consul, who was under orders to assist the Germans, nor the captain of the American warship then in port, who was very friendly with a German captain, were inclined to stand up to the German moves:

> There remains the American consul-general, Harold Marsh Sewall, a young man of high spirit and a generous disposition. He had obeyed the orders of his government with a grudge, and looked back on his past with regret almost to be called repentance. From the moment of the declaration of war against Laupepa, we find him standing forth in bold, consistent, and sometimes rather captious opposition, stirring up his government at home with clear and forcible despatches, and on the spot grasping every opportunity to thrust a stick into the German wheels.[8]

As a result of Harold's stirring testimony, Congress appropriated funds for the protection of U.S. interests in Samoa and set about establishing a coaling station at Pago Pago (a concession granted under an earlier treaty). President Cleveland, although by then on his way out of office, ordered the Asiatic Fleet flagship USS *Trenton* to join two smaller warships keeping watch over three German naval vessels and a British cruiser in Apia Harbor.

Surely none of the three great powers had any wish to go to war over Samoa—indeed, the U.S. Navy was then at its lowest post–Civil War ebb—yet the state of affairs on Upolu grew increasingly volatile, dangerous, and unpredictable. Then, almost providentially, the standoff was defused in a matter of hours by a March hurricane that wrecked all of the German and American ships, the British cruiser *Calliope* being the only vessel to get clear of the entrapping harbor. The wrecked ships were thrown ashore after the flooded river washed away the sediment that had provided the harbor bottom with a veneer of anchoring ground. (Ironically, it was the river which had created the harbor, so-called, by keeping open a passage through the coral reef with its freshwater outflow.)

Perhaps no one owed more thanks to the fickle river than did Harold, for had there been war, instead of being lionized, he would likely have been excoriated.[9]

Later that year, in Berlin, at a convention of the now-mollified rivals, a three-way condominium plan of government was agreed upon. The American commission, led by the new Republican secretary of state, James G. Blaine of Maine, included Harold Sewall as disbursement officer. In 1890 Harold was reappointed as consul-general to Apia by President Harrison. A clipping of an editorial from an unidentified newspaper, pasted into one of Harold's scrapbooks, reads:

> It is not too much to say that Consul General Sewall did more to preserve the honor and dignity of the United States, at the critical time in our relations with Germany over the Samoan question, than any other individual or influence. To his clearness of head, firmness, and fearlessness is due the fact that the interests and credit of this country were not overborne and swept aside by German intrigues and aggression in the South Seas.

After serving one year in Apia, Harold took another leave of absence, this time traveling in Southeast Asia, China, and Japan, before resigning for the second time in 1892, but not before Arthur had accompanied him in January on his return to the islands. Harold's timing was deft, as Samoan politics soon descended again into disorder and bloodshed.

Harold, always a collector, returned from his travels with many souvenirs. Recalling the episode of Dan the groom, a letter from Arthur Sewall in March 1893 to Captain T. P. Gibbons, of the Bath ship *John R. Kelley*, then at New York, bears some irony:

> I have just returned from a fortnight's absence and I find the Jap question a rather serious one for me. Harold engaged him and arranged for you to bring him home with the view of using him himself, intending to settle here. He has just now left for the Pacific. . . . It is uncertain when he comes back. . . .
>
> My difficulty here is that Mrs. Sewall is decidedly opposed to taking him

and does not want him, and it will be disagreeable to her if I take him for a house servant. It would relieve me very much if you could make some other disposition of him that would be just right all round and not embarrassing to you.

Where Harold was going was to Hawaii, and that is where we will later meet up with him.

His habits on shore have not been as I could wish

On October 4, 1886, Captain Alpheus Boyd of Wiscasset, master of the ship *Solitaire*, wrote the Sewalls from Acapulco, Mexico, where he had discharged a cargo of Welsh steam coal for the Pacific Mail Line. Fever had struck down most of his crew, and Boyd had also been sick. He would hire help from shore to raise the anchor. In a postscript he noted that two more men had been taken sick. On October 9 he wrote:

> One of the Panama boats [a Pacific Mail steamer] are here and has promised to tow us out and am going. The crew are all in a bad way, very weak, six can hardly stand but I hope will get stronger after we get to sea. This has been terrible, details of which would be painful to read. But I trust the worst is over.

Ten days later *Solitaire* finally departed for Nanaimo, British Columbia. She broke passage and put into San Francisco, where Boyd wrote Bath that he could not continue and was going home, leaving the ship in the care of Captain Baker.

As it happened, Captain Baker had recently written Arthur of the advisability of getting his new son-in-law, Ned Sewall, away from his "sponging associates" in "this abominable place." Arthur responded by giving Ned trial command of *Solitaire*.

Captain Joe Hamilton—whose own ship, *Undaunted*, was idle—would take *Solitaire* north to Nanaimo and Ned would bring her back. (Making a departure from Nanaimo was much safer than making an approach.) Ned promised Captain Baker that he would turn over a new leaf and economize.

Ned joined *Solitaire* at Nanaimo on December 6, made a good passage to San Francisco, and was given permanent command. Captain Baker wrote Ned a heartfelt five-page letter pleading with him to mend his ways: "Arthur Sewall & Co.," he warned, "will not allow any such extravagances." Ned made a successful round trip to Nanaimo, then asked Arthur to help send Susie out so that she could join him—ordinarily a request by a fledgling captain to have his wife on board would not have been well received at the House of Sewall, but doubtless it was hoped that Susie would be a good influence. Poor Susie was seasick for the entire passage north.

On March 6, 1887, Oscar Sewall wrote Arthur from the office of Williams, Dimond & Co. apologizing for *Solitaire*'s missing accounts, which he said must have been mislaid—one suspects that he might have been covering for his brother. And he had a much more serious matter to report:

As far as sailing his ship is concerned I think Ned has done very well, but his habits on shore have not been as I could wish and they must be changed if he expects to retain the command of any ship. He does the same as many other captains do in port, but only married a year and with his wife with him, it is very surprising to me. . . . In this connection I am exceedingly sorry to mention Capt. Hamilton. He hasn't rendered him much assistance or given him much good advice, but you are aware of his own failings . . . leaving this out, he is one of our best masters.

The previous Saturday Ned and Captain Hamilton had gone to the races together. Neither returned home that night—or on Sunday or Sunday night. Monday morning stevedore "Commodore" Allen, who had been searching "all the dives and houses," and Oscar, found them in a "house." Oscar told Ned that if he did not return to his ship he would be put out of her. The two miscreants first went aboard *Solitaire*, and then to a hotel, and did not return to their wives—who were "nearly crazy"—until Tuesday. Ned had since made up with Susie and Mrs. Baker, promising to do right. To Oscar he cited the example of Captain Thompson, who, Oscar admitted, "goes it pretty fast here some-times."[10] What particularly troubled Oscar was that he knew that Ned had been unfaithful to his wife, and not for the first time. "If it does not stop," he concluded, "she cannot live with him."

In February 1888 *Solitaire* was at New York, in from San Francisco with a cargo of sugar, to load a general cargo for San Francisco. Ned was in trouble again, having used ship's monies for personal use. Arthur gave him the choice of mending his ways or giv-ing up the ship. Ned remained in the ship. In July Arthur sent a letter to meet *Solitaire* informing Ned that his ship was in debt to the firm. From San Francisco *Solitaire* car-ried wheat to Dunkirk, France.

On April 16, 1889, Sam Sewall wrote home from Philadelphia, where he had gone to meet *Solitaire*, just arrived with empty petroleum barrels atop ballast. No officers were to be found aboard the ship, Ned and the mates having "thought it prudent to leave town" due to trouble on the passage. According to the account printed some years later in *The Red Record* (see pp. 360–63), abuses committed on the passage included Second Mate Robbins having struck two men when aloft, causing both to fall. One was killed. On the passage to Dunkirk, First Mate Ryan was said to have knocked a sailor down and then jumped on his breast, killing him. Captain Sewall was accused of beating two men for talking while at work. The second mate allegedly beat a boatswain with "knuckle-dusters" for not addressing him as "Sir," and both boatswains were beaten by the mates for not beating the sailors. A sick sailor was sent aloft. And so on. The complaining sailors reportedly bore "marks of their sufferings."

On April 19 Sam reported that a marshal had padlocked the ship—evidently it was thought that Ned was an owner. The story had appeared in the papers, and the judge who would be handling the case was the same one who had imprisoned Captain Percy.[11] Ned would surely be imprisoned if he showed up. Sam had paid the carpenter to leave town after the carpenter told him about the man killed on the outward passage. Sam was sure that Ned would never have countenanced such actions, yet Ned was responsible for what happened aboard his ship, and it would have to stop—had the ship entered a foreign port with such troubles she could not be protected by her friends.

On top of all this Sam discovered that Ned had kept no regular accounts, and had spent about twice his salary for personal use. It was plain that he could not have given his ship proper attention. Sam wrote that he would rather pay his share of what Ned "wastes & gives away" than to see him lose his command, "as I don't see what else he can do for a living." But he acknowledged that Ned could never sail for another owner. According to *The Red Record*'s account, "It is reported that Captain Sewall 'healed the wounds of all complainants' with $440 cash. . . ."

In May Ned signed an agreement with Arthur Sewall & Co. to end his monetary misdeeds, acknowledging that this was his final trial. Ned and Susie sailed for Hiogo—ships sailed "for Hiogo," but "arrived" or were officially "entered" at neighboring "Kobe"—with case oil. In heavy weather off the Cape of Good Hope it had been necessary to jettison 1,500 cases.

In February 1890, writing from Hakodate, Japan, where *Solitaire* was discharging the remainder of her cargo, Ned wrote that he had had trouble with sailors in Kobe, and that the day after two were released from jail the ship was "fired." Smelling smoke, Ned rushed into the hold and found a fire burning at the base of the mizzenmast, and extinguished it. With 8,000 cases of oil still aboard, disaster was but moments away. Ned did not elaborate beyond noting that the solder was melting out of nearby tins. Captain Baker, in a later letter to Arthur, related that Susie had written that Ned had "seized that burning mass in his arms & thus saved the ship," and praised his heroism.[12] *Solitaire* arrived at San Francisco on April 5 with a cargo of sulphur.

On April 11 Captain Baker, from aboard his fine new Sewall command, the rebuilt four-masted bark *Kenilworth*, lying at Port Costa, wrote Arthur:

Now about Ned & the *Solitaire*. As Oscar has written you fully in regards to his behavior the first three days of his arrival I will not repeat it. . . . We got poor Ned to himself again yesterday & I left him this afternoon a penitent man. . . . He swears he will never touch another drop. . . . At sea his wife tells me he never touches liquor but it seems as though the devil reigns as soon as he lands.

On April 12 Ned wrote Bath:

My accounts from Japan and the long delay here has been caused by reasons which you know and which I now very much regret. It is the same old story but whatever happens I hope it is the end and as far as my interest in the estate goes I have placed it out of my reach for the benefit of my wife. And I intend to stand on my own ground in the future whatever I may be obliged to do for a living. I cannot ask any more of your firm but at the same time it will be hard to obtain work here.

On August 2, 1890, with *Solitaire* chartered to carry wheat to London, Arthur wrote Liverpool broker William Beach:

The ship *Solitaire* you are aware, is bound to London and the firm has sent the ship to your friends [i.e., friendly fellow brokers]. Captain Sewall of this ship, perhaps you may know, is a nephew of mine, a young man, and his habits are not quite as we would wish them to be and we have not the confidence in him that I hope to have later. I want to ask you to follow his every daily movement while he is in London, do it in such a way that he may not know it, and in case you find him neglecting the ship's business or squandering his own money or the ship's, you must go there yourself and protect his interests and yours in such a way as you may think best; but whatever means you are obliged to take, you must prevent any serious waste of money or neglect of ship's business.

From London *Solitaire* carried chalk to New York, then general cargo to Astoria, there to load grain. A similar cautionary letter was sent to Captain Fred Bosworth, who had retired from the sea to become a marine surveyor in Portland, Oregon. (A telegram sent to *Solitaire*'s Portland agents read: "Make no further payments Captain Sewall pending his explanation.")

When *Solitaire* arrived at Havre Ned neglected to wire his arrival. Nor did he send a letter in response to Arthur's wire expressing his displeasure. *Solitaire* arrived at New York in ballast on June 6, where Ned was replaced by Captain Edward H. Thompson. Ned would never command another square-rigger.

I commenced to get discouraged

Captain Fred Blair of Bowdoinham was born in 1850. He took command of the 396-ton three-masted schooner *Carrie S. Bailey* in 1884. On New Year's Day, 1886, he wrote Sam Sewall from Tecolutta, Mexico, on the Gulf of Campeche, where the *Bailey* had sailed from Aspinwall [Colon] to load "logwood," a dye wood. Colon was notorious for its fevers—yellow (often called "Colon" or "isthmus" fever) and malaria. Captain Blair's letter is worth reading, especially when considering the size of the schooner:

As this is not exactly a business letter I will write it to you personally. I left Colon the 18th of Nov. . . . The next morning [of the fourth day] at 4 o'clock I wore ship to go on my course. . . . I put a man at the spanker boom tackle to slack it over easy. He either did not have strength enough to hold it or was careless about it. But the boom came over with such force as to break it in two places & tore the spanker considerable in getting it down. I let the vessel go for the land & the next day at 12 o'clock we anchored about two miles from the Mosquito Coast, fixed our boom & repaired the spanker. Was there three days. I got under way the next morning at 6 A.M. The crew were from 6 A.M. until noon getting the anchor on the bow. I commenced to see then that the men were half sick. That day one took to his bed and never came out alive. The next day another went into the forecastle sick. . . . A couple of days [later] we got a north gale. We got the sails down & reefed but were unable to hoist them & they tore to pieces considerable. . . . In furling the foresail the mate fell off the forward house on deck, that laid him up. All I had left was two sailors, the second mate having deserted the day we sailed. The next day one of them commenced to have the fever & laid up sick. That left myself & one man & from 10 to 15 days we worked the vessel with some assistance from the steward. About that time I commenced to feel the fever . . . but I took large doses of quinine & when I got so played out I couldn't stand it any longer I would take some kind of stimulant. . . . [On] 14 Dec. on the NE edge of Campeche Banks, we got another norther. All I could do was lower the sails down on deck and let them lay & run the vessel before the wind under forestay sail. The next forenoon we got a reef in the spanker & hauled the vessel to the wind. That afternoon I sighted Cape Antone again, went to leeward of the island & hove to. That day I got the mate out and made him steer. That night was the first night I had gone to bed for 16 days. . . . The next day it still was blowing a strong gale & I commenced to get discouraged. I couldn't run for Jamaica. . . . I made my mind to . . . if the wind was favorable to go to Key West & ship a new crew but the wind was too far to the NE. . . . So I shaped my course for Tuxpan. . . . I would steer in the day time & the mate & man nights, and I can say that I have seen all I want to of Colon in the fall of the year. I have a mate & three men on board and they are not worth the salt that goes into their food.

On August 23, 1886, Dr. R. D. Murray, surgeon at the U.S. Marine Hospital at Ship Island, Mississippi—a major lumber-loading port—wrote the Sewalls:

I feel it to be my duty to inform you that Capt. F. L. Blair is not fit to go to sea in the sc. *Carrie S. Bailey*. He is very feeble from the effects of Phthis Pulmonalis and Colon fever. His spirits are bright and determination fixed but his days are about numbered. . . .

"Phthis Pulmonalis" could refer to several conditions, but likely here was a fancy name for tuberculosis. Captain Blair died. A letter from the Sewalls to his widow, Delia, in September 1886, described him as a "smart and faithful shipmaster." The Sewalls also—surely wisely—attempted to dissuade her from having the body shipped back to Maine: "We know by experience in these matters that many obstructions are in the way, causing much annoyance and probably resulting in disappointment [and] heavy expense, and we would not advise you to undertake it."

Among Captain Blair's effects on board the schooner were three planes, three saws, one drawknife, one monkey wrench, three large augers, two chisels, one square, one brace and set of bits, one oilstone, one crosscut saw, and one cabin lamp. Total value: ten dollars.

Blair had three young children. In November (year not given) Delia wrote Arthur:

Knowing you as the late employer and kind friend of Capt. Blair I have ventured to ask a favor of you in behalf of his little son. The little fellow is eight years old, bright and intelligent. His eyes are in a bad condition caused by humor. I have taken him once to see Dr. Holt in Portland. He said that he could be cured and he prescribed a medicine to be applied to his eyes twice a week. The physician here charges me $1.00 for each application which in my limited circumstances is more than I can afford. His friends in Bath advised me to apply to you for a Railway Pass so that I could take him twice a week to the Eye and Ear Infirmary at Portland where the services are free. I do so hoping to meet with your kind consent and approval, shall anxiously await your reply.

Arthur, then president of Maine Central Railroad, answered promptly, and doubtless the pass was sent.

It is a cold, cold business

In 1882 Arthur Sewall was named president of the Boston-based Eastern Railroad, which connected with the Maine Central Railroad at Portland. (In addition to being well known by Boston shipping and railroad men—many were one and the same—Arthur was a director of Boston's Pacific Bank, just then going belly-up, as it happened, and had speculated in a Boston-area seaside resort. The following item was clipped from an unidentified newspaper:

> The intimate relations which exist between the Eastern and Maine Central, makes the person who is the President of the Eastern Road necessarily an important personage to the people of Maine. Mr. Arthur Sewall who has recently been promoted to this position, is a native of, and resident of Bath. He is 47 years of age. . . . Mr. Arthur Sewall, familiar with the ocean-carrying trade, naturally turned his attentions to the great questions of travel and transportation by land. He has been for some time a large owner of the stock of the Maine Central and Eastern roads, and for some years been a director in both roads. . . . He has for several years been recognized in railroad circles as one of the ablest railroad men in New England . . . .

The Eastern had a long history of mismanagement. Beginning in 1873, after signing an onerous contract with the Maine Central, $1,220,538 was secretly expended buying a controlling interest in its tormentor in order to break the deal. Certain Maine Central insiders, including President Richard Rice, made out extremely well, while others, likely including the Sewalls, made out very well indeed. The Eastern then paid nearly as much for two Boston waterfront lots, found later to be separated by a narrow—and very costly—strip. The absurd price of $38,500 was paid for a wharf in Bar Harbor on the rumor that the Boston & Maine might be about to horn in on the Eastern's steamboat service to the rising resort.

Detail of the formal builder's portrait of the locomotive Arthur Sewall, *built by the Portland Company for the Maine Central Railroad, of which Arthur Sewall was a direcctor, in 1877. In the hit-or-miss days of railroading the crews of other engines were particularly alert for the sight of the smoke or headlight of the oncoming* Sewall, *which had a clock that ran notoriously fast. The* Sewall *was the last "named" Maine Central locomotive.*
DETAIL, MAINE HISTORICAL SOCIETY, COLL. 242

In 1884, in a financial maneuver intended to benefit its stockholders, the Eastern leased itself to the Boston & Maine, a hick country cousin with a mattress stuffed with money. The last order issued by the Eastern Railroad, announcing its delivery into the hands of the Boston & Maine, was signed by Arthur Sewall, president, and Payson Tucker, general manager. Sewall and Tucker then moved on to became president and general manager, respectively, of the Maine Central, which, in fact, was now controlled by the Boston & Maine, although for a while it was allowed to operate independently.

By 1884, in large part through leasing distressed smaller roads, the Maine Central operated on 524 miles of right-of-way—the largest in New England—and owned a steamboat line as well. The road was entering a period of continued expansion, modernization, and profitability, gaining a reputation as one of the more progressive roads of·its size in the nation.

By 1889 the Maine Central's trackage had increased to 650 miles—the maintenance "of way" on such a road was in itself a major managerial undertaking. Regular daily traffic included 85 passenger trains and 46 freights, powered by a stable of 119 locomotives. Traffic was controlled by telegraph, and no train could move without written orders, hundreds of which—accuracy was essential—were issued every day. There were 30,000 possible ticket combinations between 167 stations, all carefully accounted for. Freight agents tracked the movement of every freight car in the system, including those from other roads. A great vault in the Portland office housed the railroad's deeds. The workforce of 2,500 to 3,000 surely made the Maine Central the state's largest single employer by far.

Daily operations of the road were overseen by General Manager Payson Tucker, who, being an experienced practical railroad man, called himself Arthur Sewall's "Old Pastor." Despite his expressed belief that his "modesty" had been a "drawback" to his career, Tucker was one of the most gregarious and best-known men in Maine, and surely the only person in the history of the planet to have had a barkentine, a hose company, and a cigar named after him.

As president, Arthur's primary areas of responsibility would have involved strategic planning, and financial, legal, and political matters, at which Arthur was very adept. It was through railroading, not shipping, that Arthur Sewall dealt with some of the truly big-time movers and shakers, and makers and takers, of American industry, business, politics, and finance. .

Following the style of big out-of-state roads, Maine Central management strove to favorably impress wealthy summer visitors that this was no hayseed outfit. To this end the Maine Central ended the practice of naming locomotives—the last had been the *Arthur Sewall*—and fancy scrollwork, now deemed dated and provincial, was removed. Brasswork—once each fireman's pride—and even the red driving wheels, were painted a sober, businesslike black. Passengers for Bar Harbor transferred to a steamer for the last, brief leg of their journey to the magical "isle," and the Bath-built *Sappho*, a steamer of great beauty, put into service in 1886, was a fit consort for the Pullman-service Bar Harbor Express, which became a famous train.

Built in 1888, Portland's imposing French chateau-style Union Station, where the Boston & Maine met the Maine Central, was intended to impress not the wide-eyed upcountry Granger, but rather, the sophisticated out-of-state Gilded Ager. (Conveniently, a quarry owned in part by railroad officers provided its granite. The Maine Central was, as well, a good customer of schooner-delivered hard pine purchased from Arthur Sewall & Co.)

The Maine Central's attorney, a very important man, was Orville Dewey Baker, who, for four years, was as well Maine's part-time attorney general. Baker, whose client list included the Boston & Maine and Western Union, not only continued his private law practice while in office, but used stationery headed "Office of the Attorney General." Baker was also an investor in the Maine Central, and in November 1886, he asked Arthur to assist him with some insider trading:

> *Confidentially*, is it the understanding that if the preferred scheme succeeds the surplus earnings of this past year will be divided on the common? . . . If you

understand it will be divided for this past year please add the word yes at the end of your telegram. On the other point, if not to be divided now, please add the word no, and much oblige.

Baker and Arthur were also fellow speculators in a Bar Harbor real estate venture, and Baker also summered at Small Point, where he died in 1908.

Joseph H. Manley, a high Republican Party leader and arguably Maine's slickest political operator of all time—no small distinction—was a Small Pointer as well, and also a Sewall relative by marriage.[13] (Manley was one of the founders of Small Point's summer colony, which initially was composed largely of people from Augusta.) A power in Washington as well as Augusta, Manley was a key aide both to James G. Blaine, and. later to "Czar" Thomas B. Reed, two of the most powerful men of their times. In the later 1880s Manley was awarded the plum appointment of postmaster at Augusta, which was then one of the nation's busiest post offices, thanks to the carload upon carload of fodder for the nation's outhouses cranked out by the city's publishers, who were among the country's leading producers of mass-circulation magazines of astonishing vapidness. E. C. Allen, the largest of Augusta's bottom-feeding press barons, was a major investor in the Sewall fleet. Augusta's grand old granite post office building is a monument to the influence and affluence of Augusta's publishers.

In the legislature, Manley worked to advance the interests of the Maine Central. In February 1885, at the close of the session, he proudly wrote Arthur:

Every measure which you desired to have prevented from becoming a law also has been defeated. There is only one thing remaining for us to watch and defeat, that is the Heath bill. . . . If we kill it I shall feel that the winter's work has been one of great success. We have no lobby here and everything has been accomplished with very little expense. It is really a great contrast to the days when Judge Rice and others used to keep a lobby of thirty or forty men on hand all the time.

In Congress, Manley worked to rescue the Maine Central's annual $30,000 mail contract and assured Arthur that the ten-hour workday would not apply to railroads. Manley also joined Arthur in Bar Harbor real estate affairs. In February 1888 Manley wrote Arthur in regard to a Bar Harbor water company whose charter he had pushed through the legislature in opposition to the established water company: "There are 15,625 shares which are to be issued to you."

The Maine Central's 1888 lease of the bankrupt Portland & Ogdensburg Railway, and the subsequent leasing of connecting routes into Quebec, was later judged the most serious mistake of the company's history.[14] Intended to be a trunk line to the west, the cobbled-together route, hampered by steep grades, never amounted to much more than a summer tourist line from Portland to Crawford Notch. Railroad historian Edward Chase suspected that this great burden was placed upon the neck of the Maine Central by its Boston & Maine rulers, whose only interest was to deprive any rivals of the route. Whatever Arthur's role was or was not in this decision, he worked hard to get the enabling legislation passed, and then to unload the various issues of securities upon gullible commercial bankers

On December 15, 1893, Fred Richards, a Portland investment banker closely associated with the Maine Central, regarding rumors that Arthur Sewall and Payson Tucker were to be turned out at the upcoming annual meeting, quoted an unnamed lawyer of high standing as saying: "The fact is, the Maine Central Railroad is today very popular on account of the personal popularity of these two gentlemen. It is their personal following, and their able management, which enables the Maine Central to keep its hold upon the people of this state. . . . " Nevertheless, the headline of the December 23, 1893 Bath *Enterprise* trumpeted: "Sewall is Out of the M. C. R. R. Directory."

An unusually large turnout of stockholders at the annual meeting, representing 32,650 shares, indicated that something was up. Despite maneuvering by Joe Manley, new directors closely associated with the Boston & Maine's president Lucius Tuttle—Tuttle had worked under Arthur and Tucker as the Eastern's ticket agent—were voted in. Five incumbents, including Arthur, were out. And by 1897 Payson Tucker also was out. In 1899 Lucius Tuttle added the presidency of the Maine Central to his titles, and the Massachusetts takeover of the Maine Central was complete.

In 1894 Arthur had written his confidant Erskine Phelps, "The time has gone by when you can find any warmth in railroad circles. It is a cold, cold business all the time, and nothing else. We must look upon now for all our warmth and genuine congeniality, in our friendly associations, entirely outside and independent of our business circles."

i thought i would write & Aske A Request of you

A wearer of many hats, Arthur Sewall was asked for many favors. And he dispensed many favors, some with strings attached. Many of these involved railroad passes.

Railroad fares were expensive, and a pass, as one politician succinctly put it, was "a very nice thing to have." Indeed, only Captain Jarvis Patten of Bath, who had lost his position as commissioner of navigation due to Arthur's behind-the-doors political manipulations, is on record returning a pass. The giving of passes for interstate travel was finally ended in 1906 by the Hepburn Act, while one of Harold Sewall's achievements when he served in the Maine legislature was the abolishment of in-state passes—he knew firsthand their corrupting influence.

In November 1884 Joe Manley asked Arthur for passes for Secretary of State James G. Blaine and his family on "the Eastern road." This was a relatively modest request, considering that in October, at Manley's request, Arthur had dispatched an entire special train to transport Mr. and Mrs. Blaine from Portland to Augusta. (According to an old story, Speaker of the House Thomas Brackett Reed once telegraphed a request to the Maine Central asking for a special train to "meet a large party" at a certain station. The "large party" was the amply-girthed Tom Reed himself.)

In May 1885 former governor (and Civil War hero) Joshua Chamberlain wrote to thank Arthur for his annual pass. After the December 30, 1885, *Lewiston Evening Journal,* a paper published by ex-governor Nelson Dingley, editorialized against discriminating railroad rates, Joe Manley wrote Arthur: "Don't Dingley have a pass?" In March 1887 Joe Manley requested a pass for Mrs. Marble, the wife of state senator (and future governor) Sebastian S. Marble, who had enabled Manley to "quietly kill the [railroad] tax bill, and he will help me on every measure that we have."

In January 1889 Manley wrote that former Governor Frederick Robie wanted another pass, and Manley thought that he should get one: "You know the Governor's position as the head of the Grange . . . and I know he is inclined to reciprocate any favor extended to him. . . ." When Senator William Frye sent a note asking Arthur for various passes over various roads Frye concluded that he had "done enough for these rail roads to quiet my modesty in this regard. I am now trying to get the mails for the Redington road. You needn't file this letter."

In August 1888 Arthur wrote out by hand the ultimate pass, giving the owner of a private rail car the right to have his car attached to the rear of Maine Central trains of his choice, free of charge—the wealthy and powerful are indeed different:

Conductor, Maine Central RR. Upon presentation of this order you may haul the private car of Shreve, V. P. N.Y. & N.E. R. R. and pass free the occupants over the line of the road as Mr. Shreve may desire.

In July 1887 Father N. Charland, a parish priest from Waterville, which had a large French-Canadian population, wrote Arthur asking for a pass for His Lordship, Bishop Healy of Portland, so that Healy might better visit parishes on the line. A month later, Charland thanked Arthur for the bishop's pass, and added that his adopted son Henry would try once again to visit Arthur. He enclosed a recent photograph of Henry:

He met, as you will see, with an accident. In playing with a little cannon, it kind of exploded, and the powder burned and marked his face. . . . Henry wants to intercede for his father John B. Trial. He would like, if it were possible, to get him a place as a foreman or something of the kind. . . . He has a large family to support, and he does not earn much in the mills.

Charland later wrote that Henry now wondered if Arthur could get his father a job firing the locomotive of engineer James Marquis. Furthermore, Henry's father would like, if employed, to be able to be at home evenings. A January 1889 letter from Charland finally makes reference to the mysterious political matter that had evidently brought him and Arthur together in the first place:

I believe that it is safe now for me to state that we will be able to settle for you the matter in which you are deeply interested in this city. . . . The matter is a delicate one and needs to be treated with a great deal of care and prudence. This we are doing and have been doing. Depend upon it, dear Sir, anything I can ever do for you or Mr. Tucker I will do. . . .

Passenger Manager Boothby provided the good Father Charland with passes to Montreal and Three Rivers, for which he was grateful. And as regards passes for the clergy, in July 1883 the Reverend Frank Sewall, who was always crying poverty, wrote from Urbana, Ohio:

> Some time ago I wrote to you about some R.R. passes and I am afraid my letter never reached you—could you send me a season pass on the Maine Central and on the Boston & Maine or the Eastern RR. I intend to be coming east early in August. . . . If you could send me a trip pass from "Cleveland to Boston" (via N. Y. Central & Boston & Albany) it would be a very considerable favor. . . . I then intend to make a tour in the Adirondacks. . . . The trip pass must allow a stop over at Albany to be of use. . . .

Writing from San Francisco in March 1885, Captain Parker H. Morrison of Phippsburg, master of the ship *Indiana*, wrote Arthur:

> Will you kindly grant my daughter Alice P. Morrison a pass to and from Portland. She is trying to fit herself in music to teach. As I am & have not been making a living for the past three years it would be thankfully received.

As for doing favors for other people's needy children, among the crosses that Arthur bore was trying to find a suitable position for Payson Tucker's insufferable, ne'er-do-well son "H. R." In August 1884 H. R. wrote Arthur on Maine Central stationery from Bar Harbor:

> Mrs. Stevens, stewardess on steamer *Sebenoa* [one of the railroad steamers which operated between Mt. Desert Ferry and Bar Harbor] got her back up a little because I wanted her to go on the *Frances* [another railroad ferry] one trip in place of the stewardess there to accommodate the steward so I discharged her. This reduces our payroll forty dollars ($40) a month more.

Perhaps this act was what ended H. R.'s career with the Maine Central. In February 1885 H. R. wrote from New York asking for a good word for him with Charlie Russell, as H. R. wished for a position in the Brower House hotel that Russell had just purchased, renaming it The Carlton. H. R. reported himself as being in "a bad fix," adding, "I regret deeply that I have acted so disgracefully and abused the many generous privileges so kindly granted me." He resolved not to return until he was a credit to his father.

In April H. R. wrote, "Captain Russell has intimated to me that you have some idea of buying an interest in The Carlton, and allowing me to represent that interest. Such an act of kindness on your part would be of course greatly to my advantage." The financial stability of the hotel, he reported, was now in question because the bookkeeper had made false trial balances, omitting the partners' indebtedness.

January 1886 found H. R. in San Francisco, writing Arthur once again that he intended to do his "level best to try to make some amends for the past. And make myself some comfort to my dear Father & Mother in their declining years." He had secured a position—apparently with Arthur's help—as brakeman on the Southern Pacific Railroad, and had resolved to stick it out although he expected a long, hard struggle.

In his next letter, from Tulare, California, he wrote that the superintendent told him that the only job available would be on a freight, but that a man would have to be discharged to make room for him:

> I feel very reluctant to go on a freight not from any desire to get a softer job, but . . . walking over freight cars when they are standing on a turnout is all that I care to do, much less than when they are running. Now, if they have got to necessarily discharge a man to give me a job, it seems as if it might as well be from a passenger train. . . . I wish you would speak to Mr. Pratt once more and see if he can make some arrangements.

Also very hazardous was connecting the primitive link-and-pin couplers—a freight brakeman's job was among the most dangerous in an era of dangerous jobs. Maimed brakemen were traditionally pensioned out as crossing guards. A Bath crossing guard named Connally had a request for President Arthur Sewall—Mr. Connally's letter has not been edited for the reason that to do so would substantially subtract from its charm:

October 1891
Mr. Suil, Dear sir i thought i would write & Aske A Request of you to gete me A little house At the crossing to Seate in to when waiting for trains.

 Mr Stiles said I Could Build one on my own Expense But my shattered health & Small monthly pay wll not Allow me to Build one.

 the Company wll give me one thrue your Entreesson. plasse let me no by Return of Male. yours With Respect Wm Connally

They feel that I have been duped

Arthur Sewall's masterminding of the acquisition of the Knox and Lincoln Railroad by the Maine Central Railroad, of which he then was president, has never been revealed.

 Since the Knox & Lincoln's opening in 1871, having exacted from its owners—Bath, Rockland, and the towns along its line—twice its estimated cost, paid for by local bonding, the road's revenues had never covered the interest on its debt. The consequences— including, perhaps, contributing to the untimely demise of Edward Sewall—were severe. Bath was impoverished for decades. Wiscasset was bankrupted.

In the early 1880s the Maine Central made overtures for the Knox & Lincoln, which, if upgraded, would allow Pullman cars to connect with steamboats at Rockland—the managers could be excused for thinking that railroads (including electric lines) and steamboats would dominate transportation until, well, forever. But the towns' voters—suspicious farmers fearful of being taken advantage of once again—voted the offers down. In 1888, under Arthur Sewall's instigation, Portland investment banker Fred Richards—likely Maine's foremost financier—began negotiations with the towns. By 1890, the majority of the towns had agreed to sell the road to a syndicate of investors, recruited by Arthur and Richards, for $200,000 cash and the assumption of $1,300,000 of their bonds. Of the process in Bath, Richards wrote:

> I regard [Bath mayor Capt. Charles] Patten the great obstacle now in the way and you & General Hyde must somehow prevent any hitch by him. . . . [Former mayor] Wakefield should be seen and kept under the surface somehow. . . . It would be better now for all concerned if he could appear . . . very indifferent on the streets of Bath, I think.

The "associates" Arthur recruited included people closely tied to the Maine Central; Richards's recruits included local people who thought they were helping the communities, and who feared that they had been deceived by sharpers. In January 1891 Richards wrote that his associates now believed the property to be worth "a good many hundreds of thousands more than we paid for it." In a letter following up on a conversation between the himself and Arthur, Richards appears to be trying to get their stories straight:

> The underlying basis of the agreement between ourselves when the negotiations were commenced was that you and I should manage the Knox and Lincoln property without the interference from either your or mine associates. . . . That as soon as we came into possession of the road, we should improve the property and put on a new ferry boat, make all necessary changes to accommodate Pullman trains, and for that purpose we should issue "second preference bonds. . . . "

A month later he wrote:

> I regret to say that their [his associates'] feeling is intense in its bitterness at the position taken by the co-purchasers of the Knox & Lincoln. . . . I know you have been entirely straight-forward, honest, and upright towards myself throughout these negotiations but to convince them is quite another thing. . . . They believe that the Maine Central [planned] . . . to use us as tools and then reward us with a stone. . . . They feel that I have been duped to an extent which is not complimentary to my personal sagacity, and I think they look upon me with a degree of contempt such as they might entertain towards an idiot. . . .

The record does not fully explain what then happened. We do know that the Knox & Lincoln briefly vanished into a legal construct known as the Penobscot Shore Line Railroad, formed by Richards, with a charter to extend the tracks to Bangor, although apparently the immediate plan was to reach Camden—prudently, Richards and Arthur first sought to gain control of a competing trolley line. In 1891, with its old name restored, the Knox & Lincoln was leased to the Maine Central, and in 1901 the two roads were "merged."

The Maine Central subsequently made extensive improvements on the line, although with the arrival of the automobile age but a few decades later, one doubts the costs were ever recouped.

1. Torrey, from Richmond, was the proprietor of Bath's Torrey Roller Bushing Company. His Washington Street manse became the Harold Sewall home.

2. This book's author complained to his editor about the very same thing as he tried to read Arthur's handwriting. Unfortunately, Chesebrough is long dead. —Ed.

3. It was common in large ports for certain agents and brokers to seek the business of ships of certain flags, and obviously being a fellow countryman was a great advantage. The Skolfield of the Liverpool brokerage house of Ross, Skolfield was the veteran Captain Alfred Skolfield, of Brunswick, Maine.

4. Chester Lloyd Jones, *The Consular Service of the United States*, University of Pennsylvania, Series in Political Economy and Public Law, 1906., p. 17. No definition of "unofficial fees" is given, although the sums realized "at a few posts like London and Paris has come to be enormous."

5. Marienbad, in Bohemia, was the most famous of European health spas.

6. Arthur G. Staples, *The Inner Man* (Lewiston, ME: Lewiston Journal Press, 1923), p. 77.

7. In July 1886 Harold reported that the leading Liverpool underwriter of wheat cargoes had thoroughly inspected the *Reed* and expressed great satisfaction with the ship. And indeed the *Reed* was evidently a superior ship, much praised by her captains—Captain Work reported that her model could not be improved upon, while Captain Starkey called her "a Bully Ship." She carried a figurehead of Thomas M. Reed, who, shortly after her 1880 launching, hosted a dance for seventy-five guests in the *Reed*'s 'tweendecks which lasted until "the moon looked pale" (*Bath Independent*, May 22, 1880). In February 1888, also at night, while at Bramley Moore dock at Liverpool where she was being loaded with coal, the ship was destroyed by a dramatic fire which illuminated the whole vicinity. It was believed to have started from candles used by the coal trimmers in the hold.

8. Robert Louis Stevenson, *In the South Seas: A Foot-Note to History* (New York: Charles Scribner's Sons, 1903), p. 433. See also J. C. Furnas, *The Life of Robert Louis Stevenson* (New York: William Sloane Associates, 1951).

9. For recent treatments of Harold Sewall see Paul T. Burlin, "Maine Migrations: Arthur and Harold Sewall in the Pacific," *Maine History*, vol. 35, no. 112, Summer-Fall, 1995; also, Paul T. Burlin, *Imperial Maine and Hawai'i* (Lanham, MD: Lexington Books, 2006); David M. Pletcher, *The Diplomacy of Involvement: American Economic Expansion Across the Pacific, 1784–1900* (Columbia, MO: University of Missouri Press, 2001), p. 90.

10. Captain Edward H. Thompson of Topsham, who was then master of *Challenger*.

11. Captain N. E. Percy of the Phippsburg ship *Standard,* who was pardoned by President Cleveland. One wonders if Arthur played a role.

12. A number of Sewall ships experienced fires, some fatally. One which was believed to have been set was that which destroyed the ship *George Stetson,* Captain Frank Patten, off the Loo Choo Islands in the East China Sea in September 1899. After fighting the fire in vain, the ship's company escaped in the boats, with no casualties. Captain Patten suspected that the sailmaker, who had been aboard *Kenilworth* when there were two set fires, and who was the only one to save all his clothes, had done the deed. The possibility of spontaneous combustion existed as well. The crew list, curiously, lists five members of the twenty-two-man crew as natives of Iowa and Nebraska. Indeed, twelve men claimed American birth, a number which strains belief.

13. Manley was said to be the chief beneficiary, possibly to the tune of $100,000, of the wartime "Paper Credit Fraud." See Neil Rolde, *Continental Liar from the State of Maine* (Gardiner, ME: Tllbury House Publishers, 2007), pp. 127–28. Also Louis C. Hatch, *Maine, A History* (Somersworth, NH: New Hampshire Publishing Co., 1974), p. 500–04.

14. Edward E. Chase, *Maine Railroads* (Portland, ME: A. J. Huston, 1926), p. 91.

PART NINE

Captain Dunphy of ship Occidental *is succeeded by his mate, John Williams, who is stabbed to death. His widow will not be sending Christmas cards to Arthur. We see how schooners fare in deep water. Captain Dunphy's new ship, the* Willie Rosenfeld, *is launched. We see Arthur as the romantic, and learn of his plans for the "Big Four," to be the largest, and among the very last, wooden square-riggers ever built. The ship* Chesebrough *has a tragic wreck, the Sewalls enjoy a Pullman vacation, and there are more interesting letters.*

Taking my own chance of landing, as usual

In 1874 the Sewalls built the 1,500-ton ship *Occidental* for the command of Captain William Dunphy, a native of Gardiner. Dunphy, who had been master of the old fashioned, kettle-bottomed ship *Henry S. Sanford*, built at Bowdoinham, Maine, in 1869, must have been delighted with his handsome new command.

Dunphy had paid his dues. During his long and distinguished career he quelled three mutinies; in one, after being shot in the head, he had to threaten force against his mates to protect his assailant.[1] He first went to sea in 1856 at age thirteen. In 1867, while captain of the brig *Nellie Mitchell*, four days after leaving Aspinwall (Colon), his crew was struck down with "isthmus fever," leaving all but Dunphy and one man helplessly ill. Fifty miles from their destination of Swan Island, Cuba, they, too, were stricken. Before collapsing, Dunphy wrote a letter explaining what had happened. Three days later, Dunphy, in agony, regained just enough strength to crawl about, nursing his men and manning the helm. Rescued by another vessel, Dunphy spent a year recuperating.[2]

While under Dunphy's command, aside from two guano voyages, *Occidental* was steadily employed in the San Francisco grain trade. John Williams, a Swede, served as Dunphy's first mate for about a dozen years. That any master and mate could maintain such a long relationship spoke well for both. In February 1885 the Sewalls offered Dunphy the command of the new *Willie Rosenfeld*, then still on the stocks, and Dunphy suggested that "Mr. Williams, my old mate," be given command of *Occidental*.

Dunphy described Williams as "one of the best seamen, and he takes good care of a ship. Also he is honest and sober. . . . I hope you will try him as he has been expecting to get the *O* if I left her." Given that Williams had been in the Sewalls' employ as first mate of a fine ship for a decade, it is interesting that in this and other letters Dunphy took care to explain who Williams was. Williams, who had taken leave during Dunphy's final year in *Occidental* in order to attend "commercial school" in Europe, took command of *Occidental* in Liverpool in November 1885.

On November 13 *Occidental* departed Liverpool for San Francisco with coal. Also aboard were Williams's wife Alice and their two young children, and a friend of the Williamses, a rigger named H. Peletier who was also an unlicensed, part-time St. George's Channel pilot. As was customary, the pilot signed a contract that read:

Liverpool, 13th November, 1885
I, the undersigned, H. Peletier, hereby agree to act as channel pilot, per ship *Occidental*, from Liverpool Bar to Cape Clear (taking my own chance of landing, as usual, and charging nothing extra if carried off by stress of weather) for the sum of nine pounds (£9).
H. Peletier
Witness: H. Beach

On March 23, 1886, Captain Williams wrote the Sewalls from San Francisco, having arrived after a passage of 129 days. He had planned to send a letter for them ashore with the pilot, but due to heavy gales the pilot had had to remain aboard the ship:

He then wanted me to land him at Cape Verde Islands but I thought that I was not justified in doing so as it would detain the ship and would probably make me pay port charges for landing there so had to carry him out here but I had a written contract with him so that he has no claim on the ship unless you wish to allow him something. I supplied him with clothes and tobacco during the passage out of the slop chest.

On the 25th Williams wrote that he was afraid that the pilot was going to cause trouble; he wanted 10 shillings 5 pence per day of the passage, and would "go to law" to get it. Williams and Mr. Chesebrough had talked with a lawyer who advised them that he did not think that the pilot had any claim on the ship. Mr. Chesebrough was sure that he was not entitled to anything and "will go to law when he sends in his claim."

Mr. Chesebrough should not have been so sanguine. On April 6 Williams wrote that the pilot had libeled (sued) the ship for $5,000, that a marshal had been put on board, and the ship bonded for $10,000. The case was heard by Judge Hoffman in the District Court of the United States for the Northern District of California in Admiralty. The lawyers on both sides did themselves proud, spinning the dispute out in the most tedious and protracted manner, filling hundreds of pages of transcript.

The preponderance of testimony supported the captain's position that the conditions had been too rough for Peletier to have been put off near Cape Clear or Fastnet Rock. Contradicting his explanation given to the Sewalls, however, Captain Williams testified that on the day preceding sighting San Antonio Island, of the Cape Verdes, which he had sailed out of his way to reach, Peletier said that he would prefer to take his chances on finding a homeward-bound vessel, and that furthermore, he did not much care about returning home, and would prefer to go to San Francisco, it being a new country. He had made a life-saving invention and thought that he could probably do better in San Francisco than in Liverpool, where he had been on the verge of starvation. Williams further testified that off Pernambuco, on the coast of Brazil, a great many fishing catamarans were around the ship, but Peletier declined to go ashore on one.

Voluminous testimony was presented by both sides regarding the possibility that Peletier could have been put aboard any of the several ships that were sighted in the Atlantic. Peletier claimed that on repeated occasions when there was such an opportunity Williams's response was some version of, "You God dam'd son of a bitch. . . . By God, I can carry you all over the world on the strength of that contract!" His attempts to sway the captain by informing him that his wife was nearing confinement had no effect. And he claimed that the mate had altered an entry in the log regarding weather conditions off Tusker Rock.

Mr. Sullivan, representing the ship, stated; "We will not call him a liar, but, in the language of a celebrated satirist, we think the testimony will show beyond question that he deserves that epithet." He further remarked:

> We shall allude hereafter to other portions of libellant's testimony, wherein he says the Captain repeatedly called him vile names . . . simply remarking . . . it seems, considering the long acquaintance existing between the family of Captain Williams and the libellant, utterly improbable, not to say incredible, such language could have been used by Captain Williams. . . . *Nemo repente turpissimus fuit*.[3]

To cast doubt on Peletier's claims of great financial loss, a Captain Mills of Liverpool testified that unlicensed pilots such as Peletier "in many instances are employed . . . from motives of charity." Lawyer Sullivan described them as "broken-down branch [licensed] pilots, old shipmasters, or fishermen who are only too anxious to get a job to take vessels to sea, and willing to take chances to return home."

Occidental, meanwhile, having been bonded, had sailed. Writing from Queenstown on November 1, Captain Williams wrote the Sewalls:

> I am very sorry that the pilot case is not settled yet. It has worried me all the passage. I could not help bringing him out there as he refused to be landed at Cape De Verde. All the pilots in S. Francisco are working against us and supplying him with money.

Judge Hoffman's decision found that Peletier should have been put off on either the bark *Julia* or at an island. Captain Williams was found to have "stood upon the letter of his bond with a hard and almost brutal indifference to the feelings of the Libellant, or his claims upon his consideration or sense of justice." Also: "The owners of the ship had rejected all demands upon them for compensation, not even offering Peletier the means of defraying his transportation to Liverpool." A summary judgment of $4,000 and costs was entered against *Occidental*'s owners, which was reduced on appeal to $3,000, plus $259.43 costs. The total cost of the affair to the owners was $6,010.88.⁴ It was noted in an appeal that the pilot had only been in San Francisco for a short time before he had taken out citizenship papers.

A defensive Captain Dunphy pointed out to the Sewalls that other ships of theirs had also carried pilots away. He held Captain Williams blameless, inferring that a ship could not get a fair shake in a San Francisco court.⁵

He has stabbed me through the heart

Occidental's misfortunes continued on her second voyage under Captain Williams. On November 1, 1886, she arrived at Queenstown from San Francisco with wheat, "for orders," under a jury rig, having been substantially dismasted in an Atlantic gale. Captain Williams would receive a cash reward and commendation from the insurers of the cargo for bringing the crippled ship to port. Ordered to proceed to Havre, where the wheat was discharged, *Occidental* was there repaired by Captain Wilder Cooper, a Kennebecker from Pittston, whose yard, complete with dry-dock, was well patronized by American ships.

On January 4, 1887, *Occidental*, in ballast, departed Havre for Cardiff to load coal for Acapulco. Mrs. Williams, her two young children, plus a baby, and a girl hired as a helper, were in the cabin. Mrs. Williams was in a "delicate" condition from her last childbirth. Her oldest child was three.

On May 12 the Sewalls received a cable from their Liverpool brokers reading: "CAPT. OCCIDENTAL MURDERED. SHIP PROCEEDING DESTINATION. WRITING." The news had been telegraphed from the captain of the steamer *Willowbank*, just arrived at Hamburg, who had spoken to the second mate of *Occidental* who had come alongside the steamer at sea on March 24 in a small boat, while the ships lay hove-to.

In the follow-up letter from the brokers it was reported that *Occidental* had been making a long passage, and that Mrs. Williams was well. The steamer's captain suggested that *Occidental*'s first mate must be "a man of little determination or energy from what the 2nd mate told me and from the fact of his not having put the murderer in chains." The Sewalls asked the brokers to do some checking on the mate, who was thought to have come from the Isle of Man, but nothing was turned up.

On March 23 *Occidental*'s first mate, John Craine, had put a letter to the Sewalls aboard a passing homeward-bound ship. According to Craine, the murder had taken place on March 16 at latitude 13.02 degrees north, longitude 25.13 degrees west, or, south of the Cape Verdes.

All the crew were busily engaged setting up the fore rigging and stays. Capt. Williams was superintending a few of the men on the forecastle head. He had some angry words with one of the men named Johnson when the latter suddenly drew his knife and stabbed the Capt. in the breast the knife puncturing the heart causing death almost immediately after. I had the man secured at once and placed in irons, and he is now prisoner on board. Whilst I was about securing him several of the crew surrounded him with drawn knives to protect him but the man Johnson stepped out and gave himself up quietly saying he was willing to suffer for what he had done. After deliberating for the best of all concerned [and] having a master's certificate, I have determined to proceed on our voyage to our port of destination which I hope to reach in due time if the crew do their duty in future in an orderly manner which I think they will.[6]

The murder, he continued, had been a great shock to the Williams family, and so far it had been a very long and tedious passage with light headwinds and calms.

On May 13, Wilder Cooper, at Havre, received a letter written at sea by Mrs. Williams, which she asked to be forwarded to the Sewalls—during *Occidental*'s repairs Captain and Mrs. Williams and Cooper had become good friends. She described what happened after Johnson stabbed her husband:

My husband jumped off the forecastle and called out Mr. Craine catch that man he has stabbed me through the heart. My poor husband struggled to get aft but dropped at my feet saying Oh Alice; and died in less than two minutes. The mate went to secure the murderer, and he said Mr Craine I will go quietly don't ill use me. The mate said he would not. He put him into the tool locker with out as much as a lock on the door and no irons on him not even his knife taken from him, going in and out when he likes walking the deck with his pipe in his mouth and his arms folded. I am very sure every one on board will try to get the murderer off, for they say the man did it in the heat of passion, but such is not the case. It was the most deliberate cold blooded murder ever committed, and if there is any justice done the wretch will be hung. May the widows and orphans curse rest on any one that try to get him off. I am left destitute with three helpless infants. . . . Oh gentlemen whoever reads this help me, and see justice is done, and God will bless and reward you. . . . People often told [my husband] if he walked about the deck [on the poop] instead of working he would be thought more of [by the crew], but he said the owners were paying him to work to their interest and he would do it to the best of his ability and he did. If ever an honest man lived it was him.

Her father was now all that she had left for support, she continued, and he was barely able to support himself. After paying for her family's passage home— she would be living in Dublin—she would have but fifty dollars left. Her husband had spent money too freely, not expecting to be taken from his family in the prime of life, or he would have been more saving.

In his cover letter to the Sewalls, Cooper expressed his great admiration for Captain Williams, and suggested that authorities on both coasts of South America be alerted in case the crew took over the ship and put in somewhere.

On June 16, having doubled Cape Horn, *Occidental* put into Valparaiso, Chile. Through agents Grace & Co., Craine asked for instructions. Evidently the response from the Sewalls was brief—telegrams between the United States and Chile went via Europe, and were very expensive, even when shortened by the use of code. We can presume that the Sewalls authorized Craine's continued command and instructed him to proceed to Acapulco.

On June 25, the day of departure from Valparaiso, Craine wrote the Sewalls to apologize for having broken passage, but explained that although the crew had behaved well rounding the Horn, upon reaching fair weather they had become "mutinous and refractory." They were backed up by the second mate, who had been helping them steal cabin stores, leaving Craine no choice. He believed that it was their intention to get the murderer "out of the ship at all risks by seizing the boats and leaving the ship when near land." The murderer was now imprisoned, and Craine had discharged "the whole of the crew," and signed on a new one. A later account in the press held that the carpenter and two sailors from the old crew had sailed with the ship.[7]

Occidental arrived at Acapulco on August 6, to be met by one of the Sewalls' veteran masters, Captain William Taylor of Wiscasset. Taylor's former ship, *Harvester*, had recently been sold at San Francisco, and he was dispatched to take command of *Occidental*. Captain Taylor, who had been awaiting *Occidental*'s arrival for some time, had not been enduring his sojourn without complaint.

A May 2 letter from Arthur Sewall to Mrs. Williams, addressed to Acapulco, expressed shock and deep sympathy for her loss. Arthur suggested that it would probably be best for her and her family to return home, since any legal proceedings against members of the crew would be very expensive and probably futile. "The owners of the ship feel that in paying your expenses home they will do all they can at present as they have had a great loss in the Peletier lawsuit at San Francisco."

Mrs. Williams responded that she would be leaving for Liverpool via Panama as soon as the next steamer called. She said that she would have left at Valparaiso but "it would have left Mr. Craine in a bad position as he had no charts or nautical instruments" and could not afford to buy them from her. And Mr. Craine thought it would have caused an extra bill for the ship were the ship to have purchased them from her, and suggested that she remain on board until they had heard from the Sewalls. She gave thanks for having the passage home paid for. "Please gentlemen do what you can for me as I am left in a very destitute condition with three little children."

Captain Taylor wrote shortly after that he had sent Mrs. Williams and family to San Francisco for $112, plus $35 cash, as he did not have the $350 required to send them to Europe via Panama. She had wanted $100 cash but he needed funds for the ship, which had arrived very low on stores, with the flour sour and the bread full of worms. He had put seven crewmen in jail—the American consul would later remark that this was the worst crew he had ever dealt with.

In a later letter, Captain Taylor credited the new mate shipped at Valparaiso for having taken charge, else there would have been nothing left in the ship's stores. According to the carpenter there had been but two bad men in the crew, the rest being "green Dutchmen" (i.e., Germans). Taylor had decided to send Craine to San Francisco and keep the new mate. Regarding Craine, he wrote, "I don't think I want him. I don't hear any good reports of him in Valparaiso & Mrs. Williams. Don't know whether there is anything in it or not." Following up on August 21, he wrote:

I think Mrs. Williams acted very queer leaving her things in his [Craine's] charge when she knew I had come to take charge. I have them all the same. I did not let them go. There is two chronometers on board. She says one of them belongs to Capt Williams & a desk of dishes. The ship is very short of dishes. His charts are here & some books. They say Craine had the most of his charts & tell hard stories of them so I will leave you to judge for yourself. They was both strangers to me.

You have defrauded a helpless woman

On October 26 , 1887, an article appearing in the Dublin *Evening Telegraph*, picked up from the New York *Herald*, purported to relate the events that had occurred aboard *Occidental* on "one of the most thrilling and exciting voyages that has taken place in many years." The article was based on information said to have been provided by officers and crew at Port Townsend, Washington, after *Occidental*'s arrival from Acapulco. In truth, there were apparently but two members of the original crew on board, the carpenter having died on the difficult passage north. The account matched the versions related by Craine and Mrs. Williams, but there was also this:

The crew allege that Craine was intimate with Mrs. Williams, and that such proceedings were continued until Valparaiso was reached, where both parties were seen on numerous occasions to enter saloons and to appear intoxicated on the streets. . . . [At Acapulco] Craine was attacked with delirium tremens, and sent to San Francisco with Mrs. Williams.

Captain Taylor had not reported Craine doing any drinking, and Mrs. Williams and family had departed for San Francisco before Craine did. After the article appeared, Mrs. Williams wrote the American consul in Acapulco begging him to write to the *Herald* to correct the story: "It is a terrible disgrace to have my name mixed up with a man who is a complete stranger to me. I was almost employed as a stewardess on the Dublin steamers when this appeared and now I cannot be employed unless my name is cleared."

On November 12, Consul R. W. Longhery, responding to an earlier letter from Mrs. Williams, wrote Arthur Sewall & Co. that baggage—evidently including Captain Williams's navigational items—had not been put aboard the steamer to San Francisco. Mr. Longhery believed that Arthur Sewall & Co. should do something for Mrs.

Williams. His response to Mrs. Williams's second letter was printed in the Dublin *Telegraph* on December 28, and read in part:

> You can well imagine what a painful experience it must have been, and how she must have felt returning to her native land penniless, with three small children to provide for. Was that not enough without coupling her name with slander? . . .
> She is charged in the extract from the *Telegraph* referred to with undue intimacy with the mate, John Craine, who, it is alleged, accompanied her to San Francisco. I am satisfied that these statements are without foundation. . . . Her conduct while here was marked by the strictest propriety. She seemed to me a modest, refined, good woman. Only once did she come ashore during that time and remained only an hour or two. Craine abandoned the ship after it got here and took a room at the hotel. He did not obtrude himself on her, and always spoke of her in terms of respect. . . . She writes to me deeply grieved to shield her from this calumny, based upon the testimony of seamen seven of whom I had to have arrested for insubordination.

In thanking Longhery for his kindness, Mrs. Williams added that some weeks previously she had written Arthur Sewall & Co. asking that money due her from her husband's account be sent to her. She estimated this sum to be about $1,300, not counting the cost of her board, which "they said they charge as a fair sum to captains who took their wives to sea, but everyone said that under the circumstances . . . they would not charge for."

On January 17, 1888, Mrs. Williams wrote the Sewalls reminding them that she had written them two months previously asking them to do something for her, as she was in great need. She added that a certain party in San Francisco—doubtless a lawyer—had offered to pay her passage there on "speculation," but she would prefer not to put Arthur Sewall & Co. to "trouble and expense."

On January 26 Consul Longhery wrote the Sewalls a four-page letter defending Mrs. Williams's honor against the word of mutineers, and criticized the Sewalls for not having sent any instructions regarding her disposition. He noted that there was disagreement as to whether Captain Williams was owed money or was in debt to the ship, and criticized the Sewalls' lack of response to Mrs. Williams's letters. Arthur responded with a soothing letter, assuring Longhery that all would be properly attended to.

On February 27 Mrs. Williams wrote to the Sewalls challenging their claim that Captain Williams was in debt to the ship, "unless you kept his hard earned wages to defray the pilot's expenses." She denied any blame for going home via San Francisco, pointing out that Mr. Craine had no authority to draw funds to send her home from Valparaiso, and that Captain Taylor had taken her off the steamer to Panama when he learned the cost:

> You state in the letter to me that you have given Capt. Dunphy authority to settle with me. You do not consider how I and my poor children are to live until

his arrival in England and if my husband was so much in your debt as you state it is hardly worth waiting for. I have had advice from San Francisco this week and they are only waiting for my consent to commence the suit and send me the money to go there. It is not for the wages but for compensation for the loss of my husband who lost his life in your service. I am very sorry for having to trouble you so often but I think you might have done something for me. You would not have missed $10,000 and it would have started me in life. If it goes to law it will cost you more than double and it won't hurt me for I have nothing to lose and the lawyers are willing to take all chances.

Threatening Arthur Sewall was rarely an effective tactic. He responded that while he thought that it would be best for her to wait and go over the account with Captain Dunphy [upon his expected arrival at Liverpool in the *Willie Rosenfeld*], since she desired that the account be sent at once, it was enclosed. "As regards our charge for board [it] may not be exactly correct but they are as accurate as we can make them from what we have at hand at the office. . . . " If she found any errors they would be pleased to modify them. Arthur Sewall was a patient and well-practiced adversary.

The account showed that despite Arthur's promise, the travel expenses from Acapulco to San Francisco to Dublin, $372 in all, had been charged against Captain Williams's estate. The board for Alice Williams, her children, and her helper, which ended only when they left the ship at Acapulco, amounted to $572. Captain Williams's estate therefore owed the ship $63.04.

On June 12, writing on black-bordered stationery marking the recent death of his wife, Captain Dunphy informed the Sewalls that the *Willie Rosenfeld* had arrived at Liverpool, having "beat the fleet this passage, some fourteen vessels." He had not slept for two days. Regarding "Alice's people," he wrote that he had met her father and step-mother once in Dublin when he was in *Occidental*:

Alice is a woman that wants to do what is fair. But her step mother . . . is a different person. She is half Italian and well educated [and] well up on business. The father is a quiet sort of man and was a petty officer in the English army in India. I am sorry that I will have to leave my ship under the circumstances. . . . I will run on to Dublin and find out what Alice's idea is & explain everything to her [and] get her lowest figure. . . .

"In regards to Capt. Williams," Dunphy wrote, still defending his having urged the Sewalls to give him the ship, "he was an officer with me for about twelve years & he was a good mate." He thought him unlucky as a captain, and that the lawyer for the ship on the pilot case "is the biggest fraud in S. F." Dunphy's reluctance to leave the ship to go to Dublin was due in part to the fact that his mate was likely to be under the influence of liquor in port—"In fact there is not three mates in the American fleet but what is about the same. My mate is a good man at sea." On June 19, Dunphy wrote:

I went to Dublin and settled with Mrs. Williams. Paid her $170. . . . She seemed very bitter against your firm. . . . She said when Mr. Craine was sleeping she keeped a watch nights, that is watched what course the ship was making. Also was ready to call him if there was any sign of the men coming in the cabin. The crew intended to put the ship ashore on the coast of Chile & I suppose to kill the mate. The steward & 2nd mate was with the crew. So, had Mrs. Williams gone to San Francisco she had a pretty good case. I arrived in Dublin at 9 P.M. and I was not able to get her to settle until 12 P.M. I don't think she would settle with any other person. . . . There was two lawyers in San Francisco offered to pay her passage out. Her father did not want her to go to S.F. She is in poor circumstances. I gave her 15 dollars of my own after settling with her. She thinks Capt. Williams paid some of the ship's bills with the money he drawed at different ports.

Presumably the $170 was the balance due for the value of Captain Williams's navigational items. On June 12 Oscar Sewall had written Bath that he had sold Captain Williams's chronometer for $100, and still had two barometers and one "mecurial" [barometer] yet to sell. On July 5, Mrs. Williams wrote the Sewalls a final letter:

Captain Dunphy called a few days ago . . . to settle with me according to your instructions. It was much against my will I done so, but as Capt. Dunphy and his wife were always friends to me I accepted the sum of one hundred and seventy dollars $170 on his account and I think it was a mean ungentlemanly action to take advantage of his friendship. . . . However, if your own conscience is satisfied on the subject let the matter rest. But you must feel in your hearts that you have defrauded a helpless woman and three little children of their rights for there was over one hundred pounds due to my poor husband. . . . You promised to pay my passage home but you did not do so. . . . You were ready to believe everything a lot of mutineers said about me. I made enemies for myself trying to help you for the *Occidental* would not have reached port only I watched with and helped the mate for he could not trust anyone on board and they were all against him. Perhaps you will prosper for the way you have treated me but I don't see how you can.
 Respectfully,
 Alice Williams

John Johnson was found guilty of manslaughter and was sentenced to ten years in Folsom Prison and a $1,000.00 fine.

In astonishment the big craft stops

When the ship *John Rosenfeld* slid into the Kennebec in June 1884, a keel ten feet longer than the *Rosenfeld*'s had already been "stretched." It was rumored that the new

The ship Willie Rosenfeld, *Captain William Dunphy, at New York, after her January 1896 arrival from Tacoma via Valparaiso and Caleta Buena, Chile. Rough seas have scrubbed black paint off her topsides, revealing the white lead undercoat. Charges of brutality on the voyage, reported in the press, would be reprised when Arthur Sewall became a vice-presidential candidate. Departing New York for San Francisco in April, the* Rosenfeld *foundered off the coast of Brazil. It is obvious why the "Willie" was considered a very handsome ship, although the figurehead added nothing to her good looks. Softwood fenders hang alongside.*

ship would have four masts, but Captain William Dunphy, who would command her, requested that she carry the same rig as the *John Rosenfeld*. He did, however, want a larger cabin.

The new ship, which would later be named the *Willie Rosenfeld*, would measure 2,455 tons and was a long time building, with work stopping in the winter. Shipping rates were low and investors were wary. In light of his interests in *Occidental* and the *Babcock*, Dunphy wished to be allowed to buy but a $1/16$ share of the new ship, since by spreading out his investments he would not feel compelled to insure them—this was the Sewalls' usual practice as well.

The Bath *Daily Times*'s headline for September 24, 1885, proclaimed: "The Largest and Handsomest Ship Ever Launched from Local Yard,—A Description of the Beauty." As it happened, this would be the last full-rigger built at Bath until 1891. The editorial struck a reflective note:

> When one looks over the noble ship that was launched yesterday, and appreciates the fine workmanship, the result of years of experience, that is put into her construction, and thinks of the great industry of wooden shipbuilding brought to its

present perfection by so many epochs of persevering hard work, it is difficult to concede that the time is coming when if Bath wishes to remain in the van of marine architecture the product of the hard-pine forest must be abandoned for that of the iron mine.

The reporter covering the launching perhaps had literary aspirations that went beyond reporting the local news:

Regardless of the miserable light rain which made the day one most unpleasant for outdoor pursuits, a large crowd gathered at the A. Sewall & Co. yard yesterday forenoon to see launched the largest ship that has ever hailed from Bath. The crowd convened fully an hour too soon, and in shivering groups enjoyed the exhilarating influence that a discouraging rain storm is wont to exercise over the souls of men and women.

As the carpenters "struck up their chorus on the wedges" the spectators crowded closer. With but a few keel blocks remaining under the keel:

A tremble runs through the system of the huge ship and a small boy in the crowd informs the multitude that "There she goes." In astonishment the big craft stops, and with searching eyes (alongside the foot of the bowsprit) looks over the crowd to find who dares foretell her movements.

Having discouraged the small boy element she concludes to proceed with the launching. Shortly there is the sound of crushing wood, and the ship seems to start. She increases her speed and the ways begin to send up clouds of smoke. They grow more heated and in places flames are seen. It is only for a moment, for the ship has left the realms of the terrestrial and plunged into the realms of the aquatte.

The water boils at her stern, the crowd shouts, the steam whistles set up a shriek, the flags in long lines from the bulwarks to trucks, flutter with excitement and then the bow drops down from the ways into the water.

The tension on the lines at quarter and bow, one to a wharf above, and the other to the [tug] *Ice King* below grow taught and rigid as the terrible strain comes upon them, and the chain of the anchor, just dropped, becomes as straight as a line under the tension. At last she swings around with the tide and the launching is pronounced a success.

After the ship was brought alongside and our intrepid reporter had boarded the beauty, he observantly noted "the long sweep of deck, each plank of equal width and parallel to its neighbor," with her lofty masts "tapering from deck to truck." Descending into the "Egyptian darkness" of the vast and empty hold, he reported that the distance from the main deck to the bottom of the keelson was almost twenty-eight feet. When topside again, he noted that the wheelhouse was of unusual size, but neglected to mention that it contained, in addition to the wheel room, a chartroom, storeroom, and WC.

The climax of our virtual tour was his visit to the cherry-paneled, Queen Anne–style cabin, with its red plush sofas, "inviting in their luxurious depths. . . . Every door has a dozen pretty little square panels and composition door knobs, the rich colors of the wood being relieved in good effect by the bright hue of the metal. . . . The captain's stateroom is fitted up with an eye to both comfort and style, being complete in all that can contribute to make homelike his retreat where for a short season the ship's governor may find time to withdraw from the cares of his position to the comforts of his private apartment."

Of the ship's model, the reporter opined: "While Mr. Pattee has modeled many a handsome ship, he has never before succeeded in combining so well the lines essential to carrying capacity, speed, beauty, and sea-going qualities. Almost broad and having a wide, flat bilge, she is at the same time very sharp and yacht-like."

And indeed, the model of the *Willie's* hull, as cut by William Pattee, was said to be a graceful departure from the usual more burdensome models favored by the Sewalls.

Willie, a young son of John Rosenfeld, had died early in 1885, and it was Arthur who had proposed naming the ship after him, and having her carry a figurehead that was a likeness of the boy. John Rosenfeld, after some hesitation, would become her largest single owner—at least on her register—with a $1/8$ share. Regarding the figurehead, Rosenfeld wrote in May:

> I would prefer to have it made at San Francisco, as then could see that it is made as natural as possible from the photograph. When done I will send it on by rail. Please send me a diagram of the shape of the bow, also please let me know what dimensions you would recommend for the figurehead. Many thanks for expressions of sympathy in the great bereavement which has befallen me.

While surely not unmindful of the prospects of having John Rosenfeld buy into a ship named for his dead son, no doubt Arthur was also sincere in making a kindly gesture. In 1864 he and Emma had lost their third child, Dummer, or "Dosie," at age two, and Arthur's brother Edward and wife had lost a son, William, age nine months. Nevertheless the bow of the *Willie* was not stylistically suited for the addition of a figurehead, which thus looked like an awkward afterthought, if not an unwanted growth.

But I will get more insurance

On October 16, 1885, Captain Alpheus Boyd, a Wiscasset native, in Captain Dunphy's absence, took the new *Willie Rosenfeld* to Baltimore where she would load coal for San Francisco. At Baltimore Captain Boyd was chloroformed while asleep in his cabin, and relieved of his watch, chain, and a considerable sum of money.[8] On November 13, finally under command of Captain Dunphy, the *Willie Rosenfeld*, laden with 3,692 tons of coal, departed Baltimore for San Francisco, arriving on March 22, 1886, after a passage of 128 days. From San Francisco Captain Dunphy wrote the Sewalls:

On leaving Cape Henry and getting all sail set I noticed the ship had a heavy ungainly motion. . . . She started all the tiles in the galley floor, very little sea on. She commenced to ship seas up on the poop deck. . . . I thought perhaps she had too much cargo in the lower hold so took up 10 tons in the upper tween decks but it did not make any difference. I had no bad weather until off Cape Horn. There I had strong winds but no bad gales. She acted terrible bad. With a strong wind I could not carry but very little canvas. She would ship heavy seas and flood the main deck. . . . She disabled several of the men. . . . I think if I had encountered a severe gale she would have washed bulwarks, houses away. Perhaps gone down. She would settle down like a block of marble. The cabin worked awful bad. . . . She started the oakum out of her butts outside. A vessel could not behave worse. . . . In Lat. 10 North Pacific I had a strong breeze for a few hours and took in the topgallant sails. When clewing up the main topgallant sail she shipped a sea and washed the watch in to the lee side, nearly killed five men. I have had to send them into the hospital. . . . She cannot carry over 3,500 tons of coal & 3,550 tons of wheat. You know by the cargoes I have carried while in *Occidental* that I will put in all the cargo a ship can carry. But if you say put in 3,700 tons I will do so. But I will get more insurance on my part for the first severe gale she encounters she will come to grief. She is a different model from all your ships. The *A. G. Ropes* is but 11 tons smaller and all the wheat she carried was 3,520 tons.9 The *Willie Rosenfeld* is something like her.

Evidently she was overloaded, and with her finer model did not tolerate it as well as did fuller-modeled ships.

At San Francisco the *Rosenfeld* was called "the finest modeled ship that has ever come to this port." Her decks were crowded with admirers. But Dunphy wrote that he was "very much disappointed both in her carrying & sailing." Comparing tracks and dates with his old mate, Captain John Williams, on the smaller *Occidental*, he determined that the two ships were not fifty miles apart for the last forty-eight days, despite a "good strong whole sail breeze." He believed that the *Willie*'s upper sails were too light, and that her fore and main topgallants and lower topsails were "ever so much too small." Also the jibs didn't set well. And "after the palm oil got washed out" of the running rigging it looked like "it was made from grass."

And he had more complaints, the last being that the water closets were not fit for a sailing ship—when the ship settled down in a sea "the water spurts up through the bowl three feet." He did allow that she was a very good steering ship, and "looks as gay as she can look," but "I think the *John Rosenfeld* model is a more profitable one. She was a good sailor and a good carrier and was a fine heavy weather ship." Seeing her "wreckage"—salvaged gear brought to San Francisco for auction—he felt badly for the loss of "this fine, noble ship."

The *Willie* then made a 119-day passage to Liverpool carrying 3,625 tons of wheat, and another 60 tons of stores, dunnage, and so on. Dunphy reported that in bad weather the ship "behaved about the same as on the outward passage. . . . She requires more watching in heavy weather than any vessel I ever was in."

In a letter in the September 16, 1886, *Journal of Commerce*, a correspondent who went by the name of "Old Argus" praised the *Willie* as "the most magnificent wooden ship afloat." She sat in the dock "surrounded by the iron denizens of the briny deep—all sorts of ugly ancient and modern shapes—as though gazing upon her as the greatest and last of a vanquished race."

Captain Dunphy was said by Argus to be "well known in former days of the American packet service." His "massive forehead, genial countenance, and weather-beaten brow indicate the intelligent navigator and seaman brave. . . . " Dunphy told Argus of a gale met on the passage which nearly submerged the ship until "with one bound she shook herself free. . . . I thought she would do it; but if we had been on board some of those long, narrow gun-barrel things that I saw in Frisco, not one of us would have been left to tell the tale." Dunphy was referring to British "iron" ships, which had less beam and less buoyancy than did American wooden ships.

Vice Consul Harold Sewall, forgetting his advice to build no more wooden ships, swelled with pride: "The queen of the fleet came in the river today, her colors flying and her spars glistening, a vessel to be proud of. . . . I never saw a ship in such condition. Of course it all comes back to the captain [Dunphy] and I do not think a finer one treads the deck."

The condition of the *Willie*'s wheat cargo was a matter of great interest, given the discrimination in insurance rates imposed against wooden ships by Liverpool underwriters. It was disheartening, indeed, when some damaged cargo was found. The source was a mystery until two auger holes were discovered in the floor of the mate's room, by which means he had drained several inches of storm water. Although it meant that the ship could not make an insurance claim, Harold advised Dunphy to reveal the truth, thereby saving the ship's good name.

Dunphy described the already discharged mate as "a fraud and an un-responsible man," who was no seaman, had yarned with the men, and, as mate of the *W. R. Grace*, had helped Captain Black drink himself to death. Dunphy would have gotten rid of him at San Francisco if he could have found another mate. Had he discovered the holes while at sea the mate would not have remained in very good health.

With more passages under her keel, Dunphy gained more confidence in the *Willie*, although he could not resist writing the Sewalls of all the ships that passed him by—even the big-bellied Thomaston carrier *Edward O'Brien* sailed her out of sight to windward in sixteen hours. "The *Willie* is no good on the wind, but with a free wind she sails very well. I don't understand why she is not a faster ship."

In 1887 Dunphy was all but undone by the death of his wife. Captain Wiley Dickinson of Bath took over for a Liverpool–San Francisco coal passage while Dunphy went home to tend to his three children.

In February 1891 Dunphy's caution when approaching the Golden Gate likely saved his ship and the lives of those aboard. Off Point Reyes the barometer fell very rapidly, and Dunphy immediately headed offshore, splitting some sails in the process. The three-skysail ship *Elizabeth*—one of the ships that had once shown the *Willie* her heels—built at Newcastle, Maine, and owned at Searsport, Maine, stood in, attempting to make port. Although two tugs were fast to her, hurricane-force winds from the southeast and heavy seas drove her ashore near the Golden Gate, drowning eighteen, including Captain Colcord. A British ship narrowly escaped a similar fate by anchoring and cutting away some spars.

In January 1894, bound from San Francisco to Queenstown, the *Rosenfeld* was running before a moderate gale under lower fore and main topsails near the Western Islands, or the Azores, when, at 9:30 P.M., a terrific sea pooped the ship. The sea lifted the big wheelhouse from its fastenings and drove it against the after cabin, breaking the wheel. The house, adrift, shifted back, then to port, then to starboard. Dunphy had been standing in the wheelhouse watching the steering, and, along with four sailors, was pinned under the wreckage. Two men and the second mate had been standing outside the house; one man was killed outright, the other had his leg broken in two places.

After feeling "as though life was almost crushed out of me," Dunphy crawled out from under the house, his right leg dislocated, his left leg bleeding badly, and his body bruised and cut. He ordered the topsail sheets let go so that the ship would not broach to and sink stern-first. The men were got out from under the house, the tiller was lashed, the yards braced, and the after hatch secured. With the help of the cabin boy Dunphy got onto the after house and lashed himself to the mizzenmast. With a line stretched along the spanker boom, the boy managed to pull Dunphy's leg back into the socket. Dunphy then went below where he set all the sailors' broken bones. In all, eight men were severely injured and one was killed.

Fortunately Dunphy had an excellent mate (at least at sea, when he was sober) named Gillespie, who "did all he possibly could to get the ship along," shaking the rest of the men out of a state of paralysis. The following day it blew a "regular hurricane," harder than anything Dunphy had ever experienced in nineteen years at sea. His extended account of working the stricken ship to Queenstown over the next two weeks, in the face of continual gales, is exhausting just to read.

The *Willie* was towed to Havre where she was repaired. She then sailed to Newport News in ballast, and there Captain Dunphy requested a few days off to go see his children, whom he had not seen for over two years.[10]

The bravest men and the best citizens

In 1887 Arthur Sewall was quoted by a reporter for the *Boston Herald*:

> It is often asked by people who are ignorant of the national bearings, the national importance of this issue. . . . "Why build ships if other nations will do our carrying trade cheaply enough now?" That question is best answered by another: Why should we not permit some other nation—England, for instance— to control our railroads, manage our domestic mails, our telegraph and express

companies, nay, even the business of government itself. . . ?

The question whether the ship owner makes a small profit or none at all is a minor one, for the ship owners are the ship builders, the very mechanics themselves, and the building of ships and maintaining them supports a hundred industries. . . . And without a merchant marine we are without sailors! It is idle to assume that modern warships do not need experienced sailors. . . .

The bravest men and the best citizens are those who follow the sea and those who build ships. There is no healthier mechanical occupation, physically, morally and mentally, than that of shipbuilding. For proof of that, see our ship mechanics of Bath. A sturdier, steadier, better set of men never breathed. They are industrious, frugal, intelligent and highly skilled. Ten thousand ship mechanics are immeasurably superior as men and citizens to 10,000 factory operatives. Ship building makes men, not machines.

It is impossible to build ships successfully where they are not largely owned, where there is not a maritime community. It has been tried time after time, and every time it has failed. . . . If the present state of things continues, America will, in less than a quarter of a century, lose all knowledge of the art of shipbuilding. If we are to be a maritime nation again, we must build iron ships. To build iron ships we must be relieved of the burdens and obstacles imposed by the government. That is the whole thing in a nutshell.[11]

While it is unlikely that the reporter's version was word perfect, the sentiments expressed are pure Arthur Sewall, and one suspects that Arthur believed all of this with all of his heart, at least while he proclaimed it. The homage to the stellar qualities of "those who follow the sea" would surely surprise many of the hard-pressed sailors aboard Sewall ships.

A strong sentimental streak runs through Arthur's remarks, suggesting that for all the cold calculation, the penny-pinching, and even the bloodied decks of some of his ships, there beat in Arthur Sewall the heart of a romantic, longing for a return to a lost golden era.

On the other hand, his concerns for the future of shipbuilding—and for the future of Bath—were surely well-founded. While the building of wooden deepwater square-riggers at Bath had been, for the time being, replaced by the building of big wooden schooners, in twenty-five years shipbuilding at Bath—as Arthur had known it all through his life, and through his father's life as well—would indeed be all but ended.

There was surely also a whiff of nativism—very much a part of the times —here as well. Arthur's nostalgia is for the day before foreign ships stole away America's trade, when red-blooded American sailors served in American ships—never mind that foreigners had long been in the crews of American ships, or why American sailors had now all but vanished. He was calling up, as well, the days before foreign-born mill operatives crowded Maine's mill towns—never mind that Arthur was invested in some of these mills and sat on their boards, and that these great mills, now largely dependent on foreign-born workers, were very good customers of the Maine Central Railroad, of which Arthur was president.[12]

In 1887 Arthur Sewall & Co.'s fleet consisted of twelve ships and five schooners, and—with the fleets of Chapman and Flint having been divided in 1880—constituted the largest fleet of American-flag square-riggers sailing deepwater. (In 1890 Flint & Co. had eleven square-riggers and two schooners; I. F. Chapman had eleven full-riggers.) But the two newest Sewall ships had been built in 1885 and 1882, the oldest in 1869, and all were getting older and also relatively smaller. If new and larger ships were not added the Sewalls would soon face having to leave the business which had fitted them so well for nearly sixty years.

And while Arthur recognized the inevitability of moving to the building of iron ships—a letter received back in 1883 from a Philadelphia iron broker indicates that Arthur even then had been considering the switch to iron—this was evidently not yet that day.[13] But building more wooden ships looked to many like a dead end. In the 1890s Arthur would make the move to steel, but not before building, as if for a last hurrah, four outsized wooden ships bearing the melodic and romantic Indian names of southern rivers, *Rappahannock, Shenandoah, Susquehanna,* and *Roanoke,* launched in June 1890, December 1890, September 1891, and August 1892, respectively. According to the *Bangor Daily Commercial,* November 5, 1898, they were named for "events of the war with the South."

Whereas *Rappahannock* was an oversized three-masted full-rigged ship, the others were far more sensibly rigged as four-masted barks, although they were still called "ships," as had been the three previous American four-masted barks, *Great Republic, Ocean King,* and the *Frederick Billings.* (The Bureau of Navigation called them "four-masted ships," and in some quarters they were called "shipentines.") The resistance to calling them barks ran deep, since in New England maritime culture the bark had always been viewed as possessing inferior status to the ship.

Indeed, it is interesting that previous to *Shenandoah,* E. & A. Sewall and Arthur Sewall & Co. had built forty-one ships and only three barks, one of which was quickly sold. Yet, as the resourceful New Bedford ship owner William H. Besse—whose fleet was largely built next-door to the Sewalls—in particular, had well demonstrated, big barks were fully the equal of ships in performance. Indeed, they were handier and also cheaper to build, to maintain, and to man.[14] It would seem that here the Sewalls' obsessive concern with economy was overridden by a greater concern for status, perhaps combined with sentiment, habit, and—dare it be suggested of the man who so eschewed excessive ornamentation—romance. Even if the four big ships were conceived as a calculated stopgap measure, and in the expectation that Congress would soon pass a shipping bounty bill being pushed by Maine's Senator Frye, Arthur Sewall's under-the-table die-hard romantic streak surely played a role as well.

For their big wooden ships, the Sewalls attracted some investors with no previous connection to the world of shipping—known as "dry owners"—a practice which would be continued with their steel ships. These very big ships were intended to be manned by crews smaller even than those carried in the past by very much smaller ships, although the ships' greater size was not compensated for by any great addition of labor-saving devices. Instead, so critics charged, their crews were overdriven by bucko mates. Instead of proving the viability of ever-larger wooden ships, the "Big Four" demonstrated their practical limits, romance or no romance.

I become, at times, a trifle bitter

In November 1888, as an experiment, the Sewalls sent the 1887 schooner *Carrie A. Lane* west around Cape Horn to San Francisco. In January 1889 they sent the new four-masted schooner *Douglas Dearborn* eastward past the Cape of Good Hope to Sydney, Australia, and, eventually, around the world, doubling Cape Horn going from west to east. While "coasting" schooners had for years been making numerous European, West African, and South American voyages, relatively few had ventured beyond the two great capes.

Given the small crews used to man these two schooners, in large part due to the use of a steam "donkey" engine to hoist and trim sails (for various reasons, steam could not be practically applied to square-rig), they were sailed very economically, at least in regard to wages. However, the schooner rig was vulnerable in both a rolling calm, where the schooner's fore-and-aft sails slatted destructively, and in very heavy weather, when the reefed-down schooner's sails were blanketed in the wave troughs. Square-riggers, by contrast, used their lower topsails as storm sails.

The *Lane*, being, at 760 tons, more than a hundred tons larger than the Sewalls' next-largest three-masted schooner, was something of an experiment herself, testing the outer limits of manageable size with her rig. With coal from Baltimore, it took her 165 days to reach San Francisco, having spent forty-seven days doubling the Horn. Meeting a series of powerful westerly gales, she suffered blown-out sails, a flooded cabin, and mutiny. Four times she passed the Horn, only to be blown back to the east. Finally arrived at San Francisco, Captain Fred Dyer, a native of North Haven Island, Maine, wrote Bath:

> It is a mistake to think that this rig on a schooner as large as the *Lane* and heavy rigged can make good time around Cape Horn. The sea there . . . when it falls calm as it did many times with me, the wear and tear to sails and rigging is something dreadful. My peak halyard blocks are all broke down. Will have to have new sheaves, most of running rigging will have to be new. . . . I feel greatly disappointed in having to come back again.

Captain Dyer had thought that she would be staying on the West Coast, and was very unhappy at being told to turn around, but Oscar Sewall thought her too small for the coastal coal trade, and not well configured for carrying a deckload of lumber. He also thought she should have been a four-master. For a return cargo, she loaded dyewood at Altata, Mexico. After her departure from Altata, Oscar wrote from San Francisco:

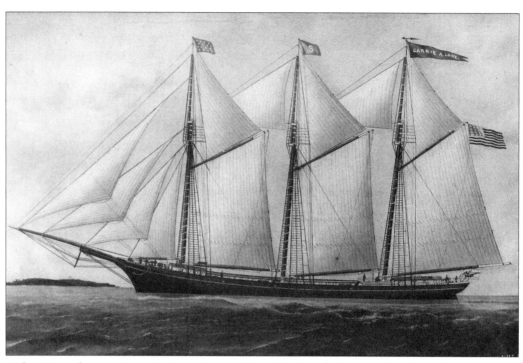

The 1887 schooner Carrie A. Lane. *Several New England artists produced vessel portraits in this semi-primitive style—this rendition was probably the work of S. F. M. (Solon Francis Montecello) Badger, of Charlestown, Massachusetts. Captains were prime customers of these paintings, and this one belonged to Captain Richard Quick, the* Lane *having been his first command. A very big three-master, the 760-ton* Lane *was converted to a four-master in 1900.*

The captain took from here a good mate, but he did not remain with him after arrival at Altata. He advanced his second mate to mate, and took one of the crew as second mate. I understand that this present mate knows nothing of navigation, and that when the vessel left, had it not been for the agent of the company, who was on board, she might have gone ashore, as the mate, who was at the wheel, being cursed by the captain, seized a hammer, left the wheel, and chased the captain about the decks. The agent meanwhile took the wheel.

Dyer, Oscar reported, was thought by some to drink excessively and to exhibit more bluster than spine. The charterer, under the circumstances, thought it prudent to fully insure the cargo. Nevertheless, the *Lane* completed her round voyage after an uneventful 145-day passage.

The *Lane* was named for the wife of the New York agent of the Pacific Mail Steamship Co. with whom the Sewalls had dealt when chartering ships carrying coal to Acapulco. In gratitude, Mr. Lane had bought a $1/16$ interest—$2,500—in the schooner, and, as was traditional, presented her with a "set of colors, i.e., flags. In 1899, after twenty-eight years of service with the "old P. M.," Mr. Lane was forced out. The direc-

Sparmakers (and river fishermen) John, Frank, and Edwin Parris, flanked by two employees, at the Sewall yard. The Parris brothers were sons of sparmaker Albion K. Parris, who first made spars for the Sewalls circa 1860. The men are in the process of tapering, rounding, and smoothing "Oregon pine" (Douglas fir) mast timbers, shipped as cargo aboard a square-rigger via Cape Horn. Such timbers usually arrived eight-sided. Possibly they are for the three-masted schooner Agnes E. Manson, *launched in September 1889—if so, the large vessel in frame beyond would be* Rappahannock. MAINE MARITIME MUSEUM

tors, he wrote, "regretted that the financial condition of the company precluded the possibility of a pension." Mr. Lane, who was evidently a native of England, observed that the English handled such matters better than did the Americans. "As my breakdown was caused by *over* work in the Co.'s interest, I become, at times, a trifle bitter," he wrote.

Mr. Lane had previously written to the Sewalls inquiring as to the possibilities of selling his interest: "Your firm wrote me that 'if I would advise them my price for my interest they would let me know, in case they saw an opportunity of disposing of same.'. . . Will you not for the sake of old relations kindly interest yourself in this matter. . . ?" The Sewalls did not reply. In 1900, when rebuilt after being wrecked, the *Lane* was re-rigged as a four-master. In 1902 she was sold.

———

In January 1889 the four-masted schooner *Douglas Dearborn* was launched and immediately towed to Boston, there to load case oil and general cargo for Sydney, Australia,

The four-masted schooner Douglas Dearborn *awaits her launching in January 1889*
MAINE MARITIME MUSEUM

for Henry W. Peabody & Co.'s venerable "Australasian Line." Peabody was alarmed to discover that the Sewalls intended to send the *Dearborn* off without a square-sail on her foremast. "All the schooners which we have sent out to Australia have been so rigged and this sail has been found to be of great advantage. . . . We hope you will conclude to have one made for your vessel." The Sewalls responded that they had considered this matter and had decided against one.

The *Dearborn* made a creditable passage of ninety-nine days, only about a month slower than record clipper times. In June, writing from Newcastle, New South Wales, where she was loading coal for Acapulco, Captain F. B. Welch, of Portland, wrote: "The vessel sails well and is a good sea boat. I have had a great deal of trouble to get seamen here as everyone thinks I do not carry crew enough, but four [sailors] is a plenty to man her."

From Acapulco the *Dearborn* sailed in ballast to Port Townsend, Washington, and there loaded lumber for Philadelphia, which she reached in 134 days. She spent the remainder of her brief career on the Atlantic coast, being wrecked on Cuttyhunk Island in February 1893.

At far left, the four-masted schooner Agnes E. Manson *of New Haven, Connecticut, built in 1889 by Arthur Sewall & Co. for Captain Magnus Manson, of New Haven. An unknown three-master is tied alongside her; two four-masters are ahead; all are being towed up the Kennebec River (by the tug at far right) to load ice. In June 1873 the Sewalls' schooner* Satilla *was in just such a tow when the schooner she was lashed to ran aground, and the schooners towing behind them ran into their sterns.* MAINE MARITIME MUSEUM

In March 1894 the Ross & Howell Towboat Co. of Bangor, Maine, sent the Sewalls a fourth request for payment of a bill for $60.76 for towing the ice-laden *Douglas Dearborn* to sea in 1892—the bill for towing the schooner down the river to the bay had been paid by the ice shipper, but the schooner was responsible for any towing thereafter. Although the first notice had been sent before the schooner was lost, the Sewalls responded in May 1892 that had the bill been promptly sent it would have been paid. They gave no indication that they now planned to do so.

Give the monkeys a chance

Deep-sea vessels were more often lost ashore than at sea. The classic fatal situation was for an embayed vessel to be driven by a gale onto a lee shore, and such was the fate of the ship *Chesebrough*, wrecked on the northern end of the main island of Japan on October 30, 1889.

The ship Chesebrough *fitting out, July or August 1878. Her first master, Samuel Dinsmore, wrote: "I am highly pleased with the sailing qualities of the* Chesebrough.*" For her first voyage* Chesebrough *was chartered by the Tudor Company of Boston to load ice at Wiscasset, on the deep Sheepscot River, for Bombay, India. Ice was carried halfway around the world at a low rate in lieu of sailing in ballast. Except for such cargoes carried by newly launched Maine square-riggers, most of the ice carried to the Far East was Massachusetts ice that departed from Boston.* MAINE MARITIME MUSEUM

The fine ship *Chesebrough,* of 1,461 tons, was launched in July 1878, being the last vessel launched by E. & A. Sewall. Thomas M. Reed of Phippsburg, with 15/32, was her largest registered owner.

The *Chesebrough's* first master was Captain S. B. Dinsmore, late of the ship *Undaunted.* He was succeeded in 1884 by Captain Peter Erickson, then about age thirty-four. Erickson wrote long letters in a legible hand, his diction but faintly revealing that English was a second language. He was by all accounts an able and prudent shipmaster. Erickson had been informally adopted when twelve years old as a cabin boy by Captain Lemuel Soule of Woolwich to help take care of his young son Fred. Loretta Soule Carter, who grew up referring to Peter as her cousin, wrote Mark Hennessey that Peter was cruelly beaten and half-starved by his father, who was glad to be rid of him.

She also claimed that he was Portuguese, without explaining how he came to have a Nordic name.

Mrs. Carter lost two actual cousins in the wreck along with Peter—twenty-three-year-old James "Bert" Bailey, the first mate, and twenty-two-year-old Fred Soule, who was Peter's surrogate brother, and who was third mate. (Both were six feet two inches tall, Bert's body being positively identified by his red beard. Peter was but five feet four, which is how his corpse was identified.)

In an 1891 letter to the Honorable Nathan Webb of Portland, in regard to probate, Arthur wrote of Captain Erickson: "He was a foreigner by birth, and has no relation or heirs in this country to my knowledge. I do not know what part of Europe he came from, or where you could find his heirs. He was unmarried." Arthur added: "I do not understand why any money should be with Captain Erickson's personal effects, excepting what small amount he might have had on his person. If any considerable amount has been sent you, it should belong to the ship." He promised to look further into the matter. Mrs. Carter wrote that thirty years after Peter's death, Peter's father put in a claim for "every dollar Peter left."

The *Chesebrough* departed Philadelphia in March 1889, with a cargo of case oil for Hiogo, Japan. In September, having discharged the cargo and taken on ballast, she had sailed to Hakodate, on the north island, to load sulfur for New York. She arrived partially dismasted after a three-day tussle with a typhoon, and was there re-rigged. Her departure, after loading 2,330 tons of sulfur, was delayed for nine days by a series of heavy gales.

On October 28 Erickson thought he had a fair chance to make an offing sailing west through Tsugaru Strait toward the Sea of Japan. However, shortly before she would have cleared the strait, the wind headed the ship, and Erickson anchored for the night. The following morning the wind had freshened to a gale, and it was necessary to up anchor. With hindsight, the ship should have turned-to and sailed east, into the Pacific. However, Erickson apparently thought that the ship would be able to fetch clear of the land on the port tack. But soon it was evident that the ship was being set upon the northern shore, and the ship was tacked.

During the night the mizzen topgallant mast and headsails were lost, and, being set down on the southern shore by a rising nor'west gale and a strong current, the ship—dull and unresponsive with its heavy dead-weight cargo—was brought back on the port tack by wearing around, or by bringing the wind across her stern, rather than across her bow as when tacking. Much ground is lost when wearing ship, yet she nearly weathered the last point lying between disaster and the open sea, but could not. Both anchors were dropped but they dragged and she soon went aground, turning broadside to and careening toward the crashing seas. The wreck lay about one mile off the beach of the fishing village of Shariki.

The wind and the water were both numbingly cold. No boat could live in the furious seas between the disintegrating ship and the distant shore. Men, stripped-down, clung to the mizzen rigging until the mast fell, killing outright or fatally injuring some, and throwing others into the sea, where they were blinded by the floating

Portland, Oregon, January 1886. Two views of the ship Chesebrough, *Captain Peter Erickson, "hove down" for repairs after dragging onto Clatsop Spit at the mouth of the Columbia River on Christmas Day, 1885. With her cargo of wheat discharged and lower masts braced with spars, she was "hove down" by three heavy tackles, one rigged to each masthead. A hole, plugged with sand and chips—which would have sunk her—was discovered on the port side of the keel. Note the aft-pointing tiller aft of the simple rope-and-spindle steering gear and the octagonal binnacle, typical of Sewall ships.* MAINE MARITIME MUSEUM

sulphur. Men also died when struck by wreckage as three particularly large seas swept over them. Of the twenty-three aboard the ship, only four men made it to shore alive, and two of them had temporarily lost their minds. Three of the survivors were sailors—an American, a Liverpudlian, a Finn—and the fourth was eighteen-year-old Victor Beck of Philadelphia, a passenger.[15]

The bodies, both alive and dead, were pulled from the seas by fishermen. The villagers aided the survivors in every way possible, dressing them in kimonos and wrapping them in blankets by a fire. When one of the sailors, Henri Wilson, appeared to be in critical condition, Mrs. Han Kudo, the wife of a fisherman, took off her clothes and hugged him to warm him. Mr. Wilson revived.[16] The survivors were then carried to a house; the next day two were so sore as to be unable to move.

On the following day they were taken by horseback and carriage in a procession of policemen to Aomeri, eighteen miles away, and were fed meat from a drowned pig washed ashore from the ship. They then traveled back to Hakodate and took a steamer to Yokohama, where they boarded a steamship for the United States. Before departing, Victor Beck stated: "I cannot give fitting expression to the gratitude my comrades and myself feel towards the Japanese people and authorities who displayed every possible proof of sympathy and kindness."

For the people of Shariki the *Chesebrough*'s flotsam contained many treasures and surprises. The sweet canned fruit gave them headaches; they enjoyed the potatoes but feared that the smarting fumes of onions would blind their children, and promptly buried them. A pear tree grown from seed from a sweet fruit found on the beach grew much larger than Japanese pear trees, and in the 1970s its first fruit was still ceremoniously offered to the graves of the nineteen drowned men. A toilet seat, thought to be a work of art, was hung on a wall with pride. During World War II sulfur from the cargo was used to make matches; sails were made into aprons.

The *Chesebrough*'s crew, signed on at Philadelphia, had consisted of—in addition to the three surviving sailors, Captain Peter Erickson, the mate Bert Bailey, and third mate Fred Soule—the second mate, from New York; the carpenter, from Sweden; the steward, from Philadelphia; the cook, from Rhode Island; the boy, from Antwerp; and sailors from Nova Scotia, London, Norway, Sweden (three), Ireland (two), Scotland, Philadelphia, and Vermont.

That unfortunate Captain Erickson was a kindhearted man is quite evident from the following incident telling, as it does, that in the midst of disaster and when his crew and himself were in the greatest possible danger he had thought for the dumb. Said Boeck [*sic*] to his interviewer: "Just before we went into the mizzen rigging the captain shouted the order, 'Open the lazerette and give the monkeys a chance.' This was done but the monkeys were evidently killed for they did not respond. Could there be any finer epitaph in memory of Captain Erickson, we ask, than 'Open the lazerette and give the monkeys a chance!'"
— *The Japan Gazette*, November 14, 1889

Monkeys and exotic birds were often acquired by sailors and officers to be sold at home as private "adventures."

Including wines and cigars

In October 1889 Arthur Sewall rented the parlor car "Idlewild" from Pullman's Palace Car Co. for a seventeen-day family rail tour from Bath to Vancouver, British Columbia, and return. The car rental was $425, commissary service, $269.80, for a total bill of $694.80.

No one went hungry—the commissary account includes grouse, teal duck, turkey, bluefish, oysters, cod, mackerel, sirloin beef, roast beef, lamb, mutton, sausage, liver, veal, bacon, ham, pork, baked beans, codfish balls, clam chowder, lambs' tongues, mincemeat, sardines, shrimp, asparagus, cucumbers, celery, corn, eggplant, lettuce, mushrooms, parsnips, parsley, peas, potatoes, sweet potatoes, radishes, squash, tomatoes, turnips, apples, bananas, grapes, oranges, peaches, pears, cherries, cranberries, pineapple, plum pudding, cherry preserves, strawberry preserves, brown bread, Graham bread, Vienna bread, toast bread, butter, cake, coffee, milk, chocolate, Edam cheese, eggs, lemons, syrup, ice cream, oatmeal, olives, onions, raisins, rice, French mustard, and so on. Nor did they go thirsty.

Given that Arthur was a railroad president, to say nothing of a personal friend of Mr. Pullman's, it is not surprising that it was noted on the bill that "the rate for use of the car is a very low rate, namely $25 a day, and we have charged you only for actual time that the car was absent, and the commissary service we have furnished at cost, wholesale rates. . . . Including wines and cigars the bill only averages about $1.75 a meal. . . . "

On December 14 a second letter was sent, the Pullman district supervisor noting that as "nothing has ever been heard from you in regard to the matter, and thinking that the bills may have been lost or missent . . . will you please let us hear from you. . . ?" The bill was then promptly paid.

The letter of acknowledgment for the payment ended, "Also please find enclosed a check for $10, being money the Porter borrowed from you to make commissary purchases."

Another Selection of Interesting Letters

From Joseph Foster, United States Navy Yard, Portsmouth, New Hampshire, June 9, 1891:

> Herewith please find my check No. 10012 on the First National Bank of Portsmouth N. H. for twenty and 25/100 dollars as per annexed statement, being your deposit on account of the sale of condemned stores at this navy yard June 3rd 1891. Your bids not being the highest for any lot.

From Arthur Sewall & Co. to John B. Worth, Esq., Bath, October 19, 1890:

We enclose check to your order for $464.34 in payment of following bills, say—
  Jan. 13 vs. Schooner *Carrie A. Lane* $150.93
  " 14 vs. Ship *Shenandoah* $313.42
By notes in pencil on these bills you will observe that your charges were in excess of what others were charging us for similar goods at the same time; $8.16 on first bill, $15.37 on other. This will account for our delay in remitting for same.
  We regret that your prices will not permit us to buy stores for our vessels from you any longer, as we have saved money going elsewhere.

———

From W. M. Belcher & Co., Boston, New England agents for the Caligraph typewriter, June 28, 1890:

In reply would say that have been trying to get a young man to go to Bath, but we find that those that are willing would want $15 per week. Have only a few at that price. Have a number of young ladies who would like the position, that are competent stenographers and type-writers, at a salary $8 or $10 per week. . . .

From Miss Alice Rollins, Portland, Maine, January 30, 1892:

Since coming home I have considered what you said in regard to paying $8.00 to start with. Do I understand that is what I am to receive? $9.00 was the price named by you to Mr. Richards and the price at which I accepted the situation. . . . I do not feel like taking the position at less than the price named in the first place. If you are willing to pay me $9.00 I shall be ready to go at any time you wish to have me. Deducting a dollar a week from my salary for a time and paying so many car fares makes more difference with me than you would at first realize.

———

From Arthur Sewall, December 10, 1894, to Captain R. E. Fletcher, schooner *Talofa*:

This will be handed to you by Harry Smith, a young tramp, in whom I have taken a little interest.
  I want you to take him on board your vessel and keep him two months, if he behaves himself and proves worthy, then I will take him for other work. Give him

$5.00 per month and spend all of that yourself in clothes for him. Treat him well, but work him hard.

Do not know whether he is honest or not, but I am inclined to think he may be. I want you to find out what his habits are, if they are not good in every respect let him go. If they are good take good care of him, and as I said, work him hard.

Send him back to me in a couple of months if you have him then. Write me if you receive him all right, and what you think of him after you have worked him a few days.

———

From J. S. Jackson & Sons, tackle block manufaturers, Bath, May 12, 1894:

The amount we have carried to your account [is] a just bill & we expect payment of the same and unless it's paid by a check, and you ever have anything more of us, it will be in the bill whether you can see it or not. We warn you now that unless you wish to pay it, don't ever order anything more of us.

And Some Letters Displaying Charity

In May 1892 Arthur wrote George Dearborn to thank him for canceling, at Arthur's request, a San Francisco coal charter for the ship *Hecla*, owned by John Marr, an old-time Bath ship owner. Arthur apologized for "what most naturally appears to you as an interference on my part with your business." He explained:

In brief, yesterday morning I was sent for by some of my friends to go see Mr. Marr and if possible help him out. I found a very sick man and a great trouble on his mind, and it was preventing sleep, was the complication which he had innocently gotten into with *Hecla*. I saw at once that he ought to be relieved of this and as a duty to my neighbor and friends here I assured to ask you to do as you did. . . . If you should suffer any pecuniary loss by it, I should make it up to you.

———

In July 1899 Arthur received a letter from C. H. Greenleaf, tax collector of the city of Bath:

Horace Littlefield informs me that you are disposed to assist in the payment of the tax on his real estate. Enclosed is the bill. . . . As the city is about to sue for all back taxes it is a good time to settle & avoid costs. I want to help Horace out as far as possible.

Horace Littlefield was a caulker.

In April, 1901 Israel Eastman, a ship carpenter, wrote the Sewalls: "Please accept the sincere thanks of myself and family for the generous check received, as an expression of your sympathies for me in my unfortunate accident, also for the good wishes for my speedy restoration."

On April 21, 1906, Arthur Sewall & Co. telegraphed Williams, Dimond & Co., San Francisco, that $1,000 had been deposited to their credit "to be used for suffering and needy" resulting from the earthquake and fire. Of the general situation, Williams, Dimond, wrote: "It is useless for us to attempt to describe anything of the nature of this calamity at present. . . . " They had relocated their office to the American-Hawaiian Steamship Co. pier. Williams, Dimond thought that the money could best be spent sometime in the future, as immediate needs were being covered by the general relief fund. Mrs. Mary Merrill, the wife of a Dr. John Merrill, distributed $250 from the Sewalls' relief fund to twelve individuals from December 1906 to March 1907. Ten of the recipients were women, and most of the money was spent toward clothing. One of the two male recipients received a double truss.

1. Frederick C. Matthews, *American Merchant Ships, 1850–1900*, Series 1 (Salem, MA: Marine Research Society, 1930), p. 218.
2. Bath *Daily Times*, June 30, 1874.
3. "No man ever becomes a villain all at once." Juvenal
4. Arthur Sewall, Edward Sewall, William D. Sewall [estate], William P. Lincoln, William H. Dunphy, Peter G. Bradstreet, Frank P. Dunphy, Thomas M. Reed, Charles K. Coleman, George E. Foster, the claimants, and T. H. Allen and Daniel Foster, sureties, had put up the bond.
5. In December 1876, as *Indiana* was towing out of Chesapeake Bay bound for San Francisco behind the Baltimore tug *Mary Shaw*, the pilot fell and was paralyzed. The injured pilot was put on the tug to be taken to Baltimore and the tug's skipper, Captain William Shaw, remained aboard *Indiana* to serve as pilot. A fair wind offered before the tug could return, and *Indiana* sailed with Shaw aboard. On March 7, 1877, Captain Alexander Jones, owner of the towing company, wrote to Arthur Sewall:

> Dear Friend, I now think that Wm. H. Shaw will most likely go to San Francisco in your good ship *Indiana*. I hope you will direct Capt. Drummond to send him home as soon as he arrives. I need him very much and have suffered very much this winter not having him in the boat. I had to hire a capt. in his place which is not of half the value of Wm. I pay Wm. $100 per month and I see by the Pilot Law when a pilot is carried to sea the ship has to pay one until his death or return which includes passage [home] if any.

On April 5 Alexander wrote *Indiana*'s Captain Drummond in expectation of the ship's arrival at San Francisco, stating that he had had no reply from the Sewalls, but wanted Captain Shaw sent back overland. He expected to be paid by the Sewalls for Shaw's time and transportation home. A settlement must have been reached, as Jones's tugs would continue to tow Sewall ships from Baltimore. According to an item in the Bangor *Industrial Journal*, Aug. 28, 1885, the ship *Benj. F. Packard*—then not yet a member of the Sewall fleet—carried a Liverpool pilot to Victoria, B. C., on a 150-day passage.

6. Craine's master's certificate was likely British, since no certificate was required aboard American sailing ships. "Setting up" the standing rigging was a routine procedure commonly undertaken in calm latitudes; it involved adjusting mast rake and rigging stretch.

7. Dublin *Evening Telegraph*, October 26, 1887.

8. Bangor *Industrial Journal*, November 20, 1885.

9. The ship *A. G. Ropes*, launched by John McDonald at Bath in November 1884 for I. F. Chapman & Co., was considered a prime example of the superior vessels that constituted the final generation of big American square-riggers. Under Captain Dave Rivers of Thomaston, who remained in her throughout her long career, in 1885–86 she made a passage of 104 days from San Francisco to Cork, then was but nineteen days from Liverpool to New York, and 104 days back to San Francisco.

10. Dunphy's handwritten account of this incident survives in the Sewall Family Papers, but is all but illegible. The description given here is thus derived primarily from the protest, and also from the account given in Matthews, *American Merchant Ships*, p. 372. Evidently Matthews interviewed, or corresponded with, Captain Dunphy.

11. Reprinted in the Bangor *Industrial Journal*, September 16, 1887.

12. French-speaking, Catholic French-Canadians composed the predominant workforce in Maine's textile and paper mills. It is worth noting that English-speaking Protestant "Provincials" from the Maritime Provinces, who were relatively indistinguishable from the local Yankees, were fast infiltrating the ranks of Bath shipwrights. When times were slow at Bath in the late 1880s, many shipwrights left town for work on the Great Lakes, sometimes taking the jobs of striking French-Canadian shipwrights.

13. From Charles W. Mathews, a Philadelphia iron dealer, dated May 31: "At the insistence of Mr. Starbuck of New York who informs me that you are about entering into iron shipbuilding, I beg to say that I make a specialty for the necessary iron requirements." In December 1883 E. C. Allen, the very wealthy Augusta, Maine, publisher, a major owner in Sewall ships, had written Arthur regarding buying into the *John Rosenfeld*: "I have been looking over the situation, and I must confess that my courage regarding wooden ships is weaker and weaker. . . . I have all that I want in wooden ships."

14. Captain William Besse's ships and barks were built by the Sewalls' waterfront neighbor, Goss & Sawyer, and that firm's subsequent corporate manifestations. Besse's niches included pioneering in the "coolie trade" from Hong Kong to the West Coast, and the shipment of West Coast timber to the East Coast. It is worth noting that Besse's full-rigged ships were named after large investors, such as the ship *William J. Rotch* which, according to a Besse cousin writing in 1882, outclassed the Sewall ship *Iroquois*, which lacked a donkey engine or a long poop. See W. H. Bunting, *Sea Struck* (Gardiner, ME: Tilbury House, 2004), p. 122. On the other hand, Arthur Sewall, inspecting his new purchase, the Goss, Sawyer & Packard–built ship *Benj. F. Packard*, opined that while she was good, she was not the equal of a Sewall-built ship.

15. *The Japan Gazette*, November 14, 1889, spelled his name Boeck. In his account published in Matthews, *American Merchant Ships*, pp. 67–69, the name is spelled Beck.

16. Research by Kou Ootaka, from a speech delivered at Aomeri, Japan, October 5, 1997.

PART TEN

The famous Big Four, Rappahannock, Shenandoah, Susquehanna, *and* Roanoke, *are built. Captain Jim Murphy becomes the celebrity captain of the celebrated* Shenandoah. *Joe Sewall is back. The mighty ship* Roanoke *has a shocking surprise—we meet her young Captain Thompson. And then there is just one.*

Crew trouble has been adjusted

In mid-August 1889, President Benjamin Harrison, who was vacationing at Bar Harbor, visited Bath and walked the recently laid keel of what was to quickly grow into the second ship *Rappahannock*. (Traveling with the presidential party was Harold Sewall, Washington insider.) At 278 feet, the keel was one hundred feet longer than was the keel of the first *Rappahannock*, considered a marvel of her age, and which the then-future president, General Harrison—Benjamin's father—admired in 1841. The 1889 *Rappahannock* was the first full-rigger to be built at Bath since 1885, and her construction attracted considerable attention from summer visitors.

The model, or hull shape, of *Rappahannock* has been described by the naval architect and historian William A. Fairburn as following not the perfected sailing model best exemplified by the great ship *Henry B. Hyde*, but rather the "box-modeled with rounded ends" hull of the steam tramp, driven forward by the "sheer force" developed by very large sail plans. In fairness, the big clippers of Donald McKay had proved that box-like midsections were not in themselves detrimental to speed, if combined with sufficiently long ends. And although the Sewall ships ended abruptly, their ends were modeled with enough artistry to give them a handsome profile. The longer the hull, however, the higher the potential speed, provided that sufficient power was applied, and indeed, despite their small crews, these ships were fitted with very large rigs, including skysails (which the Sewalls had generally eschewed), and even studdingsails. In light winds, however, they generally frustrated their masters.

Wooden vessels were designed, or "modeled," by way of carved half-models, rather than drawings. *Rappahannock*'s model was "cut" by William Potter Pattee for fifty dollars—in fact, Pattee designed, or "modeled" the vast majority of vessels built at Bath

A clambake to honor Arthur Sewall, held at Foster's Point, West Bath, on August 14, 1889. A six-foot-tall marble and bronze "hall ornament," made in Paris and bearing the inscription "A Token to the Public Spirit of ARTHUR SEWALL By a few Friends, August 14, 1889" was delivered to the Sewall mansion. Although Arthur Sewall had few close friends, he evidently did not lack for acquaintances and would-be friends. Arthur had taken a leading position in the installation of a waterworks for Bath, with water piped—not without some setbacks— from Nequasset Pond in Woolwich, across the bottom of Long Reach. He subsequently became an investor in other Maine waterworks projects.

The back of Arthur's head was as distinctive as was its front. Emma sits at Arthur's left, Governor Burleigh, to his right. This was one of three tables seating altogether more than two hundred guests. The elegant carriage at far right, drawn by two flashy white horses, was very likely Arthur's. General Thomas Hyde and his wife Annie attended, and Annie wrote a blistering letter to the editor attacking "a certain class of men approaching middle age, whose highest idea of enjoyment seems to be to linger around the flowing bowl" drinking a "remarkable punch," the "ingredients of which are known only to the concocters thereof and his Satanic majesty. . . . "

Governor Edwin Burleigh was a Republican who had entered public life clerking for his father, the state land agent, and ended up in Congress. William R. Pattangall, the acerbic Democratic editor of the Machias Union, *wrote of Burleigh in* The Meddybemps Letters: *"Maine once owned large tracts of timberland. Maine does not own any timberland now. Mr. Burleigh was once without any timberland. He owns considerable timberland now. . . . "*

Maine Maritime Museum

after the Civil War. A Bath native, Pattee apprenticed under the gifted Boston naval architect Dennison Lawlor and was credited with having had some seven hundred vessels built to his designs. Of course, every model began with consideration of the owner's requirements and desires, as translated into three dimensions by the artful Pattee. Although all were carved by Pattee, models often bore a family, or fleet, resemblance.

With remarkable dispatch, *Rappahannock* was completed and launched on January 6, 1890. Her hull had consumed 700 cubic tons of Maryland oak and 1,200,000 feet of hard pine. She sported a tubular steel spike bowsprit—a first for Bath—fifty-six feet long; at only five tons it weighed but one-third as much as a conventional wooden bowsprit and jibboom. Measuring 3,185 tons, *Rappahannock's* registered dimensions were 287.2 x 48.9 x 28.7 depth of hold. Said to be the largest wooden sailing vessel then in the world by 456 tons, she was reportedly also the largest three-masted full-rigged ship ever built.

Rigged with double topgallants and three skysails, *Rappahannock* crossed twenty-one yards. Her main yard was ninety-five feet long, and even her main skysail yard measured forty-three feet. Incredibly, this huge, heavily rigged ship was to be manned with but twenty men before the mast. By contrast, in 1869 E. & A. Sewall advised the master of the 1,327-ton ship *Matterhorn*—nearly 2,000 tons smaller and one hundred feet shorter than *Rappahannock*—that twenty-one men was her normal crew.

Costing $160,000, *Rappahannock* originally had eighteen owners. Arthur, Will, and Sam were listed on the register with but 1/64 apiece, while George Dearborn was listed with 16/64, the greater part of which doubtless, in fact, belonged to the Sewalls.

Exactly one month after her launching, *Rappahannock*, ballasted with paving stone, was towed down the Kennebec to set sail off Seguin for Delaware Breakwater. Her master for the brief passage, Captain John Dickinson, reported that she steered very nicely, sailed fairly well, and "worked"—tacked and wore—as well as could be expected, i.e., while sailing in ballast. At the breakwater she "took steam" and towed up the bay and river to Philadelphia, where the "great white bird" was greeted by a chorus of whistles. At the Atlantic Refining Company's extensive Point Breeze terminal she commenced loading a record cargo of case oil for Hiogo

Rappahannock's actual master was Captain John's brother, Wylie Dickinson, who had been detained while undergoing surgery, and who joined the ship at Philadelphia along with his wife and two teenaged daughters, who would accompany him on the voyage. It had been announced in the Bath papers that *Rappahannock* would load 120,000 cases of oil—each case weighing sixty-five pounds—but at Philadelphia the local advice was that 115,000 cases would be plenty, and Captain Dickinson agreed. However, Arthur, from 411 Front Street, directed that the cargo should be as advertised.

On March 21 Dickinson wrote that all 120,000 cases were aboard, with the ship drawing twenty-six feet, nine inches aft, and a few inches less forward. And she had but four feet "of a side out"—that is, she had but *four feet* of freeboard (the distance from the waterline to the deck)—as measured at the forward end of the poop. Arthur, while

Rappahannock, *ready to depart on her maiden sail for the Delaware, February 1890.*
The stack of a tug on her starboard quarter sticks up above the poop.
MAINE MARITIME MUSEUM

surely pleased at the $40,800 freight, did not then know how much this overloading would soon cost the ship. In fact, her keel was surely a foot or more deeper amidships, given the "camber," "roach," or "rocker," it would have been built with to counteract the inevitable "hogging," or drooping, of the hull ends once in service.

On March 22, with a crew rounded up at the last minute from boardinghouses in Philadelphia and Baltimore—reportedly sailors were scarce everywhere, but surely the smart ones would have wanted nothing to do with this oversized, undermanned, and overloaded "workhouse"—*Rappahannock* began her tow down the river. She did not get far before running aground for the first of numerous times, thus beginning an expensive and exhausting twenty-five-day debacle that would live on much longer in protracted arbitration to determine how much the owners of the ship owed the Red Star towing company.

A detailed account of the untoward events that unfolded would make for tedious reading; suffice it to say that Dickinson initially rejected the pilot's and the two tugboat captains' advice to lighter off part of the cargo, evidently on Arthur's orders, because the expense would not have been covered by insurance. But after futile efforts, in which the ship at one point was stuck athwartship to the channel, about 10,000 cases were taken off, but even then the ship could not move while awaiting higher water.

The crew, once sobered up, no doubt soon tired of handling cases, and, realizing how few they numbered and how big this ship was, had second thoughts about going to sea in her. (Some of them—perhaps the ones imported from Baltimore—had been told that they were joining a pilot schooner—surely "crimp" humor at its outrageous best.) On March 26 Dickinson wrote Bath of his concerns that the crew would desert. Two days later he wrote from Wilmington, Delaware, just below Philadelphia:

> I telegraphed you this morning that ship is anchored at Deep Water Point waiting higher tides. She floated this A.M. tide. Will proceed as soon as the pilot will risk his reputation but I told him that I did not want to use the ship to sound out the channel with, that is, ground at high tide and risk damaging the ship. . . . The crew have kicked. Think will get them straightened out today. There has been a great deal of night work and they are a miserable lot not inclined to stand good treatment.

The next day, after reporting that the hull had created an eddy which had built up a blocking shoal, Dickinson ended with the cryptic "crew trouble has been adjusted." According to the captain of the tug *Hercules*, as quoted in the subsequent arbitration transcript:

> We anchored the ship, and her men were sent below a little after 4 o'clock in the morning to get their coffee and take a rest. . . . At 6 o'clock they were called out to turn to do their duty, and revolted—mutinied—drew their knives on the captain. I went aboard of the ship alongside of him, with my knuckles and revolver, and stood by him, and told him that my crew were at his disposal.

Dickinson then went up to Philadelphia in the tug *Hercules* to get reinforcements, while the tug *Argus* stood by to protect the Dickinson women if necessary. *Hercules* returned with some policemen and a crew of boardinghouse runners to do battle. According to the bill tendered by shipping agent William Smith, the ship was charged thirty dollars for "taking 6 runners to Deep Water Point to make sailors work on ship." Or, as the captain of the tug *Argus* testified, "some officers and runners came down aboard the ship to straighten things out, which they did." On April 12 a U.S. marshal came aboard and arrested Captain Dickinson for a hearing before the U.S. Shipping Commissioner, who promptly dismissed charges. Dickinson summed it up to Arthur:

> Marshal came onboard, arrested me and took out three men (witnesses). Had a hearing yesterday and was acquitted. Got the men back again. It was brought about by stevedore's man and sailor who was ringleader in the mutiny which took place the 28th ultimo [of last month]. Sailors union was the instrument which made the report and brought me before the court. The whole thing was a

farce, but of course ship pays costs and all that. . . . Sailor will try to desert as long as he can see land on two sides.

According to the version of events in *The Red Record*, published several years later, the gang of boardinghouse runners beat up the sailors, put them in irons, and locked them in the forecastle, where they were imprisoned for the next two weeks, on but little food. The marshal had found one sailor suffering with a broken arm, and another with his head "smashed." Case dismissed on grounds of "justifiable discipline." Obviously the "two weeks" detention reference was in error, since *Rappahannock* towed to sea four days later, on April 16, with a greatly relieved Wylie Dickinson and a very sore and unhappy crew.

On September 23, 1890, the ship arrived at Kobe, minus a German sailor who had fallen from aloft and was killed, an American sailor who had been washed overboard and drowned, and two deserting sailors who had risked death by sharks or by drowning while swimming ashore in the Sunda Strait.

Captain Dickinson wrote Arthur that the lengthy passage had been the result of light winds and the fact that the ship was a "dull sailer." Of the many ships sighted on the passage, only two had not "gone away from us." She was overloaded, and with her low ends (from not having much sheer) she was very wet in heavy weather—in a severe gale off the Cape of Good Hope, "she was under water most of the time." It fact, she had reminded Dickinson of Fuller's Rock, a ledge off of Small Point, in a heavy sea, except that of the two, the rock was "the most buoyant."

In a typhoon in the China Sea the ship was "drowned wholly" but "done nobly" for a ship so deeply loaded. "She would put the bowsprit under sometimes ten feet," washing the jibs away. When the stern dipped, four feet of water would wash into the wheelhouse windows. And in a bad sea she steered very hard, requiring two men at the wheel—the tiller was too short. Also too short was the bowsprit. The caulking about the deck was poor. And so on. "Trusting this will reach you in season to profit by the small shortcomings in the R."—this in reference to *Shenandoah*, then under construction. Finding more faults, in a followup letter he assured Arthur that he did not wish to be seen as writing in the spirit of a fault-finder. "Perhaps [*Shenandoah*] will be finished while the weather is fine; a winter-finished vessel seldom gets all attended to; some cracks and corners are slighted."

I felt as if I was being roasted in a bright fire

On November 12, 1890, *Rappahannock* departed Kobe for San Francisco loaded with coal and also curios intended for the Christmas season. She arrived too late, on December 30.

In late November *Shenandoah* had been launched at Bath.

A young American named David Kindell, evidently signed aboard *Rapphannock* as ordinary seaman—well-educated young adventurers who shipped as boy or as ordinary seaman were housed in a room apart from the other sailors—described the passage in an account published in his Girard College alumni publication.[1]

According to Kindell, the first mate, Mr. Merriman (he was from Topsham), broke his leg while getting the anchor. Rather than take the time to send Mr. Merriman ashore to a hospital, Captain Dickinson departed with the fair wind, and the mate spent the passage in his room. Dickinson, in his letter to Bath after arrival at San Francisco, wrote that the mate had "hurt" his leg, and that he, Dickinson, "got along better without him." Merriman, he wrote, was a "poor thing for a mate," albeit a "good, honest man."

Kindell wrote that the ship, taking the northern route toward Alaska, encountered gale upon gale, culminating, after ten days, in a "tornado," by which he presumably meant a cylonic disturbance. With the wind howling, the decks swept by seas, and sails blown to ribbons, men were forced to cling to the rigging. Between boarding seas, the pumps were worked by use of ropes led to the poop. After the lower topsails blew out, the ship rolled madly and was in peril, and at this interesting juncture Kindell, standing at the base of the foremast, was struck by lightning. "There was a crash aloft, followed by a blinding light which dazed me—a burning sensation then overcame me and I felt as if I was being roasted in a bright fire. . . ." He awoke in his bunk a day later, with the captain moistening his lips with whiskey. He remained an invalid for most of the remainder of the passage.

Dickinson, in his letter to Bath, reported: "Lost two lower topsails coming from Japan by the hooks in the sheets breaking. It blew with a terrific force. The worst lasted only about three hours, quite long enough." The ship, he wrote, had been too stiff, with too much cargo weight in the lower hold: "She can roll with anything that sits in the water. Heavy water on deck washed everything, including men, about like straws. She appears to be the wrong size to fit the lumps [seas]." There were broken-in doors, damaged joinery, and injured men. And he went on:

> I want your permission to put ten feet on to the bowsprit. . . . She does not balance. The longing of the bowsprit ought to help the matter. She runs up into the wind and hangs for some time then will yaw way off. To better illustrate you have seen some horses drive right up on a rein following right after their head. Another kind is one where you haul his head nearly at right angles before the body pays any attention. The last covers our case when sea and wind do not harmonize.

It is interesting that Dickinson seemed to think that Arthur would best understand the problem if framed in regard to horses. Arthur's curt response: "We hope some time to receive a favorable report of *something* connected with ship *Rappahannock* from you. So far we must confess, reports have been largely to the contrary. Of course we want to know of defects there may be in any of our vessels, but at the same time we would like to hear that *something* is satisfactory." And he did not want any alterations made in costly San Francisco.

San Francisco was the port of discharge for the crew. From *The Red Record*: "Beating, kicking, belaying-pins and pistols were used from the day of sailing. . . . Crew refused to go to law about it, as they said it was no use to bother the courts." Neither Dickinson nor, significantly, Kindell, mentioned any crew problems. Possibly neither had any incentive to do so, or possibly the sailors were getting even for past incidents.

In February 1891 *Rappahannock* departed for Liverpool with 4,553 tons of wheat.[2] Evidently properly loaded for a change, she sailed almost like a different ship. Coming north in the South Atlantic, in the course of one day she out-sailed one unknown ship and two British ships that were known to be fast. Dickinson reported himself "puffed up" with pride for the "*Rappie*," as his girls called her. In light wind, however, "she still sticks in the water." *Rappahannock* arrived at Liverpool on June 16, 130 days out. Arthur wrote:

> I was much pleased this morning to hear of your safe arrival at Liverpool. . . .
> I trust you will realize the importance of making as quick time as possible in
> Liverpool, thus making your ship available for Dec. canceling or loading in San
> Francisco. . . . I should not load deep with your coal freight, saving your courage
> for deep draft for your return passage. I shall feel very anxious about the condi-
> tion in which you discharge your cargo until we hear. This is a critical point for
> the future of the ship. . . . It will be very gratifying for us to make the dividend as
> large as possible, hence I must ask you to practice the utmost economy. . . . I hope
> that by this time you have gained confidence in your ship and that your letters
> will be toned with confidence and favor rather than the reverse, as some hereto-
> fore have been.

Before she could unload, while still at anchor on June 20, *Rappahannock* was run into by a steamer which carried away her head gear and part of her stem. But she did turn out a good cargo. Captain Dickinson had gone so far as to caulk seams in the "built" hard-pine masts to prevent water from getting below by that route. Finally, on July 29, with a cargo of Birkenhead coal aboard, she sailed for San Francisco.

In September 1891 *Susquehanna*, the third member of the Big Four, was launched at Bath.

On November 27, 411 Front Street received this telegram:

> Valparaiso—Sewall Bath, Maine
> *Rappahannock* burned and sunk Juan Fernandez. All hands
> Saved. Disaster caused by spontaneous combustion.
> Credit required for 400 pounds sterling. Dickinson.

The big ship had had a slow, tough time doubling Cape Horn, being forty days sail-ing from 50 South to 50 South, during which she had been stripped of most of her can-vas, and three times had passed Cape Horn, twice being driven back. And then, just as conditions were at last looking up, disaster struck. On November 18, 1891, a week after the loss of his ship, Captain Dickinson, sitting on Juan Fernandez Island off the coast of Chile, wrote a difficult letter to the Sewalls:

Captain Wiley R. Dickinson, 1845–1918, with his wife, Emma Powers (whose sister married Wiley's look-alike brother, Captain John) and daughter Bessie Emma, aboard the ship Aryan. Aryan, built by C. V. Minott of Phippsburg, Maine, in 1893, was the last wooden full-rigged ship built in the United States. At left is the side of the wheelhouse. The photo was taken at San Francisco. MAINE MARITIME MUSEUM

I have now to chronicle one of the hardest facts that has ever been my lot to be a party to (viz) the burning of the good ship *Rappahannock* here at this place, an island, on the 11th. Where we anchored at noon the 10th on fire. Just how long the ship had been on fire no one knows. On the 8th there was vaporous gas in the hatches but not sufficient to cause one to suspect fire especially with Liverpool loaded coals well ventilated in a perfectly tight ship. . . . On the 9th there was no doubt that our ship was in great danger and I made for this island. . . . After anchoring got a hawser fast to shore so that we could keep fire forward, the wind being from the land. This enables us to save some stores . . . there being none on the island, no breadstuff or other stores except fish and goats. . . . At 12 midnight had an explosion in the midships. . . . Kept picking up such stores and anything handy. At about 2 A.M. of the 11th had a second explosion. . . . We got down into

the boats only a short while when the mizzen hatch house was blown up. . . .
Carpenter cutting hole in the side of the ship to scuttle ship, then *another* explosion took place, blowing the whole deck forward into the air. . . . A general conflagration was next to follow forward. . . . Both ends of the ship were now in flames. A few minutes later flames burst from the hatch forward of the after house and the three were apparently striving for mastery. In a short time the rigging was on fire and the masts and sails burning one after another from the lower yards to the royal. The fire seemed determined to take everything. The [first] masts fell at 10 A.M. . . . The fire lightened the ship so fast that where we had cut was soon out of water. . . . She sunk in six fathoms forward, four aft.

Juan Fernandez, made famous by the story of Robinson Crusoe, was then being exploited for charcoal, and was inhabited by two dozen or so friendly folk. The day after Dickinson wrote his letter *Rappahannock*'s mate was taken aboard a small Chilean bark bound for Valparaiso. A few days later contact was made with a small Chilean dispatch boat, which was searching for another lost crew. Eventually she took aboard and delivered the thirty-three marooned *Rappahannock* refugees to Valparaiso, from whence they were picked up by the USS *Baltimore* and delivered to San Francisco.

Typically, Arthur received the news of the loss of the "great white bird" with stoic equanimity, promptly contacting David Dearborn to express the hope that his interests were insured. Captain Jim Murphy of *Shenandoah* would write from Havre:

Today I heard of the loss by fire of the *Rappahannock*. I truly sympathize with you in the loss of such a ship. The energy etc. in building such a ship is in a short time entirely destroyed. But I know you will feel it deeply but still raise and say nothing shall conquer me.

The following note was received from one Thomas Waring:

Having seen in the papers a short account of the calamity that over came the *good ship Rappahannock,* I am desirous of obtaining a more complete account. . . . I was a boy on the *Rappahannock* on her maiden trip to Japan and I will always have a warm place in my heart for the ship and its able and kind master, Capt. W. R. Dickinson.

Rappahannock was one of six vessels that had loaded coal at Birkenhead that month and burned on passage to San Francisco.

In 1893 Wylie Dickinson became the first master of the ship *Aryan,* built by C. V. Minott of Phippsburg, which was to be the last wooden full-rigged ship built in the United States. He commanded her for seven years. Before taking command of *Rappahannock,* Dickinson had commanded the bark *C. S. Rogers,* the schooner *Bessie E. Dickinson,* the bark *Halcyon,* the ship *Yorktown,* and the Sewall ships *Willie Rosenfeld, McNear,* and *W. F. Babcock.*

Captain Jim Murphy made *Shenandoah* famous, and *Shenandoah* made Jim Murphy famous. As master of the ship *W. F. Babcock*, Jim Murphy had made the Sewalls good money, and with *Shenandoah* he brought them fame as well.

James F. Murphy was born in Woolwich in 1850 to Captain James K. and Mary Jane (Sewall—but no known relation) Murphy. Weighing but one and a half pounds at birth, in his prime Jim weighed 280; and after his prime he surely weighed more. Jim's father was a shipmaster, as was his younger brother Ebed, who would command the Sewall ships *Henry Villard* and *George Stetson*.

Jim first went to sea in 1864 at age thirteen with his father in the barkentine *Australia*, sailing to Port Adelaide, Australia. In a letter written to a friend at the conclusion of the passage, young Jim described Adelaide as a sandy place offering little in the way of entertainment for him, as the three sailors' dance houses "ain't fit for a decent sailor." During the lengthy passage of 134 days two strong gales were met, one having staved in the forward house. Jim wrote that he had learned how to find a ship's position, that he now weighed 120 pounds and was stronger than when he left. He liked the sea "first rate," although not as much as he thought he would.

Due to fear of capture by a Confederate raider, the barkentine was sold in Australia, and Jim and his father took passage aboard a returning English vessel for the first leg home. At St. Helena, however, Jim joined a homeward-bound New Bedford whaler. Returned to Bath, Jim made a brief attempt at attending school before joining the schooner *Orville*. After the *Orville* was wrecked on the coast of New Brunswick, Jim joined the Houghton Brothers' ship *Crescent City* as third mate. After two guano voyages he left her as second mate.

Murphy then served in three Bath barks, quickly rising to first mate. One of them, the *Annie Kimball*, was commanded by his cousin, Captain Bill Lincoln.

In 1872, at age twenty-two, Jim left the *Annie Kimball* at Liverpool to take command of the Searsport ship *David Brown*, whose captain had broken his leg. Jim made a passage of seventy-seven days to Melbourne—this was clipper time—where he obtained a cargo for San Francisco. From San Francisco he carried wheat back to Liverpool. There he abruptly left the *Brown* and made haste to Bath to win the hand of the beautiful Maria Higgins, who was being hotly courted by Bill Lincoln. Or so wrote Doc Briry, who attended the wedding at the Winter Street Church, since his mother was Maria's sister.

The honeymooners sailed away in the Bath ship *Alexander* to the highly unromantic guano ports of Peru. A difference of opinion with an obnoxious port captain at Mollendo would likely have escalated after Jim tossed the official, gilt braid and all, into the harbor, had it not been for the fortuitous arrival of the frigate USS *Omaha*.[3] In Mollendo the Murphys lost an infant son.

Maria would suffer a number of failed pregnancies, which no doubt made their two surviving children—Mary Jane, born aboard the *Alexander* in 1877, who would attend

Captain James Frederick Murphy, 1850–1912, and Maria S. Higgins, possibly at the time of their marriage in September 1874. MAINE MARITIME MUSEUM

Smith College; and James Wilder, born in 1879 at Bath—all the more cherished. Maria did not like going to sea and stuck cotton in her ears during storms, but she was devoted to her husband. Interviewed in 1892, Maria reported that she had been around the Horn fifteen times.[4]

In 1877, unable to find a paying freight at Rio, Jim was ordered to bring the *Alexander* to New Orleans in ballast. As Murphy was sailing on primage, he made but twenty dollars a month when the ship was sailing empty. He obediently brought the ship north, but when her managing owner, a Bath jeweler named Hayden, wired for the balance of the outward freight money, Murphy replied that there was none left, he having claimed it as his fee for the delivery. Hayden threatened to have Murphy arrested if he ever returned to Bath, but when that happened cooler heads would prevail. So wrote Doc Briry.

Bath's Houghton Brothers then gave Murphy command of their ship *Northampton*, from which he shifted to the Richmond, Maine, ship *Yorktown*, and made much money with her. In March 1882, when Murphy was thirty-three, the Sewalls dangled the possible command of their new ship *W. F. Babcock* in front of him, to which he responded:

Aboard Shenandoah, *likely at South Street, New York. Captain Jim Murphy is front and center. The top-hatted black man to his left is surely the Murphys' long-time steward, "T. G. Northey." (Doc Briry credited Jim's "intelligent steward" for very likely saving Jim's life by his careful treatment of a dangerous carbuncle on the back of Murphy's neck.) Maria Murphy stands at Jim's right. The woman next to Maria looks to be related, and could be her sister May, who was Doc Briry's mother. The young woman at left looks like the Murphys' daughter Jane. Note that the deck has been sheathed with boards to protect it from being marred while in port.* ANDREW NESDALL

Will here solicit and ask from you the captaincy of the new ship whose model you kindly showed me at your office. I may have taken too much liberty in asking you for such a ship, but my excuse is that I should like to command the largest and best ship out of the river.

It worked. Murphy reported back after his first passage that the *Babcock* was so unbalanced that she had to be sailed with her helm hard-up, and that she should have had her foremast stepped eight feet forward. But evidently he learned how to compensate for this and spent the next eight or so years in her, during which time the *Babcock* never once called at an East Coast port. Murphy did well with the *Babcock*, and in 1889 he was invited to return home to oversee the construction of *Shenandoah*, his new command.

Jim Murphy put *Shenandoah* in the newspapers. Already larger than life, when he strode ashore at New York after a fast passage he wore the top hat, the waist coat, and the swagger of an old-time clipper captain headed for the Astor House. And Jim

Murphy was a reporter's dream, although, according to Doc Briry, "My Uncle Jim Murphy went through life known at times as a Great Liar." While his stories may have lost nothing in the telling, Murphy had much to honestly crow about. A superb seaman—at least when in his prime—he was able to extract the full potential of *Shenandoah* and of his crews. While not a man to be crossed, Jim Murphy was no bucko, and he enjoyed a reputation that attracted good sailors.

Jim's relationship with Arthur Sewall was unique among Sewall captains. Probably no other captain was given so much authority to act as he thought best for the ship, even to fixing charters under the noses of Williams, Dimond & Co., who were not amused. Doc Briry told this classic tale about the Arthur Sewall–Jim Murphy relationship; by way of background, Arthur Sewall was renowned for the quality of his stable, and notorious for his fast driving between Bath and Small Point in the summer.

Senior Sewall owned a span of horses which could take [him] to Small Point within sixty minutes. . . . I do not know whether Mr. Sewall sent this span of horses one summer forenoon to Murphy's High Street [home] out of courtesy to give Murphy and wife a ride, or whether Mr. Sewall had malice aforethought in his heart. It is barely possible that these two men had discussed horse flesh the day before at the A. Sewall & Co. office. Possibly Captain Jim told Arthur Sewall that a man who had faced "Cape Stiff" as many times as he, Murphy, had faced it, wasn't afraid of anything in the horse line which Mr. Sewall had to offer.

As I recall the incident, Captain Murphy and wife decided to accept Mr. Sewall's generosity that morning by driving to Brunswick to take dinner at the old Tontine Hotel and then return home. This span of black hounds could not have weighed more than 1,000 pounds each. But Murphy soon found they were "American clippers" for making fast trips.

While the reins were on the dashboard and the Sewall stable men were [standing] by on the sidewalk, all was well. Captain Murphy helped his wife to a comfortable seat and then reached for the reins. But hardly had he thrown his left leg into the buggy when this span of black horses started off on the run just as if started by some racetrack gun. Murphy was taken completely by surprise. He was not expecting anything of that kind out of a bright summer sky. It was Murphy's intention to turn from High Street into North then follow the Brunswick Road. But good seamanship told him not to attempt it when he shot by that turn. Passersby remarked that Captain Murphy was almost standing in position with several turns of the reins around his wrists. While Mrs. Murphy, looking kind of scared, was holding down her bonnet with her hands as they flew by.

It was not until this flying outfit was nearing Center Street that Murphy, now having learned a point about horses' steering gear, dared to make the two quick turns from High Street into Center and then into Lincoln Street. It was not until this "Out Riding for Pleasure" party had reached the top of Peterson's Hill that Murphy felt he was captain of the buggy, and the span of black clippers were his sailors. The next day the following dialogue is said to have taken place in

Sewall's office: "How did you like your ride yesterday? How did you like my span of horses?" Mr. Sewall is said to have asked Captain Murphy, who is said to have replied:

"Maria and I had a bully ride. We thank you very much for your kindness and thoughtfulness in sending the horses around. You had told me something about owning a span of horses which would land at Small Point within an hour. I was very much disappointed in your span of horses. I have at times gotten some speed out of your ships, but all the way to Brunswick and back I thought I was driving a couple of goats."

Mr. Sewall at this point is said to have reached for a fresh cigar, but did not offer Murphy one.[5]

But, the ship does leak

Thousands gathered to witness the noontime launching of *Shenandoah*, christened by Miss Jane Murphy on the day before Thanksgiving 1890. Built to the same model as *Rappahannock*, but with four frames added amidships, her registered length was 299.7 feet (she was 322 feet on deck), and, at 3,406 measured tons, was then the largest wooden vessel in the world.

Shenandoah had twenty-eight owners, and if one were to believe her official register, Arthur, Will, and Sam owned but $2/128$ apiece, while David Dearborn owned $23/128$. However, the Sewalls' private accounts credit David Dearborn with but $1/32$, the remainder presumably being hidden there from the taxman by the Sewalls. This likely was also the case with the $1/8$ shares in Oscar and Frank Sewall's names.

Undaunted by the *Rappahannock*'s problems, it had been the Sewalls' intention to rig *Shenandoah* as an even bigger three-masted ship. Jim Murphy, however, realized the folly of this, and, given the authority to design *Shenandoah*'s rig, made her a four-masted bark (although she was always called a "ship"). He also planted her four masts in what turned out to be exactly the right places to achieve perfect balance. If Murphy had been the only one to brag that she handled like a knockabout sloop it would have been one thing, but her other captains were equally enthusiastic.

Shenandoah's square-rigged masts were of equal height, with matching yards on each mast. Figures cited by writers for the height of her main truck above her deck range from 170 feet to 217 feet—the 170 figure was surely the correct one, with her main truck 189 feet above her light load waterline, or three feet shorter than *Rappahannock*'s. According to her sailmaker, Alexander Cutler, 12,000 yards of canvas duck were used to make her suit, which included studdingsails.[6] Her yards were shorter, and the sails thus smaller, than were *Rappahannock*'s, and were therefore more manageable. She crossed single topgallant yards. *Shenandoah* carried four more sailors than did *Rappahannock*, still but a fraction of the size of crews carried aboard the old clippers.

The longer a ship's hull, the greater the stresses created. The natural tendency, particularly with a wooden hull, was for the ends to droop, or hog. Other elements being

Shenandoah *under construction. The Sewall office building, 411 Front Street, is at the extreme left. An unusual feature of* Shenandoah's *construction was the close spacing of her (hard pine) deck beams, each one of which was ultimately tied to bilge keelsons by "wing" stanchions so closely spaced that shifting boards were not required for coal cargoes. Note the hewn vertical oak top timbers, which, after being "dubbed" fair by adze, will support the bulwarks.* MAINE MARITIME MUSEUM

SHIP SHENANDOAH, of BATH, MAINE. 3,406.78 Tons.
LAUNCHED NOV. 26, 1890.
ARTHUR SEWALL & CO. Builders.   JAMES F. MURPHY, Master.

Future schooner masts lie in the foreground. See page 263. Andrew Nesdall

equal, the most effective means of adding longitudinal stiffness to a hull was to install diagonal iron strapping. John McDonald, who had built strapped ships when a foreman for Donald McKay, introduced strapping to Maine in 1865 with the long-lived Thomaston-built ship *Pactolus*, and strapped the ships *Henry B. Hyde, John McDonald,* and likely others.7

The Sewalls employed the logical and more economical approach, which was simply, as ships got longer, to add ever more wood. *Shenandoah's* keel and keelson were through-bolted into a backbone twelve feet deep. The Big Four were all fitted with beams for three decks, although the "lower 'tweendeck" was not planked. With the Big Four, the Sewalls were entering uncharted territory—veteran ship owner I. F. Chapman believed that his 1884 ship *A. G. Ropes,* of 2,342 tons, 258 x 44.7 x 28.5, which was heavily timbered but not strapped, represented the practical limit of wooden construction.

One feature of *Shenandoah's* construction which was possibly unique, at least among the Big Four, was the addition of extra deckbeams in place of carlins—fore-and-aft timbers placed between deckbeams—combined with rows of "wing," or "quarter stanchions" that connected each deckbeam to a bilge keelson. Although most ships had

Aboard Shenandoah. *From left, Will Sewall, Arthur Sewall (holding cigar), Jim Murphy (cupping cigar), and Sam Sewall. Likely December 1890, while the ship was being rigged before sailing to New York. Fog foreshortens the perspective.* MAINE MARITIME MUSEUM

but one run of stanchions placed atop the keelson, wing stanchions were not new—*Undaunted* had them—but perhaps in no other vessel were they spaced so closely together. Indeed, the Sewalls did not feel that shifting boards, normally installed to keep bulk cargoes like coal from moving at sea—were necessary with *Shenandoah*. How much this feature contributed to her longitudinal strength is arguable, but they were surely a great nuisance when working cargo.

The Big Four all had long poop decks extending over the main deck forward of the mizzenmast. Their hulls would have been appreciably stronger if the deck had been continued right to the bow, making them flush-deckers, but, among other drawbacks, this would have made the deckhouses dark holes. While a long poop provided some buoyancy aft, and strengthened the after portion of the hull, this feature exacerbated the inherent tendency of the forward part of the ship to "work," or flex, as if hinged, in heavy going. Also, the long poops tended to leak.

On December 11 *Shenandoah* sailed for New York, arriving safe and sound after being blown off the coast. Jim Murphy reported that the ship handled very well. She was soon "on the line" at South Street, resplendent in her lofty massiveness for all to admire, loading general cargo (over a bed of railroad iron and coal) for San Francisco.

Shenandoah *at South Street, New York, in February 1892, at the completion of her first round voyage, New York to San Francisco to Havre to New York. The photographer was standing atop the forward end of the cabin. The white railing seen beyond the upturned boat marks the break of the long poop, abaft the mainmast. The jigger mast, which is stepped through the cabin, is out of sight behind and to the left, but one can visualize how, by sighting along these three masts, any independent movement of the foremast due to the flexing of the hull forward of the poop would be all too obvious.* Maine Maritime Museum

William Webb, the grand old man of American naval architecture, stopped by for a look, and was favorably impressed:

> The presence in these times at our wharves of such a vessel as the *Shenandoah*, exceeding 3,000 tons register, and costing nearly $175,000, shows wonderful enterprise on the part of her owners, Messrs. Arthur Sewall & Co. of Bath, Me. It is in accordance however, with the record of this house in the good olden time. . . . May the construction of the *Shenandoah* prove, as I trust it will, a presage of the future of our too long neglected mercantile marine.[8]

Shenandoah arrived at San Francisco on May 25, 1891, after a passage of 126 days. Murphy reported to Arthur:

The ship was loaded just right. . . . She is masted to perfection, showing great speed. . . . She works and handles very easy, wearing and tacking full as well, if not better, than my *Babcock*. The only *bad* feature . . . is her *rudder*. Why it is so hard to hold I can't tell. Nearly killed one man the third day out and he is crippled for life by being knocked down by the wheel.9 I have now 12 blocks on her tiller and in heavy weather have to put two men at the wheel. . . . There is no work [flexing] whatever to the ship. Even in the heaviest of weather her scarfs [joints] are so tight and never work.

Her copper sheathing, however, had sheets wrinkled, broken, and missing. Murphy opined: "My idea is this. After the launch, if you remember, the scarfs were a trifle apart. When we loaded our great weight the ship came together and so remained and will remain."

On November 20 *Shenandoah* arrived at Havre with 5,026 tons of wheat after a passage of 109 days. Murphy wrote: "We have had no damage or lost anything during the voyage (except losing a very fine sailor overboard off Cape Horn)." Near the Western Islands the ship had been "completely submerged" during a powerful cyclonic storm. "Cabins very wet, the poop full of water. Don't like this long poop at all. In any sort of sea, water more or less is constantly there." Murphy suggested that the next ship that the Sewalls built should be strengthened on the main deck alongside the hatches. "We work a great deal through center of ship, and hatch combings, the ends of house sills working in a seaway."

Shenandoah arrived three days ahead of the new Rockport, Maine-built ship *S. D. Carlton*; both departed Havre before two British ships, which had also left San Francisco at the same time, had arrived. This was the beginning of *Shenandoah*'s much heralded racing career, Jim Murphy being a very competitive man.

On January 30, 1892, *Shenandoah* arrived at New York, having experienced a very hard passage but having beaten the British four-masted bark *Swanhilda*. Murphy was distressed to discover a dozen wing stanchions started from the beams "from 2 in to fully 10 inches. Will try with screws [jacks] to get some back. I feel much concerned. If you remember I wrote you from San Francisco that I thought this grooving beams for stanchions wrong. . . . The center of these ships must be made stronger." One beam had been broken where joined to its stanchion, and a number of beams were cracked. Arthur suggested that the beams, not the ship, were defective. He also wondered how the stanchions could have moved, since they had been strapped and bolted.

Arrived at San Francisco on July 13, having beaten the very fast British ship *Old Kensington*, Murphy wrote of a worrisome leak which had developed off the Horn. Also, he noted that the "ship's center line is moving in heavy seas, [when] driving in heavy seas, and [it] is hard and trying for a captain to look forward and see the movement of his ship." Arthur responded that the center of the ship could be made stronger.

Things were to get worse. From Liverpool in December, after sailing dead heats against the British four-masted barks *Wanderer* and *Brackdale*, Murphy reported:

> We lost neither carried away anything the whole passage, *but,* the ship does leak and I feel thankful enough to bring her safely to port and not make a broken passage. *My crew deserve* great credit the way they have worked even under compulsion.

For the final leg of the passage it had been necessary to pump fully half of the time. And there had also been problems with the pumps.

> It [the water] simply runs right into her. . . . I never want the same experience again. I know this passage has aged me years. [For the sake of the ship's reputation] I could not feel like making a broken voyage and felt and acted to my crew that it was either Liverpool or to our boats. . . . The ship from her poop forward works and bends both sideways and up and down and to my mind is getting worse every passage. Have seen her bow certainly lift 3 feet then fall back. This work must be all from the bottom. Then in running in heavy rolling seas have seen her bow go sideways then sighting the masts in line [with] the foremast head go out of line and back from head of mainmast 4 feet. I do not know how you could fully strengthen this ship.

Arthur suggested that likely what the ship needed was a good caulking to tighten her up—caulking was indeed a vital structural component. Even when at rest in the dock the ship leaked freely, needing to be pumped out (by steam) in four ninety-minute sessions, day and night. Murphy announced that he was going to add a second set of pumps—had the pumps failed completely on the last passage the ship would have sunk within four days. He also wrote that in an attempt to stiffen the ship at Havre he had wedged the 'tweendeck planking, the seams being too open to be caulked.

And Murphy asked the Sewalls to find some other master to buy out his 1/8 interest, even at a loss.

The Spaniards were looking for me

Just when all looked dark, there came some light. Amazingly, *Shenandoah's* cargo turned out in perfect order, with not a single stained bag. Murphy's courage was revived, even after finding a "pond of water" in the hold a foot over the skin after ceasing pumping for eighteen hours. "Why no damage has been done to bottom tiers [of bags] speaks well for my men," he wrote Arthur.

When the ship was finally in dry-dock and her metal stripped off, three bad planking butts were found from which "water poured out"—six feet of water had been run into the hold from a hydrant. Several lesser leaks were located as well, and the caulking on the bottom was found to be generally slack. In addition to recaulking and re-metaling (extra copper strips were nailed over the offending butts), eight inches was taken off the trailing edge of the rudder, which greatly improved her steering.

Refloated, *Shenandoah* loaded a cargo of salt—carried for nominal freight, salt cargoes were, in effect, ballast—for New York, which she eventually made in the face of severe westerly gales. All had gone well with the ship, however. She cleared for San Francisco in May, making a very long passage, as did nine other first-class ships. It was this passage that would later put Jim Murphy and *Shenandoah* into *The Red Record*, to wit:

> *Shenandoah*, Captain Murphy, arrived at San Francisco, October, 1893. One seaman, M. Bahr, fell overboard from the royal yard and no effort was made to save him. Captain acknowledged this, but excused himself on the ground of rough weather. Ship had topgallant sails set to the wind. A passenger reports that food was a revelation (to him), being meager in quantity and bad in quality. Cruelty and constant abuse charged to the officers. Captain Murphy refused to see these goings on or to interfere when complained to.

No doubt this originated with a story titled: "A Sailor Lad's Fall," published in the San Francisco *Examiner* October 19, 1893, in which two passengers alleged that the seaman Bahr could be seen swimming after the ship for fifteen minutes, and that Murphy "made ten times more fuss over the loss of a fish from his line trailing astern than he made over the loss of that sailor who was a mere lad of eighteen years of age." Also, that the sailors' food was unfit to eat, and that the hungry men stole slush grease (as was used on the masts and rigging) to use for butter, and so on.

Jim Murphy's end-of-passage letter to the Sewalls, dated October 17, 1893, struck a very different note:

> We came to anchor this morning after a long tedious passage of 151 days. We had light fair winds to 19 north when we had a siege of 12 days of calms. Had to beat down the Brazilian coast using up a great deal of time. Had very heavy weather off Cape Horn but had no damage. From the Equator to port many long days of calm, in fact, the whole passage has been a series of delays. Will write more fully after being ashore. Had no accidents whatever, and ship never behaved better.

While Captain Zack Allen once forgot to mention a man lost on a passage, Jim Murphy was no Zack Allen. There was no mention of the charges in the *Chronicle*, nor any mention of the story in any correspondence between Williams, Dimond & Co. and the Sewalls. And no charges were filed against Murphy nor any of his mates. Unless some corroborating accounts surface, it would appear that the story holds no water. Oftentimes passengers on a long voyage under sail were addicts of some sort seeking to distance themselves from temptation. They did not necessarily depart as best of friends with the captain, and possibly this story was concocted in the spirit of revenge. In any event, nothing appears to have come from it.

Writing after arrival off Liverpool on April 14, 1894, Murphy reported that the ship had performed well: "Does not seem to strain as much as former passages and is perfectly tight." But arriving at Liverpool one year later, on March 26, 1895, Murphy reported that in very heavy weather met only days before, the ship had been badly strained and was leaking. "The ship has been so tight since we last coppered that this starting a leak again was a great blow to me." After docking, Murphy wrote that the metal was found to be in the worst condition he had ever seen, with 500 sheets gone altogether, the remainders, ragged. (The normal service life of a suit of metal exposed to warm water was about three years.) The new leak was found under the mizzenmast, but all the butts aft of the midships house were found to be "*very* bad."

The most obvious explanation for these woes was the excessive working of the hull, likely made worse by being hard-driven. Much like the teenaged boy returning the family sedan without saying anything about drag racing, Murphy made no mention to Arthur about his race with the fast British four-masted bark *California*. *California*, it seems, had departed San Francisco ten days before *Shenandoah*. When approaching the Irish coast in boisterous conditions, *Shenandoah*, setting a main skysail, came up from astern and forged ahead of *California*, which dared set nothing above her topgallants.[10]

Loading coal for San Francisco at Birkenhead May 1, 1895, Murphy left the next charter in the Sewalls' hands. "We have the last three voyages been so disappointed with our high hopes. My courage is about done." The next San Francisco cargo was barreled wine and tinned salmon for New York. *Shenandoah* arrived in February 1896 after twisting her rudderhead and having lost one man in a violent gale off Cape Hatteras. However Murphy was pleased to learn that *Shenandoah*'s image was to be used on the new United States register certificate.

On *Shenandoah*'s next passage to San Francisco the cargo shifted, and the ship again commenced to leak. Murphy supposed that the bottom butts were getting slack again. In May 1897, while towing up to Baltimore after arriving from Liverpool, Murphy wrote: "I have made up my mind to remain at Bath for a passage, as I think a summer around home would do me good." He was pleased with the Sewalls' selection of Captain Dunphy, whose ship *Willie Rosenfeld* had foundered the previous summer, as his replacement.

Arrived at San Francisco, Captain Dunphy had nothing but praise for *Shenandoah*, which he described as a "perfect yacht," and as the most comfortable vessel he had ever been in. In fact, he wished to make a deal with Murphy to be able to sail her for three years. But Jim wanted to return to sea. With son Wilder as first mate, *Shenandoah* arrived at Liverpool on April 30, five days after Congress had declared war on Spain. Murphy wrote Bath:

Off Queenstown, I heard of the war by a passing Cork steamer, and he told me the Spaniards were looking for me. I thought considerable of it during the night. The next morning another S. S., the *Rathlin*, came near and told me again that the torpedo boats & cruisers were in the Channel. I asked him if he would tow us up. . . . He agreed to tow us to Liverpool, or until I could get a Liverpool tug, for

300 pounds. You probably will think I have been foolish, as I do myself NOW. But . . . it would have been easy to capture us, and I thought I was doing the best for all concerned.

A week earlier the *New York Herald* had printed a story headlined: "The *Shenandoah* Reported Caught," which claimed that *Shenandoah* had been captured by the Spaniards. Both the Sewalls and David Dearborn dismissed the story as a fake. Likewise, the persistent story that Jim Murphy, instead of buying war risk insurance, had mounted two four-inch guns on his ship and had exchanged shots with a pursuing Spanish cruiser while dashing off at fifteen knots under a tremendous press of sail, is, sad to say, completely fictitious.

Jim Murphy wrote before leaving Liverpool:

What a wretched thing for us, and for our whole country this war is. Nothing to gain. Good many lives will be sacrificed, a big debt for a set of half-breeds who can't govern themselves. Why couldn't they have been left to kill each other off without us having anything to say?

Bath went into something of a war panic. Submarine mines were laid at Popham to guard against any raiding Spanish cruisers, and Sam wrote Oscar, who was now at Williams, Dimond's New York office, suggesting that it might be wise to send securities to New York for safekeeping.

He watches his ship as a cat watches a mouse

Aboard *Shenandoah* on Sundays Maria Murphy added to her chain letter to be posted to her sister, May, Doc Briry's mother, when port was reached. On a passage from San Francisco to Liverpool in 1896 she wrote:

We have been amusing ourselves as usual playing cribbage, and whist in the evening. You would laugh to see us sometimes with our chairs tied to the table, bobbing and lurching about. . . . I hear steward popping corn. He makes excellent caramels and peppermints. One will be so glad when we get up in steady weather—these latitudes are generally strong, or head winds. Jem [Jim} is up all times of night—he watches his ship as a cat watches a mouse. Some of the time all sail is set, and the next hour under lower topsails. He loves to carry sail but is not reckless. . . .

There were four [ships] in company that appeared this morning, but a long way off. We have passed them all. We have just finished tea and thought I would write before going for my usual walk. Would you like to know what we had for supper? [Canned] Lobster, cold roast pork, salt beef, fried potatoes, potatoes warmed over with onions, fresh bread, toasted bread, stewed dried peaches, sponge and spice cake, tea, orange jelly. . . .

Yesterday morning the English bark *Mona,* on the other tack, passed quite near, so that we saw the captain's wife and children. As we passed the crew of the M gave three cheers for the *Shenandoah,* which our boy returned lustily. It did seem good to see someone outside of our own little world. . . .

One of our men burned his foot in such a funny manner—he came to the galley for the dinner and first carried a pan of pea soup to the forecastle and set it down inside the door, while he went back for the rest of the things. On returning he had forgotten about the soup, and put one of his bare feet right into it! . . . The mate asked if it hurt the soup and he said: "Oh, no."

Later on the same passage she wrote:

Jem has been in fine health, although he says he has diabetes and today informs me he has leprosy but I think he must be mistaken. . . . The men have been caulking the quarterdeck. Now are bending heavy weather sails, getting ready for Cape Horn regime. Everybody is busy. . . . Things are going along smoothly, very smoothly in fact. The ship is a regular sailor's home this time and Jack no doubt enjoys it. . . . Our meals are about as entertaining as before. The constant flow of eloquence is something remarkable. Can only compare with the time going to San Francisco with Mr. Cole as mate. "Had a dream last night?"—"Yes." "Fine morning, isn't it?" "Yes." And so on until the inevitable result follows—an ominous silence.

In August 1898, thirty-four days out of Baltimore for San Francisco, Marie wrote:

Five weeks and more since we sailed and really the time has gone quite quickly—much more so than [on] our passage across from Liverpool. This time you see, we make up our minds to be at sea four months & probably more and soon get reconciled to it, whereas coming across [the Atlantic] this last time the time dragged so, our being so anxious to get home & see you all. . . . Nothing is so wearisome at sea or on shore to be beating about.[11]

I hardly think that he will go to sea anymore

On June 19, 1898, halfway across the North Atlantic during *Shenandoah's* passage from Liverpool to Baltimore, Wilder Murphy, age nineteen and now first mate, wrote to his mother Maria, back home in Bath:

This is the third Sunday at sea and the first really pleasant day we have had . . . for since leaving L'pool we have gone through a succession of SW and westerly gales. A most tedious and discouraging chance. . . . Hardly think the royals have been on her for more than four hours at a time since leaving. . . .

We have a very respectable crew, the only fault [I] have to find with the port

Young Wilder Murphy, at left, in the cabin of Shenandoah. *Wilder was eleven in 1890, the year* Shenandoah *was launched. A painting by an unknown Brooklyn artist shows* Shenandoah *in a powerful hurricane encountered on November 11, 1891, west of the*

watch being that two thirds of the men are old fossils and fit for Snug Harbor only. . . . In the second mate's watch he has two invalids, one with delirium tremens and cramps in his digestive apparatus, the other a half cripple—he fell down the same chain locker as my last third mate did and nearly took wings on account of it. . . .

In the culinary department we are somewhat at sea. Steward's young brother-in-law waits on the table and washes dishes aft while Mr. Northey [the Murphys' longtime black steward] takes care of the galley. The cooking is O. K. but Eddy is as mordant as the Cheshire Hills. He makes Father fearfully nervous by his manner of waiting on him at times. . . .

One week later, south and east of Halifax, Wilder continued:

It seems hard to write the same disagreeable and uncomplimentary things about the weather as last Sunday, but of all the wretched winds this W S W one takes the apple pie. . . . From last Tuesday morning right up to the present it has been howling and for the last day accompanied by a heavy, penetrating fog.

Bay of Biscay, while bound from San Francisco to Havre. The portrait is of Edward Sewall. The cabin was embellished with rosettes molded from papier-mâché—the Sewalls had never been good customers of Bath ship-carvers. MAINE MARITIME MUSEUM

Friday we enjoyed one of the pleasantest little squalls imaginable. It was about half past six in [the] morning and the second mate's watch on deck. Father was up at the time, and had just taken in the topgallant sails when glancing to windward he saw an extra dark looking squall on the rise, that is, coming up to see us—we have half a dozen of them every watch so are getting somewhat accustomed to them. Anyway, this fellow was out for blood and before we could get any more sail off of her, it was on us. How it did blow for about twenty minutes! The mainsail, fore and main upper topsails went completely. . . . Besides this all our staysails got split more or less, making things a trifle busy for a few minutes. . . .

We should truly be thankful that it is not winter and cold, and that the ship is not loaded, for had she been some of the seas we have met would have made things a trifle damp for the "say-boys" forward and, in fact, all concerned. As the ship is in ballast we hardly feel the force of the seas and nothing but spray comes on board to welcome a fellow when he comes out for another four hours from midnight on. . . .

After listing the several laid-up ill and injured sailors, Wilder wrote:

However, I hardly think that they have a very hard time of it, as it is preferable to be in a man's bunk, than to be perched up on a topsail yardarm with the wind blowing and water running a small Niagara down your back. The most of the men have but one suit of clothes and have to work and sleep in them and in their oilskins. A sailor's life has its faults as you probably found out several moons ago. . . .

Sunday, July 3 found *Shenandoah* still three hundred miles from Cape Henry, with poor prospects of getting there until the end of the week.

Last Sunday I thought surely we would be in Baltimore by the fourth. . . . I guess our celebration won't amount to much this year. Our week's work has been as follows—51, 80, 138, 88, 39, 94, and 121 miles in a zig-zag course. . . . We are getting somewhat reconciled to headwinds and rather look forward to them. . . .

Three hundred miles seems such a short distance. . . . Last passage across don't you remember, we made three-hundred in the twenty-four hours on two occasions. . . .

We are having a small-sized race with a three-masted schooner, bound the same way. We saw him first at noontime on the other tack about four miles off. We tacked ship and now at four o'clock he is about abeam and four or five miles to leeward. So you see we have beaten him considering. Our ship sails like a bird and it is a pleasure to watch [her] go with a good stiff breeze, and one forgets . . . that the wind is ahead and we are making a dead beat of it. We have been into the Gulf Stream several times and tacked ship again to clear it. . . .

On July 6, while at last towing up Chesapeake Bay, Wilder wrote:

At last the elements favored us & the wind hauled around to the eastward, only there was but very little of it. Monday & Tuesday we came down the coast before the wind passing several schooners and close in to the land. Tuesday night we were off Cape Henry and 5 o'clock in the morning we took a pilot and started to sail up the bay. We were fortunate in getting Mr. Thompson and he told us all the news.

It has rained steadily all day and all hands are just soaked. At 6 o'clock when we were about 60 miles south of Baltimore, having sailed up half the distance, the tugboat *Britannia* came alongside and took hold of us. We clewed up all sail and were glad enough to see the top-gallant sails come in for the last time.

Mr. Thompson telegraphed up from Cape Henry that we had arrived and the tow boat brought down the letters which we were glad enough to get. I will finish tomorrow as it is after midnight now and I want to get a few hours sleep before we dock in the morning. This has been rather a busy day since four o'clock this morning.

Thursday

We docked safely this morning at Baltimore. Crowds of people down to see the ship. . . . Father's in the best of health & I hardly think that he will go to sea any more.

Much love, Wilder

At this juncture we shall leave *Shenandoah* and the Murphys, to return to them later after picking up the stories of *Susquehanna* and *Roanoke*, the final members of the Big Four.

You, who pass your life on land, cannot understand

In February 1890, one month after *Rappahannock* had been launched, Eben Haggett, a ship timber contractor (and sometime shipbuilder) from Newcastle, Maine, wrote Arthur Sewall from the Eastern Shore of Maryland, where he and his crews and ox teams had been spending the winter getting out white oak frame timber for Bath builders:

> It is with great reluctance that I undertake another frame. If you knew the hardship it costs to cut and haul timber in the spring here, you would know how much work we do for little money. I shall try to get you as good frame as the last one but shall expect $18.00 [per ton]. This is what I get for all but Houghton's, and his I had early in the winter. There is a dollar difference in the cost in winter than spring. Can you send me Mr. Work to mould it or some other good men? If you could, might get it well along before the sap rises much. Would work another crew.[12]

The "last one" was *Shenandoah*'s frame. The Houghton frame was for the 2,371-ton ship *Parthia,* the Houghtons evidently having contracted a case of big-ship envy. The new frame would be moulded using *Parthia*'s moulds, although the Sewall ship would be longer and somewhat broader. Making a hull longer was simple enough—just add frames—while making a beamier hull from a set of moulds involved some ingenious Yankee geometric tricks, but was often done.

The new frame would become that of the ship (in fact, four-masted bark) *Susquehanna,* which was launched in September 1891, several months before *Parthia.* With registered dimensions of 273.6 x 45.1 x 28.1, and measured tonnage of 2,628 tons, *Susquehanna* was substantially smaller—and less expensive—than were her two predecessors, although she still exceeded I. F. Chapman's suggested maximum size.

Susquehanna's short list of owners presumably reflected worsening economic times, and also possibly cold feet among potential investors due to *Rappahannock*'s difficulties. Arthur, Will, and Sam Sewall were each listed on the register as owning but 1/64 apiece, whereas David Dearborn was credited with 16/64, exactly 15/64 more than the Sewalls' own accounts show him owning.

A social gathering in the cabin of the ship Standard, *taken by a New York photographer very likely in the late 1880s.* Standard *was built at Phippsburg in 1878 by C. V. Minott, and her longtime master was Captain Nathaniel Ellis Percy. The man sitting at left is Banforth Percy, the captain's son, who served as first mate and commanded* Standard *on one passage from Philadelphia to San Francisco. In March 1895 he was lost overboard from the coastwise steamer* Morgan City. *The man to Percy's left was identified on the back of the photo only as "stevedore," but we may imagine that he was Irish, as were many New York stevedores. Next to him is Captain Joe Sewall. The husky man at right was identified as Joe Jenks, and likely is the Sandy Hook pilot of that name. Ben Jenks, a New York shipping master, or "sailor catcher," did much business with the Dearborns and the Sewalls. Quite possibly both Jenkses were Kennebeckers. Mainers played a very large role in the workings of the great port. The finish and furnishing of the cabin are typical.* MAINE MARITIME MUSEUM

It would appear that more shares were sequestered out of state with George Dearborn ($^{15}/_{64}$), Fred Sewall ($^{15}/_{64}$), and Oscar Sewall ($^{12}/_{64}$). Captain Joe Sewall, who was to command her, later wrote to have $^{1}/_{128}$ put in the name of his mother, and $^{1}/_{64}$ put in Miss Celia Lincoln's name, in addition to taking his master's $^{1}/_{8}$, half of which was held by the estate of his brother-in-law, Captain Bill Lincoln, presumably belonging to his wife and two sisters-in-law.

Rigging the ship began in late August. *Shenandoah* had been the first "ship"— as opposed to some schooners—to have her shrouds fitted with turnbuckles, and *Susquehanna* followed suit. By September 9 the topgallant masts had been stepped, and the *Daily Times* reported that the crowd of riggers "swarmed over her like flies on a molasses barrel." Bath's riggers were of an exotic tribe, Arthur Staples recalled:

Queer, old-fashioned sailormen were these riggers, all of whom had sailed many a time across the Western Ocean as well as the other six or seven seas. I can hear them now, with their deep sea chanties, " Way Down Rio," "Blow a Man Down," "Biscay, O!" and many more, that linger only as faint memories of music, long forgot. One sturdy, tarry man, I can see now, and his voice I yet can hear across the years, rolling above the tide down the river, up the river, head-chantyman was he![13]

Riggers were often engaged as runners to man new ships on their maiden sail to a loading port, usually New York.

In December 1890 Captain Joe Sewall offered comments regarding the new ship's sail and deck plans. Joe had remained in command of the ship *El Capitan* after she was sold to DeGroote & Peck in 1883. In 1887 he made a round voyage to Calcutta in command of DeGroote & Peck's ship *Paul Revere,* in the course of which he and his wife Sadie lost their three-year-old daughter Anna to "inflammation of the bowels." From December 1890 until May 1891 Joe commanded the Sewalls' ship *Challenger,* which had been re-rigged at Bath after a total dismasting on a passage from New York to Portland, Oregon.

With easier lines than the *Rappahannock* model, *Susquehanna* was the hand-somest of the Big Four. Bath-born naval architect and historian William A. Fairburn thought that her beam, which was disproportionately narrow for a Bath-built ship, was too lean. She needed ballast to stand up safely when empty in port, and unless well bal-lasted was overly tender when carrying a case oil cargo, thus reducing her capacity. But she proved to be fast and handy. On her outward passage to San Francisco, sailing on "the line," off the River Plate she overhauled three first-class ships, including the new McDonald-built bark *Pactolus.* Arrived at San Francisco in April, Joe wrote:

The ship is complete, steers beautifully, sails well, especially with strong winds, rather dull with light breezes. Our best run, yards very nearly against back stay, 298 miles from observation to observation. 12^1/$_2$ knots per hour through the twenty-four. . . . Every kite pulling. . . . She is a noble sight under sail as she majestically marches along her trackless path. . . . She is about as near perfect as you can build and from visitors elicits nothing but praise.

Her cargo turned out well, but her topsides were caulked anyway—the Sewalls had found that it was impossible to send a new ship around the Horn to San Francisco and not have to recaulk topsides upon arrival. But to Joe's disgust, even then the ship was

*June 1896. Avonmouth, a district of the city of Bristol, England. The four-masted bark
Susquehanna, Captain Joe Sewall, in the "pontoon" floating dry-dock.* Susquehanna *had
delivered a cargo of barley and wheat from San Francisco. In dry-dock, she had her metal and
its underlying felt stripped off, all seams and butts up to the metal line caulked and
"horsed"—driven in with horsing irons—and re-felted and re-metaled. All told,* Susquehanna
*would spend £4,446.18. 3d at Bristol, and every receipt is in the Sewall Family Papers. The
steamer in the foreground may be a collier—one can understand why sailing-ship sailors
might look down upon steamship seamen with disdain.* ANDREW NESDALL

forced to take a low "wooden" rate for Liverpool. Upon *Susquehanna*'s arrival there on
September 3 Joe was in a much better mood: "We arrived safely & anchored in the
Mersey at 9 A.M. this morning, 93 days from S. F. And without boasting, I may say the
Susquehanna has retrieved herself." On the 27th, while readying for departure for
New York, he was still crowing:

> It was one of the chances of a life time; and at the present day, as also for the past
> thirty years, no ship floats that has made quicker time between these two ports
> than the *Susquehanna*. . . . You may, perhaps, think I have said too much about
> this, but you, who pass your life on land, cannot understand the affection a sailor
> feels for his ship. For, except his wife, she holds dominion of his heart.

In 1860 the record run from San Francisco to Liverpool of slightly under eighty-seven days had been established by the New York–built extreme clipper *Panama*, so Joe's boast was accurate. The denigration of his landlubber cousins was surely no accident. Also, given the subsequent rocky course of Joe's marriage, there is some irony to be found here, as well.

In March 1894, when *Susquahanna* arrived at New York after another round voyage via San Francisco and Liverpool, Joe and cousins had an ugly spat. At Liverpool, without consulting Bath, Joe, having decided that the forward house was too heavy, had shortened it by eight feet. Presumably while doing this he had been guilty of neglecting his correspondence. And at New York he took too long to get the ship ready for its case oil cargo, and had the cargo lightered to the ship, presumably to avoid having to house his topgallant masts to squeeze under the Brooklyn Bridge.

On March 14 Joe wrote his cousins in response to their criticism:

I wish to continue the pleasant relations hitherto existing between us, but I must plainly and emphatically state that I do not like this spirit of faultfinding nor am disposed to submit to it. If you feel dissatisfied with my course I would prefer to retire but should expect a fair equivalent for the interest I control in this ship, as I should need it to secure another command.

In response, Arthur wrote "My dear Joe" a four-page letter at once soothing and hard-nosed:

You know, and have always known, my . . . high regard for you and deep interest in your welfare. You now have with us a large interest; you also have a very much larger interest of ours under your command. In addition to this I know you share with me a family pride. I was extremely glad when you came back to our employ, and . . . I was desirous that you should have the best ship we had.

There was no one in our employ that I have thought more of, felt more interest in than you. . . . However, it is very important to our success and to our future relations that this condition of affairs should continue . . . unless it can be, the sooner we separate the better for both. . . . This would be an event which I would extremely regret. . . .

If, after reflection upon the above, you prefer to retire we must, of course, make the change. I hardly think, however, we could take your interest at a price satisfactory to you. Ordinarily we might, but at present with our new ship we are not disposed to buy tonnage, and I do not see that we are under any obligation to do so.

On March 22 Joe wrote two letters. To "My Dear Cousin Arthur" he apologized while yet defending all his actions and stating his belief that a shipmaster should be trusted to make certain decisions without consulting the owners at home. He foresaw more "bickerings and irritations":

Allow me to state, and believe me in earnest when I claim an interest and feeling in the name we jointly bear. . . . I am proud of the reputation of the firm, and without flattery, proud of yourself and the ability that brought you to the front. You have also a personal magnetism that attracts men. I myself with others esteem you. . . . Also let me say Sam is unfortunate in manner of greeting many people other than the masters.

And he also wrote the firm—Sam and Will—again apologizing, and again not backing down. On March 27, as he prepared to depart for Hong Kong, Joe wrote Sam to mend fences, sort of:

I want to say that whatever I may have said to you in N.Y. that wounded your feelings, I am sorry for. I was irritable and also sore over my detention and trouble in Liverpool and it needed but little to fan the flame of a temper that at times gains control of me. . . . Now I am going to say that which perhaps you may not thank me for saying. . . . I see and hear many things you could not . . . and I would like to tell you that you are estranging some of the men who would do almost anything for you. . . . Nothing would please me more, Sam, than to see the yard increase, and send off ship after ship to fly the blue S in the world's busy marts and harbors and maintain the honorable reputation and business so long established. I know you all feel blue at home, so do I. But just think how much better off you are than myself whose little all is afloat. And I have not lost my courage, though it has had some severe shocks. Well, Good Bye, I will try to get out in good time, but I am afraid she will be tender for carrying sail.

From Hong Kong, Joe reported that on this passage the ship had not "squirmed so much," indicating that some structural issues had arisen previously. In November 1895, writing from San Francisco, Joe reported that in very heavy weather off Cape Horn "the main deck worked considerable . . . she broke every main deck scupper on the waterway seam and at several places you can see the deck planks move back & forth in a bad sea." The Sewalls responded:

We . . . regret to learn that the ship shows any sign of working about the deck. As our larger ships have stood so well [!] we cannot quite understand why the *Susquehanna* should show any signs of weakness. This, of course can be easily remedied by locking say two stringers, one on each side of the hatches on the under side of the deck beams, but we would not want to do this work until reaching some port where it can be done cheaply.

The Great Brute

In January 1891 Eben Haggett agreed to deliver to Arthur Sewall & Co. on or before August 1, "a first-class white oak frame from after the moulds of ship *Shenandoah* or

Susquehanna, as may be hereafter determined by said Arthur Sewall & Co., said frame to be cut, moulded, and beveled, ready to go into frame. . . . All to be delivered at said Arthur Sewall & Co. shipyard for the sum of sixteen dollars ($16.00) per ton."

In addition to the aforesaid frame, one hundred tons of "promiscuous timber" to include stern, sternpost, and rudderpost, all finishing timber required for said ship, and fourteen pieces of keel, averaging forty-five feet in length, fourteen by sixteen inches, were to be delivered for fifteen dollars a ton, unless the shipping bill then before Congress—the Frye–Farquhar bounty bill, modeled after the French bounty system of subsidies— should pass, in which case Arthur Sewall agreed to pay fifty cents more per ton for the frame. However, the bill did not pass, and indeed, no bill subsidizing American shipping would ever pass during the lifetime of Arthur Sewall.

Haggett, then cutting timber in Maryland, had the frame ready to be shipped in March, and wanted to deliver it and be paid, but the Sewalls wrote him back:

> In regard to our timber, we want you to keep it back as long as possible. We do not want it landed in our yard before next fall as we have no place to put it, and no use for it. There were no cash advances contemplated in this contract; while we are always ready to make advances if we are in position to do so, at this time we are not in position to advance any funds.

Haggett, having paid out all the expenses involved to date, and eager to return to his Newcastle farm, would have to bide his time. The Sewalls, planning to shift to steel construction the following year, would not be requiring Eben Haggett's services again.

The frame that Haggett cut was for *Roanoke*, the final member of the Big Four. The big ship was launched without a hitch before a huge crowd of spectators on August 22, 1892. A visiting observer writing for the *New York Times* reported:

> The visitors who observe the event as a holiday alone afford the enthusiasm which makes the event memorable. They filled the shipyard to-day, and the surface of the Kennebec from bank to bank was covered with every form of Yankee pleasure craft, all adorned with bunting. Mr. Sewall and his friends and Capt. J. P. Hamilton, the master of the big ship, seemed to regard the affair as a purely business matter and manifested a stern indifference to the enthusiasm of their guests.

A further elongated version of the *Rappahannock* model, *Roanoke* was the largest wooden square-rigger ever built, only eclipsed by about 200 tons by the 1909 Bath-built schooner *Wyoming*, the largest wooden vessel ever built.[14] Called "the Great Brute" by Captain Hamilton, *Roanoke*'s registered dimensions were 311.2 x 49.2 x 20.2 depth of hold, measuring 3,539 tons. She was said to measure 345 feet overall. Her frame contained 24,000 cubic feet of white oak, and 1,250,000 board feet of hard pine. She was fastened with 98,000 locust treenails—each of which had to be bored for, driven in, split, and wedged. She was braced with 550 hackmatack knees and contained 225

Probably Roanoke, *ready for launching. One school of thought held that ships should not be metaled on the stocks, but rather after they had "found" their shape after having been afloat. Ships were commonly painted with white lead for the first year or so, which filled the grain, before switching to a dark color, usually black, which was more easily maintained.*
MAINE MARITIME MUSEUM

tons of iron fastenings. Her sailmaker recalled that he used 14,000 yards of duck to make her suit of sails.

Elisha P. Mallett, the Sewalls' longtime master builder, died in January 1892, and thus did not live to see *Roanoke* completed. Born in Topsham in 1826, at age twenty-six Mallett was master builder for Trufant, Drummond & Co., Bath builders of square-riggers. In 1869 he built the ship *Tabor* for E. & A. Sewall, and thereafter, excluding *Roanoke*, built forty-five vessels for the Sewalls. (In 1880 Mallett built two schooners for Goss & Sawyer in partnership with Arthur Sewall, who provided the use of the Sewall yard.) Arthur Sewall remarked after Mallett's death, "He could get more work out of a crew with less effort than any man I ever saw. Not that he hurried them—he didn't; carpenters always liked to work for him—but he always had his work so laid out that there was no lost time and no mistakes."[15]

The greater part of the construction of *Roanoke* was supervised by Miles M. Merry.

Above and below: Roanoke's launching, August 22, 1892 Maine Maritime Museum

The mighty Roanoke, *so new that her name does not yet appear on her stern.* DAVID E. KENNEY

Merry was a once legendary figure in Bath about whom little now seems to be known. Reportedly having built 107 vessels, he not only completed the mighty *Roanoke*, but built the monster schooner *Wyoming* as well—he thus was responsible for constructing the culminating wooden square-rigger and schooner.[16]

Also in his grave before her launching was *Roanoke*'s designer/modeler William Pattee. *Roanoke*, along with the bark *Olympic*, built next door at the New England Company (originally Goss & Sawyer), would be the last wooden square-riggers built at Bath proper, with the ship *Aryan*, built just downriver at Phippsburg in 1893, being the final wooden full-rigged ship built in the United States. A momentous era was fast drawing to a close.

Twenty-one owners were registered for *Roanoke* in August, 1892. Although the three partners were listed as owning only $2/128$ apiece, in letters Arthur repeatedly worried about how heavily invested they were in the ship. Shares registered under the Dearborns, Fred and Oscar Sewall total $80/128$, although the Sewalls' accounts show that David Dearborn, who supposedly owned $20/128$, in fact owned $1/32$.[17]

The next largest registered owner, with $10/128$—and he actually paid good money for the honor—was Daniel F. Lewis, the president of a Brooklyn streetcar company and the brother-in-law of Captain Joseph C. Hamilton, also of Brooklyn, who was to be *Roanoke*'s master. To receive the mastership Hamilton had had to raise at least a $1/8$ interest, which he did thanks to Lewis—Hamilton himself was in for but $2/128$. Citing the ship's great size, Arthur offered Hamilton only 4 percent primage unless he could raise an additional $1/16$, at which point he would receive the standard 5 percent. This he was unable to do. Poor Lewis, who had invested in good faith knowing nothing about shipping, would regret having rushed in where more knowledgeable men feared to tread.

Captain Joe Hamilton, born in New York in 1837, was the son of the captain of the extreme New York clipper ship *Eclipse*. As a young man Joe Hamilton had sailed aboard McKay's rebuilt *Great Republic*, also rigged as a four-masted bark. As first built—she partially burned before ever making a voyage—she was very nearly as large as *Roanoke*. When Hamilton began his career with the Sewalls in 1878, taking command of the ship *Hermon*, he had already spent eleven years as a captain. He later briefly commanded *Solitaire*, and commanded *Undaunted* from 1880 until she was sold in 1889. Joe Hamilton made a very good first impression on people, and was noted for the fine condition in which he kept his ships. Dron Chesebrough once wrote of him: "Like him *tip top. Never* saw the least thing wrong in him. Right after his business *all the time.*"

However, Hamilton had a known drinking problem and was likely the leader in the sordid philandering episode in San Francisco involving Captain Ned Sewall in 1887. And he had had sailor problems. Sam Sewall, always the most suspicious partner, reported in December 1887 that Hamilton had taken out more insurance than usual on his interests and personal property, and had been heard to express his discouragement in ships, and that he would not be surprised if the crew fired *Undaunted*.

In October 1891 David Dearborn had written Sam:

Hamilton has placed himself in my hands & tomorrow I go with him to White Plains where he will receive the bi-chloride of gold treatment which I have every reason to believe will permanently cure his infirmity. He will then want a ship & says that he & his friends would take a satisfactory interest in the *Roanoke* if he can go in her & think you will agree with me that Joe Hamilton without his present infirmity would be satisfactory to you.

The bi-chloride of gold treatment was the principal component of the Keeley Cure. On December 30 Hamilton declared his interest in commanding *Roanoke*, and described himself having been cured of alcoholism: "I feel now that I am proof against any temptation."[18] In January 1892 Arthur offered Hamilton terms. In his letter of acceptance, Hamilton expressed his hope that the ship would be fitted with wing stanchions:

I think a ship of the *Roanoke*'s size must carry a great deal of water on deck at times and she must have good support to her decks. I was in the ship *Great Republic* when she had her decks broke down by a sea off Cape Horn. She had only midship stanchions at the time, but as soon as she arrived in port wing stanchions were put in her.

The first person to die aboard *Roanoke* was a ship's boy who fell into the hold at New York. His father, a small-town photographer from Ansonia, Connecticut, was told that he had been injured, and only learned the sad truth when he arrived at the ship. The Sewalls covered the $111.25 funeral expenses.

On December 18, 1892, *Roanoke* sailed "on the line" for San Francisco. *Susquehanna* sailed three days later, and—122 days later—both arrived on the same day. Captain Hamilton reported that *Roanoke* was about what he had expected—a heavy ship and a fair sailer, yet she steered very well. He had no fault to find. He noted with satisfaction that the joinerwork in the cabin had creaked so much that the two passengers—who had been booked over his strong objections—could not rest at times, for which he was *"very sorry."* (It was said that the joinerwork of a new ship needed time to settle into place.)

Roanoke returned to New York in a very respectable 111 days. She began her second voyage by carrying 126,000 cases of oil to Shanghai, a record cargo for a sailing vessel. She returned to New York via Manila, where she had loaded hemp. On June 20, 1895, again sailing "on the line," she departed for San Francisco, but on September 15 broke passage by putting into Rio de Janeiro, although Captain Hamilton did not write Bath until October 27, the day the ship departed from there. Given Hamilton's history, this raised red flags, and Sam wrote Oscar in San Francisco asking him to closely interrogate members of the crew when the ship arrived.

Hamilton's explanation from Rio was that he had but ten men and five officers fit to work the ship. Three men had been killed by falling from aloft, and fifteen were laid up disabled, a heavy sea having injured the most of them by washing them about the deck, while others were covered with sores. At Rio the doctors had ordered all fifteen to be placed in the hospital. When later directed to return to the ship, they had been taken in and hidden away by boardinghouse masters. He had had great difficulty replacing them.

And then, he continued, he had been taken ill with fever and had been sent by the doctor to a hotel in the suburbs. When his delirium continued, the consul had sent him to a private hospital fifty miles away. Although still weak, he had returned to Rio on October 14, which was when he learned that the crew members who had been left on board had mutinied and had attempted to kill the mate, who, in turn, had shot two of them, one seriously. Both the mate and the mutineers were put in jail. The mate was released six days later, and six men, considered but followers, were returned to the ship, while eleven were being kept in jail on bread and water, at ship's expense. The cause of the trouble had been the carpenter, who had broached whiskey from the cargo. The second mate had been discharged for hiding in his room during the fracas. On October 27, 1895, Hamilton wrote:

After the riot I found it almost impossible to obtain sixteen men for the ship.

Although I was not well I went around day and night looking for sailors and got the last man on board today. Will proceed to sea tomorrow. . . . The only way to obtain men here is to have them stolen from other ships or men that have been discharged from the hospital. The reason I have not written you before this is that my head had troubled me severely since my arrival here that I was unable to keep my thoughts correct.

Roanoke's passage from Rio to 'Frisco was uneventful. She returned to New York with sugar from Hawaii. Her fourth voyage was made with case oil to Yokohama, again returning to New York with sugar from Hawaii. On November 11, 1897, Sam wrote Bath from New York: "*Roanoke* arrived at quarantine about 2 P.M. and while I was at dry dock the mate Mr. Thompson called at the [Dearborn's] office and reported death of Capt. Hamilton Sept. 20th on the other side of Cape Horn." Thompson appeared to Sam to be about thirty-five years old. News of Hamilton's death brought forth an unusual expression of sentiment:

For all [Hamilton's] former failings which have always been a drawback to him, I am very much afraid we will have hard work to replace him. He belonged to a type of men which is fast dying out, the old-style shipmaster, and when away from home, merchant. I am very sorry to have lost him.

Dearborn reported that soon after leaving Honolulu, Hamiliton had complained about a small sore on the back of his neck. This sore increased until it had spread over the back of his head, and finally he died of blood poisoning. Thompson, formerly second mate, had been promoted to first mate at Honolulu. "He looks like a very decent man, says he was within 3 miles of Scotland light-ship last Tuesday and was blown off. Ship is all-right in every way."

Sam was not mourning Hamilton's loss for long. He wrote the following day:

Mr. Thompson was up this morning from the ship and is a young man under 25 years of age of very good appearance and I have concluded to keep him in charge for the present as I believe he can be trusted. Ben Jenks went off to the ship with him last night and got the whole story during the night. I retract everything I have said in favor of Hamilton. He has deceived us from the start. The voyage to San Francisco via Rio he was not on deck the first 40 days out of N. Y. and at Rio he was in a private insane asylum. In Yokohama he was away from ship up in the mountains 14 days and did not get back day she was to sail until late in the afternoon and before ship got out of harbor the head wind came & made it impossible to proceed for three or four days. . . . At Honolulu he was drinking and from the time he left Honolulu he never came on deck and died from blood poisoning resulting from the carbuncle on Sept. 7th. He was drunk on ship after leaving port for weeks at a time and often violent, threatening the steward and officers with a loaded rifle and a hatchet and after drinking up all the stuff he brought on board and drunk all the alcohol & bay rum &c he could find. . . . It is a wonder the ship is now afloat. . .

Imagine a young man 24 years old, a second mate, assuming command just after leaving Honolulu with the captain drunk, sick, violent, and really insane and for the first part of the voyage at least in control of the charts & instruments so that Thompson could not have free access to them, and taking for his mate & second mate nothing more than seamen, and with all these odds, preserving good discipline and bringing that ship & cargo worth say $400,000, from Honolulu to N Y in 103 days, and Jenks says he never saw the ship in better order. . . . It is a wonder that such a man should happen to be on board in capacity of second mate.

It was surely Joe Hamilton who, if the story was true, once became so exasperated at the slowness with which the mizzen upper-topsail was being furled that he fired a gun loaded with rock salt at the sailors' behinds.[19]

The shock felt at Bath was great. Arthur wrote Sam:

You know, I have always felt a deep suspicion about this man. . . . I hope you will, personally, have a look at all of his private papers and effects before you allow them to go out of the ship. . . . They are on the ship now and really in our possession and I think we have a perfect right to examine all his papers of every nature and should do so. . . . Murphy will no doubt gladly take the ship, but doubtless if Mr. Thompson is capable and promising in every way it would be desirable, being a young man, to retain him and he no doubt would take the ship by the month on comparatively low wages. . . . With our large ownership a thousand dollars a year in the cost of sailing the ship means a good deal.

An investigation ensued on both coasts to find out who Chadwick Thompson was—the following outline is based both on intelligence received by the Sewalls, and from Thompson's own version of his life story, as related to Mark Hennessy years later.

Chadwick Thompson was born in San Francisco in 1873, one of ten or eleven children of a reputable foundryman (deceased by 1897) and a mother who greatly impressed the interviewer. Chadwick had defied his parents' wishes that he go to college by going to sea at age sixteen aboard the Bath-built three-skysail-yard ship *St. Frances,* under the gentlemanly Captain Robert Wilbur of Noank, Connecticut, for a grain passage to Havre.

At New York he joined the steamer *Cromwell* running to New Orleans. After a stint as a stevedore at New York he sailed for San Francisco as bo'sun aboard the Waldoboro, Maine–built ship *Emily Reed.* When the *Reed* put into Rio with a twisted rudderhead, Thompson caught smallpox. Finally arrived at San Francisco, Thompson made several trips aboard square-riggers employed in the Nanaimo coal trade and was aboard the Phippsburg, Maine–built ship *St. Charles* in May 1892 when she blew up from coal gas. After three days her boats landed at Cape Foulweather, where the injured Captain Chapman died in the lighthouse. Thompson then shipped in the barkentine

Captain Chadwick Thompson
MAINE MARITIME MUSEUM

Captain Jabez A. Amsbury, 1839–1912
MAINE MARITIME MUSEUM

William H. Dimond, a Honolulu packet commanded by Kennebecker Captain Edwin Drew, following which he joined the bark *Ceylon* as second mate for eighteen months.

Thompson then rejoined Captain Wilbur aboard the *St. Frances* as second mate for a Liverpool grain voyage. Back at New York he shipped as second mate aboard the bark *William Hale*, running to Havana, then joined the ship *St.* ——— (Thompson mistakenly typed "Charles") as second mate for Shanghai. Returned to New York, he spent three months in the Marine Hospital, then shipped on a hard-pine schooner. Still ill, and against doctor's advice, he shipped as second mate aboard the Mallory Line steamer *Leona* for about two years, getting a master's license for steam. (Captain Hicks of the *Leona* said that he liked Thompson, but that he was a little too free with his fists to serve in steamers.) Thompson wrote:

> I applied for a position with Captain Hamilton on the *Roanoke* bound from New York to Yokohama. He had a mate, so offered me the berth of second mate. I agreed to take this if he would let me go home from Honolulu. . . . After arriving in Honolulu, Captain Hamilton paid the mate off and insisted that I go to New York as mate.

He had told Sam that he wished to return to San Francisco to see his wife, whom he had married in secret at age nineteen. Aboard *Roanoke* Thompson had considered intervening in Hamilton's behavior, but decided that it might be difficult to explain in port.

The four-masted bark Roanoke, *South Street, New York, June 18, 1904, preparing to sail to Melbourne on what would be her final voyage, interrupted by collision in the South Atlantic, and ending in conflagration in New Caledonia. The view is looking forward toward the mainmast, as riggers bend sail. The rope yarns—called "robands"—hung on their belts*

It was decided to let Thompson make one round voyage with *Roanoke* while a captain was recruited who could buy into her. During the long and difficult passage of 141 days, three men were lost by falling from aloft and one by disease. At San Francisco Captain Thompson and his wife were married in a public ceremony, and Mrs. Thompson joined him aboard the ship. (The Thompsons were under very close observation by Frank Sewall, then at Williams, Dimond & Co., who even took notice of how many places were set for dinner, i.e., whether excessive funds were being used for entertaining.) Thompson then brought *Roanoke* back to New York in the clipper time of 102 days.

At New York the command of *Roanoke* was taken over by Captain Jabez A. Amesbury, a veteran shipmaster from Rockport, Maine, who, having just had his old ship *Willliam H. Macy* sold, had the means to buy a captain's share of *Roanoke*. He would command *Roanoke* until her loss in 1906. His most memorable experiences, aside from her loss, were sailing 2,200 miles while fighting a fire in her coal cargo in 1901, and then delivering a cargo from Seattle worth $850,000.

Captain Thompson, as a reward, was given command of the ship *Iroquois*, which he held from 1899 to 1902 when, loaded with case oil for Tsinteau, China, the ship was lost on an uncharted reef in Sappi Strait, Dutch East Indies. Captain Thompson, with two boats, rowed against wind and current for seven days to reach an island from whence

will be used to seize sails to jackstays or hanks. Inside the main fife rail are the two flywheels of the "Liverpool" pump. A ship making ready for sea was always a scene of at least apparent disorder. ROBERT WEINSTEIN

he took a steamer to Macassar. When a salvage vessel finally reached the wreck site nothing was left to salvage.

Captain and Mrs. Thompson returned to San Francisco from Singapore on the transport *Kilpatrick*. From 1903 to 1909 he commanded the 2,131-ton Belfast, Ireland–built former German four-masted bark *Homeward Bound*, ex-*Otto Guilderr-master*, which had come under the American flag. During these years Thompson became known as "Homeward Bound Thompson."

After selling the bark to the Alaska Packers Association, Thompson retired from the sea, and went into the draying business. In 1923 he became interested in aviation, and in 1927 established the Alameda Airport. He also constructed a yacht harbor using old destroyers and the four-masted bark *David Dollar* and the four-masted barkentine *Kate L. Peterson* for bulkheads.

Requiescat in pace

New Caledonia is a French Island in the Loyalty Group, lying in the Coral Sea east of Queensland, Australia, and not far west from the New Hebrides. The port of Nehoue— if a nearly deserted railhead loading facility of a mining company, entered by way of a narrow pass in the surrounding coral reef, could properly be termed a port—was the final port-of-call for both *Roanoke* and *Susquehanna*, lost within weeks of each other in August 1905. After his arrival in July, Captain Edward Watts of *Susquehanna*, her master since December 1905, had written:

> You said this island was dangerous. You bet it is. Reefs all around it, and only one light, and no anchorage outside of the reefs. . . . I could not get a chart, so had to run on my general chart. I made lots of islands coming along. The pilot told me that there was lots of ships come to grief around this island. There was one lost a few days before I come along.

Both ships had been chartered to load chrome ore at Nehoue for Delaware Breakwater. *Susquehanna* arrived from Tsingtao, China. *Roanoke* arrived from New York via Sydney, having suffered a serious collision with a steamer in the South Atlantic resulting in six months' delay for repairs at Rio. At Sydney, in anticipation of carrying the heavy ore, Captain Amesbury reinforced the ship's upperworks with timbers. (In 1902 Amesbury had been concerned about the ship's "racking movement, sideways when in a heavy sea," and at some point *Roanoke* had been fitted with a windmill pump.)

On August 12, 1905, Captain Amesbury wrote an insurance protest: "To whom it may concern: On Aug. 8th 1905 the American ship *Roanoke* took fire while at anchor in the bay, partly loaded with chrome ore, and was burned to water's edge. I therefore note my protest before the only authority available, no American consul or other chance to note or extend protest." Among the witnesses signing the protest was Captain Edward A. Watts of *Susquehanna*. *Roanoke*'s crew had been aided in their efforts by *Susquehanna*'s crew and that of a Norwegian bark. Mate Griffin of *Susquehanna* had been overcome by exhaustion. The cause of the fire does not appear in the surviving reports.

It is entirely possible that had *Roanoke* not burned she would have sunk on the way home, as did *Susquehanna*. Chrome ore was very heavy and could not be loaded directly in the bottom of the hold, but had to elevated on a platform to keep the ship from being too stiff. Ideally, the hold was fitted to contain the ore within a fore-and-aft trunk structure, keeping the weight concentrated amidships along the central backbone. It is not known how extensively *Susquehanna*'s hold was fitted, but Captain Watts wrote that 1,000 tons only amounted to a mound about 2.75 feet high piled between the foremast and the jigger mast. Watts, recognizing the danger, added in his letter to the Sewalls:

> If my part of the ship is not fully covered [by insurance], please insure its full value, for this is a bad cargo. . . . I don't think I shall load the ship down to 26 feet . . . this stuff is terrible heavy. It is heavier than copper ore, and I don't like it in these large, long ships. We will not be much over half full, and I don't think it will be that.

Susquehanna sailed on August 23 with 3,588 tons of ore, in addition to 63 tons of timber in the ore platform. Aboard were two of *Roanoke*'s sailors, and *Roanoke*'s mate Elwell and his wife, they having married in Sydney.[20] On September 17, 1905, Captain Watts wrote the Sewalls from the island of Gabuta (or Gavotu) in the Solomons: "This will be hard news for you to hear if this gets home before a cable, but I am sorry to say I had to abandon the *Susquehanna* on Aug. 26, Lat. 16.50, Lon. 162.20 at 10 A.M."

On the evening of the 23rd, with the weather breezing up, and all sail in but the foresail and topsails, Watts, who had just "layed down," awoke to a "terrible crash." The mate could find nothing the matter in the hold, and said that the ship had risen with a sea and come down with a crash. By midnight there were eleven inches of water in the well. By 2:00 A.M. there were twenty-three inches in the well, and steam was put to the pumps. At 4:00 A.M. Watts wore ship to stand back for the land. With daylight it could be seen that the stern had fallen aft of the jigger rigging. In the hold a 'tweendeck beam was found broken, and water was running in freely from a "caved-in" place.

Not wanting to strain the ship by heading back to windward, Watts put her off for the Solomon Islands. The seas were too rough to lighten the ship, and the water was gaining. By the morning of the 26th, with the pump shaft broken, the bow settling, and the waterways opening, Watts decided that it was time to abandon ship. With ten people in Watts's boat, ten in the second mate's boat, and eleven in the mate's boat, the little flotilla headed to the westward. Twice the captain's boat was filled to the thwarts.

On September 1 Watts's boat was picked up by a trading schooner, and the next day the mate's boat—which had been staved in when launched, was found. All hands were landed on Gabuta, a coaling station. The second mate's boat was found about a week later, its people having had to make their escape from a "cannibal" island. As Watts was writing his letter, a steamer was due the next day to take them to New Britain. "None of us saved only what we stood in and I think we was lucky to save our lives."

Of the Big Four, only *Shenandoah* was left.

Writing from aboard the *William P. Frye* at Philadelphia, Joe Sewall wrote:

Well, so the *Susquehanna* has gone for good. I mourn her loss, though financially I am better off. Let us pray the other wooden ships may find their grave in old ocean's bottom. She was a noble ship, and under my command established the record for time. Moreover, no American ship will ever equal it, I assert this confidently. *Requiescat in pace.*

Finally returned to his farm in Tenant's Harbor, St. George, Maine, Watts wrote the Sewalls on December 21, 1905: "Found my wife and daughter both well on arrival home, and if you want a master for one of your ships at any time I am at your service."

Captain Amesbury, age sixty-eight, did not get home to Rockport until July 12, 1906. He wrote the Sewalls:

I arrived here today. My wife is with me, and not very well and we have not been in our house for twenty years, so we will have to help clear away some. Will come to your city Monday morning next, unless you require me before, or I can go to New York at once if required.

1. The *Girard College Record*, vol. V, no. 3, April 1891.

2. *Rappahannock's* crew list for this passage listed twenty-eight men and one boy, not counting Dickinson and his family. Of officers and crew there were two mates, two boatswains, fifteen able seamen, six ordinary seamen (two had been reduced from A. B.), one boy, "Jap Sam" (steward), and "John Fat" (cook); *Lewiston Journal*, Magazine Section, January 20, February 10, 1951.

3. The Bath *Independent*, vol. 30 no. 72, December 11, 1909.

4. The Bath *Enterprise*, April 13, 1892.

5. An item in the *Daily Times*, May 28, 1903: "Last evening Dick, one of the best known and fastest driving horses in this vicinity, was shod, blanketed, and made ready for his last journey on this earth." Over thirty years old, Dick was then owned by the proprietors of a laundry, having come to them with the business. He had done his work faithfully for as long as he could. Led to the country, he was shot, and buried with all his gear, by Mr. W. H. Woodson. For many years Dick had been owned by Arthur Sewall, a "swell driver and very fast," who held the record driving the sixteen miles from Bath to Small Point in one hour and five minutes.

6. Janet Cutler Mead, *Bent Sails* (Cincinnati, OH: Mail It, Inc., 1962), p. 80. Curiously, photos taken of *Shenandoah* at Bath do not show studdingsail boom irons on her yards. Unlike British square-riggers of this era, which were rigged with lower, wider sail plans, a number of first-class American square-riggers carried fore-topmast studdingsails which were set not only in light air, but also to ease a weather helm in heavier going.

7. Bangor *Industrial Journal*, January 5, 1883.

8. Bath *Daily Times*, January 5, 1891.

9. A letter posted from a marine hospital July 2, 1891, to Captain Murphy from Hans Hansen read: "Since I have been in the hospital the doctor has formed a operation on me and I will be disabled for life all through the rudder being out of order. I hope you will do something for me as I am unable to follow my work. Please answer this letter and let me know what you intend to do." Five days later Hans sent Murphy a receipt for $200 as full settlement.

10. William Armstrong Fairburn, *Merchant Sail* (Center Lovell, ME: 1945–55), p. 1765; The *Bath Independent*, December 11, 1890. In this interview Murphy claimed that in 1894 *Shenandoah* had left Havre before the *S. D. Carlton* had arrived; Captain Amesbury asked: "If James sailed from Havre before I came in, how was it he used to come aboard the *S. D. Carlton* so often to . . . take hot biscuits out of my cook's oven?"

11. Discovered in the Murphy home, and now in the Small Manuscript Collection, Maine Maritime Museum library.

12. Letter from Mrs. Minnie McMichael Allen, dated May 26, 1937, in Hennessy Collection. Shipbuilder and timber contractor Ebenezer Haggett, of South Newcastle, Maine, along with brothers Thomas and Jotham, for many years cut white oak ship frames for Bath builders during the winter on Maryland's Eastern Shore, and along the tidal rivers of Virginia. Their crews were recruited from Newcastle, Damariscotta, and Sheepscot. They took their ox teams with them—no doubt in early years they went by vessel, but by the 1880s likely the whole outfit went by rail to as close as possible to the timber lot. At the outbreak of the Civil War, Haggett lost a winter's worth of timber on the banks of the Rappahannock, escaping under fire in an oyster boat. See appendix for additional notes.

13. Arthur Staples, *Just Talks on Common Themes* (Lewiston, ME: Lewiston Journal Publishing Co., 1918), p. 211.

14. Or, at least as can be documented—fantastical theories concerning gigantic ancient globe-circling wooden Chinese super-ships notwithstanding.

15. In October 1893 Dr. C. H. Mallett wrote Arthur inquiring about his father's tools. Arthur responded: "Our arrangement with him was that we paid him so much for services and use of his tools. . . . I cannot see that under any arrangement we had with him we are under obligation to purchase what there are left of them, and the contemplated change in our building from wood to iron of course makes the tools less valuable to us than if we were continuing the old way." He suggested that Mallett's brother Albion would be best able to identify the tools, which would then be purchased or returned.

16. For as important a personage as Merry was, very little seems to be known about him. In January 1872 Merry wrote the Sewalls from Newport, Maine, where he had just arrived to oversee the getting out and moulding of ship timber: " I thought I would rite you a few lines to let you know how we are getting along. When I got here they had 12 floors out, and 8 —— out and 3 sticks of keel and that was all. It looked hard when I git there. The moulds was mix all up. The man that commence moulding he had a bottle of whiskey to help him and you can guess how a man could mould and mark his moulds and I got all these moulds straite now and getting along —— now. . . . "

17. A notable dry owner, with $8/128$, was Arthur's friend "Freddy" Prince—Frederick H. Prince—who, when he died in 1953, was called one of the world's wealthiest men, said at one time to have owned or controlled forty-six railroads. He and Arthur Sewall were in close contact when his attempt to combine the Boston & Maine, the Philadelphia & Reading, and the New York & New England was thwarted by J. P. Morgan. He was also an owner of the Chicago Stockyards.

18. General Manager Payson Tucker, of the Maine Central Railroad, whose alcoholism had long been a worry to his friends, also took the Keeley Cure in 1891, traveling to the Dwight, Illinois, headquarters. He wrote Arthur Sewall: "This is no humbug, but a blessing to mankind. . . . Would to God I had known of this treatment ten years ago . . . King Alcohol has reigned supreme for ages, but at last has found a foeman worthy of his steel, at the hand of Dr. Keeley in the little town of Dwight. . . . there are five to six hundred patients here. . . . I have already received sixty hypodermic injections of Bi-Chloride of Gold in my right arm and I take . . . a liquid form eight times a day.. . . [The treatments] have already relieved me of a heavy burden and opened to my vision a bright sunlight. . . . Eminent judges, lawyers, and leading businessmen from all parts of the land are here with me."

19. Commander J. R. Stenhouse, *Cracker Hash* (London: Persival Marshall & Co., 1955), p. 76.

20. First mate Calvin Elwell was from Saturday Cove, Northport, Penobscot Bay. He later commanded *Kenilworth* after she was sold to the Alaska Packers Association. His wife was described as "an opera singer and a dancer" in the Belfast *Republican Journal*, March 1908.

PART ELEVEN

A cargo of wheat and an uninformed owner cause problems. The Sewalls buy a steel ship and then convert their yard to steel construction. We then learn something of Arthur Sewall's political career, including his candidacy for the office of vice president of the United States in 1896. More sailor troubles, some detailed in The Red Record, *and the* Willie Rosenfeld *sinks.*

What he may have legally is another matter

In 1893, during a spat with Dearborn & Co., Arthur Sewall wrote: "I believe in doing our business in a liberal off hand way," apparently advocating for more openness and amity in business dealings. However, the dispute and lawsuit that had then been dragging on between the Sewalls and Parker Reed since 1891, regarding a cargo of wheat in 1885, suggested that actions can sometimes speak louder than words.

Parker McCobb Reed was a brother of Thomas McCobb Reed, the Sewalls' longtime and very wealthy virtual silent partner (who had died after being kicked by a horse in 1879). In 1894, Parker, described as a journalist, published a book entitled *History of Bath and Environs*, which largely ignored the Sewalls, particularly Arthur. One possible explanation for this glaring lapse is found in two letters from Reed to Arthur in 1889 and 1890, in which Reed reminded Arthur of his promise to make a fifty-dollar contribution to aid the publication of the book. And a further explanation might be found in a dispute over the cargo of wheat.

What was not in dispute was that in 1885, rather than chartering the ship *Indiana* to carry a cargo of wheat from San Francisco to Queenstown or elsewhere at what the Sewalls considered a low rate, the Sewalls bought a cargo of wheat on speculation, betting that its value would rise during the passage. Their calculation was made on rumors that war might soon break out between Britain and Russia, but alas, peace was maintained.

The Sewalls would later claim that the purchase had been made on the ship's account, and although it did not result in any assessment—or "Irish dividend"—being made on the owners, it did result in the ship earning approximately $3,500 less than she would have if she had been chartered. Also, the Sewalls never informed the owners of the purchase or of its result.

A letter from the Sewalls to Williams, Dimond & Co. in April 1885 authorized the purchase of the wheat provided that Oscar, Will, and Dron Chesebrough signed off on it. In it they stated: "Our idea is to ship per *Indiana* should you deem advisable to purchase cargo." The Sewalls would later hold that this letter demonstrated "with perfect clearness the fact that the cargo of wheat was bought for account of Ship *Indiana* and owners."

In 1885 Parker Reed—or else his wife—was then the owner of $1/32$ of the ship *Indiana*. He was also the owner of $1/64$ of the ship *Iroquois*. The captain of *Indiana* in 1885 was Captain Parker Henry McCobb Morrison, a close neighbor of Reed's in Phippsburg, and—no surprise—a relative. In 1890, when Captain Morrison was relieved of his command at San Francisco, the parting was not a friendly one. *Indiana* had not been making money, and Captain Lewis Colley, who replaced Morrison, wrote the Sewalls that he found the ship to be in poor condition and badly "run out"—even the cabin carpet and the master's mattress were worn out. The Sewalls were quite certain that it was Morrison who had told Reed about the cargo of wheat, presumably in retribution.

Ultimately, Reed's suit was not about whether or not the Sewalls had bought the cargo for themselves, but whether Reed, as an owner, had been informed in either case. The Sewalls admitted that they had not informed the other owners about the purchase or of its result, but maintained that they must somehow have certainly told Reed about the plan, since Reed often came by the office to check on his properties. The Sewalls' explanation for not having informed the other owners was that, "we knew that by far the majority were with us, and willing to have us act as we deemed best."

The case became more complicated when it was discovered that in November 1885, Mr. Reed had had his interest in *Indiana* registered under his wife's name. Hopes in the Sewall camp that the whole mess could be dismissed thanks to a loophole were dashed when the Sewalls' lawyer, William Putnam, wrote them that, "Unfortunately, under our laws, the wife has all the rights as any other person. . . ." The matter of the somewhat arbitrary methods by which a ship's expenses were apportioned to sequential voyages also came under discussion.

Some of the Sewalls' replies to questions raised by Lawyer Putnam are of interest. No dividends, they stated, had been declared for *Indiana* from October 1884 to August 1890. It had not been the custom of either E. & A. Sewall or Arthur Sewall & Co. to send copies of a vessel's accounts to owners—owners were instead welcome to inspect a ship's accounts at the office. However, since 1889 or 1890, the Sewalls had been sending owners brief statements whenever a vessel's account was closed.

It was also revealed that it was the Sewalls' custom at times to carry insurance on the freight, or in some cases on the hull, for account of the whole ship, so that in the event that the ship was lost or seriously damaged, funds would be available to pay off the crew and settle other necessary bills. Also:

It has been our custom at times to purchase cargoes on ship's account. They have principally been coal or wheat . . . As our ships have been usually in few hands, and by our personal friends largely, we have never thought it necessary to formally advise [the other owners].

In September 1893, shortly before a hearing on Parker Reed's lawsuit was to be held in Portland, Reed's lawyers warned the Sewalls that Mr. Reed likely intended to publish the hearing "in some newspaper, and we suspect the Bath papers."

We do not mean by this that he intends to make a mere newspaper item of news of it but that he means to spread it fully in some way in the newspapers. Of course when reporters get hold of such matters it is difficult to shut them off, but we write this that you may take such steps as you desire to prevent such publication on the part of Mr. Reed.

A settlement was subsequently reached, wherein the Sewalls agreed to purchase the Reeds' interests in both *Indiana* and *Iroquois* at good prices. Explaining their decision to Parker Reed's lawyers, the Sewalls wrote: "we know as well as we can know anything that Mr. Reed's claim is not valid for one cent from a commercial point of view. What he may have legally is another matter. . . ."

On March 9, 1894, the Sewalls wrote David Dearborn:

We have settled the Reed Claim on the *Indiana* by purchasing his interest in both this ship and the *Iroquois*. As we do not wish to have our name appear in this transaction we are having the tonnage put in your name.. . . .

I am decidedly in favor of iron ships

The 2,300-ton four-masted steel bark *Kenilworth* was arguably the most artfully modeled and surely the most expensively built ship owned by the Sewalls.[1] Given the Sewalls' unwavering opposition to allowing foreign-built hulls to come under American registry, there is no little irony in the fact that *Kenilworth* was built in 1887 by John Reid & Co. of Glasgow, Scotland.

Kenilworth's Liverpool owners reportedly instructed her builders to spare no expense in her construction, and she was intended to be the finest vessel in all of the huge British sailing marine. Originally rigged as a four-masted ship, her cost has been estimated at $240,000 and features of her construction were long admired by knowledgeable critics. After making an 1888 San Francisco grain voyage in very good time, *Kenilworth* returned to San Francisco in August 1889 for a second round. However, sparks from a burning warehouse caught her ablaze, destroying her deck and houses, although causing no fundamental structural damage. Nevertheless, her owners abandoned her to the underwriters, and she was auctioned off. The winning bidder was Dron Chesebrough, acting on behalf of Arthur Sewall. She was "knocked down" for $55,100.

Chesebrough suggested giving her mastership to Captain Jim Baker, which was so done, and Baker closely supervised her entire rebuilding, which began at the Union Iron Works. Because the cost of repairs—said to be $45,000—did not amount to three-quarters of her total cost of $101,277, an act of Congress was required to place her under the American flag. The bill was passed in February 1890. No Sewall equity appeared on *Kenilworth*'s registers until 1904, and that was but for 1/64. George Dearborn was the registered owner for 76/128, his father David, 1/32, although when George sold all his Sewall properties in 1900 he only owned 5/128 of *Kenilworth*.[2]

No doubt most of George Dearborn's registered ownership belonged to the Sewalls, who, in addition to not wanting to pay Bath taxes on it, very likely may not have wanted to appear to be owners of a foreign-built vessel.

Kenilworth won her U.S. registration one month after *Rappahannock* was launched. *Shenandoah* and *Kenilworth* both had registered lengths of 300 feet, but *Shenandoah* had six feet more beam, six feet more depth, and at 3,407 tons, measured 1,114 tons larger. Operating *Kenilworth* alongside their wooden fleet gave the Sewalls a perfect opportunity to compare the two types. There was no doubt about Jim Baker's opinion—on July 26, 1890, ninety-eight days out of San Francisco, ninety miles west of Cape Clear, Baker wrote:

> The ship works well every way & steers like a yacht. She drags no dead water & leaves it clean & makes little or no fuss about it. The [inner] skin today is as dry as when we left. *I am decidedly in favor of iron ships.* I hope no more wood for me. In heavy weather large quantities of water on deck, *lots of it.* Much more than wood, but then she is iron, not much damage can be done.

Captain Baker, accompanied by Mrs. Baker and Kate, made the passage to Liverpool in the fast time of 101 days. Baker was convinced that *Kenilworth* was about the fastest ship afloat until she was out-sailed "fair & square" by the great wooden ship *Henry B. Hyde*. The only other ship to pass him, he claimed, was the British four-master *Rowena*. Surely he was only speaking of *Kenilworth*'s speed when clean-bottomed—Baker was dismayed by the dragging effect of a badly fouled bottom, a major handicap of iron and steel ships, which turned his flyer into a bale of hay.

From Liverpool, *Kenilworth* sailed to Calcutta, where she lay for four very hot months after her jute cargo caught fire and had to be replaced. Despite the heat, Kate and Mrs. Baker made the most of what would turn out to be their last voyage. Many years later Kate described the snake charmers, the zoo, and the botanical gardens:

> For some time, we were the only women among the shipping and so had every attention. It was a splendid time for me. The American Consul's daughter took me around to native schools, shops, and into a few native homes of higher class. The women were pleased to talk to us and showed us all their jewels. They loved everything glittering.[3]

Captain Baker's nine-year career in *Kenilworth* is thoroughly described in *The Sewall Ships of Steel*, and will not be here, yet there is one passage from Baker's sea letter at the conclusion of his 1893 passage to Shanghai that cannot be passed over:

> In the first place everything about the ship is okay, & have not much met with any accident as far as the ship is concerned. But we have been unfortunate enough to lose one of our seamen, who fell from the starboard main yard arm overboard and was lost. It was blowing a hard gale most of the time & the ship running under a hard press of canvas. A very high sea running & it was impossible to save him. . . . A native of England. As the ship passed him the 2nd mate threw the spanker sheet right over him, but the ship was going so fast he could not hold on & the last we saw of him he was swimming for the ship & I was obliged under the circumstances to turn my back to the poor fellow.[4]

On July 24, 1898, Victor H. Genereaux, second mate of the bark *Kenilworth*, at Valparaiso, Chile, wrote a ten-page letter to Arthur Sewall & Co., which came accompanied by the ship's log. Arthur Sewall wrote: "We call it a very good letter, but a very sad story."

> Arrived at Valparaiso after a very sad and unfortunate passage, with the deaths of Capt. Baker, Arthur B. Piper [first mate], and Henry Hobson [ship's boy] and also the ship's cargo [of sugar] on fire.
>
> Since leaving Hilo [Hawaii] everything went along very smooth, no trouble whatever with the crew, when on July 8, 40 days out from Hilo, at 3 P.M., smoke was noticed coming out of the forward ventilator on the poop deck, by first officer Mr. Piper, and upon investigation the cargo was found to be on fire, so all hands were immediately called and everything that was possible was done to extinguish the fire, but to no use.

Flames were coming out of a ventilator, and the fire became hot enough to burn the woodwork in the midships deckhouse. Water was played through the ventilators, and then everything was tightly battened down, and the ship was headed toward Valparaiso. When Mr. Genereaux went below at 11:45 to call Captain Baker, as requested, he found everyone who was in the cabin—Baker, Piper, Hobson, and a passenger—unconscious. They were immediately brought up on deck, stimulants were administered, and all

A portfolio of photographs taken in 1916 aboard the British steel four-masted bark Vimeira, *Glasgow for Melbourne, by a sailor (later a captain) named Einar Peterson.* Vimeira, *built at Glasgow in 1891, was of 2,233 tons;* Kenilworth, *built at Glasgow in 1887, was of 2,308 tons. These scenes thus represent conditions aboard* Kenilworth *as well.* ANDREW NESDALL

Opposite: The view of the lee rail looking aft from the forecastle head. The wind-filled fore course, or fore sail, bellies overhead.

Above: Furling the main topgallant sail.

Opposite: Two sailors securing the main topgallant sail.

Below: Sailors furl the main course as the bark runs before a rising gale.

Above:Sailors at the braces, keeping a weather eye for any boarding seal.

Opposite: Sailors standing on footropes furling sail.

Below: . The view forward along the lee rail.

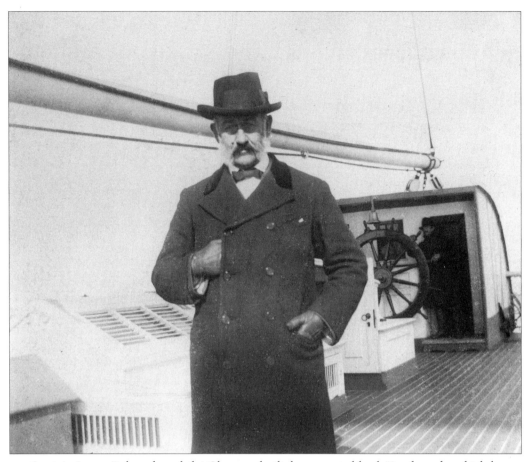

Captain James Baker aboard the Glasgow-built four-masted bark Kenilworth, *which he commanded from 1889 until his death by asphyxiation aboard her in 1898. Although British builders never adopted the full wheelhouses found on many American square-riggers (and some big schooners), some did eventually erect whaleback structures, as seen here, which protected the helmsman from the force—and the sight—of a pooping sea breaking over the stern.* MAINE MARITIME MUSEUM

hands worked to revive them. The passenger came to about 2:00 A.M., but by 3:00 A.M. the others were cold and stiff. The bodies were sewn up in canvas and buried at sea with prayers that morning. It was believed that the victims had inhaled "gas"—carbon monoxide—from the fire while asleep.

The stores and also most of the fresh water were not accessible, due to the gas and a melted pipe. The fire continued to burn, but one way and another they made do. Sixteen days later, without the use of a chronometer—all three had stopped—or a proper chart, Mr. Genereaux brought the ship to Valparaiso, and even bargained-down a towing fee. In port the cargo was discharged and the fire extinguished. Captain Jim Murphy, who had just retired from *Shenandoah*, was dispatched to the scene. He re-stowed the cargo and sailed *Kenilworth* to New York in the very fast time of sixty-six days.

The case of the late mate, Mr. Piper, was particularly sad. Having recently inherited some money which he wished to invest in a master's share, he had wanted to leave the *Kenilworth* to seek his own command, but had been persuaded by Captain Baker to make one more voyage as mate.

When Captain George Goodwin, by then captain of *Dirigo*, lying at Port Angeles, Washington, learned of the news, recalling his years as mate with the Bakers aboard *Sterling*, he wrote Arthur Sewall: "You have lost . . . a good servant and I have lost a valued friend. I . . . am more than sorry for Mrs. Baker."

In September, from their farm on Cape Cod, Mrs. Baker wrote Arthur :

Thank you for sending me a copy of the *Kenilworth*'s log. There is a certain satisfaction in knowing the sad truth of this unfortunate and terrible affair. I think great credit is due the second mate for getting the ship into port under such trying circumstances.

By using several names of our friends

There was an old saying among wooden shipbuilders that there was no "bull"—or mistake—so big or so bad that it couldn't be fixed. Wooden shipbuilding was a forgiving, pliable process, an evolved folk art even involving a good deal of sculpture. Iron and steel shipbuilding, by comparison, was a revolutionary and wholly different process, which, while not without artfulness, required precise calculation, complicated mathematics, and scientifically derived standards. That said, even in the early 1900s metallurgy was still in relative infancy, and many lessons were yet to be learned.

Whereas the capital requirements for a wooden shipyard were relatively small, and the tools, mostly hand-held, were usually owned by the workers, setting up an iron shipyard cost a great deal of money, requiring everything from a self-propelled steam crane to punching machines, boring machines, plate-bending machines, and so on, down to hammer handles by the hundreds. And hammer handles were about the only Maine inputs. Nevertheless, Arthur Sewall was determined to enter this brave new world.

In August 1891, as *Susquehanna* was nearing completion, the Sewalls contracted with Smith Brothers, a Glasgow firm, "to have you lay out ways [in our yard] suitable for building two iron vessels at the same time, preserving our present ways for wood, locating all buildings and tools and giving estimate of entire cost of plant, f.o.b., shipping port."

To Arthur's father, William D., shipbuilding was likely primarily a means to become a ship owner, owning ships being a path to wealth. But to Arthur, owning and managing ships—although a complicated business, at which he was very good—was perhaps as much the means by which he could continue to be a shipbuilder. In Bath it had always been the shipbuilder who had ruled the roost, and Arthur Sewall was not born to play second fiddle to any other Bath cocks of the walk.

The interests of shipbuilder and ship owner were often at natural odds. In Arthur

Sewall, who wore both hats, the interests of the shipbuilder took precedence. Many ship owners—and unemployed captains—supported the admission of "free" foreign-built ships to the American fleet, a proposal bitterly opposed by the Sewalls and other American shipbuilders. (Although they did support the free admission of shipbuilding materials and tools.) On this issue, as with many others, Arthur adamantly opposed fellow Democrat President Grover Cleveland. In 1894 Arthur predicted in a letter to Maine's Senator Frye that if our great President" were to have his way "we shall soon see the British tramps, from one to fifty years old, plying up and down our rivers and lakes and on our coast, passing our abandoned shipyards and worst of all, flying our flag."

Arthur saw himself as a member of the producing class—as opposed to the parasitic speculating class. He was also defending and building upon an honored heritage— the blue "S" house flag, snapping at the main truck of a new ship, was a powerful talisman. A fleet of big steel sailing ships flying the Sewall house flag would surely have guaranteed the continued status of the Sewall fleet as the largest American fleet of deepwater, foreign-going square-riggers.

Arthur was doubtless already familiar with the basic practical aspects of metal-working and steel construction through his close association with Bath's ill-fated Goss Iron Works and its successor, the growing Bath Iron Works. And Bath Iron Works, led by Arthur's good friend General Thomas Hyde, was then moving into the construction of steel naval vessels.[5] In April 1892 Arthur Sewall & Co. wrote their Liverpool broker, Robertson, Cruikshank & Co., regarding the possibility of obtaining plans and specifications for a ship of British design, and also of buying the complete stock of steel "plating, angles, beams, etc.," and tools, required to build such a ship. This material could be admitted duty free, provided that the keel pieces were rolled, and not forged.

An intriguing note from Arthur dated May 9, 1892, went to Will and Sam regarding a model he wished Bath's great "modeler" William Pattee to cut "on *H. B. Hyde* lines as near as he can, only reduce the sheer about one half, that is if she has 12 ft. of sheer make ours 6 to 8 ft. . . . " The traditional, beamier Bath ship model, as best represented by the *Henry B. Hyde*, was in certain important respects demonstrably superior to the narrow British model, and there is thus the possibility that Arthur was considering building a steel version of the traditional Bath ship, but any such ideas ended with the June 1892 hiring of J. F. Waddington, a thirty-two-year-old British naval architect, to design the new ship. Shortly afterwards Arthur embarked on a tour of British steel shipyards.

J. F. Waddington had served a full apprenticeship at Belfast's great Harland & Wolf shipyard, with practical training in all the applicable trades, including ship design. After briefly going to sea, he had, by his account, set up a shipyard near Liverpool where he had supervised the construction of nearly thirty vessels. He was completing drafting plans for the battleship *Oregon* at San Francisco's Union Iron Works, and had recently applied for American citizenship.

After knocking a hefty chunk off Waddington's asking salary, and declining to pay his fare east, the Sewalls hired him to design their new ship.[6] The positions of superintendent and foreman were left open, should Waddinton be judged fit to fill these roles. The ship that Waddington designed was, fundamentally, a standard four-masted bark of the type then being built on the Clyde and at Belfast, although her ends—her bow and stern—possessed none of the typically British graceful curves and artful touches which relieved the eye of their bulkiness. While her narrow hull was pure British, her lofty three-skysail rig was all Yankee. She would measure 3,005 tons, 312 x 45.2 x 25.6. In February 1893, as the steel plant neared completion, the tramp steamer *Buckingham* from Glasgow entered the Kennebec with a cargo that would become *Dirigo*.

Presumably because of the uncertainty of the novel enterprise, which was occurring in the midst of a national depression, Arthur, according to tradition, did not seek outside investors; he set up the steel yard and underwrote at least initial construction of the ship himself, borrowing money on collateral. Doc Briry, who had been a director of the Bath Savings Bank, recalled a visit by Will Sewall to his medical office, then located at the head of the stairs over Anderson's drug store, regarding a loan:

> The loan business was conducted along the following lines: An applicant for a loan of money would state his case to the treasurer who in turn would lay the application before the trustees at the regular weekly or semi-weekly meeting. . . . The trustees of a bank seldom ask an applicant for what use he needs the money—it is none of a bank's business to pry into a man's private affairs.
>
> Our treasurer had reported that Mr. Arthur Sewall had applied for a loan of $30,000 and our treasurer here described what securities Mr. Sewall proposed to put up to secure the loan. The statutes of the state of Maine [regarding the] kind of securities which savings banks can accept for a loan prompted me to make a motion which was quickly seconded: "that Mr. Sewall's application be turned down until such time as he could or saw fit to put up a higher grade of security for the loan."
>
> Will Sewall came into my office the next forenoon, wanted to know why A. Sewall & Company were not good for a loan of $30,000 at Bath Savings. I told Will Sewall that A. Sewall & Company were all right—and a very wealthy firm. I told him further that the grade of securities which his father proposed to put up as security for the loan was all wrong, and did not conform with the banking laws of our state.
>
> There followed a long animated discussion between Will Sewall and myself [about] just why the shares of stock in a little railroad almost bankrupt were not [collateral for] a first-class loan. Several patients then entering my office, I felt obliged to tell Will Sewall to tell his father to hunt through his safety boxes and send *something better* to [the bank] in the shape of securities. This Mr. Sewall did and Mr. Sewall promptly received his money.

Finding investors for the ship would later become a high priority. In March 1894, with the ship in the water, the Sewalls put the squeeze on Samuel Foster, a San

Francisco chandler, to buy an interest in her, intimating that otherwise they would "feel perfectly free to enter into more close relations with other parties in your line of trade in your city." When Foster pointed out that they had already promised to give him their trade after he bought into the *Willie Rosenfeld*, it was conceded in a letter from 411 Front Street to Oscar that, "Our correspondence at the time would literally seem to bear his [Foster's] construction of it, but of course we never intended [to] commit ourselves for all time.[7] On March 29, 1894, Arthur wrote to Erskine Phelps, his Chicago confidant and close friend:

> For certain reasons it is desirable for us to make up the register ownership [of *Dirigo*] by using several names of our friends out of the state and in this case have taken the liberty of using your name for 1/8th, which by our Custom House Record is now owned by you. You will, therefore, see the reason for my asking you to execute this bill of sale and return it to me.[8]

The Sewalls knew absolutely nothing

The Sewalls launched *Dirigo* in February 1894. The next launching would not be until July 1898, when *Dirigo's* near sister, the *Erskine M. Phelps*, slid into the Kennebec. With somewhat finer ends and the same lofty rig, the *Phelps* was thought by many to be the best—and fastest—of all the Sewalls' steel ships. For a dozen years her name would be associated with Captain Robert Graham, a Pennsylvanian and a strict disciplinarian whose many crew problems raised even the Sewalls' ire, but who kept his ship in perfect order.

The superintendent—a new name for master builder—of the Sewall yard from the building of the *Phelps* to the schooner *Kineo* in 1903 was Thomas Spence. Trained in the shipyards of his native Scotland, Spence first came to the United States in 1881, but soon left to build Spanish warships in the Philippines. Returning to the United States in 1890, he became a citizen and worked in various American shipyards before coming to Bath. In retirement he kept a small country store at Small Point.

The six four-masted barks that followed the *Phelps*—the *Arthur Sewall*, 1899; the *Edward Sewall*, 1899; *Astral*, 1900; *Acme*, 1901; the *William P. Frye*, 1901; and *Atlas*, 1902—were of the basic *Dirigo* model with twenty feet added amidships. Their decks were raised slightly, and they were rigged with the shorter, broader British sail plan. *Astral*, *Acme*, and *Atlas* were built under contract for the Standard Oil Co.—by being U.S.-flagged, they, unlike Standard Oil's larger fleet of British-flagged oil ships, could carry Hawaiian sugar to American ports, and cargo intercoastal, i.e., between the East and West Coasts.

As for the aesthetics of the later Sewall steel ships, Captain P. A. McDonald, not one to beat around the bush, wrote Mark Hennessy that "it would be difficult to imagine anything more ugly than those [later] Sewall steel ships." He thought *Dirigo*—and by extension, the *Phelps*—reasonably good-looking, however.

All of the Sewall-built four-masted barks had the narrow 45-foot beam established with *Dirigo*; by contrast, *Shenandoah*, of comparable 300-foot length, had a 49-foot beam. Bath-raised naval architect William A. Fairburn, a very bright young man who cut his teeth, almost literally, at Bath Iron Works and later led his class in naval architecture at Glasgow University, tried to persuade the Sewalls to adopt his beamier model of *Dirigo*, with water ballast tanks and a 47-foot beam. (The twenty feet of length added to the later Sewall barks made them proportionally even narrower and shoaler than *Dirigo*.) Fairburn never forgave the Sewalls for rejecting this opportunity to build what he was convinced would have been a very superior ship. He later wrote, likely overstating the case:

> The Sewalls knew absolutely nothing about iron [i.e., steel] ships or iron ship-building. Not a member of the firm knew anything whatsoever about naval architecture, and when the firm decided to change from wood to iron shipbuilding, the members were timid. They would not consider having the Bath Iron Works, with its staff of competent technical men, design and build iron or steel hulls for them in harmony with American experience and tradition. . . . 9

The British merchant marine early became accustomed to narrow-beamed hulls when tax laws encouraged them. Later, it was believed that narrow hulls were faster. When iron replaced wood, it was feared that the iron plates of a beamy, flat-bottomed ship would tend to buckle. According to Fairburn, however, beam was in fact much more of a limiting factor with wooden construction—fifty feet being the outer limit—than with iron construction. Beam was also the most expensive dimension for a ship, and in the highly competitive British shipbuilding industry the myth that narrow beam was better was perpetuated for economic reasons, despite a great cost in lost carrying capacity, lost ships, and lost lives.

Sewall captains who moved from beamier wooden ships to the narrow steel ships invariably wrote back after their first passage describing how much water the steel ships carried on deck. Water on deck was churned white as milk. In heavy weather, seas flowed freely over the five-foot-high bulwarks, flooding the main deck under an enormous weight of water. Working at the braces—rigging that controlled the angle of the square sails—which led to the bulwarks could be exceedingly dangerous.

The Sewall ships no doubt could have benefited enormously by installing the brace winch invented by Captain J. C. B. Jarvis, a Scotsman. Two men at a brace winch, which was mounted amidships, could do the work of a dozen or more hauling at the rail, and in far greater safety. In 1898 Captain Jarvis offered to put a winch aboard a Sewall ship for one voyage at no expense, but did not receive a response. Few were sold to British ship owners, also, although they were widely adopted by German ships. (Unfortunately, a flaw in the patent cut Jarvis out of any royalties.)

Aside from problems with rivets and broken frames in some of the ships—problems not widely known—the Sewall steel ships were reputed to have been well built. Their reputations were helped by the fact that both the Sewalls and Standard Oil believed in keeping them well supplied and maintained. They were big ships by any

The Erskine M. Phelps, *fastest of the Sewall steel barks, and the pride of Captain Robert Graham, who kept her in fine order, in dry-dock. Graham's record of crew relations was not so exemplary. The lack of any traditional ornamentation on the bow save for the truncated "chicken beak" under the bowsprit reflected the Sewalls' hard-nosed, no-nonsense style. Phelps, a Chicago shoe wholesaler, became Arthur Sewall's most intimate friend. In later years, Mr. and Mrs. Phelps, evidently with too much time on their hands, became great pests at 411 Front Street, bombarding Sam and Will with persistent questions about the ship's affairs.* MAINE MARITIME MUSEUM

reckoning, and, due to lax American regulations, they were routinely—and arguably dangerously—overloaded, which did not help their performances. They were not fast, although they tacked and wore-about handily, and they made some good runs when their bottoms were clean and it blew hard.

Some, to be certain, were shunned by good sailors for good reasons, causing the mates to come down even harder on their hapless crews, perpetuating a vicious cycle. That said, by and large the captains of these ships were men of great ability and courage. And they were proud of their ships.

The other products of the Sewalls' steel yard were the three-masted bark *Kaiulani*, 1899; an oil barge; and the five-masted schooner *Kineo*, 1903. *Kaiulani*, built to her owner's specifications for general freighting between San Francisco and Hawaii, was

The bowsprit of one of the steel Sewall-built barks overshadows Front Street. The office building at 411 Front Street is hidden from view by fence and ship. MAINE MARITIME MUSEUM

well built, very handy, and fast. Her beamier proportions were of American model.

Mark Hennessy, of course, wrote the history of the Sewalls' steel ships. Much of the information regarding the steel ships in the pages following was either unavailable to Hennessy, or did not fit the story that he was telling.

I had seen the cloven foot

Dirigo was launched during a heavy snowstorm on February 3, 1894, the white flakes contrasting with the shiny black paint slathered onto the frosted steel for the occasion.

The belief, forwarded by Hennessy, that *Dirigo* was built by local wooden shipwrights who picked up a new trade, is not credible—steel shipbuilding involved many skills wholly foreign to wooden construction, some requiring a lengthy apprenticeship. Likely most of the ironworkers who built *Dirigo* came from the yards of the Delaware. The Bath newspapers took no notice of them, but then, Bath had often absorbed influxes of shipwrights from elsewhere into her boardinghouses and spare back rooms.

A firsthand account of the construction of *Dirigo* is the decidedly jaundiced remembrance, written about twenty years afterwards, by Captain George Goodwin, *Dirigo's* first master, who definitely had an axe to grind. But he was there, and we were not.

> With the exception of a few, the men that worked on this ship were what might be called "turnpike" mechanics: foreigners, the refuse of other yards, who spend more time tramping the pike from one yard to the other than they do at work. They were insolent, indifferent workmen. The so-called wooden men and the iron workers were at loggerheads from the start to the finish. It was like building the tower of Babel—chaos, without head or tail.
>
> The old rigger would not touch the job because they would not give him a fit place to work. The man who did that part of the work was a good rigger, when he was sober. The only work done on this ship that I can, or ever did eulogize, was the joiner work in the cabin. The decks were a disgrace to any ship. The planks looked to me as if they were the refuse from the ships that had been built in the previous twenty-five years.
>
> Owing to a strike, inefficient and indifferent workmen, etc., this ship, that was to have been launched in November, did not float on the water until January. The cement and paint that was put on the steel, when it was full of frost, did not adhere; the seams of the deck were caulked more with ice than oakum.[10]

The strike was a walk-out, followed by a lock-out, of riveters protesting the farming-out of metal sparwork to an outside contractor. The riveting on *Dirigo* was done by "squads," each of which was dealt with as a separate "company," as in "Thomas Doyle & Co.," in which case Thomas Doyle hired, and paid, a second riveter, a holder-on, and a boy. Doyle himself was paid by piecework, i.e., by the finished rivet.

The striking riveters were union men, an uneasy subject in Bath. Arthur Sewall stated to the papers that he was in no hurry to get the ship done anyway, and that the solution for the future was to make Bath men into ironworkers. "We always managed our own affairs while we were building wooden ships, and we propose to do it now."

Mr. Waddington, who had been superintending the job, was eventually informed that the firm would hereby be doing its own superintending. He walked out just before he had completed the design of the next ship. The word around town was that there had been a clash between two strong personalities, but George Goodwin guessed that Waddington left due to interference from his employers, who were likely pleased to thus save the couple of hundred dollars that had been promised him as a bonus at the ship's completion. In any event, Arthur took over as superintendent for the final two months of the job.

There was history, of course, behind George Goodwin's gripes. After the ship *Sterling* had been sold by the Sewalls to John Rosenfeld in 1881, young Captain Goodwin and Arthur continued corresponding. Goodwin wished to command a new ship in which he could be an owner; Rosenfeld captains sailed on wages. In the bitter January of 1893, after Goodwin had been blown off the coast three times bringing *Sterling* into New York, he received word that Arthur wished to meet with him at Bath.

Possibly the launching of the Arthur Sewall, *February 23, 1899. Overlapping riveted joints were caulked by striking the upstanding edge with a chisel-like "splitter" which partially detached a bead of metal which was then driven against the surface of the other plate with a tool called a "maker." Before pneumatic caulking, it was important to arrange plating so that right-handed caulking could be employed as much as possible. During the* Arthur Sewall's *construction a Sewall employee fell about 30 feet from a staging—a standard shipyard accident—while counting rivets. The injured man sued the Sewalls for $10,000. In December 1899 the Sewalls prevailed in court by arguing that since the riveters, who were employed by piecework, had constructed the staging, they were to blame for the faulty plank, even though the Sewalls had provided the materials and had paid the riveters extra for the job. (The [Bangor]* Industrial Journal, *February 16, 1900).* MAINE MARITIME MUSEUM

There, Goodwin was offered the command of *Dirigo* if he would take on the master's ⅛ share. Goodwin wrote later: "I always had a great deal of admiration for Mr. Sewall so I listened to his talk and the nice things he said about me."

> Finally my ambition ran away with my judgment, so . . . I told [Arthur Sewal] that I would go in the new ship. . . . After I walked down the *Sterling*'s gangway for the last time, I felt so badly that I could not bear to go on board of her again.

She had carried me hundreds of thousands of miles safely through thick and thin. I had a great deal of sailor's pride in her. . . . Her owner [John Rosenfeld] was a man whose word was as good as his bond—the whitest man for whom or from I ever earned a dollar. His letter to me, when I resigned command of his ship, is something that I have put among the things I keep. . . .

After I had finished my business with the owners of the *Sterling*, it was suggested to me [by the Sewalls] that I buy the interest in the steel ship . . . but go in command of a wooden ship—one that I would never have taken on any consideration. It was their idea for the captain of this wooden ship to command the new steel ship. To a man who had listened to the fairy tales I had, to put it mildly, this proposition was astounding. And I did not think it could possibly have come from headquarters until I met with a frost when I went to Bath.

I had given up my ship, had put up a deposit, and an agreement was being drawn up. When I arrived at Bath this agreement did not materialize. I was told something else which knocked the props from under one of my little tin gods, that have never been replaced. You may say that I should have had more business sense, but . . . I had been sailing for a man for nearly thirteen years whose word was as good as any agreement he could sign, and I was not looking for anything else. I did not say anything but went home to wait for coming events.

Goodwin eventually read in a paper that construction was to begin on *Dirigo* and that he was to command her. He promptly removed to Bath so that he might become familiar with the ship, piece by piece, and so that she would not seem so big to him. But he eventually decided that he had been "hoodwinked." The cost of his share, $20,000, was to be paid with $10,000 cash, a $5,000 advance, and $5,000 to be carried on account, and worked off by earnings.

Any suggestion I happened to make, if it cost less . . . would be accepted, but if it cost more and the result would have been twice as good, it would be ignored. I gave up making suggestions or even giving my opinion when asked. I often thought, when I saw a cake of ice going down the river, I might as well go on it as wait for this ship. . . . I went to Bath with as much ambition, professional pride, self-respect and respect for my employers as any man could have, but the latter turned to something near disgust when I sailed away with something for which I had to pay a fancy price and all I had to show for it was a ship botched up, half fitted with what she should have had for running gear, etc.[11] I had to work like a slave for years, and spend thousands of the stockholders' dollars to make the ship what she ought to have been when she left the builder's hands.

Arthur expressed a very different view of the ship to his brother-in-law, Captain Fred Bosworth, of Portland, Oregon:

I wish very much you could inspect this ship. I believe you will say when you see her that she is as good or the best steel ship you ever examined. I feel very proud of her and have enjoyed her construction very much. . . . We have a very complete plant here and believe are in position to build steel ships certainly cheaper than anyone in this country, and can soon compete with builders abroad.

Goodwin was told that *Dirigo* had been chartered to take case oil from Philadelphia to Japan at sixteen cents a case; he later wrote that he knew this would not even pay expenses. In 1911, in a bitter letter to Will and Sam, he recalled:

The agreement [letter of instructions] which your Mr. S. S. Sewall called my attention to in Philadelphia when he was on the warpath about something I did not care what, but the beachcombers said I was going to be fired. . . . This agreement so different from what I was led to expect after listening to the fairy tales which I took for granted as I have had to do a good many times since, was signed with a mental reservation simply because I was in a position where I could not help myself. The text of this agreement abridged would read in good plain English, "We have got your money. You have got to meet with our entire satisfaction or get out."

He later wrote of this moment: "I had seen the cloven foot as had many others that had gone before me, and I felt the velvet paw as the years rolled on."

Goodwin had consulted with experienced captains of similar ships to find out how much ballast he needed with an oil cargo, and the amount specified had supposedly been put aboard before the ship left Bath. At Philadelphia the ship was loaded with 121,000 cases of oil. Meanwhile, Goodwin was getting used to the way the sound of water was transmitted through steel into his cabin: "You can hear every ripple so plain . . . it sounds as if the water was running right through her I have got up twice in the night and sounded the pumps."

My eggs were in this basket

Almost any new ship will, when first put in service, reveal many faults and oversights, especially a prototype built of an unfamiliar material in the cold of a Maine winter. And such was the case with *Dirigo*. As soon as she reached the Gulf Stream the ice melted from the seams of the decks, which leaked so much that tents had to be rigged in the cabins over the beds and furniture; in bad weather men bailed day and night. She carried a lot of water on deck, for which the wooden deckhouse doors—which served well on the wooden ships—were entirely inadequate. And so on, according to Captain Goodwin:

I have had experiences in five new ships but there were more things dropping apart in this one than in all the others put together. When I got in the trade winds and had to brace the yards forward, I found we did not have ballast enough

March 1894. Dirigo *loads sand and scrap-iron ballast at the Maine Central Railroad wharf, while ice floes pass by on the river. A rigger works aloft on the main royal yard. Bath's 1858 granite customhouse and post office is at right; the new coastal steamer* City of Lowell, *being completed at the Bath Iron Works, is at far left.* Dirigo *is lying very near the sites of the two*

to give the ship sufficient stability to carry the light sail—I had also been scrimped on the ballast. . . . When I reached the region of the "brave west winds" where I expected to make the fine runs that I had made on previous voyages, we could not push the ship because we could not steer her as she did not have enough rudder.

When off Madagascar . . . we had a hurricane. . . . The heavy black clouds had cleared leaving the sky the color of brass with the scud going like a streak of lightning. The water on the horizon gave us the first indication of wind. It was just a wall of foam. . . . We were clewing up the topsails when the wind struck the ship. The big steel yards went up and down on the topmast until I thought the mast would go over the side. The ship was on her beam ends at an angle of thirty-eight degrees and was laying over so much that it spilled the

bridges that presently span the Kennebec, and which, combined with the wall of the Route One highway viaduct, and also the massive view-blocking buildings of the present-day Bath Iron Works, have greatly altered the perceived geography of Bath in fact and in mind.
MAINE MARITIME MUSEUM

wind out of the sails and we managed to get them furled.

The men and officers, who had gone forward, could not return aft due to the extreme list, and the only man Goodwin saw until daylight was an old quartermaster, standing by the lashed helm. The ship's rigging had been "rattled down" with gas pipes instead of hemp line, and as the pipe ends had not yet been plugged, each became a flute of a different tone. This sound, along with the howling of wind "which would blow the breath back down your throat," the slatting of the torn main lower topsail, the vicious lashing of sea and spray, all "played a devil's tattoo."

I did not think it was possible for a ship to get down on her side so far and recover herself again, and she would not have done so if she had not been on the right [correct] tack. So when the wind hauled [the seas on her lee bow] pushed her up on her bottom. Everything movable was washed overboard, even the belaying pins were washed out of the rail, and the running gear and lee braces were trailing astern.

Kobe was reached in October 1894, after 151 days. Half of the cargo was damaged by salt water from the leaking deck. Arthur and Goodwin corresponded extensively regarding the ship, and Goodwin, responding to Arthur, wrote: "You say you are surprised that I think the ship will want more ballast with another oil cargo. It is a fact nevertheless, and can it be reasonably expected that a light draft ship built of the lightest material used in shipbuilding can stand up with an oil cargo the same as the *Roanoke?*" Goodwin later wrote:

> It is my belief that if you ever send a ship of the *Dirigo's* model with a cargo of oil and without ballast to sea you can say good bye for good to the ship and the people that go in her. . . . For my part I fail to see where the judgment comes in where one sacrifices every quality there is in a ship for the sake of a few tons less ballast and a few tons more cargo.

While Goodwin was entering *Dirigo* at the custom house at Kobe, a free-for-all broke out on board, the mate and most of the crew having gotten drunk on the local "kill me quick." The carpenter, his stomach ripped open, went to the hospital, and the two worst troublemakers received two years in prison.

To Goodwin's disgust, he found the ship fixed for a charter carrying "Japanese goods"—rice, ore, and general merchandise—to New York for the "magnificent" sum of $18,000, with loading not to commence until March. He knew that he would not be profiting from this voyage, "However, I was there up to my neck. My eggs were in this basket and Mark Twain's advice is 'to stay with the basket.'" He resigned himself to spending the winter in Japan. Never had he seen more desperate poverty than he witnessed among the working people of Japan at that time, during the Chinese–Japanese War.

When *Dirigo* at long last departed she made a 137-day passage to New York, very creditable under the circumstances, as she was light and so foul that she wouldn't steer and had to be sailed with the helm hard over. In dry-dock at New York the barnacles were found to be three layers deep. Here the rudder was enlarged, and other improvements made. "I had the doors fixed so that if a bucket of water was thrown against them, half of it would not go through the jamb."

On her next passage, to San Francisco, the ship proved to be well balanced, to steer and "work" well, but arrived leaking so badly from loose rivets in the stern that steam pumping was required—Goodwin ceased pumping just long enough to strike a good bargain with a tug without revealing his distressed condition—and then immediately commenced to pump again, since the water had gained considerably in the time spent dickering.

The long passage had been due to light and adverse winds—Goodwin later wrote: "A week or ten days of light airs and calms will start a growth on the bottom of a steel ship that will retard her progress one knot per hour for the remainder of the passage." *Dirigo*'s proclivity for finding such conditions became a lifelong habit. As Goodwin put it, "The *Dirigo* . . . has made some fine runs . . . but has a habit of turning around and looking at what she has been doing and spoil it all." She reminded him of a cow his family once had that "would give a good lot of milk and then kick the pail over." In May 1897, Arthur, having impatiently awaited *Dirigo*'s latest tardy arrival at San Francisco, and having been embarrassed by comments made about her slowness, wrote Sam:

> I wish you could in some way arrange for Murphy to take the *Dirigo* for one voyage. I believe under his mastership she would show better results in time. This ship is in absolutely perfect condition. Goodwin has spent his time usefully with his crew in painting, etc. She has not made a drop of water since she left New York, and I feel that we have a staunch ship in her that will work for us for the next 40 years, if we can keep her off shore and avoid collision.

And it would seem that "the Senior" expected to still be around in forty years. He later wrote: "I believe [*Dirigo*] the best steel ship afloat, barring her sailing qualities."

In June 1897 Frank Sewall (Fred's son) joined *Dirigo* on her passage from San Francisco to Liverpool. *Dirigo* made an excellent passage of 109 days, beating two English ships which had sailed about the same time by thirty-eight and forty days respectively. Frank wrote in the journal that he was keeping for Arthur: "I think it would do Captain Goodwin lots of good if you or the firm write him a good congratulatory letter. He says you talked to him very severely in 'Frisco and has brooded over it the whole passage."

I have a Republican I wish to get rid of

Arthur Sewall was very much a political animal, albeit in some respects a very unusual one. Presumably Arthur was a Democrat because that was the party into which he had been born.

Back when the Democratic Party was Jefferson's Republican Party it claimed many anti-establishmentarian followers in Maine, which was then the wilderness outcast district of stuffy Federalist Massachusetts. By the time of the Civil War, however, the party had split, with the Northern anti-slavery faction reclaiming the old Republican name for a new party, and with Southerners claiming the Democratic Party, along with a mixed bag of Northerners, including a number of Maine shipping men engaged in Southern trades.

After the Civil War the Democratic Party, particularly with the 1896 candidacy of William Jennings Bryan—Arthur, of course, was his running mate—became the party of the small southern and western farmer, the union laborer, and the immigrant. In Maine, however, the Democrats had been all but wiped out by the rise of

Arthur Sewall, probably in 1896
Maine Maritime Museum

Republicanism. With the elections of Democrat Grover Cleveland in 1884 and again in 1892, Arthur, as a Democrat leader in one of the most Republican of states—and in an era of the spoils system, graft, and political shenanigans—applied himself to the task of putting Democrats into government jobs with the same energy that he brought to all of his endeavors.

While some might have suggested that Arthur's strong disagreements with Cleveland's stands on many issues meant that Arthur was in the wrong party, Arthur held that it was Cleveland who had lost his way. Arthur's tireless and mostly fruitless politicking in opposition to "free ships," and his advocacy of various approaches for subsidizing American shipbuilding and shipping industries makes for a long and tedious story which will not be dwelt upon here.

Arthur's forays into elective politics predated the era of baby kissing, which, given his natural reserve—not to mention his disdain for the press—would likely have resulted in even less success at the polls than he enjoyed, his only elected public positions being city councilman and alderman. In 1893 he lost a hopeless bid for the U.S. Senate—senators were then elected by state legislatures. From 1872 through 1900

Arthur was either a delegate or a visitor at every Democratic national convention. From 1888 to July 1896 he served on the executive board of the Democratic National Committee, finally being turned out over his stubborn advocacy, in opposition to Cleveland, for the free coinage of silver.

An example of Arthur's political pull was his hidden role in the removal from office of Captain Jarvis Patten, Commissioner of Navigation, to make a vacancy for a political hack, even though Patten was a member of the distinguished Bath tribe of Pattens, a family with whom the Sewalls shared much common history and associations.

Patten, an erudite veteran shipmaster, was appointed in 1884 by President Chester A. Arthur to be the first U.S. Commissioner of Navigation.[12] During his brief tenure Patten merged several disorganized and ineffective maritime bureaucracies. In 1887, Patten, a Republican holdover from the Cleveland administration, was asked to resign. His replacement was a Democratic functionary from Augusta, Maine, one A. B. Morton. This was the hidden handiwork of Arthur, who wished to preserve the job of a Sewall cousin—another Republican and thus a marked man—in the Bureau of Internal Revenue, whose office at the IRS had been slated to be awarded to Morton.

William Putnam, Arthur's very well-placed lawyer and adviser, wrote Arthur in December 1886 that Morton "would not be an ideal commissioner, but I suppose he has sufficient capacity to run the bureau according to the practical standard which seems to have been adopted for it." Hardly a ringing endorsement. Putnam begged off from taking any stronger position, claiming that Jarvis Patten and Putnam's mother had been next-door Bath neighbors.

Proof of Arthur's role is found in an October 1893 letter to him from Morton in which Morton declared that their friendship was now ended by reason of Arthur's support of efforts by Joe Manley to install a crony as engineer of Augusta's post office, in opposition to the candidate backed by local Democrats. Morton wrote: "I know of no act of mine since I was Commissioner of Navigation wholly through your influence where any act of mine has been thrown against you personally or politically. I have been willing to do every thing except throw away my manhood."

A letter from Patten to Arthur in August 1887, accompanied by a clipping from a Washington newspaper alleging Arthur's key role in the purge, speaks for itself:

> I enclose an item from a Washington paper now some weeks old but which my attention was only just called to by a gentleman who inquired the truth of the report. I told him . . . the whole Sewall story must be a canard for several reasons.
>
> 1st. Because you were interested in shipping and it would be the last thing any true friend of that interest would like to see—a bureau only lately established for the benefit of ships and seamen made an object [of] plunder for the hungry & thirsty politician;
>
> 2nd. The town in which we lived was the only great shipbuilding town in Maine and the only place to take any special pride in the office, and it would be an unpopular move in any one to recommend its transfer elsewhere, and especially to a crankish kind of novice, such as my successor was said to be;

3rd. Mr. Sewall was a Swedenborgian, one of the cardinal tenets of which creed was "love for thy neighbor," and the course named was so unlike the conduct of a true-believer as to be unworthy of serious consideration. . . .

Something of Arthur's labors in Maine's political vineyards is revealed by several 1892 letters from one D. W. Parker, evidently the Maine Central Railroad's station agent at the remote eastern woodland town of Danforth. Parker, who was running for the legislature, wished to obtain cheap railroad fares for a group of foreigners—very likely French-Canadian tannery workers—to send them to Bangor for naturalization, after which they would be paid to vote the Democratic ticket in the state elections that September. On August 6, 1892, Parker wrote:

I have written Mr. Boothby about rates for the men to be naturalized. I think there will be 40 to go. I have one or two that it will cost $15.00 each to get fixed, but otherwise they will not cost us $5.50 to $6.00. . . . Do you think I should take the high priced ones?

Mr. Boothby was the Maine Central's passenger manager. One week later Parker wrote:

Everything is looking first class and I have no doubt of my election. I have 40 to naturalize. I think we can get that no. [number] through all right. I don't think the other party have 10 new ones. Do I understand that I shall sell their men tickets at the same rate ($2.00)? I shall see Hanson first of the week and do what is right about contribution. This is an expensive district to carry as you must know, and is one that [Senator Eugene] Hale is depending on, so I understand.

(On August 22 the chairman of the Democratic Committee of the central Maine town of Winthrop wrote, asking for $50 needed to naturalize "10 Frenchman" who "the Republicans would be very glad to naturalize.")

On August 25 Parker wrote that "for one reason and another" only twenty-eight men had "passed." The total cost, including hotel bill, was $178.12. The Republicans had gained fourteen or fifteen new voters. Quite a number of men still had to be brought home to vote, and he wondered if arrangements had been made for reduced rates for them. On the 27th he wrote:

I have a Republican I wish to get rid of from Forest City, Sidney Phales. Will you please send him a pass to W. E. Pritham, agt. Forest, from Forest to Portland? So he can use it Friday P.M.? I have two men to get from Pittsfield, one from Portland, two from Bangor, possibly two from Portland, two from Vanceboro, 3 or 4 to Lambert Lake. Can't you send me some blank passes to fix these men with? Everything is looking first class but we must leave no stone unturned. . . . *Ans* by *mail*, make it *personal*.

On September 2 Parker wrote that he had found no town where "Democrats will vote for my opponent, except, I fear, his 2 bro's in law & father in law. Unless they flood Princeton with money I think it is all right. I left $32.00 there, I think that ought to get them out, but they talk $5 a piece for some of our men there. . . . I shall put in a couple more days there next week. . . . Wish you would secure me 5 more passes." On September 13, Parker, victorious, reported:

> I am elected by 10 plurality. It was a very hard & expensive fight. They the (Rep.) paid $15.00 each for votes and took their chances, but we still made a gain of 18 in this town. Wish you would send me a blank pass, I have a voter to get back to Boston. Guess that will fix all of them.

This was the first election held after Maine, reflecting a national movement, adopted the secret ballot—however the politicians had quickly found ways to circumvent this annoyance.[13]

Think it must be very up by this time

The front page of the Bath *Daily Times* of October 7, 1896, featured two stories, side by side, concerned with Arthur Sewall. At far left, in relatively small type, was the headline "The Mate of the *Rosenfeld*." The brief story reported that the steamer *Carib Prince* had arrived at New York carrying Mate Gillespie, Mrs. Gillespie, the steward, and cabin boy of the foundered ship *Willie Rosenfeld*.

We will return to the story of Captain Dunphy and the ship *Willie Rosenfeld* after dealing with Arthur Sewall's quixotic quest for the vice presidency, the subject of the much larger headline to the right which read: "PROUD OF THE HONOR," and under it, "Sewall Formally Accepts Nomination Tendered by Democrats." Arthur's letter of acceptance began:

> Gentlemen, I have the honor to accept in writing . . . the nomination tendered by you, on behalf of the Democratic Party, as its candidate for vice president of the United States. And in so doing I am glad, first, to express my satisfaction that the platform of our party, which has commanded my lifelong allegiance, is honestly and fully declaratory of all its principles, and especially of the absorbing financial issue upon which, as you say, I took my stand, "When the hours of triumph seemed remote, and when arrogant money changers throughout the world boasted that the conquest of the American masses was complete."

The nomination of Arthur Sewall is among the more significant forgotten footnotes of presidential history.[14] While there was no guarantee that the Democrats could have won had someone other than an Eastern banker and railroad man been on the ticket, having an Eastern banker and railroad man on the ticket likely guaranteed that the Democrats could not have won under any circumstances. The victory of William

McKinley and Garret Hobart, representing the interests of big business, over "the Great Commoner" and "the Maritime Prince," arguably cast the shape of American presidential politics until the election of Franklin Roosevelt in 1933.[15]

The contest was held amidst great national unrest and division, the lingering legacy of the panic of 1893, which had led to wholesale bankruptcies and violent labor strife. Arthur Sewall, it would appear, had been genuinely shaken by these events. In July 1894—a truly dismal year—he had written his friend Erskine Phelps:

> I am not one of those who join the popular clamor to shoot down and stamp out this industrial [labor] element of our country that is now the great factor in the existing trouble. . . . There are none of us that would be so autocratic, and arbitrary, as not to listen to the complaints and distress of others. Every true citizen owes a duty to his family, to his neighborhood, to his community, to his country, higher and paramount to his own personal gain, or success. . . . The underlying cause of this unrest and general bad condition today in our country is the bad legislation for the last twenty years. . . . The class legislation and corruption in high places that has existed during the past is sure to bear the bitter fruit that we are eating today.

And what of the complaints of the unpaid seaweed-eating sailors of the *Nora Bailey?* People do change, and perhaps as Arthur's views on life matured and broadened he was evolving into an unusual, and admirable, political hybrid—although a more convincing case could be made if he took actions to ensure the decent treatment of sailors on his ships.

During the campaign, complex economic and social issues coalesced into a single simplistic, impassioned national debate—if a strident shouting match can be termed a "debate"—over the "free coinage" of silver. In 1873 the federal government had all but ended the minting of silver coins—known as "The Crime of '73" by the "silverites"— and which Arthur Sewall, in an 1895 letter to Fred Bosworth, called "the most unfair, unjust and wicked legislation ever enacted by our Congress."

The subsequent rise of the value of gold, along with rising interest rates and lower commodity prices, convinced the silverites—many being poor farmers from the rural West and South—that they had been victimized by the rich and manipulative "gold bugs" of Wall Street, in collusion with the "Jews of Europe."[16] Deflation had enriched the lending class while impoverishing the borrowing class, who, according to Arthur, were society's producing class.

The silverites' solution was for the government to expand the money supply by purchasing and coining silver, which, by means of some mysterious law, would find equilibrium with gold at a ratio of sixteen to one. This would encourage economic activity. Inflation would help debt-strapped farmers, presently trapped by their mortgages between deflating money and lower commodity prices.

The gold bugs, on the other hand, were convinced that such a move away from "sound currency" would quickly drain the Treasury of its gold, demoting the United

States to the level of Mexico. They spun their efforts as a noble struggle to prevent rich silver-mine owners from reaping a huge and ill-gotten windfall.

Both sides fought with all the passion of antagonists in a religious schism. A blizzard of propaganda, as dependent upon blind faith as any theological tome, was unleashed by both camps. And perhaps neither side really understood what it was talking about. The issue cut across party lines, although only the Democrats, with outgoing President Cleveland opposed to free coinage, faced being split by it. Chaos among the Democrats gave a third party, the Populists, leverage.

Arthur Sewall had long been a confirmed proponent of silver coinage. (Putting his money where his mouth was, as it were, he was also heavily invested in silver-mining stocks.) According to Portland's Democratic *Eastern Argus* (probably *circa* 1894), "Mr. Sewall's [pro silver] utterances have very little significance to anybody but himself. It is a long time since he voiced the sentiments of the Maine Democracy. He is not in sympathy with them on the tariff question (Arthur generally supported tariffs) or the currency question or the free ship question. Not a Democratic paper in Maine upholds the silver heresy."[17] And indeed, shortly before the national convention the Maine Democrats nominated a gold bug for governor, and stripped Arthur of his position as national committeeman. He believed that his political career was finished.

The national convention, held in Chicago, was a rowdy and impassioned affair quickly captured by the silver men. William Jennings Bryan, "the boy wonder of the Platte," assured victory with his ringing "Cross of Gold" speech—"You shall not press down upon the brow of labor this crown of thorns; you shall not crucify mankind upon a cross of gold."[18] The convention's final business was the selection of a vice presidential candidate. The name of Arthur Sewall was put before the weary conventioners by a California delegate. The *New York Times*, which had been covering the convention with ill-disguised contempt, reported:

> It was 3 o'clock when the last Territory voted on the ballot. The band struck up a tune. . . . Suddenly Altgeld of Illinois jumped on his chair and waved his hand. The Chairman saw him and shut off the band. Altgeld then announced that the forty-eight votes of Illinois had been transferred to Sewall. Convinced that Sewall was to be the nominee, the supporters of that convert to Populism seized banners and marched through the aisles twice. They made the circuit of the hall without exciting a cheer. The band forgot to play and the procession halted. A Louisiana delegate then moved that the nomination be made unanimous. . . . The convention ratified the nomination with a short period of excitement. The band played "Yankee Doodle" and "He's a Jolly Good Fellow, " which pleased the galleries. The banner of Pennsylvania appeared in the procession. A small boy carried it.[19]

Sewall carried on the fifth ballot, without the unanimous support of the Maine delegation. Neither he nor Bryan was in the hall at the time, and in fact the two had yet to meet. The turnabout for Sewall was stunning. The common wisdom was that Arthur, stolid eastern elder, was selected as a counterbalance to the young western demagogue.

But the eastern establishment was going to vote Republican no matter what. Arthur had no rational hope of even landing Maine's few electoral votes. And he made for a fat target.

The upstart People's, or Populist, Party, fast-growing in the West and the South, and hell-bent for free silver, held its convention at St. Louis shortly afterwards. The convention backed Bryan as a "fusion" candidate for president, but could not stomach "the bloated capitalist" Arthur Sewall, naming instead Tom Watson of Georgia as its choice for vice president.[20] Ironically, by attempting to be kingmakers, the Populists had signed their own death warrant, while also guaranteeing a Republican victory.

Bath had an alternative theory regarding Arthur's selection—alas, it is probably just a good story. Arthur Sewall sent barrels of rum (and perhaps also whiskey) to sea to be slowly rocked to aged perfection. It was said that these barrels were built into a new ship's transom, to be removed when the ship was opened up for her seven-year survey. According to the story, Arthur thoughtfully brought such a barrel to the convention at Chicago so that the Maine delegation could properly entertain other delegates, and in gratitude, Arthur was given second place on the ticket.[21]

There is record of a number of barrels of Arthur's rum going to sea in Sewall ships. Captain Baker, aboard the *John Rosenfeld* at San Francisco in November 1886 wrote: "That bbl. [barrel] of W. I. [West India] rum *still lives*. Think it must be *very up by this time*." And in January, after the *Rosenfeld* was wrecked, Baker wrote: "I have shipped by the *Sterling* the barrel of rum in good order & condition & charged Goodwin to see to it in NY & forward it on to Bath. It ought to be good by this time."

In November 1893 Captain Robert Graham of the ship *W. F. Babcock*, arrived at Philadelphia, wrote Arthur, who had requested the shipment to Bath of the rum barrels sequestered aboard the *Babcock*:

The three barrels of rum are on board, and the last time I saw them, they were in perfect condition. Have had them stowed in lazarette and walled in with three thickness of three-inch planks thoroughly spiked to prevent their being tampered with.

In September 1896 Captain Baker shipped Arthur a barrel of seasoned rum from the four-masted bark *Kenilworth* while at New York. Perhaps that was a replacement for the barrel that allegedly went to Chicago![22]

He Knows Old Sewall

When Arthur Sewall returned to Bath from Chicago on the evening of July 15 his train was met at Depot Square by a crowd of several thousand well-wishers and spectators. The city cannon roared and church bells pealed. Front Street was draped in bunting. When Arthur stepped out of the car "perfect pandemonium reigned" for several minutes. A very brief speech by the candidate was answered by the but recently devised "Sewall Yell," to wit, "Yell, yell, everybody yell, S-E-W-A-L-L!"

DON QUIXOTE AND SANCHO PANZA ARE NOW APPROACHING BOSTON.

MAINE MARITIME MUSEUM, SEWALL FAMILY PAPERS

A procession was formed, led by a platoon of Bath's policemen followed by Portland's twenty-six-piece Chandler's Band. A company of uniformed, cane-carrying young men escorted Arthur's carriage "through the crowded streets to his mansion. Red fire, rockets and bunting were on all sides." At the mansion, whose grounds were illuminated by Japanese lanterns, a general reception was held. Afterwards, the procession continued to the park, where, "during the brilliant pyrotechnic display, Sewall shook hands with the multitudes." Future Maine governor F. W. Plaisted "made a brilliant oration, non-partisan and eloquent in praise of Bath's greatest man." The crowd gave cheer upon cheer, and Arthur shook more hands again and "the band played a brilliant programme." Even the Republican *Kennebec Journal*, swept up by the gay mood, reported: "The city was crowded with people from everywhere brought by many special trains and everybody was proud and happy." The honeymoon would be brief.

The celebration of Bath's moment in the national eye was not to be confused with local support for the Democrats, for Arthur's politics, nor, even, with any great affection for the man himself. As Mark Hennessey noted, Arthur Sewall was, by nature, "not a man of the people," and was not well known personally in Bath outside of his family and a close-knit group of friends.[23]

Bath's three papers were all Republican organs, and, once the euphoria of the moment had cooled, were quick to get in their licks. The *Enterprise* noted: "People who have lived in the same town with Arthur Sewall for many years and scarcely knew he existed, now turn themselves into all sorts of positions trying to get a glimpse of him."[24] The *Times* and the *Independent* carefully distinguished their criticism of what they viewed as a disastrous Democratic platform from any disparaging comments regarding the candidate as an individual. The *New York Times* was not so circumspect. Before Arthur had even returned to Bath the paper condemned the treatment of sailors aboard Sewall ships, citing reports in *The Red Record*, and reprising a case earlier in the year of allegations of brutality aboard the *Willie Rosenfeld*.[25]

And much more was to come. The Maine Populist Party leader, Luther C. Bateman, from Auburn, in a letter to a friend in Texas that was picked up by the national press, charged that Arthur had recently fired Hallowell granite cutters who refused to work in 102-degree heat in the shade; that his last act as president of the Maine Central was to cut wages by 10 percent while the road was paying 15 percent on watered stock; and that his ships were notorious for inhuman treatment among sailors. "He is a plutocrat by birth, instinct, and education. . . . He is despised by all who know him on account of his avaricious hard hearted and cruel nature. . . . It is the most outrageous, inconsistent and wretched nomination that the entire history of American politics can disclose."[26] And so on.

For starters, Arthur Sewall neither owned nor controlled any granite quarries. Possibly Bateman was miffed by the collapse of a plan whereby the Democrats would have backed him for governor of Maine in return for his support of Arthur.

A Texas Populist paper called *The Vindicator*—Texas was a hotbed of Populism—in a story headlined "He Knows Old Sewall," published an interview with a farmer named Albro who claimed to have lived in Bath for six years, during which time he came to know the Sewalls personally. Albro claimed that the "back generations" of Sewalls were Tories, that during the Civil War the Sewalls were "black abolitionists," and that Arthur Sewall had stated that he "had rather see his daughter married to a decent Negro than a poor white man." In a party supported in large part by poor white Southern farmers, this latter charge was sure to have maximum effect, despite the facts that Arthur Sewall had no daughter to marry off to anyone, and that William D. would have been very upset at being labeled as an abolitionist of any stripe or color. (Also, of course, Dummer had supported the Rebel cause during the Revolution.)

It did not help Arthur's image that Harold, who had switched parties in 1894, gave the keynote address at the Republican state convention and actively campaigned against the Democratic platform. Someone sent Arthur two clippings—one concerning a New York millionaire who left his impudent son but a hundred dollars, and another about Harold's having just spent four weeks on the stump in eastern Maine—with some advice: "If I had such a son I would punish him." To his credit, Arthur maintained that he was proud of his son, no matter his political affiliation. Bateman viewed the situation as a case of "Heads I win, tails you lose!"

Given the likely critical role of the Populist fusionist vote to the Democrats, and the strong animosity toward Sewall among Populist voters, the question of whether Arthur would be asked, or would volunteer, to step down, became the leading question of the campaign. Bryan never quite asked Arthur to step down, and Arthur never volunteered to do so, although both gave tacit permission for the other to act as he thought best. Instead, as the *Kennebec Journal* headlined on September 1, it was a case of "Sewall Being Shelved, The Maine Man Slowly But Surely Fading Out Of Sight," as discretion was judged the better part of valor. While Bryan campaigned across the country, thereby setting a new pattern for presidential candidates, Arthur stayed home out of sight.

Allegations of abuse on Sewall ships having become an embarrassing political issue, particularly with the *New York Times*, the Sewalls were presented with an awkward situation in August with the expectation that Captain Robert Graham of the ship *W. F. Babcock*, then lying at New York, would be arrested on charges resulting from events on a passage from Honolulu when he showed up to take the ship to sea. The plan concocted, but ultimately not required—bail was arranged and the trial postponed—was to have Graham switch ships with Captain Thompson of *Solitaire*, then lying at Philadelphia. Both ships were bound for San Francisco.

One public event that Arthur could not avoid was Bryan's long-promised New England visit late in September. In Boston, where a very large crowd had gathered, Bryan quickly turned the platform over to the "man who was in favor of an income tax although he had to pay it." Arthur told the crowd that he wanted to show the people that they still had a vice-presidential candidate, and continued on in an anti-capitalistic vein that surely outraged or bemused many of his wealthy friends and associates. He then delved into some arcane economic theories regarding capital and labor that have even puzzled academics.[27]

On September 26 the two odd political bedfellows took the train to Bath. A rally had been planned for 8:00 P.M. at Custom House Square, and, once again, Bath worked itself up into a tizzy. At an earlier Bryan rally at New Haven some insolent Yale students had caused a disturbance, and, not planning to brook any such nonsense at Bath, City Marshal Kittredge arrested several Bowdoin students, including future Maine governor, James P. Baxter, as a precaution. The Bath *Daily Times* commended Kittredge for his alertness, citing a report that Portland longshoremen—i.e., tough intoxicated Irishmen—were ready to "take a hand if the students got fresh."[28] Meanwhile, pickpockets plucked a rich harvest.

Bryan spent Sunday rusticating at Small Point, attending the local Congregational church in the morning, and partaking of a seafood dinner—something sometimes challenging to a midwesterner—that evening. Bryan and his stomach were then treated to one of Arthur Sewall's breakneck carriage rides to catch the midnight train.[29]

Shortly before the election, a Russian crop failure had raised the price of American wheat, defusing much of the anger in the West. The great disparity between the two parties' war chests (despite a reported $20,000 contribution from Arthur early in October) heavily favored the Republicans. On November 3, the national election day—Maine's state elections, held in September, had been a Republican landslide—Arthur voted early. He jokingly asked Captain Charles Patten if he would not like to move up the street, as he expected to be renting out his house. Captain Patten, not missing a beat, replied that if Arthur was to rent his house then he (Patten) would have to sell his. Arthur then retired to his mansion to receive the returns over a private wire.

McKinley was elected president with 271 electoral votes to 176 for Bryan. Hobart won 271 votes for vice president to 149 for Sewall, and twenty-seven for Watson. The popular vote was 7,106,199 for McKinley, and 6,502,685 for Bryan. In Maine the vote was 80,403 to 32,204, with 2,383 votes for Bryan on the Populist ticket. Sagadahoc County voted almost three to one Republican, and the results in Arthur's own ward were even worse. Arthur was said to have appeared depressed by the results, predicting four years under a government of syndicates, trusts, and injunctions.

Arthur's personal letter book for 1896, at some point, suffered water damage. A portion of his November 4 letter to Bryan read: "The battle is over and we have lost: You ——— fight for the principles of our party, but with the ——— and money power against us, the odds were too great." And so on. A letter to James K. Jones, of Chicago, began: "The fight is over, and we have lost, chiefly ——— of our own people, by traitors in our own camp."

On November 6 an anonymous person wrote to Arthur:

As you are a professed Swedenborgian, let me recommend to you to get on your *knees* with your head covered with ashes, and pray the Lord to forgive you for being allied with the wretched *Anarchists & Populists*, [Illinois governor] *Altgold*, Jones & Co., with their *mouth* piece Bryan, and stay there till the Lord forgives your miserable sins for the harm you have done for your country. Your honored father, if he knew of your bad conduct, would turn over many times in his grave. Thank the Lord our country is saved from *ruin*.

"Ecce! Tyrannus" (Behold! The Tyrant)

The publication in December 1895 of a thin booklet entitled *The Red Record*, subtitled *Ecce! Tyrannus*, containing a collection of sixty-four cases of alleged brutality inflicted upon seamen in American ships in the previous seven years, as recorded in the *Coast Seaman's Journal*, published by the Sailors' Union of the Pacific, did not help Arthur Sewall's candidacy. The introduction read in part:

This pamphlet presents a concise and vivid view of one phase of the American seaman's life. Considerations, not only of humanity, but of business expediency, as evidenced by the growing scarcity of seamen, demand public attention to the cause and cure of brutality to seamen. . . . These cases of cruelty are so atrocious and so repellant to the sense of common decency, not to say justice, as to be almost incredible. . . . Indeed, the incidents here mentioned are of the commonest order, the exceptional features of buckoism being of such a character as to be unprintable. . . . The cause of cruelty to seamen lies in the mistaken idea of economy which obtains among ship-owners. . . . The system originated and is maintained upon the theory that brutal ships' officers can by threats and violence compel a small crew to do the work of the larger number of men required under a just system.

Fourteen of the cited cases involved Sewall ships. *Solitaire, Rappahannock, Susquehanna, Roanoke,* and the *Benj. F. Packard* each were cited twice.[30] By comparison, the combined fleet of two dozen Cape Horners of the old partners Benjamin Flint and I. F. Chapman, twice as large as the Sewall fleet, accounted for five charges, two being earned by the *M. P. Grace.* The ten Cape Horners managed by Captain William Besse, of New Bedford, figured in a single incident. An excerpt from *Roanoke's* second listing may be of interest, given the Sewalls' surprise when it was revealed that Captain Hamilton had fallen off the wagon:

Captain Hamilton arrived at New York March 13, 1895. Crew charged that while the vessel was lying in Shanghai Edwin Davis, able seaman, fell from aloft, through fright at the threats of Second Mate Taylor, and was killed. The second mate is reported to have laughed at this. . . . The day following this fatality Arthur Baker, able seaman, was working under the hatches. A bale of cotton was in danger of falling on him, and when the attention of First Mate "Black" Taylor was called to this he swore at the crew and ordered them to "go ahead.". . . The bale fell on Baker, injuring him seriously. . . . The first mate accused Frank McQueeney of being asleep on the lookout, and pounded him into insensibility with a belaying-pin. Captain Hamilton struck Carpenter Hansen on the head with a bottle, inflicting deep wounds, and afterward put him in irons and triced him up to the spanker-boom, where he was kept till nearly dead. Crew accused Captain Hamilton of drunkenness and neglect of his officers' conduct.

Fourteen deaths cited in *The Red Record* were "recorded under circumstances which justify the charge of murder." However, only three of the sixty-four cases—none involved a Sewall ship—resulted in convictions, all for "brutality." This was explained in part by the "disappearance" of officers upon a ship's arrival in port. Forty cases were reported in San Francisco alone, and but one from a foreign port. "As cases of abuse are most frequent on vessels bound to foreign ports . . . the *Record* falls far short of the actual number of happenings."

The claim by *Red Record* publisher, J. Elderkin, general secretary of the National Seamen's Union of America, that "the strictest personal investigation into both sides of [each] case" was made is belied by confusion between Ned and Joe Sewall.[31] It would appear that most accounts were taken on faith from newspaper stories, never a wise course. However, the overriding contention that American ships were often the scenes of intolerable brutality and abuse cannot be denied, along with the fact that ships of the Sewall fleet were disproportionately represented. The July 14, 1896, *New York Times* crowed:

The candidacy of Arthur Sewall of Bath, Me. . . . on a platform which makes humanity its pretense, would cause amusement among many shipping people and seamen did it not incite to a feeling of indignation at the hypocrisy of the thing. . . . Commendable as the Sewall fleet is, however, from the standpoint of commerce and art . . . it has been a tradition among sailormen that these noble vessels are floating hells, that on them men are starved and abused to a more outrageous extent than on any other American ships, and that is the same as saying on any other ships that sail the high seas.

On July 16, 1896, a letter from an Arthur S. Brunswick, Esq., 31 Park Row, New York City, was answered by 411 Front Street thusly:

Your letter addressed to our senior under date of July 15 has been handed to our firm, for reply to the inquiries you made therein. We will not undertake to answer them separately, but will merely say that we have had during the forty years we have employed labor in our Ship Yard, no trouble of any consequence. In regard to the allegations of the Red Book, as you term it, they are entirely without foundation so far as our knowledge and authority extend.
    Arthur Sewall & Co.

The December 14, 1896, Bath *Enterprise* dealt with the locally sensitive subject of *The Red Record* by reprinting an article published in the (Republican) *Kennebec Journal*:

This publication is not an entertaining one for a Maine man to read. Out of the 64 cases mentioned, at least 36 were those in which Maine vessels and officers were implicated, in several instances more than once. . . . Reputable men acquainted with seafaring have been found who admitted that they did not doubt that in the main most of these charges are true.

Politically, *The Red Record* was well timed. The Maguire Act of 1895 protected coasting seamen—but only coasting seamen—from imprisonment for desertion. This led to a Supreme Court decision in the case of the barkentine *Arago* that held that seamen were exempted from the Thirteenth Amendment, which prohibited involuntary servitude. This, in turn, led to the passage of the White Act in December 1898, which not only limited the penalty for all American seamen for desertion in American ports to the forfeiture of wages and effects left behind, but prohibited all forms of corporal punishment.[32] The LaFollate Seaman's Act of 1915 resolved most remaining grievances of sailors' labor leaders.

Old habits—of seamen as well as officers—died hard, and accounts of flying belaying pins and mates' fists aboard Sewall ships well after the passage of the White Act could be cited, one being the following by Captain Benjamin Albertson, who as a young man shipped aboard the *Erskine M. Phelps*, Captain Robert Graham, in 1907, as contained in a letter to Mark Hennessy in 1949:

Captain Robert J. Graham, 1857–1929
MAINE MARITIME MUSEUM

During fair weather and a following breeze the helmsman could use a high stool at the wheel. One night Graham came up sometime in the first watch and caught the helmsman just about to caulk off, head nodding and with wheel in becket. Graham stepped over and sent him sprawling with a slap that could be heard all over the ship. . . . We had a cabin boy who was none too bright, willing but dull. Skipper had a favorite cup, almost as big as a tankard, for his breakfast coffee. In some way the kid knocked the bottom out of it. Afraid to report it, he made repairs with the white of an egg. The old man was going ashore for his clearance and was tucked out in whites. Sat down and the boy poured his coffee. G. ate a bite before picking the thing up and, when he did, the bottom dropped out and the hot Java slopped him from shirt front to pants cuff. The boy was in pantry when it happened so did not know. He brought in something else and went to serve the old man. Just as he leaned over to set down the plate he got it, IT was a crack that drove him into the sideboard and slid him to the floor. But, if one of the crew were sick or injured he could not have been in better hands, but God help him if he was trying to put one over. . . . He sailed a tight ship, his mates did not hesitate to use a "Bunch of Fives," a foot, or, at times, a belaying pin.

Captain Albertson himself chose to leave the sea when faced with loss of master's papers for smacking an insolently disobedient seaman aboard a steamer.

About 1915, at New York, when Able Seaman Adrian Raynaud was promoted to second mate aboard the bark *Edward Sewall*, the old mate instructed him to "Never give a sailor a kind word or a break, because if you do you'll ruin him." Raynaud did not understand the wisdom of this advice until he ordered the new gang of sailors, milling about in the forecastle, to turn-to. His orders were ignored until he backed them up with a belaying pin applied to several of the sailors' "short ribs," at which point the men could not exit the forecastle fast enough.[33]

The crew all swore to a lot of lies

It may be recalled that when we last left Captain Dunphy and his ship the *Willie Rosenfeld* in January 1894, she had been pooped by a tremendous sea near the Azores, which had broken the wheelhouse adrift from its moorings, killed three men, and dislocated Dunphy's leg. Mate Gillespie's efforts to save the ship were lauded.

In May 1894 the *Willie* carried coal from Newport News to Acapulco, then sailed in ballast to Port Townsend, Puget Sound, to load lumber for Valparaiso, Chile. *The Red Record* would charge that Mate Gillespie had assaulted sailors with belaying pins, cutting their scalps, and that Second Mate Sullivan and boatswain Kelly were also guilty of abuse. Gillespie disappeared, charges were dismissed, and Sullivan became first mate.

From Valparaiso the *Willie* shifted to the port of Caleta Buena to load nitrate of soda for New York. Caleta Bueno, located north of Iquique, was, like other nitrate ports on this bold and bleak coast, an open roadstead. Nitrate was mined in the interior desert and brought out to the edge of the coastal plateau in bags by mule train. A counterbalanced inclined railway lowered the heavy nitrate to the port, from where it was carried out to the anchored ships by lighters propelled by long sweeps.

As a cargo, nitrate had many objectionable properties, including great weight and foul odor. It was water soluble, and, when brought in contact with organic matter—such as any oily residue—could form explosive compounds. Remarkably, a ship's entire cargo was stowed by a single expert stevedore. A bag being placed on the stevedore's shoulders from a stack built up under a hatch, the man would trot off, bent forward with his hand on his hips, to just the right place, and then dump the bag in precisely the right position. The bags had to be placed so as to form a mass that tapered from bottom to top. Once in place, the bags melded together, and would never shift.[34] This cargo put great strain on wooden hulls both by its weight, and by having no "life," not allowing the hull to work, or flex, in normal fashion.

The *Willie* arrived at New York on January 26, 1896. According to a crowing article in the *New York Times* the next day, she had licked the British ship *Allerton*, also laden with nitrates, which had left Caleta Buena seventeen days before the *Willie* and towed into the harbor twelve hours after the *Willie* had anchored. As she towed by the *Willie*, *Allerton*'s sailors climbed into the rigging and gave the American ship three cheers, which was answered from the *Rosenfeld*. Captain Dunphy told the reporter that he had been held up a day off Cape Horn by more icebergs than he could count.

Once ashore, the apparent good cheer of the *Willie*'s crew quickly vanished. The January 31 *New York Times* published a long story reporting the seamen's testimony to Shipping Commissioner Keenan. One sailor had a gaping head wound, caused by a blow from an iron block wielded by the second mate, that had not healed in four months. Another sailor calculated that he had been assaulted 170 times—or two or three times on every watch. Captain Dunphy was closemouthed, but claimed to have discharged Second Mate Gilman at Caleta Bueno for the iron block incident. The crew charged that three seamen had been "got rid of" so that they could not be questioned.

In a further story in the February 4 *New York Times,* the United States shipping commissioner, responding to complaints by the crew, declared the *Willie* "a floating hell," alleging that conditions on the ship during the voyage included "inhuman brutality" and "semi-starvation." Agent Williams of the Atlantic Coast Seaman's Union charged that the men had been promised twenty dollars a month, although fifteen was later written in the wages column of the articles. The sailors claimed that the slop chest markups were 50 to 100 percent, instead of the legal limit of 10 percent.

There was no doubt whose side the reporter was on—clearly there was then no firewall between the paper's editorial and news departments. The fact that Mate Gillespie had been paid off without being arrested was cited as proof that "merchant Jack, kicked, beaten, defrauded, and half starved, is at a hopeless disadvantage to find redress for his wrongs."

On February 1 Captain Dunphy wrote the Sewalls a lengthy letter from the City Hotel, Providence, Rhode Island, giving his side of the affair:

> I suppose Mr. Dearborn has written you the full particulars of the trouble of crew and commissioner. The crew all swore to a lot of lies and the commissioner favored them in every way. . . . There was a warrant out for the first mate yesterday & I did not know that they might get one out for me so I came here for a few days. The commissioner is completely in the hands of a half Negro who represents the sailors union & the news paper men also seem to favor him. . . . ."35

According to Dunphy, the trouble started over wages. Dunphy had obtained the men fair and square for fifteen dollars a month in a crew swap, exchanging his inward crew for an outward crew with a Port Townsend boarding master, and a deputy commissioner had been there when the men signed the articles. Claims that the stores were bad and that the crew didn't get enough to eat were groundless—Dunphy had a written contract made with the crew that if there were any such complaints one man from each watch could report to him, and he would rectify the problem, but no complaints had been made. Furthermore, he had fed them "extra well" on the homeward passage, knowing that he was coming into New York, only running short on coffee and beans.

Regarding the charges of brutality, when Dunphy learned that the second mate had struck a man with a block at Caleta Bueno, he "had a row with him for doing so & discharged him immediately." He later learned of another instance wherein the second mate had struck a man—but with his hand after the man drew a knife on him. "The men have sworn that there was brutality used regularly. In fact they have sworn to everything that men could think of."

In March Dunphy was served with two summonses to appear in superior court on account of two sailors who had gone to the hospital. According to Dunphy it was another "put up" job by the sailors' union, as both had been at work on the ship until the last moment. The charges included claims of deficiencies regarding the contents of the ship's medicine chest. On March 8 he wrote: "Since my last, the Sailor's Union is working up a case of the passage from Liverpool to Acapulco in 1881 in the ship *Occidental* when rigging out the jibboom, a seaman fell over board and was drowned."

On April 23 the *Willie* departed New York with general cargo for San Francisco, with Captain Dunphy and Mate Gillespie on board. (Also on board was Gillespie's wife, Dunphy having persuaded the Sewalls to relax their strict ban on having mates' wives aboard ship, as otherwise he stood to lose a good mate. The Sewalls relented, but not happily.)

On the 25th the *New York Times* published an article headlined "No Justice For Sailors" which recounted the purported facts of the case, stating that when the ship had arrived the crew had testified as a body regarding inhuman treatment "received at the hands of Captain Dunphy and his mates, showing their wounds "as mute evidence of the truth of their complaints." Captain Dunphy's "surly answers to the questions put to him by Deputy Commissioner Keenan" were seen as proof of his guilt. As the *Times* had predicted, the captain had given bonds for his appearance, and then departed aboard the ship, forfeiting the money.

On August 13, in latitude 31.23 and longitude 42—off southernmost Brazil—after heavy gales, it became necessary to abandon the sinking *Willie*. Her people left in three boats. Twelve, including Dunphy, Mate Gillespie, Mrs. Gillespie, the steward, and the cabin boy, went in the longboat. Each of the smaller boats carried seven persons. Instructions were given to proceed in the direction of Santa Catharina Island. During the night the people in the longboat lost sight of the two smaller boats. Eight days later, after much suffering, the longboat arrived at the port of Imbituba. The two smaller boats were never heard from.

In October Sam wrote Will that he thought that Dunphy's "sailor troubles" had been "largely responsible for the disaster as [Dunphy's] mind was taken off his ship and he was also obliged to be much away from her." Sam's theory was that the railroad iron in the lower hold was placed too low after the original San Francisco cargo intended for the 'tween decks was sent to *Shenandoah* instead, and heavier cargo than intended was put in the *Willie*. Had it been foreseen that the cargo would be so heavy, the rails would likely have been "built up from the bottom and ship made much easier, for it makes a vast difference whether rails are stowed closely or built up though the same weight might be distributed in hold, lower & upper between decks."

In March 1897 Captain Dunphy, writing from Portland, Maine, dismissed several lingering sailors' lawsuits against him. He predicted that if "people do not make an effort to stop the proceedings of that secretary of the Sailor's Union on South Street there will be many more cases like the *Herbert Fuller*"—the captain, his wife, and the second mate of the barkentine *Herbert Fuller* had been killed by an axe murderer while they slept. In fact the mate, rather than a sailor, was eventually convicted, although he later received a presidential pardon.

Referring to comments made by the Sewalls in the final settlement of his *Rosenfeld* accounts, Dunphy wrote, "I am inclined to think that some New York parties [have] prejudiced your mind against me." In his defense, he cited instances where he had acted for the Sewalls' benefit. He concluded, "Therefore, if at any time you need a master I hope you will not leave me on the shelf. I am willing to invest in a decent sized ship."

Apparently the Sewalls bore Dunphy no great ill will, as he soon returned to their employ, serving as master of *Shenandoah* from that May until the following January.

1. For more about *Kenilworth* see Mark W. Hennessy, *The Sewall Ships of Steel* (Augusta, ME: Kennebec Journal Print Shop, 1927); John Lyman, "The Star of Scotland, ex-*Kenilworth*," *American Neptune, vol. I, pp. 333–35. See also* Harold D. Huycke, "The Great Star Fleet," *Yachting*, February and March, 1960.

2. In January 1900 George Dearborn's interests in Sewall vessels consisted of 5/128 in *Kenilworth*, 1/64 in *Shenandoah*, 1/64 in *Susquehanna*, 1/16 in the *Henry Villard*, and 1/64 in the *Erskine M. Phelps.* In 1905, attorney W. L. Putnam sold his 1/32 shares in *Shenandoah* and the *Erskine M. Phelps* to Harold Sewall. Below is an excerpt from his letter of February 16, 1905 to Sewall regarding this vessel property:

> One thirty-second of the *Shenandoah* cost me, in 1890 . . . $5,275.05. I find that she stands on my list of assets at . . . $2,500. She is, of course, valued subject to her indebtedness . . . of something in excess of . . . $3,000. . . . A purchaser would assume one thirty-second of that indebtedness. My one thirty-second of the *Phelps* cost me in 1898 . . . $4,263.68, less an item of interest of . . . $56.95, making net . . . $4,206.75. I find she is valued on my list of assets at . . . $3,300. . . . I have the *Shenandoah* left at a valuation. . . to represent substantially what she has earned in fifteen years. . . . The *Phelps* will probably pay for herself with the present freight, leaving the valuation of . . . $3,300 to represent the net earnings in seven years, being about . . . $475 a year; a quite large return if I had not insured myself.

3 Mildred P. Paine, *Harwich Men of the Sea* (Harwich MA: Harwich Historical Commission, 1977), p. 44.

4. Joe Hamilton, aboard *Undaunted*, arrived at Yokohama in March 1883, struck a somewhat different note: " . . . long passage and it has been a hard one although the ship has stood it much better than the Old Man. . . . I have had no accident except my usual luck of losing a sailor overboard."

5. The significance of a curious letter from General Hyde to his wife Annie, dated December 19, 1891, is not known: "I am having difficulty with A. Sewall & ——— which is too long to write. It will come out all right, but some people cannot get along without bulldozing & I won't be bulldozed even if I am sick. I am too old, don't you think? I think I had money enough to be ——— president of [Bath?]. Will & Art S. I fear not. There is lots of mean jealousy in this town, but there are lots of fine fellows in our employ & they seem to like us & as long as they do what care I—it is Bath Iron Works against the world and the more fighting the better. . . ." Bowdoin College Library, Special Collections Division, M1992 Box 4 folder 15. My thanks to Bud Warren, who discovered it.

6. This would not be the first large American metal sailing ship. That distinction went to the iron ship *Tillie E. Starbuck*, built in 1883 for New York ship owner W. H. Starbuck by John Roach on the Delaware River at Chester, Pennsylvania, at the center of American iron and steel shipbuilding. She was followed by two more iron ships built in a shipyard set up specifically for that purpose. These were the *T. F. Oakes* and the *Clarence S. Bement*, launched in 1883 and 1884, respectively. All three, designed on the Delaware, were slow sailers—some said because they were too beamy and flat, others, because they weren't beamy enough. The *Oakes* would become one the most notorious ships of the era thanks to a horrific 259-day starvation passage in 1896–97 from Hong Kong to New York. There is good evidence that Mrs. Reed, the captain's wife, was really in command, purposely prolonged the passage, and refused to put in for stores. She and her husband remained well-fed. See Gladys M. O. Gowlland, *Master of the Moving Sea* (Flagstaff, AZ: J. F. Colton & Co., 1959), pp. 63–77. Arthur Sewall had previously contemplated buying the *Starbuck* and the *Oakes* from their owner, W. H. Starbuck.

7. On June 4, 1937, Herbert R. Foster, Oakland, California—presumably a descendant—wrote Mark Hennessy: "Mother and I have been through what ship pictures are remaining and I am sorry that apparently the pictures of the Sewall ships have been discarded. At the time of my Dad's death two years ago we destroyed much of such material as we got tired of having it around not knowing who would care for it."

8. Dron Chesebrough also became the "owner" of a 1/8 share. The three partners were credited with a total of but 9/16 registered ownership.

9. William A. Fairburn, *Merchant Sail* (Center Lovell, ME: Fairburn Marine Educational Foundation, 1945–55), p. 1487.

10. From Goodwin's unpublished autobiography, Maine Maritime Museum library.

11. *Dirigo* probably cost about $157,000, or, Goodwin claimed, $40,000 more than "a ship with twice the fittings from a foreign yard." Over the years he claimed to have paid out $15,000 in insurance premiums on his inflated interest in her.

12. Kenneth R. Martin and Ralph Linwood Snow, *The Pattens of Bath* (Bath, ME: Maine Maritime Museum and Patten Free Library, 1996), pp. 54–59.

13. Of course any prudent boss would want a guarantee that the money invested would produce the desired results. Accordingly, the first conspirator to enter the polls put the ballot in his pocket, and put a plain piece of paper in the ballot box. Once outside, the blank ballot would be filled out as desired and given to the next man in, who would deposit it, and bring out another plain ballot. And so on, to the last man, who would vote two ballots, thus preserving the correct count at the polls.

14. See Leonard Schlup, "Bryan's Partner: Arthur Sewall and the Campaign of 1896," *Maine Historical Quarterly*, vol. 16, no. 4, Spring, 1977. Also Richard Pitt Irwin, "Maine and the Election of 1896," Master's Thesis, University of Maine, August 1949.

15. McKinley defeated Maine's Thomas Brackett Reed for the nomination.

16. The "Jews of Europe"—meaning the great financiers, such as the Rothchilds—were standard bogymen in the worldview of the silverites, including Arthur Sewall. As but one example, in February 1895 Arthur wrote Erskine Phelps: "I hear this P.M. that your great man at the head of our Government [President Grover Cleveland] has sold $82,000,000 of 4% bonds to the Jews of Europe on a 3 3/4 basis. What do you think of this financiering? I think our Yankee schoolboys, twelve to fifteen years of age, would do better." The sale was one of several frantic efforts by the Cleveland administration to replenish the Treasury's gold supply. Yet the true villains in Sewall's mind were the homegrown gold bugs. There is no indication that Arthur Sewall was

anti-Semitic—although casual anti-Semitism was widespread—or indeed held any strong prejudices against members of other races, beliefs, or classes, "sailor lawyers" and their clients excepted. (Not that any could match a Down East Yankee, of course.)

17. Evidently in 1894, as quoted in an undated clipping from the *Brooklyn Eagle*.

18. An anonymous flyer railed against the blasphemy of Bryan's speech: "Never before, in all the political contests in this country, has an aspirant for office made use of language which so shocked the religious sentiment of Christian people, of every sect and creed. . . . No, you shall not crucify mankind upon a cross of gold. Neither was the victim of Calvary's stupendous tragedy so crucified, but He was cruelly betrayed for *thirty pieces of silver*, and the metal still smells of treachery."

19. *New York Times*, July 12, 1896.

20. Irwin, "Maine and the Election of 1896," p. 39.

21. *Log Chips*, October 1954, p. 123. John Lyman, who reported the story, wrote "whiskey."

22. In October 1891 Mr. F. A. Wilson, of Bangor, wrote Arthur to thank him for the barrel of Newburyport rum just received after three years aboard the *Henry Villard*. "I thank you for thus enabling me to be sure of a healthy drink in my old age now fast approaching." A cargo plan shows a barrel sequestered under the cabin floor of the four-masted bark *Dirigo*.

23. Mark W. Hennessy, *The Sewall Ships of Steel* (Augusta, ME: Kennebec Journal Press, 1937), p. 158.

24. Hennessy, *Sewall Ships of Steel*, p. 160.

25. *New York Times*, July 12, 14, 1896.

26. Sewall Family Papers, Box 582, folder 16. All the campaign material quoted hereafter is from this box.

27. Irwin, "Maine and the Election of 1896," p. 97, quoting the *Daily Eastern Argus*, September 26, 1896.

28. Bath *Daily Times*, October 17, 1896.

29. Arthur's official campaign biography described his mansion in Bath as both his town and country house, and stated Arthur's purported belief that a man should have but one home. The Bath mansion was described as being such a house as could be found "numerously in every city in New England." (Arthur had not yet built his Small Point "cottage" and the Sewalls had likely been staying with Joe Manley or renting a cottage.)

30. The third edition, published in 1898, included nine new cases against Sewall ships, including four additional cases against the *W. F. Babcock*, Captain Graham, for a total of five.

31. In an expanded list of eighty-eight cases published in 1898 by the *Coast Seaman's Journal*, twenty-two involved Arthur Sewall & Co. ships, not counting the ship *Benjamin Sewall*, whose Captain A. Sewall was from another branch of the family (despite his being identified as also having been captain of *Solitaire* and *Rappahannock*, the editor obviously having confused the three Sewalls). Three cases cited against Captain Goodwin, one on *Sterling*, and two on *Dirigo*, raise questions—the *Sterling* case, alleging poor food, scurvy, and "brutal treatment from the officers" in 1890, gives no month, nor does an 1897 charge against First Mate Elwell on *Dirigo*. Poor food provided by vendors was usually a circumstance beyond the control of the master. The case of a crew deserting *Dirigo* at Honolulu in 1896 might not bear much scrutiny—there were many alluring attractions at Honolulu, a consul unfriendly to Sewall ships, and some very active crimps whose business plan depended upon persuading sailors to desert their ships.

32. Elmo Paul Hohman, *History of American Merchant Seamen* (Hamden CT: Shoe String Press, 1956), p. 30–31.

33. Captain Adrian F. Raynaud, talking at the Tenth Annual Symposium of Maine Maritime Museum, May 1, 1982.

34. Captain Vincent Large and Desmond Jackson, *Windjammer 'Prentice* (London: Jarrolds, 1971), p. 94.

35. The "half Negro" was James H. Williams, a union organizer who was a native, ironically, of Fall River. Some of Williams's autobiographical writings were collected in a volume titled *Blow the Man Down!* (Warren F. Kuehl, editor, New York: E. P. Dutton & Co., 1959). One of his accounts involves his experiences in 1884 aboard a ship he calls *Inquisition:* "The *Inquisition* was a large, stately clipper, a perfect specimen of that most graceful, elegant, and beautiful of all sailing craft, the American East Indiaman. In every detail of her construction and equipment she showed, in its highest development, the subtle cunning and wondrous skill of the shipmaster's art—light, lofty, tapering masts and spars towering majestically on high above her snow-white decks; erect in stays, symmetrical in design, correct in rake and alignment, perfect in general proportion and complete in artistic finish, with sheer, high, graceful bows and gilded scrollwork on her classically carved contour of her exquisitely rounded ends. What a pity that such an inspiring marvel of elegant perfection, delicate grace, usefulness, and majestic power should be made a floating torture-house, a 'blood-packet,' a beautifully sculptured shelter for human misery, grief, and despair, inhuman, fiendish cruelty, and wanton, unrestricted barbarities." P. 48.

PART TWELVE

We meet Joe Sewall again. The Edward Sewall. Shenandoah *goes to a "boy" captain. A new ship is named for Arthur. The Murphys suffer a grievous loss. Arthur's death ends Bath's era of fame, fortune, and productivity. We learn more about Emma Sewall. Harold in Hawaii lends a hand to history. And Jim Murphy should never have invested with Brother Charlie in Texas.*

It has been a terrible strain on me

The winter North Atlantic from Cape Hatteras north can be one of the most dangerous regions of all the oceanic world. It was especially so for ships arriving on the coast fresh from the tropics, whose crews might not be prepared for what they were to receive. On February 18, 1895, Captain Joe Sewall arrived at New York from Hong Kong with *Susquehanna* on the return leg of a case-oil voyage, loaded with matting and firecrackers. At Hong Kong he had successfully gotten rid of his expensive New York crew and had signed on an entire Japanese crew just before departure. He wrote Bath:

> We arrived safely yesterday at dock at 7 P.M. Ship in good condition but crew pretty well demoralized. We had terrible weather off the coast, the worst I ever had. Feb'y 8 took the blizzard in about 38.00 N. and 73.00 W and got all frozen up with snow and ice. My Jap crew were useless. Terrified and benumbed. Up to Feb'y 4 when we were off Hatteras we had a fine quick passage 89 days, and I looked forward to getting in in 94 days, which was not at all impossible, but from that time the wind howled from the N. W. & W. with but little intermission. The *Susquehanna* rode it out nobly and we lost not a rope yarn nor made any water. I lost one man overboard off [the] main yard, benumbed, I suppose, with the cold, and had three others injured by seas knocking them down. And to get our canvas off with such a miserable set was trying work. Our braces got frozen in the blocks and we couldn't haul the yards around for some time until we got thawed out. . . . I myself am pretty well played out with strain and fatigue, hence this scrawl.

(Private) In the height of the blizzard Feb'y 9 Mrs. S—— was confined and gave birth to a fine large hearty boy. Everything went well, except the cold was severe and the ship tossing about on large seas. Feb'y 14 the baby suddenly took an ill turn and in a few hours strangled to death with croup. Mrs. S. naturally grew worse and last night I sent her to the hospital in an ambulance very very low. She will recover, I hope, and the Dr. says he can bring her up all right but two days more at sea she would have died of blood poisoning. It has been a terrible strain on me.

Hastily, J. E. Sewall

You had better not ask for my story

Susquehanna was twice listed in *The Red Record* when under command of Joe Sewall, in April 1893 and November 1895, with the crew charging the "usual ill treatment against the captain and officers." The specific charges—once charges against Ned Sewall mistakenly ascribed to Joe are removed—are relatively tame. However, Doc Briry wrote:

> Captain Joe continued his vicious ways on his crews that he practiced during his school days upon boys younger than himself. He became very brutal at sea. . . . [On one occasion] Captain Joe Sewall did not dare to go on board his ship, then ready for sea at Philadelphia, because of still more cruelty at sea. An oceangoing tug with Captain Joe on board met his ship *Susquehanna* somewhere off the coast.

Two men who, when young, had sailed aboard *Susquehanna* under Captain Joe Sewall described Joe's shipboard behavior in very different ways. In 1941 Mr. A. J. Thornley of Montebello, California, wrote Mark Hennessy that in 1898 he had sailed from San Francisco to New York aboard *Susquhanna*, which was carrying canned salmon and wine. During the course of this passage the Spanish-American War began and ended. An Englishman, Thornley had found times very hard in California, and as he could not get ahead, he wished to return home. He met a sailors' boardinghouse master who, of course, said that he could get him a place as seaman aboard a ship headed for New York.

Once aboard *Susquehanna* Thornley quickly realized from talking with the sailors that he was not competent to be rated able seaman, and the next morning he asked to speak with the captain. Joe Sewall asked him if he wished to stay aboard or go ashore, and he elected to stay, promising to do the best he could. He later wrote a lengthy poem about trying to do the best he could which began:

> The shades of night were falling fast
> As up the ratlines there passed
> A youth who swore mid rain or dust
> He'd reach the skysail yard or bust.

Thornley recalled: "Captain Sewall and the mates seemed to enjoy it."

Susquehanna's company consisted of the captain and two mates, a bo'sun for each watch, the carpenter, a Chinese cook, a Japanese (he thought) steward, and ten men in each forecastle. The sailors consisted of one Frenchman ("Frenchy"), an Irishman ("Liverpool"), an American, a Swede, a Chilean, a Dane, an Englishman (Thornley), and others whom he had forgotten, including one lost overboard, leaving Thornley's watch one man short; to even things up, the port watch lost a man to a rupture.

As the junior man in his watch it was Thornley's job to overhaul buntlines on the square sails each morning, so he soon became comfortable aloft.[1] The food was good and plentiful. "Liverpool," the best seaman, took Thornley under his wing and taught him seamanship. It was winter when they arrived off the Horn, and whereas they should have had fair westerly gales, it took them two weeks to get around, facing one continuous easterly storm.[2]

> Two men were at the wheel, all gear, ratlines, halyards, etc., were coated with ice, waves were dashing over the ship. There were ropes stretched over the decks to hang on to so we would not be swept overboard. While we all had oilskins on these were only good to keep the wind out as we were all wet through. . . . The door on our focs'le swept open and our donkey's breakfast [beds] and all our dunnage were soaked by another good old wave. However, while we did not average four hours a day sleep during the storm, Captain Sewall kept the cook serving our coffee good and hot whenever possible, together with a drink of rum occasionally. . . . Captain Sewall was on deck almost all the time and was such an inspiration to all of us that I did not personally feel the least fear nor did I hear a word of fear from any of the crew. We knew we were in good hands.

Once they got into better weather it was necessary to cut off their salt-caked underwear. And Thornley soon found the equatorial doldrums to be worse even than Cape Horn:

> For about two weeks it was one continual all hands on deck to wear ship, to catch every little zephyr of air that the mate felt or thought they felt coming up. Standing by the halyards in ice-cold rain showers while you are roasting under a tropical sun, aching bones, torn and blistered hands from eternal pulling the yards round, racing aloft to take in the skysails and royals if a squall came up, and the crowning misery of all, the studding sails. . . . If you never helped to put studding sails on a windjammer, you never experienced anything. Talk about Yo ho and a bottle of rum, you would wish you had a bottle of cyanide before you finished the job.
>
> But even the Doldrums didn't last for ever and then we got into the trade winds and clear sailing to New York. We painted and cleaned ship nearly all the way and she sure looked beautiful when we got to the harbor. . . . Captain Sewall asked me if I would care to stay on the ship as watchman until we were paid off,

which was about a week. I was glad to, and slept in the focs'le and I had my meals in a neighboring restaurant. I dined once in the cabin with Captain Sewall, and when I was paid off I was given a good discharge as A. B. I have never forgotten Captain Sewall and I am happy to have had the honor of sailing with that splendid seaman and gentleman.

In 1937, from 30 Rockefeller Plaza in New York, Robert L. Hague had responded very differently to Mark Hennessy's inquiry about Joe Sewall's behavior at sea:

With regard to my experiences on the *Susquehanna* and with Captain Joe Sewall, I am afraid my recollections are unprintable and, in fact, not at all friendly, because those down-East skippers did not hesitate to lay a hand or foot on any part of the anatomy they could reach. So with this in mind, you had better not ask for my story.

Robert Hague was a man whose observations should carry weight. A Rhode Islander, young Hague had left Worcester Tech to join a fishing schooner, then signed on as an "apprentice" aboard *Susquehanna* on a case oil voyage to Yokohama. After "a rough career with sailing vessels" he learned the machinist's trade, becoming a locomotive fireman and engineer. He returned to sea by way of the engine room, and by 1937 had became general manager of the Standard Oil fleet, which increased under his tenure from 81 vessels to 205, making it the world's largest privately owned fleet.

According to a March 9, 1939, clipping from the *Worcester Telegram* regarding his unexpected and untimely death at age fifty-eight, Hague was described as having been a friend to many prominent politicians as well as to "half the police force of New York City" as well as sailors, publishers, and locomotive engineers. He backed many Broadway plays, and was a noted collector of ship models. He was said to have earned $100,000 a year and to have spent every cent of it.

There is no satisfactory way to explain the dichotomy of Joe Sewall's behavior. Perhaps he had a good crew on Thornley's passage—usually good sailors who did their jobs were not the targets for abuse. It was also Joe's last passage in command of the wooden *Susquehanna* before becoming the first captain of the steel four-masted bark *Edward Sewall*, a promotion he had much desired.

I do not remember of being discourteous

Captain Joe Sewall's initial experience in steel, in command of the new *Edward Sewall*, was brief and troubled. While awaiting the loading of coal at Baltimore in November 1899 his ejection of a customs official from his cabin initially resulted in a five-hundred-dollar fine for "obstructing an officer in performance of duty," although his appeal to friends in high places in Washington reduced it to twenty-five dollars. In a magnanimous mood, he sent Sam instructions for the distribution of two cases of cigars he had brought from Manila on his last voyage. Sam was to take a thousand himself. Mr. Frye was to get three hundred "good ones." Ned was to get three hundred. His father, in Boston, was to get five hundred. "Give Cousin Arthur & Will some." But the Sewalls were not willing to forget and forgive so readily. Joe's story then changed, and as was customary, ended with a threat to quit:

> I notice you use the term "Put the officer out of the cabin," which is misleading. I asked him quietly to withdraw after answering his question and after he would not, ordered him out. You do not regret publicity of such affairs more than myself. . . . I do not remember of being discourteous to even the humblest individual on any ship I ever commanded. . . . I feel, at present, that it would be a happy relief if I could abandon a sea life.

The *Edward Sewall* finally sailed from Baltimore for San Francisco with coal on January 18, 1900. Sixty-eight days out Joe put into Montevideo with a heated cargo. He wished to sell the coal there, but orders from Bath were to shovel it out, turn it over, and re-stow it. He arrived at San Francisco from what he termed "Manana Land" 208 days after leaving Baltimore. He then carried grain to Liverpool, from where he wrote in March: "You have built a good ship in the *Edward Sewall*." He thought the riveting good, aside from some weeps. She did "spring some" amidships, breaking rail connectors, but nothing to worry about. "There is a new French barque here, ex S. F. and she is fragile compared with us, and will need considerable in repair, broken rivets, started beam ends, etc." He later wrote:

> Now as regards load line. I think we were deep enough. . . . I have lost a man washed off the boom, and had a few others more or less injured around decks by water and we have had no serious weather. These ships are wet. Call this ship a fine sea boat. If you covered the main deck in 'midships for a space of 70 or 80 feet, give them a sheer, it would be a great improvement."

A rail-to-rail midships house, which William Fairburn had also advocated, was added to the *Frye*. This reduced the weight of water on deck, elevated the pinrails, and reduced the "fetch" of seas on deck. After a prolonged passage of thirty-eight days in ballast for New York, arriving in May, 1901, Joe Sewall quit the sea in disgust, despite learning that the shortage of cargo discharged at Liverpool—cases of canned fruit were missing—had been due to thieves in San Francisco who had cut a hole in the wharf and were robbing from underneath, an old trick of harbor pirates.

Perhaps—in retrospect—due to domestic strains, Joe quickly un-retired and took a master's share and command of the new *William P. Frye* four months later. Arriving at New York in January 1903, after two case-oil voyages to Shanghai, Joe stayed ashore for a passage for a rest, rejoining the *Frye* at San Francisco. Arriving at Delaware Breakwater with sugar, he wrote: "I hope you will allow me to fix the rudder as I suggested last year. The ship steers badly and very hard. She nearly broached to with us off the cape in a gale. . . . . Lost one man overboard off the cape."

The four-masted bark William P. Frye *under construction. The presence of women and children on board, the party gathered aft, and the crowd which can just be glimpsed on the wharf at left, indicate that this is her scheduled launching day, October 2, 1901. Unfortunately she refused to budge until the following day, although the christening ceremonies were carried out nonetheless. The* Frye *was fitted with a 68-foot "bridge deck" house—we are looking at it here—which extended from rail to rail, taking the place of the forward and midships houses on the earlier steel ships. In addition to adding strength and buoyancy, it served to break the run of heavy seas on deck.* Maine Maritime Museum

Joe then made case oil voyages to Shanghai and also to Manila, arriving back at Philadelphia in March 1907, where he gave up the sea for good. There had been fair warning—back in 1903 he asked that his insurance policies on his interests in Sewall ships not be renewed, as his primage did not cover the premiums, and in 1905 he had asked to be bought out of his interests in the ships. He was not dissatisfied with Will and Sam, he explained, but with all that had to be contended with. "Your ships are not safe at sea, with the cattle manning them. . . . Sell the whole fleet and give it up."

It will be recalled that Joe had married Sadie Lincoln after she and her sister Mary had sailed on their brother Bill's ship, *El Capitan*, with Joe as mate. In 1938 old Doc Briry wrote regarding this union:

A sailor's knot—often called a square knot—is supposed to be everlasting. The matrimonial knot which bound Captain Joe to Miss Sadie Sewall commenced to slip a little, following Captain Joe's retirement for good from the *William P. Frye*.

Captain Joe commenced spending his summers at East Bowdoinham on the Captain Jack farm. As the years—fourteen in all—passed by, Captain Joe went to Bowdoinham earlier and earlier, and remained later and later. Captain Jack, now dead, at one time was a Sewall ship commander.³ He and his wife had died, leaving an only daughter, Miss Marie Jack, to run the farm and accept a boarder if she wished.

Captain Joe Sewall spent his winters at Bath. One evening when calling on my sister and myself, Captain Joe relieved his heart—and threw a lot of stuff off his chest—that had to do with the whole Lincoln family—not sparing two or three Lincoln generations back. Captain Joe stated that Captain Bill Lincoln put one over on him when he persuaded him to become his mate on the *El Capitan*, and then took two of his sisters to sea at the same time. And he—Joe Sewall—fell in love, or thought he fell in love—with Sadie, the youngest sister. But had now found the mistake. . . .

Mary Lincoln was the first Lincoln sister to die. She never married. I think she would have married Captain Joe, had he offered himself to her, and not to her sister Sadie. Sarah Lincoln died a few years ago—died brokenhearted, I am inclined to think. I have heard her say she "hated Miss Jack." Then Captain Joe brought Miss Jack to Bath to take care of himself and the surviving sister, Celia Lincoln.

Celia Lincoln was found dead in her bed one morning with an enormous bruise and gash on her temple.

Captain Joe surprised Sister and myself during one of his many calls by stating with tears in his eyes that he was standing on the edge of his grave. . . . It took about eighteen months for Captain Joe's three cancers [in his intestines] to do their work. . . . Can not one well call Captain Joe's treatment of his wife a continuation of the ——— and cruelty that was in his blood in his youth?

You can form your own conclusions

We left *Shenandoah* arrived at Baltimore in July 1898, with Wilder Murphy predicting that Jim Murphy would now retire. Murphy backed and filled, trying to make up his mind about what to do. He decided against the Sewalls' idea that he take command of the new steel ship *Erskine M. Phelps* while selling half his interest in *Shenandoah* to Captain Robert Graham.

Graham, who had done well in the *W. F. Babcock*, had been promised the next steel ship if he took *Shenandoah* for a while. Graham, meanwhile, had heard stories about *Shenandoah*'s structural problems, and was getting cold feet as well, to which the Sewalls responded: "We do not like such complaints as this and hope you will be careful in the future so we shall have no more of them." But this was now beside the point, as Jim Murphy had another plan:

I don't feel like accepting the new ship, not knowing fully about her and at my age don't care to have a big debt. I wish to remain at home for a time, and I trust when the *Shenandoah* gets to San Francisco, you will allow my brother to command her. Wish you would allow my son to take the ship out to San Francisco. He is young and that is all there is against him. He has plenty of ability and good judgment and, of course, knows the ship fully. He is diffident and don't forward himself, but he is quick to see things and a perfect sailor.

Arthur Sewall & Co. responded that while Jim's request would have their careful consideration, it would be better for Wilder to remain as mate for a year or two longer. After all, Wilder was but nineteen. One wonders if Jim Murphy's ever-competitive spirit had been goaded by the appointment some months previously of twenty-five-year-old Captain Chadwick Thompson to the command of *Roanoke*, a larger ship even than *Shenandoah*.

Captain William Starkey—"Stutterin' Starkey"—of Woolwich was asked to take *Shenandoah* to San Francisco. Starkey was a well-respected shipmaster who had commanded many ships, including both the *Thomas M. Reed* and *Iroquois* for the Sewalls. Sixty-five years old, this passage would end a career as shipmaster of forty-two years without losing a ship. His stuttering, it was said, never interfered with the giving of critical orders.

On July 13 the Sewalls sent Murphy a letter informing him that Starkey had been engaged, that they wanted Wilder to remain as mate, and that Jim's brother Ebed could take command of *Shenandoah* at San Francisco. Before the letter could reach him Jim had telegraphed Bath: "Shall remain in ship. Captain Starkey remain home." The Sewalls responded that Starkey was already on his way, and that, "If you could have decided a little earlier, it would have saved considerable trouble and expense." They left Murphy to sort it out with Starkey, and by the time the Starkeys arrived Jim had decided to retire after all. And so *Shenandoah* sailed from Baltimore with a load of coal and with Captain and Mrs. Starkey in the cabin.

Sailing under a new regime aboard the ship in whose cabin he had in good part grown up was a new experience for Wilder. At sea on August 1 he wrote his mother:

It is two o'clock in the morning now, and I am writing by the aid of a full moon. It is a flat calm and one of those nights when a graveyard watch (from 12 to 4) drags fearfully so I thought I would write a bit to you.

We are eleven days out from Baltimore. . . . It seems much longer and I miss Father dreadfully. However, I am getting rather used to things now and get accustomed to washing in the same water for two or three days in succession, and other little things. It seemed really odd at first, not to feel at liberty to run down in the cabin for anything I wanted or to be down in the "old man's" room during a dog watch if it seemed convenient. Captain & Mrs. S—— are very pleasant and we get along in good shape. It is not at all difficult talking with him and only at times does he seem to have trouble with the flow of his silvery speech. Mrs.

Starkey tried to get that game of Halma together, but there are so many pieces missing that I guess it will be impossible to do much with it.

Mrs. Starkey had joined the ship so quickly that she had neglected to bring sufficient reading matter or sewing work, so Wilder lent her some of his books.

We have but two cats now, old Tom, who is just as indifferent as ever, and a little Liverpool kitten. Tell Father that the gray kitten got himself into serious complications with the main brace when we were slacking it away and went over the side, where I suppose he still is unless rescued by some passing ship.[4] Well I must close for tonight and I will try and write before the next full moon. . . .

Meanwhile, Jim Murphy's brief period of relaxation at home was rudely ended by a telegram received from Valparaiso informing Arthur Sewall & Co. of the death of Captain Baker and his mate aboard *Kenilworth*. Murphy happened to be in the office at 411 Front Street when the stunning telegram arrived, and soon was making a hurried departure south as a special agent to attend to the affairs of the ship.

Arrived at San Francisco, Captain Starkey wrote the Sewalls: "*Shenandoah* is a daisy. I never was on board a better ship." On December 3, after one day of discharging her coal, fire—caused by spontaneous combustion—was detected deep in the cargo in the area of the port bilge, forward. It appeared to finally be extinguished on the 5th, only to break out again. After it seemed to have been extinguished again, Captain Starkey wrote: "This is a hard pill that we can only regret and swallow. . . . Am going to bed for the first time since the fire was discovered. This fire is a bad one, the worst accident I ever had."

On the 14th fire again broke out, this time sixty feet aft from where it had been before. The damage was considerable, the fire at the forward location, under the waterline, having burned through ceiling, frames, and planking to the copper sheathing. Once again the Sewalls called on Captain Jim to deal with a disaster, and he arrived in San Francisco on Christmas Day to find the situation far worse than he had expected. He soon came up with a clever plan for repair, implementing heavy timber reinforcements and diagonal iron strapping to minimize the number of long pieces that had to be replaced, satisfying the surveyors and keeping the repair bill to about $25,000.

On December 29 Jim learned of the sudden death by pneumonia of his younger brother Ebed at Portland, Oregon. Ebed had lately been master of the ship *Henry Villard*, and had been indicted, along with his mate, Mr. James Harvey, on a charge of cruelty. Mr. Harvey's case had been dismissed, and Ebed's had been continued, allowing him to make a voyage, and the plan had been for Ebed and Mate Harvey to take *Shenandoah* on a round voyage to Australia, while Wilder joined his father on the new steel *Arthur Sewall*.

With Ebed removed from the scene, Jim renewed his efforts to have Wilder appointed master of *Shenandoah*. Captain Starkey thought that Wilder was qualified. So did Oscar and his brother Frank, then at Williams, Dimond & Co., while Sam was

Captain (James) Wilder Murphy, 1879–1901
MAINE MARITIME MUSEUM

strongly opposed and Will evidently agreed with him. But Arthur consented to his old friend's wish, although Wilder's pay was to be $125 a month, as was customary for first-time captains—Jim, bold as brass, had requested that Wilder be allowed to sail the ship "on the same terms and instructions as I have from you."

The news about "Young Captain Murphy" was picked up by the press, and in the papers his age was given as nineteen, not twenty. Before Wilder (with Frank) went to the San Francisco Custom House to put his name on the ship's register, Jim instructed him, if he was asked his age, to say that he was "going on twenty-two." When Wilder did as instructed, he was told by an official that if he had been under twenty-one he would not have been a legal citizen of the United States, and thus could not have taken command of the ship. When then asked what year he was born in, Wilder replied, falsely, "1877," and his name was put on the register.

Jim, suffering from a rare case of nerves, wrote Arthur: "I never thought his age would be questioned. . . . His name is on the register as master of the ship, and perhaps everything would go right ninety out of a hundred, but they could easily ascertain his age. I think it best all around that he should not go a master of this ship." Arthur, in a confidential letter to the commissioner of navigation, explained the circumstances, and Commissioner Littlefield replied that there was no age requirement on citizenship.

Wilder would sail as captain, and Mr. Harvey would go as mate.

Shenandoah was chartered to load lumber in Puget Sound for Port Pirie in southern Australia, to return to San Francisco with a cargo of coal from Sydney. On the passage north a sailor was lost overboard during a gale. The stevedore at Port Blakely complained that *Shenandoah* was not well suited to the cargo, leaving much wasted space due to knees and beams and the long poop.5 She sailed with 2,427,358 feet, with a deck load up to the rail tops. Although timber cargoes invariably made a ship tender, Wilder did not sail her that way. A report received at Bath:

> Captain Johnson [of the bark *Roderick Dhu*] reports the wind as N. N. E. about 45 miles per hour. Captain J. was under short sail, but the young man was going along with three skysails heading about S. S. W. and Capt. J. thinks she was going at the rate of 14 knots. In fact, he thinks she was going as fast as ever she did go. Wind on the quarter with everything drawing and the ship was standing up to her work in good shape. In fact Captain Johnson remarked to his chief officer that she could not have much of a deck load.

Shenandoah arrived at Port Pirie on June 26. With her deep draft, some of her cargo had to be lightered off before she could go alongside a wharf. On August 15 Wilder wrote Williams, Dimond & Co.:

> I expected to be away by this time at my last writing, but we have not been able to get very good dispatch. . . . Nobody is in a hurry here. I am taking 115 tons of flour to Sydney at 2/6 per ton. This will save my buying ballast here. . . . Everything on board is running smoothly and we have had no trouble to speak of with the crew. We shall want seven or eight men but I think there will be no trouble getting them as the ship seems to have a good name and attracts a great deal of attention. . . . The *Arthur Sewall* will be about due when this reaches S. F. and I hope will make a fine passage. . . .

Shenandoah did not depart Sydney for San Francisco until November 15. Meanwhile, aboard the *Arthur Sewall*, bound from Philadelphia to San Francisco, Maria Murphy wrote in her sea letter on June 25: "We have enjoyed these beautiful moonlit evenings on deck, thinking of our absent ones, and wondering what they are doing and have accomplished." In October, having arrived at San Francisco, Maria wrote to her sister May, Doc Briry's mother:

> We were amazed to see T. G. Northey walk in Friday afternoon. He had come up on the Australian steamer. Said he left Wilder well. There had been a strike on in Sydney for four months, and he [Wilder] had been waiting three weeks, but hoped to get the first load [of coal] the next day. Wilder wrote a brief letter. I expect the poor boy is lonely and discouraged to be detained so long in both ports, and misses seeing us here. He must be on the way now but there isn't the

shadow of a chance that we will meet. He has had too much care put on his young shoulders but possibly it will make a man of him.

Northey, the Murphy's longtime and loyal black steward aboard *Shenandoah*, was being diplomatic regarding the circumstances of his departure. Wilder, according to Oscar in a letter to Bath written in January 1900, had discharged Northey, and "wrote a strong letter to his father stating that he hoped he would not employ this man again; notwithstanding Captain Murphy Sr. immediately employed him. You can form your own conclusions."

It seems most likely that wise old Northey had tried to save young Wilder from making a fool and a failure of himself.

Stewed rivets à la Sewalls' shipyard

Two Sewall vessels disappeared at sea without a trace. The first was the schooner *Carrie S. Bailey*, lost in December 1889 while on a passage carrying hard pine from Darien, Georgia, to Bath. The other was the big four-masted bark *Arthur Sewall*, which disappeared on a Cape Horn passage departing Philadelphia with coal for Seattle in April 1906. Very likely the *Bailey* capsized, and that has often been suggested as a likely explanation for the loss of the *Arthur Sewall* as well. But there are other possibilities.

The third steel four-masted bark built at the Sewall yard, the *Arthur Sewall* was launched in February 1899. She was twenty feet longer than her predecessor, the *Erskine M. Phelps*, thanks to added frames amidships. Her rig was an ungainly looking departure, crossing no skysails, and with novel fixed upper topsail yards crossed beneath double topgallants. Although the rig was said to perform satisfactorily, and to be economical, it was not to be repeated

A letter from the Sewalls to Williams, Dimond & Co. in October 1898 predicted that the ship, then under construction, would cost no more than forty-five dollars per ton. At current rates she could stock $67,000 for a round voyage from New York to San Francisco and back again via Honolulu, with a sugar cargo.

In May 1899 the *Arthur Sewall* departed Philadelphia for San Francisco on her maiden voyage, carrying naval steam coal. Joining Captain Jim in the cabin were wife Maria and daughter Jane. From Maria's fifth installment of her Sunday sea letter to her sister May, written on June 25, at latitude 2.14 degrees north, longitude. 29 degrees west:

4 P.M. We have just come in from the top of the house where we have been entertained by our crew in honor of a visit from Neptune and wife. We are not across the "line," but expected to be if we had favorable winds, but as the men had made their preparations, it was thought best to go on with them. Well, it was the funniest sight I ever witnessed on board ship. Of course Neptune came up over the bow with a shout . . . joined by his bride, and the procession started aft—first came the

Aboard the Arthur Sewall *at Philadelphia, looking from the main deck aft toward the poop. The mizzenmast is in the foreground. Running rigging is seized to the shrouds to get it out of the way. The open door behind the man—very likely he is the steward, often the only member of the crew to remain aboard at the completion of a voyage—led into the forward cabin, the portion of the cabin where the officers, the steward, and any passengers lived, and where the dining saloon and pantry were located. The captain's quarters were farther aft, in the after cabin. The deckhouse on the poop contained the chartroom and served as the captain's office, with rolltop desk and settees where the captain could nap during bad weather and where his wife could pass the time knitting.* Maine Maritime Museum

police, with big badges, then Neptune and wife, followed by the barber with a razor about a yard long, then the doctor, scribe, etc. For music they had a guitar, mandolin, banjo, concertina, triangle, and harmonica. . . . The bride was too funny for anything—I laughed til I cried.

An artistically rendered three-page "Programme," displaying elegant calligraphy, listed the day's gala events. Activities scheduled in the second "spasm" of events included "Shaving of eight victims inter-mingled with select music furnished by Professor Sousa. Opening Chorus—Break the News to Mother, by entire ship's company." Featured dishes in the "Grand Menu" included "fried oakum with sea foam,"

The four-masted bark Arthur Sewall *at Philadelphia. The view is forward from the poop. At right is the flying bridge, leading first to the midships house, and then to the forward house, and on to the topgallant forecastle deck, a very much appreciated feature when the main deck was awash. The standard compass atop the midships house was used for taking bearings and as a check on the steering compass.*
MAINE MARITIME MUSEUM

"fricasse jigger with gaff," and "stewed rivets à la Sewalls' shipyard."

The arrival of the *Arthur Sewall* at San Francisco in October after a leisurely passage of 127 days proved to be a memorable occasion—Oscar Sewall described it in a letter to his Uncle Arthur almost in amazement:

> It was a pleasure to see the crew leave the ship, and the good feelings existing between master and men. It was really quite a touching sight. After the ship dropped her anchor the crew all mustered amidships and sang a good bye song, then gave three cheers for Captain Murphy, and Mrs. Murphy and daughter and the *Arthur Sewall,* then with hats off all marched on the poop where we were all gathered and shook hands with the Captain and ladies and we all went ashore in launches together. This made a very good impression on the waterfront [and] gave the ship a good name.

Aside from the fact that her hull was stripped of paint—the mill scale and dirt of the shipyard made it impossible keep the first coat of paint attached on a Cape Horn passage—Oscar praised the "perfect condition of the ship in every respect." However, Captain Murphy "seemed to be kind of blue. Said she would never make the speed the *Shenandoah* would, and could not trust same as that ship, had to pump all the way from the Horn, etc. Wished he had never put any money into her and had gone into tramp steamers. . . ." Oscar, as would Sam and Arthur, dismissed the leak as but the usual few loose rivets in a new ship.

However Jim Murphy's letter to the Sewalls, i.e., to Arthur, written shortly before arriving at San Francisco, left no doubt as to the strength of his feelings. The ship began to leak on the fifth day out, and for most of the passage had required three to six hours of pumping a day, and these pumps "heaved" twice as much water as did the *Shenandoah's.* "I thought I had a strong, able ship and was through pumping, but now have not much faith in this ship. This ship 'works' in a big sea. . . . Coming around the Cape she broke all the copper over her pin-rail joints. . . . These steel ships better have an extra set [of pumps]."

Murphy judged the arrangements of all the deckhouses to be wrong, and the steering gear to be too light. But he thought the ship "a splendid sea boat, good in a head sea, and much drier than I expected. Sails well, works easily." The novel rig, which Murphy had designed, "is fine."

On October 2 Arthur responded: "We are particularly disappointed to note you do not appear to be quite satisfied with her. . . . [It is] not unusual to have some loose rivets in a new ship, especially when built in the winter, and the frost acting on the rivets."

On October 18, with the ship dry-docked, Murphy reported that thirty-two loose or headless rivets had been replaced in the starboard bow, and that there were some loose rivets in the port bow. Another fifty loose rivets would be found below the water-line between the main and mizzen masts. A few days later he wrote: "The ship must strain and work a great deal. She gives me great care and uneasiness." Arthur responded: "We do not think it possible for the ship to work any. . . . If she really did strain there would be more than twenty-five or fifty rivets on the side that show signs of looseness." Although all ships "work," or flex, to some degree, excessive working could have the most serious implications, particularly in a ship of conventional transverse framing, which was literally held together by her riveted skin.

On her next passage, from San Francisco to London with wheat, the ship survived what Jim Murphy described as the heaviest gale and the biggest sea in his experience. One giant wave flooded the decks, washing away both boats and the standard compass, yet the ship remained "perfectly tight," and Murphy wrote: "I trust her rivets now are all right." But a number of rivets in gusset plates would later be found broken.

At Honolulu Murphy had kicked when the insurance surveyor ruled that due to the ship's greater length, her loaded freeboard could not be less than six feet, four inches—had their decklines had more sheer, the Sewall barks would have been allowed to load deeper. And in fact, after the severe conditions experienced on the passage to London, Murphy decided that it was well that she had not been loaded deeper.

Jim Murphy at London was not a happy man. The London charter, which he had brokered, had been criticized by the Sewalls; Wilder's brief career as master of *Shenandoah*—as we shall presently learn—had ended in costly disgrace. And problems with the *Edward Sewall*, in which he had invested, caused him to grouse that he might end up a pauper in Sailor's Snug Harbor. And then, to make matters worse, the *Arthur*, in ballast, had had to beat against headwinds all the way across the North Atlantic, taking a tedious forty-three days to make the passage.[6] And he obviously never liked the ship. Arrived at New York in July 1900, Murphy announced that he wished to be relieved of the command of the *Arthur*.

An interview with Maria back in 1892, aboard *Shenandoah*, no doubt revealed her husband's unease with iron or steel ships: "Why," she said, "if there's a hole in an iron ship . . . she's gone." [7]

He has always been a dutiful son

We were surprised enough to see Wilder yesterday, and so rejoiced to see him again. He has had a hard time. It is so hard for such a boy to have such a load to carry, but I thank God he is honest and has done nothing wrong. Somebody forged his name and drew from the bank in Sydney quite an amount of money. The poor boy was not successful when he went to the bank and found it out. He put a detective at work but thinks he was no good. He kept quiet about it, thinking it would come out better. He has had this on his mind all these weeks. Jem feels terribly about it, but he knows Wilder has done the best he could. The Sewalls hold Jem responsible for this money. Don't say anything about this until I write again. I only hope and pray that people will not think he has been dishonest. Those who know him will not.

So wrote Maria Murphy aboard the *Arthur Sewall*, just arrived in London in

April 1900, to her sister, May Briry, home at Bath.

Back in January, *Shenandoah* had finally arrived at San Francisco from Sydney. Awaiting Captain Wilder was a letter from Arthur Sewall & Co. regarding his accounts—missing from the Sydney accounts was any mention of the £1,700 freight from Port Pirie. Arthur Sewall & Co.—no doubt Sam—was not happy. Frank Sewall saw Wilder shortly after his arrival, and thought that he looked and seemed well, but several days later, without warning, Wilder left town on the "overland" train, headed to Bath. Oscar wrote:

> Frank visited the ship at Oakland this morning, and everything appears all right, and [mate] Harvey seems perfectly capable of taking charge during the captain's absence. Evidently he [Wilder] decided to leave in a great hurry, for all his clothes and things are strewn about the cabin and he took nothing excepting a small hand satchel. . . .
>
> The ship continues to leak and makes 30 inches of water in twenty-four hours. . . . She is evidently very open on her topsides, and must be thoroughly caulked. . . . Some of the scarfs amidships have opened up considerably. They will probably regulate themselves when she has finished discharging. Mr. Harvey states that on passage they had to keep loosening and tightening the rigging on account of the strain. . . .
>
> It was a mistake in the first place putting so young a man in so large a ship, giving him charge of such a valuable property, but this of course you fully understood at the time. . . . You are aware of course that it will ruin his prospects to take him out of the ship at this time. . . . However, it is not right to jeopardize your property for this reason. . . .

Sam wrote Oscar on the 29th that Wilder's accounts were short £894. Wilder's explanation was that he had bet on a yacht race at Sydney and had lost £75, for which he had given a check. He believed that his signature on that check was used to forge additional checks. He had hired a detective but had not notified the bank. He had no checks, no receipts, had kept no record of the account, and had destroyed both the checkbook and stubs. Sam found the story to be unbelievable and declared that Wilder had no future with the company.[8]

On April 4, Jim Murphy, after receiving the distressing news, wrote from London:

> You will please cancel my son's draft of $3,235.78 on myself and charge same to my account. This I do with a good heart, knowing my son is honorable, upright and not one lie have I ever known him to tell me. The boy's carelessness let him to be an easy prey to some forging scoundrel. No doubt the one he gave foolishly that check for £69.10 was the one. Next fault is Wilder kept everything to himself and not consulting good advice. . . . I do wish you would let him continue in command of the *Shenandoah*. . . . You can all know my feelings knowing that my son has been a victim. It is a great blow.

Shenandoah departed San Francisco for Sydney on March 16, 1900, with redwood lumber and general cargo, under the command of former mate Harvey. (A letter to Harvey from the Sewalls, written in January 1899, stated that they planned to name him to *Shenandoah's* command after he had made a few voyages as mate.) The best that can be said for Captain George Harvey's tenure is that by comparison he made Wilder's look good. An anonymous letter from Sydney stating that Harvey had been imprisoned for drunkeness confirmed suspicions raised by the "well worded" typed letters ostensibly from Harvey stating that all was well, but which appeared to have been written by someone else.

Discreet inquiries brought word to the Sewalls that Harvey had indeed been seen drunk, and also that his paperwork on departure had been muddled. Confirmation was received in spades in October: "We note your inquiry as to Captain Harvey of American ship *Shenandoah*, and we can only say that he was drunk every day while in port, and we consider him a disgrace to his flag."

Captain Jim Murphy, breaking his retirement yet again, headed west (by way of Marfa, Texas, and brother Charles's store) to take command of his old *Shenandoah* once more. On October 20 *Shenandoah* arrived off the bar, but Captain Harvey was not on board, having jumped overboard four days after leaving Sydney, never receiving the letter awaiting him at San Francisco severing his relationship with Arthur Sewall & Co.

Word was sent ashore from the ship for men to help pump—she had thirty-four inches of water in her, and a tube was gone in the boiler. Upon seeing the run-out condition of his old love, Murphy wrote: "I only wish I could see Mr. Harvey alone for an hour—a worse man would be hard to find."

Captain Harvey's mother Olive wrote from Brooklyn, Hart's County, Nova Scotia:

We sorrowed over the death of Mr. Arthur Sewall [Arthur had died on September 5] not knowing that our own was so near. He has always been a dutiful son, and made friends wherever he went and his death is a great blow to me. Any information or particulars regarding him will be thankfully received by his widowed mother. If Captain James Murphy is in San Francisco . . . he would gladly forward any of his things as he [Harvey] was mate in the *Geo. Stetson*[9] for a long time of which a brother of Mr. Murphy was captain, and my son nursed him through his last illness and took his remains over to California for burial. . . . I never received a line from him all the time he was in Australia although I was daily expecting a check but it never came. . . .

She later wrote Andronicus Chesebrough inquiring after £30 15s. that the mate had written her had been found among Harvey's effects, and had been turned over to Mr. Chesebrough. She repeated that she was a poor widow, and that her son had been her only support. Dron Chesebrough replied with regret that as Captain Harvey's Sydney accounts showed a considerable shortage beyond his wages, the money was to be credited to the owners.

In August, 1899 Arthur Sewall & Co. received a letter from Manley Sargeant, of Sheepscot, a village in the town of Newcastle:

> I received your letter with dollar; many thanks. I did not ask anything for the [saw]horses. I meant them as a free gift, for I have worked in your yard a good deal in the past. They was no good to me as I see no work in the yards in Bath for me at joiner work. Hoping it may not be out of place to mention; I would again vote for Mr. Sewall for the highest office. I have a kindly remembrance of Mr. Edward Sewall when working on one of his barques. I worked on these vessels and others many of whose names I have forgotten.

Sargeant listed the *Freeman Clark, Solitaire, Iroquois, Willie Rosenfeld, W. F. Babcock, Iroquois, Willie Rosenfeld, Thomas M. Reed, Henry Villard, Alice Archer,* and a barque [bark] and four schooners whose names he had forgotten.

Manley was a master joiner and a local character. After feuding with his brother Henry and his sister-in-law, he moved out of the family house and built himself a one-room cabin. One day, so the story went, he showed up with a wife and her daughter, who moved in with him. So tight had he built the cabin that after an argument with his wife he slammed the door hard and blew out the windows. Manley was also a poet. Even today anyone looking across the Kennebec toward Woolwich from the riverfront at Bath will see what Manley saw:

> The Woolwich Hills
>
> The crest of a hill has a
> charm to me
> Outlined on the sky's arched
> blue.
>
> It looks at rest in repose,
> and free,
> While its evergreen trees
> of somber hue
> Tossing their boughs seem
> to beckon me.
>
> This is a bright,
> sunshiny day
> In April, but 'tis
> more like May;

Manley Sargeant, his wife and stepdaughter, at his Sheepscot, Maine, home.
MAINE MARITIME MUSEUM

The whistle just blew,
then I stop'd my plane
For the noontide hour's
a very short time
To banquet, to dine and
muse in rhyme.

By the charm of the whistle
in the mill
The work in the yard is
stopped and still,
And while in the hush
of a midday lull
A nooning I took
And a wishful look
Away to the crest of the
Woolwich hill.[10]

When I was a boy I wanted to be like Robin Hood

Arthur Sewall died on Wednesday, September 5, 1900, at his newly completed and more than ample "cottage" called The Dunes, at Small Point. He had been "stricken with apoplexy"—a stroke—the previous Sunday, and had never regained consciousness. Arthur had not been in good heath for about two years, said to be suffering from Bright's Disease, a condition then frequently diagnosed, characterized by high blood pressure and albumin in the urine. His recent trip to Hawaii had been made in the hope that it would improve his health. Given his vast and varied accomplishments, it comes as a shock to realize that "the Senior" was but sixty-four years old.

Even Victorian America's fascination with death does not explain the Bath *Daily Times*'s almost hysterical reaction to the passing of a man who even then was conceded to have been well known by but few in town. Indeed, one doubts that the second coming would have been covered more diligently, including details of Arthur's affliction, the bedside vigil, and even the undertaker's schedule for picking up the remains. It was speculated that the crisis might have been brought on by Arthur's overeating just before going to bed. One suspects that editor, reporters, and readers all recognized that Arthur Sewall's death, aside from the passing of a most remarkable local figure, also symbolized the passing of Bath's great age of shipbuilding.

> Scarcely had the streets of the city begun to assume their early morning bustle today when all were saddened by the untimely news of the death of the Hon. Arthur Sewall. . . . It was not a shock to the community, for for two days we from the sunlit paths of life and happiness have seen him wandering in the gloom of the Valley of the Shadow of Death. There was no hope that he could return and the shock which was suffered by the community on Monday when the news of Mr. Sewall's danger first reached here gave place to calm deep sorrow when the news arrived that the great shipbuilder had breathed his last.
>
> In Arthur Sewall Bath loses her ablest and best known citizen, her greatest shipbuilder, her leading financier, and a man whose sterling worth was generally recognized even by those who were not his friends. Everybody esteemed and honored Arthur Sewall. . . .

The paper interviewed a number of leading citizens for reactions. According to the Reverend F. W. O'Brien: "To many he appeared distant, austere, and aristocratic, but contact with him swept all that away. Under a granite exterior there lay a tender and sympathetic nature, a heart moved as easily as a little child's, ready to respond to the call of suffering and need."

For three days after Arthur's death, all work at the yard, where the Standard Oil Company's four-masted bark *Astral* was taking shape, ceased, by the workers' decision. On Saturday morning a procession of 150 shipbuilders, bearing a flower ship eight feet long by five feet high, marched from the Boilermaker's Hall to the mansion on Sewall

Arthur Sewall in the Bath mansion, by Emma Sewall. MAINE MARITIME MUSEUM

Hill. As the line filed past the coffin, each man placed a single flower on it. Will and Sam, in a reciprocal demonstration of respect, paid the men for the three days' lost wages.

Newspapers far and wide covered the story. The *Bangor Daily News* reprinted Arthur's 1894 interview in which he addressed the subject of "free ships," a part of which read:

Why, it seems to me that it ought to be worth millions to us to have our flag carried around the world. From the patriotic standpoint, aside from that of commercial expediency, I cannot see how the thought of the American flag flying over anything that is not American can fail to be offensive.

The *Boston Post* noted: "As a humorist he belonged to a type found only in Maine. He originated the prevailing sarcasm in the State concerning inferior ships. He was shown a new type of vessel and remarked: 'The week's wash must be pretty big when they need that.' . . . Mr. Sewall resembled Abraham Lincoln in being able to tell a story that bore upon any subject at hand. Some of his most effective anecdotes were of his boyhood days":

When I was a boy I wanted to be like Robin Hood. I thought it must be very nice to be at the head of a robber band, doing what you please and levying tribute on the people. So I resolved that when I became a man I'd be a Robin Hood. Now that I'm a man I find so many others in the business that there's no room for me. That's what comes of being under a protective tariff.

The people of this nation are called the salt of the earth. Why don't they mingle with the salt of the sea? The other day I heard a man poking fun at the people of Kentucky because they did not know that water is good for them. Why, right here, we don't seem to know that water is good for ships.

These "witticisms" were said to be even funnier when he told them, "because he had a slow, calm way of talking that was the very wit of silence."

A column by "The Smoker" in the September 15 Bath *Independent* broached the subject then on many minds:

Since the death of Arthur Sewall citizens naturally have been wondering what effect that great loss would have on business of the firm on which, to a considerable extent, the prosperity of Bath depends and the Smoker finds it to be the general opinion of Bath businessmen that the surviving members of the firm, Wm. D. and S. S. Sewall, inherit in a great degree the business ability of their fathers, respectively, Arthur and Edward Sewall. . . . The only fear expressed is that the young men will work too hard in the conduct of their extensive business affairs. The only expressions of business men of Bath as to the two young men are complimentary and confident.

As word sooner or later reached the captains of the fleet, in ports about the globe, each sent a brief note of condolence. Always before, when writing Arthur Sewall & Co., they had really been writing for the eyes of Arthur Sewall. But no more.

Arthur's estate was divided among his three heirs, Emma, Harold, and Will. The sum of $15,000 was left to the city of Bath, the interest from which was to go to the worthy poor, and to support a bed at Maine General Hospital. His grave in the Sewall family cemetery within the grounds of the Oak Grove Cemetery, occupying old Sewall land, is marked by a large, spare granite monolith, appropriately devoid of ornamentation.

But I can see it distinctly now

Mrs. Sewall, his wife, has been by his bedside nearly all the hours since Sunday evening and has borne up with wonderful calmness and fortitude. Immediately after Mr. Sewall's death she broke down and did not leave her room until after dinner.

—Bath Daily Times, September 5, 1900

Emma Sewall is well deserving of special mention. She was born in 1836 to Bath ship-builder and merchant-turned-botanist Charles Crooker and Rachel Sewall Crooker. After graduating from the Bath schools Emma spent a year of finishing at the rigorous Ipswich Female Seminary at Ipswich, Massachusetts, which she reveled in. In 1859 she married Arthur Sewall. In 1860, 1861, and 1864 respectively, she bore sons Harold, William, and Dummer, Dummer dying at age two.

To historians of early New England photography, Arthur Sewall was Emma Sewall's husband and photo subject.[11] The arrival about 1884 of the revolutionary dry photographic plate opened up the world to amateur photography, and Emma was among the small but vital cadre of genteel New England women who, having perhaps gained an artistic eye when taught ladylike sketching, were creatively empowered by photography's magic.

Rural coastal New England in the late nineteenth century was an ideal stage for members of the so-called naturalistic school of photography, which had a special appeal to these women. Working in the tradition of the Barbizon school of French painting and British photographer Peter Henry Emerson, naturalistic photographers sought to capture scenes depicting the picturesque, supposedly simpler world of old-fashioned and fast-vanishing folk of sea and shore and farm. Behind this romantic and antiquarian vision was a distaste for, and distrust of, industrialism and commercialism.

While Chansonetta Stanley Emmons of Kingfield, Maine, is perhaps today the best known of these women, Bostonian Emma Lewis Coleman, who often photographed in Maine, and Emma Sewall, known for her iconic images of the farmers and fishermen of Small Point, were artistically and technically every bit her equal, although less of their body of work has survived. Far from being isolated by her Maine residence, Emma was a member of the Boston Camera Club and the winner of prizes in Paris exhibitions.

An introverted and idiosyncratic woman, Emma's reclusive nature mystified many in her larger family circle. She was not fond of living in the Bath mansion, described by one visitor as being decorated with walnut carvings, elegant bronzes, moose antlers, luxurious upholstery, "and the countless beauties and comforts accessible to a man of fortune." Before the Sewalls began to summer at Small Point about 1892, Emma spent many summers away from Arthur at inland lake and mountain resorts. Her letters to Arthur, while more formal than playful or intimate, are familiarly affectionate.

Behind the sand dunes, Morse's River, Small Point, by Emma Sewall
MAINE MARITIME MUSEUM

Emma's bizarre behavior in 1899 regarding the efforts of the Boston "high-grade" coach-maker Ferdinand French to build her a suitable carriage is at such a variance with our expectations as to at least raise the question whether the suspicion among family members that she had a problem with alcoholism might not have been valid. Mr. French wrote:

We have duly received your favor of the 2nd inst. which was preceded by the return of the phaeton. . . . You can well imagine that it is very disappointing to us to have the third carriage returned from you and especially when we feel with an experience of 37 years and supplying a great number of the most particular people in the country has not enabled us to understand your wants sufficiently to produce a satisfactory result. . . . We only regret that you had not written us before returning the carriage that it was all right save the [seat]back, and we would have gladly sent our best trimmer to Bath, at our expense. . . . Before sending it we had at least half a dozen people, most of them women, try the back to see if it was comfortable. . . . We ourselves have been quite the sufferers, as the first buggy . . . was sold by us at quite a little loss, and the second one at a very much greater loss and this phaeton will not be . . . an easy one to dispose of at even the cost of making, hence we should like your further consideration, if possible, to make it suit you, and we will cheerfully bear the expense of freights to and from and all cost of making the changes.

After Arthur's death, and also the death of his niece, Alice Cutler, who had lived with the Sewalls for many years and had been Emma's close companion, Emma retreated further into herself, becoming a true recluse, spending much time pursuing Sewall genealogy, and also the history of Small Point. She remained at The Dunes as late in the season as possible before returning to Bath for the winter. She died at her beloved Small Point in September 1919, before another long winter in town had descended. The Washington Street mansion would remain uninhabited until it was demolished in the 1930s.

Emma's efforts to record the magic of Small Point, both by camera and pen, were truly remarkable. A peninsula in the peninsular and, not coincidentally, insular town of Phippsburg, Small Point was located between Popham and West Point, an enclave of quaint fisherfolk known for "rocking" touring rusticators whose carriages intruded into their territory—shore fishing communities, as a rule, are notoriously suspicious of outsiders. Native Small Point fishermen farmers, while more accepting than the West Pointers, were yet of a tribe of Mainers distinct from that of summering plutocrats, even those from nearby Bath.

Not only the people, but the appearance of Small Point was then very different than now. With the original forest having been long since cut off, and the second growth not yet reclaiming the uplands, the Point offered broad vistas of the sail-rimmed sea, of breaking surf on outlying ledges, of islands, and of the saltwater marshes.

After Emma's death, appreciative members of the family collected some of her Small Point writings, *circa* 1905, into an elegant little slipcased volume entitled *The Rivers and Marshes of Small Point*. The following excerpt describes the region of marshes and sandbars, once the old path of the Kennebec, now traversed by two narrow saltwater rivers, lying between the Kennebec and Small Point:

I have often wondered why it is that the inhabitants of the seashore are so much more superstitious than those of the mountains. I suppose it must be from the mystery and uncertainty which always surrounds the sea. I do not think it possible that anything inland could have inspired the awe, which as a child I felt in crossing this marsh which has filled in the western arm of the Kennebec.

Imagine, if you can, this place. On one side huge sand drifts and dunes and the thundering of the unseen sea; on the other side—ruin and desolation—the road itself, a zigzag cart-path in which our wheels cut deep, and from which the sand fell as they revolved slowly, winding in and out among drift stuff and wreckage of every kind. It is sixty years since I saw it, but I can see it distinctly now. Stumps of giant trees with bleached roots like whitened bones; fragments of masts with rusty irons still attached; the broken stern of a schooner half buried in the sand, its gaping companionway with one door still swinging, showing traces of the light blue paint which had once adorned it; logs with the owners' marks cut on their sides, their ends rounded and battered by beating on the rocks and rolling in the surf; a piece of a broken windlass; slabs; an old deck bucket, made from a cask, with its frayed rope handle; a broken oar; bits of sheathing; parts of a vessel's frame; dangling strips of black kelp; bushes long ago washed from their native earth; seaweeds and shells—everything piled in confusion as the drifting high tides from the river or the heavy surf from the ocean had left it, save where it had been pushed or dragged aside to clear the road. Over all was a cloudy sky and a howling wind. Little wonder that the effect produced on my childish mind has never been effaced.[12]

A transparent fraud and humbug

Early in 1893, after the overthrow of Hawaii's Queen Liliuokalani's royal government by the so-called "Sons of Missionaries," representing the interests of the *haoles*— white foreigners—Harold Sewall, the former Samoan consul, arrived at Honolulu as a correspondent for the *New York Sun*. A treaty of annexation that had been hurriedly negotiated between the Republic of Hawaii—led by Sanford Dole, the son of a missionary from the Kennebec Valley—and the United States during the final months of President Harrison's administration was withdrawn by the incoming Cleveland administration. Harold, once again, was disgusted by what he saw as Cleveland's weak-kneed policies regarding strategic islands in the Pacific.

This was not the first attempt to annex Hawaii. The islands—whose populations suffered devastating mass die-offs following the introduction of European diseases— came under American influence in the early 1800s, thanks to resupplying and recreating New England whalers. And in the whalers' wake followed no-nonsense Calvinistic New England missionaries, including some Mainers of significance to Hawaiian history.[13] In 1843 Daniel Webster vowed that the United States would never allow the islands to become possessions of another power, and a subsequent treaty of annexation failed only because the islands were to be made a state. A reciprocity treaty signed in 1875, eliminating duties on Hawaiian sugar, led to a great expansion of the sugar industry that had been established by missionary sons. The demand for plantation labor eventually resulted in the influx of large numbers of workers from China, Japan, Portugal, and Puerto Rico.

Having returned to the United States in September 1893 Harold married Camilla Ashe, the daughter of a wealthy San Francisco family. Arthur and Emma gave the couple an around-the-world honeymoon trip. While taking passage aboard a Dutch colonial steamer from Manila to Singapore the newlyweds survived a shipwreck on the island of Bentang. In his account of the disaster, in which the Dutch captain, whose wife

Harold Marsh Sewall, United States minister to Hawaii, 1897–98 MAINE MARITIME MUSEUM

was also aboard, died, Harold praised Camilla's calm bravery, while leaving no doubt as to his own admirable behavior.

Back home at Bath, in 1894, Harold seized upon an invitation to be a Democratic convention delegate as the appropriate occasion to announce his switch to the Republican Party. Arthur, responding to a friend who had written on the news, accepted Harold's move with typical equanimity:

> I fear he has made a sad mistake, but believe that everyone should follow and act their own convictions in politics. Am very glad that he has your support. I am too old to change my religion, or politics. The older I grow the more thoroughly attached I become to the principles of both.

Harold's bolt paid off with McKinley's victory in 1896. With Senator Frye's assistance, Harold was appointed minister to the Republic of Hawaii, moving there with Camilla in June 1897. The April 24 *New York Sun* editorialized:

> Mr. Sewall represents, perhaps, as notably as any other American man alive, the policy and ideas of Blaine and Stevens[14] with regard to the extension of American influence in the Pacific for the sake of American commercial supremacy in that

ocean in the twentieth century. On that line of Jingoism he may almost be regarded as the original Jingo of the Pacific; for the whole discussion of that great question of national policy originated in his patriotic performances in the Samoan Islands ten years ago. . . .

The editorial quoted a portion of one of Harold's speeches, spoken as a true believer in Manifest Destiny:

I am here to speak for the honor and glory of the American flag, for the protection of American citizens and American interests wherever they are, and for the extension of this great republic wherever in this western hemisphere natural right and national destiny have decreed that it shall go.

During Harold's brief term a principal concern in Washington was the heavy immigration of Japanese plantation laborers, viewed as the possible precursor of a Japanese takeover either by overwhelming numbers or possibly by force. Paranoia over the supposed threat of teeming "Asiatics" was reflected in American and Canadian Chinese exclusion acts, and was a significant factor in the growing sentiment pushing for annexation; the strategic location of the islands, made apparent by the Spanish-American War, sealed the deal.

Harold also kept his ear to the ground for intelligence of use to Arthur Sewall & Co. regarding sugar charters—the sugar people were well organized and drove hard bargains. He also kept well posted on the doings of the fleet. In June 1898 Harold wrote Bath:

I hope you will try to arrange not to have Graham come back here in the *Babcock*. The ship has a bad name here, and if Graham comes in her she is certain to have a repetition of her old troubles. You will understand that these troubles make it very embarrassing for me.

In July 1898 President McKinley signed the Hawaiian annexation bill; on August 12, in an impressive ceremony at Iolani Palace, Harold officially accepted the transfer of sovereignty from President Sanford Dole of the Hawaiian Republic, and assisted in the raising of Old Glory. Few native Hawaiians attended what they considered a day of mourning, and the name of Harold Sewall is today still anathema to many in the native Hawaiian community. Harold surely had no second thoughts, however. In July 1898 Harold wrote Arthur: "The first thing the Government ought to do here . . . is to appoint a United States Shipping Commissioner here. . . . You ought to be able to control this important appointment." Writing Commissioner of Navigation Chamberlain, Harold opined in classic imperialist style:

We need here badly the extension of our laws. These people have now practically no duties to pay, no war taxes, no restriction to American bottoms for the sugar

During the prayer at the annexation ceremony, Iolani Palace, Honolulu, August 12, 1898. A balding Harold Marsh Sewall, the American minister to the soon-to-be defunct Hawaiian Republic, standing next to Admiral Miller, holds the papers of annexation under his arm. Harold personally hoisted the American flag at the climax of both the ceremony (which he had planned) and his diplomatic career. The onlookers contained very few native Hawaiians, most considering this to be an occasion of sorrow. MAINE MARITIME MUSEUM

trade due entirely to our markets, and no restrictions on the importation of Asiatic contract labor, a very fine thing for them, while we protect them against foreign or domestic violence.

It would take Congress more than a year to organize the territory, and Harold stayed on as a "special agent." As such, he continued to agitate against the practice of placing foreign ships (iron and steel ships, of course) under Hawaiian registration—

"a transparent fraud and humbug"—in the expectation that they would in time receive American registration, which did indeed happen.[15]

Harold also began to invest in the islands—in December 1899 Arthur, from San Francisco, wrote Will at Bath: "I also note that Harold is getting wild in his finances again, but you will honor his drafts and requests until you hear from me to the contrary." When Arthur himself later reached Hawaii—his plans to sail further into the Pacific were thwarted by an outbreak of bubonic plague—he too spent heavily on island investments.

Harold very much wanted to be appointed governor, and had convinced himself that he would best represent the interests of all islanders. While at Samoa he had become interested in Polynesian culture—he sent seven cases of Samoan "curiosities" home—and doubtless was acquainted with the attractive and charming half-Hawaiian, half-Scot Princess Kaiulani, before her untimely death in 1899. Likely for political reasons, the Sewalls named their island-born daughter Emma Kaiulani, reportedly much to the displeasure of his mother, Emma. Harold also tried to persuade Williams, Dimond & Co. to mount a figurehead of the princess on their new Sewall-built bark *Kaiulani*, but they correctly pointed out that the bark's bow was not shaped so as to be able to properly mount a sculpture.

In May 1900 the governorship went to Sanford Dole. Joe Manley, in the thick of the fight for Harold—at least by his account—explained the smoke-filled-room turn of events:

> At the last moment the Committee on Conference got a provision in the bill that the Governor should be a citizen of Hawaii. We did not object because we believed Harold was a citizen. . . . The President was inclined to hold that Harold was a citizen; the Attorney General decided that he could not have acquired citizenship because he was holding a United States position, and this absolutely cut him out of the nomination.

Harold later tried to gain an appointment through President Teddy Roosevelt, with whom he had overlapped at Harvard. Perhaps because they shared too many terrier-like qualities, however, Teddy had formed a dislike for Harold and turned him down.

Returned to Bath, among various useful, if less than all-consuming activities, Harold served several sessions in the state legislature, where he was known as an effective reformer. He failed in a run for Congress. As Bath's city forester he was devoted to the care of the city's trees.

Life's a failure. Charley has fixed us all

In October 1900, having "retired" from the *Arthur Sewall*, Jim Murphy went to Marfa, Texas, to visit his older brother Charlie and his younger brother Will.

Charlie Murphy had become an important man in Marfa. Once the mate on a ship commanded by his father, Charlie was one of many former Maine mariners who ended up in unlikely inland locations. He arrived at Eagle Pass in the barren West Texas country in 1882, and was initially involved with an Englishman named Humphris in a stock-raising and storekeeping venture. Drought would send them to Marfa, a water stop on the Southern Pacific Railroad connecting San Francisco and New Orleans, which was completed in 1883.

Humphris & Co. established a general store in Marfa which quickly grew into one of the biggest concerns in the Big Bend region, occupying an entire block, with six branch stores, a bank, and a stage line. In 1900 Humphris became overextended with credit problems, and was bought out by Charlie and his nephew-in-law, James Walker, who incorporated as Murphy & Walker. Will Murphy was part of management.

Jim Murphy was so impressed with the business that he wrote the Sewalls from Marfa that he had given a draft on his account for $16,000 to Murphy & Walker. This was a very considerable amount of money. He apparently also persuaded other family members—including nephew Doc Briry—to invest in the firm, and may have put more of his own money in as well.

After taking *Shenandoah* from San Francisco to Liverpool to New York in 1901, Jim retired once again, but, in 1903, was persuaded to take the steel four-masted bark *William P. Frye* on a passage from Baltimore to San Francisco as a favor to Captain Joe Sewall, who was tired and feeling out of sorts.

In February 1907 Jim, despite diabetes and obesity, succeeded the retiring Captain Joe Sewall in command of the *Frye*, and remained with her until 1909, during which time he made three round Cape Horn voyages (including one to Honolulu). In November 1907, aboard the *Frye* in San Francisco, Murphy wrote in his personal log: "Bad news from Charley. Have lost $28,000. . . . "$28,000 lost by a brother. Life's a failure. Charley has fixed us all." Possibly a major flood that inundated the business section of Marfa was a factor.

But all was not lost. Murphy & Walker went into receivership, to emerge in 1909 with Will as general manager. And from aboard the *Frye* at Philadelphia in June 1909, explaining why he would be leaving her command, Jim Murphy wrote the Sewalls that he had $20,000 for which he wished to find suitable places to invest. It would appear, however, that in 1908 Murphy very likely thought that all, in fact, had been lost, and this should be borne in mind when considering the account of the memoir of M. Francis Cushing, who sailed aboard the *Frye* in that year, which follows.

1. Buntlines were lines that helped to furl the body, or bunt of a square sail. To keep them from chafing the sail they were overhauled, or pulled up from aloft enough to give them some slack, and then tied off with rotten twine, which could be parted with a sharp tug from on deck.

2. This was very unusual Cape Horn weather, with the normal westerly gales supplanted by easterly gales. See the account by Carleton Allen who was there on board the Bath-built bark *Guy C. Goss* in W. H. Bunting, *Sea Struck* (Gardiner, ME: Tilbury House, 2004).

3. Captain Robert Jack, born in Bowdoinham in 1812, was said to be the last man to sail a ship into Liverpool. He was the Sewalls' longest-serving captain. After being mate on *Rio Grande*

from 1846 to 1880, he commanded *Macedonia, Wm. D. Sewall, Adriatic, Ocean Scud,* and *Indiana.*

4. The Murphys were very fond of their shipboard pets. When aboard the *Arthur Sewall* Jim once sent a boat's crew off in a failed attempt to rescue a kitten overboard. Their dog Jug on the *Sewall* was a favorite of the sailors, but of one aboard *Shenandoah* Jim wrote in his personal log: "Dog died. *Poisoned.*"

5. Big wooden schooners and barkentines, built especially for the Pacific lumber trade, were much more efficient lumber carriers than were square-riggers, and traded successfully to Australia and China.

6. Captain George Goodwin did not believe in beating across the North Atlantic, especially in winter. Instead, he put the ship on the starboard tack and let her go south until he reached the northeast tradewinds. When he reached the strong trades he turned west, on a parallel of 10 to 20 degrees, until meeting the track of north-bound West Indiamen. Such passages, made in warm, flying-fish weather, could take but half the time that other ships spent beating their heads against bitter westerly gales.

7. Bath *Enterprise,* April 12, 1898.

8. Sam's letter book, January 29, 1900, courtesy of Gene Reynolds.

9. Captain Ebed Murphy was master of the ship *George Stetson* when the Sewalls bought her in 1898. Murphy then was shifted to the *Henry Villard.*

10. Provided by the late Charlotte Donnell.

11. Abbie Sewall, *Message Through Time, The Photographs of Emma D. Sewall, 1836–1919* (Gardiner, ME: Harpswell Press, 1989).

12. Emma D. Sewall, *The Rivers and Marshes of Small Point* (Bath, ME.:The Times Company, n.d.), pp. 28–29.

13. Paul T. Burlin, *Imperial Maine and Hawaii* (Lanham, MD: Lexington Books, 2006). A remarkable work of original scholarship.

14. Maine's James G. Blaine, secretary of state during the Harrison administration, and Harrison's minister to Hawaii, John L. Stevens—another Mainer from the Kennebec Valley—were both sympathetic to the desire of the American *haoles*—a small minority—who were the principal landowners, planters, and the business elite—to have the islands annexed by the United States.

15. Three square-riggers which would later be preserved as museum ships, *Star of India, Balclutha,* and *Falls of Clyde,* gained U.S. registry in this manner.

PART THIRTEEN

Alas, the Sewalls miss out on the deal of the new century. We catch up with Ned. The Arthur Sewall *goes missing,* Shenandoah *is still floating. Captain Jim is in decline aboard the* Frye, *but then makes a final Cape Horn passage with* Shenandoah. *We meet the prickly, prideful Captain Quick.*

I appreciate very much your hearty good wishes

With thousands of square-riggers yet sailing the seas, with American imperialism on the ascent, and with the recent rise in shipping rates, Arthur Sewall likely died believing that by boldly converting the yard to steel he had put the Sewall fleet on a sound path for the future. However, Flint & Co.'s 1899 decision to sell their fleet of ten aging Cape Horners—once the finest fleet of wooden ships ever built—and to put the proceeds into building the first steamer of the American–Hawaiian Steamship Company, proved far shrewder.

In November 1898 George Dearborn wrote Arthur about incorporating his steamship proposition, to be called the American–Hawaiian Steam Navigation Company: "Tomorrow afternoon a meeting will be held . . . at which Messrs. Flint and Burnham, Sam, Oscar, and I will be present." Sam soon dropped out, due to demands at Bath—had the Sewalls then wished to join in, they could have. And had they only had old wooden ships in their fleet and in their future, very likely they would have.[1]

The official version, *circa* 1954, of the founding of American–Hawaiian, credits George Dearborn, the company's first president, with having first had the idea for converting the intercoastal trade from sail to steam traversing the Strait of Magellan back in 1882, when he was twenty-four years old.[2] Indeed, in 1851 his father David had been purser aboard the first steamer to take that route. Beginning in 1891 George Dearborn; his cousin Henry E. D. Jackson (a partner in Dearborn & Co.); and Dearborn's brother-in-law, Lewis H. Lapham, the head of one of the nation's largest leather companies, were credited with masterminding that idea into reality.

The newly created firm of Flint, Dearborn was to be the line's general agent, with Williams, Dimond & Co. handling the West Coast and Hawaiian ends of the business.

Andronicus Chesebrough was second vice president and Oscar Sewall was a director.3 In April 1899, George Dearborn wrote Sam Sewall: "I appreciate very much your hearty good wishes for the success of our steamship service, and will frankly say right here that I should feel happier and would be better pleased with our outfit were you interested and actively one of us. . . . "

Dearborn predicted to Sam—or politely pretended—that putting steamers into the intercoastal trade would boost business for sailing vessels by bringing attention to the route. Yet his business plan depended on capturing the majority of the Hawaiian sugar trade, which was the key to obtaining eastbound cargoes for sail as well. And in January 1902 Sam wrote Captain Joe Sewall that the American–Hawaiian steamers had taken all "the Line" business. The 1903 offer by Sam and Will to sell their entire fleet of sailing ships to the Hawaiian sugar planters was surely an expression of the frustration they were then experiencing.

The majority stockholders of American–Hawaiian were Flint & Co., H. G. Lapham & Co., Williams, Dimond & Co., and George S. Dearborn. The remaining shares were held by the officers and closely associated firms and individuals, including sugar planters who guaranteed cargoes. In 1901 the Flints had to sell out their position to cover personal losses on the stock market. In 1923 former Flint & Co. partner Charles R. Flint wrote: "The shareholders of this corporation realized over 500 percent profit on their investment—the most successful American steamship company ever organized."4

Prime credit for the operational success of the line lay with Captain W. D. Burnham, Flint & Co.'s old marine superintendent. Three of the first four steamers, which went into operation in the winter of 1900, were commanded by former masters of Flint sailing ships. Transit time, via the strait, was soon reduced to fifty days. The line pioneered the burning of oil, and the Texas Company—Texaco—which would later lease the Sewall shipyard property to build tankers, and in which some fortunate Sewalls invested early, was created in American–Hawaiian's boardroom to take over oilfields in which Lapham was heavily interested.

Beginning in 1907, to block the threat of a competing rail-steamer combine, freight was transshipped across Mexico's Isthmus of Tehuantepec via the Tehuantepec National Railway, running between Puerto Mexico and Salina Cruz. By 1914 the line was operating twenty-six steamers in two separate Atlantic and Pacific fleets. American–Hawaiian was profitable from the beginning, and during the World War I shipping boom dividends rose to $395 per share.

As if the rise of American-Hawaiian, and the failure of the passage of any meaningful shipping legislation were not enough, Will and Sam also faced ruinous competition from a mushrooming fleet of steel French "bounty ships."5 The first French shipbuilding and operating bounty dated from 1881, but the effects were not really felt until after the temporary increase in shipping rates at the turn of the century gave rise to a great expansion of the fleet.

Bounty ships needed to carry cargo for only two-fifths of a voyage to receive a full subsidy, based on mileage sailed—not surprisingly, ships often took circuitous routes, such as sailing to the West Coast of South America by way of the Cape of Good Hope. Subsidy reenactments lasted for ten years, and ten years after the 1903 reenactment, France supported a fleet of 140 fine, new, big sailing ships, against which no other national fleet was able to compete on an equal basis in unprotected trade.

There were a couple of attempts to organize the remnants of the American Cape Horn "clipper fleet," most notably by the firm of Bates & Chesebrough, "Chesebrough" being Dron's son, Arthur Sewall Chesebrough. Old David Dearborn was their New York agent. Relations between Bates & Chesebrough and Sam and Will Sewall soon collapsed in acrimony. When Bates & Chesebrough attempted in 1909 to create a line of small steamers operating in conjunction with the Panama Railroad, George Dearborn, using his Washington connections, acted quickly to put the firm into bankruptcy.[6]

To some cottagers, the annual summer arrival of Oscar and family at Small Point, with a small retinue of servants, must have been galling enough. But then came George Dearborn who, after visiting with Harold Sewall about 1911, bought nearby land, upon which he constructed a compound which included several cottages, guesthouses, housing for the help, a greenhouse, a powerhouse, and a ten-car garage filled with expensive automobiles. George cruised to Maine aboard his 189-foot steam yacht *Colonia*, said by locals to have been manned by a crew of twenty-five, and for which he was said to have turned down an offer of $1 million.[7]

History, of course, is written by the victors, but in 1971 David Sutton, the son of Woodruff Sutton of Sutton's Dispatch Line, and the grandson of old E. B. Sutton, the pioneer of the California "line" trade, provided an alternative version of the founding of American–Hawaiian:

> Woodruff Sutton, my father, seeing that sail could not compete with steam, started, with two or three associates, to organize the American Hawaiian Line when he was suddenly stricken with apoplexy and died. Among his associates was one George Dearborn who finished what my father had started and cut my family out of any interest in the new line. I was a small boy at that time and my brothers were in college and knew nothing of business, so we lost everything.[8]

Every thing we have ever done seems to be to no avail

When last we considered Captain Ned Sewall's ongoing troubles, his marriage to Captain Baker's daughter Susie was failing. They were evidently separated by April 1893. On April 22 Susie wrote:

> Dear Uncle Arthur,
> In the absence of my father and feeling that I cannot disclose this matter with any one else I come to you for advice. Ned has written me that you and the family think advisable to have the trust deed cancelled, for each to hold our respective share, that it is to secure employment he wishes this done. I am willing if it is

going to benefit Ned. I ask for the money coming to me to be in my own name—*absolutely mine*—and in case Ned should spend or in any way use his part that he cannot come to me or demand any of my money. I wish the trust company to hold my part which Ned says is ten thousand dollars and receive the income just the same as I do now and if at any time I may think best to invest any of the principal to do so, also to pay one half of the lawyers' expenses for drawing up the papers and half of any other expenses which you think I ought to pay. I hope you may not think I ask too much but if this matter is settled this way it will be *perfectly satisfactory to me.*

    With kindest regards to you and Aunt Emma I remain very sincerely yours,
    Susan B. Sewall

(A margin note in Arthur's hand: "Ans. May 2. Advise not to break trust.")

Despite all the broken promises, in July 1893 Ned was permitted to buy a $1/_{32}$ interest in, and take command of, the schooner *Carrie A. Lane*. He promised not to misuse vessel funds, and not to use intoxicating liquor or have any on board. Oscar wrote Arthur that he was glad to learn of this development. He added that he had "rather lost confidence in Susie," and if she and Ned were not to live together again, he would advise divorce. A letter dated February 2, 1894, from a Boston lawyer to a Bath lawyer stating that Mrs. Sewall "does not want the trust discharged until the family strongly desire it" may mark the date of the divorce.

In September 1893, in lowering daylight, the *Lane* collided with the anchored schooner *Three Marys* in Delaware Bay. There was substantial damage. Before submitting his logbook to the insurance adjusters Ned wrote home that he had to "straighten" it up a little—but a logbook is a legal document that must never be straightened up, not even a little.

In January 1894, Oscar wrote Arthur:

I regret that Ned could not continue in the *Lane* or in employ of Arthur Sewall & Co. I cannot see, however, how you could do otherwise & everything we have ever done seems to be to no avail. I am afraid he will give Mother much trouble & unhappiness. I have written him a very plain letter & told him he better get away somewhere where he was not known & do something for himself. We have all talked this over so much that it is no use to say more now.

Oscar also discussed the state of the sugar business, in which he had become involved: "Our little [sugar] factory, costing $250,000, will make and divide this year $100,000." He was sending Arthur four half-barrels of brandy on the Thomaston ship *R. D. Rice.*

A letter of reference dated May 19, requested by Ned, stated that he had been in Arthur Sewall & Co.'s employ, serving from boy to master, from 1880 until 1893, and that "during all this time, we have had no occasion to find fault with your seaman-ship or navigation, and we shall feel very much gratified if this letter proves of any assis-

Captain Edward "Ned" Robinson Sewall, 1863–1926
MAINE MARITIME MUSEUM

tance whatever to you in the new line of steam navigation." What was unsaid spoke volumes.

The Dearborns, as a favor, succeeded in getting Ned a berth as second mate with the Morgan Line, a coastal steamship line operating between New York and New Orleans. In September Ned's services were loaned to the government to pilot the *Ericsson,* a new and yet to be commissioned 120-ton torpedo boat built at Dubuque, Iowa, from New Orleans to New York.9

As of December 18, 1894, the E. R. and Susan B. Sewall Trust was valued at $19,876.17, including $3,327.38 worth of "ship property." The other major assets were marine insurance stock and various railway stocks and bonds. The trust was finally discharged in 1896, with Sam serving as the assignee of Ned's half.10

One cannot follow Ned's subsequent trail in any great detail. In September 1897 Arthur wrote his brother Frank that, except for Ned, the family was "very well fixed." That November Ned wrote Arthur that he was still living in New York, had "not found anything yet," and asked to be given command of *Roanoke* for her next passage, New

York to San Francisco. "I could get her out there as safe as anybody else and under any terms you would make." There is no record of a reply from Arthur.

The following April Oscar wrote Sam regarding Ned's having been arrested, of the $2,000 cash bail demanded, and of an associated lawsuit, but provided no details. The $2,000, Oscar concluded, would have to come from their mother. Ned was then sailing on the Morgan Line steamer *El Monte* "in his old position. He is giving good satisfaction to the company and no doubt if he continues will be advanced."

On December 27, 1898, Ned wrote Sam asking for a loan of "another" fifty dollars. "I am getting pretty low in funds now and am living as cheap as I can. I am in hopes to be well enough to go in my ship when she gets back. I am feeling better and don't have such bad days as I had a week ago and am getting some strength back. Hope you and the family had a pleasant Christmas." The contrast between the brothers' financial and domestic circumstances could not be missed. In August 1900 Ned married Katherine White of Chicago; this marriage is believed to have ended in divorce.

In February 1901 Sam wrote Frank that he understood that Frank had been sending money in response to Ned's requests, and that Ned had also been obtaining money from their mother. As long as he could gain an income without working, wrote Sam, so long would he continue to loaf. Dearborn had found him several available positions.

On June 22, 1901, Ned wrote Sam asking for another loan. His steamer, *El Sud*, was sailing that day for New Orleans, and he would be leaving his wife sick in bed "with no one with her in one room. With the sickness and $18 rent a month it leaves me in a position that I can not see my way through on a salary of $45 a month." On June 30 Ned thanked Sam for the loan, adding that he had left but six dollars at home, and worried about what he would do if his ship was laid up for repairs.

In June 1902 Ned was elated to learn that he still owned an interest in *Carrie A. Lane*, which had been sold, and asked Sam to debit his account for sums advanced by "Mother and yourself," together with the $250 that Oscar had just advanced him against his coming windfall. Sam explained to Oscar that he had previously sold just enough of Ned's interest in the *Lane* to cover repair assessments, and had thought it best for Ned not to know that he still owned a 1/32 share. He feared that Ned's credit of $879.32 would "melt away as all credits heretofore have done."

By way of contrast, in June 1904 Oscar—further enriched by his interest in American–Hawaiian Steamship Company and now living in Englewood, New Jersey—wrote Sam of plans for bringing his family to Small Point for summer vacation. Oscar asked for a two-horse truck (there would be "considerable baggage") to meet the Bar Harbor Express on July 6. Also, another truck would have to meet the noon train from Boston to pick up three of the family's four servants—there should be one conveyance to take his family down, and another for the servants, and he did not want the servants to have to wait for the afternoon stage. He wanted arrangements to be made for milk and ice, coal, wood, and kindling;

> My present intention is to have my man Thomas follow us down later, and if so I shall not need to employ Kelly. . . . If I do . . . need to employ Kelly . . . under no

consideration will I feed him the same as last year. . . . If you could arrange [with a man] to have a fire in the range and be present on our arrival, I would appreciate it. . . . I received a letter from Mother the other day, inquiring about Ned, and as she is worrying a good deal about him and knows that things are not going all right, I have written what I know. . . . I understand he is at the Fulton Ferry Hotel and out of employment. . . . Hoping you are all well and having a good time and hoping to see you very soon.

The next word of Ned, in September 1908, is from E. D. Douglas of Williams, Dimond's New York office for Sam. In Oscar's absence, Douglas had given Ned an order on Fulton Supply for sea clothes and a sextant. A ticket for Savannah would be purchased for him. If Ned called at the office just before his steamer sailed he would be given thirty-five dollars in cash. "This, altogether, makes $160, which is the $150 you authorized and a weekly payment about due, which will be absorbed in a board bill he owes."

Finally, a letter to Sam from H. B. Driver, assistant trust officer of the Old Colony Trust Company, Boston, June 1923, regarding the Edward R. Sewall Trust, suggests that in order to remit Ned $650 without drawing on the principal, a check for $275 from Sam would be required. Sam sent the check.

He is great hearted, kind, and generous

With Jim Murphy's re-retirement, a new master for the *Arthur Sewall* needed to be found in a hurry. A telegram sent to Williams, Dimond & Co. requesting recommendations brought the response: "We have thought of no master that will fill your requirements except it may be Captain Gaffry, formerly of the *Tacoma* and now in port here in command of *Berlin* . . . ."[11] Thomas Burton Gaffry was a native of St. Stephen, New Brunswick, the town right across the St. Croix River from Calais, Maine.

On August 6 Sam Sewall, after having turned the *Arthur Sewall* over to Captain Gaffry, wrote Will from New York:

I gave him [Gaffry] to understand that we might sell 1/16 for $12,000 but could not allow 5 percent primage on so small an interest and in fact appeared rather indifferent about selling just now. He may mention it to you as he is obliged to go to Bath tonight to settle with Minott who owes him some $6,000.

Any share sold to Gaffry was to come from Arthur's interests.[12] A price of $12,000 for a 1/16 interest figures out to sixty dollars a ton. According to a letter from Oscar to Sam in April 1899, however, she had cost the original owners just under forty-five dollars a ton, which figure presumably included the Sewalls' profit, claimed to prospective buyers of shares to be 10 percent. Obviously, Arthur would be profiting much more handsomely on any share sold to Gaffry. Likely such a hefty advance in price would have been justified as representing the ship's higher replacement cost.

Captain Thomas Burton ("Burt") Gaffry, on the poop deck of the four-masted bark Arthur Sewall. San Francisco Maritime NHP, Charles Page Collection

Gaffry's first voyage in the *Arthur Sewall* began with a passage to Yokohama with case oil. A recent Yale graduate, Charles Page, who was planning to study for law school when at sea, was a passenger. In a letter written at Yokohama to a friend who had accompanied him to the ship at New York, Page wrote:

[The captain] has proved himself a splendid character. As a man he is great hearted, kind, and generous to passenger, officer, and men alike, and I may say that with the exception of two malcontents . . . all hands feel for him not only respect but an affection. If you know of the ways of American ships and officers—it is the boast of some captains that they would not hand anything to a sailor but would always kick it to him—you would recognize in this a tribute to the man. He is all "every inch a sailor" even to that Cape Horn roll he gets into his walk and is equally a navigator. As to his treatment of me there is little I can say—had it not been for the awkward right of ownership in the vessel vested in Arthur Sewall & Co., of Bath, I might have had her long ago.[13]

Of the first mate, who Murphy had praised to the Sewalls, Page wrote: "Oily and pleasant enough when you saw him, he soon showed up in his true colors as a coward, a liar, and a brutal bully of the first water. . . . 'I'll show you who I am, I'm McKay from way down East and don't you forget it.' . . . The captain . . . has dressed him down for his conduct and informed him that he is a fool, liar, etc. . . ." McKay was possibly a Nova Scotian, of which there were many among the officers in the oil fleet, and more than one named McKay.

On the other hand, Page greatly admired the second mate, Mr. George, a New-foundlander:

That New York hoodlum whom you saw aboard gave this officer a bit of back slack the second evening out and had the pleasure of spending the next ten minutes insensible in the lee scuppers. This one incident nipped in the bud any fractiousness that may have been growing among the men and from then on they have given him *unlimited respect*. In addition to his other qualities he is a singer—he has what I call a magnificent voice could it have been trained—and is always ready with a sea-song or chanty, and as for a sailor's hornpipe he is a daisy.

Of the twenty sailors aboard there was one American, two Filipinos, one Filipino-Chinese, one Japanese, two Malays, one "kanaka" from Guam, "a number of Swedes and Danes," two Spaniards, one Greek, and "sundry Russian Finns."

Major events of the lengthy 161-day passage included a brush with the tail of a powerful Atlantic hurricane which brought the fore-topgallant mast crashing to the deck. The storm also started a leak in the bluff of the bow—Gaffry wrote: "I was quite startled at first, as there was about 12 feet of water in the 'fore hole' [no doubt the fore peak] before we discovered it." Thereafter, in calm weather the leakage measured in the pump well amounted to about five inches a day.

During a severe gale in the Indian Ocean the cargo shifted—this was not supposed to happen with case oil—imparting a 12 degree list to starboard. At the first opportunity—one week later—hatches were opened and cases from starboard were stowed in the midships deckhouse, and "everything heavy" on deck was moved to port, to almost right the ship. After "running his easting down" east of the Cape of Good Hope, Gaffry elected to enter the Pacific by way of the Ombay and Gilolo passages through the East Indian archipelago. Page marveled at the great skill and also good luck required to navigate the big ship safely through these perilous, unmarked, reef-strewn waters, particularly during fierce, dark squalls that suddenly descended.

The crew of the Arthur Sewall *posing for a portrait at Hiogo, Japan, 1902. Group photos of crews on American ships are rare. The* Arthur *had very nearly reached port when only 114*

The *Arthur* arrived at Yokohama January 21, 1901. There, Gaffry learned of the death of Arthur Sewall. He wrote Bath: "Mr. Sewall looked so strong and robust when I last saw him, it seemed impossible he should be carried off so suddenly. . . . We do not like to lose our friends, and Mr. Sewall has been a friend that has shown me many favors."

Charles Page left the ship at Yokohama, writing home that during the five-month passage he had gained in health, flesh, and strength, and had found something to enjoy at all times. "In one thing I failed—and failed most lamentably and that was in reading law." In fact, he wondered if he might be better suited for the ministry—he had earlier

days out of Philadelphia, but then had battled fierce "northers" for another seventeen days before finally anchoring. ANDREW NESDALL

written that Christians might more productively spend their efforts on saving the souls of sailors, leaving the heathen Chinese "to the quiet enjoyment of their faith."

On February 24 the *Arthur Sewall* sailed in ballast to Honolulu, there to load sugar for Delaware Breakwater for orders. At Honolulu on March 25 Gaffry wrote the Sewalls:

The sailors made such a cry in Yokohama about the ship leaking it came to the ears of the surveyors. Had the ship repaired and surveyed . . . thought I was alright but coming across we started more rivets, aft under the run. . . . When the ship would settle, the water came in a stream. I have kept it quiet and getting them put in as cheaply as possible. There is a number of rivets in the between decks that need seeing to also. . . . This is an American port now and all my crew claimed their discharge. They are all so drunk now they will not report anything but I am very anxious about the surveyor.

Gaffry reported that the riveters "idea" was that the entire ship should be "riveted all over." After repairing cement work in the bilges, preparatory to lining the hold with wood—which Gaffry likened to building a ship within a ship—Gaffry groused: "Think it would pay you to hire a small boy to pick up the old bolts and scrap iron before you plank over the limbers." He ended with: "How is it the Standard Oil people allow a captain to carry their wives free and Arthur Sewall & Co. make them pay $4 a week?"

The *Arthur* sailed April 18. Arriving at Delaware Breakwater on August 6, 1901, she received orders to proceed to Philadelphia to discharge. On August 27 Gaffry wrote Bath: "I can see a smile illuminate your thoughtful countenance when I ask for four days to go home and get married. Hoping you will grant my request."

Members of the Sewall family frequently asked captains to shop for them, particularly when calling at Asian ports. Gaffry was not only charged by Harold Sewall with buying wine for him at Honolulu, but was also to bring home Harold's Honolulu furniture. One senses that Harold rubbed Gaffry the wrong way, and Gaffry was clearly annoyed by Harold's complaints regarding the condition in which his furniture arrived at Bath:

Mr. Sewall's furniture left the ship in the same condition I received it. That was in good order. Some of it was only protected by burlaps. Saw it go over the rail and on the lighter. And Mr. Elwell saw it from the lighter to the steamboat wharf. . . . The way goods on trains and steamboats is handled, think you ought to be satisfied to receive the pieces.

You may lose a valuable ship and cargo

In September 1901 the *Arthur Sewall* departed on another case-oil passage, this time for Hiogo, arriving in March 1902, then departing in ballast for Honolulu. And once again she would sail from Honolulu with sugar for Delaware Breakwater, arriving in September 1902. Gaffry wrote Bath: "We have two lady passengers on board. They are not very agreeable people. . . . I grow old and learn but forget as fast as I learn, but there is one thing that will cling to me as long as life lasts, and that is to beware of lady passengers."

At Philadelphia Gaffry found eleven broken frames and about sixty broken rivets in the deckbeam knees, along with "a good many rivets so loose I could turn them around with my thumb & finger." Repairs were made.

The *Arthur*'s fourth voyage was from New York to Shanghai with oil, then back to Honolulu for sugar for Philadelphia, where she arrived in November 1903. On

November 12, Gaffry, responding to a nagging circular letter sent to all captains from 411 Front Street—"We have also concluded it true economy to employ only such masters as have the ability to command the highest compensation for their services"—wrote:

> Your letter of economics received. I was well aware before you informed me that you paid your masters well. The Standard Oil pay their masters from 100 to 125 per month with the full benefit of the slops and the privilege of carrying wife free of charge. Also a perquisite at the end of every successful voyage. I never considered myself anything but ordinary and a poor ordinary at that, so the sooner you reduce my wages to a level with my capacity the better it will be for all concerned.

Not for the first time Gaffry's dry Down East humor eluded the cousins, who responded in affronted alarm. In response to a second Front Street circular reminding captains of their instructions to credit "all savings for commissions and perquisites" to the ship, Gaffry wrote:

> As to commissions it is hard for a master to get them, as you have agents at principal ports of the U.S. or otherwise transact the ships' business by letter from your own office. I can truthfully say the ship owes me—a thing that will never occur again, as [I] am very well convinced [that] the masters who look after himself are the ones who gets the most credit. . . . As to the luxuries you mention, I am at a loss. However there is a store list on board of my provisions last year . . . so if you have not one will copy it and send it to you. So you can cross out the articles you think luxurious.

In February 1904 the *Arthur Sewall* again left New York with case oil for Shanghai, arriving June 22. Gaffry's wife had been sick the entire passage, and he had to send her home by steamer with an attendant, a costly business. On July 14 Gaffry wrote of his attempts to get clear of his sailors after the Sewalls ordered the ship to be laid up awaiting better business: "When we first arrived I gave the sailors all that was due them, thinking they would clear out. But the rascals simply took a week's drunk, and came back for something to eat and medical treatment."

In August the *Arthur* sailed in ballast to Puget Sound, where she loaded a cargo of lumber for Shanghai at Port Gamble, Washington. Loading lumber was a difficult job with a square-rigger, which lacked the lumber ports of a schooner. Gaffry wrote the Sewalls: "As far as a stevedore is concerned, Rothschild knows no more about the loading of this ship than you do." Port Gamble, with its white Cape houses, sugar maples, and a copy of the East Machias, Maine, "Congo" church, was a transplanted version of that Down East settlement, the hometown of its founders, A. J. Pope and Fred Talbot, and many of its residents. Gaffry observed:

The four-masted bark Arthur Sewall *at Port Gamble, Washington, loading lumber for Shanghai.* ANDREW NESDALL

If there was ever a monopoly the Port Gamble Mill Co. is one. They own the mill, the lumber, the village store, hotel, and the contiguous territory. Two classes of men work around the mill. One class are mill hands who get $26 per month and the mill boards them at a cook house. The others call themselves longshore men. They get $.50 per hour and have to be handled with kid gloves or they will not work at all. Of the $.50 per hour the ship pays these men Rothschild probably gets 20 percent rebate. 50 percent goes to the rum shop under the hotel, and the remaining 30 percent goes to the mill hotel and the mill store for clothes.

Arrived at Shanghai, Gaffry wrote that off Cape Flattery one man was washed overboard and drowned, and another, injured, was now under a doctor's care. A started rivet in the "fore hold" had demanded frequent bailing. On April 10: "We are having a time with drunken and sick sailors, fumigation, and smallpox. But suppose you may have troubles enough of your own without listening to my tale of woe." On April 21 Gaffry dryly observed: "The heathen refused to work today because it is Good Friday."

Once again the *Arthur* sailed from Shanghai to Honolulu for sugar, arriving June 14, 1905. Gaffry reported: "I have silks and ——— for Mrs. S. S. Sewall, segars [cigars] for Mr. S. S. Sewall, two screens for Mr. W. D. Sewall, and a dress for Mr. Dearborn, ordered by Mrs. Harold Sewall." The ship loaded 5,570 tons of sugar. From Delaware Breakwater, on November 6, Gaffry wrote: "We have had a very rough passage. The vessel has made water freely all the passage, and in heavy gales we could hardly keep her free with both pumps. You can rest assured I was heartily glad when we came to anchor." On December 4, responding to questions from the Sewalls regarding Shanghai bills, and also the fact that a number of stevedore Ah Sing's bills for provisions, chandlery, etc., were settled at a 5 percent discount, but appear at gross amount in accounts, Gaffry responded:

The items you question in my Shanghai account were used or are still on board ship. The cigars & cigarettes were bought for the slop chest. The ginger is still on board with the exception of one jar that was used on the voyage home. The whiskey, gin, and brandy was used partly at sea in stormy weather by the crew, some in port by people doing business with ship and some by myself. Ah Sing paid discount of 5 percent but cannot find in my accounts where it has been credited to the ship. The slipshod way I keep accounts will be adjusted. . . .

Any self-respecting shipmaster would have felt justified in pocketing the rebate from Ah Sing, of course, and the Sewalls knew it.

On December 12, 1905, the *Arthur Sewall* left Philadelphia loaded with "government coal"—bituminous "Eureka"—for Manila. Eureka coal had a bad record for spontaneous combustion, and the ship was fitted with a Clayton fire-extinguishing machine, accompanied by a man from the factory to operate it, as an experiment. Gaffry doubted its efficacy. Just as cargoes of naval coal had ignited in 1905 aboard *Dirigo* and the *Erskine M. Phelps*, when Gaffry wrote the Sewalls from Batavia on April 2, 1906, it was to inform them of a dangerously heated cargo, sending out smoke, under the after hatch.

Gaffry had not thought it safe to proceed to Manila from Anjer, and had had the ship towed to Batavia. "Two days before arriving at Anjer nearly lost a whole watch [from coal gas]. Some were so far gone it took half an hour to bring them back to life again." He also reported that a few days out of Philadelphia, in a fierce gale of wind, the ship had sprung a leak so bad that for a while the pumps could not keep up with it. Ordinarily she leaked but five inches a day.

The crew dug out some 400 tons of coal to expose the fire, which was then extinguished by the fireboat. The sailors could only work for twenty minutes at a time in the intense heat and smoke, then lay on the deck to recover. When the ship was finally safe, the men, not surprisingly, believed they deserved some recreation, as Gaffry surely understood, although he also surely knew the inevitable consequences:

The sailors thinking I have not trouble enough are trying to make it pleasant for me. Last Monday morning they refused to go to work unless I gave them ten guilders apiece and liberty. They are all in jail. The ship will have to go on dock before she can load sugar. She makes no water in port but in a gale of wind we

The sailors' band aboard the Arthur Sewall, *taken by Captain Gaffry. A notation on the back of the photo by Gaffry to his wife at home read: "If only Allie could hear one tune from that German band he would pass the remainder of his life in ecstasy." Allie—Thomas Alban Conley—was his brother-in-law, who had sailed in the* Sewall *as deck boy and second mate.* ANDREW NESDALL

cannot keep her free. If the rivets are not found you may lose a valuable ship and cargo.

Evidently it was believed that the fire would have been worse without the Clayton system, because machines were later installed on all the steel vessels and the *Benj. F. Packard.*

Arrived at Honolulu, Gaffry wrote that on the passage the ship had leaked worse than ever. It took about three weeks of pumping before the water was reduced enough to find the leaks, which proved to be a missing rivet and three rivets leaking freely abaft the foremast. The rivet hole was stopped with a wooden plug, the loose rivets caulked with lead.

On the back of this photo Captain Gaffry had written,
"Fine winds and fine weather." ANDREW NESDALL

Arrived at Philadelphia in March 1907, Gaffry laid the heavy loss of sails to the fact that his crew "was not the best," and of the nineteen, including ten Puerto Ricans, three Japanese, and three "kanakas"—only one man had had any experience at sea. And none could understand English. However, Gaffry was one of those captains who didn't experience serious "sailor troubles," no matter the frustrations or temptations.

On April 2, 1907, the *Arthur Sewall* left Philadelphia with coal for Seattle. After dropping her pilot off the Overfalls lightship she was never heard from again. Burt Gaffry's last letter to the Sewalls, on March 10, read: "Will you kindly send my wife

Captain Gaffry had written on this photo,
"Koly very much interested." ANDREW NESDALL

$1,000 and let her have $100 a month out of my wages. I am buying a home and would like to pay for it."

By November there was considerable concern for the overdue ship, although agents Darrah & Elwell assured the worried father of the ship's boy that they as yet had no fears for the ship's safety, while at the same time telling the Sewalls that the case looked doubtful. By Christmastime Sam and Will had concluded that the ship had been lost. They speculated that she might have collided with the Rockport, Maine, bark *Adolph Obrig*, which had sailed about the same time and had also not been heard from. On February 8, 1908, Lloyd's finally posted the *Arthur Sewall* as missing.

False reports of sightings of the missing ship cruelly raised hopes. In April 1908 a Hawaiian sailor turned up in Philadelphia and claimed to a newspaper reporter that he and three others had escaped from the burning *Arthur Sewall* off Cape Horn, and had

Captain Gaffry, sitting on a sailmaker's bench by the chart house, sailmaking.
He wrote on the back, for his wife and brother-in-law, "Does it put you in mind
of old times, lots of preparation, little work." ANDREW NESDALL

been rescued by a Norwegian bark and carried to Australia. But his story had many
holes in it, and he quickly disappeared.

The possibility of structural failure due to faulty rivets was never publicly suggested. Reminders from Arthur in letters sent home while he traveled to watch the riveting show that riveting was a matter of concern, as it certainly should have been. In
fairness, as recent research into the loss of *Titanic* has shown, there was then a great
deal yet to be learned about metallurgy. The Sewall barks were all built under the
inspection of a classification society.

Back in October, Jim Murphy, from aboard the *William P. Frye* at San Francisco,
had written Bath:

Nothing yet from the *Arthur*. Too bad. Do you suppose her rivets got loose? I have heard that many [ballast] stones were left in her bottom last voyage, and were washing around. These might have loosened her rivets.

Texteth Park Cemetery, Sec. 12, No. 546

On January 10, 1901, *Shenandoah*, with Jim Murphy in command once again, her top-sides recaulked and pumps repaired, sailed for Liverpool with grain. She arrived at the bar on May 8 after what Murphy described as "the most trying and serious passage I ever made." The first night out the ship commenced to leak badly. Forty-five days out the leak doubled, requiring one set of pumps to be worked constantly and the second set to be employed every two hours to keep her clear. "Cape Horn and its big seas looked a hard thing for me to try with a leaky ship, but I did not mean to put into any port, but stick it out until the last. Which I have done."

At Liverpool Murphy received the devastating news that the ship *John McDonald*, aboard which his son Wilder was chief mate, was presumed lost with all hands. A week after *Shenandoah* had sailed, the coal-laden *McDonald*, bowling along off the California coast headed for San Francisco, was spoken to by a British bark. The *McDonald* signaled that she was on fire, but asked for no assistance. She never arrived and was presumed to have blown up from an accumulation of coal gas. "I feel broken up, but I must have hope. Daytimes I keep busy with my ship, but the nights and being alone are bad," wrote Jim. He was also suffering a great pain in his side, initially diagnosed as appendicitis.

On May 25 *Shenandoah* was put into a graving dock. She sat comfortably with the blocks raised six inches forward and ten inches aft—evidently she still had some rocker to her keel. Three bad butts were found. Her metal looked good. And Jim would write: "Had this morning a horrible accident on board. My carpenter—a very fine fellow—whilst running the engine got caught in the shaft, and was killed instantly."

The carpenter, named George Mathieson, had been discharged but was working by the day, pending signing on for the next voyage. He was a native of Norway, and a Declaration of Intention to become an American citizen was found among his belongings. His family was not known.

Excepting a bundle of letters, cash receipts, etc., forwarded by the consul to the judge of the circuit court in New York, the carpenter's belongings were left aboard ship to be delivered to the U.S. Bureau of Shipping commissioner at New York. These effects included one lot of old papers, one violin with two bows, one suit of buckskin underwear, five neckties, one ruby lamp, one pair of dungaree pants, one hairbrush, three collars and cuffs, one old umbrella, one pillow, one old muffler, one camera, four bottles of photo solution, and two photo-toning baths.

The eleven cash deposit receipts, etc., included a promissory note for $215 signed by one Alexander Collins, at San Diego, 1895; £77 deposited in two Freemantle, Australia, banks; £35 deposited with the consul at Liverpool on May 15, 1901, for safe-

Shenandoah. *Looking aft atop her long poop deck. The structure on the forward end of the after cabin, which gave entrance to the cabin, was called the "pilothouse" or "coach house," not to be confused with the wheelhouse, aft of the cabin. Broad-beamed Jim Murphy, in white, stands at the mizzen fife rail. Note the size of the "built" mizzenmast of hard pine. Perhaps this photo was taken by ship's carpenter George Mathieson, whose belongings, after he was killed in a horrible accident at Liverpool in 1901, included a camera and developing chemicals.* ANDREW NESDALL

keeping; $815 deposited in two San Francisco banks; $194 worth of gold bullion deposited at the United States Mint, San Francisco; ten shares of the Govina Yukon Dredging and Exploitation Company, i.e., a gold-mining stock; and a deposit of $265.88 at a San Diego bank. Mathieson's tool chest contained 178 tools and accessories, including twenty-three plane irons and eleven plane frames. He was buried at the Texteth Park Cemetery, Sec.13, No. 546.[14] It is well to be reminded that there were yet to be found aboard ships some thoroughly professional and expert sailormen. Arthur Sewall believed that "Swedes"—in Maine any Scandinavian was a "Swede"—made the best sailors.

When *Shenandoah* arrived at New York, Murphy wrote asking to be relieved. "This weary waiting and hoping has affected me greatly, and I feel it my duty to remain at home for a time to try and comfort my wife and receive the same myself." *Shenandoah* leaked not at all coming to New York, and Murphy declared her to be in perfect condition.

Jabbing me in my stern sheets

At New York Jim Murphy was replaced aboard *Shenandoah* by Captain Edward Watts, a dry Yankee from St. George, Maine, who had commanded Thomaston and Waldoboro vessels. In September 1901 *Shenandoah*, under Captain Watts, sailed for Yokohama with 123,000 cases of oil plus a quantity of barreled oil—Jim Murphy had said she would require no ballast—arriving in 140 days. This was a month faster than Standard Oil's big four-masted bark *Brilliant*, or their Sewall-built *Acme*. But in heavy weather, Watts reported, *Shenandoah*'s bow would rise and fall a foot, and the scarfs in her railing would open and shut an inch.

Signed aboard as a boy was a tall fifteen-year-old named Robert Buell. In 1949 Buell reminisced about the voyage in a letter to Mark Hennessey. Buell had later sailed in a Scottish bark and the old East Boston–built (medium) clippers *Glory of the Seas* and *Spartan*, but *Shenandoah* remained his favorite.

> After leaving Bayonne, on the first night, the captain [Edward Watts—Buell had forgotten his name] had all hands called to the foot of the poop deck. . . . He gave a lecture at to what was expected from every one and he emphasized the fact that he would not tolerate any cursing or using foul language aboard his ship. No need to say, his lecture didn't mean a damn thing, considering the fact that we had a first mate who was known throughout the trade for having the foulest mouth of any mate that ever sailed. . . . After the lecture, the watches were picked and it was my good fortune to be picked by the second mate.
>
> When we had been at sea for about a week, we ran into a squall. It was the boys' job to go aloft and furl the skysail every time they took it in.[15] At this particular time, I was called by the second mate to furl the main skysail. I had some little experience in going up the rigging on the old USS *Constellation*, but never experienced anything like shinnying up the mast from the royal to the skysail. However, I went aloft and got as far as the royal yard, but wouldn't go any farther. The second mate was shouting and cursing at me from the poop deck, but I wouldn't budge.
>
> Finally, the second mate came up after me and with a long sail needle started jabbing me in my stern sheets, and every time he did this, I made a lunge to go a little higher until I made it to the skysail yard. I was tired when I reached it, and for the first time, I was homesick. He then showed me how to take in the sail and how to secure it by passing the gaskets from the yard towards the mast. . . .
>
> The first mate's name was Taylor, better known as "Skysail Yard Taylor."

Taylor was a rawboned, six-foot individual with a slow, rolling, swaggering gait, and a voice like the roar of lion. . . . I saw "Skysail Yard Taylor" let fly with a belaying pin at a young lad by the name of Goodrich. This happened when all hands were called on deck to shorten sail while in a storm. . . . I think Goodrich resented some remark passed by the mate, and the mate let fly.

The second mate's name was Graham, a well-liked sort of chap. Graham was marked with a long scar on the side of his face and he kept it covered by growing a good-sized Van Dyke beard. He was a young fellow and a good sailor. . . . We arrived in Yokohama sometime in February 1902. This I remember quite well because the USS *Kentucky* was in Yokohama at the time, and they invited the crew of the *Shenandoah* to a dinner honoring Washington's birthday, which we gladly accepted. . . .

After discharging our cargo of case oil, we took a ballast for Frisco. The *Shenandoah* was always kept neat and clean and when we pulled into Frisco, after a thirty-day run, a record for that type of ship from Yokohama, the papers came out with a story of the *Shenandoah* being the cleanest ship that ever put into that port.

I got paid off in San Francisco and took up lodging in the Sailor's Home on Mission Street. Shortly after we were paid off, I heard that a body was found among some old tin cans in an empty lot near the Sailor's Home, and that the body was that of Skysail Yard Taylor. How true that story is or was, I don't know, but I never heard of him again.

As for the Skipper, the crew had him down as a sanctimonious Down Easter, an "holier than thou" kind, and let the mate get away with all he wanted to.

Watts returned *Shenandoah* to New York, where he left her. One year later, it will be recalled, he took command of the ill-fated *Susquehannah*.

I was actually afraid she would break up

Captain Watts was replaced by the reserved and dignified Captain Omar Chapman of Newcastle, Maine. Chapman would command *Shenandoah* for the next seven years, beginning with another oil voyage to Japan, and including a coal voyage to Manila.

Omar Chapman was an unusual man. A reserved Yankee who dressed at sea like a banker, he cooly dealt with all the myriad problems that confronted the master of a big ship in this era, in addition to which, his ship was often doing its best to sink on him. That he persisted as he did likely also reflects how few opportunities there then were for even first-class shipmasters, as well as his hope of obtaining a steel ship in good time.

Of a hurricane met by *Shenandoah* in the Pacific after doubling the Horn, Chapman wrote, at sea, on April 5, 1905:

I had to run before the wind and sea for two days, as she labored and strained so

Captain Omar E. Chapman, 1854–1912
MAINE MARITIME MUSEUM

badly. . . . [When head to sea] her bow would rise and fall four or five feet and work from side to side as much or more. After we got her before the sea, the sideways motion stopped, but the up and down motion was just as bad. When the seas would run under her, first the mizzen rigging would slack up, then the main, and then the fore rigging. The mizzenmast was bent forward. . . . We could just keep her free [of water] by steam. . . . We pumped by steam up to March 17, when to save fresh water and coal, I let the steam go down. Since then, we have been pumping constantly by hand with ten minutes rest every hour and can just keep her free with one pump. . . . I can carry very little sail, as any pressure makes her leak so badly that we cannot handle it. We have pumped her constantly for 22 days, 3,250 miles. My crew are getting tired out. The pumps are getting worn badly.

Chapman put into Valparaiso to have the topsides recaulked.

On a passage from Baltimore to San Francisco in 1907 with coal, Chapman elected to go west by going east, avoiding Cape Horn. Nevertheless, he was again forced to break passage, putting into Melbourne. He wrote:

The *Shenandoah* is dangerous; she is not safe. . . . She worked frightfully, just as a raft would. I was actually afraid she would break up. . . . The way she carries away the rigging is this. When the hollow of the sea goes under her, the masts settle and slack the rigging so it hangs in the bight. Then when the crest of the wave goes under her, she comes up with a jerk, and something must go. I have used all our hawsers, chain, and wire as preventers. . . . [In port] we keep her free of water till ten o'clock at night, then let it stand til six in the morning. Then there is always four feet one inch in her.

Dry-docking in Melbourne was too expensive to be considered, so a diver was hired to attend to bottom leaks, and the topsides were caulked once again. (The ship-caulking trade, now all but extinct, was once extant worldwide.) While *Shenandoah* lay in port, Mr. Thomas Bent, the premier of Victoria, made inquiries about buying *Shenandoah* for a training ship, to be fitted out to accommodate 2,000 boys. Captain Chapman, of course, thought this a capital idea, but the newspapers killed it, patriotically objecting to the acquisition of a foreign ship for this purpose.

Shenandoah sailed in October, arriving off San Francisco on December 29, 1907, once again in a badly leaking condition. First, she had worked out the topside oakum between the fore and main masts. Then, about a month before landfall, in a head sea, she began to leak worse than ever, requiring pumping by steam all day and by hand all night. Captain Chapman, venturing down into the hold as deeply as he could get, observed that the ceiling planks above the lower deck beams worked fore-and-aft on the fastenings, and could hear water running in.

While entering the harbor under tow, *Shenandoah* grounded on Potato Patch shoal, where she pounded for an hour before being gotten off. Miraculously, the only obvious hull damage that was found when she was dry-docked was that about ten feet of keel had been canted. A lawsuit was filed against the tug company, and at the same time negotiations were entered into between agents Bates & Chesebrough and the navy regarding the possible sale of the ship as a coal hulk. Navy surveyors, taking borings, found her timbers to be sound except for a few knees rotten at the heart.[16]

The agents noted that it was a delicate matter when suing the tug people, to "run up as high as possible" any and all possible damage, alow or aloft, that might be claimed to have been caused by the stranding, while, at the same time, "when dealing with the Government we want to minimize the bottom damage." Ultimately the navy backed out of the deal, and *Shenandoah* was engaged as a store ship for $900 a month, with Captain Chapman remaining aboard as shipkeeper. He wrote of her: "She is a puzzle. She looks well, her shape is as perfect as the day she was launched. But she is so weak that it would not be safe to go another voyage."

In February 1909, following instructions from the Sewalls, Chapman had the ship put in a safe anchorage, awaiting developments. He noted that prospects of a sale on the West Coast were slim, as about two hundred vessels of different types were laid up in Oakland Creek. On May 6 he wrote: "I am sorry you asked for my opinion of the seaworthiness of the *Shenandoah*, for I do not know what to say. If she is chartered for lumber, she must be caulked from the twenty-seven foot-mark up. If windmill pumps were installed, there is a possibility that she would reach the Atlantic Coast without trouble. But I consider it extremely doubtful."

Captain Chapman was soon very pleased to be given command of *Kenilworth*, lying at San Francisco. "I am anxious to get into active service again. This laying up is, to say the least, 'cussed.'"

I kept shuddering to think what might have happened

The Sewalls received numerous inquiries from boys and young men wishing to go to sea, from fathers of boys or young men who wished to go to sea, and from the fathers or brothers of boys or young men whom they wished to *send* to sea. In February 1895 Sam Sewall wrote Joe Sewall aboard *Susquehanna* regarding the son of a "particular friend" of his—likely a Yale classmate—with a brother who was, "as you may guess, somewhat dissipated. . . . The family is a very nice one, but, as usual, there is one black sheep in it, and having tried everything else they now propose to try a sea voyage." A year later Sam was singing a different tune to his uncle, the Reverend Frank Sewall, who was inquiring on behalf of a young man:

> Our captains are always willing to take young men who want to learn something about navigating a ship and try to get ahead in that line, but they are never anxious, and usually unwilling, to take a young man of dissolute habits who is sent to sea by his parents who are unable to control him at home. . . . They are apt to have unpleasant experiences on board the ship, write doleful tales to their parents, and possibly the press, giving the ship, master, and owners the worst possible reputation.

In 1908 M. Francis Cushing, born in Bangor, Maine, sailed as "boy" at age seventeen aboard the four-masted bark *William P. Frye* from Newport News to San Francisco. He enjoyed the experience very much, but he did not think highly of Captain Jim Murphy, who was then not dealing well with setbacks in his life. Cushing did not write his tale until he was old and disabled, about two years before his death at Bangor in 1961, but he turned out a wonderful job. Published in 1963 as *I Once Knew A Ship*, Cushing's account is surely the most informative of any such narrative about sailing aboard a Sewall ship, and arguably ranks among the best such final days of sail reminiscences, of which there are a great many.[17] He wrote in his opening:

> Soon after the turn of the century I was going to high school in a small city in Maine. I had a good home and about everything a boy could ask for, but I often felt something like a captive. Too many things were decided for me which made me feel overprotected. So I wanted to get away from home to grow up, I suppose, and thus have a chance to make my own decisions.

And so he decided to go to sea, where his days would be spent following a mate's decisions. His father was then deceased and his mother was not well, which he thought kept her from opposing his wishes more effectively. As it happened, his mother related his wish to a woman she chanced to meet who was related to Maria Murphy, and Jim Murphy's ship was just then about to depart from New York.

In April 1908, young Cushing went to New York—he confused the Dearborns, whose office he was to call at for directions, with the ship's owners—and was soon aboard the *William P. Frye,* lying at Erie Basin, Brooklyn, signed on as boy for twelve dollars a month. A "boy" was not a cabin boy, but an apprentice of sorts, who bunked away from the sailors in the "half deck," or the midships house, where the bosun, cook, carpenter, and sailmaker also had their rooms.

Soon after, the *Frye* towed to Newport News, manned by a small crew of "runners" with an old mate in command, to load naval coal. Doc Briry, it may be recalled, wrote that his Uncle Jim Murphy's word could not always be fully relied upon, and sure enough, Murphy wrote to the Sewalls that "we" had left the anchorage and arrived at Newport News, although Cushing informs us that Murphy left the ship at the last moment, leaving his wife Maria and daughter Jane aboard.

At Newport News the ship lay alongside a massive coaling facility that loaded six ships at once. Coal thundered down from on high, dumped from trains of small, oddly shaped hopper cars pulled by toy locomotives driven by smiling black engineers. Perhaps they were smiling because they were not "trimmers," shoveling in the dust-choked holds.

The coaling dock was an interesting place to be—all sound and motion, and bright lights gleaming redly through the all pervading coal dust. This action took place high overhead, and was getting farther and farther away by the hour as the *Wm. P. Frye* settled deeper in the water. This loading, uninterrupted, kept up twenty-four hours a day all the duration of our stay.

Cushing's mental images had remained most vivid. Of his first impressions of Jim Murphy—who in the book he gave the pseudonym of Beal—he wrote: "He had a large frame, was overweight, had a large bullet-shaped head with clipped hair and a voice too deep to understand easily. He also had a gloomy manner plus a habit of getting in the way of busy people." Further along he wrote:

Captain [Murphy] must have been quite a wonderful man in his younger days. Many people said so, and I never heard it denied; but now he was depending on his reputation instead of his judgment to carry him through. The old man was just a shadow of his former self, albeit a fat one. The skipper had very large ears to match his large head and fleshy face, a small mouth, little button nose, and small eyes whose resentful expression sometimes seemed pathetic. He never laughed or smiled, and if we heard him talking much it was safe to assume he had been drinking.

With the ship anchored in the harbor with 5,111 tons of coal on board, Murphy's deal to sign a crew from Norfolk fell through, and his letter to Bath reports that he had asked Mr. Dearborn to send a crew from New York. According to Cushing, the crew, in a drunken state, arrived directly from New York aboard a big, handsome, white seagoing tug, with polished brass and a uniformed crew.[18] Murphy wrote that he thought he had received a good crew, a good cook, and a good steward (both were Siamese), two good mates, and an agreeable passenger. He thanked Mr. Dearborn for his kind attention.

Soon after getting under way the usual ritual was enacted—a "sea lawyer" with two sidekicks approached the poop, where Murphy was leaning against a rail smoking a long clay pipe, to demand their rights. No sooner had the sailor opened his mouth than the two mates flattened him with two blows almost too fast to be seen. The vanquished sea lawyer was carried forward by his seconds, and proper order had been established aboard the *William P. Frye*.

The crew was composed of Germans, Finns, Norwegians, Swedes, and Spaniards, with one Brooklyn Jew and one Englishman, and included a number of experienced sailors. The steward and the old sailmaker had sailed with Murphy in different ships for many years. The passenger, a Mr. Walker, was from a wealthy family which had sent him to sea to be cured of his alcoholism, not realizing that he was also a drug addict and had brought a supply with him.

Given Captain Murphy's own abuse of alcohol on the passage, Cushing credited the two mates—particularly the first mate, whom Cushing called "Mr. Mac"—for bringing the ship safely into San Francisco, and in splendid order, at that. Mr. Mac was a native of the Maritime Provinces. The second mate was a Yankee-hating Virginian whose family's wealth had been lost in the war. They were both very professional mates, each bearing the scars and even identical surgical reconstructions marking past battles. But they did not choose to rule by fear or bullying. To improve morale and teamwork among crewmembers, Mr. Mac organized rat hunts—having just carried barley, the ship was heavily infested—which the men found great sport.

But the era of good feelings was soon cut short. During a nighttime squall a wet, heavy sail was dragged over a molding of the midship house. Although no one then knew the connection, in the morning, deep slashes appeared to have been cut in the wood. As no one would confess to the vandalism, Murphy, enraged, punished the entire crew for the remainder of the passage. Water rations were reduced to the point that the men could not wash, and thus developed deep, pus-filled abscesses on their hands, which the mate treated as best he could. The watches were kept working two extra hours during the day, and were put to the most unpleasant and tortuous tasks that Jim Murphy's brooding brain could devise.

Off the Horn the *Frye* was battered for four weeks, losing one of the Finns off the bowsprit. The cargo shifted, and the mates had to resort to some driving in the dark hold to get the ship quickly back on even keel. When the ship was finally headed north, the captain's and the mate's "dead reckoning" estimation of the ship's distance off the coast—they had not been able to get any sights for eleven days—differed by over sixty miles, and one night Mr. Mac, fearing that the eastward "set," would soon put the ship ashore, told the men to sleep in their clothes. The ship was hove-to in a fog, awaiting daylight, when the breakers were heard:

> They said the Captain reached the deck quick enough but upon seeing the island, made some kind of despairing ejaculation, and disappeared below to find his courage in a bottle. The mates took charge, and since there was only one way to go, they took it. To me it was a wonderful display of seamanship to get that big ship around in such a short space with so little canvas drawing. They couldn't have made it except for the deep water close to shore. Once the *Frye* was round the end of that island she was carried by the current into a channel about a quarter of a mile wide. . . . Once committed to this channel the ship couldn't get out. . . .

Cushing held down the chart laid on the deck while the mates, on their knees, heads together, tried to identify the islands vaguely depicted. Captain Murphy returned "full of fortitude," but neither the mates nor anyone else paid any attention to him. While squeezing between a skylight and a ventilator Murphy slipped and fell—there was a very heavy groundswell running—and was stuck there by his great girth. He bellowed, he commanded, and then he pleaded for help, but was ignored. In time, when he had sobered up somewhat, he was helped to his feet.

This was a very different Jim Murphy from the man Doc Briry described as filled with "great animal courage," and who once, coming on deck at night when hove-to off Cape Horn, instantly realized that his ship was drifting down on another hove-to ship and ordered sail to be set just in time to draw clear.

> We were now drifting through a channel bordered by rather small, fairly evenly spaced, but infinitely varied islands, which stretched in both north and south directions as far as the eye could see. When the stern of a ship is alternately lifted twenty feet or more into the air, then set down into a hole in the ocean equally deep, you can't see much at a distance from on deck. But the most frightening and amazing, and in its way the most beautiful sight of the ride through that channel came at the beginning. Only the three men working at the stern and facing aft saw it, and I was lucky to be one of them.
>
> Two pinnacles of rock seemed to rise from a receding swell only about sixty feet astern. One was glossy black like obsidian. This rock spire, as slender as a church steeple, but with a jagged outline, was shedding foaming water from various places which, coursing down its surface in little streams, made it appear to be covered with white lace. The other rock, only a short distance away, was slightly less pointed, had a broader base and a dull surface. Its face and outline looked much water worn, but its distinctive feature, a dark red like a well burned brick, made it stand out from the rest. After the immediate shock and scare had worn off, I kept shuddering to think what might have happened if the *Frye* had come down on that black spear!

The four-masted bark William P. Frye *entering the Golden Gate*
ANDREW NESDALL

Until well into the afternoon the ship drifted, passing about twenty miles of islands. The second mate swept the scene with a telescope, looking for a sign of the *Arthur Sewall*, although all knew that nothing of her would have survived. When finally the ship drifted clear of the islands no one cheered or celebrated—all were in "a dazed state of wonderment."

The rest of the passage north was spent putting the ship in what Cushing described as yacht-like condition. Mr. Mac's first project was to repair a leaking seam in the hull plating that had for weeks been flooding the galley and the half deck. Rivets were heated in the galley range.

Jim Murphy's arrival telegraph, sent to Bath on September 24, read: "No trouble or accident thirty days off horn." His follow-up letter, however, did mention that they had "lost one man overboard whilst furling the jib." Other than describing the month spent off the Horn as "the hardest chance I ever had," the letter revealed nothing of the untoward events of the passage, although Murphy's handwriting was not up to his usual very legible standard. The crew and officers were paid off and disappeared, and only then did the steward learn, after talking with the steward on the previous voyage, that the slashing of the molding had occurred then, and that the dragging sail had knocked out the putty and paint which had hidden the damage.

Cushing related many interesting sidelights of life aboard the *Frye*. Under certain conditions—as Joe Sewall had reported—the ship steered very hard. Relieving tackles were often employed. Helmsmen had been badly injured when thrown over the wheel, and the scuff marks of their shoes were left untouched on the painted overhead as a warning. On one occasion Murphy's quick reaction and his great bulk pressed against the rim of the spinning wheel, aided by the second mate, kept the ship from broaching-to and possibly being lost.

When the main deck was filled with water, a space beneath the broad shelf on the inboard side of the bulwarks contained a pocket of air, up into which a submerged man working at the braces could poke his head for a breath.

The sail locker was a deep steel well filled with sails rolled as tightly as possible, stored vertically, each carefully labeled as to its identity and condition, and readily accessible.

One Saturday afternoon—which was when the slop chest was open—the steward, who was the storekeeper, opened a case of slippers with red piping and a rosette and which appeared to be well-made. Soon pleased purchasers were proudly parading about until a rogue wave soaked all, revealing the fast-disintegrating slippers to have been made of paper over pressed wood pulp, with cleverly and deceptively embossed stitching.

Her name and mine are blended together

Jim Murphy made one more Cape Horn passage with the *William P. Frye*, carrying Hawaiian sugar to Philadelphia. He appears to have sobered up and regained his courage. No doubt the news that he was not, in fact, bankrupted, helped; perhaps having Herman Kiehne as first mate, whom he was fond of and whose opinion of him he would have valued, also helped.

Towing up Chesapeake Bay in June 1909, Murphy wrote the Sewalls that on the passage he had set a compound fracture of a sailor's arm broken by a fall from aloft, and "His arm is now as perfect as ever was." And he had decided to resign the command of the *Frye*. "I am in good health and spirits. . . . I want a little time at home, to rest, to see my friends and be with my family. I feel this is due me."

But in December 1909, Captain Jim Murphy, age fifty-nine, roused himself once again and traveled to San Francisco to refit his old ship *Shenandoah* to bring her back to the East Coast, there to be sold as a coal barge. There was no market for her on the West Coast. He wrote upon seeing her:

> I have had a good look over the ship, and find a great change since I left her. She shows great signs of work[ing] from the poop forward. Aloft, she is all adrift, which speaks badly. . . . I found the ship so much worse than expected. The poor old ship herself is good, but everything is out of her.

By the end of January repairs were complete. The jigger lower mast had been fished. All the yards had been sent down to fix their bands. The rudder was banded and re-bolted, the donkey engine and sails overhauled. She loaded a cargo of scrap iron, asphaltum, wire rope reels, lumber, cased goods, and so on.

Fitted with a windmill pump, she sailed on February 16 and arrived at New York on June 24 after "a most trying passage. . . . The ship didn't sail well, all of 25 percent slow"; winds were light. However, amazingly, she leaked but three inches per hour. "The ship is in fine order. Looks as of old." On July 22, Jim Murphy wrote:

> Mr. Scully with his men looked the ship over in every part of her yesterday, and he accepted the ship, taking charge of her when the iron is out. . . . I began the career of our good ship and as a good ship I have ended it. Her name and mine are blended together and will be marine history.

Shenandoah sold for $36,000.

Thomas Scully was one of a number of barge operators who bought up old square-riggers, removed their rigs, deckhouses, and bulwarks, and towed them in strings coast-wise, bringing mid-Atlantic coal north to New York and New England in competition with coasting schooners. They often took ice south. The Morses of Bath had been pioneers in this business, buying thirteen old ships from 1885 to 1888 whose value had declined with the drying up of the German market for "petroleum klippers" for the barreled oil trade. Scully's fleet of barges included some of the finest ex-American sailing ships of all time, including the Bath-built *E. B. Sutton, Governor Robie, Helen A. Wyman* (ex *William J. Rotch*), *I. F. Chapman*, the Thomaston ship *Joseph B. Thomas*, and the ship *State of Maine*, built in 1878 by the Sewalls' ship-timber contractor, Eben Haggett, at Newcastle.

Barge crews—dismissed as tramps and hobos by real sailors—favored the old ships over purpose-built barges, glorying in the palatial cabins once the sacred realm of storied shipmasters. It was customary for ships' logs to accumulate in the cabins, and that is where many remained. In 1911 a reporter was a guest in the cabin of the Scully barge *Shenandoah*, whose captain enjoyed leafing through her old logs. Citing one entry, in April 1906, sailing from Manila to Port Blakely, the log read: "Strong breeze, heavy squalls, took fore and mizzen topgallant in. Hail and snow squalls. Sea making up. Men standing by." Noon to noon she had sailed 318 "knots."[19]

On October 29, 1915, the barge *Shenandoah* was rammed by the steamship *Powhattan* off Shovelful Shoal lightship, near Fire Island, New York, and sank, with loss of one life. Presumably the logs went with her. In 1916 the submerged hull was blown up by the government.

Jim Murphy, obese and ill, looking far older than his sixty-two years, died on April 15, 1912. Doc Briry wrote of his death:

> My uncle died one night from diabetic pneumonia, sitting on the side of his bed with my arm around him. He had robbed me—his nephew—of a thousand dollars cold cash—through a mining proposition that his oldest brother Charles Murphy was promoting at Marfa, Texas. Jim Murphy was always dishonest.

Captain Jim Murphy at home in Bath, probably in retirement following his leaving the command of the William P. Frye *in 1909. (He would die in 1912.) He is holding one of his ever-present "TD" clay pipes, which he purchased in large quantities. The substantial structure he is sitting on much resembles the twin settees commonly installed in ships' cabins. An identical settee, said to have come from* Shenandoah, *contributed by a member of the Sewall family, is in the Maine Maritime Museum collections— likely it is the same one* MAINE MARITIME MUSEUM

In the Murphy house at 1120 High Street, Bath MAINE MARITIME MUSEUM

No serious consideration of the Sewall fleet—or perhaps even of Arthur Sewall—would be complete without mention of Captain Richard Quick, born in 1868 in the Bay of Islands, Newfoundland, and whose daughter Clarabelle would someday become the mistress of Will Sewall's impressive mansion, York Hall.

Going to sea in local craft as a boy, Quick's formal education was brief. He came to the "Boston States" about 1887, becoming a sailor aboard the schooner *Carrie A. Lane*. When Ned Sewall was forced to step down from her command late in 1893, Arthur Sewall named Quick, then second mate, as her captain. Where others saw but a small, rough-cut "Newfie," Arthur astutely saw the makings of a competent shipmaster. Arthur took a personal interest in Quick's development, and his letters of correction were patient and instructional, rather than terse and critical.

In 1897 Quick made a Mediterranean voyage, carrying hard pine out, returning with cork, ginger root, and olives. That September Captain Joe Sewall, upon learning that he might be relieved for a passage in *Susquehanna* by Quick, wrote Arthur that "he does not seem a desirable man for one of your best ships and I think we are taking a great risk. This is not intended as any reflection on your judgment." Of course not. The very idea that Joe could be replaced by a semiliterate schooner skipper who had never even sailed in square-rig was simply intolerable..

Quick was instead given permanent command of the ship *Henry Villard*, then lying at Tacoma. Her departing captain, Ebed Murphy, wrote Bath that he thought that with "a little experience in square-rigged ships he will make a good ship master but at the present he has a lot to learn but I think he will soon learn as he seems very bright and has self-confidence." The *Villard*'s mate—who Quick discharged—and others were unhappy with Quick's promotion, and a tipped-over tar barrel, which damaged cargo, was likely sabotage.

The story goes that when one of the mates, in a patronizing manner, used the expression "Now, *this* is how we do it aboard a *square-rigger*" once too often, Captain Quick remarked, after felling the man with a lightning uppercut, "And *that's* how we do it aboard a *schooner!*"

Captain Quick had a successful career aboard the *Villard*, marred only by the death of his wife at sea in 1899.[20] He was impatient to get a steel ship, and in 1901 Joe Sewall had to bite his tongue as he turned over command of the *Edward Sewall* to Quick. For twenty-one years the name of Quick would become synonymous with that of the *Edward Sewall*—it would have been difficult to find a master of the largest liner who took more pride in his ship than did the small, bristly redhead from the Bay of Islands.

Keeping any steel ship in salt water free of rust stains was a task for Sisyphus, even when the topsides were painted black, but Captain Quick—like Graham in the *Phelps*—gloried in painting the *Edward* white from waterline to mastheads, and keeping her white. Sailors were put over the side on staging to paint the topsides before entering port. Captain Quick's own pastime at sea was turning out new sails by the suit

with a sailor-powered sewing machine.

Like her sister the *Arthur Sewall,* the *Edward* suffered from cracked beams and frames and loose rivets, although none seem to have resulted in bad leaks. In 1903, however, when off Cape Horn, a side port became sprung, and when discovered the ship had seven feet of water in her, which took two weeks' pumping to clear.

In 1905, becalmed amongst the Marshall Islands, the ship drifted 480 miles off course in a month's time, nearly grounding on coral reefs three times—shades of the wreck of the *Rainier.*

In 1908, off the Horn in a gale, a link to the fore-yard truss broke and the steel spar, ninety-six feet long, came down "by the board," landing about half overboard, with the big sail dragging in the water and the ship rolling heavily. After four days' work at the forge, Captain Quick had rebuilt the truss as good as new. After waiting eight more days for the seas to calm sufficiently, the yard was re-crossed.

In 1909 off the Horn in a winter blizzard, the second mate—a fine young man—was washed overboard. The mate, badly injured, was laid up for four weeks and then went crazy. And a sailor had gone crazy in the gale. In his inimitable style, Quick wrote—to alter Quick's spelling would not do justice to this self-taught man's pluck—"i tail you i had my hands full fer a wile." Seeing that he had no officers to back him,

The four-masted bark Edward Sewall *loading coal, possibly at Newport News in 1907, from whence she sailed to Honolulu. Although her devoted captain Richard Quick was wont to fondly call her his "white yacht," no one would mistake her here for anything but a big, utilitarian bulk carrier.* MAINE MARITIME MUSEUM

the crew "staerted to get funie with me" but with the help of his six-shooter and "a big bluff I got the best of their game." In this gale he had fifteen sails "bloed to pesis"—the first blast stripped the ship of foresail and three lower topsails, all the sail that she then had set.

On a passage from Newport News to Honolulu with coal in 1910, the coal spontaneously ignited around the base of the foremast, settling it eighteen inches. At Honolulu, instead of giving the repair job to contractors who were licking their chops, Quick borrowed jacks and sufficient ties for blocking from the railroad, and with hired Japanese laborers and his carpenter, sent down all the yards and the topgallant mast, and lifted and repaired the mast and keelson.

Lawrence C. Howard, a school ship graduate, made a Cape Horn passage on the *Edward Sewall* in 1911–12, quickly experiencing a North Atlantic storm that flooded out the midship house, and blew both the foresail and the mainsail out of their gaskets and to destruction. Fourteen beams were found to have been cracked. Of Captain Quick he wrote:

> He was small of stature, had a red mustache and small eyes. He was well named, too, for he was quick of his decisions and actions. . . . He . . . believed that the

In the hold of the four-masted bark Edward Sewall, *at Honolulu, 1910,
looking at the heat-distorted base of the foremast, atop the keelson.
(What appear to be portholes are holes punched in the photograph.)*
Maine Maritime Museum

Above: Clarabelle Quick and Susan Estelle Quick aboard the four-masted bark Edward Sewall. Maine Maritime Museum

Right: Susie Quick and Captain Quick play dress-up. Maine Maritime Museum

men under him must be kept in line through threats, curses, and punishments. I came to know him well and believe that underneath this hardness there was a gentler vein. . . . I remember one occasion when it was freezing cold and blizzard weather when Captain Quick ordered me in very rough language to come to the cabin. I went fearful of having done something wrong and was told to go into the wheelhouse. There stood Mrs. Quick with a steaming bowl of hot chocolate. I drank it and the Captain ordered me gruffly to "get forward where I belonged."[21]

Quick's second wife was the sister of his first wife. His son Randall, by his first wife, a fine lad, died at about age eleven from the effects of a fall aboard ship. His two surviving of seven children were Susan and Clarabelle, both of whom were aboard ship in 1911.

The academy-educated Howard questioned Quick's skills as an exact navigator, but the ship made a perfect landfall after 127 days at sea. However, Howard wrote, Quick was totally hopeless with signal flags. Howard also thought that an incident when an enraged Quick grabbed the mate about the neck and called him a liar in front of the crew most unprofessional. But he found much to admire as well.

Howard, who continued to follow a career at sea, termed all the sailors in the *Edward's* crew—a Hollander, a Newfoundlander, Germans, Scandinavians, Irish, and

The after cabin—captain's quarters—of the Edward Sewall. *By contrast, the first mate's rooms in the Sewall steel barks were likened to a monks' cells.* MAINE MARITIME MUSEUM

Yankees—save two, "the finest seamen I have ever known, really masters of their trade," despite their inebriation on shore.

The passage from Philadelphia to Seattle with coal which commenced on October 10, 1913, would be Quick's greatest test. Twice the ship put into Bahia Blanco, Argentina, to repair a broken bowsprit. She was then fully sixty-seven days doubling the Horn, during which time she passed the Horn three times, once being 300 miles to the west of it before being blown back forty miles to the east of it. Quick put into Honolulu for one day to replenish stores, finally reaching Seattle on August 7, 1914. While at Honolulu, Quick wrote the Sewalls:

> In steded of the fine yars work we started out an it has been a compleat failure and wile it hirt your good salvs frum anxhity. No body have suffard so mich as I have my self. I have lost the top of 3 fingers one in B Blanco and 2 off the Horn. I have stayed on deke 42 hairs at a time and have went aloft and helped firal top-sails when my min wre layed up sick and I stude the mats and 2d mate watch for 27 days in all whin that min got hurted. I tryed my very best and failed in the very best ship that could be bilt and it braks harth to think of it. . . . I have tryed my very best baut my best is not good anough to sail this ship with every thing against me.

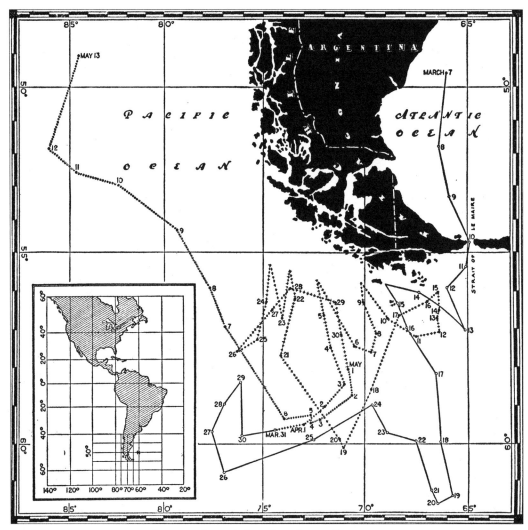

The Rounding of the Edward Sewall *in 1914,*
shown in Felix Rosenberg's Cape Horn *(New York: Dodd Mead & Co., 1939)*

At Seattle he received reassurance from the Sewalls: "We well know you have tried hard and have done your best to get the ship around, and that is all we can ask or expect. We are not discouraged ourselves, and you must not be, but we will hope from now on your old time luck will return."

The *Edward's* next passage would be her last by way of Cape Horn, the next-to-last Cape Horn voyage—the *William P. Frye* made the last one—by an American square-rigger.

Captain A. F. Raynaud, second mate under Quick, stated many years later: "Captain Quick was a very able seaman, a fine shipmaster, and a fearless one. He worked hard for the ship and the owners and expected everyone else to do so. The ship was first and last in his thoughts."[22] Raynaud also praised the Sewalls for not stinting the ship of necessary supplies, despite the difficult financial times.

York Hall, Will Sewall's 1897 neo-Georgian mansion on Sewall Hill, at Edward and Washington Streets, which overlooked the old home of his grandfather, William D. Sewall.
MAINE MARITIME MUSEUM

The opening of the Panama Canal in 1914 ended intercoastal trading under sail. In 1916 the *Edward* was sold to the Texas Company, which intended to convert her to a motor ship, but ended up keeping her under sail with Captain Quick in command. In 1922 she was sold to the Alaska Packers, and Captain Quick, leaving his "fine white yacht" after twenty-one years, went into steam, to spend the next twenty years or more in command of Texas tankers. He died at Bath in 1947.

Clarabelle Quick married G. Baer Connard, a high official of Bath Iron Works. The Connards bought York Hall, Will Sewall's grand Sewall Hill mansion.

1. The Flint fleet then consisted of nine wooden ships and one steel ship converted from a steamer. The first American–Hawaiian steamer was ordered from Union Iron Works, San Francisco, at a price of $400,000; the second and third, ordered from Roach, on the Delaware, were to cost $425,000. These prices were considered "very near the bottom," leaving "practically no margin of profit." Letter from George Dearborn to Sam Sewall, April 6, 1899. Andrew Nesdall has a table drawn up by Flint & Co. in 1898 showing that the average age of their ten ships was fourteen years (omitting two schooners). The average cost when new was $94,892. The average return over cost was $27,451, or 29 percent. The average dividend in 1897 was 13.2 percent. The estimated value of the ships averaged $27,000, although given that the *M. P. Grace*, estimated at $27,000, sold for $32,000, these figures may well have been conservative—a testi-

mony to their fine construction and upkeep. In 1898, however, only five ships paid dividends. All of the ships built by Chapman & Flint (by John McDonald) after 1865 that went into the Flint fleet—including two that went missing, two that burned up, one that went ashore, and one that was condemned—had lasted an average of nineteen years before the fleet was liquidated, a remarkable achievement.

2. Thomas C. Cochran and Ray Ginger, "The American–Hawaiian Steamship Company, 1899–1919," *The Business History Review*, vol. 28, no. 4 (December 1954), pp. 342–65.

3. Oscar's close ties to the Hawaiian sugar industry would prove helpful in establishing trade agreements for the line. His heavy sugar interests also made him spout some rather obnoxious opinions regarding sugar plantation laborers. He wrote Harold on July 8, 1901: "If the [Japanese] laborers who are now there would work, they would have a sufficient supply, but they will not work, for the simple reason that they are earning too much and can afford to lay off for half the time." He backed unsuccessful attempts to bring in Puerto Rican and Louisiana Italian laborers.

4. Charles R. Flint, *Memories of an Active Life* (New York: G. P. Putnam's Sons, 1923), p. 21.

5. Alan Villiers and Henri Picard, *The Bounty Ships of France* (New York: Charles Scribner's Sons, 1973), p. 21.

6. Cochran, American–Hawaiian Steamship Company, p. 356.

7. Stanwood C. and Margaret Gilman, *Small Point (circa* 1965), p. 61; the present David Dearborn regrets that his forebears had spent all their money before his turn came.

8. Letter to Andrew Nesdall, August 30, 1971. In a letter to John Lyman, July 30, 1968, Sutton elaborated. He wrote, "My father came down to our country home in West Islip, Long Island, on a weekend in June 1896, and I remember he was in a very happy mood, for all the papers had been drawn, the financing all arranged, and everything was to be signed on the following Monday to launch the steamship line, when Sunday afternoon a great tragedy struck. . . . [He] died that night. . . . His brothers just folded up the business. The so-called friends, Dearborn, et al., carried the organization through . . . and did not even give one share of stock to my mother. To make it more ironical, my uncle, because of his name, Effingham B. Sutton [who "did nothing"] was elected to the Board of Directors . . . knowing nothing of business. I don't think he received anything worthwhile out of it." David Sutton also recalled that his grandfather, Effingham B. Sutton, had had close ties with Collis P. Huntington of the Southern Pacific Railroad and, after shipping out material for the road's construction, received a good deal of the road's "slow freight" to send by ship.

9. Bath *Independent*, September 15, 1894.

10. In January 1898 Susie's Boston lawyer wrote Oscar, at Williams, Dimond & Co., to inquire if any dividends were expected from the vessels in which Susie held interests as a beneficiary. Oscar replied that there had been no dividends paid since December 1896. The only remaining tonnage was in the ships *Iroquois*, *Reaper*, and *Indiana*, the bark *Xenia* and ship *Solitaire* having been sold. Oscar made it understood that he had nothing to do with the management of this tonnage, and that dividends were declared by the managing owners, Messrs. Arthur Sewall & Co., Bath, Maine.

11. The ship *Tacoma*, built in 1881 by the Sewalls' upriver neighbors, Goss, Sawyer & Packard, was considered one of the finest vessels in the American merchant fleet. Her managing owner was Charles Davenport of Bath. In 1897 Arthur Sewall, with a sharp nose for a good bargain, bought a controlling interest in her at San Francisco for $28,000 and sold her the following year for a good profit to the Alaska Packers Association. She was soon chartered by the U.S. Government to transport army horses to Manila, with Captain Gaffry evidently still in com-

mand. Her existing condenser was enlarged to produce 2,000 gallons of water a day; a large house was built over her deck; windmills and even electric fans were installed. Despite predictions of disaster, she made one horse-passage to Honolulu and two to Manila, including weathering a typhoon, landing the horses in excellent condition. Frederick C. Matthews, *American Merchant Ships* (Salem, MA: Marine Research Society, 1931), pp. 324–26. The ship *Berlin* was built just downriver from Bath in 1882 by Charles V. Minott of Phippsburg. Minott was also her managing owner until 1890, when she was sold to Captain George Plummer, another Kennebecker—probably from Dresden—who built up a large West Coast fleet composed mostly of Maine-built ships. Burt Gaffry had completed one voyage in *Berlin* when he left San Francisco for New York for a bigger fish to fry.

12. Arthur officially owned but $^2/_{128}$ of the ship, but that was fiction.

13. Charles R. Page, "An Account of a Voyage Aboard the Square-Rigged Sailing Ship *Arthur Sewall* from New York to Yokohama," *Log of Mystic Seaport*, vol. 27, no. 2, August 1975.

14. Sewall Family Papers, 22-461-6.

15. Since *Shenandoah* was carrying no ballast under her cargo of case oil, her fore and mizzen skysail yards may well have been on deck.

16. The Chesebrough in Bates & Chesebrough was Arthur Sewall Chesebrough, Andronicus's son.

17. M. Francis Cushing, *I Once Knew a Ship* (Bangor, ME: Furbish-Roberts Co., 1963). Cushing's obituary in the *Bangor Daily News*, January 12, 1961, is all too brief. He was born in Bangor, the son of Malzar and Lucy Cushing. He attended Bangor and Skowhegan schools, graduated from Bangor High School and the New York Electrical School, and was a veteran of World War I. He was survived by his wife Ruth, and a cousin, Mrs. Edward Getchell. It shold be noted for the record that the foremost authority—and admirer—of Jim Murphy is the noted historian Ralph Linwood Snow, who takes strong exception to Cushing's account. In a note to W. H. Bunting, "Lin" Snow wrote: "You know my views on that callow youth, Francis Cushing, trying to recall the most exciting days of his life fifty years later. A *teenager* who probably thought anyone over thirty was stupid, silly, and beyond redemption. There, I feel better now."

18. This was likely the tug *Britannia*, or else her sister *Columbia*, owned by the Baker Whitley Coal Company of Baltimore, the Sewall's favored tugs for towing the steel ships. Perhaps the tug had indeed come from New York as Cushing claimed—he had gained the impression that Murphy was in great haste to leave because his ship was overloaded—but normally a crew would have been put aboard a coastal steamer, under the close eyes of a couple of "watchers," and then transferred to a local tug for delivery to a waiting ship.

19. *Bangor Daily News*, November 2, 1911.

20. In October 1900, Arthur Sewall & Co. submitted an inventory of Captain Richard Quick's personal effects, which he wished to insure, to the Merchants Insurance Company, Bangor, Maine. Captain Quick commanded the ship *Henry Villard*, then lying at Savannah, bound to Honolulu: One chronometer, $150; one sextant, $50; one barometer, $50; books of sailing directions, $45; charts of the world, $165; typewriter, $75; music box, $65; wearing apparel, $200; gold watch & chain, $85. Total: $855.00. The Sewalls proposed that the risk be taken at $3^1/_2$ percent.

21. Lawrence C. Howard, *The Log of the Edward Sewall, 1911–1912* (Lawrence C. Howard, 1958), p.135.

22. Notes from an interview in 1956. Captain Raynaud also spoke at the Maine Maritime Museum in 1982 about his experiences aboard the *Edward Sewall*.

PART FOURTEEN

We come to the end of our story of the maritime Sewalls. Captain Goodwin gets in the last word. The Kineo *makes a disastrous voyage. The Londons sail aboard* Dirigo *with Captain Chapman and Mate Mortimer. The business is wound up, but the war saves the bacon. Other maritime Sewalls pass away. In 1935 Sam, the last surviving maritime Sewall, dies. In 1939 the bark* Kaiulani *is the last Sewall-built ship to make a passage under sail.*

It was like peeling an onion

However strained matters between George Goodwin and Arthur Sewall had become, Goodwin's relationship with Will and Sam was worse, particularly after they had fixed a 1902 charter that disregarded the state of the monsoon, placing *Dirigo* in an almost impossible position to make a canceling date for a Hawaiian sugar charter from Hong Kong. Goodwin wrote the two cousins on the fifty-first day after his departure, having spent forty-four days beating against wind and current with a foul ship in ballast:

> I fully realized what I had before me when I left Hong Kong—steamers were coming in every day with their smokestacks white with salt clear to the top where they had been bucking against the monsoon coming up the [China] Sea.... It has been a heart-breaking job, and we have pulled the life out of my best sails and running gear.... With the wind dead on end the *Dirigo* would not beat to windward a mile in a month.... Three months in the China Sea has fouled her so she can hardly get out of her own way.... I have done the best I could with a voyage planned as this one has been.... The only piece of luck I had was in having a good lot of sailors, the best have had in years.... We wore ship fifty-one times in the China Sea, and thirty times since then.[1]

It would be a mistake, however, to dismiss George Goodwin as a sour malcontent—at least not yet. In 1908 he had so enjoyed socializing in Honolulu that he extended the

Captain George William Goodwin, 1848–1916, taking a sight with a sextant aboard the four-masted bark Dirigo. MAINE MARITIME MUSEUM

good feelings by keeping a journal—a guided tour of his long road home—for his island friends.

Honolulu was always a difficult place to sign up a decent crew for a cold Cape Horn passage, and Goodwin wrote that he gathered up "any old thing that came along," with not an American among them. He instructed his mates to go easy on the men until they had become acclimated. Of training a green crew, Goodwin wrote, "When I see results I rather enjoy it." Two weeks later he wrote:

You would not know this crew of men if you could have seen them the day we sailed and could see them now after having the City Front whiskey worked out of them, and living on good wholesome food. . . . They are washed and shaved and with clean clothes on, look something like human beings. This is about the time they begin to make good resolutions not to drink anymore. They won't until the first land shark gets them the day they are paid off. My carpenter spent $250 in one saloon in Honolulu. My sailmaker was paid off with $240. He spent it all in drink, joined the ship again, took a month's wages in advance to pay his debt, and came to me yesterday to get underclothes to change with. Both of these men are much better than the average . . . such is the life of the sailor that is easily led. They are never so well off as they are at sea on board of a good ship.

Goodwin's thoughts kept returning to the good times he had enjoyed in Honolulu—during moonlit nights, he wrote, he very much wished there was someone aboard who he could talk with.

When approaching the Horn, at about the latitudes where "the brave west winds" were supposed to begin to blow, *Dirigo* instead met ten days of easterly gales, blowing up to seventy miles per hour, that "made the old man feel a little down by the head." After one of his Japanese sailors fell from the main topsail yard to the deck while reefing sail, Goodwin wrote: "It shook him up a bit but he had so many clothes on that there was not any bones broken. It was like peeling an onion getting the clothes off of that fellow to find out how badly hurt he was." A week later the sailor was back on duty.

With a bitterly cold wind blowing from the Antarctic, Goodwin wrote: "It was rough on [the crew] last night. They had to keep shaking the braces to keep them from freezing up. . . . I would like to be in Honolulu long enough to take a sun bath today. . . . This makes fifty-five times that I have passed Cape Horn going and coming. I have said several times lately I'll never go there any more."

Sunday, August 30, at latitude. 6.35 degrees north, longitude 41.32degrees west, in the South Atlantic, having come through the doldrums without much difficulty, Goodwin wrote: "How are all the friends that push, and the girl that pulls this bright sunshiney day. You did nobly during the past week. . . . The ship looks as trim and clean as a yacht with her new coat of paint and her brass work shining and everything ready for the first tub of coal to smother it all up." But any chance for the hoped-for hundred-day passage was now gone—to do that, one needed a crew with which one could hold onto sail to the last minute, and then quickly set it again when the threat had passed. He had made a hundred-day passage once. And in those good old times he had signalized from a dozen to twenty ships in one day off Cape St. Roque, that great ocean crossroads off the bulge of Brazil for sailing ships headed north or south, coming from or going to either Cape Horn or the Cape of Good Hope. "This is the longest section of the voyage to me" wrote Goodwin, "I get restless and cannot sleep or eat and two weeks look longer to me now than two months did when we left Honolulu." On Sunday, September 13, when east of the Bahamas, Goodwin predicted a West India hurricane. And on Thursday he wrote: "We have had our hurricane and it did blow like a man." On September 28, after 128 days, Delaware Breakwater was finally made:

> The *Fong Suey* [*Foohng Suey*][2] which sailed about ten days before we did, anchored about an hour before we did. She lost some of her spars in the hurricane. I have just read a letter from Mrs. Goodwin and it is a relief to get into port again and find all well. I have taken a little pleasure in keeping this journal and if you do the same in reading it I shall be satisfied. I enjoyed the cigars you gave me and many pleasant thoughts of you all went up with the smoke.

In January 1909, on Goodwin's next—and final—passage, deep-loaded with coal from Baltimore bound for Honolulu, *Dirigo* put into Rio with a cracked plate in her stern twelve feet below the waterline. Fortunately the crack could be reached from inside, and the flow slowed, but it could not be stopped. And Goodwin feared that it might grow larger, as this area of the ship worked. This was exactly the type of failure that hidebound wooden-ship men believed explained the disappearance of many iron ships—a leaking wooden ship, they argued, took no one by surprise and could usually be pumped into port, or, at the very least, sank slowly. It was due only to Goodwin's insistence that the well be sounded every watch that there was not more than two-and-a-half feet of water in her when the leak was discovered.

Sam and Will wired Goodwin: "Do not discharge any more cargo than necessary. Tip the ship." But to have followed this plan in a harbor subject to fierce squalls would have endangered the ship, and Goodwin testily replied: "It made me ask myself the question—do you give me the credit of having the sense I was born with?" He had calculated that 2,500 tons of coal would have to be discharged in order to bring the leak up high enough to be repaired, and, in fact, 2,538 tons was what it took. A good repair was made. In further correspondence, both Goodwin and the Sewalls took care to be polite to each other, lest relations be even further strained.

When *Dirigo* finally arrived at Honolulu in May 1909, George Goodwin wrote: "It is utterly impossible for me to remain in the ship. I have to get out and have a rest. That leak and the hell hounds that I have had for a crew have made me a nervous wreck. I have just received your cablegram that Captain Chapman will relieve me and it was very welcome news." Chapman, who had finally been rewarded for his perilous years in *Shenandoah* with the command of *Kenilworth*, only to have that ship sold out from under him, received the command of *Dirigo* in compensation and with gratitude.

That is the way WE do business

Two years after retiring, Goodwin, upset by claims against *Dirigo*'s owners for damaged cargo which Goodwn believed could have been avoided, asked the Sewalls to either buy out his interests in *Dirigo*, the *Edward Sewall*, and the *William P. Frye* for $8,000, or let him return to command of *Dirigo*. Turned down on all counts, he responded:

> Your ultimatum with the great big *WE* are not disposed to give you the command of this ship received. . . . How familiar I am with your methods, and what a man has got to do to meet with your entire approbation, how you have used them that have gone before, both men and women. . . . I would rather go down in pauper's alley and black boots for a living than go to sea under existing conditions. . . . I have known from my very first time I went to Bath after resigning command of the *Sterling* and you did not find me as pliable as you wished that you did not have any use for me. . . . You have belittled me in many ways since. . . .
>
> I could not very well go out to sea if I wanted to as I have signed another agreement, and am writing a book from the time that Captain Clark left off in his

book.3 It will take in my views as I see them on the decline of the merchant marine, the so-called famous ships and what they were famous for, in fact it will take in everything from the builders, managers and his handy billies to the sailor catchers. I have data enough to have it published in the near future.

Goodwin never completed his book, more's the pity, but he did make a good start at writing an autobiography in which his criticisms of the Sewalls caused his lawyer to forbid him ever attempting to publish it. We have no such fears today, and, on the chance that Captain Goodwin's ghost might yet be haunting 411 Front Street, it seems only fair to finally give some of his complaints the light of day, so that the old shell-back's spirit might at last be able to complete its final passage to Valhalla.

Why do we not have an American merchant marine? It is largely owing to the greedy, narrow-minded, and short-sighted men who only want to see the dollars they are going to get to-day. Men who want one hundred percent profit to build a ship, sell all but enough so that they and their henchmen can manage it, and their uncles and cousins can furnish the stores. The dry owners can have the pleasures of seeing their money go to repairing the slop jobs done in the building of the ship.

The dry owners have suffered from the methods and brilliant management of these people. . . . It is the price you pay for building commissions and cost of managing that make a ship under the American flag so expensive to run. . . . What have these shipbuilders ever done that their interests should be protected to the detriment of the American merchant marine? . . . Did you ever see any of them wearing . . . a Grand Army button?4 They are not built that way. When it comes to fighting, they stay home and "Let George do it," and pick up the crumbs that are gathered from their country's misfortunes. In looking after political snaps is where they shine, and if they are not found on one side of the fence they will crawl over to the other side. . . .

No one ever knows what it costs these people to build a ship. They are their own time-keepers, their own book-keepers, and their own auditor, and if you do not want to become unpopular you must not ask questions. If you do you will not receive any satisfaction. They may condescend to tell you that that is the way WE do business, and you will be treated the same as others. They will send you a statement to sign that you will have to take for granted is correct because there is nothing to verify it, with a supplement saying, "If this statement is not returned in —— days we will enter it on our books as correct." . . . [The master] can make out his requisition and they will send the goods to the ship, but not the bill and the master never knows what the things cost yet he is asked to sign a statement at the end of the voyage about which he does not know a thing.

These people, or their agents, charter the ship, employ the stevedore and freight clerk. The shipping orders go to the last named who will receive anything that comes along regardless of its fitness to go into the ship. . . . The captain is

Dirigo *lying at Howard Street Wharf, San Francisco, 1910. The French "bounty ship" barks astern and across the wharf, have dressed ship for Bastille Day, July 14. The bark lying across the wharf from* Dirigo *is the* Marechal de Villars, *2,198 tons, launched at Nantes in 1899. She, like* Dirigo, *would be sunk by a German submarine in World War I.* ANDREW NESDALL

ignored entirely. If he knows what is due his position as master and part owner of the ship, he will probably walk around feeling like something marked down from thirty cents. However, if the cargo does not turn out all right . . . he is the man who is jumped on and his primage is curtailed to the extent of five per cent of the reclamation paid on the damaged cargo. . . .

When I was in the *Sterling* we had to carry cargoes at a lower rate than the steel ships, but [with *Dirigo*'s second voyage] . . . the conditions were reversed. The *Dirigo* was loading at the same dock, getting our cargo on many occasions out of the same lighter, part for us and part for the other ship, which was built of wood and nearly twenty years old, chartered by the same people, and consigned to the same people in San Francisco; yet this wooden ship was getting one dollar and a half more per ton than the *Dirigo*. I never received any satisfaction when I asked about it at the time or since. But I have learned more about some of the methods used in high finance. . . . I also believe the time is coming when a man, who has given his employer the best there is in him during the best years of his life, will have a pension according to his position. This will go further towards getting better services and bringing capital and labor together than anything on earth.

What he must have been in the heyday of his youth

Captain Omar Chapman, who in 1909 took command of *Dirigo*, was born in 1854, probably in Damariscotta, Maine. Chapman had commanded the Bath ship *Alameda* and the splendid three-skysail ship *John R. Kelley* until 1899, when she dragged ashore and was wrecked in the Falkland Islands. Chapman left the islands as captain of the big Thomaston ship *Cyrus Wakefield*, which had sought refuge while carrying the body of Captain Fred Henry, a man much disliked and who had died under mysterious circumstances.

In 1911 Chapman "stopped" at home due to illness in the family, and *Dirigo* was taken for a round voyage by Captain Walter Mallett of Topsham (Walter was master builder Elisha Mallett's nephew). In December Captain Chapman, at his home in Newcastle, Maine, while awaiting *Dirigo*'s arrival at New York from San Francisco, learned that the writer Jack London, with wife, servant, and dog, would likely be joining *Dirigo* for her next passage, carrying coal from Baltimore to Seattle. The gentlemanly Chapman was concerned:

> In view of the kind of officers and crews we are obliged to carry now, I fear his impressions . . . would receive a sad jolt. . . . As you know the cabin furniture and fixtures are getting worn, especially the bath room. The tub has a hole in it and is out of commission, and the toilet would have to be fixed if a lady is to use it. . . . Please be sure to tell him under what difficulties we have to sail ships now.

A week later Chapman wrote that he was trying to find a "suitable" mate:

> There is one in Baltimore who came east in the *Aryan*. He has got on a drunk and left his ship there. I believe he is a good man at sea. He was master of Mighel & Budrow's[5] ships for several years, until whiskey got the best of him. I think perhaps he is the best man [I] can find. I am not sure of him either.

This description perfectly fit Fred Mortimer, the epitome of the Down East mate, who had, in fact, been the mate on *Dirigo*'s westward passage under Mallett. In *The Mutiny of the Elsinore*,[6] Jack London's novel based on his *Dirigo* experience, the first mate, Mr. Pike, is drawn from Fred Mortimer, while Captain Chapman was the model for the *Elsinore*'s Captain West. Both were great men, the Londons concluded, and also unfathomable.

At Baltimore the Londons were disillusioned by the appearance of the crew—the only member who met their expectations as to how a sailor should look was a cadet from a school ship. Captain Chapman, however, thought them good enough, despite there being but few real sailors in their number. The novel's narrator wrote:

> They did not walk. They slouched and shambled; some even tottered, as from weakness or drink. But it was their faces . . . ships always sailed with several lunatics or idiots in their crews. But these looked as if they were all lunatics or feeble-minded. . . . There was something wrong with all of them. Their bodies twisted, their faces distorted, and almost without exception they were undersized.

The basic premise of London's blatantly racist novel is the contrast drawn between the tall, resolute, and civilized fair-haired American Aryans of the cabin, and the cowardly, sawed-off, brutish, dark-haired Euro-trash of the forecastle. An evil trio of troublemakers, ex-jailbirds, included "a hybrid Irish-Jew," and another "in whose veins ran God alone knows what Semitic, Babylonish, and Latin strains."

Although he drank too much ashore, and had several other failings, in the narrator's eyes Mr. Pike clearly belonged to the superior species:

> Mr. Pike, on these delicious [trade wind] nights, stands his first watch after midnight in his pajamas. He is a fearfully muscular man. Sixty-nine years seem impossible when I see his single, slimpsy garments pressed like fleshings against his form and bulged by heavy bone and huge muscle. A splendid figure of a man! What he must have been in the heyday of youth two score years and more ago passes comprehension.

Jack London made Pike older than Mortimer then was, perhaps to be able to place him aboard true clippers in his youth, great ships manned by true sailors of old, "brisk, devilish, able-bodied men; who fought their officers . . . who killed and were killed, but who did their work as men." In a letter to Mark Hennessy, London's wife Charmian wrote of Mortimer:

> Mortimer . . . was the absolute pink of a bucko mate. We secretly laughed when at times his grim contempt of the poor material at his command wished the modern laws were not so strict about disciplining. We came to realize that his ability and judgment were beyond question. He was an incredibly powerful man, each year signing on a year or two younger than his age. . . . Strong as a gorilla, he was seamed and lined, weather-baked of face to mahogany hue. And his eyes were those of an eagle and missed nothing. Those enormous paws I likened to the "block" fists one draws from in art school. Mighty hands, and one shivered at the thought of the unfortunates who must have run afoul of their sleepmaking blows.

Of Captain Chapman, as met on a cold Baltimore wharf, she wrote:

Taken aback does not describe our emotions when that tall, remotely lofty gentleman, impeccable in winter greatcoat and hat, detached from the knot. He advanced unhurriedly, his ascetic, chiseled countenance suddenly rippling over with fine wrinkles in a welcoming smile. A faultlessly gloved hand clasped ours with mild hospitable pressure. There was even a twinkle of geniality in the light-blue regard that swept us.[7]

And here is Jack's version of the moment from the novel:

Captain West advanced to meet me, and before our out-stretched hands touched, before his face broke from repose to greeting . . . got the first astonishing impact of his personality. Long, lean, in his face a touch of race I as yet could only sense, he was as cool as the day was cold, as posed as a king or emperor, as remote as the farthest fixed star, as neutral as a proposition of Euclid.[8]

Once at sea, the narrator was perplexed by the distance that Captain West maintained from the everyday affairs of the ship, but in time came to understand:

He is the brains of the *Elsinore*. He is the master strategist. There is more to directing a ship on the ocean than in standing watches and ordering men to pull and haul. They are pawns, and the two officers are pieces, with which Captain West plays the game against sea and wind and season and ocean current. He is the knower. They are the tongue by which he makes his knowledge articulate.

Captain Chapman was dying of undiagnosed stomach cancer. Slowly starving to death, he was eventually unable to eat much more than egg whites from the few hens remaining in the shipboard flock. He was also missing his wife. Distracted, his normal caution failed him, and he was seduced into taking the treacherous Cape Horn shortcut of the Strait of Le Maire, from which his ship but narrowly escaped.

The following night, in an incident eerily similar to Jim Murphy's nearly fatal mistake aboard the *Frye* in 1908, Chapman also misjudged the strength of the easterly drift and nearly put his ship on bleak Walliston Island. She was saved thanks only to Mr. Mortimer's superb seamanship. The next morning found Captain Chapman looking, according to Charmian, "tragically drawn, and unapproachable." For the remainder of the passage he slowly withdrew from the world, although never losing his dignity nor his innate commanding presence. Eventually he could not leave his big brass bed.

Mr. Mortimer filled the void, and delivered *Dirigo* to Seattle in splendid order, 148 days out of Baltimore. Captain Chapman, shrunken to a skeleton, was gently carried to an ambulance, and thence to hospital, where he died two days later, having held on to life until his ship was safely in port. Charmian watched Mortimer watching the captain being carried ashore:

The great, rugged First Mate, best of his kind, stood expressionless, the weathered image of an Easter Island stone figure. His mighty fists hung loose by his sides. What emotions or hopes were within him he doubtless never did express. A great mate.

The Sewalls did not give Mortimer command—they had had enough of drunks in the cabin—and instead gave him a hundred-dollar bonus. Captain Mallett took *Dirigo* again, and Mortimer stayed on as mate. He reappears in another book when, with a typhoon threatening, Mallett ordered him not only to send the upper yards down on deck, but to lower and lash aloft the topgallant masts—a Herculean act of seamanship which was accomplished in short order.[9]

According to Charmian, a newspaper item reported that Fred Mortimer was killed in 1927 by a homicidal maniac aboard a rum-running schooner. His age was said to be seventy, but how could anyone have known for certain?

Cannibalism is what must occur

The diligent searcher in Jack London's *The Mutiny of the Elsinore,* a novel of questionable value, is, however, rewarded with pithy glimpses of, and insights into, life aboard *Dirigo*:

> I can see, now, that the problem of sailing a ship with five thousand tons of coal around the Horn is more serious than I had thought. So deep is the *Elsinore* in the water that she is like a log awash. Her tall, six-foot bulwarks of steel cannot keep the seas from boarding her. She has not the buoyancy one is accustomed to ascribe to ships. On the contrary, she is weighted down until she is dead, so that, for this one day alone, I am appalled at the thought of how many thousands of tons on the North Atlantic have boarded her and poured out through her spouting scuppers and clanging ports.[10]

Dirigo had delivered a cargo of barley to New York.

> Life is cruel. Among the *Elsinore*'s five thousand tons of coal are thousands of rats. There is no way for them to get out of their steel-walled prison, for all the ventilators are guarded with stout wire-mesh. On her previous voyage, loaded with barley, they increased and multiplied. Now they are imprisoned in the coal, and cannibalism is what must occur among them. Mr. Pike says that when we reach Seattle there will be a dozen or a score of survivors, huge fellows, the strongest and the fiercest. Sometimes, passing the mouth of one ventilator that is in the after wall of the chart-house, I can hear their plaintive squealing and crying from far beneath in the coal.[11]

After viewing the ship from one of its boats at sea:

I chanced to lift my eyes, and the glorious spectacle of the *Elsinore* burst upon me. I had been so long on board of her that I had forgotten she was a white-painted ship. So low to the water was her hull, so delicate and slender, that the tall, sky-reaching spars and masts and the hugeness of the spread of canvas seemed preposterous and impossible, and insolent derision of the law of gravitation. It required effort to realize that that curve of hull inclosed and bore up from the sea's bottom five thousand tons of coal. And again it seemed a miracle that the mights of men had conceived and constructed so stately and magnificent an element-defying fabric. . . .[12]

The wear and tear has been something enormous

Arthur Sewall died in 1900 presumably believing that a prosperous future awaited his growing fleet, yet 1903 saw the closing of the storied Sewall shipyard after the launching of the five-masted schooner *Kineo*, and in retrospect it should have been obvious that the days of the Sewall fleet were numbered

During the winter of 1903–04 Sam and Will worked in support of legislation that would give preference to American-flag ships carrying American coal to American naval bases on foreign soil, i.e., the Philippines, and to restrict commerce between the United States and the Philippines to American-flag ships. The "supply" bill became law, but restrictive provisos, Navy Department obstructionism, and a dearth of suitable American tonnage prevented it from becoming the hoped-for panacea.

The Philippine bill, initially passed, ultimately met fatal opposition from powerful interests, including cordage manufacturers, despite Sam's assurance that the Sewall fleet alone could provide sufficient tonnage for their needs. The Manila hemp trade, pioneered by Boston ship owner William F. Weld, had long been a mainstay of Boston ship brokers Henry W. Peabody & Co., who wrote the Sewalls in January 1904:

> So far as our hemp trade from the Philippines is concerned, you are doubtless aware that it is improbable that sailers will be employed for some years to come, if ever. Hemp is on a very high level and consequently manufacturers desire to get their hemp into their mills as soon as possible. . . . Our firm have used American sailers in our trade with the Antipodes for two generations, and our interests and desires lay in a continuance of that form of transportation. The change to steamers came against our will and to our detriment. . . . However, the employment of steam was inevitable, and we have been obliged to so recognize it.

And "steam," at the time, meant foreign-flag ships.

The story of *Kineo* is one of the oddest chapters in the Sewall saga. The development by Maine—mostly Bath—builders of massive multimasted wooden schooners for the East Coast coal trade began in the 1880s, reaching its peak in the early 1900s. The profitability of these schooners came in good part from their low operating expenses, i.e., small crews, made possible by using steam power even to trim sheets, and large demurrage earnings in congested mid-Atlantic coal ports. Despite the inherent disadvantages of the fore-and-aft rig offshore, not to mention structural issues more severe than those experienced by the Big Four, the Sewalls tried to persuade schooner owners to join them in bidding on coal cargoes for the Philippines, but the schooner men showed better sense.

Kineo, of 2,128 tons and fitted with water ballast tanks, was intended for both coastal and deepwater service. She performed reasonably well coastwise, although Captain Frank Patten complained that her lack of a raised poop, along with her fine stern, made her dangerously wet aft and forced him to heave-to when "we ought to be making 240 miles a day." Her disastrous circumnavigation in 1905–06, carrying naval coal to Manila from Norfolk, ended any illusions the Sewalls may have entertained regarding the replacement of square-riggers by schooners. Captain Patten's letter after arriving at Philadelphia with Hawaiian sugar in November 1906 summed up the experiment:

> I made fair progress from time of sailing until reaching 29 S Lat. and then my troubles commenced. We had continued bad weather then until reaching around north of the River Platte.
>
> The seas were heavy and the ship has been dismantled five different times. Sails gone and unable to make repairs for weeks at a time owing to the fact of the seas making such breach right over the ship. To make matters worse our tubes in boiler gave out and everything had to be done by hand with no means aboard for heaving. Crew and officers both unaccustomed to handle this class of craft. The wear and tear has been something enormous and both sails and ropes are now in very bad condition. All our time nearly has been spent in repairing and patching to enable us to get along. We had a fore sail washed away by a sea breaking into it while set reefed. . . .
>
> During one gale she shipped a very heavy sea over stern, smashing boat to small pieces and bending and twisting davits, starting stern to leaking, filling lazarette full of water, destroying stores, washing away everything about decks, destroying gear, causing after house to leak badly. . . .
>
> There is not a mast hoop left on the ship. She has shot them to pieces. . . . The foretopmast is gone badly, the spanker topmast struck by lightning and pole shattered. . . . In all we have lost 14 sails this trip. And for the most time while running our 6,000 miles of Easting down the *Kineo* has been under water so the chances to make repairs to sails have been extremely rare. Oftentimes the schooner has been obliged to steer N. E. when her course was S. E., and my experience in the *Kineo* off Cape Horn is a repetition of what the *Gov. Ames* went through, and what every other big schooner will go through that is unfortunate enough to go there.[13]

Patten had had to put into Melbourne in distress with the entire ship's company—save his small daughter and the ship's boy—reduced to crawling due to the effects of *beri beri* after stores were destroyed by a typhoon and tropical rot.

Although the five-masted barkentine—square-rigged on the foremast—which the Sewalls had Boston naval architect B. B. Crowinshield design for them, would surely have performed better than *Kineo*, it, too, would have been unsuited for working through the doldrums or doubling Cape Horn. The Sewalls would build no more ships. And although Sam's letter book for these years would contain far more correspondence concerned with his other investments, Arthur Sewall & Co. would doggedly carry on the management of the fleet until patience would be rewarded by the high prices offered for even old tonnage by the World War I shipping boom.

It should be noted that, during the lean years leading up to the war, when many of the world's surviving square-riggers had been sold to single-ship corporations dedicated to squeezing out the last possible profits by means of stinting on every possible expenditure, Sam and Will, while by no means turning into spendthrifts, continued to spend the money necessary to maintain their ships in the manner to which they were accustomed. Whereas for many years Sewall ships had been ships that many sailors avoided, now they were among the best-found ships sailing.

Far below the humming traffic

In 1900, at Arthur Sewall's death, there were but sixty-eight square-riggers remaining under the American flag. The Sewall fleet, the largest fleet of American square-riggers engaged in world trade, consisted of eleven square-riggers and two schooners. Yet to come were the four-masted bark *William P. Frye* and the five-masted schooner *Kineo*. Of these vessels, the fates of the schooner *Alice Archer*, the four-masted barks *Arthur Sewall*, *Roanoke*, *Shenandoah*, and *Susquehanna*, and the ship *Iroquois*, have already been dealt with. The final chapters of the lives of other members of the fleet now follow:

The ship *Henry Villard* was sold in Honolulu in 1901 for $42,500. Reduced to a barge, she was burned at Seattle in 1926 (as was the old Sewall ship *Oriental*).

The four-masted schooner *Carrie A. Lane* was sold in 1902, and was wrecked on the Ivory Coast, Africa, in 1918.

In 1898 the four-masted bark *Kenilworth* had been returned to New York by Jim Murphy, who had been dispatched to Valparaiso upon word of the death of Captan Jim Baker. Her long career with the Sewalls ended ignominiously with her notorious twice-broken passage from Philadelphia with coal to San Francisco, which began under Captain Jabez Amesbury in August 1906. In February 1907, after 181 days—two months of which was spent off Cape Horn—*Kenilworth* put into Montevideo in distress, with sails blown away, yards and steering gear broken, and crew battered and demoralized. On April 5, although now very foul, she set out again.

On September 4 *Kenilworth* turned up back at Rio, her crew again battered and demoralized, having failed to round Cape Horn or to reach San Francisco by way of the Cape of Good Hope. Captain Amesbury, who was worried about corroded bow plates, was done with her, and Joe Sewall was sent down to tend to her—he claimed that the

Ship W. F. Babcock *at New York at the turn of the century. A bow port, installed for loading West Coast timber, appears below the hawsepipe. Built in 1882, the* Babcock *was owned by the Sewalls until 1907. According to Mark Hennessy, who evidently had access to the ship's log kept on a passage from San Francisco to Philadelphia in 1905–06, Captain M. T. Bailey made an entry describing an amazing two weeks, beginning sixteen days out of port, when the ship was accompanied by an immense school "of the tunny [tuna] tribe," extending as far as the eye could see. At one point, in light weather, the fish were so dense that the* Babcock *was brought to a standstill. All together the school accompanied the* Babcock *for over 2,000 miles until a ship that crossed their bow became the new attraction. In 1912 a surveyor found the* Babcock *to be in remarkably good condition; she was cut down to a barge a year or two later.* Mariners Museum

job almost killed him. In December she set sail once again for 'Frisco, under Captain Will Taylor, arriving in eighty-eight days. At San Francisco, after being promised to Omar Chapman, she was sold to the Alaska Packers Association and renamed *Star of Scotland*. In 1942, having been re-rigged as a six-masted schooner, she was torpedoed off Southwest Africa.

The ship *W. F. Babcock* was sold in 1907 for $30,000. In 1913 she was barged at New York.

The ship *Benj. F. Packard*—like *Kenilworth*, she was not built by the Sewalls—was sold in 1909 to the Northwestern Fisheries Co. for employment in the Alaskan salmon-packing business. She made her last trip to Alaska in 1924. In 1925, loaded with lumber, she was towed to New York by way of the Panama Canal. In 1939, after a number of years on display as a "pirate ship" at Playland, the Rye Beach, New York, amusement park, the old ship, her sheer still fair, was scuttled off Eaton's Neck, Long Island, in Long Island Sound.[14] Before her scuttling the panels and furniture of her after cabin were removed and have been restored and reassembled for display at Mystic Seaport.

The four-masted bark *Erskine M. Phelps*, the "clipper" of the Sewalls' steel ships, was sold in 1913 for $100,000 to the Union Oil Co. and turned into a schooner barge. After use as a depot barge at Manus Island in the Pacific during World War II she was scuttled by the navy in 1945.

The four-masted bark *Dirigo* was sold for $140,000 in 1915, and in 1917 was sunk by a German submarine off the Irish coast.

The four-masted bark *Edward Sewall* was sold in 1916 to the Texas Company, which sold her to the Alaska Packers in 1922, who renamed her *Star of Shetland*. In the late 1920s she was laid up along with others in the fleet, as the Packers shifted to steam. In 1936, loaded with salt and scrap metal, she was sailed to Japan and presumably was soon scrapped, following in the wake of two Sewall-built sisters, the *Star of Lapland*, ex-*Atlas*, and *Star of Zealand*, ex-*Astral* (the third Sewall-built Standard Oil bark, *Star of Poland*, ex-*Acme*, had been lost in 1917 on the coast of Japan).

The five-masted schooner *Kineo* was sold to the Texas Company in 1916 and was converted to the motor ship *Maryland*.

The bark *Kaiulani*, built by the Sewalls in 1899, was never a member of the Sewall fleet. She became *Star of Finland* in the Alaska Packers' fleet, and, being a great favorite, was retained by the association for some years after it laid up its sailing fleet, and appeared in some movies. In 1939 she was sold for a good price and put back to sea—the last Sewall-built vessel known to be under sail—carrying lumber to Durban. At Hobart, Tasmania, she was bought by the U.S. Army, which barged her. She ended up in the Philippines and was finally broken up *circa* 1974. Parts of her are preserved in San Francisco.

On January 28, 1915, in the South Atlantic, the four-masted bark *William P. Frye*, Captain Herman Kiehne, was sunk by the German raider *Prinz Eitel Friedrich*. The *Frye* was the first American ship sunk in World War I. In 1922, for reparations, $157,066.65 was awarded for her loss, the owners, after deductions for insurance paid and government charges, dividing $140,653.07. She was believed to have cost $150,000 when new.

Although the 1876 ship *Indiana* had been sold in 1898 for $20,000 to the Alaska Packers Association, she deserves inclusion here not only for her long service to the Sewalls, but because we met her at the beginning of this book while she was still on the ways, as Cleveland Preble was finishing off Captain John Delano's walnut secretary. It will be recalled that Captain Delano did not remain with her. After *Indiana*'s maiden passage to San Francisco, Captain John Drummond wrote the Sewalls that "she is the best ship in every respect that I have ever sailed in. She is all I can ask for. . . ." Drummond claimed that she had entered San Francisco Bay at fourteen knots, outrunning a pilot schooner.

In 1925, in a world vastly changed from that of 1876, *Indiana* went to Hollywood,

The 1876 ship Indiana, *a relic from a vanished world, in 1931 during the filming of the movie* The Suicide Fleet, *in which the ship* Bohemia, *built by the Houghtons in 1875, was sunk by gunfire and explosive charges. Note that* Indiana's *lower topsail yards have been removed, and that her lower topsails have been sewed to her upper topsails for a previous movie role in which she portrayed a vessel of an earlier era. Remarkably, after fifty-five years, many spent in the punishing Cape Horn trade,* Indiana's *sheerline appears to be about as fair as it was that day in 1876 when Arthur Sewall ordered Cleveland Preble to take his hatchet to Captain Delano's elegant walnut secretary.* ANDREW NESDALL

appearing in *The Colonial Dame* and *The Yankee Clipper*. In the latter she played alongside the ship *Bohemia*, which had been built by the Houghtons in 1875 for Captain Delano. Delano made only one voyage in her, presumably leaving her in anticipation of moving into the cabin of the fine new ship *Indiana*, being built by his brother-in-law, Arthur Sewall. In 1936 *Indiana*, still afloat at age sixty, and with here rig intact, blew ashore at Long Beach and later that year was burned to celebrate Harbor Day.

In 2008 the remains of the hull of the 1874 ship *Occidental*—Captain William Dunphy's pride, and aboard which Captain Williams was stabbed to death—can yet be viewed in a shallow cove on Kill Van Kull, at Port Johnson, Bayonne, New Jersey. According to an article in the January 3, 1999, *New York Times*, the old ship's bones lay

Harold Marsh Sewall's library at 963 Washington Street, Bath Maine Maritime Museum

Opposite: Two views of the Sewall shipyard property during its lease to the Texas Company, 1916–21. Both views include the Sewalls' 411 Front Street office building, overlooking the activity. The northerly view shows something of the massive infrastructure erected in the old New England—formerly Goss & Sawyer and, before that, Johnson Rideout—yard. The Texas Company built thirty-five vessels, including ten steam tankers, large-sized for their day. Concrete foundations are all that remain of the complex today. The old Sewall yard is presently slated for a residential development. Maine Maritime Museum

"far below the humming traffic crossing the Bayonne Bridge." Her hull has been burned to the waterline—to the level of the lower 'tweendeck beams—and in the 1980s her stern was wantonly removed to make room for a pipeline structure.

Not one of them besides our own is alive

In 1907 some of the shipyard tools were sold. From 1916 to 1922 the yard was leased to the Texas Company for the building of tankers. In 1924 Mark Hennessy began his association with the Sewalls, serving as office boy at 411 Front Street. In 1929 the firm's account with Baring Brothers was closed out, after more than a hundred years.

Oscar Trufant Sewall died of pneumonia at Greenwich, Connecticut, January 19, 1914. He was fifty-four.

William Dunning Sewall II, 1861–1930
MAINE MARITIME MUSEUM

Samuel Swanton Sewall, 1858–1935
MAINE MARITIME MUSEUM

Harold Marsh Sewall died October 28, 1924, in New York City, where he had undergone an operation. He was sixty-four. Before leaving Bath he left his family an informal will. Of the spacious "homestead" on Washington Street, he wrote: "Every article and every book is in its appropriate place, and to disrupt this arrangement is to destroy the harmony and the fitness of it all." (One can well believe a description of Harold by a family member as having been a small man who smoked cigarettes and who possessed something of a glove fetish.) His old friend Arthur Staples, who liked Harold very much and was in awe of his intellect, wrote of him that it a was shame that with Harold's great abilities he had not "been kept continually in public service."

> He was born to wealth. He has always had it and has enjoyed it though consumed by ambition unfulfilled. . . . If he had been born poor and compelled to work as some of us he would have been far more in accord with the general voter and far happier.[15]

Ned Sewall died in Bath on July 7, 1926, age sixty-three, apparently having been brought there to die by the family from an out-of-state old sailors' home. His death certificate stated that he died of stomach cancer, although family members of a later generation were told that he had died of syphilis. They had also been told of an incident in which Ned had dangled a prostitute from a balcony of the Plaza Hotel in New York,

April 1889. The ship Benj. F. Packard *departs New York for San Francisco, with Captain Zaccheus Allen in command for his first of many voyages in her cabin. The handsome and long-lived* Packard *was built in 1883 by Goss, Sawyer & Packard, the Sewalls' northerly neighbors. She was owned by the Sewalls from 1888 until 1909. Her original cabin interior has been reassembled for display at Mystic Seaport, Mystic, Connecticut.*
MAINE MARITIME MUSEUM

which possibly lay behind the aforementioned $2,000 bail. Ned would today probably be diagnosed as a classic manic-depressive, for starters. Given that manic-depression is often inherited, Ned's very much more extreme behavior may shed some light on his father Edward's difficulties as well.

On April 25, 1930, Will Sewall—William Dunning Sewall II—age sixty-nine, died at Kittery, Maine, as a result of an accident with his chauffeured automobile. In the Bath *Times* story on his death he was described as "Prominent Banker, Former Shipbuilder, Honored Citizen, and Man of Highest Integrity." An editorial noted: "Possessed of much wealth, Mr. Sewall was always among the foremost to open his purse generously for all worthy causes and his service and contributions to the Bath City Hospital at the time of its direct need will never be forgotten."

Samuel Swanton Sewall retired to an orange grove in Redlands, California, where he died on February 10, 1935. In January 1900 he had written his brother Oscar:

Perhaps critics will explain how it happens that of all of the firms in the country which were in our business of managing *deep water* ships, not one of them besides our own is *alive* in the same business today. All the others, without exception, have been unable to maintain the efficiency of their fleets and those still nominally in the business are simply wearing out their old ships.

As it happened, of course, this was probably just the time that the Sewalls should have cashed in their fleet and joined George Dearborn, Oscar, Dron Chesebrough, and the Flints in American–Hawaiian Steamship Co. Instead, they stayed with the ship, reaping fame as the last of the old order, rather than fortune with the new.

The books of Arthur Sewall & Co. finally closed on March 31, 1963.

Although we are concerned here with the maritime Sewalls, and not their wives or children, an exception will be made for Will and Mary Sewall's son Sumner, 1897–1965, the most notable Sewall of his generation. Sumner withdrew from Harvard to serve in the American Ambulance Field Service in France and later became a decorated pilot in the U.S. Army Air Corps, shooting down seven enemy planes and two balloons. He then became involved in organizing the first commercial airmail carrier. After service in the Maine legislature he was the wartime governor of Maine from 1941 to 1945, and later served as a military governor in Germany. He married a Russian countess, Helen Elena (Embach) Evans, the vivacious mistress of York Hall.

Capt. Allen never suggested cutting the finger off

We cannot leave this story without laying Captain Zack Allen to rest. We last saw Zack in command of the Sewalls' ship *Harvester*. In 1884 Zack took command of the ship *Charles Dennis*, built and owned at his hometown of Richmond. Then, from 1889 to 1896 and from 1897 to 1904, Zack commanded the three-skysail-yard ship *Benj. F. Packard*, built next door to the Sewalls in 1883, and purchased by them in 1887.

Employed primarily in the Cape Horn trade, the *Packard* under Zack gained a reputation as the "battleship of the American merchant marine," and Zack became known as "Tiger" Allen. The *Packard* was twice in *The Red Record*, although considering Zack's notoriety one would have expected many more entries. One of the cases involved the 1894 story of two young men, named Day and Nicoll, both from well-to-do families, who had shipped as "boys" for a Cape Horn passage, and who, according to *The Red Record*, charged the first mate—Zack's son Joe—and the second mate—a Mr. Turner—with extreme abuse. Nicoll was said to have been seriously injured by being kicked by Joe Allen.

A sensational story published by the *New York Herald*, October 13, 1894, was far less restrained than *The Red Record* entry, describing a nonstop orgy of violence and said to have been based on entries from Day's diary. Additionally, the food was said to have been very bad. Oscar Sewall made inquiries and in a letter to Bath deemed the reports "very much exaggerated," claiming that the two young men were reprobates sent to sea for their own good. In fact, Nicoll later wrote and signed a statement that read:

Captain Zaccheus "Tiger" Allen when master of the ship Benj. F. Packard, *1889–96, 1897–1904.* MAINE MARITIME MUSEUM

Second mate Tom Turner of the ship Benj. F. Packard.
Captain Zack Allen's son Joe was first mate; both mates were reputed to be "buckos." RICHMOND HISTORICAL AND CULTURAL SOCIETY

In regard to the statement made in the *N. Y. Herald* as to the treatment of the boys on the *B. F. Packard*, I as one of them wish to deny the ill-treatment. It is true that I injured my leg & finger but that might happen to anyone & I had all the care the circumstances would allow. Capt. Allen never suggested cutting the finger off although we both agreed that it might have been done on shore. This is the first statement on this subject made by me. J. H. Nicoll.

Zack stayed ashore for a voyage in 1896 in order to appear as witness in a suit brought by the Sewalls against the San Francisco towboat company whose tug, in December 1895, towed the *Packard* onto Mission Bay Rock, causing considerable damage to her bow and keel. The question was not the fault of the company, but whether a larger and more valuable tug that had tied up to the *Packard's* side had then been adding propulsion. This was a crucial legal point, since the company's liability was limited to the value of the towing boat or boats. Despite persuasive evidence to the contrary, Zack testified that both tugs were in use. The court found otherwise, and the *Packard* lost heavily.

In 1899 Zack was found not guilty in a New York court for having made no effort to rescue a sailor fallen overboard.[16] The July 15, 1902, Bath *Daily Times* printed a story plucked from an unnamed New York daily regarding the upcoming amputation of part of the infected hand of the *Packard's* bosun, injured while hitting a seaman being held by Mate Joe Allen. The altercation reportedly began when the seaman coiled a line too slowly.

The April 19, 1904, the *Daily Times* published an interview with the retired Zack at his home in Richmond wherein the identity of the ship *Eric the Red* was confused with the Richmond ship *Red Cross*, and Ned Sewall was confused with Harold Sewall. Better yet, Zack was credited with having lashed Harold to a mast—evidently saving Harold was considered more praiseworthy than saving Ned. By 1959 the story had evolved within the family to the point where Zack, holding Harold by his left arm, swam for a day through shark-infested waters. This was said to be the cause of Zack's swollen left arm. It will be recalled that Ned, a strong swimmer, had saved himself.

In April 1910 Zack won a long court fight to ban baseball playing by boys on a field within ball-range of his house, where baseball had been played for twenty-five years. Zack died in 1915. It appears that son Joe, once the mate of the *Packard*, may have taken the well-trodden path to perdition earlier taken by Ned Sewall. Younger son Tom became a druggist.

One may mar a tale like this

When Arthur Sewall died in 1900 he was probably still dreaming of seeing the Sewall house flag snapping at the main trucks of a large fleet of big, steel, world-ranging barks. By 1907, however, the Belfast *Republican Journal* lamented: "Of Sewall's magnificent fleet of ships, only a remnant remains."[16] Arthur's legacy fladed quickly—Louis C. Hatch's 1919 900-page tome, *Maine, A History*—admittedly very thin on shipping—

contained a single citation for "Archer" [*sic*] Sewall, and that referred to the 1896 election.[17]

The Down Easters, published in 1929, a potboiler by the British writer Basil Lubbock, who had swallowed some of Jim Murphy's whoppers whole, began the resurrection.[18] In 1930–31 Frederick C. Matthews' two-volume seamark *American Merchant Ships, 1850–1900*, appeared, which included brief histories of about thirty wooden Sewall vessels.[19] In 1937 Mark Hennessy's *The Sewall Ships of Steel* hoisted the Sewall house flag on high. Old Arthur Staples wrote an over-the-top review of *Ships of Steel*, which appeared in the January 13, 1938 *Lewiston Evening Journal*:

> This book . . . is admirable in every way as a literary work. Of course we may not call recital of such matters "literature." But one may mar a tale like this. I am amazed at the diction, the style and the tact in the story.
>
> I knew Arthur Sewall "The Maritime Prince" very well as a lad. He gave me a railroad pass between Bath and Brunswick in 1877 without which I never could have gone to college. I remember his father quite distinctly—William D. Sewall. I knew Edward Sewall by sight, brother of Arthur. I was brought up as a playmate with Mark and Ned and Oscar, sons of Edward; Harold and Will were my beloved friends.
>
> Mark Hennessy has done a masterful job in characterizing Arthur Sewall; and it is no eulogy or biography or appeal to aristocratic forbears. Arthur Sewall was aristocratic enough without an ancestor. He was not a popular man; but he was indeed a prince. . . . How well I see Arthur Sewall and his few cronies, he had not many—John Ballou, Charles W. Larrabee, Gen. Tom Hyde, in a four-seater beach wagon behind a great gray horse setting out for Small Point. . . .

John Ballou was Bath's longtime police chief, a man so respected that being arrested by him was said to be an honor; Charles W. Larabee was a retired printer; General Tom Hyde was president of the Bath Iron Works.

> I do think that somebody—perhaps somebody in the Sewall family of today has recalled enough of the Sewalls of Arthur and Edward's day to tell the severe truth about a family of great adventurers, masterful courage, undaunted determination—the greatest shipbuilders on the American continent. It is a proud heritage—and never a stigma on the proud name. . . .
>
> Let us remember always that here were two dynasties of this life of the maritime prince. . . . His brother Edward was killed accidentally in the old Windsor Hotel in New York by falling down stairs in the great marble corridor. Edward's son, Samuel Swanton Sewall, a strange red-Sewall, red haired and freckled, reticent and powerful, carried on. Sewall & Co. had him as partner.

While it would be petty to nit-pick an old man's rosy-hued memorial to both the Sewalls and his youth, Staples's endorsement of Hennessy's generally fawning characterization of Arthur Sewall merits note. Doc Briry, also a playmate of the Sewall boys, and with no particular axe to grind regarding Arthur, endorsed, instead, a phrenologist's assessment—phrenology was a pseudo-science whereby character was supposedly divined by the shape and protuberances of the skull—commissioned by the *New York Herald* during the campaign of 1896.[20] Whether the conclusions resulted more from a close reading of the press rather than of Arthur's prominent protuberances, Briry judged it to be "finely worded and well thought out—a very true description of Mr. Sewall." A small portion, to wit:

> Both Bryan and Sewall are men of great courage, but that of Sewall is bulldog courage. . . . You would get bruised each time you ran up against him. That is, he would be about as easy to disturb as a block of granite. He is a money getter. His is the commercial nose all over. No one would ever get the best of him in a bargain. . . . You see his sagacity by his large, long nose; his acquisitiveness by its fullness about the nostrils. . . .
>
> Were it not for his large moral and logical faculties, he would be a selfish, grasping man. . . . His acquisitiveness and his ability to get the better of the men with whom he comes in contact would always be coming in collision with his sense of what is right and fair.

So who was Arthur Sewall, really? Letters exchanged between Arthur and Erskine Phelps, a wealthy Chicago shoeman who was the most intimate friend among Arthur's correspondents—they had met in a hotel when Arthur approached the stranger next door to borrow a clean shirt—shed further confusion. In July 1894, with the nation crippled by labor unrest, the gleaming stucco "White City" of the 1893 Chicago Columbian Exposition burned, possibly at the hands of striking Pullman workers, and an alarmed Phelps wrote Arthur: "It staggered, it reeled, all red and smoking hot, and then came the crash and thunder. . . . To-day we are waiting, watching, fearing what an angry howling mob will do at the gates of our city."

Arthur's response was as noteworthy for who he didn't blame as for whom he did:

> To-day that conflagration, that destruction of the White City seems to me to be the withdrawal of the purpose for which it was built: a second declaration to the world that the stability and greatness of our government is yet in doubt, that corruption infects our National Council, that patriotism is wanting when most needed, that personal ambition and greed govern when concession and compromise should be a factor. . . .

And yet, this was the very man whose ships would continue to be singled out for brutality. America's Gilded Age, of course, was also a Golden Age of Hypocrisy, and Arthur Sewall was nothing if not a man of his times. Although Arthur presented the retiring Reverend Dike with an around-the-world tour, there is no evidence that his business decisions were guided by religious conviction—especially if no one was watching—or that he wrestled with his conscience. Indeed, Arthur appears to have been entirely comfortable in his own skin, which fact—despite his refusal to court popularity—may well have lain at the core of the magnetism which, Joe Sewall noted, so attracted other men.

Arthur's rise in prominence and prosperity was limited by his stubborn—and even romantic—loyalty to the obsolete, demoralized, and fast-disappearing American sailing marine. Compared to many far-wealthier, more powerful, and also more ruthless men of industry and finance, with whom he sometimes dealt, Arthur was but a small-town, dry-humored, even quaint Down East nabob. Yet his name lives on. As unflappable and phlegmatic as ever—an enigma wrapped in a veil of pungent cigar smoke—Arthur smugly signed off to Phelps:

> Enough of this: I have now been at home about a fortnight, have my busines all snugged up and ready for a long period of dullness and inactivity and so far I am enjoying it very much. . . . I had a delightful [European] trip and have returned more fully convinced than ever that this is the spot in the whole world to live and die in.

The Shenandoah was running free

The celebrity of *Shenandoah*, the fabled flexible flyer, and of Captain Jim Murphy, great seaman and great showman, have been central to the survival of the Sewall legacy. In *Under Sail*, his classic account of a Cape Horn passage in Flint & Co.'s three-skysail-yard, Bath-built ship *A. J. Fuller*, Captain Felix Riesenberg—he had then been an ordinary seaman—did his part. His description of the 1897 meeting some seventy miles southwest of the great cape, of *Shenandoah*, speeding eastward, and the *Fuller*, slogging westward, concludes our tale:

> When south of Diego Ramirez, we passed the American ship *Shenandoah*, Captain "Shotgun" Murphy, bound from 'Frisco to Liverpool, with a cargo of grain. She was racing two English four-masted barks, and we were told that she dropped her hook in the Mersey a month ahead of them.
>
> When sighting the *Shenandoah* we were close to the wind on the starboard tack, standing about due west: the *Shenandoah* was running free, with the wind two points abaft her port beam, carrying everything to t'gans'ls, stays'ls, and jigger, a truly magnificent sight and the first sail we had seen since leaving the *Tam O'Shanter* off Cape Horn.
>
> When abeam we exchanged courtesies of the sea, dipping our ensign from the monkey gaff, and running aloft our "number," the gay string of lively colored flags, pennant, and burgee—J. V. G. B. of the International Code—the universal language of the sea.
>
> The *Shenandoah* also ran up her number, a spot of color in the beautiful spread of white cotton canvas on her yards. The sky was dull, but the clear air set

November 20, 1897. Shenandoah, *Captain William Dunphy, from Baltimore with coal, approaching San Francisco with a bone in her teeth.* ANDREW NESDALL

her off with cameo like distinctness against the grey background of the horizon. The deep blue of the sea smothered white under her bow and, as she rolled gracefully, the yellow gleam of her copper flashed along under her sleek black side, or else we caught a glimpse of her white decks over the line of her bulwarks, as she dipped to leeward.

We had sighted the sail ahead, and having our starboard tacks aboard, were accorded the right of way. . . . In obedience to this Law of the Sea, the four-masted ship *Shenandoah* starboarded a point, passing the *Fuller* well to windward and some five miles south of the Island of Diego Ramirez.[21]

1. A ship wore around to the opposite tack by falling off before the wind, rather than coming about by tacking with the wind from ahead.

2. *Foohng Suey*, a Glasgow-built bark owned by the old Boston–Hawaiian trading house of Brewer & Co., came under the American flag with the annexation of Hawaii.

3. Arthur H. Clark, *The Clipper Ship Era* (New York: G. P. Putnam, 1910).

4. Goodwin enlisted in the army in 1864 at age sixteen "for one year or so during the war." He

said he got all the soldiering he wanted, but no fighting.

5. William A. Mighell was the head of the California Shipping Company, organized in 1899. Charles Boudrow was a principal stockholder. By 1900 the company was said to be the largest owner of sailing tonnage in the world, with twenty-eight vessels, including former Flint & Co. ships *May Flint, Henry B. Hyde, S. D. Carlton, Pactolus, John McDonald, R. D. Rice, St. Francis, A. J. Fuller, St. James*, and *St. David*. Eleven other vessels previously managed by Mighell included the former Sewall ship *Carrollton*.

6. Jack London, *The Mutiny of the Elsinore* (New York: McKinlay, Stone & Mackenzie, 1913).

7. Hennessy Collection, library of the Maine Maritime Museum, 53-2-22.

8. *Elsinore*, p. 5.

9. Claire Rankin, *The Tall Voyagers* (Los Angeles: Ward Ritchie Press, 1965), p. 106.

10. London, *Elsinore*, p. 76.

11. London, *Elsinore*, p. 161.

12. London, *Elsinore*, p. 128.

13. Built in Waldoboro, Maine, in 1888, the *Gov. Ames*, the first East Coast five-masted schooner, had a difficult time off the Horn when sailing from Cape Henry to San Francisco in 141 days, later returning to the East Coast by way of the Horn and Liverpool.

14. Paul C. Morris, *A Portrait of a Ship, The Benj. F. Packard* (Orleans, MA: Lower Cape, 1987).

15. Arthur G. Staples, *The Inner Man* (1933), pp. 77–79; *Lewiston Evening Journal*, October 29, 1924.

16. Belfast *Republican Journal*, July 11, 1907.

17. Louis Clinton Hatch, *Maine, A History* (Somersworth, NH: New Hampshire Publishing Co., 1974). Originally published in three volumes. Incidentally, Googling "swedenborgian shipbuilder" in January 2008 resulted in 265 hits, all apparently repeating the claim that John McCain's selection of Sarah Palin was the most dunderheaded choice of a vice-presidential candidate since that of Arthur Sewall.

18. Basil Lubbock, *The Down Easters* (Glasgow: Brown, Son & Ferguson, 1929).

19. Frederick C. Matthews, *American Merchant Ships, 1850–1900* (Salem, MA: Marine Research Society, 1930–31). Matthews despised Lubbock, whose quick-and-sloppy book had scooped his far more substantial work.

20. Mark W. Hennessy, *The Sewall Ships of Steel* (Augusta, ME: Kennebec Journal Press, 1937), p. 6. Would that a phrenologist had had a go at Jim Murphy's bristly noggin!

18. Felix Riesenberg, *Under Sail* (New York: Harcourt, Brace & Co, 1918), pp. 120–23. The explanation for the fact that *Shenandoah* altered her heading to port after she "starboarded a point" is that steering orders were given in reference to the orientation of a forward-facing tiller, not the rudder. In Riesenberg's popular *Cape Horn* (New York: Dodd, Mead & Co, 1939), pp. 332–33, his account of the meeting is far more dramatic and includes different, unlikely, and even impossible details. In this later version *Shenandoah* "seared close by our stern, her colors snapping forward, and far aft stood the famous Captain Murphy, who waved his hand once in salute, returning the similar gesture of our captain." Perhaps Reisenberg was ordered by his editor to juice it up a bit—that he did so is a small blot on distinguished careers at sea and in letters. One does learn from this, however, that a special storm-weight ensign was carried.

APPENDICES

1. The Sewall Family Papers

One of the prime reasons that members of the Sewall family supported the creation of *Live Yankees* was to make the existence of the Sewall Family Papers, one of the outstanding collections of business papers in the world, better known and more frequently used by scholars and others.

With documents dating from 1761 to 1965—the bulk of the collection dating between 1840 and 1916—the Sewall Family Papers occupy more than 647 boxes in the library of the Maine Maritime Museum. The three main sections of the collection consist of Company Papers (216 boxes), Vessel Papers (336 boxes), and Family Papers (82 boxes). In 1991 the papers were donated to the Maine Maritime Museum by grandchildren and great-grandchildren of William D. Sewall II. Among this group, Nicholas Sewall had the most hands-on history with the collection and its preservation.

The papers survived thanks to the stewardship of several generations of Sewalls, and through great good fortune—fires in the old shipyard in 1934 and 1936 narrowly spared the old office building at 411 Front Street, where the papers then resided. In the 1950s a part of the collection was dumped in the Kennebec on the outgoing tide—it washed back again on the flood—and later some papers were burned at the Bath dump, but presumably these were but check stubs and other culch. While the surviving papers are far from complete—some vessels are represented by many boxes of documents, others, not at all—a very great deal has survived, and much of it is of great rarity, of much interest, and of inestimable value.

The late Mark Hennessy enjoyed a long and intimate relationship with the collection, and some documents from the collection appear to have migrated to the Hennessy Collection, also held at the library of the Maine Maritime Museum. Additionally, the Hennessy Collection contains the fruit of Mark Hennessy's many years of careful research into the Sewall collection. The two collections should thus be considered mutually complementary.

For all its treasures, the collection would be of very limited use to researchers were it not organized. Aided by thousands of hours of work contributed by volunteers, the mastermind who accomplished the daunting task of putting some 450,000 items in their proper place was archivist Elizabeth S. Maule. And when this was done, a 553-page catalog, *Inventory for Manuscript Collection MS-2, Sewall Family Papers,* was assembled, and published in 1995. Overseeing all was Senior Curator Nathan Lipfert. The author of *Live Yankees* acknowledges his great debt to all who had a hand in this process.

2. The Sewall Ships

Clark & Sewall, 1823–54
Brig 1 *Diana* 1823
Brig 2 *Orbit* 1823
Brig 3 *Lewis* 1825
(Brig *Charles* rebuilt 1827)
Brig 4 *Dummer* 1827
Brig 5 *Pleiades* 1828
Sch (2) 6 *Emulous* 1829
Ship 7 *Emperor* 1831
Ship 8 *Girard* 1831
Ship 9 *Tropic* 1832
Ship 10 *Ceylon* 1833
Ship 11 *Roger Sherman* 1835
Ship 12 *Diadem* 1838
Ship 13 *Ville de Paris* 1837
Ship 14 *Pennsylvania* 1840
Ship 15 *Genesee* 1841
Ship 16 *Rappahannock* (1) 1841
Ship 17 *Detroit* 1843
Ship 18 *Macedonia* 1845
Ship 19 *Rio Grande* 1846
Ship 20 *Switzerland* 1847
Ship 21 *John C. Calhoun* 1847
Brig 22 *Marcia* 1848
Ship 23 *Wm. D. Sewall* 1848
Ship 24 *Adriatic* 1850
Ship 25 *Sarah G. Hyde* 1851
Ship 26 *Erie* 1851
Ship 27 *Commerce* 1852
Ship 28 *Lady Franklin* 1853
Ship 29 *Samaritan* 1854

E. & A. Sewall, 1854–78
Ship A *Holyhead* (possibly Clark & Sewall) 1845
Ship B *Kineo* (1) 1855
Ship C *Hellespont* 1856
Ship D *Leander* 1857
Ship E *Valentia* 1858
Ship F *Vigilant* 1859
Ship G *Villafranca* 1859
Ship H *Ocean Scud* 1860
Ship I *Vancouver* 1862
Ship J *Vicksburg* 1863
Brig K *Glendale* 1863
Ship L *Intrepid* 1864
Bark M *Volant* 1864
Ship N *Ocean Signal* 1864
Ship O *Freeman Clark* 1865
Bark P *Frank Marion* 1865
Ship Q *Matterhorn* 1866
Bark R *Wetterhorn* 1866
Ship S *Hermon* 1868
Ship T *Tabor* 1869
Ship U *Undaunted* 1869
Ship V *Eric the Red* 1871
Ship W *Humboldt* 1872
* Ship X *Sterling* 1873
* Ship Y *Carrollton* 1872
Ship Z *El Capitan* 1873
Sch (3) 1 *Satilla* 1873
Ship 2 *Granger* 1873
Ship 3 *Occidental* 1874
Ship 4 *Oriental* 1874
Ship 5 *Continental* 1875
Ship 6 *Harvester* 1875
Ship 7 *Reaper* 1876
Ship 8 *Thrasher* 1876
Ship 9 *Indiana* 1876
Ship 10 *Challenger* 1877
Ship 11 *Thomas M. Reed* (1) 1877
Sch (3) 12 *Carrie S. Bailey* 1878
Ship 13 *Chesebrough* 1878
* Out of sequence as listed by E. & A. Sewall.

Arthur Sewall & Co. 1879–1903
Ship 14 *Solitaire* 1879
Ship 15 *Thomas M. Reed* (2) 1880
Sch(3) 16 *Belle Higgins* 1880
Sch(3) 17 *Kate Markee* 1880
Sch(3) 18 *S. M. Thomas* 1881
Ship 19 *Iroquois* 1881
Sch(3) 20 *B. L. Burt* 1881
Ship 21 *Henry Villard* 1882
Sch(3) 22 *Nora Bailey* 1882
Ship 23 *W. F. Babcock* 1882
Sch(3) 24 *Alice Archer* 1882
Ship 25 *Rainier* 1883
Ship 26 *Blanche Allen* 1883
Ship 27 *John Rosenfeld* 1884
Sch (3) 28 *Ada Bailey* 1884
Ship 29 *Willie Rosenfeld* 1885
Sch (3, later 4) 30 *Carrie A. Lane* 1887
Sch (4) 31 *Douglas Dearborn* 1889
Sch (4) 32 *Talofa* 1889

Sch (3) *Agnes E. Manson* 1889
Ship 34 *Rappahannock* (2) 1890
Sch (3) 35 *Aloha* 1890
Bark (4) 36 *Shenandoah* 1890
Sch (3) 37 *Tofa* 1891
Bark (4) 38 *Susquehanna* 1891
Bark (4) 39 *Roanoke* 1892
Bark (4) 40 *Dirigo* 1894
Bark (4) 41 *Erskine M. Phelps* 1898
Bark (4) 42 *Arthur Sewall* 1899
Bark (4) 43 *Edward Sewall* 1899
Bark 44 *Kaiulani* 1900
Bark (4) 45 *Astral* 1900
Bark (4) 46 *Acme* 1901
Bark (4) 47 *William P. Frye* 1901
Bark (4) 48 *Atlas* 1902
Barge 49 *S. O. Co. No. 93* 1902
Sch (5) 50 *Kineo* (2) 1903

Acme, Agnes E. Manson, Astral, Atlas, B. L. Burt, Diana, Dummer, Emperor, Henry Villard, Intrepid, Kaiulani, Kate Markee, Lewis, Ocean Signal, Orbit, Pleiades, S. M. Thomas, S. O. Co. NO. 93, and *Vicksburg* were either built on contract for other parties or were sold on the stocks or shortly afterwards.

Vessels owned and managed by the Sewalls which were purchased, or built under contract by another builder included brig *Almira,* 1847, ship *Champion* (P. R. Curtis for Clark & Sewall), ship *America* (Johnson Rideout for E. & A. Sewall); ship *Benj. F. Packard* (Goss, Sawyer & Packard, purchased by Arthur Sewall & Co.); *Bullion* (Brown & Stantial, Bath, purchased by Arthur Sewall & Co.); brig *Charles* (rebuilt by Wm. D. Sewall); sch. *Dicky Bird*, ex-*William C. French* (rebuilt by Arthur Sewall & Co.); ship *George Stetson* (A. Hathorn, purchased by Arthur Sewall & Co.); ship *J. B. Walker* (Edward O'Brien, purchased by Arthur Sewall & Co.); *McNear* (Henry McGilvery, purchased by Arthur Sewall & Co.); ship *Tacoma* (Goss, Sawyer & Packard, purchased by Arthur Sewall & Co.); bark *Olympic* (New England Co., purchased by Arthur Sewall & Co.); ship *Eclipse* (Goss, Sawyer & Packard), purchased and briefly owned by Arthur Sewall & Co.

Based on the lists in Sewall Family Papers inventory volume, and other sources.

3. LETTER OF INSTRUCTION

Dated December 13, 1869, addressed to Captain W. O. Frazier, sent to meet the arrival of the bark *Frank Marion* at Liverpool, and offering First Mate Frazier command of the ship *Matterhorn*:

To: Capt. W. O. Frazier:

Dear Sir.

We hereby give you command of the Ship "Matterhorn" now discharging at Antwerp subject only to instructions you may hereafter receive from us. On receipt of this we wish you to proceed immediately and take command of this ship either at Antwerp or Cardiff as you may reach her. This Ship is now under charter to Callao and back to U. K., from Cardiff. Charter-party will be handed you by Capt. Curtis, which charter you will proceed to execute on your part. In future while you hold command of this Ship, you will engage such business (in the absence of positive instructions from us), as in your judgement will net the most earnings.

We wish you personally to effect and attend to the business of the ship, exercising strict economy in your disbursements, making all possible dispatch in *Port and at Sea*: settling all her bills and accounts before leaving port, sending copies of same with Duplicates, with corrections, if any, from next port, writing us as often as once a week while in port and keeping us fully advised of all your proceedings. In case of disaster you will act for all concerned, making full protests, and having all her bills and accounts for repairs, &c duly vouched, that we may make due claim on our underwriters. Should you require funds for disbursements, with no freight on board to draw against, or in case of disaster & funds are required, and you cannot otherwise so well obtain them, and in your judgement you deem it best, you may draw upon us at not less than thirty days sight, for amount required, always being particular to advise us in duplicate of all Drafts, at time you draw. The balance of all freight & passage money, after reserving sufficient to cover your disbursements, you will remit, if in the U. States to Messrs. E. & A. Sewall, of Bath, Maine, if in a foreign port to Messrs. Baring Brothers & Co., London, Engd, to be placed three quarters (3/4) to the Cr. of E. & A. Sewall, Bath, Me., and one quarter (1/4) to the Cr. of Thomas M. Reed, Phippsburg, Me., making your remittance in Cash or approved bills, and as early after arrival as possible. Your compensation as master it is hereby mutually agreed shall be twenty dollars U.S. Currency pr. month wages and two & one half (2 1/2) pr. cent primage for present voyage, and five pr. cent for all future voyages, on all freight and passage money received after deducting all comss. [commissions] paid for procuring & collecting the same, together with all discounts for interest and short cargo, and bills paid for compressing, baling, and baging cargo, this to be in full for all your services, and for all savings of comms., and perquisites of every kind. You are at liberty while aboard to draw from Ship's funds, such amounts from time to time as you may require for your own personal expenditure, the balance of your account with the Ship to be paid by us, on the settlement of your accounts at Bath.

Wishing you every success, with safe and speedy passages.

We are Yours Truly

E. & A. Sewall

The form of this letter generally followed the letters of instruction issued by Clark &

Sewall, if somewhat longer. (Arthur Sewall & Co. letters were longer yet.) A second letter, no doubt reflecting the unusual circumstances of Frazier's promotion, added that twenty-one men all told was considered sufficient for the ship, that the ship was to be loaded "as deep as you consider safe," that the ship was to be kept well salted and ventilated, and that the ship was insured for this voyage for $30,000 on a valuation of $60,000.

4. WATKINS' CODE

Telegrams were expensive. The most common code used by American shipowners, brokers, and captains was The Ship Brokers' Telegraphic Code by E. T. Watkins, first published in Boston in 1881. Watkins wrote in his preface:

> It has been the aim of the author of this work, to compile a code for the use of ship brokers and others engaged in chartering vessels, that would be concise and explicit, and to effect a saving in the cost of telegraphing. . . . At the commencement, the words were taken from the English and Spanish languages only; but, upon checking over the proofs, many objectionable ciphers were discovered, and it was found necessary to replace these with Italian or French words. . . .

For reasons of secrecy, brokers (and others) had their own private codes. The Watkins code was designed to be used in conjunction with private codes:"VESUVIAN 348" would mean that the third, fourth, and eighth words of the message were taken from your private code, and the remainder from Watkins' code.

Code words, listed alphabetically, were divided into sections of application, i.e., negotiations for charter, state of markets, supply of tonnage, prospects, grain charters, livestock, cotton freights, lumber, East Indian freights, salt freights, coal freights, capacities and quantities, guano freights, position of ship, captain and crew, standing of firms, and so on and so forth

Below is a telegram in Watkins' code sent to Bath by Captain F. B. Perkins, ship *Henry Villard*, at Portland, Oregon. September 24, 1890:

Text	Translation
Estimated damage	
(Vacuum)	$4,000.00
Require	
(Uvular)	$1,300.00
(Timbalear)	Ship paying 2$^1/_2$% commission on advance and cost of insurance.
(Vindicatif)	She will sail in about three days.

5. SQUARE HALVES

Captains of schooners commonly sailed under what was known as "square halves," as set out below in an excerpt from the letter of instruction for Captain Fred L. Blair:

> Bath, Maine October 18, 1884
> Dear Sir:
> We give you command of schooner *Carrie S. Bailey* now at Wilmington, Del. on date of your joining her at that port, to be sailed by you subject to our instructions only and so long as your services shall prove satisfactory to us. . . . [Boilerplate re. engaging business, remitting freights, not contracting debts on the schooner's credit, sending statements, telegraphing arrivals, writing letters, etc.]
>
> As to your compensation as master you hereby agree to the following terms, to wit you are to victual & man the vessel and furnish labor to keep the hull & rigging of schooner in good repair. You are to pay one half pilotage and towage and wharfage bills & all stevedore bills. You are to receive one half of gross freight earned less all commissions paid for procuring & collecting same . The vessel pays all bills for material & repairs and other bills not above specified to be paid by Capt.
>
> You will receive advices and instructions from us from time to time. Wishing you safe & speedy passages and all success.
> Yours truly
> Arthur Sewall & Co.

Square halves à la the Sewalls differed slightly from the usual arrangement in that they required a schooner captain making an offshore passage to provide (usually by hire) his own chronometer. Square-riggers were outfitted with one chronometer.

6. PROTESTS AND AVERAGES

The ships' files in the Sewall Family Papers contain many "protests" and "average" statements. "Noted" protests are sworn statements entered by a captain with the consul or appropriate local authorities shortly after his arrival in a port, briefly describing damage to ship or cargo and the circumstances responsible, and actions taken. In effect, the protest was against the ship's owners being held accountable through any fault of the ship or the master, officers, or crew for damage or loss, by protesting against "all and every person and persons whom it doth or may concern, and against the winds, and waves, and billows of the seas," and so forth, which are claimed to have been responsible.

Protests were also entered if a passage had been broken by putting into an intermediate port, as this could otherwise negate insurance policies, or against a charterer or consignee who had cost the ship money by not meeting their obligations.

An extended protest, following up on the noted protest, typically was a lengthy document filling in all the details, as part of an average adjuster's statement, was usually written in elegant longhand or printed to appear as such, and nicely bound. The average adjuster was engaged to negotiate a settlement with the other interested parties, hopefully avoiding legal action.

A claim for "average"—in this usage "average" meant "loss" or "expense" in Medieval

Latin—came under either "general" average or "particular" average, both involving the apportioning of losses or expenses among the interested parties. A claim under "general average" required some form of sacrifice for the greater good, the classic example being the cutting away of masts in a storm to save a vessel, in which case the owner of the cargo (or his insurance underwriter) would be expected to help compensate the ship's owner for the loss. If, on the other hand, high winds dismasted the ship, the loss would come under "particular average," to be borne by the owner or his underwriter. Needless to say, log entries played a significant role in determining which form applied.

An extraordinary expense voluntarily or reasonably incurred at a time of peril to preserve property endangered in a common adventure qualified as a sacrifice for general average. General average cases were often exceedingly complicated, as they were often international in scope, and therefore most charter parties, bills of lading, and insurance policies specified compliance with the York–Antwerp Rules. The appraised value of the vessel also figured prominently in average settlements, it being desirable for the owner to obtain as low a figure as possible so as to lessen the vessel's proportion of contributory interest, and so that the value of the vessel did not exceed the insurance coverage.

A very simple case of general average involved a loss that befell the schooner *Alice Archer*, loaded with hard pine, when being towed up the Kennebec to Bath in February 1896. The schooner struck a heavy sheet of ice on the port bow, staving in the covering of a lumber port and filling her with water. Being loaded with lumber, she floated with rails awash but too deep to be brought alongside the wharf. She was gradually worked up onto the flats by the stevedore until, at low tide, the port could be covered and the schooner pumped out. For this loss the Sewalls made a claim under general average.

The bill from stevedore J. C. Mulligan—the Sewalls' old office manager—was $90.25. The Knickerbocker Steam Towage Company was paid $30.00 for pumping, and the captain paid another $7.00 labor for hand pumpng. The materials for boarding up the port cost $2.70, a carpenter's labor cost $1.50. The total "extraordinary" expenses which the Sewalls claimed came under general average was thus $131.45.

The Sewalls claimed that the schooner was valued at $10,000. The freight for 387,000 board feet at $5 per thousand was $1,935, although only one-half—$968—was considered, indicating that this was the amount of an advance paid on freight, the other half being as yet uncollected. The cargo was valued at $4,760, for a total of $15,728. Arthur Sewall & Co. proposed that the proportion of the $131.45 loss which the vessel should be liable for was $83.58.

In November 1891, after the *Carrie A. Lane*, bound from Philadelphia to Bath, had been obliged to put into Norfolk in distress, the firm of Johnson & Higgins, Philadelphia average adjusters, "in accordance with the arrangements made by our representative with you" agreed to give Arthur Sewall & Co. the commissions for collecting any bills for services should they send a representative to Norfolk, in addition to 25 percent of their adjuster's fee.

7. Southern Ship Timber

(See Note 12, p. 322.)

Clippings from the Rockland *Courier Gazette, circa* December 1888:

A. E. Wentworth of Rockport leaves today with a crew of twenty men for the Chickahominy River, Virginia, where he will labor for six months or so getting out ship timber. He takes six yokes of cattle and has chartered a car straight through to Richmond. He will get out timber for two schooners to be built by H. M. Bean, Camden, and is talking with the Sewalls of Bath about a frame for a 2500-ton ship which they are contemplating constructing.

Joseph Bisbee of West Camden, of the firm of Bisbee Bros., shipped a carload of twelve fine working oxen to Virginia last week in charge of William Martin of Appleton and T. J. Bisbee of Rockland. Joseph Bisbee left on Monday morning's train accompanied by his wife and daughter. He expects to meet his oxen in Richmond. Bisbee Bros. will do a rattling business getting out ship timber this coming winter.

In November 1949 Lieut. W. J. L. Parker, USCG, interviewed Ben Bisbee, son of William Bisbee. Both Bisbees were engaged for many years in "getting out" ship timber in the South, mostly from derelict Virginia plantations. The southern white oak did not have the acid of northern red oak. During the Civil War operations were shifted to Delaware. They took provisions, moulds, oxen, hay, and men with them; for a large frame twenty-five to thirty men would comprise the gang. Some of these men worked in shipyards in the summer. Ben's mother was cook, and Ben had a brother born in a camp. A camp with foreman's cabin, bunkhouse, cookhouse, and ox hovel (i.e., stable) would be built. Two men would fell timber, two more would trim tops, then the moulder would mould the timber before the teamster hauled it to the river, often two to seven miles away. St. George (i.e., Thomaston, Tenant's Harbor) schooners did most of the carrying for the trade.

In November 1951, Parker interviewed Harold Vinal of Thomaston, Maine. Vinal was the son of Ira Vinal, master builder of the Washburn yard. In 1904 Ira first went to Virginia to get out frames. Contractors bought stumpage rights. At this time only a cook and several key men went south, the remainder of the crew—half white, half black—being hired locally. Black choppers, he recalled, often sang to their axes while at work. One or two men (Ira and his father) did the "lining," marking shape of timber with chalk. Timber, having been "sided" with broadaxes, was then "moulded" with a pencil or race knife as guide for hewing, or "getting out," the desired piece. Bevels taken from a bevel board were hewn, and the frame as shipped was almost ready for assembly, save that the ends of the futtocks (pieces) had to be sawed off on the framing stage when the frame was assembled.

Stumpage was purchased by the contractor. Contents were figured by the ton, a ton being one foot square by forty feet.

8. Frame Contract

A contract, dated January 10, 1881, between Arthur Sewall & Co. and David Pratt of Maitland, Hant's County, Nova Scotia, for providing the frame of a three-masted schooner, no doubt the *B. L. Burt*, launched in December 1881, built under contract for J. B. Phillips of Taunton, Massachusetts:

> I hereby agree to furnish Arthur Sewall & Co. a first class Frame for a Sch. of about 450 Tons Reg. more or less said frame to be cut & bevelled by mould to be furnished by said Arthur Sewall & Co.
>
> Keels, Floors & Navals [navels—the lowest frame futtocks, amidships] to be hard wood the balance of frame to be of good quality Hacmatac, all to be delivered at Bath for the price of $13.50 thirteen & $^{50}/_{100}$ Dollars per ton & or before June 1st 1881.

9. Framing Contract

A memorandum of agreement between E. & A. Sewall and John Billings for setting up ready for "dubbing"—fairing and smoothing outer frame surfaces by adz—the frame of "Ship #5," and also building staging, dated May 23, 1874. Ship # 5 was launched as the ship *Continental*, January 25, 1875.

> Mem. of Agreement made this day by & between "John Billings" of Damariscotta & E. & A. Sewall of Bath, Me.
>
> The said Billings here by agree for the Consideration herein after named to do the following work for said Sewall
>
> To take the material as it now lays in yard & make & block up the keel and put the Ship Called No. 5 in frame, ribbon [ribband] her & build two good Stages around her, timber out the Stern & put in four tiers of main keelson Meaning to take the timber as furnished by said Sewalls. Completely timber out the Ship leaving her plumb & fair ready for dubbing, to furnish all the Labor & do all the fastening.
>
> Said Sewalls agree to find all yard tools & rope required & furnish what team is necessary & to pay said Billings for above Job when fully Completed to their Satisfaction, the sum of twenty two hundred dollars, payments to be made as the work progresses say from time to time 75% of the estimated amt due, the balc. or 25% to be paid when Job is Completed—
>
> Said Billings agree to do all the work in a first class manner & fully equal to the same job on Ship No. 4 & under the general direction of said Sewalls or their Master-workman E. P. Mallett. The above Job of work to be Completed within Eight weeks after Ship No. 3 is Launched.

10. Split Commissions and Confidential Rebates

An excerpt from a letter from Arthur Sewall & Co. to Messrs. S. B. Marts & Co., Baltimore, November 4, 1898, re: chartering of the four-masted bark *Edward Sewall*:

> As you know, our arrangement is that [chartering] commissions are to be divided, unless otherwise agreed upon. All we insist upon now is that we shall share equally with yourselves, the commissions on this charter. In case you were obliged to recognize a third party if you will kindly advise us of the party's name, and the amount paid him, we will rectify our account making the commissions between us equal.

An excerpt of a letter from the Baltimore Ship Building and Drydock Co. to Arthur Sewall & Co. , December 19, 1904, re: dry docking and painting the four-masted bark *Edward Sewall*:

> We beg to acknowledge receipt of your telegram as follows: "Telegraph lowest bid, painting immediately, Ship *Edward Sewall*, two coats Van Hovelings Composition to nine foot water line, covering Dockage, material, labor," and beg to confirm our reply wired immediately, as per enclosed confirmation, in the sum of $621.50— less *confidential rebate* of two (2) cents per net ton to you, equaling a rebate of $58.32.

11. Account Statement

Harriet Hyde (Sewall) Cutler, Trustee E. & A. Sewall, in account with Arthur Sewall & Co. 1881. Harriet was the oldest of William D. and Rachel Sewall's seven surviving children.

1881				
April 7	By ⅛		sch. *Satilla* a/c	$65.75
May 14	"		ship *El Capitan* a/c	361.17
"	"		" *Sterling* a/c	377.23
June 30	"		sch *Satilla* a/c	125.00
July 25	"		ship *Occidental* a/c	567.05
"	"		" *Oriental* a/c	1,072.79
Aug. 30	"		sch. *Satilla* a/c	195.69
Sept. 12	"		ship *Sterling* a/c	2,424.56
Oct. 21	"		sch. *Satilla* a/c	40.03
Nov. 30	"		ship *Oriental* a/c	4,874.77
Dec. 31			Interest paid on above	124.49
				$10,139.63

12. CHARTER AGREEMENT

An "agreement for charter of ship *Indiana*," a charter being a contract for the employment of a vessel. In this instance, however, the ship owner, E. & A. Sewall, owned the cargo until it was purchased after delivery.

> E. & A. Sewall of Bath Maine agree to sell and the Pacific Mail Steamship Company of New York agree to buy the cargo of two thousand one hundred and sixteen (2,116) tons (more or less) of Brymbo Welsh Hartley Steam Coals shipped on board the ship "Indiana" as per Bill of Lading dated in Birkinhead Jany 25th 1879, at thirty-eight /38/-/ shillings per ton at Acapulco, Mexico, to the Agent of the Pacific Mail Steamship Company at that port. The coal to be taken delivery of at the rate of not less than seventy-five (75) tons for each working lay day and demurrage at the rate of one hundred and fifty dollars ($150) per day to be paid for every day's detention beyond the time so required to discharge the ship.
>
> Payment for the coal to be made as follows viz: one ($1) dollar per ton U. S. gold coin advance at the port of Acapulco, for the needful disbursements of the ship, and the balance to be paid in cash at the office of the Pacific Mail Steamship Company in San Francisco at the rate of $4.86 to the pound sterling, on presentation of a certificate of the true delivery of the cargo from the Agent of the Company at Acapulco.

W. H. Lane, Witness to signature   John Riley
of the vice president.   Vice President PMSSCo.

13. MASTER'S STATEMENT

Ship *El Capitan* & Owners in a/c J. E. Sewall, Master. Oct 22, 1883.

Gross freight Philadelphia to Portland as per Freight List	$20,958.35
Less 7¹/₂ % commission on same	1,571.88
	19,386.47
5% Primage on Net Freight	969.32

Gross Freight Portland to Hull [England]per freight list	£3,793.16.6 4.82	
		$18,286.23
Less Commission in Portland $716.21		
" Hull £94-16-1 @4.82		1,173.35
		17,112.88
5% on net freight		855.64

Gross Freight Hull to Philadelphia 741 tons @ 6/		£222.8
5% on £222.8 @ 4.82 $1,071.97		53.60

Wages from June 8th 82 to Oct. 22 83 16 m. 14 @ $20,   329.25

Balance due Self from Slop a/c as rendered   269.24

                                                                             Cr. $2,477.05

By cash Phila. $66.28
    Portland $418.56
    Hull 19.00 $91.58
    Phila. $207.00
                                 783.39   783.39
                                        Balance due Self to date $1,693.66

14. RIGGER'S CONTRACT

An agreement between Samuel. H. Wade and Arthur Sewall & Co. to rig the four-masted bark *Arthur Sewall*, November 28, 1898.

> I hererby agree to rig the new Ship now being built by Arthur Sewall & Co., (called the "ARTHUR SEWALL") doing everything required by the builders, the same as the last ship, for the sum of sixteen hundred and fifty dollars ($1,650.).
>
>   I further agree not to drink any liquor, or allow my men to, while I am doing this job, and in case I violate this pledge, I agree to discount on the price two hundred dollars ($200.) making for the job, say fourteen hundred and fifty dollars ($1,450.).

Wade, a native of Calais, Maine, had been the principal foreman for leading Bath riggers Francis A. Deloche and Frank A. Palmer. According to one version, when Palmer balked at raising *Dirigo*'s long, one-piece lower masts (which included the length of the topmasts), Arthur Sewall asked Wade if he could do the job, and Wade replied, "Mr. Sewall, I'll lift that whole ship up if you want me to," thus ending Palmer's further employment by the Sewalls.* George Goodwin's version was somewhat different: "The old rigger would not touch the job because they [the Sewalls] would not give him a fit place in which to work. The man who did that part of the work was a good rigger, when he was sober."**

* William Avery Baker's *A Maritime History of Bath, Maine, and the Kennebec River Region*, Vol. 2 (Bath, Maine: Marine Research Society, 1973), p. 804.
** From George Goodwin's unpublished autobiography at the Maine Maritime Museum library, p. 101.

15. A Live Yankee Bargain

In July 1889 Arthur Sewall purchased at auction, for $1,800, the stranded three-masted schooner *William C. French*, of Newburyport. The *French* was fast atop a tidal ledge off Small Point, having defied the owner's salvage efforts. After a Boston firm also failed to dislodge her, Arthur made a shrewd bargain with L. E. Lunt, of Portland, who had approached Arthur about salvaging materials from the wreck. On August 19, Lunt wrote Arthur:

> As we understand our agreement made this day to remove Schooner *Wm. C. French* from Glover's Rocks is as follows. We are to endeavor to remove the Schooner from the rocks and deliver her at Bath on the Railway. You to pay expense of hauling the Schooner. We to receive on delivery of Schooner at Railway in Bath the sum of Four Thousand dollars ($4,000). In case of our failure to remove the Schr. from the rocks we are to receive from you one-half the amount of expenses that we have paid out in actual expense to us for material Labor & tools necessary on the work not to include any chains or anchors that we may use on the work. We further agree to proceed with the work until we shall have expended the sum of twenty-five hundred dollars ($2,500) and then should we want to give the job up to be at our option of same.

Despite legal threats from a Small Point shooting club, composed of Bostonians, which claimed possession of the rock and that blasting was scaring off seabirds, and a storm that caused the re-launching ways to be rebuilt, in mid-October the *French*, caulked in part with four cords of rockweed, floated free. Repairs were expected to cost no more than $5,000. Arthur, in a moment of whimsy, renamed the schooner *Dicky Bird* after the manner in which she had been perched atop the rock.

INDEX

Citations for topics that appear in great number have been selected to hopefully include the most important references. The names of a number of non-Sewall ships, and of persons, places, and firms that appear but fleetingly, have not been included. Mates, sailors, or even ship's boys who served as captains at some point in their careers, are cited as such. Rig notations following the names of vessels are "sp" for ship, "bk" for bark, "bkt" for barkentine, "br" for brig, "sch" for schooner, and "str" for steamer. Thus, a "3msch" would be a three-masted schooner.

St. Helena Island, 94–96, 285

Standard Oil Co., 338, 339, 375, 416, 417

Standard sp, 304

Staples, Arthur, 8, 18, 199, 220, 221, 305, 466, 470, 471

Starkey, Capt. William, 241, 379, 380

stenographer, 271

Sterling sp, ii, 135, 139, 155, 176, 342, 343, 370, 453, 485, 477

Stevenson, Robert Louis, 225

Stinson, Capt. Frank, 82

sugar trades, 43, 44–46, 121, 328, 334, 335, 338, 398, 400, 406

Sumter, CSS, 72

Susie P. Oliver 3msch, 113

Susquehanna 4mbk, 120, 127, 260, 303–07, 309, 314, 320–22, 362, 372–75, 438, 478

Sutton & Beebe, 120

Sutton & Co. (Sutton's Dispatch Line), 120, 124, 127, 130, 136, 204, 407, 446

Sutton, David, 407, 446

Sutton, Effingham, 124, 407, 446

Sutton, Woodruff, 124, 407, 446

Swedenborgian church, 70, 360

T. F. Oakes sp, 368

Tabor sp, 51, 84, 85, 120, 130, 131, 155, 161, 162, 212, 310, 477

Tacoma sp, 446

Talofa 3msch, 187, 271, 272, 478

Tapley, Capt. Robert, 165

Taylor, Capt. P. H., 51, 84, 85

Taylor, Capt. William, 248, 249, 461

Texas Co., 406, 445, 462–64

Thomas M. Reed (1) sp, 159, 161, 171, 477

Thomas M. Reed (2) sp, 120, 126, 157, 200, 222 , 241, 478

Thomaston, 29, 71, 81, 82, 86, 114, 483

Thompson, Capt. Chadwick, 315–19

Thompson, Capt. E. H., 217–19, 359

Thompson, Rachel Fannie, 166

Thornely, A. J., 373–74

Thrasher sp, 2, 87, 55, 162, 171, 207, 477

timber, shipbuilding, 30, 31, 33, 34, 56, 68, 78–81, 91, 112–16, 187, 303, 308, 309, 322, 483

Tofa 3mch, 188

Torrey, Francis B., 145, 211

Trott, Capt Mitchell, 45, 63

Tucker, H. R., 238, 239

Tucker, Payson, 213, 233, 234, 236, 238, 323

Turner, Tom, 469

Undaunted sp, 130, 133, 142, 143, 155, 191, 227, 312, 313, 477

Valentia sp, xi, 47, 75, 168

Valparaiso, 248, 249, 282, 334

Van Vleck & Co. (Robt. B.), 124, 126, 127, 212

Vancouver sp, 93

Vicksburg sp, 73

Vigilant sp, 72, 73, 93

Villafranca sp, 75, 93, 477

Ville De Paris sp, 25

Vimeira 4mbk, 328–33

Volant bk, 70, 477

votes bought, 352, 353

W. F. Babcock sp, 129, 201, 284–87, 359, 400, 461, 478

W. R. Grace & Co.,124, 127. *See also* Grace, William R.

Waddington, J. F., 336, 337, 342

Wade, Samuel H., 487

Watkin's Code, 480

Watts, Capt. Alfred, 30

Watts, Capt. Edward A., 320, 321, 426, 427

Watts, Samuel B., 29

Webb, Watson, 76

Webb, William, 293

West Gardiner, 9

West India trade, 5, 22, 43–46

Wetterhorn bk, 130–34, 155, 477

wheat. *See* grain trade.

Whitmore, Capt. Dexter, 198

Whitmore, Capt. Parker, 67, 88

William C. French 3msch. *See Dicky Bird.*

William D. Sewall sp, 58, 159, 404, 477

William P. Frye 4mbk, 6, 338, 376–78, 403, 423, 430–35, 444, 452, 456, 460, 462, 478

Williams, Alice (Mrs. John), 244, 246–52

Williams, Blanchard & Co., 104, 121, 123

Williams, Dimond & Co., 121, 122, 142, 143, 273, 402, 405, 406, 411

Williams, James H., 367, 370–71

Williams, Capt. John, 243–47, 251, 256

Williams, Reuel, 60, 61

Willie Rosenfeld sp, 243, 251, 253–58, 284, 297, 338, 353, 365–68, 478

Wilson, Capt. Arthur, 188

Work, Capt. Abel, 200, 223, 241

Wyoming 6msch, 21, 309, 312

Youngren, Capt. J., 164